Henry F. Kett

The voters and tax-payers of De Kalb County, Illinois; containing,

also, a biographical directory

A history of the county and state, map of the county, a business directory, an

abstract of every-day laws - Vol.

Henry F. Kett

The voters and tax-payers of De Kalb County, Illinois; containing, also, a biographical directory
A history of the county and state, map of the county, a business directory, an abstract of every-day laws - Vol.

ISBN/EAN: 9783337714048

Printed in Europe, USA, Canada, Australia, Japan

Cover: Foto ©ninafisch / pixelio.de

More available books at **www.hansebooks.com**

VOTERS AND TAX-PAYERS

OF

DEKALB COUNTY, ILLINOIS

CONTAINING, ALSO, A

*BIOGRAPHICAL DIRECTORY OF ITS TAX-PAYERS AND VOTERS; A HISTORY OF
THE COUNTY AND STATE; MAP OF THE COUNTY; A BUSINESS DIREC-
TORY; AN ABSTRACT OF EVERY-DAY LAWS; OFFICERS
OF SOCIETIES, LODGES, ETC., ETC.*

PREFACE.

But few can realize the task involved in the publication of a work of this kind. We have to contend against ignorance, prejudice and selfishness. Ignorance of some people as to our objects, many refusing to give their names, for fear they will be used for some swindling purpose, or their politics, lest it be used to their discredit; or how much property they own, fearing it is to increase their taxes. Prejudice of people who have subscribed through agents for publications, and, not having received what they expected, have forever thereafter sworn warfare against all agents, without discriminating, or taking into consideration the absolute necessity of employing men under certain circumstances as the media between publisher and people. Selfishness by citizens who expect to have published, gratuitously, every thing they see fit to send us, which usually is of a personal nature, or not relevant matter, and if published would be of no general interest, therefore we deem best to suppress it, thereby receiving their outspoken enmity. For this work we do not claim perfection; that would be an impossibility. Most townships have been gone over by the third man, but still there are undoubtedly errors, mostly in spelling names and in dates. We have several cases in DeKalb County where members of the same family spell their names in different ways, and a number of cases where the dates of births, of marriages, or when they came into the county, were improbable, and when brought to their notice, they had made a mistake generally of ten years in calculation. We give our agents the most positive instructions to be especially careful in getting names and dates, but ofttimes men are indifferent in *giving* required information, and when met on the road, at the threshing machine, or in the rain or cold, the information is given hurriedly or carelessly, and our agents are obliged to put it down as given them, and when copied, mistakes necessarily occur.

We have endeavored to get the names of all tax-payers and voters. We have about 6,800 names, the vote being about 6,000, which shows we could not have missed many. In our History of the County we have endeavored. to give an interesting, condensed, and correct sketch. Our History of Illinois will give the reader some interesting and valuable historical facts. Our Laws should be carefully read by every business man or farmer; they contain invaluable information. In fact we have toiled long and at great expense, and have far exceeded our promises to make every thing in these pages interesting and valuable, and all you could expect or wish, and in your criticisms, please to bear in mind that in gathering, compiling and publishing a volume of this kind, perfection would be an impossibility.

Contents.

MISCELLANEOUS.

	PAGE
Agricultural Statistics of DeKalb	138
Population of DeKalb Co	131
Population of the United States	82
Population of Fifty Principal Cities	82
Population and Area of the United States	85
Population of Principal Cities in the World	83
Population of Illinois	84 & 85
Township Organization	135
Village Corporation	137
Town Government	137
Officials of Societies, Lodges, etc	139
Pioneers of DeKalb Co	132
Interest Table	82
Miscellaneous Table	82
Map of DeKalb Co	Front Page
Business Directory	338
Too Lates and Changes	152

PORTRAITS.

Shabbona	Frontispiece
Glidden J. F	184
Ellwood E	80
Marsh W. W	151
Marsh C. W	151
Miller Wm. A	16
Hopkins Thos. M	128

HISTORICAL.

History of Illinois	13
History of DeKalb County	86
Physical Features	87
Indians of the Country	89
Early Settlement	90
Claim Association	91
Organization of Co	92
First Courts, Court House, etc	94
New Court House	97
Towships Organized	98
Rapid Entry of Land	98
DeKalb and the Rebellion	99
Sketch of U. P. Church, Somonauk	101
" Sycamore	102
" Sandwich	119
" DeKalb	111
" Cortland	124
" Somonauk	113
" Malta	123
" Genoa	125
" Kingston	130
" Kirkland	130
" Hinckley	130
" Shabbona	129
" Waterman	130

TOWNSHIP DIRECTORIES.

Afton	248
Clinton	330
Cortland	221
DeKalb	180
Franklin	271
Genoa	312
Kingston	292
Malta	241
Mayfield	299
Milan	286
Paw Paw	232
Pierce	256
Shabbona	320
South Grove	279

P. E.

Squaw Grove	261
Sycamore	153
Somonauk	194
Victor	306

BIOGRAPHIES.

Ellwood Reuben	144
Glidden James F	145
Marsh C. W. & W. W	151
Miller Wm. A	145
Hopkins Thos. M	149
Waite Campbell W	148
Boles Henry Lawson	147
Robertson Gilbert H	147
Winne Dr. C	146
Bloodgood Henry F	150
Post L. H	149
West Chas. A	150

ABSTRACT OF LAWS OF ILLINOIS.

Bills of exchange and promissory notes	45
Interest	45
Descent	45
Wills and estates	46
Taxes	48
Jurisdiction of Courts	48
County Courts	49
Limitation of action	49
Married women	49
Exemption from forced sale	50
Estrays	51
Deeds and mortgages	51
Game	52
Weights and measures	52
Millers	53
Marks and brands	53
Adoption of children	54
Surveyors and surveys	54
Roads	55
Drainage	57
Paupers	58
Fences	60
Damage from Trespass	61
Landlord and Tenant	61
Liens	64
Definition of Commercial Terms	65
Church Organization	79
Suggestion to Persons purchasing Books by Subscription	80
Form of Blank Note	66
" Order	66
" Receipt	66
" Bills of Purchase	66
" Articles of Agreement	67
" Clerk for Services	67
" Bills of Sale	68
" Bonds	68
" Chattel Mortgage	69
" Lease of Buildings	71
" Landlord's Agreement	72
" Tenant's "	72
" Notice Tenant to Quit	73
" Tenant's Notice to Quit	73
" Real Estate Mortgage to Secure Money	73
" Warranty Deed	74
" Quit Claim Deed	75
" Release	76
" Form of Will	77
" Codicil	79

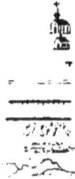

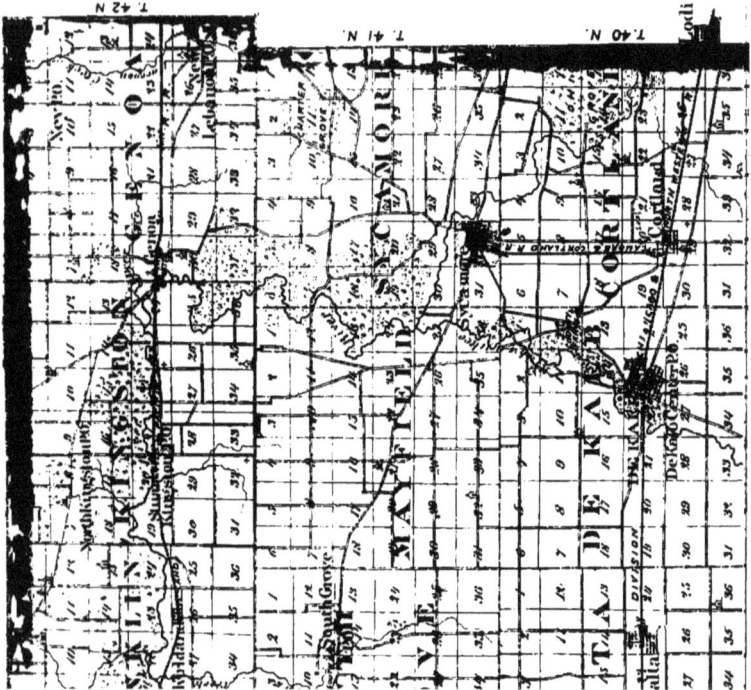

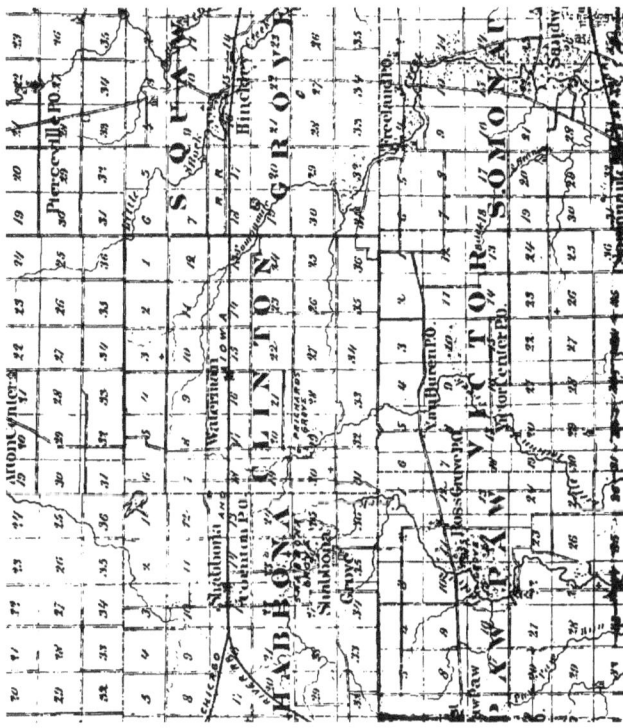

HISTORY OF ILLINOIS.

The name of this beautiful Prairie State is derived from *Illini*, a Delaware word signifying Superior Men. It has a French termination, and is a symbol of how the two races—the French and the Indians—were intermixed during the early history of the country.

The appellation was no doubt well applied to the primitive inhabitants of the soil whose prowess in savage warfare long withstood the combined attacks of the fierce Iroquois on the one side, and the no less savage and relentless Sacs and Foxes on the other. The Illinois were once a powerful confederacy, occupying the most beautiful and fertile region in the great Valley of the Mississippi, which their enemies coveted and struggled long and hard to wrest from them. By the fortunes of war they were diminished in numbers, and finally destroyed. "Starved Rock," on the Illinois River, according to tradition, commemorates their last tragedy, where, it is said, the entire tribe starved rather than surrender.

EARLY DISCOVERIES.

The first European discoveries in Illinois date back over two hundred years. They are a part of that movement which, from the beginning to the middle of the seventeenth century, brought the French Canadian missionaries and fur traders into the Valley of the Mississippi, and which, at a later period, established the civil and ecclesiastical authority of France from the Gulf of St. Lawrence to the Gulf of Mexico, and from the foot-hills of the Alleghanies to the Rocky Mountains.

The great river of the West had been discovered by DeSoto, the Spanish conqueror of Florida, three quarters of a century before the French founded Quebec in 1608, but the Spanish left the country a wilderness, without further exploration or settlement within its borders, in which condition it remained until the Mississippi was discovered by the agents of the French Canadian government, Joliet and Marquette, in 1673. These renowned explorers were not the first white visitors to Illinois. In 1671—two years in advance of them—came Nicholas Perrot to Chicago. He had been sent by Talon as an agent of the Canadian government to

call a great peace convention of Western Indians at Green Bay, preparatory to the movement for the discovery of the Mississippi. It was
deemed a good stroke of policy to secure, as far as possible, the friendship and co-operation of the Indians, far and near, before venturing upon
an enterprise which their hostility might render disastrous, and which
their friendship and assistance would do so much to make successful;
and to this end Perrot was sent to call together in council the tribes
throughout the Northwest, and to promise them the commerce and protection of the French government. He accordingly arrived at Green
Bay in 1671, and procuring an escort of Pottawattamies, proceeded in a
bark canoe upon a visit to the Miamis, at Chicago. Perrot was therefore the first European to set foot upon the soil of Illinois.

Still there were others before Marquette. In 1672, the Jesuit missionaries, Fathers Claude Allouez and Claude Dablon, bore the standard
of the Cross from their mission at Green Bay through western Wisconsin
and northern Illinois, visiting the Foxes on Fox River, and the Masquo-
tines and Kickapoos at the mouth of the Milwaukee. These missionaries
penetrated on the route afterwards followed by Marquette as far as the
Kickapoo village at the head of Lake Winnebago, where Marquette, in
his journey, secured guides across the portage to the Wisconsin.

The oft-repeated story of Marquette and Joliet is well known.
They were the agents employed by the Canadian government to discover
the Mississippi. Marquette was a native of France, born in 1637, a
Jesuit priest by education, and a man of simple faith and of great zeal and
devotion in extending the Roman Catholic religion among the Indians.
Arriving in Canada in 1666, he was sent as a missionary to the far
Northwest, and, in 1668, founded a mission at Sault Ste. Marie. The
following year he moved to La Pointe, in Lake Superior, where he
instructed a branch of the Hurons till 1670, when he removed south, and
founded the mission at St. Ignace, on the Straits of Mackinaw. Here
he remained, devoting a portion of his time to the study of the Illinois
language under a native teacher who had accompanied him to the mission
from La Pointe, till he was joined by Joliet in the Spring of 1673. By
the way of Green Bay and the Fox and Wisconsin Rivers, they entered
the Mississippi, which they explored to the mouth of the Arkansas, and
returned by the way of the Illinois and Chicago Rivers to Lake Michigan.

On his way up the Illinois, Marquette visited the great village of
the Kaskaskias, near what is now Utica, in the county of LaSalle. The
following year he returned and established among them the mission of
the Immaculate Virgin Mary, which was the first Jesuit mission founded
in Illinois and in the Mississippi Valley. The intervening winter he
had spent in a hut which his companions erected on the Chicago River, a
few leagues from its mouth. The founding of this mission was the last

act of Marquette's life. He died in Michigan, on his way back to Green Bay, May 18, 1675.

FIRST FRENCH OCCUPATION.

The first French occupation of the territory now embraced in Illinois was effected by LaSalle in 1680, seven years after the time of Marquette and Joliet. LaSalle, having constructed a vessel, the " Griffin," above the falls of Niagara, which he sailed to Green Bay, and having passed thence in canoes to the mouth of the St. Joseph River, by which and the Kankakee he reached the Illinois, in January, 1680, erected Fort *Crevecœur*, at the lower end of Peoria Lake, where the city of Peoria is now situated. The place where this ancient fort stood may still be seen just below the outlet of Peoria Lake. It was destined, however, to a temporary existence. From this point, LaSalle determined to descend the Mississippi to its mouth, but did not accomplish this purpose till two years later—in 1682. Returning to Fort Frontenac for the purpose of getting materials with which to rig his vessel, he left the fort in charge of Touti, his lieutenant, who during his absence was driven off by the Iroquois Indians. These savages had made a raid upon the settlement of the Illinois, and had left nothing in their track but ruin and desolation. Mr. Davidson, in his History of Illinois, gives the following graphic account of the picture that met the eyes of LaSalle and his companions on their return :

" At the great town of the Illinois they were appalled at the scene which opened to their view. No hunter appeared to break its death-like silence with a salutatory whoop ot welcome. The plain on which the town had stood was now strewn with charred fragments of lodges, which had so recently swarmed with savage life and hilarity. To render more hideous the picture of desolation, large numbers of skulls had been placed on the upper extremities of lodge-poles which had escaped the devouring flames. In the midst of these horrors was the rude fort of the spoilers, rendered frightful by the same ghastly relics. A near approach showed that the graves had been robbed of their bodies, and swarms of buzzards were discovered glutting their loathsome stomachs on the reeking corruption. To complete the work of destruction, the growing corn of the village had been cut down and burned, while the pits containing the products of previous years, had been rifled and their contents scattered with wanton waste. It was evident the suspected blow of the Iroquois had fallen with relentless fury."

Touti had escaped LaSalle knew not whither. Passing down the lake in search of him and his men, LaSalle discovered that the fort had been destroyed, but the vessel which he had partly constructed was still on the stocks and but slightly injured. After further fruitless search, failing to find Touti, he fastened to a tree a painting representing himself and party sitting in a canoe and bearing a pipe of peace, and to the painting attached a letter addressed to Touti.

Touti had escaped, and, after untold privations, taken shelter among the Pottawattamies near Green Bay. These were friendly to the French. One of their old chiefs used to say, "There were but three great captains in the world, himself, Touti and LaSalle."

GENIUS OF LaSALLE.

We must now return to LaSalle, whose exploits stand out in such bold relief. He was born in Rouen, France, in 1643. His father was wealthy, but he renounced his patrimony on entering a college of the Jesuits, from which he separated and came to Canada a poor man in 1666. The priests of St. Sulpice, among whom he had a brother, were then the proprietors of Montreal, the nucleus of which was a seminary or convent founded by that order. The Superior granted to LaSalle a large tract of land at LaChine, where he established himself in the fur trade. He was a man of daring genius, and outstripped all his competitors in exploits of travel and commerce with the Indians. In 1669, he visited the headquarters of the great Iroquois Confederacy, at Onondaga, in the heart of New York, and, obtaining guides, explored the Ohio River to the falls at Louisville.

In order to understand the genius of LaSalle, it must be remembered that for many years prior to his time the missionaries and traders were obliged to make their way to the Northwest by the Ottawa River (of Canada) on account of the fierce hostility of the Iroquois along the lower lakes and Niagara River, which entirely closed this latter route to the Upper Lakes. They carried on their commerce chiefly by canoes, paddling them through the Ottawa to Lake Nipissing, carrying them across the portage to French River, and descending that to Lake Huron. This being the route by which they reached the Northwest, accounts for the fact that all the earliest Jesuit missions were established in the neighborhood of the Upper Lakes. LaSalle conceived the grand idea of opening the route by Niagara River and the Lower Lakes to Canadian commerce by sail vessels, connecting it with the navigation of the Mississippi, and thus opening a magnificent water communication from the Gulf of St. Lawrence to the Gulf of Mexico. This truly grand and comprehensive purpose seems to have animated him in all his wonderful achievements and the matchless difficulties and hardships he surmounted. As the first step in the accomplishment of this object he established himself on Lake Ontario, and built and garrisoned Fort Frontenac, the site of the present

WILLIAM A. MILLER
DE KALB
PIONEER OF DE KALB COUNTY

city of Kingston, Canada. Here he obtained a grant of land from the French crown and a body of troops by which he beat back the invading Iroquois and cleared the passage to Niagara Falls. Having by this masterly stroke made it safe to attempt a hitherto untried expedition, his next step, as we have seen, was to advance to the Falls with all his outfit for building a ship with which to sail the lakes. He was successful in this undertaking, though his ultimate purpose was defeated by a strange combination of untoward circumstances. The Jesuits evidently hated LaSalle and plotted against him, because he had abandoned them and co-operated with a rival order. The fur traders were also jealous of his superior success in opening new channels of commerce. At LaChine he had taken the trade of Lake Ontario, which but for his presence there would have gone to Quebec. While they were plodding with their bark canoes through the Ottawa he was constructing sailing vessels to command the trade of the lakes and the Mississippi. These great plans excited the jealousy and envy of the small traders, introduced treason and revolt into the ranks of his own companions, and finally led to the foul assassination by which his great achievements were prematurely ended.

In 1682, LaSalle, having completed his vessel at Peoria, descended the Mississippi to its confluence with the Gulf of Mexico. Erecting a standard on which he inscribed the arms of France, he took formal possession of the whole valley of the mighty river, in the name of Louis XIV., then reigning, in honor of whom he named the country LOUISIANA.

LaSalle then went to France, was appointed Governor, and returned with a fleet and immigrants, for the purpose of planting a colony in Illinois. They arrived in due time in the Gulf of Mexico, but failing to find the mouth of the Mississippi, up which LaSalle intended to sail, his supply ship, with the immigrants, was driven ashore and wrecked on Matagorda Bay. With the fragments of the vessel he constructed a stockade and rude huts on the shore for the protection of the immigrants, calling the post Fort St. Louis. He then made a trip into New Mexico, in search of silver mines, but, meeting with disappointment, returned to find his little colony reduced to forty souls. He then resolved to travel on foot to Illinois, and, starting with his companions, had reached the valley of the Colorado, near the mouth of Trinity river, when he was shot by one of his men. This occurred on the 19th of March, 1687.

Dr. J. W. Foster remarks of him : " Thus fell, not far from the banks of the Trinity, Robert Cavalier de la Salle, one of the grandest characters that ever figured in American history—a man capable of originating the vastest schemes, and endowed with a will and a judgment capable of carrying them to successful results. Had ample facilities been placed by the King of France at his disposal, the result of the colonization of this continent might have been far different from what we now behold."

EARLY SETTLEMENTS.

A temporary settlement was made at Fort St. Louis, or the old Kaskaskia village, on the Illinois River, in what is now LaSalle County, in 1682. In 1690, this was removed, with the mission connected with it, to Kaskaskia, on the river of that name, emptying into the lower Mississippi in St. Clair County. Cahokia was settled about the same time, or at least, both of these settlements began in the year 1690, though it is now pretty well settled that Cahokia is the older place, and ranks as the oldest permanent settlement in Illinois, as well as in the Mississippi Valley. The reason for the removal of the old Kaskaskia settlement and mission, was probably because the dangerous and difficult route by Lake Michigan and the Chicago portage had been almost abandoned, and travelers and traders passed down and up the Mississippi by the Fox and Wisconsin River route. They removed to the vicinity of the Mississippi in order to be in the line of travel from Canada to Louisiana, that is, the lower part of it, for it was all Louisiana then south of the lakes.

During the period of French rule in Louisiana, the population probably never exceeded ten thousand, including whites and blacks. Within that portion of it now included in Indiana, trading posts were established at the principal Miami villages which stood on the head waters of the Maumee, the Wea villages situated at Ouiatenon, on the Wabash, and the Piankeshaw villages at Post Vincennes; all of which were probably visited by French traders and missionaries before the close of the seventeenth century.

In the vast territory claimed by the French, many settlements of considerable importance had sprung up. Biloxi, on Mobile Bay, had been founded by D'Iberville, in 1699; Antoine de Lamotte Cadillac had founded Detroit in 1701; and New Orleans had been founded by Bienville, under the auspices of the Mississippi Company, in 1718. In Illinois also, considerable settlements had been made, so that in 1730 they embraced one hundred and forty French families, about six hundred "converted Indians," and many traders and voyageurs. In that portion of the country, on the east side of the Mississippi, there were five distinct settlements, with their respective villages, viz.: Cahokia, near the mouth of Cahokia Creek and about five miles below the present city of St. Louis; St. Philip, about forty-five miles below Cahokia, and four miles above Fort Chartres; Fort Chartres, twelve miles above Kaskaskia; Kaskaskia, situated on the Kaskaskia River, five miles above its confluence with the Mississippi; and Prairie du Rocher, near Fort Chartres. To these must be added St. Genevieve and St. Louis, on the west side of the Mississippi. These, with the exception of St. Louis, are among the oldest French towns in the Mississippi Valley. Kaskaskia, in its best days, was a town of some two or three thousand inhabitants. After it passed from the crown of France its population for many years did not exceed fifteen hundred. Under British rule, in 1773, the population had decreased to four hundred and fifty. As early as 1721, the Jesuits had established a college and a monastery in Kaskaskia.

Fort Chartres was first built under the direction of the Mississippi Company, in 1718, by M. de Boisbraint, a military officer, under command of Bienville. It stood on the east bank of the Mississippi, about eighteen miles below Kaskaskia, and was for some time the headquarters of the military commandants of the district of Illinois.

In the Centennial Oration of Dr. Fowler, delivered at Philadelphia, by appointment of Gov. Beveridge, we find some interesting facts with regard to the State of Illinois, which we appropriate in this history:

In 1682 Illinois became a possession of the French crown, a dependency of Canada, and a part of Louisiana. In 1765 the English flag was run up on old Fort Chartres, and Illinois was counted among the treasures of Great Britain.

In 1779 it was taken from the English by Col. George Rogers Clark. This man was resolute in nature, wise in council, prudent in policy, bold in action, and heroic in danger. Few men who have figured in the history of America are more deserving than this colonel. Nothing short of first-class ability could have rescued Vincens and all Illinois from the English. And it is not possible to over-estimate the influence of this achievement upon the republic. In 1779 Illinois became a part of Virginia. It was soon known as Illinois County. In 1784 Virginia ceded all this territory to the general government, to be cut into States, to be republican in form, with "the same right of sovereignty, freedom, and independence as the other States."

In 1787 it was the object of the wisest and ablest legislation found in any merely human records. No man can study the secret history of

THE "COMPACT OF 1787,"

and not feel that Providence was guiding with sleepless eye these unborn States. The ordinance that on July 13, 1787, finally became the incorporating act, has a most marvelous history. Jefferson had vainly tried to secure a system of government for the northwestern territory. He was an emancipationist of that day, and favored the exclusion of slavery from the territory Virginia had ceded to the general government; but the South voted him down as often as it came up. In 1787, as late as July 10, an organizing act without the anti-slavery clause was pending. This concession to the South was expected to carry it. Congress was in session in New York City. On July 5, Rev. Dr. Manasseh Cutler, of Massachusetts, came into New York to lobby on the northwestern territory. Everything seemed to fall into his hands. Events were ripe.

The state of the public credit, the growing of Southern prejudice, the basis of his mission, his personal character, all combined to complete one of those sudden and marvelous revolutions of public sentiment that once in five or ten centuries are seen to sweep over a country like the breath of the Almighty. Cutler was a graduate of Yale—received his A.M. from Harvard, and his D.D. from Yale. He had studied and taken degrees in the three learned professions, medicine, law, and divinity. He had thus America's best indorsement. He had published a scientific examination of the plants of New England. His name stood second only to that of Franklin as a scientist in America. He was a courtly gentleman of the old style, a man of commanding presence, and of inviting face. The Southern members said they had never seen such a gentleman in the North. He came representing a company that desired to purchase a tract of land now included in Ohio, for the purpose of planting a colony. It was a speculation. Government money was worth eighteen cents on the dollar. This Massachusetts company had collected enough to purchase 1,500,000 acres of land. Other speculators in New York made Dr. Cutler their agent (lobbyist). On the 12th he represented a demand for 5,500,000 acres. This would reduce the national debt. Jefferson and Virginia were regarded as authority concerning the land Virginia had just ceded. Jefferson's policy wanted to provide for the public credit, and this was a good opportunity to do something.

Massachusetts then owned the territory of Maine, which she was crowding on the market. She was opposed to opening the northwestern region. This fired the zeal of Virginia. The South caught the inspiration, and all exalted Dr. Cutler. The English minister invited him to dine with some of the Southern gentlemen. He was the center of interest.

The entire South rallied round him. Massachusetts could not vote against him, because many of the constituents of her members were interested personally in the western speculation. Thus Cutler, making friends with the South, and, doubtless, using all the arts of the lobby, was enabled to command the situation. True to deeper convictions, he dictated one of the most compact and finished documents of wise statesmanship that has ever adorned any human law book. He borrowed from Jefferson the term "Articles of Compact," which, preceding the federal constitution, rose into the most sacred character. He then followed very closely the constitution of Massachusetts, adopted three years before. Its most marked points were:

1. The exclusion of slavery from the territory forever.

2. Provision for public schools, giving one township for a seminary,

and every section numbered 16 in each township; that is, one-thirty-sixth of all the land, for public schools.

3. A provision prohibiting the adoption of any constitution or the enactment of any law that should nullify pre-existing contracts.

Be it forever remembered that this compact declared that "Religion, morality, and knowledge being necessary to good government and the happiness of mankind, schools and the means of education shall always be encouraged."

Dr. Cutler planted himself on this platform and would not yield. Giving his unqualified declaration that it was that or nothing—that unless they could make the land desirable they did not want it—he took his horse and buggy, and started for the constitutional convention in Philadelphia. On July 13, 1787, the bill was put upon its passage, and was unanimously adopted, every Southern member voting for it, and only one man, Mr. Yates, of New York, voting against it. But as the States voted as States, Yates lost his vote, and the compact was put beyond repeal.

Thus the great States of Ohio, Indiana, Illinois, Michigan and Wisconsin—a vast empire, the heart of the great valley—were consecrated to freedom, intelligence, and honesty. Thus the great heart of the nation was prepared for a year and a day and an hour. In the light of these eighty-nine years I affirm that this act was the salvation of the republic and the destruction of slavery. Soon the South saw their great blunder, and tried to repeal the compact. In 1803 Congress referred it to a committee of which John Randolph was chairman. He reported that this ordinance was a compact, and opposed repeal. Thus it stood a rock, in the way of the on-rushing sea of slavery.

With all this timely aid it was, after all, a most desperate and protracted struggle to keep the soil of Illinois sacred to freedom. It was the natural battle-field for the irrepressible conflict. In the southern end of the State slavery preceded the compact. It existed among the old French settlers, and was hard to eradicate. The southern part of the State was settled from the slave States, and this population brought their laws, customs, and institutions with them. A stream of population from the North poured into the northern part of the State. These sections misunderstood and hated each other perfectly. The Southerners regarded the Yankees as a skinning, tricky, penurious race of peddlers, filling the country with tinware, brass clocks, and wooden nutmegs. The Northerner thought of the Southerner as a lean, lank, lazy creature, burrowing in a hut, and rioting in whisky, dirt and ignorance. These causes aided in making the struggle long and bitter. So strong was the sympathy with slavery that, in spite of the ordinance of 1787, and in spite of the deed of cession, it was determined to allow the old French settlers to retain their slaves. Planters from the slave States might bring their slaves, if they would give them a chance to choose freedom or years of service and bondage for their children till they should become thirty years of age. If they chose freedom they must leave the State in sixty days or be sold as fugitives. Servants were whipped for offenses for which white men are fined. Each lash paid forty cents of the fine. A negro ten miles from home without a pass was whipped. These famous laws were imported from the slave States just as they imported laws for the inspection of flax and wool when there was neither in the State.

These Black Laws are now wiped out. A vigorous effort was made to protect slavery in the State Constitution of 1817. It barely failed. It was renewed in 1825, when a convention was asked to make a new constitution. After a hard fight the convention was defeated. But slaves did not disappear from the census of the State until 1850. There were mobs and murders in the interest of slavery. Lovejoy was added to the list of martyrs—a sort of first-fruits of that long life of immortal heroes who saw freedom as the one supreme desire of their souls, and were so enamored of her that they preferred to die rather than survive her.

The population of 12.282 that occupied the territory in A.D. 1800, increased to 45,000 in A.D. 1818, when the State Constitution was adopted, and Illinois took her place in the Union, with a star on the flag and two votes in the Senate.

Shadrach Bond was the first Governor, and in his first message he recommended the construction of the Illinois and Michigan Canal.

The simple economy in those days is seen in the fact that the entire bill for stationery for the first Legislature was only $13.50. Yet this simple body actually enacted a very superior code.

There was no money in the territory before the war of 1812. Deer skins and coon skins were the circulating medium. In 1821, the Legislature ordained a State Bank on the credit of the State. It issued notes in the likeness of bank bills. These notes were made a legal tender for every thing, and the bank was ordered to loan to the people $100 on personal security, and more on mortgages. They actually passed a resolution requesting the Secretary of the Treasury of the United States to receive these notes for land. The old French Lieutenant Governor, Col. Menard, put the resolution as follows: "Gentlemen of the Senate: It is moved and seconded dat de notes of dis bank be made land-office money. All in favor of dat motion say aye; all against it say no. It is decided in de affirmative. Now, gentlemen, I bet you one hundred dollar he never be land-office money!" Hard sense, like hard money, is always above par.   ⋅

This old Frenchman presents a fine figure up against the dark background of most of his nation.. They made no progress. They clung to their earliest and simplest implements. They never wore hats or caps.

They pulled their blankets over their heads in the winter like the Indians, with whom they freely intermingled.

Demagogism had an early development. One John Grammar (only in name), elected to the Territorial and State Legislatures of 1816 and 1836, invented the policy of opposing every new thing, saying, "If it succeeds, no one will ask who voted against it. If it proves a failure, he could quote its record." In sharp contrast with Grammar was the character of D. P. Cook, after whom the county containing Chicago was named. Such was his transparent integrity and remarkable ability that his will was almost the law of the State. In Congress, a young man, and from a poor State, he was made Chairman of the Ways and Means Committee. He was pre-eminent for standing by his committee, regardless of consequences. It was his integrity that elected John Quincy Adams to the Presidency. There were four candidates in 1824, Jackson, Clay, Crawford, and John Quincy Adams. There being no choice by the people, the election was thrown into the House. It was so balanced that it turned on his vote, and that he cast for Adams, electing him; then went home to face the wrath of the Jackson party in Illinois. It cost him all but character and greatness. It is a suggestive comment on the times, that there was no legal interest till 1830. It often reached 150 per cent., usually 50 per cent. Then it was reduced to 12, and now to 10 per cent.

PHYSICAL FEATURES OF THE PRAIRIE STATE.

In area the State has 55,410 square miles of territory. It is about 150 miles wide and 400 miles long, stretching in latitude from Maine to North Carolina. It embraces wide variety of climate. It is tempered on the north by the great inland, saltless, tideless sea, which keeps the thermometer from either extreme. Being a table land, from 600 to 1,000 feet above the level of the sea, one is prepared to find on the health maps, prepared by the general government, an almost clean and perfect record. In freedom from fever and malarial diseases and consumptions, the three deadly enemies of the American Saxon, Illinois, as a State, stands without a superior. She furnishes one of the essential conditions of a great people—sound bodies. I suspect that this fact lies back of that old Delaware word, Illini, superior men.

The great battles of history that have been determinative of dynasties and destinies have been strategical battles, chiefly the question of position. Thermopylæ has been the war-cry of freemen for twenty-four centuries. It only tells how much there may be in position. All this advantage belongs to Illinois. It is in the heart of the greatest valley in the world, the vast region between the mountains—a valley that could feed mankind for one thousand years. It is well on toward the center of the continent. It is in the great temperate belt, in which have been found nearly all the aggressive civilizations of history. It has sixty-five miles of frontage on the head of the lake. With the Mississippi forming the western and southern boundary, with the Ohio running along the southeastern line, with the Illinois River and Canal dividing the State diagonally from the lake to the Lower Mississippi, and with the Rock and Wabash Rivers furnishing altogether 2,000 miles of water-front, connecting with, and running through, in all about 12,000 miles, of navigable water.

But this is not all. These waters are made most available by the fact that the lake and the State lie on the ridge running into the great valley from the east. Within cannon-shot of the lake the water runs away from the lake to the Gulf. The lake now empties at both ends, one into the Atlantic and one into the Gulf of Mexico. The lake thus seems to hang over the land. This makes the dockage most serviceable; there are no steep banks to damage it. Both lake and river are made for use.

The climate varies from Portland to Richmond; it favors every product of the continent, including the tropics, with less than half a dozen exceptions. It produces every great nutriment of the world except bananas and rice. It is hardly too much to say that it is the most productive spot known to civilization. With the soil full of bread and the earth full of minerals: with an upper surface of food and an under layer of fuel; with perfect natural drainage, and abundant springs and streams and navigable rivers; half way between the forests of the North and the fruits of the South; within a day's ride of the great deposits of iron, coal, copper, lead, and zinc; containing and controlling the great grain, cattle, pork, and lumber markets of the world, it is not strange that Illinois has the advantage of position.

This advantage has been supplemented by the character of the population. In the early days when Illinois was first admitted to the Union, her population were chiefly from Kentucky and Virginia. But, in the conflict of ideas concerning slavery, a strong tide of emigration came in from the East, and soon changed this composition. In 1870 her non-native population were from colder soils. New York furnished 133,290; Ohio gave 162,623; Pennsylvania sent on 98,352; the entire South gave us only 206,734. In all her cities, and in all her German and Scandinavian and other foreign colonies, Illinois has only about one-fifth of her people of foreign birth.

PROGRESS OF DEVELOPMENT.

One of the greatest elements in the early development of Illinois is the Illinois and Michigan Canal, connecting the Illinois and Mississippi Rivers with the lakes. It was of the utmost importance to the State. It was recommended by Gov. Bond, the first governor, in his first message. In 1821, the Legislature appropriated $10,000 for surveying the route. Two bright young engineers surveyed it, and estimated the cost at $600,000 or $700,000. It finally cost $8,000,000. In 1825, a law was passed to incorporate the Canal Company, but no stock was sold. In 1826, upon the solicitation of Cook, Congress gave 800,000 acres of land on the line of the work. In 1828, another law—commissioners appointed, and work commenced with new survey and new estimates. In 1834–35, George Farquhar made an able report on the whole matter. This was, doubtless, the ablest report ever made to a western legislature, and it became the model for subsequent reports and action. From this the work went on till it was finished in 1848. It cost the State a large amount of money; but it gave to the industries of the State an impetus that pushed it up into the first rank of greatness. It was not built as a speculation any more than a doctor is employed on a speculation. But it has paid into the Treasury of the State an average annual net sum of over $111,000.

Pending the construction of the canal, the land and town-lot fever broke out in the State, in 1834–35. It took on the malignant type in Chicago, lifting the town up into a city. The disease spread over the entire State and adjoining States. It was epidemic. It cut up men's farms without regard to locality, and cut up the purses of the purchasers without regard to consequences. It is estimated that building lots enough were sold in Indiana alone to accommodate every citizen then in the United States.

Towns and cities were exported to the Eastern market by the ship-load. There was no lack of buyers. Every up-ship came freighted with speculators and their money.

This distemper seized upon the Legislature in 1836–37, and left not one to tell the tale. They enacted a system of internal improvement without a parallel in the grandeur of its conception. They ordered the construction of 1,300 miles of railroad, crossing the State in all directions. This was surpassed by the river and canal improvements. There were a few counties not touched by either railroad or river or canal, and those were to be comforted and compensated by the free distribution of $200,000 among them. To inflate this balloon beyond credence it was ordered that work should be commenced on both ends of

each of these railroads and rivers, and at each river-crossing, all at the
same time. The appropriations for these vast improvements were over
$12,000,000, and commissioners were appointed to borrow the money on
the credit of the State. Remember that all this was in the early days of
railroading, when railroads were luxuries; that the State had whole
counties with scarcely a cabin ; and that the population of the State was
less than 400,000, and you can form some idea of the vigor with which
these brave men undertook the work of making a great State. In the
light of history I am compelled to say that this was only a premature
throb of the power that actually slumbered in the soil of the State. It
was Hercules in the cradle.

At this juncture the State Bank loaned its funds largely to Godfrey
Gilman & Co., and to other leading houses, for the purpose of drawing
trade from St. Louis to Alton. Soon they failed, and took down the
bank with them.

In 1840, all hope seemed gone. A population of 480,000 were loaded
with a debt of $14,000,000. It had only six small cities, really only
towns, namely: Chicago, Alton, Springfield, Quincy, Galena, Nauvoo.
This debt was to be cared for when there was not a dollar in the treasury, and when the State had borrowed itself out of all credit, and when
there was not good money enough in the hands of all the people to pay
the interest of the debt for a single year. Yet, in the presence of all
these difficulties, the young State steadily refused to repudiate. Gov..
Ford took hold of the problem and solved it, bringing the State through
in triumph.

Having touched lightly upon some of the more distinctive points in
the history of the development of Illinois, let us next briefly consider the

MATERIAL RESOURCES OF THE STATE.

It is a garden four hundred miles long and one hundred and fifty
miles wide. Its soil is chiefly a black sandy loam, from six inches to
sixty feet thick. On the American bottoms it has been cultivated for
one hundred and fifty years without renewal. About the old French
towns it has yielded corn for a century and a half without rest or help.
It produces nearly everything green in the temperate and tropical zones.
She leads all other States in the number of acres actually under plow.
Her products from 25,000,000 of acres are incalculable. Her mineral
wealth is scarcely second to her agricultural power. She has coal, iron,
lead, copper, zinc, many varieties of building stone, fire clay, cuma clay,
common brick clay, sand of all kinds, gravel, mineral paint—every thing
needed for a high civilization. Left to herself, she has the elements of
all greatness. The single item of coal is too vast for an appreciative

handling in figures. We can handle it in general terms like algebraical signs, but long before we get up into the millions and billions the human mind drops down from comprehension to mere symbolic apprehension.

When I tell you that nearly four-fifths of the entire State is underlaid with a deposit of coal more than forty feet thick on the average (now estimated, by recent surveys, at seventy feet thick), you can get some idea of its amount, as you do of the amount of the national debt. There it is! 41,000 square miles—one vast mine into which you could put any of the States; in which you could bury scores of European and ancient empires, and have room enough all round to work without knowing that they had been sepulchered there.

Put this vast coal-bed down by the other great coal deposits of the world, and its importance becomes manifest. Great Britain has 12,000 square miles of coal; Spain, 3,000; France, 1,719; Belgium, 578; Illinois about twice as many square miles as all combined. Virginia has 20,000 square miles; Pennsylvania, 16,000; Ohio, 12,000. Illinois has 41,000 square miles. One-seventh of all the known coal on this continent is in Illinois.

Could we sell the coal in this single State for one-seventh of one cent a ton it would pay the national debt. Converted into power, even with the wastage in our common engines, it would do more work than could be done by the entire race, beginning at Adam's wedding and working ten hours a day through all the centuries till the present time, and right on into the future at the same rate for the next 600,000 years.

Great Britain uses enough mechanical power to-day to give to each man, woman, and child in the kingdom the help and service of nineteen untiring servants. No wonder she has leisure and luxuries. No wonder the home of the common artisan has in it more luxuries than could be found in the palace of good old King Arthur. Think, if you can conceive of it, of the vast army of servants that slumber in the soil of Illinois, impatiently awaiting the call of Genius to come forth to minister to our comfort.

At the present rate of consumption England's coal supply will be exhausted in 250 years. When this is gone she must transfer her dominion either to the Indies, or to British America, which I would not resist; or to some other people, which I would regret as a loss to civilization.

COAL IS KING.

At the same rate of consumption (which far exceeds our own) the deposit of coal in Illinois will last 120,000 years. And her kingdom shall be an everlasting kingdom.

Let us turn now from this reserve power to the *annual products* of the State. We shall not be humiliated in this field. Here we strike the secret of our national credit. Nature provides a market in the constant appetite of the race. Men must eat, and if we can furnish the provisions we can command the treasure. All that a man hath will he give for his life.

According to the last census Illinois produced 30,000,000 of bushels of wheat. That is more wheat than was raised by any other State in the Union. She raised last year 130,000,000 of bushels of corn—twice as much as any other State, and one-sixth of all the corn raised in the United States. She harvested 2,747,000 tons of hay, nearly one-tenth of all the hay in the Republic. It is not generally appreciated, but it is true, that the hay crop of the country is worth more than the cotton crop. The hay of Illinois equals the cotton of Louisiana. Go to Charleston, S. C., and see them peddling handfuls of hay or grass, almost as a curiosity, as we regard Chinese gods or the cryolite of Greenland; drink your coffee and *condensed milk;* and walk back from the coast for many a league through the sand and burs till you get up into the better atmosphere of the mountains, without seeing a waving meadow or a grazing herd: then you will begin to appreciate the meadows of the Prairie State, where the grass often grows sixteen feet high.

The value of her farm implements is $211,000,000, and the value of her live stock is only second to the great State of New York. Last year she had 25,000,000 hogs, and packed 2,113,845, about one-half of all that were packed in the United States. This is no insignificant item. Pork is a growing demand of the old world. Since the laborers of Europe have gotten a taste of our bacon, and we have learned how to pack it dry in boxes, like dry goods, the world has become the market.

The hog is on the march into the future. His nose is ordained to uncover the secrets of dominion, and his feet shall be guided by the star of empire.

Illinois marketed $57,000,000 worth of slaughtered animals—more than any other State, and a seventh of all the States.

Be patient with me, and pardon my pride, and I will give you a list of some of the things in which Illinois excels all other States.

Depth and richness of soil; per cent. of good ground; acres of improved land; large farms—some farms contain from 40,000 to 60,000 acres of cultivated land. 40,000 acres of corn on a single farm; number of farmers; amount of wheat, corn, oats and honey produced; value of animals for slaughter; number of hogs; amount of pork; number of horses —three times as many as Kentucky, the horse State.

Illinois excels all other States in miles of railroads and in miles of postal service, and in money orders sold per annum, and in the amount of lumber sold in her markets.

Illinois is only second in many important matters. This sample list comprises a few of the more important: Permanent school fund (good for a young state); total income for educational purposes; number of publishers of books, maps, papers, etc.; value of farm products and implements, and of live stock; in tons of coal mined.

The shipping of Illinois is only second to New York. Out of one port during the business hours of the season of navigation she sends forth a vessel every ten minutes. This does not include canal boats, which go one every five minutes. No wonder she is only second in number of bankers and brokers or in physicians and surgeons.

She is third in colleges, teachers and schools; cattle, lead, hay, flax, sorghum and beeswax.

She is fourth in population, in children enrolled in public schools, in law schools, in butter, potatoes and carriages.

She is fifth in value of real and personal property, in theological seminaries and colleges exclusively for women, in milk sold, and in boots and shoes manufactured, and in book-binding.

She is only seventh in the production of wood, while she is the twelfth in area. Surely that is well done for the Prairie State. She now has much more wood and growing timber than she had thirty years ago.

A few leading industries will justify emphasis. She manufactures $205,000,000 worth of goods, which places her well up toward New York and Pennsylvania. The number of her manufacturing establishments increased from 1860 to 1870, 300 per cent.; capital employed increased 350 per cent., and the amount of product increased 400 per cent. She issued 5,500,000 copies of commercial and financial newspapers—only second to New York. She has 6,759 miles of railroad, thus leading all other States, worth $636,458,000, using 3,245 engines. and 67,712 cars, making a train long enough to cover one-tenth of the entire roads of the State. Her stations are only five miles apart. She carried last year 15,795,000 passengers, an average of 36½ miles, or equal to taking her entire population twice across the State. More than two-thirds of her land is within five miles of a railroad, and less than two per cent. is more than fifteen miles away.

The State has a large financial interest in the Illinois Central railroad. The road was incorporated in 1850, and the State gave each alternate section for six miles on each side, and doubled the price of the remaining land, so keeping herself good. The road received 2,595,000 acres of land, and pays to the State one-seventh of the gross receipts. The State receives this year $350,000, and has received in all about $7,000,000. It is practically the people's road, and it has a most able and gentlemanly management. Add to this the annual receipts from the canal, $111,000, and a large per cent. of the State tax is provided for.

THE RELIGION AND MORALS

of the State keep step with her productions and growth. She was born of the missionary spirit. It was a minister who secured for her the ordinance of 1787, by which she has been saved from slavery, ignorance, and dishonesty. Rev. Mr. Wiley, pastor of a Scotch congregation in Randolph County, petitioned the Constitutional Convention of 1818 to recognize Jesus Christ as king, and the Scriptures as the only necessary guide and book of law. The convention did not act in the case, and the old Covenanters refused to accept citizenship. They never voted until 1824, when the slavery question was submitted to the people; then they all voted against it and cast the determining votes. Conscience has predominated whenever a great moral question has been submitted to the people.

But little mob violence has ever been felt in the State. In 1817 regulators disposed of a band of horse-thieves that infested the territory. The Mormon indignities finally awoke the same spirit. Alton was also the scene of a pro-slavery mob, in which Lovejoy was added to the list of martyrs. The moral sense of the people makes the law supreme, and gives to the State unruffled peace.

With $22,300,000 in church property, and 4,298 church organizations, the State has that divine police, the sleepless patrol of moral ideas, that alone is able to secure perfect safety. Conscience takes the knife from the assassin's hand and the bludgeon from the grasp of the highwayman. We sleep in safety, not because we are behind bolts and bars—these only fence against the innocent; not because a lone officer drowses on a distant corner of a street; not because a sheriff may call his posse from a remote part of the county; but because *conscience* guards the very portals of the air and stirs in the deepest recesses of the public mind. This spirit issues within the State 9,500,000 copies of religious papers annually, and receives still more from without. Thus the crime of the State is only one-fourth that of New York and one-half that of Pennsylvania.

Illinois never had but one duel between her own citizens. In Belleville, in 1820, Alphonso Stewart and William Bennett arranged to vindicate injured honor. The seconds agreed to make it a sham, and make them shoot blanks. Stewart was in the secret. Bennett mistrusted something, and, unobserved, slipped a bullet into his gun and killed Stewart. He then fled the State. After two years he was caught, tried, convicted, and, in spite of friends and political aid, was hung. This fixed the code of honor on a Christian basis, and terminated its use in Illinois.

The early preachers were ignorant men, who were accounted eloquent according to the strength of their voices. But they set the style for all public speakers. Lawyers and political speakers followed this rule. Gov.

Ford says: "Nevertheless, these first preachers were of incalculable benefit to the country. They inculcated justice and morality. To them are we indebted for the first Christian character of the Protestant portion of the people."

In education Illinois surpasses her material resources. The ordinance of 1787 consecrated one thirty-sixth of her soil to common schools, and the law of 1818, the first law that went upon her statutes, gave three per cent. of all the rest to

EDUCATION INSTEAD OF HIGHWAYS.

The old compact secures this interest forever, and by its yoking morality and intelligence it precludes the legal interference with the Bible in the public schools. With such a start it is natural that we should have 11,050 schools, and that our illiteracy should be less than New York or Pennsylvania, and only about one-half of Massachusetts. We are not to blame for not having more than one-half as many idiots as the great States. These public schools soon made colleges inevitable. The first college, still flourishing, was started in Lebanon in 1828, by the M. E. church, and named after Bishop McKendree. Illinois College, at Jacksonville, supported by the Presbyterians, followed in 1830. In 1832 the Baptists built Shurtleff College, at Alton. Then the Presbyterians built Knox College, at Galesburg, in 1838, and the Episcopalians built Jubilee College, at Peoria, in 1847. After these early years colleges have rained down. A settler could hardly encamp on the prairie but a college would spring up by his wagon. The State now has one very well endowed and equipped university, namely, the Northwestern University, at Evanston, with six colleges, ninety instructors, over 1,000 students, and $1,500,000 endowment.

Rev. J. M. Peck was the first educated Protestant minister in the State. He settled at Rock Spring, in St. Clair County, 1820, and left his impress on the State. Before 1837 only party papers were published, but Mr. Peck published a Gazetteer of Illinois. Soon after John Russell, of Bluffdale, published essays and tales showing genius. Judge James Hall published *The Illinois Monthly Magazine* with great ability, and an annual called *The Western Souvenir*, which gave him an enviable fame all over the United States. From these beginnings Illinois has gone on till she has more volumes in public libraries even than Massachusetts, and of the 44,500,000 volumes in all the public libraries of the United States, she has one-thirteenth. In newspapers she stands fourth. Her increase is marvelous. In 1850 she issued 5,000,000 copies; in 1860, 27,590,000; in 1870, 113,140,000. In 1860 she had eighteen colleges and seminaries; in 1870 she had eighty. That is a grand advance for the war decade.

This brings us to a record unsurpassed in the history of any age,

THE WAR RECORD OF ILLINOIS.

I hardly know where to begin, or how to advance, or what to say. I can at best give you only a broken synopsis of her deeds, and you must put them in the order of glory for yourself. Her sons have always been foremost on fields of danger. In 1832-33, at the call of Gov. Reynolds, her sons drove Blackhawk over the Mississippi.

When the Mexican war came, in May, 1846, 8,370 men offered themselves when only 3,720 could be accepted. The fields of Buena Vista and Vera Cruz, and the storming of Cerro Gordo, will carry the glory of Illinois soldiers along after the infamy of the cause they served has been forgotten. But it was reserved till our day for her sons to find a field and cause and foemen that could fitly illustrate their spirit and heroism. Illinois put into her own regiments for the United States government 256,000 men, and into the army through other States enough to swell the number to 290,000. This far exceeds all the soldiers of the federal government in all the war of the revolution. Her total years of service were over 600,000. She enrolled men from eighteen to forty-five years of age when the law of Congress in 1864—the test time—only asked for those from twenty to forty-five. Her enrollment was otherwise excessive. Her people wanted to go, and did not take the pains to correct the enrollment. Thus the basis of fixing the quota was too great, and then the quota itself, at least in the trying time, was far above any other State.

Thus the demand on some counties, as Monroe, for example, took every able-bodied man in the county, and then did not have enough to fill the quota. Moreover, Illinois sent 20,844 men for ninety or one hundred days, for whom no credit was asked. When Mr. Lincoln's attention was called to the inequality of the quota compared with other States, he replied, "The country needs the sacrifice. We must put the whip on the free horse." In spite of all these disadvantages Illinois gave to the country 73,000 years of service above all calls. With one-thirteenth of the population of the loyal States, she sent regularly one-tenth of all the soldiers, and in the peril of the closing calls, when patriots were few and weary, she then sent one-eighth of all that were called for by her loved and honored son in the white house. Her mothers and daughters went into the fields to raise the grain and keep the children together, while the fathers and older sons went to the harvest fields of the world. I knew a father and four sons who agreed that one of them must stay at home; and they pulled straws from a stack to see who might go. The father was left. The next day he came into the camp, saying: "Mother says she can get the crops in, and I am going, too." I know large Methodist churches from which every male member went to the army. Do you want to know

what these heroes from Illinois did in the field? Ask any soldier with a
good record of his own, who is thus able to judge, and he will tell you
that the Illinois men went in to win. It is common history that the greater
victories were won in the West. When everything else looked dark Illinois was gaining victories all down the river, and dividing the confederacy.
Sherman took with him on his great march forty-five regiments of Illinois
infantry, three companies of artillery, and one company of cavalry. He
could not avoid

GOING TO THE SEA.

If he had been killed, I doubt not the men would have gone right on.
Lincoln answered all rumors of Sherman's defeat with, "It is impossible;
there is a mighty sight of fight in 100,000 Western men." Illinois soldiers
brought home 300 battle-flags. The first United States flag that floated
over Richmond was an Illinois flag. She sent messengers and nurses to
every field and hospital, to care for her sick and wounded sons. She said,
" These suffering ones are my sons, and I will care for them."

When individuals had given all, then cities and towns came forward
with their credit to the extent of many millions, to aid these men and
their families.

Illinois gave the country the great general of the war—Ulysses S.
Grant—since honored with two terms of the Presidency of the United
States.

One other name from Illinois comes up in all minds, embalmed in all
hearts, that must have the supreme place in this story of our glory and
of our nation's honor; that name is Abraham Lincoln, of Illinois.

The analysis of Mr. Lincoln's character is difficult on account of its
symmetry.

In this age we look with admiration at his uncompromising honesty.
And well we may, for this saved us. Thousands throughout the length
and breadth of our country who knew him only as "Honest Old Abe,"
voted for him on that account; and wisely did they choose, for no other
man could have carried us through the fearful night of the war. When
his plans were too vast for our comprehension, and his faith in the cause
too sublime for our participation; when it was all night about us, and all
dread before us, and all sad and desolate behind us; when not one ray
shone upon our cause; when traitors were haughty and exultant at the
South, and fierce and blasphemous at the North; when the loyal men here
seemed almost in the minority; when the stoutest heart quailed, the bravest
cheek paled; when generals were defeating each other for place, and
contractors were leeching out the very heart's blood of the prostrate
republic: when every thing else had failed us, we looked at this calm,
patient man standing like a rock in the storm, and said: "Mr. Lincoln

3

is honest, and we can trust him still." Holding to this single point with the energy of faith and despair we held together, and, under God, he brought us through to victory.

His practical wisdom made him the wonder of all lands. With such certainty did Mr. Lincoln follow causes to their ultimate effects, that his foresight of contingencies seemed almost prophetic.

He is radiant with all the great virtues, and his memory shall shed a glory upon this age that shall fill the eyes of men as they look into history. Other men have excelled him in some point, but, taken at all points, all in all, he stands head and shoulders above every other man of 6,000 years. An administrator, he saved the nation in the perils of unparalleled civil war. A statesman, he justified his measures by their success. A philanthropist, he gave liberty to one race and salvation to another. A moralist, he bowed from the summit of human power to the foot of the Cross, and became a Christian. A mediator, he exercised mercy under the most absolute abeyance to law. A leader, he was no partisan. A commander, he was untainted with blood. A ruler in desperate times, he was unsullied with crime. A man, he has left no word of passion, no thought of malice, no trick of craft, no act of jealousy, no purpose of selfish ambition. Thus perfected, without a model, and without a peer, he was dropped into these troubled years to adorn and embellish all that is good and all that is great in our humanity, and to present to all coming time the representative of the divine idea of free government.

It is not too much to say that away down in the future, when the republic has fallen from its niche in the wall of time ; when the great war itself shall have faded out in the distance like a mist on the horizon ; when the Anglo-Saxon language shall be spoken only by the tongue of the stranger ; then the generations looking this way shall see the great president as the supreme figure in this vortex of history.

CHICAGO.

It is impossible in our brief space to give more than a meager sketch of such a city as Chicago, which is in itself the greatest marvel of the Prairie State. This mysterious, majestic, mighty city, born first of water, and next of fire ; sown in weakness, and raised in power ; planted among the willows of the marsh, and crowned with the glory of the mountains ; sleeping on the bosom of the prairie, and rocked on the bosom of the sea ; the youngest city of the world, and still the eye of the prairie, as Damascus, the oldest city of the world, is the eye of the desert. With a commerce far exceeding that of Corinth on her isthmus, in the highway to the East ; with the defenses of a continent piled around her by the thousand miles, making her far safer than Rome on the banks of the Tiber ;

with schools eclipsing Alexandria and Athens; with liberties more conspicuous than those of the old republics; with a heroism equal to the first Carthage, and with a sanctity scarcely second to that of Jerusalem—set your thoughts on all this, lifted into the eyes of all men by the miracle of its growth, illuminated by the flame of its fall, and transfigured by the divinity of its resurrection, and you will feel, as I do, the utter impossibility of compassing this subject as it deserves. Some impression of her importance is received from the shock her burning gave to the civilized world.

When the doubt of her calamity was removed, and the horrid fact was accepted, there went a shudder over all cities, and a quiver over all lands. There was scarcely a town in the civilized world that did not shake on the brink of this opening chasm. The flames of our homes reddened all skies. The city was set upon a hill, and could not be hid. All eyes were turned upon it. To have struggled and suffered amid the scenes of its fall is as distinguishing as to have fought at Thermopylæ, or Salamis, or Hastings, or Waterloo, or Bunker Hill.

Its calamity amazed the world, because it was felt to be the common property of mankind.

The early history of the city is full of interest, just as the early history of such a man as Washington or Lincoln becomes public property, and is cherished by every patriot.

Starting with 560 acres in 1833, it embraced and occupied 23,000 acres in 1869, and, having now a population of more than 500,000, it commands general attention.

The first settler—Jean Baptiste Pointe au Sable, a mulatto from the West Indies—came and began trade with the Indians in 1796. John Kinzie became his successor in 1804, in which year Fort Dearborn was erected.

A mere trading-post was kept here from that time till about the time of the Blackhawk war, in 1832. It was not the city. It was merely a cock crowing at midnight. The morning was not yet. In 1833 the settlement about the fort was incorporated as a town. The voters were divided on the propriety of such corporation, twelve voting for it and one against it. Four years later it was incorporated as a city, and embraced 560 acres.

The produce handled in this city is an indication of its power. Grain and flour were imported from the East till as late as 1837. The first exportation by way of experiment was in 1839. Exports exceeded imports first in 1842. The Board of Trade was organized in 1848, but it was so weak that it needed nursing till 1855. Grain was purchased by the wagon-load in the street.

I remember sitting with my father on a load of wheat, in the long line of wagons along Lake street, while the buyers came and untied the bags, and examined the grain, and made their bids. That manner of business had to cease with the day of small things. Now our elevators will hold 15,000,000 bushels of grain. The cash value of the produce handled in a year is $215,000,000, and the produce weighs 7,000,000 tons or 700,000 car loads. This handles thirteen and a half ton each minute, all the year round. One tenth of all the wheat in the United States is handled in Chicago. Even as long ago as 1853 the receipts of grain in Chicago exceeded those of the goodly city of St. Louis, and in 1854 the exports of grain from Chicago exceeded those of New York and doubled those of St. Petersburg, Archangel, or Odessa, the largest grain markets in Europe.

The manufacturing interests of the city are not contemptible. In 1873 manufactories employed 45,000 operatives; in 1876, 60,000. The manufactured product in 1875 was worth $177,000,000.

No estimate of the size and power of Chicago would be adequate that did not put large emphasis on the railroads. Before they came thundering along our streets canals were the hope of our country. But who ever thinks now of traveling by canal packets? In June, 1852, there were only forty miles of railroad connected with the city. The old Galena division of the Northwestern ran out to Elgin. But now, who can count the trains and measure the roads that seek a terminus or connection in this city? The lake stretches away to the north, gathering in to this center all the harvests that might otherwise pass to the north of us. If you will take a map and look at the adjustment of railroads, you will see, first, that Chicago is the great railroad center of the world, as New York is the commercial city of this continent; and, second, that the railroad lines form the iron spokes of a great wheel whose hub is this city. The lake furnishes the only break in the spokes, and this seems simply to have pushed a few spokes together on each shore. See the eighteen trunk lines, exclusive of eastern connections.

Pass round the circle, and view their numbers and extent. There is the great Northwestern, with all its branches, one branch creeping along the lake shore, and so reaching to the north, into the Lake Superior regions, away to the right, and on to the Northern Pacific on the left, swinging around Green Bay for iron and copper and silver, twelve months in the year, and reaching out for the wealth of the great agricultural belt and isothermal line traversed by the Northern Pacific. Another branch, not so far north, feeling for the heart of the Badger State. Another pushing lower down the Mississippi—all these make many connections, and tapping all the vast wheat regions of Minnesota, Wisconsin, Iowa, and all the regions this side of sunset. There is that elegant road, the Chicago, Burlington & Quincy, running out a goodly number of branches, and reaping the great fields this side of the Missouri River. I can only mention the Chicago, Alton & St. Louis, our Illinois Central, described elsewhere, and the Chicago & Rock Island. Further around we come to the lines connecting us with all the eastern cities. The Chicago, Indianapolis & St. Louis, the Pittsburgh, Fort Wayne & Chicago, the Lake Shore & Michigan Southern, and the Michigan Central and Great Western, give us many highways to the seaboard. Thus we reach the Mississippi at five points, from St. Paul to Cairo and the Gulf itself by two routes. We also reach Cincinnati and Baltimore, and Pittsburgh and Philadelphia, and New York. North and south run the water courses of the lakes and the rivers, broken just enough at this point to make a pass. Through this, from east to west, run the long lines that stretch from ocean to ocean.

This is the neck of the glass, and the golden sands of commerce must pass into our hands. Altogether we have more than 10,000 miles of railroad, directly tributary to this city, seeking to unload their wealth in our coffers. All these roads have come themselves by the infallible instinct of capital. Not a dollar was ever given by the city to secure one of them, and only a small per cent. of stock taken originally by her citizens, and that taken simply as an investment. Coming in the natural order of events, they will not be easily diverted.

There is still another showing to all this. The connection between New York and San Francisco is by the middle route. This passes inevitably through Chicago. St. Louis wants the Southern Pacific or Kansas Pacific, and pushes it out through Denver, and so on up to Cheyenne. But before the road is fairly under way, the Chicago roads shove out to Kansas City, making even the Kansas Pacific a feeder, and actually leaving St. Louis out in the cold. It is not too much to expect that Dakota, Montana, and Washington Territory will find their great market in Chicago.

But these are not all. Perhaps I had better notice here the ten or fifteen new roads that have just entered, or are just entering, our city. Their names are all that is necessary to give. Chicago & St. Paul, looking up the Red River country to the British possessions; the Chicago, Atlantic & Pacific; the Chicago, Decatur & State Line; the Baltimore & Ohio; the Chicago, Danville & Vincennes; the Chicago & LaSalle Railroad; the Chicago, Pittsburgh & Cincinnati; the Chicago and Canada Southern; the Chicago and Illinois River Railroad. These, with their connections, and with the new connections of the old roads, already in process of erection, give to Chicago not less than 10,000 miles of new tributaries from the richest land on the continent. Thus there will be added to the reserve power, to the capital within reach of this city, not less than $1,000,000,000.

Add to all this transporting power the ships that sail one every nine minutes of the business hours of the season of navigation ; add, also, the canal boats that leave one every five minutes during the same time—and you will see something of the business of the city.

THE COMMERCE OF THIS CITY

has been leaping along to keep pace with the growth of the country around us. In 1852, our commerce reached the hopeful sum of $20.000,000. In 1870 it reached $400,000.000. In 1871 it was pushed up above $450,000,000. And in 1875 it touched nearly double that.

One-half of our imported goods come directly to Chicago. Grain enough is exported directly from our docks to the old world to employ a semi-weekly line of steamers of 3,000 tons capacity. This branch is not likely to be greatly developed. Even after the great Welland Canal is completed we shall have only fourteen feet of water. The great ocean vessels will continue to control the trade.

The banking capital of Chicago is $24,431,000. Total exchange in 1875. $659.000,000. Her wholesale business in 1875 was $294,000,000. The rate of taxes is less than in any other great city.

The schools of Chicago are unsurpassed in America. Out of a population of 300,000 there were only 186 persons between the ages of six and twenty-one unable to read. This is the best known record.

In 1831 the mail system was condensed into a half-breed, who went on foot to Niles, Mich., once in two weeks, and brought back what papers and news he could find. As late as 1846 there was often only one mail a week. A post-office was established in Chicago in 1833, and the post-master nailed up old boot-legs on one side of his shop to serve as boxes for the nabobs and literary men.

It is an interesting fact in the growth of the young city that in the active life of the business men of that day the mail matter has grown to a daily average of over 6,500 pounds. It speaks equally well for the intelligence of the people and the commercial importance of the place, that the mail matter distributed to the territory immediately tributary to Chicago is seven times greater than that distributed to the territory immediately tributary to St. Louis.

The improvements that have characterized the city are as startling as the city itself. In 1831, Mark Beaubien established a ferry over the river, and put himself under bonds to carry all the citizens free for the privilege of charging strangers. Now there are twenty-four large bridges and two tunnels.

In 1833 the government expended $30,000 on the harbor. Then commenced that series of manœuvers with the river that has made it one of the world's curiosities. It used to wind around in the lower end of the town, and make its way rippling over the sand into the lake at the foot of Madison street. They took it up and put it down where it now is. It was a narrow stream, so narrow that even moderately small crafts had to go up through the willows and cat's tails to the point near Lake street bridge, and back up one of the branches to get room enough in which to turn around.

In 1844 the quagmires in the streets were first pontooned by plank roads, which acted in wet weather as public squirt-guns. Keeping you out of the mud, they compromised by squirting the mud over you. The wooden-block pavements came to Chicago in 1857. In 1840 water was delivered by peddlers in carts or by hand. Then a twenty-five horse-power engine pushed it through hollow or bored logs along the streets till 1854, when it was introduced into the houses by new works. The first fire-engine was used in 1835, and the first steam fire-engine in 1859. Gas was utilized for lighting the city in 1850. The Young Men's Christian Association was organized in 1858, and horse railroads carried them to their work in 1859. The museum was opened in 1863. The alarm telegraph adopted in 1864. The opera-house built in 1865. The city grew from 560 acres in 1833 to 23,000 in 1869. In 1834, the taxes amounted to $48.90, and the trustees of the town borrowed $60 more for opening and improving streets. In 1835, the legislature authorized a loan of $2,000, and the treasurer and street commissioners resigned rather than plunge the town into such a gulf.

Now the city embraces 36 square miles of territory, and has 30 miles of water front, besides the outside harbor of refuge, of 400 acres, inclosed by a crib sea-wall. One-third of the city has been raised up an average of eight feet, giving good pitch to the 263 miles of sewerage. The water of the city is above all competition. It is received through two tunnels extending to a crib in the lake two miles from shore. The closest analysis fails to detect any impurities, and, received 35 feet below the surface, it is always clear and cold. The first tunnel is five feet two inches in diameter and two miles long, and can deliver 50,000,000 of gallons per day. The second tunnel is seven feet in diameter and six miles long, running four miles under the city, and can deliver 100,000,000 of gallons per day. This water is distributed through 410 miles of water-mains.

The three grand engineering exploits of the city are: First, lifting the city up on jack-screws, whole squares at a time, without interrupting the business, thus giving us good drainage; second, running the tunnels under the lake, giving us the best water in the world; and third, the turning the current of the river in its own channel, delivering us from the old abominations, and making decency possible. They redound about equally to the credit of the engineering, to the energy of the people, and to the health of the city.

That which really constitutes the city, its indescribable spirit, its soul, the way it lights up in every feature in the hour of action, has not been touched. In meeting strangers, one is often surprised how some homely women marry so well. Their forms are bad, their gait uneven and awkward, their complexion is dull, their features are misshapen and mismatched, and when we see them there is no beauty that we should desire them. But when once they are aroused on some subject, they put on new proportions. They light up into great power. The real person comes out from its unseemly ambush, and captures us at will. They have power. They have ability to cause things to come to pass. We no longer wonder why they are in such high demand. So it is with our city.

There is no grand scenery except the two seas, one of water, the other of prairie. Nevertheless, there is a spirit about it, a push, a breadth, a power, that soon makes it a place never to be forsaken. One soon ceases to believe in impossibilities. Balaams are the only prophets that are disappointed. The bottom that has been on the point of falling out has been there so long that it has grown fast. It can not fall out. It has all the capital of the world itching to get inside the corporation.

The two great laws that govern the growth and size of cities are, first, the amount of territory for which they are the distributing and receiving points; second, the number of medium or moderate dealers that do this distributing. Monopolists build up themselves, not the cities. They neither eat, wear, nor live in proportion to their business. Both these laws help Chicago.

The tide of trade is eastward—not up or down the map, but across the map. The lake runs up a wingdam for 500 miles to gather in the business. Commerce can not ferry up there for seven months in the year, and the facilities for seven months can do the work for twelve. Then the great region west of us is nearly all good, productive land. Dropping south into the trail of St. Louis, you fall into vast deserts and rocky districts, useful in holding the world together. St. Louis and Cincinnati, instead of rivaling and hurting Chicago, are her greatest sureties of dominion. They are far enough away to give sea-room,—farther off than Paris is from London,—and yet they are near enough to prevent the springing up of any other great city between them.

St. Louis will be helped by the opening of the Mississippi, but also hurt. That will put New Orleans on her feet, and with a railroad running over into Texas and so West, she will tap the streams that now crawl up the Texas and Missouri road. The current is East, not North, and a seaport at New Orleans can not permanently help St. Louis.

Chicago is in the field almost alone, to handle the wealth of one-fourth of the territory of this great republic. This strip of seacoast divides its margins between Portland, Boston, New York, Philadelphia, Baltimore and Savannah, or some other great port to be created for the South in the next decade. But Chicago has a dozen empires casting their treasures into her lap. On a bed of coal that can run all the machinery of the world for 500 centuries; in a garden that can feed the race by the thousand years; at the head of the lakes that give her a temperature as a summer resort equaled by no great city in the land; with a climate that insures the health of her citizens; surrounded by all the great deposits of natural wealth in mines and forests and herds, Chicago is the wonder of to-day, and will be *the city of the future.*

MASSACRE AT FORT DEARBORN.

During the war of 1812, Fort Dearborn became the theater of stirring events. The garrison consisted of fifty-four men under command of Captain Nathan Heald, assisted by Lieutenant Helm (son-in-law of Mrs. Kinzie) and Ensign Ronan. Dr. Voorhees was surgeon. The only residents at the post at that time were the wives of Captain Heald and Lieutenant Helm, and a few of the soldiers, Mr. Kinzie and his family, and a few Canadian *voyageurs*, with their wives and children. The soldiers and Mr. Kinzie were on most friendly terms with the Pottawattamies and Winnebagos, the principal tribes around them, but they could not win them from their attachment to the British.

One evening in April, 1812, Mr. Kinzie sat playing on his violin and his children were dancing to the music, when Mrs. Kinzie came rushing into the house, pale with terror, and exclaiming: "The Indians! the Indians!" "What? Where?" eagerly inquired Mr. Kinzie. "Up at Lee's, killing and scalping," answered the frightened mother, who, when the alarm was given, was attending Mrs. Barnes (just confined) living not far off. Mr. Kinzie and his family crossed the river and took refuge in the fort, to which place Mrs. Barnes and her infant not a day old were safely conveyed. The rest of the inhabitants took shelter in the fort. This alarm was caused by a scalping party of Winnebagos, who hovered about the fort several days, when they disappeared, and for several weeks the inhabitants were undisturbed.

On the 7th of August, 1812, General Hull, at Detroit, sent orders to Captain Heald to evacuate Fort Dearborn, and to distribute all the United States property to the Indians in the neighborhood—a most insane order. The Pottawattamie chief, who brought the dispatch, had more wisdom than the commanding general. He advised Captain Heald not to make the distribution. Said he: "Leave the fort and stores as they are, and let the Indians make distribution for themselves; and while they are engaged in the business, the white people may escape to Fort Wayne."

Captain Heald held a council with the Indians on the afternoon of the 12th, in which his officers refused to join, for they had been informed that treachery was designed—that the Indians intended to murder the white people in the council, and then destroy those in the fort. Captain Heald, however, took the precaution to open a port-hole displaying a cannon pointing directly upon the council, and by that means saved his life.

Mr. Kinzie, who knew the Indians well, begged Captain Heald not to confide in their promises, nor distribute the arms and munitions among them, for it would only put power into their hands to destroy the whites. Acting upon this advice, Heald resolved to withhold the munitions of war; and on the night of the 13th, after the distribution of the other property had been made, the powder, ball and liquors were thrown into the river, the muskets broken up and destroyed.

Black Partridge, a friendly chief, came to Captain Heald, and said: " Linden birds have been singing in my ears to-day: be careful on the march you are going to take." On that dark night vigilant Indians had crept near the fort and discovered the destruction of their promised booty going on within. The next morning the powder was seen floating on the surface of the river. The savages were exasperated and made loud complaints and threats.

On the following day when preparations were making to leave the fort, and all the inmates were deeply impressed with a sense of impending danger, Capt. Wells, an uncle of Mrs. Heald, was discovered upon the Indian trail among the sand-hills on the borders of the lake, not far distant, with a band of mounted Miamis, of whose tribe he was chief, having been adopted by the famous Miami warrior, Little Turtle. When news of Hull's surrender reached Fort Wayne, he had started with this force to assist Heald in defending Fort Dearborn. He was too late. Every means for its defense had been destroyed the night before, and arrangements were made for leaving the fort on the morning of the 15th.

It was a warm bright morning in the middle of August. Indications were positive that the savages intended to murder the white people; and when they moved out of the southern gate of the fort, the march was like a funeral procession. The band, feeling the solemnity of the occasion, struck up the Dead March in Saul.

Capt. Wells, who had blackened his face with gun-powder in token of his fate, took the lead with his band of Miamis, followed by Capt. Heald, with his wife by his side on horseback. Mr. Kinzie hoped by his personal influence to avert the impending blow, and therefore accompanied them, leaving his family in a boat in charge of a friendly Indian, to be taken to his trading station at the site of Niles, Michigan, in the event of his death.

The procession moved slowly along the lake shore till they reached the sand-hills between the prairie and the beach, when the Pottawattamie escort, under the leadership of Blackbird, filed to the right, placing those hills between them and the white people. Wells, with his Miamis, had kept in the advance. They suddenly came rushing back, Wells exclaiming, " They are about to attack us; form instantly." These words were quickly followed by a storm of bullets, which came whistling over the little hills which the treacherous savages had made the covert for their murderous attack. The white troops charged upon the Indians, drove them back to the prairie, and then the battle was waged between fifty-four soldiers, twelve civilians and three or four women (the cowardly Miamis having fled at the outset) against five hundred Indian warriors. The white people, hopeless, resolved to sell their lives as dearly as possible. Ensign Ronan wielded his weapon vigorously, even after falling upon his knees weak from the loss of blood. Capt. Wells, who was by the side of his niece, Mrs. Heald, when the conflict began, behaved with the greatest coolness and courage. He said to her, " We have not the slightest chance for life. We must part to meet no more in this world. God bless you." And then he dashed forward. Seeing a young warrior, painted like a demon, climb into a wagon in which were twelve children, and tomahawk them all, he cried out, unmindful of his personal danger, " If that is your game, butchering women and children, I will kill too." He spurred his horse towards the Indian camp, where they had left their squaws and papooses, hotly pursued by swift-footed young warriors, who sent bullets whistling after him. One of these killed his horse and wounded him severely in the leg. With a yell the young braves rushed to make him their prisoner and reserve him for torture. He resolved not to be made a captive, and by the use of the most provoking epithets tried to induce them to kill him instantly. He called a fiery young chief a *squaw*, when the enraged warrior killed Wells instantly with his tomahawk, jumped upon his body, cut out his heart, and ate a portion of the warm morsel with savage delight!

In this fearful combat women bore a conspicuous part. Mrs. Heald was an excellent equestrian and an expert in the use of the rifle. She fought the savages bravely, receiving several severe wounds. Though faint, from the loss of blood, she managed to keep her saddle. A savage raised his tomahawk to kill her, when she looked him full in the face, and with a sweet smile and in a gentle voice said, in his own language, " Surely you will not kill a squaw !" The arm of the savage fell, and the life of the heroic woman was saved.

Mrs. Helm, the step-daughter of Mr. Kinzie, had an encounter with a stout Indian, who attempted to tomahawk her. Springing to one side, she received the glancing blow on her shoulder, and at the same instant seized the savage round the neck with her arms and endeavored to get hold of his scalping knife, which hung in a sheath at his breast. While she was thus struggling she was dragged from her antagonist by another powerful Indian, who bore her, in spite of her struggles, to the margin of the lake and plunged her in. To her astonishment she was held by him so that she would not drown, and she soon perceived that she was in the hands of the friendly Black Partridge, who had saved her life.

The wife of Sergeant Holt, a large and powerful woman, behaved as bravely as an Amazon. She rode a fine, high-spirited horse, which the Indians coveted, and several of them attacked her with the butts of their guns, for the purpose of dismounting her; but she used the sword which she had snatched from her disabled husband so skillfully that she foiled them; and, suddenly wheeling her horse, she dashed over the prairie, followed by the savages shouting, "The brave woman! the brave woman! Don't hurt her!" They finally overtook her, and while she was fighting them in front, a powerful savage came up behind her, seized her by the neck and dragged her to the ground. Horse and woman were made captives. Mrs. Holt was a long time a captive among the Indians, but was afterwards ransomed.

In this sharp conflict two-thirds of the white people were slain and wounded, and all their horses, baggage and provision were lost. Only twenty-eight straggling men now remained to fight five hundred Indians rendered furious by the sight of blood. They succeeded in breaking through the ranks of the murderers and gaining a slight eminence on the prairie near the Oak Woods. The Indians did not pursue, but gathered on their flanks, while the chiefs held a consultation on the sand-hills, and showed signs of willingness to parley. It would have been madness on the part of the whites to renew the fight; and so Capt. Heald went forward and met Blackbird on the open prairie, where terms of surrender were soon agreed upon. It was arranged that the white people should give up their arms to Blackbird, and that the survivors should become prisoners of war, to be exchanged for ransoms as soon as practicable. With this understanding captives and captors started for the Indian camp near the fort, to which Mrs. Helm had been taken bleeding and suffering by Black Partridge, and had met her step-father and learned that her husband was safe.

A new scene of horror was now opened at the Indian camp. The wounded, not being included in the terms of surrender, as it was interpreted by the Indians, and the British general, Proctor, having offered a liberal bounty for American scalps, delivered at Malden, nearly all the wounded men were killed and scalped, and the price of the trophies was afterwards paid by the British government.

Abstract of Illinois State Laws.

BILLS OF EXCHANGE AND PROMISSORY NOTES.

No *promissory note, check, draft, bill of exchange, order, or note, negotiable instrument* payable at sight, or on demand, or on presentment, shall be entitled to *days of grace*. *All other bills of exchange, drafts or notes* are entitled to *three days of grace.* · All the above mentioned paper falling due on *Sunday, New Years' Day, the Fourth of July, Christmas,* or any day appointed or recommended by the *President of the United States* or the *Governor of the State* as a day of *fast or thanksgiving,* shall be deemed as due on the day previous, and should two or more of these days come together, then such instrument shall be treated as due on the day *previous* to the first of said days. *No defense* can be made against a *negotiable instrument* (*assigned before due*) in the hands of the assignee without notice, *except fraud was used* in obtaining the same. To hold an *indorser,* due *diligence* must be used *by suit,* in collecting of the maker, unless suit would have been unavailing. Notes payable to *person named* or to order, in order to absolutely *transfer title,* must be indorsed by the *payee.* Notes payable to *bearer* may be *transferred by delivery,* and when so payable *every indorser* thereon is held as a *guarantor of payment* unless otherwise expressed.

In computing interest or discount on negotiable instruments, a *month* shall be considered a *calendar month or twelfth of a year,* and for less than a month, a day shall be figured a *thirtieth* part of a month. Notes *only bear interest* when so expressed, but after due they draw the legal interest, even if not stated.

INTEREST.

The *legal rate* of interest is *six per cent.* Parties *may agree in writing* on a rate not exceeding *ten per cent.* If a rate of interest greater than ten per cent. is contracted for, it works a *forfeiture of the whole of said interest,* and only the principal can be recovered.

DESCENT.

When *no will is made,* the property of a deceased person is distributed as follows:

First. *To his or her children and their descendants in equal parts;* the descendants of the deceased *child or grandchild,* taking the share of their deceased parents in equal parts among them.

Second. When there is *no child* of the intestate, *nor descendant of such child,* and *no widow* or *surviving husband,* then to the parents, brothers or sisters of the deceased, and their descendants, in equal parts among them, allowing to each of the parents, if living, a *child's part,* or to the survivor of them if one be dead, a *double portion;* and if there is no parent living, then to the brothers and sisters of the intestate, and their descendants.

Third, When there is *a widow or surviving husband, and no child or children,* or descendants of a child or children of the intestate, then (after the payment of all just debts) one-half of the real estate and the whole of the personal estate shall *descend to such widow or surviving husband* as an absolute estate forever.

Fourth. When there *is a widow or surviving husband,* and *also a child or children,* or descendants of such child or children of the intestate, *the widow or surviving husband* shall receive as his or her absolute personal estate, *one-third* of all the personal estate of the intestate.

Fifth. If there *is no child of the intestate,* or descendant of such child, and no parent, brother or sister, or descendant of such parent, brother or sister, and no widow or surviving husband, then such estate shall descend in *equal parts* to the *next of kin* to the intestate, in equal degree (computing by the rules of the civil law), and there shall be no representation among collaterals, except with the descendants of brothers and sisters of the intestate; and in no case shall there be any *distinction between the kindred of the whole and the half blood.*

Sixth, If any intestate leaves a *widow or surviving husband and no kindred,* his or her estate shall *descend to such widow or surviving husband.*

WILLS AND ESTATES OF DECEASED PERSONS.

No exact form of words are necessary in order to make a will good at law. *Every male* person of the age of *twenty-one years,* and every *female of the age of eighteen years, of sound mind and memory,* can make a valid will; it must be in *writing,* signed by the testator or by some one in his or her presence and by his or her direction, and *attested by two* or more *credible witnesses.* Care should be taken that the *witnesses are not interested* in the will. *Persons knowing themselves to have been named in the will* or appointed executor, must within *thirty days* of the death of deceased cause the will to be proved and recorded in the proper county, or present it, and *refuse to accept;* on failure to do so are *liable* to forfeit the sum of *twenty dollars per month.* *Inventory* to be made by executor or administrator within *three months* from date of letters testamentary or of administration. Executors' and administrators' *compensation* not to exceed six per cent. on amount of personal estate, and three per cent. on money realized from real estate, with such additional allowance as shall be reasonable for extra services. *Appraisers' compensation* $2 per day.

Notice requiring all claims to be presented against the estate shall be given by the executor or administrator *within six months* of being qualified. Any person having a claim *and not presenting it* at the time fixed by said notice is required to have summons issued notifying the executor or administrator of his having filed his claim in court : in such cases the costs have to be paid by the claimant. *Claims* should be filed within *two years* from the time *administration* is granted on an estate, as after that time they are *forever barred*, unless *other estate is found* that was not inventoried. *Married women, infants, persons insane, imprisoned* or without the United States, in the employment of the United States, or of this State, have *two years* after their disabilities are removed to file claims.

Claims are *classified* and *paid out* of the *estate* in the following manner:
First. Funeral expenses.

Second. The *widow's award*, if there is a widow ; or *children* if there are children, *and no widow*.

Third. *Expenses* attending the *last illness*, not including physician's bill.

Fourth. *Debts due* the *common school* or *township fund*.

Fifth. All expenses of *proving the will* and taking out letters testamentary or administration, and settlement of the estate, and the *physician's bill* in the last illness of deceased.

Sixth. Where the *deceased* has received *money in trust* for any purpose, his executor or administrator shall pay out of his estate the amount received and not accounted for.

Seventh. All *other debts* and demands of whatsoever kind, without regard to *quality or dignity*, which shall be exhibited to the court within *two years* from the granting of letters.

Award to Widow and Children, exclusive of debts and legacies or bequests, except funeral expenses :
First. The *family pictures* and *wearing apparel, jewels* and *ornaments* of *herself* and *minor children.*

Second. *School books* and the *family library of the value of* $100.
Third. *One sewing machine.*

Fourth. *Necessary beds, bedsteads* and *bedding* for herself and family.

Fifth. The *stoves* and *pipe* used in the family, with the necessary *cooking utensils*, or in case they have none, $50 in money.

Sixth. *Household* and *kitchen furniture* to the value of $100.

Seventh. *One milch cow and calf for every four members of her family.*

Eighth. *Two sheep* for each member of her family, and the fleeces taken from the same, and *one horse, saddle and bridle.*

Ninth. *Provisions for herself and family for one year.*

Tenth. *Food for the stock above specified for six months.*

Eleventh. *Fuel for herself and family for three months.*

Twelfth. *One hundred dollars worth* of other property suited to her condition in life, to be *selected by the widow.*

The *widow if she elects* may have in lieu of the said award, the same personal property or money in place thereof as is or may be *exempt from execution* or attachment against the *head of a family.*

TAXES.

The owners of real and personal property, on the *first day of May* in each year, are *liable for the taxes* thereon.

Assessments should be completed before the *fourth Monday in June,* at which time the town board of review meets to examine assessments, *hear objections,* and make such *changes* as ought to be made. The county board have also power *to correct or change assessments.*

The tax books are placed in the hands of the town collector on or before the tenth day of December, who retains them until the tenth day of March following, when he is required to return them to the county treasurer, who then *collects all delinquent taxes.*

No *costs accrue* on real estate taxes *till advertised,* which takes place the first day of April, when three weeks' notice is required before judgment. Cost of advertising, twenty cents each tract of land, and ten cents each lot.

Judgment is usually obtained at *May term* of County Court. Costs six cents each tract of land, and five cents each lot. Sale takes place in June. Costs in addition to those before mentioned, twenty-eight cents each tract of land, and twenty-seven cents each town lot.

Real estate sold for taxes may be *redeemed* any time before the *expiration of two years* from the date of sale, by *payment* to the *County Clerk* of the amount for which it was sold and twenty-five per cent. thereon if redeemed within six months, fifty per cent. if between six and twelve months, if between twelve and eighteen months seventy-five per cent., and if between eighteen months and two_years one hundred per cent., and in addition, all subsequent taxes paid by the purchaser, with ten per cent. interest thereon, also one dollar each tract if notice is given by the purchaser of the sale, and a fee of twenty-five cents to the clerk for his certificate.

JURISDICTION OF COURTS.

Justices have jurisdiction in all civil cases on *contracts* for the *recovery of moneys for damages for injury to real property,* or taking, detaining, or *injuring personal property; for rent;* for all cases to recover damages done real or personal property by railroad companies, in actions of *replevin,* and in actions for damages for *fraud* in the *sale, purchase,* or *exchange of personal property,* when the amount claimed as due is not over $200. They have also *jurisdiction* in all cases for *violation* of the *ordinances* of *cities, towns* or *villages.* A *justice of the peace* may *orally* order an *officer or a private person* to *arrest* any one committing or attempting to commit a *criminal offense.* He *also* upon complaint can issue his warrant for the arrest of any person *accused of having committed a crime,* and have him brought before him for examination.

COUNTY COURTS

Have jurisdiction in all *matters of probate,* settlement of estates of *deceased persons,* appointment of *guardians* and *conservators,* and settlement of their accounts; all matters relating to *apprentices;* proceedings for the *collection of taxes* and *assessments,* and in proceedings of *executions, administrators, guardians and conservators for the sale of real estate.* In *law* cases they have concurrent jurisdiction with Circuit Courts in all cases where Justices of Peace now have when the amount claimed shall *not exceed $500,* and in all criminal offenses where the punishment *is not imprisonment in the penitentiary or death,* but no *appeal* is allowed from Justice of the Peace to County Courts.

Circuit Courts—Have unlimited jurisdiction.

LIMITATION OF ACTION.

Accounts five years. Notes and written contracts *ten years. Judgments twenty years. Partial payments* or new promise in writing, within or after said period, will *revive the debt.* Absence from the State deducted, and when the cause of action is barred by the law of another State, it has the same effect here. *Slander and libel, one year. Personal injuries, two years. To recover* land or make entry thereon, *twenty years. Action to foreclose mortgage* or trust deed, or make a sale, *within ten years.*

All persons in *possession of land,* and *paying taxes for seven* consecutive *years,* with color of title, and all persons paying taxes for seven consecutive years, with color of title, on vacant land, shall be held to be the *legal owners to the extent of their paper title.*

MARRIED WOMEN

May sue and be sued. Husband and wife not liable for each other's debts, either before or after marriage, but both are liable for expenses and education of the family.

4

She may contract the same as if unmarried, except that in a partnership business she can not, without consent of her husband, *unless he has abandoned or deserted her*, or is idiotic or insane, or confined in penitentiary ; she is entitled and can recover her own earnings, but neither husband nor wife is entitled to compensation for any services rendered for the other. At the death of the husband, in addition to widow's award, a married woman has a dower interest (one-third) in all real estate owned by her husband after their marriage, and which has not been released by her, and the husband has the same interest in the real estate of the wife at her death.

EXEMPTIONS FROM FORCED SALE.

Home worth $1,000, *and the following Personal Property :* Lot of ground and buildings thereon, occupied as a residence by the debtor, being a householder and having a family, to the value of $1,000. *Exemption continues after the death* of the householder for the benefit of widow and family, some one of them occupying the homestead until *youngest child shall become twenty-one years of age, and until death of widow.* There is *no exemption from sale for taxes*, assessments, debt or liability incurred for the *purchase or improvement of said homestead.* No release or waiver of exemption is valid, unless in writing, and subscribed by such householder and wife (if he have one), and acknowledged as conveyances of real estate are required to be acknowledged. The *following articles of personal property* owned by the debtor, are exempt from *execution, writ of attachment, and distress for rent :* The necessary *wearing apparel* of every person ; *one sewing machine ;* the *furniture, tools and implements necessary to carry on his trade* or business, *not exceeding* $100 in value ; the implements or *library of* any *professional man*, not exceeding $100 in value ; *materials* and *stock* designed and procured *for carrying on his trade* or business, and intended to be used or wrought therein, *not exceeding* $100 *in value ;* and also, when the debtor is the head of a family and resides with the same, *necessary beds, bedsteads, and bedding, two stoves and pipe, necessary household furniture not exceeding in value* $100, *one cow, calf, two swine, one yoke of oxen, or two horses in lieu thereof, worth not exceeding* $200, with the harness therefor, *necessary provisions and fuel* for the use of the family *three months*, and necessary *food for the stock* hereinbefore exempted for the same time ; the *bibles, school books* and *family pictures ;* the *family library, cemetery lots*, and *rights of burial*, and *tombs* for the repositories of the dead ; *one hundred dollars' worth of other property*, suited to his condition in life, selected by the debtor. *No personal property is exempt from sale* for the *wages of laborers or servants. Wages of a laborer* who is the head of a family can not be garnisheed, except the sum due him be in excess of $25.

DEEDS AND MORTGAGES.

To be valid there must be a valid consideration. Special care should be taken to have them signed, sealed, delivered, and properly acknowledged, with the proper seal attached. *Witnesses* are not required. The *acknowledgement* must be made in this state, before *Master in Chancery, Notary Public, United States Commissioner, Circuit or County Clerk, Justice of Peace, or any Court of Record having a seal, or any Judge, Justice, or Clerk of any such* Court. When taken before a *Notary Public, or United States Commissioner,* the same shall be *attested* by his *official seal,* when taken before a *Court or the Clerk* thereof, the same shall be attested by the *seal* of such *Court,* and when taken before a *Justice of the Peace* residing out of the county where the real estate to be conveyed lies, there shall be added a certificate of the *County Clerk* under his seal of office, *that he was a Justice of the Peace* in the county at the time of taking the same. A deed is good without such certificate attached, but can not be used in evidence unless such a certificate is produced or other competent evidence introduced. Acknowledgements made out of the state must either be executed according to the laws of this state, or there should be attached a certificate that it is in conformity with the laws of the state or country where executed. Where this is not done the same may be proved by any other legal way. Acknowledgments where the *Homestead* rights are to be waived must state as follows: "Including the release and waiver of the right of homestead."

Notaries Public can take acknowledgements any where in the state.

Sheriffs, if authorized by the mortgagor of real or personal property in his mortgage, may sell the property mortgaged.

In the case of the *death of grantor or holder of the equity of redemption* of real estate mortgaged, or conveyed by deed of trust where equity of redemption is waived, and it contains power of sale, must be foreclosed in the same manner as a common mortgage in court.

ESTRAYS.

Horses, mules, asses, neat cattle, swine, sheep, or goats found straying at any time during the year, in counties where such animals are not allowed to run at large, or between the last day of October and the 15th day of April in other counties, *the owner thereof being unknown, may be taken up as estrays.*

No person *not a householder* in the county where estray is found *can lawfully* take up an estray, and then only *upon or about his farm* or place of residence. *Estrays should not be used before advertised,* except animals giving milk, which may be milked for their benefit.

Notices must be posted up within five (5) days in three (3) of the most public places in the town or precinct in which estray was found, giving the residence of the taker up, and a particular description of the estray, its age, color, and marks natural and artificial, and stating before what justice of the peace in such town or precinct, and at what time, not less than ten (10) nor more than fifteen (15) days from the time of posting such notices, he will apply to have the estray appraised.

A copy of such notice should be filed by the taker up with the *town clerk*, whose duty it is to enter the same at large, *in a book* kept by him for that purpose.

If the *owner* of estray shall not have appeared and *proved ownership*, and taken the same away, first paying the taker up his reasonable charges for taking up, keeping, and advertising the same, the taker up shall appear before the justice of the peace mentioned in above mentioned notice, and make an affidavit as required by law.

As the *affidavit has to be made before the justice*, and all other steps as to appraisement, etc., are before him, who is familiar therewith, they are therefore omitted here.

Any person taking up an estray at any other place than about or upon his farm or residence, or *without complying with the law, shall forfeit and pay a fine of ten dollars with costs.*

Ordinary diligence is required in *taking care of estrays*, but in case they die or get away the taker is not liable for the same.

GAME.

It is *unlawful to hunt, kill or in any manner interfere with deer, wild turkey. prairie chicken, partridge or pheasants between the first day of January and the fifteenth day of August;* or any *quail*, between the first day of *January* and the first day of *October;* or any *woodcock*, between the *first day of January and the first day of July;* or any *wild goose, duck, Wilson snipe, brandt, or other water fowl, between the fifteenth day of April and the fifteenth day of August, in each and every year. Penalty:* Fine not less than $10 nor more than $25, and costs of suit, and shall stand committed to county jail until fine is paid. but not exceeding ten days.

It is *unlawful* to hunt with *gun, dog or net*, within the inclosed grounds or lands of another, *without permission. Penalty:* Fine not less than $3 and not exceeding $100, to be paid into school fund.

WEIGHTS AND MEASURES.

Whenever any of the following articles shall be contracted for, or sold or delivered, and no special contract or agreement shall be made to the contrary, the weight per bushel shall be as follows, to-wit:

	Pounds.			Pounds.
Stone Coal, - - - -	80	Buckwheat, - - -	- 52
Unslacked Lime, - -	80	Coarse Salt, - - -	50
Corn in the ear, - -	- 70	Barley, - - - -	- 48
Wheat. - - - -	60	Corn Meal, - - -	48
Irish Potatoes, - -	- 60	Castor Beans, - -	- 46
White Beans, - - -	60	Timothy Seed, - -	- 45
Clover Seed, - ' - -	- 60	Hemp Seed, - - -	- 44
Onions, - - - -	57	Malt, - - - -	- 38
Shelled Corn, - -	- 56	Dried Peaches, - -	- 33
Rye, - - - - -	56	Oats, - - - -	- 32
Flax Seed, - - -	- 56	Dried Apples, - -	- 24
Sweet Potatoes, - -	55	Bran, - - - - -	20
Turnips, - - - -	- 55	Blue Grass Seed, - -	- 14
Fine Salt, - - - -	55	Hair (plastering), - -	8

Penalty for giving less than the above standard is double the amount of property wrongfully not given, and ten dollars addition thereto.

MILLERS.

The owner or occupant of every public grist mill in this state shall grind all grain brought to his mill in its turn. The *toll* for both *steam* and *water* mills, is, for grinding and bolting *wheat, rye,* or *other grain,* one *eighth part;* for grinding *Indian corn, oats, barley* and *buckwheat* not required to be *bolted,* one *seventh part;* for grinding *malt,* and *chopping* all kinds of grain, one *eighth part.* It is the duty of every miller when his mill is in repair, to *aid* and *assist* in *loading* and *unloading* all grain brought to him to be ground, and he is also required to keep an accurate *half bushel measure,* and an accurate set of *toll dishes* or *scales* for weighing the grain. The *penalty* for neglect or refusal to comply with the law is $5, to the use of any person to sue for the same, to be recovered before any justice of the peace of the county where penalty is incurred. Millers are accountable for the safe keeping of all grain left in his mill for the purpose of being ground, with bags or casks containing same (except it results from unavoidable accidents), provided that such bags or casks are distinctly marked with the initial letters of the owner's name.

MARKS AND BRANDS.

Owners of cattle, horses, hogs, sheep or goats may have *one ear mark* and one brand, but which shall be *different* from his *neighbor's,* and may be *recorded* by the county clerk of the county in which such property is kept. The *fee* for such record is fifteen cents. The *record* of such shall be *open* to examination free of charge. In cases of *disputes* as to marks or brands, such *record* is *prima facie evidence.* Owners of cattle, horses, hogs, sheep or goats that may have been branded by the *former owner,* may be re-branded in presence of one or more of his neighbors, who shall certify to the facts of the marking or branding being done, when done, and in what brand or mark they were re-branded or re-marked, which certificate may also be recorded as before stated.

ADOPTION OF CHILDREN.

Children may be adopted by any resident of this state, by filing a petition in the Circuit or County Court of the county in which he resides, asking leave to do so, and if desired may ask that the name of the child be changed. Such petition, if made by a person having a husband or wife, will not be granted, unless the husband or wife joins therein, as the adoption must be by them jointly.

The petition shall state name, sex, and age of the child, and the new name, if it is desired to change the name. Also the name and residence of the parents of the child, if known, and of the guardian, if any, and whether the parents or guardians consent to the adoption.

The court must find, before granting decree, that the *parents of the child*, or the survivors of them, have *deserted his or her family* or such child for one year next preceding the application, or if neither are living, the guardian; if no guardian, the next of kin in this state capable of giving consent, has had notice of the presentation of the petition and consents to such adoption. If the child is of the *age* of *fourteen years* or upwards, the adoption *can not* be made *without its consent.*

SURVEYORS AND SURVEYS.

There is in every county elected a surveyor known as county surveyor, who has power to appoint deputies, for whose official acts he is responsible. It is the *duty* of the *county surveyor*, either by himself or his deputy, to make *all surveys* that he may be called upon to make within his county as soon as may be after application is made. The necessary chainmen and other assistance must be employed by the person requiring the same to be done, and to be by him paid, unless otherwise agreed; but the chainmen must be disinterested persons and approved by the surveyor and sworn by him to measure justly and impartially.

The County Board in each county is required by law to provide a copy of the United States field notes and plats of their surveys of the lands in the county to be kept in the recorder's office subject to examination by the public, and the county surveyor is required to make his surveys in conformity to said notes, plats and the laws of the United States governing such matters. The surveyor is also required to keep a record of all surveys made by him, which shall be subject to inspection by any one interested, and shall be delivered up to his successor in office. A certified copy of the said surveyor's record shall be *prima facie* evidence of its contents.

The fees of county surveyors are six dollars per day. The county surveyor is also *ex officio inspector of mines*, and as such, assisted by some practical miner selected by him, shall once each year inspect all the mines in the county, for which they shall each receive such compensation as may be fixed by the County Board, not exceeding $5 a day, to be paid out of the county treasury.

ROADS.

Where practicable from the nature of the ground, persons traveling in any kind of vehicle, *must turn to the right* of the center of the road, so as to permit each carriage to pass without interfering with each other. The *penalty* for a violation of this provision is $5 for every offense, to be recovered by the *party injured;* but to recover, there must have occurred some injury to person or property resulting from the violation. The *owners* of any carriage traveling upon any road in this State for the conveyance of passengers who shall *employ* or continue in his employment as driver any person who is addicted to *drunkenness*, or the excessive use of spiritous liquors, after he has had notice of the same, *shall forfeit*, at the rate of $5 per day, and if any *driver* while actually engaged in driving any such carriage, shall be guilty of *intoxication* to such a degree as to *endanger* the safety of *passengers*, it shall be the duty of the owner, on receiving *written notice* of the fact, signed by one of the *passengers*, and *certified* by him *on oath*, forthwith to discharge such driver. If such owner shall have such driver in his *employ within three months* after such notice, he is liable for $5 per day for the time he shall keep said driver in his employment after receiving such notice.

Persons *driving* any *carriage* on any public highway are prohibited from *running their horses* upon any occasion under a *penalty* of a fine not exceeding $10, or imprisonment not exceeding sixty days, at the discretion of the court. Horses *attached* to any *carriage* used to convey *passengers* for hire must be *properly hitched* or the lines placed in the hands of some other person before the driver leaves them for any purpose. For violation of this provision each driver shall *forfeit twenty dollars*, to be recovered by action, to be commenced within six months. It is understood by the *term carriage* herein to mean any carriage or vehicle used for the transportation of passengers or goods or either of them.

The commissioners of highways in the different towns have the care and superintendence of highways and bridges therein. They have all the powers necessary to lay out, vacate, regulate and repair all roads, build and repair bridges, divide their respective towns into as many road districts as they shall think convenient. This is to be done annually, and ten days before the annual town meeting. In addition to the above, it is their duty to erect and keep in repair at the forks or crossing-place of the most important roads post and guide boards with plain inscriptions, giving directions and distances to the most noted places to which such road may lead; also to make provisions to prevent thistles, burdock, and cockle burrs, mustard, yellow dock, Indian mallow, and jessamine weed from seeding, and to extirpate the same as far as practicable, and to prevent all rank growth of vegetation on the public highways, so far as the same may obstruct public travel, and it is in their discretion to erect watering places for public use for watering teams at such points as may be deemed advisable. Every able-bodied male inhabitant, being above the age of twenty-one years, and under the age of fifty, excepting paupers, idiots, lunatics, trustees of schools and school directors, and such others as are exempt by law, is required to labor on highways in their respective road districts, not less than one or more than three days in each and every year. Three days' notice must be given by the overseer of the time and place he requires such road labor to be done. The labor must be performed in the road district in which the person resides. Any person may commute for such labor by paying at the rate of $1.50 per day, if done within the three days' notice, but after that time the rate is $2 per day.

Any person liable for work on highways who has been assessed two days or more and has not commuted, may be required to furnish team, or a cart, wagon or plow, with a pair of horses or oxen and a man to manage them, for which he will be entitled to two days for each day's work. Eight hours is a day's work on the roads, and there is a penalty of twenty-five cents an hour against any person or substitute who shall neglect or refuse to perform. Any person remaining idle, or does not work faithfully or hinders others from doing so, forfeits to the town $2.

Every person assessed *and duly notified*, who has not commuted and refuses or neglects to appear, shall forfeit to the town for *every day's* refusal or neglect, the sum of $2; if he was required to furnish a team, carriage, man or implement, and neglects or refuses to comply, he is liable to the following fines:

First. For wholly failing to comply, $4 each day.

Second. For omitting to furnish a pair of horses or oxen, $1.50 each day.

Third. For omitting to furnish a man to manage team, $2 each day.

Fourth. For omitting to furnish a wagon, cart or plow, 75 cents each day.

The Commissioners estimate and assess the highway labor and road tax. The road tax on real and personal property can not exceed forty cents on each hundred dollars' worth. The labor or road tax in villages, towns or cities, is paid over to the corporate authorities of such, for the improvement of streets, roads and bridges within their limits. Commissioners' compensation $1.50 per day. The Treasurer, who is one of their number, is entitled to 2 per cent. on all moneys he may receive and pay out.

Overseers. Their duties are to repair and keep in order the highways in their districts; to warn persons to work out their road tax at such time and place as they think proper; to collect fines and commutation money, and execute all lawful orders of the Commissioners of Highways; also make list, within sixteen days after their election, of the names of all inhabitants in his road district liable to work on highways. For refusal to perform any of his duties, he is liable to a fine of $10. The compensation of overseers is $1.50 a day, the number of days to be audited by the Highway Commissioners.

As all township and county officers are familiar with their duties, it is only intended to give the points of the law that the public should be familiar with. The manner of laying out, altering or vacating roads, etc., will not be here stated, as it would require more space than is contemplated in a work of this kind. It is sufficient to state that, the first step is by petition, addressed to the Commissioners, setting out what is prayed for, giving the names of the owners of lands if known, if not known so state, over which the road is to pass, giving the general course, its place of beginning, and where it terminates. It requires not less than twelve *freeholders* residing within three miles of the road who shall sign the petition. Public roads must not be less than fifty feet wide, nor more than sixty feet wide. Roads not exceeding two miles in length, if petitioned for, may be laid out, not less than forty feet. Private roads for private and public use, may be laid out of the width of three rods, on petition of the person directly interested; the damage occasioned thereby shall be paid by the premises benefited thereby, and before the road is opened. If not opened in two years, the order shall be considered rescinded. Commissioners in their discretion may permit persons who live on or have private roads, to work out their road tax thereon. Public roads must be opened in five days from date of filing order of location, or be deemed vacated.

DRAINAGE.

Whenever one or more owners or occupants of land *desire to construct a drain* or ditch across the land of others for *agricultural* or *sanitary purposes,* the proceedings are as follows:

1st. File a petition with the *clerk* of the *town board* of *auditors* in counties where there is township organization, or in counties not so organized with the clerk of the County Court, stating the necessity of the same, its starting point, route and terminus; and if it shall be deemed necessary for successful drainage that a levee or other work be constructed, a general description of the same shall be made.

2d. *After filing, two weeks'* notice must be given by posting notices in three of the most public places in such township through which the drain, ditch or other work is proposed to be constructed; and also, by publishing a copy thereof in some newspaper published in the county in which petition is filed, at least once each week for two successive weeks. The notice must state when and before what board such petition is filed, the starting point, route, terminus and description of the proposed work. On receipt of the petition by the clerk of either board as before mentioned, it is his duty to immediately give notice to the board of which he is clerk, of the fact, and that a meeting of the board will be held on a day to be fixed not later than sixty days after the filing of said petition, to consider the prayer of the same; and it is further the duty of the clerk, to publish a notice of the filing of the petition and the meeting of the board to consider it, by posting the same in the three most public places in the township or county. On the hearing, all parties may contest the matter, and if it shall appear to the board that the work contemplated is necessary, or is useful for the drainage of the land for agricultural and sanitary purposes, they shall so find and shall file their petition in the County Court, reciting the original petition and stating their finding, and pray that the costs of the improvement be assessed, and for that purpose three commissioners be appointed to lay out and construct the work. The costs of the hearing before the town board is to be paid by the petitioners. After commissioners are appointed, they organize and proceed to examine the work; and if they find the benefits greater than the cost and expense of the work, then it is their duty to have the surveyor's plans and specifications made, and when done report the same to the court, before which parties can be heard prior to confirmation. The commissioners are not confined to the route or plan of the petition, but may change the same. After report of commissioners is confirmed, then a jury assess the damages and benefits against the land damaged or benefited.

As it is only contemplated in a work of this kind to give an abstract of the laws, and as the parties who have in charge the execution of the further proceedings are likely to be familiar with the requirements of the statute, the necessary details are not here inserted.

PAUPERS.

Every poor person who shall be unable to earn a livelihood in consequence of any *bodily infirmity, idiocy, lunacy* or *unavoidable cause*, shall be supported by the father, grand-father, mother, grand-mother, children, grand-children, brothers or sisters of such poor person, if they or either of them be of sufficient ability; but if any of such dependent class shall have become so from *intemperance*, or other *bad conduct*, they shall not be entitled to support from any relation except parent or child.

The children shall first be called on to support their parents, if they are able; but if not, the parents of such poor person shall then be called on, if of sufficient ability; and if there be no parents or children able, then the brothers and sisters of such dependent person shall be called upon; and if there be no brothers or sisters of sufficient ability, the, grand-children of such person shall next be called on; and if they are not able, then the grand-parents. Married females, while their husbands live, shall not be liable to contribute for the support of their poor relations except out of their separate property. It is the duty of the state's (county) attorney, to make complaint to the County Court of his county against all the relatives of such paupers in this state liable to his support and prosecute the same. In case the state's attorney neglects, or refuses, to complain in such cases, then it is the duty of the overseer of the poor to do so. The person called upon to contribute shall have at least ten days' notice of such application by summons. The court has the power to determine the kind of support, depending upon the circumstances of the parties, and may also order two or more of the different degrees to maintain such poor person, and prescribe the proportion of each, according to their ability. The court may specify the time for which the relative shall contribute—in fact has control over the entire subject matter, with power to enforce its orders. Every county (except those in which the poor are supported by the towns, and in such cases the towns are liable) is required to relieve and support all poor and indigent persons *lawfully* resident therein. Residence means the *actual* residence of the party, or the place where he was employed; or in case he was in no employment, then it shall be the place where he made his home. When any person becomes chargeable as a pauper in any county or town who did not reside at the commencement of six months immediately preceding his becoming so, but did at that time reside in some other county or town in this state, then the county or town, as the case may be, becomes liable for the expense of taking care of such person until removed, and it is the duty of the overseer to notify the proper authorities of the fact. If any person shall bring and leave any pauper in any county in this state where such pauper had no legal residence, knowing him to be such, he is liable to a fine of $100. In counties under township organization, the supervisors in each town are ex-officio overseers of the poor. The overseers of the poor act under the directions of the County Board in taking care of the poor and granting of temporary relief; also, providing for non-resident persons not paupers who may be taken sick and not able to pay their way, and in case of death cause such person to be decently buried.

FENCES.

In counties under township organization, the *town assessor* and commissioner of highways are the fence-viewers in their respective towns. In other counties the County Board appoints three in each precinct annually. A *lawful fence* is *four and one-half feet high*, in good repair, consisting of rails, timber, boards, stone, hedges, or whatever the fence-viewers of the town or precinct where the same shall lie, shall consider equivalent thereto, but in counties under township organization the annual town meeting may establish any other kind of fence as such, or the County Board in other counties may do the same. Division fences shall be made and maintained in just proportion by the adjoining owners, except when the owner shall choose to let his land lie open, but after a division fence is built by agreement or otherwise, neither party can remove his part of such fence so long as he may crop or use such land for farm purposes, or without giving the other party one year's notice in writing of his intention to remove his portion. When any person shall enclose his land upon the enclosure of another, he shall refund the owner of the adjoining lands a just proportion of the value at that time of such fence. The value of fence and the just proportion to be paid or built and maintained by each is to be ascertained by two fence-viewers in the town or precinct. Such fence-viewers have power to settle all disputes between different owners as to fences built or to be built, as well as to repairs to be made. Each party chooses one of the viewers, but if the other party neglects, after eight days' notice in writing, to make his choice, then the other party may select both. It is sufficient to notify the tenant or party in possession, when the owner is not a resident of the town or precinct. The two fence-viewers chosen, after viewing the premises, shall hear the statements of the parties, in case they can't agree, they shall select another fence-viewer to act with them, and the decision of any two of them is final. The decision must be reduced to writing, and should plainly set out description of fence and all matters settled by them, and must be filed in the office of the town clerk in counties under township organization, and in other counties with the county clerk.

Where any person is liable to contribute to the erection or the repairing of a division fence, neglects or refuses so to do, the party injured, after giving sixty days notice in writing when a fence is to be erected, or ten days when it is only repairs, may proceed to have the work done at the expense of the party whose duty it is to do it, to be recovered from him with costs of suit, and the party so neglecting shall also be liable to the party injured for all damages accruing from such neglect or refusal, to be determined by any two fence-viewers selected as before provided, the appraisement to be reduced to writing and signed.

Where a person shall conclude to remove his part of a division fence, and let his land lie open, and having given the year's notice required, the adjoining owner may cause the value of said fence to be ascertained by fence-viewers as before provided, and on payment or tender of the amount of such valuation to the owner, it shall prevent the removal. A party removing a division fence without notice is liable for the damages accruing thereby.

Where a fence has been built on the land of another through mistake, the owner may enter upon such premises and remove his fence and material within six months after the division line has been ascertained. Where the material to build such a fence has been taken from the land on which it was built, then before it can be removed, the person claiming must first pay for such material to the owner of the land from which it was taken, nor shall such a fence be removed at a time when the removal will throw open or expose the crops of the other party; a reasonable time must be given beyond the six months to remove crops.

The compensation of fence-viewers is one dollar and fifty cents a day each, to be paid in the first instance by the party calling them, but in the end all expenses, including amount charged by the fence-viewers, must be paid equally by the parties, except in cases where a party neglects or refuses to make or maintain a just proportion of a division fence, when the party in default shall pay them.

DAMAGES FROM TRESPASS.

Where stock of any kind breaks into any person's enclosure, the fence being *good* and *sufficient*, the owner is liable for the damage done ; but where the damage is done by stock *running at large, contrary to law*, the owner is liable where there is not such a fence. Where stock is found trespassing on the enclosure of another as aforesaid, the owner or occupier of the premises may take possession of such stock and keep the same until damages, with reasonable charges for keeping and feeding and all costs of suit, are paid. Any person taking or rescuing such stock so held without his consent, shall be liable to a fine of not less than three nor more than five dollars for each animal rescued, to be recovered by suit before a justice of the peace for the use of the school fund. Within twenty-four hours after taking such animal into his possession, the person taking it up must give notice of the fact to the owner, if known, or if unknown, notices must be posted in some public place near the premises.

LANDLORD AND TENANT.

The owner of lands, or his legal representatives, can sue for and recover rent therefor, in any of the following cases :

First. When rent is due and in arrears on a lease for life or lives.

Second. When lands are held and occupied by any person without any special agreement for rent.

Third. When possession is obtained under an agreement, written or verbal, for the purchase of the premises and before deed given, the right to possession is terminated by forfeiture on con-compliance with the agreement, and possession is wrongfully refused or neglected to be given upon demand made in writing by the party entitled thereto. Provided that all payments made by the vendee or his representatives or assigns, may be set off against the rent.

Fourth. When land has been sold upon a judgment or a decree of court, when the party to such judgment or decree, or person holding under him, wrongfully refuses, or neglects, to surrender possession of the same, after demand in writing by the person entitled to the possession.

Fifth. When the lands have been sold upon a mortgage or trust deed, and the mortgagor or grantor or person holding under him, wrongfully refuses or neglects to surrender possession of the same, after demand in writing by the person entitled to the possession.

If any tenant, or any person who shall come into possession from or under or by collusion with such tenant, shall willfully hold over any lands, etc., after the expiration the term of their lease, and *after demand made in writing* for the possession thereof, is liable to pay *double rent.* A tenancy from year to year requires sixty days notice in writing, to terminate the same at the end of the year; such notice can be given at any time within four months preceding the last sixty days of the year.

A tenancy by the month, or less than a year, where the tenant holds over without any special agreement, the landlord may terminate the tenancy, by thirty days notice in writing.

When rent is due, the landlord may serve a notice upon the tenant, stating that unless the rent is paid within not less than five days, his lease will be terminated; if the rent is not paid, the landlord may consider the lease ended. When default is made in any of the terms of a lease, it shall not be necessary to give more than ten days notice to quit or of the termination of such tenancy; and the same may be terminated on giving such notice to quit, at any time after such default in any of the terms of such lease; which notice may be substantially in the following form, viz:

To ——. You are hereby notified that, in consequence of your default in (here insert the character of the default), of the premises now occupied by you, being etc. (here describe the premises), I have elected to determine your lease, and you are hereby notified to quit and deliver up possession of the same to me within ten days of this date (dated, etc.)

The above to be signed by the lessor or his agent, and no other notice or demand of possession or termination of such tenancy is necessary.

Demand may be made, or notice served, by delivering a written or printed, or partly either, copy thereof to the tenant, or leaving the same with some person above the age of twelve years residing on or in possession of the premises; and in case no one is in the actual possession of the said premises, then by posting the same on the premises. When the tenancy is for a certain time, and the term expires by the terms of the lease, the tenant is then bound to surrender possession, and no notice to quit or demand of possession is necessary.

Distress for rent.—In all cases of distress for rent, the landlord, by himself, his agent or attorney, may seize for rent any personal property of his tenant that may be found in the county where the tenant resides; the property of any other person, even if found on the premises, is not liable.

An inventory of the property levied upon, with a statement of the amount of rent claimed, should be at once filed with some justice of the peace, if not over $200; and if above that sum, with the clerk of a court of record of competent jurisdiction. Property may be released, by the party executing a satisfactory bond for double the amount.

The landlord may distrain for rent, any time within *six months* after the expiration of the term of the lease, or when terminated.

When rent is payable wholly or in part, in specific articles of property, or products of the premises, or labor, the landlord may distrain for the value of the same.

Landlords have a lien upon the crops grown or growing upon the demised premises for the rent thereof, and also for the faithful performance of the terms of the lease.

In all cases where the premises rented shall be sub-let, or the lease assigned, the landlord shall have the same right to enforce lien against such lessee or assignee, that he has against the tenant to whom the premises were rented.

When a tenant abandons or removes from the premises or any part thereof, the landlord, or his agent or attorney, may seize upon any grain or other crops grown or growing upon the premises, or part thereof so abandoned, whether the rent is due or not. If such grain, or other crops, or any part thereof, is not fully grown or matured, the landlord, or his agent or attorney, shall cause the same to be properly cultivated, harvested or gathered, and may sell the same, and from the proceeds pay all his labor, expenses and rent. The tenant may, before the sale of such property, redeem the same by tendering the rent and reasonable compensation for work done, or he may replevy the same.

Exemption.—The same articles of personal property which are by law exempt from execution, except the crops as above stated, is also exempt from distress for rent.

LIENS.

Any person who shall by *contract*, express or implied, or partly both, with the owner of any lot or tract of land, furnish labor or material, or services as an architect or superintendent, in building, altering, repairing or ornamenting any house or other building or appurtenance thereto on such lot, or upon any street or alley, and connected with such improvements, shall have a lien upon the whole of such lot or tract of land, and upon such house or building and appurtenances, for the amount due to him for such labor, material or services. If the contract is *expressed*, and the time for the *completion* of the work is *beyond three years* from the commencement thereof; or, if the time of payment is beyond one year from the time stipulated for the completion of the work, then no lien exists. If the contract is *implied*, then no lien exists, unless the work be done or material is furnished within one year from the commencement of the work or delivery of the materials. As between different creditors having liens, no preference is given to the one whose contract was first made; but each shares pro-rata. Incumbrances existing on the lot or tract of the land at the time the contract is made, do not operate on the improvements, and are only preferred to the extent of the value of the land at the *time of making the contract.* The above lien can not be enforced *unless suit is commenced* within *six months* after the last payment for labor or materials shall have become due and payable. Sub-contractors, mechanics, workmen and other persons furnishing any material, or performing any labor for a contractor as before specified, have a lien to the extent of the amount due the contractor at the time the following notice is served upon the owner of the land who made the contract:

To ——, You are hereby notified, that I have been employed by—— (here state whether to labor or furnish material, and substantially the nature of the demand) upon your (here state in general terms description and situation of building), and that I shall hold the (building, or as the case may be), and your interest in the ground, liable for the amount that may (is or may become) due me on account thereof. Signature, —— Date, ——

If there is a contract in writing between contractor and sub-contractor, a copy of it should be served with above notice, and said notice must be served within forty days from the completion of such sub-contract, if there is one; if not, then from the time payment should have been made to the person performing the labor or furnishing the material. If the owner is not a resident of the county, or can not be found therein, then the above notice must be filed with the clerk of the Circuit Court, with his fee, fifty cents, and a copy of said notice must be published in a newspaper published in the county, for four successive weeks.

When the owner or agent is notified as above, he can retain any money due the contractor sufficient to pay such claim ; if more than one claim. and not enough to pay all, they are to be paid pro rata.

The owner has the right to demand in writing, a statement of the contractor, of what he owes for labor, etc., from time to time as the work progresses, and on his failure to comply, forfeits to the owner $50 for every offense.

The liens referred to cover any and all estates, whether in fee for life, for years, or any other interest which the owner may have.

To enforce the lien of *sub-contractors*, suit must be commenced within *three months* from the time of the performance of the sub-contract, or during the work or furnishing materials.

Hotel, inn and *boarding-house keepers*, have a lien upon the baggage and other valuables of their guests or boarders. brought into such hotel, inn or boarding-house, by their guests or boarders, for the proper charges due from such guests or boarders for their accommodation, board and lodgings, and such *extras* as are furnished at their request.

Stable-keepers and other persons have a lien upon the horses, carriages and harness kept by them, for the proper charges due for the keeping thereof and expenses bestowed thereon at the request of the owner or the person having the possession of the same.

Agisters (persons who take care of cattle belonging to others), and persons keeping, yarding, feeding or pasturing domestic animals, shall have a lien upon the animals agistered, kept, yarded or fed, for the proper charges due for such service.

All persons who may furnish any railroad corporation in this state with fuel, ties, material, supplies or any other article or thing necessary for the construction, maintenance, operation or repair of its road by contract, or may perform work or labor on the same, is entitled to be paid as part of the current expenses of the road, and have a lien upon all its property. Sub-contractors or laborers have also a lien. The conditions and limitations both as to contractors and sub-contractors, are about the same as herein stated as to general liens.

DEFINITION OF COMMERCIAL TERMS.

$—— means *dollars*, being a contraction of U. S., which was formerly placed before any denomination of money, and meant, as it means now, United States Currency.

£—— means *pounds*, English money.

@ stands for *at* or *to*. ℔ for *pound*, and bbl. for *barrel;* ℔ for *per* or *by the.* Thus, Butter sells at 20@30c ℔ ℔, and Flour at $8@12 ℔ bbl.

℀ for *per cent* and ℥ for *number.*

May 1.—Wheat sells at $1.20@1.25, "seller June." *Seller June*

5

means that the person who sells the wheat has the privilege of delivering it at any time during the month of June.

Selling *short*, is contracting to deliver a certain amount of grain or stock, at a fixed price, within a certain length of time, when the seller has not the stock on hand. It is for the interest of the person selling "short," to depress the market as much as possible, in order that he may buy and fill his contract at a profit. Hence the "shorts" are termed "bears."

Buying *long*, is to contract to purchase a certain amount of grain or shares of stock at a fixed price, deliverable within a stipulated time, expecting to make a profit by the rise of prices. The "longs" are termed "bulls," as it is for their interest to "operate" so as to "toss" the prices upward as much as possible.

NOTES.

Form of note is legal, worded in the simplest way, so that the amount and time of payment are mentioned.

$100.   Chicago, Ill., Sept. 15, 1876.
  Sixty days from date I promise to pay to E. F. Brown, or order, One Hundred dollars, for value received.

               L. D. LOWRY.

A note to be payable in any thing else than money needs only the facts substituted for money in the above form.

ORDERS.

Orders should be worded simply, thus:

Mr. F. H. COATS: Chicago, Sept. 15, 1876.
  Please pay to H. Birdsall, Twenty-five dollars, and charge to

               F. D. SILVA.

RECEIPTS.

Receipts should always state when received and what for, thus:

$100.   Chicago, Sept. 15, 1876.
  Received of J. W. Davis, One Hundred dollars, for services rendered in grading his lot in Fort Madison, on account.

            THOMAS BRADY.

If receipt is in full it should be so stated.

BILLS OF PURCHASE.

W. N. MASON,   Salem, Illinois, Sept. 15, 1876.
       Bought of A. A. GRAHAM.

4 Bushels of Seed Wheat, at $1.50	-	-	-	-	$6.00
2 Seamless Sacks " .30	-	-		.60

       Received payment, $6.60

            A. A. GRAHAM.

ARTICLES OF AGREEMENT.

An agreement is where one party promises to another to do a certain thing in a certain time for a stipulated sum. Good business men always reduce an agreement to writing, which nearly always saves misunderstandings and trouble. No particular form is necessary, but the facts must be clearly and explicitly stated, and there must, to make it valid, be a reasonable consideration.

GENERAL FORM OF AGREEMENT.

THIS AGREEMENT, made the Second day of October, 1876, between John Jones, of Aurora, County of Kane, State of Illinois, of the first part, and Thomas Whiteside, of the same place, of the second part —

WITNESSETH, that the said John Jones, in consideration of the agreement of the party of the second part, hereinafter contained, contracts and agrees to and with the said Thomas Whiteside, that he will deliver, in good and marketable condition, at the Village of Batavia, Ill., during the month of November, of this year, One Hundred Tons of Prairie Hay, in the following lots, and at the following specified times; namely, twenty-five tons by the seventh of November, twenty-five tons additional by the fourteenth of the month, twenty-five tons more by the twenty-first, and the entire one hundred tons to be all delivered by the thirtieth of November.

And the said Thomas Whiteside, in consideration of the prompt fulfillment of this contract, on the part of the party of the first part, contracts to and agrees with the said John Jones, to pay for said hay five dollars per ton, for each ton as soon as delivered.

In case of failure of agreement by either of the parties hereto, it is hereby stipulated and agreed that the party so failing shall pay to the other, One Hundred Dollars, as fixed and settled damages.

In witness whereof, we have hereunto set our hands the day and year first above written.   JOHN JONES,
                                                    THOMAS WHITESIDE.

AGREEMENT WITH CLERK FOR SERVICES.

THIS AGREEMENT, made the first day of May, one thousand eight hundred and seventy-six, between Reuben Stone, of Chicago, County of Cook, State of Illinois, party of the first part, and George Barclay, of Englewood, County of Cook, State of Illinois, party of the second part —

WITNESSETH, that said George Barclay agrees faithfully and diligently to work as clerk and salesman for the said Reuben Stone, for and during the space of one year from the date hereof, should both live such length of time, without absenting himself from his occupation;

during which time he, the said Barclay, in the store of said Stone, of Chicago, will carefully and honestly attend, doing and performing all duties as clerk and salesman aforesaid, in accordance and in all respects as directed and desired by the said Stone.

In consideration of which services, so to be rendered by the said Barclay, the said Stone agrees to pay to said Barclay the annual sum of one thousand dollars, payable in twelve equal monthly payments, each upon the last day of each month; provided that all dues for days of absence from business by said Barclay, shall be deducted from the sum otherwise by the agreement due and payable by the said Stone to the said Barclay.

Witness our hands.   REUBEN STONE.
                                            GEORGE BARCLAY.

BILLS OF SALE.

A bill of sale is a written agreement to another party, for a consideration to convey his right and interest in the personal property. The purchaser must take actual possession of the property. Juries have power to determine upon the fairness or unfairness of a bill of sale.

COMMON FORM OF BILL OF SALE.

KNOW ALL MEN by this instrument, that I, Louis Clay, of Princeton, Illinois, of the first part, for and in consideration of Five Hundred and Ten dollars, to me paid by John Floyd, of the same place, of the second part, the receipt whereof is hereby acknowledged, have sold, and by this instrument do convey unto the said Floyd, party of the second part, his executors, administrators, and assigns, my undivided half of ten acres of corn, now growing on the farm of Thomas Tyrrell, in the town above mentioned; one pair of horses, sixteen sheep, and five cows, belonging to me, and in my possession at the farm aforesaid; to have and to hold the same unto the party of the second part, his executors and assigns, forever. And I do, for myself and legal representatives, agree with the said party of the second part, and his legal representatives, to warrant and defend the sale of the afore-mentioned property and chattels unto the said party of the second part, and his legal representatives, against all and every person whatsoever.

In witness whereof, I have hereunto affixed my hand, this tenth day of October, one thousand eight hundred and seventy-six.

                                            LOUIS CLAY.

BONDS.

A bond is a written admission on the part of the maker in which he pledges a certain sum to another, at a certain time.

COMMON FORM OF BOND.

KNOW ALL MEN by this instrument, that I, George Edgerton, of Watseka, Iroquois County, State of Illinois, am firmly bound unto Peter Kirchoff, of the place aforesaid, in the sum of five hundred dollars, to be paid to the said Peter Kirchoff, or his legal representatives: to which payment, to be made, I bind myself, or my legal representatives, by this instrument.

Sealed with my seal, and dated this second day of November, one thousand eight hundred and sixty-four.

The condition of this bond is such that if I, George Edgerton, my heirs, administrators, or executors, shall promptly pay the sum of two hundred and fifty dollars in three equal annual payments from the date hereof, with annual interest, then the above obligation to be of no effect; otherwise to be in full force and valid.

Sealed and delivered in
    presence of   GEORGE EDGERTON. [L.S.]
WILLIAM TURNER.

CHATTEL MORTGAGES.

A chattel mortgage is a mortgage on personal property for payment of a certain sum of money, to hold the property against debts of other creditors. The mortgage must describe the property, and must be acknowledged before a justice of the peace in the township or precinct where the mortgagee resides, and entered upon his docket, and must be recorded in the recorder's office of the county.

GENERAL FORM OF CHATTEL MORTGAGE.

THIS INDENTURE, made and entered into this first day of January, in the year of our Lord one thousand eight hundred and seventy-five, between Theodore Lottinville, of the town of Geneseo in the County of Henry, and State of Illinois, party of the first part, and Paul Henshaw, of the same town, county, and State, party of the second part.

Witnesseth, that the said party of the first part, for and in consideration of the sum of one thousand dollars, in hand paid, the receipt whereof is hereby acknowledged, does hereby grant, sell, convey, and confirm unto the said party of the second part, his heirs and assigns forever, all and singular the following described goods and chattels, to wit:

Two three-year old roan-colored horses, one Burdett organ, No. 987, one Brussels carpet, 15x20 feet in size, one marble-top center table, one Home Comfort cooking stove, No. 8, one black walnut bureau with mirror attached, one set of parlor chairs (six in number), upholstered in green rep, with lounge corresponding with same in style and color of upholstery, now in possession of said Lottinville, at No. 4 Prairie Ave., Geneseo, Ill.;

Together with all and singular, the appurtenances thereunto belonging, or in any wise appertaining; to have and to hold the above described goods and chattels, unto the said party of the second part, his heirs and assigns, forever.

Provided, always, and these presents are upon this express condition, that if the said Theodore Lottinville, his heirs, executors, administrators, or assigns, shall, on or before the first day of January, A.D., one thousand eight hundred and seventy-six, pay, or cause to be paid, to the said Paul Ranslow, or his lawful attorney or attorneys, heirs, executors, administrators, or assigns, the sum of One Thousand dollars, together with the interest that may accrue thereon, at the rate of ten per cent. per annum, from the first day of January, A.D. one thousand eight hundred and seventy-five, until paid, according to the tenor of one promissory note bearing even date herewith for the payment of said sum of money, that then and from thenceforth, these presents, and everything herein contained, shall cease, and be null and void, anything herein contained to the contrary notwithstanding.

Provided, also, that the said Theodore Lottinville may retain the possession of and have the use of said goods and chattels until the day of payment aforesaid; and also, at his own expense, shall keep said goods and chattels; and also at the expiration of said time of payment, if said sum of money, together with the interest as aforesaid, shall not be paid, shall deliver up said goods and chattels, in good condition, to said Paul Ranslow, or his heirs, executors, administrators, or assigns.

And provided, also, that if default in payment as aforesaid, by said party of the first part, shall be made, or if said party of the second part shall at any time before said promissory note becomes due, feel himself unsafe or insecure, that then the said party of the second part, or his attorney, agent, assigns, or heirs, executors, or administrators, shall have the right to take possession of said goods and chattels, wherever they may or can be found, and sell the same at public or private sale, to the highest bidder for cash in hand, after giving ten days' notice of the time and place of said sale, together with a description of the goods and chattels to be sold, by at least four advertisements, posted up in public places in the vicinity where said sale is to take place, and proceed to make the sum of money and interest promised as aforesaid, together with all reasonable costs, charges, and expenses in so doing; and if there shall be any overplus, shall pay the same without delay to the said party of the first part, or his legal representatives.

In testimony whereof, the said party of the first part has hereunto set his hand and affixed his seal, the day and year first above written. Signed, sealed and delivered in

   presence of   THEODORE LOTTINVILLE. [L.S.]
SAMUEL J. TILDEN.

LEASE OF FARM AND BUILDINGS THEREON.

THIS INDENTURE, made this second day of June, 1875, between David Patton of the Town of Bisbee, State of Illinois, of the first part, and John Doyle of the same place, of the second part,

Witnesseth, that the said David Patton, for and in consideration of the covenants hereinafter mentioned and reserved, on the part of the said John Doyle, his executors, administrators, and assigns, to be paid, kept, and performed, hath let, and by these presents doth grant, demise, and let, unto the said John Doyle, his executors, administrators, and assigns, all that parcel of land situate in Bisbee aforesaid, bounded and described as follows, to wit :

[Here describe the land.]

Together with all the appurtenances appertaining thereto. To have and to hold the said premises, with appurtenances thereto belonging, unto the said Doyle, his executors, administrators, and assigns, for the term of five years, from the first day of October next following, at a yearly rent of Six Hundred dollars, to be paid in equal payments, semi-annually, as long as said buildings are in good tenantable condition.

And the said Doyle, by these presents, covenants and agrees to pay all taxes and assessments, and keep in repair all hedges, ditches, rail, and other fences ; (the said David Patton, his heirs, assigns and administrators, to furnish all timber, brick, tile, and other materials necessary for such repairs.)

Said Doyle further covenants and agrees to apply to said land, in a farmer-like manner, all manure and compost accumulating upon said farm, and cultivate all the arable land in a husbandlike manner, according to the usual custom among farmers in the neighborhood ; he also agrees to trim the hedges at a seasonable time, preventing injury from cattle to such hedges, and to all fruit and other trees on the said premises. That he will seed down with clover and timothy seed twenty acres yearly of arable land, ploughing the same number of acres each Spring of land now in grass, and hitherto unbroken.

It is further agreed, that if the said Doyle shall fail to perform the whole or any one of the above mentioned covenants, then and in that case the said David Patton may declare this lease terminated, by giving three months' notice of the same, prior to the first of October of any year, and may distrain any part of the stock, goods, or chattels, or other property in possession of said Doyle, for sufficient to compensate for the non-performance of the above written covenants, the same to be determined, and amounts so to be paid to be determined, by three arbitrators, chosen as follows: Each of the parties to this instrument to choose one, and the two so chosen to select a third : the decision of said arbitrators to be final.

In witness whereof, we have hereto set our hands and seals.

Signed, sealed, and delivered

in presence of   DAVID PATTON.   [L.S.]

JAMES WALDRON.   JOHN DOYLE.   [L.S.]

FORM OF LEASE OF A HOUSE.

THIS INSTRUMENT, made the first day of October, 1875, witnesseth that Amos Griest of Yorkville, County of Kendall, State of Illinois, hath rented from Aaron Young of Logansport aforesaid, the dwelling and lot No. 13 Ohio Street, situated in said City of Yorkville, for five years from the above date, at the yearly rental of Three Hundred dollars, payable monthly, on the first day of each month, in advance, at the residence of said Aaron Young.

At the expiration of said above mentioned term, the said Griest agrees to give the said Young peaceable possession of the said dwelling, in as good condition as when taken, ordinary wear and casualties excepted.

In witness whereof, we place our hands and seals the day and year aforesaid.

Signed, sealed and delivered   AMOS GRIEST.   [L.S.]

in presence of

NICKOLAS SCHUTZ,   AARON YOUNG. [L.S.]

Notary Public.

LANDLORD'S AGREEMENT.

THIS certifies that I have let and rented, this first day of January, 1876, unto Jacob Schmidt, my house and lot, No. 15 Erie Street, in the City of Chicago, State of Illinois, and its appurtenances ; he to have the free and uninterrupted occupation thereof for one year from this date, at the yearly rental of Two Hundred dollars, to be paid monthly in advance ; rent to cease if destroyed by fire, or otherwise made untenantable.

PETER FUNK.

TENANT'S AGREEMENT.

THIS certifies that I have hired and taken from Peter Funk, his house and lot, No. 15 Erie Street, in the City of Chicago, State of Illinois, with appurtenances thereto belonging, for one year, to commence this day, at a yearly rental of Two Hundred dollars, to be paid monthly in advance ; unless said house becomes untenantable from fire or other causes, in which case rent ceases ; and I further agree to give and yield said premises one year from this first day of January 1876, in as good condition as now, ordinary wear and damage by the elements excepted.

Given under my hand this day.   JACOB SCHMIDT.

NOTICE TO QUIT.

To F. W. ARLEN,

Sir: Please observe that the term of one year, for which the house and land, situated at No. 6 Indiana Street, and now occupied by you, were rented to you, expired on the first day of October, 1875, and as I desire to repossess said premises, you are hereby requested and required to vacate the same. Respectfully Yours,

P. T. BARNUM.

LINCOLN, NEB., October 4, 1875.

TENANT'S NOTICE OF LEAVING.

DEAR SIR:

The premises I now occupy as your tenant, at No. 6 Indiana Street, I shall vacate on the first day of November, 1875. You will please take notice accordingly.

Dated this tenth day of October, 1875. F. W. ARLEN.

To P. T. BARNUM, ESQ.

REAL ESTATE MORTGAGE TO SECURE PAYMENT OF MONEY.

THIS INDENTURE, made this sixteenth day of May, in the year of our Lord, one thousand eight hundred and seventy-two, between William Stocker, of Peoria, County of Peoria, and State of Illinois, and Olla, his wife, party of the first part, and Edward Singer, party of the second part.

Whereas, the said party of the first part is justly indebted to the said party of the second part, in the sum of Two Thousand dollars, secured to be paid by two certain promissory notes (bearing even date herewith) the one due and payable at the Second National Bank in Peoria, Illinois, with interest, on the sixteenth day of May, in the year one thousand eight hundred and seventy-three; the other due and payable at the Second National Bank at Peoria, Ill., with interest, on the sixteenth day of May, in the year one thousand eight hundred and seventy-four.

Now, therefore, this indenture witnesseth, that the said party of the first part, for the better securing the payment of the money aforesaid, with interest thereon, according to the tenor and effect of the said two promissory notes above mentioned; and, also in consideration of the further sum of one dollar to them in hand paid by the said party of the second part, at the delivery of these presents, the receipt whereof is hereby acknowledged, have granted, bargained, sold, and conveyed, and by these presents do grant, bargain, sell, and convey, unto the said party of the second part, his heirs and assigns, forever, all that certain parcel of land, situate, etc.

[Describing the premises.]

To have and to hold the same, together with all and singular the Tenements, Hereditaments, Privileges and Appurtenances ther unto belonging or in any wise appertaining. And also, all the estate, interest, and claim whatsoever, in law as well as in equity which the party of the first part have in and to the premises hereby conveyed unto the said party of the second part, his heirs and assigns, and to their only proper use, benefit and behoof. And the said William Stocker, and Olla, his wife, party of the first part, hereby expressly waive, relinquish, release, and convey unto the said party of the second part, his heirs, executors, administrators, and assigns, all right, title, claim, interest, and benefit whatever, in and to the above described premises, and each and every part thereof, which is given by or results from all laws of this state pertaining to the exemption of homesteads.

Provided always, and these presents are upon this express condition, that if the said party of the first part, their heirs, executors, or administrators, shall well and truly pay, or cause to be paid, to the said party of the second part, his heirs, executors, administrators, or assigns, the aforesaid sums of money, with such interest thereon, at the time and in the manner specified in the above mentioned promissory notes, according to the true intent and meaning thereof, then in that case, these presents and every thing herein expressed, shall be absolutely null and void.

In witness whereof, the said party of the first part hereunto set their hands and seals the day and year first above written.

Signed, sealed and delivered in presence of

JAMES WHITEHEAD,   WILLIAM STOCKER. [L.S.]
FRED. SAMUELS.   OLLA STOCKER. [L.S.]

WARRANTY DEED WITH COVENANTS.

THIS INDENTURE, made this sixth day of April, in the year of our Lord one thousand eight hundred and seventy-two, between Henry Best of Lawrence, County of Lawrence, State of Illinois, and Belle, his wife, of the first part, and Charles Pearson of the same place, of the second part,

Witnesseth, that the said party of the first part, for and in consideration of the sum of Six Thousand dollars in hand paid by the said party of the second part, the receipt whereof is hereby acknowledged, have granted, bargained, and sold, and by these presents do grant, bargain, and sell, unto the said party of the second part, his heirs and assigns, all the following described lot, piece, or parcel of land, situated in the City of Lawrence, in the County of Lawrence, and State of Illinois, to wit:

[*Here describe the property.*]

Together with all and singular the hereditaments and appurtenances thereunto belonging or in any wise appertaining, and the reversion and reversions, remainder and remainders, rents, issues, and profits thereof; and all the estate, right, title, interest, claim, and demand whatsoever, of the said party of the first part, either in law or equity, of, in, and to the above bargained premises, with the hereditaments and appurtenances. To have and to hold the said premises above bargained and described, with the appurtenances, unto the said party of the second part, his heirs and assigns, forever. And the said Henry Best, and Belle, his wife, parties of the first part, hereby expressly waive, release, and relinquish unto the said party of the second part, his heirs, executors, administrators, and assigns, all right, title, claim, interest, and benefit whatever, in and to the above described premises, and each and every part thereof, which is given by or results from all laws of this state pertaining to the exemption of homesteads.

And the said Henry Best, and Belle, his wife, party of the first part, for themselves and their heirs, executors, and administrators, do covenant, grant, bargain, and agree, to and with the said party of the second part, his heirs and assigns, that at the time of the ensealing and delivery of these presents they were well seized of the premises above conveyed, as of a good, sure, perfect, absolute, and indefeasible estate of inheritance in law, and in fee simple, and have good right, full power, and lawful authority to grant, bargain, sell, and convey the same, in manner and form aforesaid, and that the same are free and clear from all former and other grants, bargains, sales, liens, taxes, assessments, and encumbrances of what kind or nature soever; and the above bargained premises in the quiet and peaceable possession of the said party of the second part, his heirs and assigns, against all and every person or persons lawfully claiming or to claim the whole or any part thereof, the said party of the first part shall and will warrant and forever defend.

In testimony whereof, the said parties of the first part have hereunto set their hands and seals the day and year first above written.

Signed, sealed and delivered

in presence of   HENRY BEST, [L.S.]

JERRY LINKLATER.   BELLE BEST. [L.S.]

QUIT-CLAIM DEED.

THIS INDENTURE, made the eighth day of June, in the year of our Lord one thousand eight hundred and seventy-four, between David Tour, of Plano, County of Kendall, State of Illinois, party of the first part, and Larry O'Brien, of the same place, party of the second part,

Witnesseth, that the said party of the first part, for and in consideration of Nine Hundred dollars in hand paid by the said party of the second part, the receipt whereof is hereby acknowledged, and the said party of the second part forever released and discharged therefrom, has remised, released, sold, conveyed, and quit-claimed, and by these presents does remise, release, sell, convey, and quit-claim, unto the said party of the second part, his heirs and assigns, forever, all the right, title, interest, claim. and demand, which the said party of the first part has in and to the following described lot, piece, or parcel of land, to wit:

[*Here describe the land.*]

To have and to hold the same, together with all and singular the appurtenances and privileges thereunto belonging, or in any wise thereunto appertaining, and all the estate, right, title, interest, and claim whatever, of the said party of the first part, either in law or equity, to the only proper use, benefit, and behoof of the said party of the second part, his heirs and assigns forever.

In witness whereof the said party of the first part hereunto set his hand and seal the day and year above written.

Signed, sealed and delivered   DAVID TOUR. [L.S.]
    in presence of
THOMAS ASHLEY.

The above forms of Deeds and Mortgage are such as have heretofore been generally used, but the following are much shorter, and are made equally valid by the laws of this state.

WARRANTY DEED.

The grantor (here insert name or names and place of residence), for and in consideration of (here insert consideration) in hand paid, conveys and warrants to (here insert the grantee's name or names) the following described real estate (here insert description), situated in the County of ―― in the State of Illinois.

Dated this ―― day of ―― A. D. 18――.

QUIT CLAIM DEED.

The grantor (here insert grantor's name or names and place of residence), for the consideration of (here insert consideration) convey and quit-claim to (here insert grantee's name or names) all interest in the following described real estate (here insert description), situated in the County of ―― in the State of Illinois.

Dated this ―― day of ―― A. D. 18――.

MORTGAGE.

The mortgagor (here insert name or names) mortgages and warrants to (here insert name or names of mortgagee or mortgagees), to secure the payment of (here recite the nature and amount of indebtedness, showing when due and the rate of interest, and whether secured by note or otherwise), the following described real estate (here insert description thereof), situated in the County of ―― in the State of Illinois.

Dated this ―― day of ―― A. D. 18――.

RELEASE.

KNOW ALL MEN by these presents, that I, Peter Ahlund, of Chicago, of the County of Cook, and State of Illinois, for and in consideration of One dollar, to me in hand paid, and for other good and valuable considerations, the receipt whereof is hereby confessed, do hereby grant, bargain, remise, convey, release, and quit-claim unto Joseph Carlin of Chicago, of the County of Cook, and State of Illinois, all the right, title, interest, claim, or demand whatsoever, I may have acquired in, through, or by a certain Indenture or Mortgage Deed, bearing date the second day of January, A. D. 1871, and recorded in the Recorder's office of said county, in book A of Deeds, page 46, to the premises therein described, and which said Deed was made to secure one certain promissory note, bearing even date with said deed, for the sum of Three Hundred dollars.

Witness my hand and seal, this second day of November, A. D. 1874.

PETER AHLUND. [L.S.]

State of Illinois, }
Cook County. } ss.

I, George Saxton, a Notary Public in and for said county, in the state aforesaid, do hereby certify that Peter Ahlund, personally known to me as the same person whose name is subscribed to the foregoing Release, appeared before me this day in person, and acknowledged that he signed, sealed, and delivered the said instrument of writing as his free and voluntary act, for the uses and purposes therein set forth.

[NOTARIAL SEAL]

Given under my hand and seal, this second day of November, A. D. 1874.

GEORGE SAXTON, N. P.

GENERAL FORM OF WILL FOR REAL AND PERSONAL PROPERTY.

I, Charles Mansfield, of the Town of Salem, County of Jackson, State of Illinois, being aware of the uncertainty of life, and in failing health, but of sound mind and memory, do make and declare this to be my last will and testament, in manner following, to wit:

First. I give, devise and bequeath unto my oldest son, Sidney H. Mansfield, the sum of Two Thousand Dollars, of bank stock, now in the Third National Bank of Cincinnati, Ohio, and the farm owned by myself in the Town of Buskirk, consisting of one hundred and sixty acres, with all the houses, tenements, and improvements thereunto belonging; to have and to hold unto my said son, his heirs and assigns, forever.

Second. I give, devise and bequeath to each of my daughters, Anna Louise Mansfield and Ida Clara Mansfield, each Two Thousand dollars in bank stock, in the Third National Bank of Cincinnati, Ohio, and also each one quarter section of land, owned by myself, situated in the Town of Lake, Illinois, and recorded in my name in the Recorder's office in the county where such land is located. The north one hundred and sixty acres of said half section is devised to my eldest daughter, Anna Louise.

Third. I give, devise and bequeath to my son, Frank Alfred Mansfield, Five shares of Railroad stock in the Baltimore and Ohio Railroad, and my one hundred and sixty acres of land and saw mill thereon, situated in Manistee, Michigan, with all the improvements and appurtenances thereunto belonging, which said real estate is recorded in my name in the county where situated.

Fourth. I give to my wife, Victoria Elizabeth Mansfield, all my household furniture, goods, chattels, and personal property, about my home, not hitherto disposed of, including Eight Thousand dollars of bank stock in the Third National Bank of Cincinnati, Ohio, Fifteen shares in the Baltimore and Ohio Railroad, and the free and unrestricted use, possession, and benefit of the home farm, so long as she may live, in lieu of dower, to which she is entitled by law; said farm being my present place of residence.

Fifth. I bequeath to my invalid father, Elijah H. Mansfield, the income from rents of my store building at 145 Jackson Street, Chicago, Illinois, during the term of his natural life. Said building and land therewith to revert to my said sons and daughters in equal proportion, upon the demise of my said father.

Sixth. It is also my will and desire that, at the death of my wife, Victoria Elizabeth Mansfield, or at any time when she may arrange to relinquish her life interest in the above mentioned homestead, the same may revert to my above named children, or to the lawful heirs of each.

And lastly. I nominate and appoint as executors of this my last will and testament, my wife, Victoria Elizabeth Mansfield, and my eldest son, Sidney H. Mansfield.

I further direct that my debts and necessary funeral expenses shall be paid from moneys now on deposit in the Savings Bank of Salem, the residue of such moneys to revert to my wife, Victoria Elizabeth Mansfield, for her use forever.

In witness whereof, I, Charles Mansfield, to this my last will and testament, have hereunto set my hand and seal, this fourth day of April, eighteen hundred and seventy-two.

Signed, sealed, and declared by Charles Mansfield, as and for his last will and testament, in the presence of us, who, at his request, and in his presence, and in the presence of each other, have subscribed our names hereunto as witnesses thereof.

CHARLES MANSFIELD. [L.S.]

PETER A. SCHENCK, Sycamore, Ills.

FRANK E. DENT, Salem, Ills.

CODICIL.

Whereas I, Charles Mansfield, did, on the fourth day of April, one thousand eight hundred and seventy-two, make my last will and testament, I do now, by this writing, add this codicil to my said will, to be taken as a part thereof.

Whereas, by the dispensation of Providence, my daughter, Anna Louise, has deceased November fifth, eighteen hundred and seventy-three, and whereas, a son has been born to me, which son is now christened Richard Albert Mansfield, I give and bequeath unto him my gold watch, and all right, interest, and title in lands and bank stock and chattels bequeathed to my deceased daughter, Anna Louise, in the body of this will.

In witness whereof, I hereunto place my hand and seal, this tenth day of March, eighteen hundred and seventy-five.

Signed, sealed, published, and declared to us by the testator, Charles Mansfield, as and for a codicil to be annexed to his last will and testament. And we, at his request, and in his presence, and in the presence of each other, have subscribed our names as witnesses thereto, at the date hereof.

CHARLES MANSFIELD. [L.S.]

FRANK E. DENT, Salem, Ills.
JOHN C. SHAY, Salem, Ills.

CHURCH ORGANIZATIONS

May be legally made by *electing* or *appointing*, according to the *usages* or *customs* of the body of which it is a part, at any meeting held for that purpose, *two* or *more* of its *members* as trustees, wardens or vestrymen, and may adopt a *corporate* name. The chairman or secretary of such meeting shall, as soon as possible, make and file in the office of the recorder of deeds of the county, an affidavit substantially in the following form:

STATE OF ILLINOIS, ⎱ ss.
——— County. ⎰

I, ———, do solemnly swear (or affirm, as the case may be), that at a meeting of the members of the (here insert the name of the church, society or congregation as known before organization), held at (here insert place of meeting), in the County of ———, and State of Illinois, on the ——— day of ———, A.D. 18—, for that purpose, the following persons were elected (or appointed) [*here insert their names*] trustees, wardens, vestrymen, (or officers by whatever name they may choose to adopt, with powers similar to trustees) according to the rules and usages of such (church, society or congregation), and said ———

adopted as its corporate name (here insert name), and at said meeting this affiant acted as (chairman or secretary, as the case may be).

Subscribed and sworn to before me, this —— day of ——, A.D. 18—.   Name of Affiant,—— ——

which affidavit must be recorded by the recorder, and shall be, or a certified copy made by the recorder, received as evidence of such an incorporation.

No certificate of election after the first need be filed for record.

The term of office of the trustees and the general government of the society can be determined by the rules or by-laws adopted. Failure to elect trustees at the time provided does not work a dissolution, but the old trustees hold over. A trustee or trustees may be removed, in the same manner by the society as elections are held by a meeting called for that purpose. The property of the society vests in the corporation. The corporation may hold, or acquire by purchase or otherwise, land **not** exceeding ten acres, for the purpose of the society. The trustees **have** the care, custody and control of the property of the corporation, and can, *when directed* by the society, erect houses or improvements, and repair and alter the same, and may also when so directed by the society, mortgage, encumber, sell and convey any real or personal estate belonging to the corporation, and make all proper contracts in the name of such corporation.' But they are prohibited by law from encumbering or interfering with any property so as to destroy the effect of any gift, grant, devise or bequest to the corporation; but such gifts, grants, devises or bequests, must in all cases be used so as to carry out the object intended by the persons making the same. Existing societies may organize in the manner herein set forth, and have all the advantages thereof.

SUGGESTIONS TO THOSE PURCHASING BOOKS BY SUBSCRIPTION.

The business of *publishing books by subscription* having so often been brought into disrepute by agents making representations and declarations *not authorized by the publisher;* in order to prevent that as much as possible, and that there may be more general knowledge of the relation such agents bear to their principal, and the law governing such cases, the following statement is made:

A subscription is in the *nature of a contract* of mutual promises, by which the subscriber agrees to *pay a certain sum* for the work described; the *consideration is concurrent* that the publisher shall *publish the book named*, and deliver the same, for which the subscriber is to pay the price named. *The nature and character of the work is described in the prospectus and by the sample shown.* These should be *carefully examined before subscribing*, as they are the basis and consideration of the promise to pay,

R. ELLWOOD
SYCAMORE

and not the too *often exaggerated statements of the agent*, who is *merely employed* to *solicit subscriptions*, for which he is usually *paid a commission* for each subscriber, and has *no authority* to *change or alter* the conditions upon which the subscriptions are authorized to be made by the publisher. Should the *agent assume* to agree to make the subscription conditional or *modify or change the agreement of the publisher*, as set out by prospectus and sample, in order to *bind the principal*, the *subscriber* should see that such conditions or changes are stated *over or in connection with his signature*, so that the publisher may have notice of the same.

All persons making contracts in reference to matters of this kind, or any other business, should remember *that the law as to written contracts is*, that they can *not be varied, altered or rescinded verbally, but if done at all, must be done in writing.* It is therefore *important* that all *persons contemplating subscribing should distinctly understand that all talk before or after the subscription is made, is not admissible as evidence, and is no part of the contract.*

Persons employed to solicit subscriptions are known to the trade as canvassers. They are agents *appointed to do a particular business in a prescribed mode*, and *have no authority* to do it in any other way to the prejudice of their principal, nor can they bind their principal in any other matter. They *can not collect money*, or agree that payment may be made in *anything else but money.* They *can not extend* the time of payment *beyond the time of delivery, nor bind their principal* for the *payment of expenses* incurred in their buisness.

It would save a great deal of trouble, and often serious loss, if persons, *before signing* their names to any subscription book, or any written instrument, would *examine carefully what it is ;* if they can not read themselves, should call on some one disinterested who can.

6

INTEREST TABLE.

A Simple Rule for Accurately Computing Interest at Any Given Per Cent. for Any Length of Time.

Multiply the *principal* (amount of money at interest) by the *time reduced to days ;* then divide this *product* by the *quotient* obtained by dividing 360 (the number of days in the interest year) by the *per cent.* of interest, and *the quotient thus obtained* will be the required interest.

ILLUSTRATION.   *Solution.*

Require the interest of $462.50 for one month and eighteen days at 6 per cent. An interest month is 30 days ; one month and eighteen days equal 48 days. $462.50 multiplied by .48 gives 222,0000 ; 360 divided by 6 (the per cent. of interest) gives 60, and $222.0000 divided by 60 will give you the exact interest, which is $3.70. If the rate of interest in the above example were 12 per cent., we would divide the $222.0000 by 30 (because 360 divided by 12 gives 30) ; if 4 per cent., we would divide by 90 ; if 8 per cent., by 45 ; and in like manner for any other per cent.

$$
\begin{array}{r}
\$462\ 50 \\
.48 \\
\hline
370000 \\
185000 \\
\hline
6)360 \\
60)\ \$222.0000(\$3.70 \\
180 \\
\hline
420 \\
420 \\
\hline
00
\end{array}
$$

MISCELLANEOUS TABLE.

12 units, or things, 1 Dozen.	56 pounds, 1 Firkin of Butter.
12 dozen, 1 Gross.	24 sheets of paper, 1 Quire.
20 things, 1 Score.	20 quires paper 1 Ream.
196 pounds, 1 Barrel of Flour.	4 feet wide, 4 feet high, and 8 feet long, 1 Cord
200 pounds, 1 Barrel of Pork.	of Wood.

POPULATION OF THE UNITED STATES.

STATES AND TERRITORIES.	Total Population.
Alabama	996,992
Arkansas	484,471
California	560,247
Connecticut	537,454
Delaware	125,015
Florida	187,748
Georgia	1,184,109
Illinois	2,539,891
Indiana	1,680,637
Iowa	1,191,792
Kansas	364,399
Kentucky	1,321,011
Louisiana	726,915
Maine	626,915
Maryland	780,894
Massachusetts	1,457,351
Michigan	1,184,059
Minnesota	439,706
Mississippi	827,922
Missouri	1,721,295
Nebraska	122,993
Nevada	42,491
New Hampshire	318,300
New Jersey	906,096
New York	4,382,759
North Carolina	1,071,361
Ohio	2,665,260
Oregon	90,923
Pennsylvania	3,521,791
Rhode Island	217,353
South Carolina	705,606
Tennessee	1,258,520
Texas	818,579
Vermont	330,551
Virginia	1,225,163
West Virginia	442,014
Wisconsin	1,054,670
Total States	38,113,253
Arizona	9,658
Colorado	39,864
Dakota	14,181
District of Columbia	131,700
Idaho	14,999
Montana	20,595
New Mexico	91,874
Utah	86,786
Washington	23,955
Wyoming	9,118
Total Territories	442,730
Total United States	38,555,983

POPULATION OF FIFTY PRINCIPAL CITIES.

CITIES.	Aggregate Population.
New York, N. Y	942,292
Philadelphia, Pa	674,022
Brooklyn, N. Y	396,099
St. Louis, Mo	310,864
Chicago, Ill	298,977
Baltimore, Md	267,354
Boston, Mass	250,526
Cincinnati, Ohio	216,239
New Orleans, La	191,418
San Francisco, Cal	149,473
Buffalo, N. Y	117,714
Washington, D. C	109,199
Newark, N. J	105,059
Louisville, Ky	100,753
Cleveland, Ohio	92,829
Pittsburg, Pa	86,076
Jersey City, N. J	82,546
Detroit, Mich	79,577
Milwaukee, Wis	71,440
Albany, N. Y	69,422
Providence, R. I	68,904
Rochester, N. Y	62,386
Allegheny, Pa	53,180
Richmond, Va	51,038
New Haven, Conn	50,840
Charleston, S. C	48,956
Indianapolis, Ind	48,244
Troy, N. Y	46,465
Syracuse, N. Y	43,051
Worcester, Mass	41,105
Lowell, Mass	40,928
Memphis, Tenn	40,226
Cambridge, Mass	39,634
Hartford, Conn	37,180
Scranton, Pa	35,092
Reading, Pa	33,930
Paterson, N. J	33,579
Kansas City, Mo	32,260
Mobile, Ala	32,034
Toledo, Ohio	31,584
Portland, Me	31,413
Columbus, Ohio	31,274
Wilmington, Del	30,841
Dayton, Ohio	30,473
Lawrence, Mass	28,921
Utica, N. Y	28,804
Charlestown, Mass	28,323
Savannah, Ga	28,235
Lynn, Mass	28,233
Fall River, Mass	26,766

POPULATION OF THE UNITED STATES.

STATES AND TERRITORIES.	Area in square Miles.	POPULATION.		Miles R. R. 1872.	STATES AND TERRITORIES.	Area in square Miles.	POPULATION.		Miles R. R. 1872.
		1870.	1875.				1870.	1875.	
States.					*States.*				
Alabama...........	50,722	996,992	....	1,671	Pennsylvania....	46,000	3,521,791	....	5,113
Arkansas.........	52,198	484,471	....	25	Rhode Island....	1,306	217,353	258,239	136
California.........	188,981	560,247	....	1,013	South Carolina..	29,385	705,606	925,145	1,201
Connecticut......	4,674	537,454	....	820	Tennessee.........	45,600	1,258,520	....	1,520
Delaware.........	2,120	125,015	....	227	Texas.............	237,504	818,579	....	865
Florida...........	59,268	187,748	....	466	Vermont..........	10,212	330,551	....	675
Georgia...........	58,000	1,184,109	....	2,108	Virginia..........	40,904	1,225,163	....	1,490
Illinois...........	55,410	2,539,891	....	5,904	West Virginia....	23,000	442,014	....	485
Indiana...........	33,809	1,680,637	....	3,529	Wisconsin........	53,924	1,054,670	1,236,729	1,725
Iowa.............	55,045	1,191,792	1,350,544	3,160					
Kansas...........	81,318	364,399	528,349	1,760	*Total States......*	1,950,171	38,113,253	....	59,587
Kentucky.........	37,680	1,321,011	....	1,123					
Louisiana	41,346	726,915	857,039	539	*Territories.*				
Maine............	31,776	626,915	....	871	Arizona...........	113,916	9,658	....	......
Maryland........	11,184	780,894	....	820	Colorado..........	104,500	39,864	....	392
Massachusetts...	7,800	1,457,351	1,651,912	1,606	Dakota...........	147,490	14,181	....	......
Michigan*........	56,451	1,184,059	1,334,031	2,235	Dist. of Columbia.	60	131,700	....	*
Minnesota,......	83,531	439,706	598,429	1,612	Idaho............	90,932	14,999	....	......
Mississippi......	47,156	827,922	....	990	Montana..........	143,776	20,595	....	......
Missouri.........	65,350	1,721,295	....	2,580	New Mexico......	121,201	91,874	....	......
Nebraska.........	75,995	123,993	246,280	828	Utah.............	80,056	86,786	....	375
Nevada...........	112,090	42,491	52,540	593	Washington.......	69,944	23,955	....	......
New Hampshire.	9,280	318,300	....	590	Wyoming	93,107	9,118	....	498
New Jersey......	8,320	906,096	1,026,502	1,295					
New York........	47,000	4,382,759	4,705,208	4,710	*Total Territories.*	965,032	442,730	....	1,265
North Carolina..	50,704	1,071,361	....	1,190					
Ohio	39,964	2,665,260	....	3,740					
Oregon	95,244	90,923	....	159	Aggregate of U. S..	2,915,203	38,555,983	....	60,852

* Last Census of Michigan taken in 1874.   * Included in the Railroad Mileage of Maryland.

PRINCIPAL COUNTRIES OF THE WORLD;

POPULATION AND AREA.

COUNTRIES.	Population.	Date of Census.	Area in Square Miles.	Inhabitants to Square Mile.	CAPITALS.	Population.
China......................	446,500,000	1871	3,741,846	119.3	Pekin............ ..	1,648,800
British Empire...............	226,817,108	1871	4,677,432	48.6	London.............	3,251,800
Russia......................	81,925,490	1871	8,003,778	10.2	St. Petersburg......	667,000
United States with Alaska...	38,925,600	1870	2,603,884	7.74	Washington	109,199
France	36,469,800	1866	204,091	178.7	Paris..............	1,825,300
Austria and Hungary........	35,904,400	1869	240,348	149.4	Vienna	833,800
Japan......................	34,785,300	1871	149,399	232.8	Yeddo.............	1,554,900
Great Britain and Ireland....	31,617,100	1871	121,315	262.3	London.............	3,251,800
German Empire..............	29,906,092	1871	160,207	187.	Berlin.............	825,400
Italy.......................	27,439,921	1871	118,847	230.9	Rome..............	244,484
Spain......................	16,642,000	1867	195,775	85.	Madrid............	332,000
Brazil......................	10,000,000	......	3,253,029	3.07	Rio Janeiro........	420,000
Turkey.....................	16,163,000	......	672,621	24.4	Constantinople	1,075,000
Mexico.....................	9,173,000	1869	761,526	....	Mexico	210,300
Sweden and Norway	5,921,500	1870	292,871	20.	Stockholm.........	136,900
Persia.....................	5,000,000	1870	635,964	7.8	Teheran...........	120,000
Belgium....................	5,021,300	1869	11,373	441.5	Brussels...........	314,100
Bavaria....................	4,861,400	1871	29,292	165.9	Munich............	169,500
Portugal...................	3,995,200	1868	34,494	115.8	Lisbon............	224,063
Holland	3,688,300	1870	12,680	290.9	Hague.............	90,100
New Grenada,..............	3,000,000	1870	357,157	8.4	Bogota............	45,000
Chili......................	2,000,000	1869	132,616	15.1	Santiago...........	115,400
Switzerland................	2,669,100	1870	15,992	166.9	Berne.............	36,000
Peru......................	2,500,000	1871	471,838	5.3	Lima..............	160,100
Bolivia....................	2,000,000	......	497,321	4.	Chuquisaca........	25,000
Argentine Republic..........	1,812,000	1869	871,848	2.1	Buenos Ayres......	177,800
Wurtemburg	1,818,500	1871	7,533	241.4	Stuttgart..........	91,600
Denmark...................	1,784,700	1870	14,753	120.9	Copenhagen........	162,042
Venezuela..................	1,500,000	......	368,238	4.2	Caracas...........	47,000
Baden.....................	1,461,400	1871	5,912	247.	Carlsruhe..........	36,600
Greece....................	1,457,900	1870	19,353	75.3	Athens............	43,400
Guatemala	1,180,000	1871	40,879	28.9	Guatemala	40,000
Ecuador...................	1,300,000	......	218,928	5.9	Quito	70,000
Paraguay..................	1,000,000	1871	63,787	15.6	Asuncion..........	48,000
Hesse.....................	823,138	......	2,969	277.	Darmstadt.........	30,000
Liberia....................	718,000	1871	9,576	74.9	Monrovia	3,000
S an Salvador,..............	600,000	1871	7,335	81.8	Sal Salvador	15,000
Hayti.....................	572,000	......	10,205	56.	Port au Prince.....	20,000
Nicaragua..................	350,000	1871	58,171	6.	Managua...........	10,000
Uruguay...................	300,000	1871	66,752	4.5	Monte Video.......	44,500
Honduras..................	350,000	1871	47,092	7.4	Comayagua	12,000
S an Domingo..............	136,000	......	17,827	7.6	San Domingo.......	20,000
Costa Rica.................	165,000	1870	21,505	7.7	San Jose..........	2,000
Hawaii....................	62,950	......	7,633	80.	Honolulu...........	7,633

POPULATION OF ILLINOIS,
By Counties.

COUNTIES.	AGGREGATE.					
	1870.	1860.	1850.	1840.	1830.	1820.
Adams	56362	41323	26508	14476	2186	....
Alexander	10564	4707	2484	3313	1390	626
Bond	13152	9815	6144	5060	3124	2931
Boone	12942	11678	7624	1705	....	....
Brown	12205	9938	7198	4183	....	....
Bureau	32415	26426	8841	3367	....	....
Calhoun	6562	5144	3231	1741	1090	....
Carroll	16705	11733	4586	1023	....	....
Cass	11580	11325	7253	2981	....	....
Champaign	32737	14629	2649	1475	....	....
Christian	20363	10492	3203	1878	....	....
Clark	18719	14987	9532	7453	3940	931
Clay	15875	9336	4289	3228	755	....
Clinton	16285	10941	5139	3718	2330	....
Coles	25235	14203	9335	9616	......	....
Cook	349966	144954	43385	10201	....	*23
Crawford	13889	11551	7135	4422	3117	2999
Cumberland	12223	8311	3718	....	....	....
De Kalb	23265	19086	7540	1697	......	....
De Witt	14768	10820	5002	3247	....	....
Douglas	13484	7140	....	....	....	....
Du Page	16685	14701	9290	3535	....	....
Edgar	21450	16925	10692	8225	4071	....
Edwards	7565	5454	3524	3070	1649	3444
Effingham	15653	7816	3799	1675	....	....
Fayette	19638	11189	8075	6328	2704	....
Ford	9103	1979	....	....	....	....
Franklin	12652	9393	5681	3682	4083	1763
Fulton	38291	33338	22508	13142	1841	....
Gallatin	11134	8055	5448	10760	7405	3155
Greene	20277	16093	12429	11951	7674	....
Grundy	14938	10379	3023	....	....	....
Hamilton	13014	9915	6362	3945	2616	....
Hancock	35935	29061	14652	9946	483	....
Hardin	5113	3759	2887	1378	....	....
Henderson	12582	9501	4612	....	....	....
Henry	35506	20660	3807	1260	41	....
Iroquois	25782	12325	4149	1695	....	....
Jackson	19634	9589	5862	3566	1828	1542
Jasper	11234	8364	3220	1472	....	....
Jefferson	17864	12965	8109	5762	2555	691
Jersey	15054	12051	7354	4535	....	....
Jo Daviess	27820	27325	18604	6180	2111	....
Johnson	11248	9342	4114	3626	1596	843
Kane	39091	30062	16703	6501	....	....
Kankakee	24352	15412	....	....	....	....
Kendall	12399	13074	7730	....	....	....
Knox	39522	28663	13279	7060	274	....
Lake	21014	18257	14226	2634	....	....
La Salle	60792	48332	17815	9348	......	....
Lawrence	12533	9214	6121	7092	3668	....
Lee	27171	17651	5292	2035	....	....
Livingston	31471	11637	1553	759	....	....
Logan	23053	14272	5128	2333	....	....

POPULATION OF ILLINOIS—Concluded.

COUNTIES.	AGGREGATE.					
	1870.	1860.	1850.	1840.	1830.	1820.
Macon	26481	13738	3988	3039	1122	
Macoupin	32726	24602	12355	7926	1990	
Madison	44131	31251	20441	14433	6221	13550
Marion	20622	12739	6720	4742	2125	
Marshall	16950	13437	5180	1849		
Mason	16184	10931	5921			
Massac	9581	6213	4092			
McDonough	26509	20069	7616	5308	(b)	
McHenry	23762	22089	14978	2578		
McLean	53988	28772	10163	6565		
Menard	11735	9584	6349	4431		
Mercer	18769	15042	5246	2352	26	*21
Monroe	12982	12832	7679	4481	2000	1516
Montgomery	25314	13979	6277	4490	2953	
Morgan	28463	22112	16064	19547	12714	
Moultrie	10385	6385	3234			
Ogle	27492	22888	10020	3479		
Peoria	47540	36601	17547	6153	(c)	
Perry	13723	9552	5278	3222	1215	
Piatt	10953	6127	1606			
Pike	30768	27249	18819	11728	2396	
Pope	11437	6742	3975	4094	3316	2610
Pulaski	8752	3943	2265			
Putnam	6280	5587	3924	2131	r1310	
Randolph	20859	17205	11079	7944	4429	3492
Richland	12803	9711	4012			
Rock Island	29783	21005	6937	2610		
Saline	12714	9331	5588			
Sangamon	46352	32274	19228	14716	12960	
Schuyler	17419	14684	10573	6972	b2959	
Scott	10530	9069	7914	6215		
Shelby	25476	14613	7807	6659	2972	
Stark	10751	9004	3710	1573		*5
St.Clair	51068	37694	20180	13631	7078	5248
Stephenson	30608	25112	11666	2800		
Tazewell	27903	21470	12052	7221	4716	
Union	16518	11181	7615	5524	3239	2362
Vermilion	30388	19800	11492	9303	5836	
Wabash	8841	7313	4690	4240	2710	
Warren	23174	18336	8176	6739	308	
Washington	17599	13731	6953	4810	1675	1517
Wayne	19758	12223	6825	5133	2553	1114
White	16846	12403	8925	7919	6091	4828
Whitesides	27503	18737	5361	2514		
Will	43013	29321	16703	10167		
Williamson	17329	12205	7216	4457		
Winnebago	29301	24491	11773	4609		
Woodford	18956	13282	4415			
Total	2539891	1711951	851470	476183	157445	*49 55162

History of DeKalb County.

This county is named after Baron DeKalb, a distinguished French officer, who came to this country with LaFayette, and fell in the battle of Camden during the Revolutionary War. He was eminently worthy the perpetuation of his name and memory in so many of the towns and counties of different States; for he was a noble friend of liberty and the rights of man. Born in 1732, in Alsace, then a German province of France, he entered the French army in which he rose to the rank of brigadier general and Knight of the Order of Merit. The French government sent him as a secret agent to the American colonies in 1762. While on this visit he learned to love the free spirit of the American people, which even then foreshadowed the Declaration of Independence; and when the War of the Revolution broke out he proceeded at once to offer his services to Benjamin Franklin and Silas Deane, our ministers at that time at the French Court. He was accepted, and the following year sailed with LaFayette and ten other French officers to this country.

Congress, September 15, 1777, appointed him a major general. He soon joined the main army under Washington at Philadelphia, and during the two following years served with honor and distinction in the campaigns in Maryland and New Jersey.

The most arduous campaign of the war, in which he was engaged, was that of his southern march to reinforce Major Lincoln at Charleston, South Carolina. In 1780, this post was threatened by the British, and Gen. DeKalb was chosen by Washington, with the approbation of Congress, to march with a force for its relief across the wilderness of the Carolinas. The force was conveyed to Petersburg, Virginia, by boats, and thence commenced its weary and destitute march across the country. A few poor and scattering settlers were all their dependence; for the commissaries had neither stores nor credit. They were obliged to collect their own supplies by impressing lean cattle from the canebrakes, and Indian corn, the only grain which the country produced.

At Deer River, DeKalb was overtaken by Gen. Gates, who had been appointed by Congress to the command of the Southern Department, and the army moved on through a barren and disaffected country towards Camden. It had by this time been augmented by reinforcements from the Carolinas and Virginia, so that on its approach to Camden it numbered nearly 6,000 men: but they were mostly raw militia, weakened by disease and their arduous marches, having to subsist on unripe peaches and green corn instead of bread. The army of Lord Cornwallis, though considerably less in numbers, were veterans, and so situated that defeat would have been their destruction. Both armies moved forward on the night of the 6th of August—Cornwallis with the intent to attack and surprise Gates, the latter intending to occupy a position nearer Camden. The advance of the two armies encountered each other unexpectedly in the woods. A council of war was immediately called; DeKalb cautioned Gates against a general attack, and recommended that the army should fall back to a more favorable position. Gates scorned the advice. Said he: "I would not give a penny to be insured a breakfast in Camden to-day with Lord Cornwallis a captured prisoner at my table." Vain conceit. The rash Gates insinuated that the caution of DeKalb was occasioned by fear. "Well, sir," said DeKalb, "a few hours will prove who is brave."

The British rushed with charged bayonets on Gates' center and left, when his troops broke and fled, leaving their guns on the ground. Gates went with them, and did not cease his flight till he reached Charlotte, eighty miles from the field of battle. The brave DeKalb, at the head of the right wing, manfully stood his ground, and contended against the whole British army more than an hour. Hundreds of his devoted troops had fallen around him, when, at last, he fell, pierced by seven bayonet wounds. At the entreaty of his aid, the British officers interposed to prevent his immediate destruction, but he survived only a few hours. He died with these words to a British officer who kindly sympathized with him in his last moments:

"I thank you for your generous sympathy, but I die the death I have always prayed for—the death of a soldier fighting for the rights of man; and though I fight no more in this world, I trust I may still be of some service to the cause of freedom."

Many years after Gen. Washington visited the grave of the departed hero at Camden, and after gazing sadly awhile, exclaimed: "So here lies the brave DeKalb! the generous stranger who came from a distant land to fight our battles, and water with his blood the tree of liberty."

Such is a brief sketch of the brave soldier who gave his life to the cause of human liberty, and whose name is perpetuated in DeKalb County and one of its principal towns.

PHYSICAL FEATURES.

DeKalb County is within a few hours' ride by rail of the city of Chicago; its county seat, Sycamore, being about sixty miles distant. The county is traversed by four lines of railway: the Chicago & Pacific, which crosses it from east to west on its northern tier of townships; the Chicago & Northwestern, which crosses it in the same direction near the center; the Chicago & Iowa, which crosses it east and west through the second range of townships from the south; and the Chicago, Burlington & Quincy, which passes diagonally in a southwestern direction across the southeast corner, extending across the township of Somonauk.

Of course, the county has unusual railroad facilities; and the construction and operation of these great lines have had a wonderful influence in the development of the country along them from a wilderness to the garden of fertility, culture and beauty which it now is, and of crowding it with a wealthy, prosperous and enlightened population.

The surface of DeKalb County has but few peculiar and distinctive features. It has no great rivers, no elevated peaks, no deep and narrow valleys; but is only a parallelogram of rich, rolling prairie, dotted with a few groves, and watered by a few small streams. It is eighteen miles broad, and thirty-six miles long. The county occupies the elevated ground between the Fox and Rock Rivers. These streams are noted for their purity and beauty. The Fox River empties into the Illinois River, at Ottawa, and the Rock into the Mississippi River, at Rock Island.

The central portion of the county contains but little timber, and only few running streams. There is more timber and water in the northern and southern parts of the county. The largest stream in the county is the south branch of the Kishwaukee River. In the early history of the county, this stream was called the Sycamore River. This stream heads in the town of Shabbona, and flows through the towns of Milan, Afton, DeKalb, Mayfield, Sycamore, Genoa, Kingston and Franklin; and empties into the Rock River, in Winnebago County. It has several branches, one of which heads in the town of Virgil, Kane County, and flows through Cortland and Sycamore Townships, and enters the main branch in the town of Mayfield. There are several small creeks that flow through the northern part of the county, which are valuable to the farms which they water. Along the banks of the Kishwaukee, in the northern half of the county, stretches one continuous forest, composed principally of white, red and burr oak trees, and some maple, butternut, black walnut and hickory. This grove furnishes the north half of the county with fuel and fencing timber. The rolling prairies occupy almost the entire surface of the central portion of the county. The early settlers of the county made their claims in close proximity to the timber and water, and could hardly believe that the distant prairies would ever serve any other purpose than that of a large range for stock. They felt sure that no farmer could live there, so far away from the timber. They little thought that many of them would live to see it all settled and occupied by man. Some of the wealthiest farmers and the most productive farms of the county are now found on the prairies. The central portion of the county has but little water, except that which is furnished by sloughs or swamps, which always connect, one with the other, until they form brooklets, which flow north and south, and ultimately become our larger creeks. The southern portions of the county, like the northern, are better watered and timbered than those towns which occupy the center. The towns of Paw Paw and Shabbona are watered by the Big Indian Creek, while Shabbona Grove and Ross Grove furnish its timber. The Little Indian Creek waters the towns of Victor, Paw Paw and Clinton; while Somonauk and Squaw Grove Townships are watered by Somonauk Creek; and along this stream will be found timber enough to supply the wants of the surrounding country. Hardly a ledge of rocks pierces the surface in any part of the county. Some limestone is found in Kingston, Franklin and Afton Townships. The whole county is unfortunately destitute of rock suitable for building purposes.

But it is easily transported on the lines of railway, which run to all the principal towns. The county is more than compensated by other advantages, which constitute the source of its wealth and prosperity. Its advantages for agriculture and stock-raising are unsurpassed, and it stands on the record as the banner dairy county of the State.

INDIANS OF THE COUNTRY.

Prior to the Spring of 1835, the territory at present embraced in DeKalb County was occupied by the Pottawattamie tribe of Indians. Their territory extended west to Rock River, which stream divided them from the Winnebagos. These two tribes spoke different dialects, and emigrated from different parts of the continent. The Pottawattamies spoke the Algonquin language, which was originally the tongue of most of the tribes north of the Potomac and east of the Mississippi. This tribe came originally from Canada. In 1835, there were villages of them near Ohio Grove ; on section 3, in the township of Cortland ; in Kingston, on section 21 ; at Coltonville ; a large settlement at Shabbona Grove, under the good chief, Shabbona ; and another at Paw Paw Grove, under a chief of yet higher rank, called Waubansie. There were some forty wigwams at Coltonville, but they were not all inhabited in 1835. Their manners and customs, as observed by the white settlers, were somewhat as follows :

The settlers found them making maple sugar from the adjoining grove. Their sap-buckets were hewn troughs and the backs of turtles. In their manner of manufacturing sugar and syrup, they were very filthy.

Most of them buried their dead in shallow graves, depositing with them their guns, bows and arrows, and various trinkets. A space was selected upon some conspicuous mound, and a square about six feet by ten fenced in by high palisades. Within this the body was placed, braced up in a sitting posture, with knives, rifle, blankets, pipe, and a good supply of tobacco, and all were thus left to molder and decay.

At the first settlement of the country, a chief of the Pottawattamies, whose name has not been preserved, was enshrined in the above manner on the farm of Calvin Colton, in Mayfield. His skeleton, with the bullet in it which caused his death, was afterwards obtained by Dr. Richards, of the St. Charles Medical School.

They disposed of the bodies of their dead children by covering them with bark, binding them with withes in halves of hollow logs, and suspending them in the horizontal branches of trees. Calvin Colton reports that as late as 1839, when he moved to his location at Coltonville, there were as many as fifty pappooses thus suspended in the grove adjoining his residence.

The Indians cultivated small patches of corn upon the bottom lands near the streams and on the borders of the groves. The squaws did all the work. They kept their seed corn by stringing it upon poles and hanging it in little bark-lined cellars in the ground. These deposits were always sacred, and no Indian, however nearly starved, would ever touch them.

Their chief reliance for food was upon the game—deer, rabbits, woodchuck, etc., which were then plentiful in the country. The buffalo had disappeared, but many of their bones were yet to be found. Near the present town line between Clinton and Shabbona, could be seen twenty years ago, around a living spring which there bubbled up when all the rest of the wide prairie was dry, the bones and skulls of hundreds of buffalo. It is supposed that these were the bones of the old and feeble which had been driven thither by the drought for drink, and died at the spring.

Shabbona, the old chief, used to say that about the year 1810 there was an unusually severe winter, during which multitudes of the Indians perished, and the buffalo all died and were never afterwards seen in this section.

The village of Shabbona, at Shabbona Grove, was the most noted Pottawattamie settlement in the county. Here lived the "good old chief Shabbona," so noted in the early annals of the country. Here was held many a council of peace and of war, during those border conflicts which agitated the country far beyond this remote wilderness, but in which the savages were prominent actors. From this place, after the surrender of General Hull, Fort Mackinaw, and the Chicago massacre, Shabbona and his braves, accompanied by Waubansie and his warriors, went to join the forces of Tecumseh and the Prophet, in aid of the British arms against the United States, in the war of 1812.

It having been noised abroad, in the Spring of 1835, that the Indians were about to be removed west of the Mississippi, no further attempt was made to restrain the immigration of the whites, and they poured into the country in great numbers.

EARLY SETTLEMENT.

Probably few, if any, white men ever visited the territory of DeKalb County till about the time of Major Stillman's defeat by the Indians, on a branch of the Kishwaukee, near the northwest corner of the county, during the Blackhawk War, in 1832.

In 1836, the county of Kane, embracing the entire territory now included in DeKalb, was organized. Capt. Eli Barnes, representing the interests of the Kishwaukee country, was re-elected one of the County Commissioners; but the settlers in the Kishwaukee country still felt that they were too far from a county seat. A company of capitalists, known afterwards as the New York Company, had already laid out a town on the east fork of the south branch of the Kishwaukee River, between the Norwegian and Big Grove.

In 1834, a mail route from Chicago to John Dixon's residence, on the Rock River, was established, which crossed the southern end of DeKalb County, and during the Summer a log hut was built for a station, on this line, at the crossing of Somonauk Creek. This was probably the first habitation of a white man erected in the county; but was abandoned in the Fall. Wm. Sebree seems to have been the first settler, and became a permanent resident of the county.

It was in the Spring of 1835, when the treaty with the Indians which followed the Blackhawk war, had bound them to leave this country for the wilderness beyond the great Father of Waters, that the first considerable body of white settlers came into the county. This section of country was then known as the Kishwaukee country, and was a part of the great county of LaSalle; which extended from the Illinois River, on the south to the line of Wisconsin Territory on the north, and on the east to Cook County. A commission was procured from Ottawa, then as now the county seat, for the election of two Justices of the Peace, and in June, 1835, an election was held, and Stephen Mowry and Joseph Collier were chosen Justices — the first public officers ever elected in this section of country. In the year 1836, but few settlers came in. The timbered lands of the county had nearly all been claimed during the previous year, and those who were not able or willing to pay the prices demanded by claimants, were forced to go further west.

In 1836, the first house was built at Shabbona Grove, by Edmund Town, assisted by David Smith. While building this house, they lived in the deserted wigwams of the Indians, who had gone west about three months before. The Indians never after made a permanent home at this place, but came and went every year or two. During this time, many whites had been attracted to the grove, and became settlers at this place, and were on friendly terms with the Indians, and ever since that time, the country surrounding the grove has improved very fast. At a general election, held in August, 1836, Henry Madden, who resided in what was called the Brush Point settlement, in the present town of Mayfield, was elected as Representative to the State Legislature. His district took in a large amount of territory, but a very small population. Most of the population, at this time, was in the southern part of the state, excepting the settlements at Ottawa, LaSalle, Joliet and Galena. Chicago, at that time, consisted only of a few log houses, clustered around Fort Dearborn, on the banks of the Chicago River.

Most of the details of the early settlement in various parts of the county have been purposely omitted here and embodied in the different town histories.

CLAIM ASSOCIATION.

Before the lands of the county came into market, and while multitudes of land-hunters were rushing in and seizing upon claims, each eager to secure the best, and not over-scrupulous of the rights of their neighbors, it became necessary that some measures should be adopted for the protection of the rights of all concerned ; and in this necessity originated the Claim Association of the early settlers.

On the 5th of September, 1835, a settlers' meeting was called at the cabin of Harmon Miller, on the east bank of the Kishwaukee River, in what was afterwards the town of Kingston, for the purpose of adopting such laws and regulations for self-government as the exigencies of the times and country demanded.

Happily, the best possible spirit prevailed. The Hoosier from the Wabash, the Buckeye from Ohio, the hunter from Kentucky, the calculating Yankee, impelled by a sense of mutual danger, here sat down in grave council, to dictate laws to Kishwaukee and " the region lying round about."

Levi Lee was chosen to preside over this august assemblage, where the three great departments of free government—the executive, the legislative and the judicial, were most happily united, and Capt. Eli Barnes was appointed Secretary. Speech after speech, setting forth the wants and woes of the settlers, the kind of legislation demanded by the crisis, went the rounds. At last, ripe for immediate action, a committee was selected to draft and present to the meeting a constitution and by-laws, by which the settlers upon the public lands should be governed. After some little deliberation back of the shanty, around the stump of a big white oak, which served as a writing desk, said committee reported a preamble, constitution and by-laws, which for simplicity, brevity and adaptation to necessity, it would be hard for any modern legislature to surpass. The common sense, law and logic, as well as patriotism, contained in this constitution and by-laws were instantaneously recognized to be the very things demanded by the crisis, and were adopted with unparalleled enthusiasm, each subscribing his name thereto, with his own hand; thereby pledging " Life, Fortune and Sacred Honor," to carry out the provisions of the code. It is not known that a copy of this unique document is now extant; still there may be. As nearly as can be recollected, its provisions were somewhat as follows : A Prudential Committee was to be then and there chosen, whose duty it should be to examine into, hear and finally determine, all disputes and differences then existing, or which hereafter might arise, between settlers, in relation to their claims, and whose decisions, with certain salutary checks, where to be binding upon all parties, and to be carried out at all hazards, by the three departments of government, consolidated in aid of the executive. Each settler was solemnly pledged to protect every other settler in the association in the peaceful enjoyment of his or her reasonable claim, as aforesaid; and further, whoever, throughout all Kishwaukee, or the suburbs or coasts thereof, should refuse to recognize the authority of the aforesaid association, and render due obedience to the laws enacted by the same from time to time, to promote the general welfare, should be deemed a heathen, a publican, and an outcast, with whom they were pledged to have no communion or fellowship. Thus was a wall, affording protection to honest settlers, built in troublous times. Hon. Levi Lee, Hon. Geo. H. Hill, Captain Eli Barnes, James Green and Jesse C. Kellogg, were chosen to be the Settlers' Committee, and who, as may well be supposed, had business on hand for some time, in order to restore and ensure domestic tranquility, and promote the general welfare. The thing worked like a charm, and similar associations were formed and maintained in other portions of the country, until the lands came into market. This event took place in Chicago, in 1843 ; when all DeKalb County, except the northern tier of townships, was sold to the highest bidder.

ORGANIZATION OF THE COUNTY.

In the Winter of 1836-7, the Legislature being in session at Vandalia, the Hon. Henry Madden, then representing the interests of the settlers of LaSalle, Kane and sundry other counties, not then organized, and on the 4th day of March, 1837, a bill was passed, through the influence of Mr. Madden, to create the County of DeKalb, from the west half of the county of Kane, provided a majority of the legal voters in Kane should on a given day vote for such new county. Therefore, in pursuance of organic law, the Commissioners' Clerk of Kane County ordered an election to be held at the house of Frederick Love, for the election of county officers in the new county of DeKalb, July 3, 1837. The day of the election of county officers at last arrived, and Levi Lee, Rufus Colton and Robert Sterrett were elected County Commissioners ; Joseph C. Lander, Sheriff; Jesse C. Kellogg, Recorder. The County Commissioners elect immediately repaired to the house of Rufus Colton, where each administered the oaths of office to the other, as authorized in the Act to

Create the County of DeKalb: appointed Jesse C. Kellogg, Clerk of the County Commissioners' Court; Eli Barnes, County Surveyor; and Lysander Darling, County Treasurer: ordered a special term to be held in a few days, at the same place, to lay off the county into Justices' Districts and Election Precincts; and before the guns of the glorious 4th came booming over "the land of the free and the home of the brave," DeKalb was a sister in the sisterhood of counties in the great State of Illinois.

An act was passed by the Legislature, that all that tract of country, beginning at the southeast corner of township thirty-seven north, range two east of the principal meridian, thence north to the northeast corner of township forty-two north, range two east of the third principal meridian, and thence along the northern boundary of township forty-two, in ranges three, four and five, east of the third principal meridian; then south, on the southeast corner of township thirty-seven north, range five east, thence west on said township line, to the place of beginning, shall form a county, to be called DeKalb. Section eight, of the same act: for the purpose of fixing the permanent seat of justice, for the County of DeKalb: Benj. Thurston, of LaSalle County; James Walker, of Cook County; and Germanicus Kent, of Winnebago County, are hereby appointed Commissioners, who, or a majority, being first duly sworn before some Justice of the Peace of this State, as is required by the fifth section of this act, shall meet at the house of Frederick Love, in said county, on the first Monday in June next, or as soon thereafter as may be, and shall proceed in all respects as is required in the fifth section of this act, provided, that the qualified voters of Kane County shall meet at the usual places of holding elections in said county, on the first Monday in May next, and vote for or against the County of DeKalb; and if a majority of said voters shall be in favor of making the said county, then the County of DeKalb shall be created; but if it should appear that there is a majority against the division, then the said county shall remain as it now is. The election was held, resulting in the establishment of the new county and the election of its officers. On Tuesday, the 11th day of July, 1837, the first regular session of the County Commissioners' Court, for DeKalb County, was held at the house of Rufus Colton, and continued to be held there until the location of the county seat. The first formal action of the Board was to select and appoint Jesse C. Kellogg, as Clerk of their Court, and the next was the important business of laying out five Election Precincts and Justices' Districts. They were: First, Kingston District and Precinct, commencing at the northwest corner of the county, running south twelve miles, thence northeast, crossing the Sycamore River, so as to include Benj. Stevens' land, and then north to the county line. It was ordered that elections be held in this precinct, at the residence of Levi Lee. Geo. H. Hill, John Whitney and James Hait, were appointed its Judges. The second was Sycamore Precinct, including the northeast corner of the county, and extending as far south as Chartres Grove, but not including the present village of Sycamore. The elections were to be held at a school house near Lysander Darling's, and Wm. A. Miller, James A. Armstrong and Samuel Cary were made its Judges. The third was named Orange District, and comprised the territory south of the Sycamore District, as far as Lost Grove, in the present Town of Cortland. Elections for this district were ordered at Rufus Colton's house, and F. Love, James Root and Eli Barnes, were made its Judges. The fourth was named Somonauk District, and comprised the territory south of Orange District, ten miles in width and about twenty in length, to the south line of the county. Elections were ordered to be held at the houses of Messrs. Woodruff and Lane. Wm. Davis, T. A. Witherspoon and Simon Price, were made Judges. The fifth district was called Paw Paw, and comprised the southeast portion of the county. No recorded provisions were made for elections in this district, and it was subsequently abolished; but afterwards, upon the indignant protest of some of its people, was re-established.

In October, 1837, the Commissioners appointed by the Legislature, to fix the county seat, met at the house of Mr. Frederick Love, as directed by the law of organization. On the third day of their meeting, the Commissioners determined upon placing it where the court house now stands. They set a long pole upon the green prairie, placed on it a streaming flag, and declared it to be the location for the county seat of the new County of DeKalb. Capt. Eli Barnes now advanced, and christened the new town Orange. No objection was raised to this, and for some years thereafter the point was called by that name. Through the advice of J. S. Waterman it was changed to Sycamore.

FIRST COURTS—COURT HOUSE, ETC.

At the February term of the Commissioners' Court, it was ordered that, as no court house was yet built, the first term of the Circuit Court should be held at Rufus Colton's residence. The following jurors were selected: Grand Jurors—George H. Hill, Nathan Billings, Wm. A. Miller, Lysander Darling, John Whitney, John Esterbrooks, Wm. Miles, Henry Madden, Eli Barnes, Phineas Stevens, Alpheus Jenks, Russell D. Crossett, John Maxfield, Wm. Davis, Maltby B. Cleveland, D. S. Bullard, Zachariah Wood, Ralph Wyman, Benj. Stevens, Joseph A. Armstrong, Henry B. Barber, Reuben Nichols and Justin Crafts. Petit Jurors—C. W. Branch, E. F. White, Abner Jackson, Peter Lamoise, Clark Wright, John Elliott, Clark L. Barber, Joseph A. McCollum, Russell Huntley, Ora A. Walker, John Corkins, Solomon Wells, H. N. Perkins, Jacob Cox, Lyman Judd, Henry Durham, F. A. Witherspoon, John Sebree, Marshall Stark, Jeremiah Burleigh, John Riddle, Wm. Russell, Watson Y. Pomeroy and Ezra Hanson. Three of these are yet living, viz: H. N. Perkins, Marshall Stark and Ezra Hanson.

The total county tax levied on the first year of its existence, as a county, was two hundred and sixteen dollars and fifty cents; but Mr. James Phillips, the Deputy Sheriff, who was also collector, reported that after a hard winter's work in collecting, he had been able to get together and pay into the treasury, eighty-four dollars and thirty-seven cents. In August, of the same year, three new Commissioners were elected—E. G. Jewell, Burage Hough and Henry Hicks. They were all in favor of the county seat then located, and issued an order that the October term of the Circuit Court be held at a house now being erected by Eli Barnes, at or near the seat of justice in this county; but the house did not get completed in time for the fall term, therefore the court was not held at this place. A meeting of the Commissioners was held in

September, at which they considered the expediency of building a court house and jail; but no definite plan was devised. Mr. Madden, who was still a member of the Legislature, had, during the last winter's session, caused the passage of an act providing that a vote should be taken first for or against the removal of the county seat from Orange. The vote was finally taken, and was voted down, by seventeen majority, in the whole county. At a meeting of the County Commissioners in December of the same year, they took action to find upon what section of land the county seat had been located. The county had not yet been surveyed by the United States. For this purpose the Commissioners duly authorized and directed Eli G. Jewell to obtain the services of a surveyor, and bring a line or lines from some survey made under the authority of the United States, down to the county seat, and there cause a number of town lots, not exceeding eighty, to be laid out, platted and recorded.

Frederick Love was appointed first School Commissioner, and was also granted a license to keep a hotel. Love's log cabin was said to be as public a place as any in the county. He called it Centreville, and hoped that at some future day it would become the county seat. In September of this year, Shabbona, the old Indian chief, employed Mr. James S. Waterman to survey the two sections of land which the government had granted him. During this year, the firm of Jenks & Co. built a mill on the Kishwaukee, in the present Town of DeKalb. There was a large frame barn built near this point. It was one of the first frame buildings in the county, and was used on several occasions for the religious services of the quarterly meetings of the Methodists. In this year, Henry Durham, of Genoa, was granted a merchant's license. A few years later the village of Genoa had become the largest and most lively village in the county; but at this time very little business is done at this point, as the county seat is too near by.

During the year 1839 a new court house was erected, and the survey of lines, ordered by the County Commissioners, had been brought down from Winnebago County, where some government surveying had already been done, and the village of Sycamore was staked out by James S. Waterman and Capt. Eli Barnes, who deserve a great deal of credit for the beautiful wide streets. The first building erected in this village was built for a hotel, by Capt. Eli Barnes, and is used to this day as a hotel. The County Commissioners ordered Mr. Jewell to sell lots at public auction, and with the proceeds to contract for building a court house and jail.

When the time arrived for the June session of the Circuit Court, a two-story building, twenty feet by thirty, had been erected, and the County Commissioners were summoned together and ordered their clerk of the court to notify the judge of the Circuit Court that the new court house was ready for occupancy, and requested that he direct the circuit clerk to keep his office in the court house. Capt. Barnes served the order upon the judge, sitting in court at Coltonville, and there was a large crowd of citizens assembled, to see what the judge would do. When the judge decided that the court must be removed to Sycamore, a shout of triumph went up from the Sycamore crowd. Judge Ford took his record under his arm, State's Attorney Purple bundled up his papers, the sheriff, the lawyers, juries, and the balance of the crowd, followed suit, and, led by Capt. Barnes, took up their line of march for the new court house at Sycamore. On their arrival, a public dinner, at the new hotel, was served up in good style.

When the party arrived at the new court house, they found that the Commissioners' declaration was rather more than its condition warranted. It had no doors nor windows, and the floor was laid with some loose boards covering one-half of the upper story. A question arose whether, process having been made returnable at Coltonville, suits could not be tried at another locality; and, except a few agreed cases, no litigations were had, and the court soon adjourned.

At the June session of the Commissioners' Court, the county was divided into three assessment districts. Franklin, Kingston and Kishwaukee constituted the first district, and H. G. Page was chosen assessor. Sycamore, Orange and Ohio constituted the second district, of which Austin Hayden was chosen assessor. Somonauk and Paw Paw constituted the third district, Stephen Arnold, assessor. Each assessor was paid for three days' service, for assessing his share of the entire property of the county. The land in the towns of Franklin, Kingston and Genoa, which had previously been surveyed by the United States and put into market, belonged to the Rockford or Polish survey.

During this year an act was passed authorizing a vote upon the removal of the county seat. The laws in these early times were not circulated till six months after the sitting of the Legislature; and before any opponents of removal were aware of the existence of such an act, the time had arrived for a vote upon the question. A poll-book was opened at Coltonville, a dozen votes or so were cast for removal to that place, and the terms of the law were considered complied with. The seat of justice *technically* was removed. But J. C. Kellogg, the County Commissioners' Clerk, refused to deliver the books. He was arrested and tried before Justice Harvey Maxfield, and, after a war of words, was discharged.

The grand struggle for the county seat was finished at the August election of 1840, by a defeat of the opponents of Orange, now Sycamore. The village of Sycamore contained about twelve houses. The hotel, kept by Capt. Barnes, was the great center of population. The court house was occupied for a school house, and also for religious meetings. An act had been passed on the 3d of January, to "permanently locate the seat of justice for the county of DeKalb." The County Commissioners ordered the following report to be placed upon their records, which explains the final settlement of the vexed question of the county seat: "I, John R. Hamlin, Clerk of the County Commissioners' Court of said county of DeKalb, and Frederick Love, Probate Justice of the Peace, and Harvey Maxfield, Justice of the Peace, in and for said County of DeKalb, do hereby certify that, at an election held in the several precincts of said county, on the third Monday in August, A. D. 1840, in pursuance of an act entitled 'An Act Permanently to Locate the Seat of Justice of the County of DeKalb,' approved January 3, 1840, there were given two hundred and forty votes in favor of the removal of the seat of justice of DeKalb County from Coltonville. There were given one hundred and forty-three votes against the removal of the seat of justice from Coltonville; showing a majority in favor of the removal of the seat of justice from Coltonville of ninety-seven votes; and there were also given at that election two hundred and seven votes in favor of Sycamore to be the seat of justice of DeKalb County; and there were given at said election one hundred and thirty-seven votes in favor of Brush Point, to be the seat of justice of DeKalb County ; showing a majority of seventy votes in favor of Sycamore to be the seat of justice.

It is likely that a test of this kind brought out all the voters. It is supposed that three hundred and eighty-four was about the number of voters then in the county. John Riddle, one of the early settlers of the town of Franklin, was this year appointed assessor of District No. 1 ; Frederick Love, of District No. 2, and Stephen Arnold, of District No. 3. They were only six days each in assessing the whole county. A tax of $334.70 was collected by Amos Story, county collector.

In 1840 a stage route was established from St. Charles to Oregon, and Timothy Wells and Charles Waterman were the proprietors. The State Road from Ottawa to Beloit, Wisconsin, running through DeKalb County, was laid out in 1841, by J. S. Waterman.

In this year Andrew J. Brown, Esq., the first resident lawyer in the county, was admitted to practice, the County Commissioner's Court certifying that he was of good moral character. He settled in Sycamore.

In 1842, E. L. Mayo, receiving a similar certificate from the county board, became the second resident lawyer, and was elected the first county judge.

During 1842 the State Bank failed, and overwhelmed the people in destitution and ruin. The public officers found it difficult to get enough money out of the treasury to pay their salaries and the postage on letters. John R. Hamlin was Clerk of the Commissioners' Court, Recorder and Postmaster, and out of these combined offices managed to get money enough to pay his board. But this state of things did not long continue. Not more than a dozen years had passed when it became necessary for the Recorder to employ four or five assistants. At this time the Recorder's office was considered worth eight thousand dollars per annum.

The Circuit Court held its session in September, 1842, and was presided over by Judge John D. Caton, since the most eminent judge of the Supreme Court of Illinois, an able amateur scientist and author, and now a resident of Chicago. S. B. Farwell was State's Attorney ; Jesse C. Kellogg, Clerk, and Morris Walrod, Sheriff. Judge Ford, afterwards Governor Ford, was the first Judge of the Circuit Court of this County, was a warm and true friend of the West.

The first brick dwellings in the county were erected at Sycamore by J. S. Waterman and the brothers Mayo, in 1846. This year DeKalb County, upon the call of the President of the United States, furnished quite a number of men for the Mexican War.

NEW COURT HOUSE.

At the March term of the County Commissioners' Court, in 1849, the building of a new court house was discussed at length, and three Commissioners were appointed to contract for the building. E. P. Young, Kimball Dow, and Jesse C. Kellogg were appointed. It was to be placed where the court house now stands, and to cost not exceeding six thousand dollars. But this was only to be done on condition that individual citizens should contribute fifteen hundred dollars of the amount.

7

The Commissioners also passed an order authorizing the erection of a county jail by the same committee, at a cost not exceeding fifteen hundred dollars ; but nothing seems to have been done under this order.

The required amount was raised for the new court house, and the work commenced at once. The building committee was also authorized to sell the old court house and town lots owned by the county at auction, and to apply the proceeds to the payment of the county orders issued for the construction of the new building.

TOWNSHIPS ORGANIZED.

At the election in 1849, 750 votes were cast in favor of the adoption of the township organization, and only one against it. Marshall Stark was elected Sheriff ; W. H. Beavers, County Clerk ; William Fordham, Recorder ; Sheldon Crossett, School Commissioner ; and E. L. Mayo, Probate Judge. But a new election was held in November, under the provisions of the new constitution, at which Martin M. Mack was elected Circuit Clerk and Recorder ; U. B. Prescott, County Clerk ; William Sheppardson, County Treasurer ; and James H. Beveridge and George Hill, Justices of the Peace.

In December, the County Commissioners appointed William A. Miller, William J. Hunt and Robert Sterritt, to divide the county into townships. They divided it into thirteen towns, as follows : Genoa, Kingston, Franklin, Vernon, Liberty, Sycamore, Richland, Orange, Shabbona, Clinton, Squaw Grove. Somonauk and Paw Paw. Some of these township names have been changed : Vernon belonged to the present town of South Grove ; Orange to DeKalb and some adjoining territory ; Liberty, to Mayfield ; and Richland, to Cortland and Pierce.

The township organization being now complete, a Board of Supervisors was elected to take the place of the County Commissioners, who had hitherto managed the county business. The first Board of the county consisted of thirteen members, as follows : Henry Durham, Genoa ; John Sheeley, Kingston ; Clark Bliss, Franklin ; John S. Brown, Vernon ; Mulford Nickerson, Liberty ; James Harrington, Sycamore ; D. F. Finley, Richland ; Thomas R. Hopkins, Orange ; William Marks, Shabbona ; Reuben Pritchard, Clinton ; Abram L. Hemenway, Squaw Grove ; Lyman Bacon, Somonauk ; Pierpont Edwards, Paw Paw.

The first meeting of the Board was held at Sycamore, in October, 1850. Among its first acts was the changing of the names of Orange Township to DeKalb, Richland to Pampas, Liberty to Mayfield, and Vernon to South Grove. The reason why these changes were made was that other towns in the state had already appropriated the first chosen names.

During this year the new court house was completed, and was considered a very fine structure for those days.

RAPID ENTRY OF LAND.

During the year 1852 the most rapid entry of land occurred in the history of the county, being stimulated by the prospect of railroads. In view of this, settlers and speculators rushed in and purchased nearly all the Government lands remaining in the county.

During this year the first Agricultural Society of the county was organized and held an exhibition.

The railroad running from Chicago to Dixon was built in 1853, and gave a powerful forward impulse to the county.

This year the Board of Supervisors resolved to purchase a County Poor Farm. Messrs. Taffan and Tindall were appointed a committee and were authorized to locate a County Farm in one of the two middle tiers of townships. The farm of A. H. Cartwright, on the road between Sycamore and DeKalb, was purchased for that purpose.

DeKALB COUNTY AND THE REBELLION.

The following summary of the services of DeKalb County in the War of the Rebellion is taken from Mr. Boies' valuable History of the County, embracing nearly the whole of the first general chapter of Part Second of that work:

" Decidedly the most interesting, most honorable and most eventful portion of the History of the County of DeKalb, is that which relates to the gallant deeds of her brave sons, their sacrifices and sufferings in that tremendous struggle for the life of the nation—the War of the Great Rebellion. * * * * The political character and predilections of the great majority of the inhabitants of our county impelled them to espouse with more than ordinary fervor the cause of the Government in its struggle with the Slaveholders' Rebellion. From the first settlement of the county, it had been the home of a strong, active, zealous party of anti-slavery men ; men who were avowed abolitionists, who gloried in that name when it was a term of reproach ; who not only voted for, but labored and expended their money for the freedom of the slave. Scattered here and there over the whole county, were numerous well-known stations on the " under-ground railroad ;" homes of thrifty, hard-working, God-fearing haters of oppression, in which, it was well understood, the panting fugitive escaping from Southern slavery, would be sure of finding rest, refreshment, a safe shelter, a warm welcome and means to help him on to other stations on the route to what was then his only safeguard, the flag of England on Canadian soil.

The homes of the Beveridges and the Hubbards, of Somonauk ; of the Townsends, of Mayfield ; David West's, of Sycamore ; and E. S. Gregory, at Genoa, were well known as homes and places of refuge for the fugitive negroes ; and many an interesting story of their experiences in aiding and secreting these oppressed people, are now told with a freedom that, before the downfall of American slavery, would have been dangerous.

Long before the formation of the Republican party, whose corner-stone was hostility to slavery extension, the majority of the voters of the county were of that class who made hatred of slavery the cardinal principle of their political creed. It was natural that when the devotees of the slave system sought to rend in twain the Union of the States, in order to protect their institution, and with fratricidal hand attacked the defenders of their country's flag, these men should rally to its defense with earnest enthusiasm. But their zeal for the defense of the country was only more fervent than that of their political opponents. Inspired by the noble utterances of their great leader, Stephen A. Douglas, whose patriotic devotion to his imperiled country burst the bonds of party, and shed over the last months of his too short life a sublime eternal radiance, the great mass of the Democratic party in the country, with some noted exceptions, rallied at the first outbreak of the war to the defense of the country, gave their support to the government, enlisted for their country's defense, or encouraged their enlistments, and gave their services, with patriotic sincerity, to the work of preserving the Union.

The echoes of the first guns that were fired upon Fort Sumter had scarcely died away, when, in the principal towns of DeKalb County, hundreds of her sons sprang to arms, began drilling and preparing for service, and earnestly demanded the privilege of being led to battle against the rebel foe. Their earnestness was constantly repressed by the government, which, embarrassed by the want of suitable laws to meet such an unlooked-for emergency, and apparently failing to appreciate the real magnitude of the contest, hesitated and drew back from the impending conflict, refused to call out a sufficient number of troops, and checked instead of encouraging, the patriotic ardor of the people.

When at last two companies of volunteers from this county gained permission to serve in her armies against the rebellion, their privilege was at a premium. Some of those who had been accepted, but from various causes found it difficult to disentangle themselves from the ties which bound them to their homes, sold out their places in the ranks to others whose eagerness could not be repressed. But as the conflict broadened and deepened, as our armies met the enemy and failed to conquer their legions, the government found use for all the men who were willing to serve her. The calls of the President for troops were as follows:

April 16, 1861—75,000 for three months.
May 4, 1861—64,748 for five years.
July, 1861—500,000 for three years.
July 18, 1862—300,000 for three years.
August 4, 1862—300,000 for nine months.
June, 1863—300,000 for three years.
October 17, 1863—300,000 for three years.
February 18, 1864—500,000 for three years.
July 10, 1864—200,000 for three years.
July 16, 1864—500,000 for one, two and three years.
December 21, 1864—300,000 for three years.

It must ever be a source of pride to the county of DeKalb, that each successive demand made during the first three years of the war, was promptly filled by volunteers. The Summer of 1862—how memorable and exciting! In the July previous half a million of men were called out, and DeKalb County promptly met the call. In August, 1862, 600,000 more were asked for. It was in the midst of the busy harvest season. The county had already been drained of more than fifteen hundred of its able-bodied men, and was suffering for help to gather its bountiful harvest; yet, without a murmur, six hundred of the very best men of the county sprang into the ranks of the 105th Regiment, and perhaps half as many more into other organizations. It was not until July, 1864, that a draft was finally required in this county, to fill the repeated and exhausting demands of the service.

What gallant and honorable service these citizen soldiers performed for their country! * * * Not one of the great battles of that long and bloody war was fought in which the loyal sons of DeKalb did not bear an honorable part. The history of their campaigns is a history of the war. DeKalb County boys opened the first battle in the seven days' fight on the Virginia Peninsula, and were the first to attack Lee's rebel host at Gettysburg. Some loaded their guns for the first time while under the fire of Fort Donelson. They swept with the great Sherman on the grand march to the sea. They were the heroes of the day at the first assault upon Vicksburg. They bore a most honorable part in its final capture. They saved, by a gallant charge, the defeated army of Banks on Red River. They were first at the capture of Mobile. In the campaigns in Texas, Missouri, Arkansas, Tennessee, and indeed wherever a rebel army was to be found, there were men of DeKalb County to meet them in the deadly conflict."

SKETCH OF THE U. P. CHURCH, SOMONAUK.

The first white man's house in DeKalb County stood on the east bank of Somonauk Creek, near the present United Presbyterian Church. This was the station between Chicago and John Dixon's residence on Rock River. This station was a five-room log house, known as the " Five-room Tavern." Mr. George Beveridge, from Washington County, New York, purchased this house and the claim on which it stood, in 1837.

His house became the nucleus around which seceders seeking a home in the West, gathered. It was for many years home, hotel and church for all such, and was always open to them. In a year or two others came, and by the years 1841–2, when Mr. Beveridge returned from the East with his family, enough had arrived to petition the Synod of Illinois for an organization. Two years after, in 1844, the Rev. James P. Miller, a minister from New York, preached a few Sabbaths for them. The Summer following a Mr. McMillan preached here. In the Fall the Rev. R. H. Pollak, late of Wooster, Ohio, was sent to this church by the Home Mission Board, and in the Spring the Rev. R. W. French. He organized the church on the 18th of March, 1846, with nineteen members, seven of whom are living—five of these are still in the congregation, viz: William Patten, David M. Dobbin, John Walker, William French and Mrs. Mary Patten. Rev. William Oburn came the following Summer and Fall, remaining a greater portion of the Winter. Rev. R. W. French returned in the Spring of 1847, and administered the first communion. At this time services were held in the school house then situated about one-half mile east of the church. The organization had been effected in the house of Mr. Beveridge, and all services had been held here. A call was made at this communion for the Rev. Oburn, which he held for some time, but finally decided in the negative. In the Spring of 1849, Rev. French returned from his charge in North Henderson, Illinois, and accepted the call given him here. He was installed as pastor November 19, 1849. Rev. G. D. Henderson preaching the installation sermon. At this time the number of members had increased to twenty-nine, with Messrs. David M.

Dobbin and William Patten as ruling elders. In 1852 Mr. Joseph Thompson was added to the session.

The following ministers had preached to this little band prior to their organization: In 1842. Rev. James Templeton, a few Sabbaths, afterwards Rev. J. N. Smith and Rev. George Vincent, next Rev. George Law; in 1843 and in the Summer of 1844, Rev. J. P. Miller, after him the Rev. Forsythe; and in the Fall of 1845, Rev. McMillan and Rev. R. H. Pollock, Rev. R. W. French coming the time stated.

A short time after the settlement of Mr. French, the church was built, and in this they worshiped until about the year 1866, when it was enlarged, and was used in that condition till July, 1875, when the congregation having grown large, and wealthy, the present beautiful building was erected. It cost the congregation in all near $12,000, and is said to be one of the finest country churches in the State. Rev. French remained as pastor until the years 1859 or '60, when he gave up his charge and removed to Peotone, Illinois. The present pastor. Rev. W. T. Moffitt, was called in 1861 or '62, and is still in charge. This church now has near 300 communicants, and is most favorably known in the church at large. It has given many thousands of dollars to the various church boards, and to benevolent charities, besides always paying a liberal salary to its ministers. It has sent three ministers into the field, all of whom are doing good work. A division at one time occurred in the church, which resulted in the forming of the Reformed Church, whose building still stands; but the members have almost all returned, and the division is now most happily healed.

SYCAMORE.

The township of this name, containing the thriving city of Sycamore, the county seat, is agreeably diversified in surface, and unusually favored with an abundance of timber and running streams. Its soil is particularly rich, black and unctuous, destitute of sand or gravel, and hardly as productive as that of some other portions of the county. This, however, may be due to its having been longer tilled; for when Erasmus Walrod first came here, in 1835, he raised ninety bushels of corn to the acre, on the upturned prairie sod.

FIRST SETTLERS.

The first settler of the township was probably Lysander Darling, who came in 1835. Dr. Norbo, a Norwegian, came the same year, and claimed Norwegian Grove, which thus received its name. Also Mr. Chartres, a Frenchman, who gave name to Chartres Grove. J. C. Kellog, E. F. White, Zechariah Wood, and Peter Lamois, were also among those who made their homes within the borders of what now constitutes this township, in the first year of its settlement by the whites.

In 1836, the New York Company, composed of Christian Sharer, a wealthy New Yorker, Evans Wherry, Clark Wright, and Mark Daniels, under the firm name of Sharer & Co., claimed two square miles of land, running from Marshall Stark's farm on the north to the south line of the town. They laid out a village plat at the north of the creek, dammed the Kishwaukee River, built a mill, enclosed with a high, heavy rail fence a tract of sixty rods wide and two miles long, whose west line was on what is now Somonauk Street, and prepared to build up a town.

This was in the flush times, when wild-cat money in abundance filled every one's pockets, and the speedy growth of great cities in the West was confidently expected.

When these bubbles had burst, and hard times came on, the company, although they had expended a large amount of money, abandoned their claim, dissolved their co-partnership, and never "entered" their land.

VILLAGE OF SYCAMORE.

The old town of Sycamore, north of the creek, consisted of two or three log cabins, in some of which Esquire Jewell kept a blacksmith and wagon shop, and J. C. and Charles Waterman kept a store. It was abandoned next year for the higher land where the present village of Sycamore stands.

Capt. Eli Barnes built the first house in this village—the large tavern now the Sycamore Hotel. The construction of so extensive a structure was considered a wild, extravagant expenditure of his means; but it did much to establish the town, and retain the county seat, which it was then thought would soon be removed. The captain was full of zeal for the welfare of this village, and for years labored, perhaps more than any other man, to secure friends and votes to counteract the numerous efforts to procure the removal of the seat of justice.

A little framed house had before this been moved down from the Hamlin farm, and was occupied by Dr. Bassett, the first physician of the place. It stood, till 1855, where D. B. James subsequently built a handsome residence, and was then burned down, on suspicion that it had been used for the sale of liquor.

The old court house was built in 1839, nearly opposite the present structure, and in 1840 the dreary little village consisted of a dozen houses, scattered over considerable land, but without fences, and with but one well. John C. & Charles Waterman, were the first merchants, 1839.

The town was laid out in 1839, by Capt. Eli Barnes, county surveyor. In 1840 it was quite a little village, containing, among others, the following houses and buildings: The main streets were State, running east and west, and Main Street, north and south. On the northeast corner at the intersection of State and Main Streets stood the old Mansion House, built by Capt. Eli Barnes; opposite was a house built by Charles Waterman; east of this, on the same side of State Street, was the house of D. Bannister; and south, on the next block, the residence of Jesse C. Kellogg; across Main Street, opposite Kellogg's, was the house of E. H. Barnes; north of this was the residence of Eli G. Jewell; and on the northeast corner, at the intersection of State and Main Streets, Stood the building of F. Love; west of this, on State Street, was the court house: and farther west, Wells' and Barnes shoe shops. C. Lattin had a house farther west on the north side of State Street, and a few rods farther west were the houses of Joseph Sixbury, and L. D. Walrod.

The Mansion House, called the Nunnery, at this time contained a large part of the population of the place.

A Congregational church was organized in 1840 with eleven members. In 1841, Rev. David Perry became pastor, and held service in the

court house. Capt. Barnes gave the church the lot on which their edifice
now stands; the building was erected in 1844, but not completed till two
years later.

A Methodist church was built the same year, on a lot given by Carlos
Lattin. The Episcopal church was built in 1856, and the Baptists, Uni-
versalists, and Roman Catholics, built churches two or three years after.

Marcus Walrod was the first boy born in the place, and Mrs. W. R.
Thomas the first girl.

Eli G. Jewell and Capt. Barber did most of the law business for
many years; but in 1841 Andrew J. Brown opened an office—the first
regular lawyer. He was succeeded by Mr. Masters, and he, in 1842, by
E. L. Mayo. W. J. Hunt practiced law here in 1844. There were then
eighteen houses in Sycamore.

In 1848 the population of the village was 262; in 1849 it was 320;
in 1850, 390; and in 1851, 435.

Much of the land now included in the village was still owned by
government in 1843. During that year, Mr. J. S. Waterman entered his
fine farm, and W. J. Hunt took up a quarter-section north and east of the
village, and eighth-section in 1848.

In 1855 there were in Sycamore six dry goods stores, two hardware
stores, two cabinet ware-rooms, one drug store, four grocery and provision stores, two saloons, three taverns, one banking and exchange office,
two wagon shops, one livery stable, two harness shops, two tin shops, one
jeweler shop, three shoe shops, four blacksmith shops, one shingle manufactory, one tailor shop, one meat market, one cooper shop, seven lawyers,
four physicians, ten carpenters, four painters, three circulating libraries,
three churches, and one steam saw-mill. The population of the township at this time was 1646.

In 1858 Mr. D. B. James erected the fine brick block now called
George's Block, which was dedicated with an old-settlers' celebration and
festival. During the same Winter a series of interesting lectures was
delivered there by Horace Greeley, Bayard Taylor, George Sumner, and
other distinguished speakers.

In the following year the Sycamore and Cortland Railroad was built,
at a cost of about $75,000. Its cost was a heavy expense to the citizens,
for the times were hard and money scarce; but it has proved a source of
great advantage to the business and growth of the town, which has
steadily flourished and increased from that time to the present. The
receipts of the road, which were only $4,500 in 1860, have increased to
over $12,000 in 1867, and to $17,000 in 1875.

THE CITY.

The City of Sycamore is one of the most attractive of its size in the
western country. It contains many fine residences, and a population
wealthy, enterprising and remarkably social. Present number of inhabitants 3,500.

Among its leading citizens are the brothers Waterman, six of whom
have, at times, resided here, and been among its most active business
men, since the first settlement of the county. Mr. James S. Waterman,
the first banker in the county, has become its wealthiest citizen, and

his elegant mansion has ever been the seat of a hospitality almost unlimited.

Of the Ellwood family of six sturdy brothers, noted for unbounded energy and enterprise, shrewdness and *bonhomie*, four have resided here, and two at DeKalb. Mr. Reuben Ellwood was a citizen of the place in 1838, but subsequently removed to New York, where he filled some important public positions. He was presented as the candidate of this county for Congress, in 1868.

Hon. E. L. Mayo, a lawyer of marked ability, moved to this place from Vermont in 1842, has held many public offices, and was a candidate for Congress in 1854.

Hon. D. B. James, formerly a lawyer in Lyndon, Vermont, removed to this place from California in 1852. He built a number of the best buildings in the place; has been an especially active member of the Republican party of the county since its organization; was appointed aid-de-camp to Gov. Oglesby, with the rank of colonel, delegate to the National Convention of 1864, and was chosen judge of the County Court in 1865.

Gen. Daniel Dustin, formerly of Lyndon, Vermont, removed to California in 1850; was a member of the Legislature of that State, moved to Sycamore in 1856; raised a company for Farnsworth's cavalry in 1862; was chosen colonel of the One Hundred and Fifth Infantry in 1863; served two years as commander of a brigade, and made one of the most faithful and popular officers in the service.

Gen. Charles Waite, one of six worthy sons of Hon. Daniel Waite, of Sycamore, enlisted at twenty-three years of age as a private in the Twenty-seventh Michigan Infantry, fought his way up to the colonelcy of that rough, ungovernable band of miners, whom he alone ever succeeded in reducing to proper discipline, was severely wounded in service in Virginia, and received the star of the brigadier for gallantry displayed in the battle of the Wilderness.

Gen. E. F. Dutton enlisted at twenty years of age in Company F, of the Thirteenth Infantry, of which he was made first lieutenant. In 1863 he was chosen major of the One Hundred and Fifth, rose to the rank of lieutenant colonel, and served through the war with that regiment. He was breveted brigadier for gallantry on the march to Atlanta, and in the battle of Goldsboro, North Carolina.

Sycamore is credited on the State record with 807 men furnished for the suppression of the rebellion. Many gave their lives to their country, and many have returned maimed and crippled; but the record of casualties is not now attainable.

Among other prominent and worthy citizens may be mentioned Judge Luther Lowell, of the County Court, who came from Vermont and became a resident in 1855.

Charles Kellum, Esq., was born in Pennsylvania, and came to the town in 1855. He has been a prominent lawyer for many years, and stands high as a public speaker.

Hon. R. L. Divine, now Mayor of the city, came here in 1858. He has been prominent as a lawyer and a man of remarkable energy. Is now proprietor of one of the banks of the city.

Rev. W. S. Harrington came here when a child about five or six years old—in 1843. He is a son of Dr. James Harrington, and one of a large and worthy family; was educated at Mt. Morris, Illinois; entered the ministry of the M. E. Church at an early day; has been presiding elder for some years; and in 1876 was put forward by his county as a candidate for Congress from the fourth congressional district. He resides at Sycamore and is presiding elder of the Dixon Conference.

Jesse C. Kellogg—Deacon Kellogg, as he is familiarly called—who died in 1873, was for nearly forty years a prominent citizen of Sycamore. No man was better informed in the early history of the county, and no man had its interests, both moral and physical, more at heart. He came from Vermont and settled here among the first, in 1835, and his example throughout his long life was worthy of imitation. As a zealous and consistent supporter of the moral and religious interests of the town, he was especially active in connection with the Congregational Church and the temperance cause. He served as clerk of the first board of county commissioners in 1837, and in 1842 was clerk of the Circuit Court, holding the office till 1849.

Henry L. Boies, now Postmaster and editor and proprietor of the *True Republican*, came to the county in 1854, and to Sycamore in 1858. He is a native of Massachusetts, and a man of marked integrity and ability. He has conducted the *True Republican* consecutively for thirteen years, and in 1868 prepared and published a History of DeKalb County, from which considerable of the matter in this History has been taken. In 1871–72 he was Secretary of the State Senate.

James S. Waterman began life here as a surveyor under the government. He has been a very liberal and enterprising citizen—a merchant, a banker, and a dealer in real estate, and has accumulated the most ample fortune of any man in the county ; and he has also benefited it as largely, probably, as any other man.

John C. Waterman, his brother, has also been a prominent and influential merchant in the place for at least forty years.

Marshall Stark, living on a farm near the city, is one of the remaining worthy pioneers. He came here September 14, 1835; was one or two terms Sheriff of the county. Besides his beautiful and valuable farm near the city, he owns large tracts of pine land in Michigan, and is engaged extensively in the lumber business at Sycamore.

We have not space for a complete list of all the old settlers, but mention, in connection with those above given, Zechariah Wood (deceased) and his two sons, Thomas H. and Henry Wood; E. D. Walrod, G. A. Maxfield, Alvin Dayton, Spafford Smith, and Joseph Sixbury.

SUPERVISORS.

Of the supervisors of this town Dr. James Harrington served from its organization in 1850, until 1856, when E. L. Mayo was elected. D. B. James succeeded him, serving in 1857–58 ; James Harrington followed in 1859–60–61 : Roswell Dow in 1862–63–64 ; Samuel Alden in 1865–66; Henry Wood in 1867 ; N. S. Cotrell in 1868; Henry Wood in 1869; John G. Smith in 1870–71 ; E. B. Shurtleff in 1872–73; Nathan Lattin in 1874–75–76.

INCORPORATION AND OFFICERS.

In 1858 the Village of Sycamore was incorporated ; and, in accordance with the provisions of the charter, has been represented upon the

Board of Supervisors by the president of its board of trustees. These have been: For 1859, E. L. Mayo; 1860, C. M. Brown; 1861, Alonzo Ellwood; 1862, C. O. Boynton; 1863, Alonzo Ellwood; 1864–65, Chas. Kellum; 1866, Luther Lowell; 1867–68, C. O. Boynton; 1869–70, Reuben Ellwood; 1871, Moses Dean; 1872, Richard A. Smith; 1873–74, John B. Harkness; 1875–76, Richard L. Divine.

Incorporated as a city March 4, 1869.

CITY COUNCIL FOR 1876.

Mayor—R. L. DIVINE.
Clerk—PRESTON K. JONES.
Treasurer—A. C. COLTON.

Aldermen.

First Ward—JOHN S. BROWN, MILO DAYTON.
Second Ward—N. C. WARREN, WM. C. BLACK.
Third Ward—MOSES DEAN, J. C. FULKERSON.

GRADED SCHOOLS.

The public school of the city is graded in ten departments, culminating in a high school, according to the Chicago plan. It has a fine building, erected in 1863, which cost about $16,000. It is a wooden structure, well furnished and fitted up for school purposes.

The number of persons of school age in the city is about 1,200 ; enrolled, 729 ; average attendance, 510.

WILLIAM WHITESIDE, *Superintendent.*
MISS ADELIA HUNT, *Principal High School.*

BOARD OF EDUCATION.

HON. LUTHER LOWELL, *President.*
P. M. ALDEN, *Secretary.*
DANIEL DUSTON.
CHARLES BROWN.
CHARLES O. BOYNTON.
WILLIAM BLACK.

CHURCHES.

Sycamore has eight churches, viz. :

St. Peters (Episcopal)—Rev. W. E. Toll, rector.
Methodist Episcopal—Rev. J. H. Moore, pastor.
Wesleyan Methodist—Rev. J. L. Clark, pastor.
Baptist—Rev. Watson Clark, pastor.
Congregationalist—Rev. W. F. Gallagher, pastor.
Catholic—Rev. Father Dun, pastor.
Universalist—Rev. S. F. Gibb, pastor.
Swedish Lutheran—

NEWSPAPERS OF SYCAMORE.

The True Republican—Weekly and semi-weekly ; Republican in politics. Boies & Armstrong, publishers.

The City Weekly—A weekly newspaper, published by V. Hix.

The Free Methodist—Organ of that denomination in the United States: Baker & Arnold, publishers.

The DeKalb County Democrat—Weekly Democratic paper; published by Waite & Bassett.

The Pearl, The Lily, and *The Pilgrim*—Monthlies, published by Baker & Arnold.

BANKS.

First National—James S. Waterman, President; C. W. Marsh, Vice President.

Private Banks—Divine & Co.; Pierce & Dean.

GROWTH OF THE CITY.

The following from the *True Republican* of January, 1876, shows the progress of building in Sycamore during the preceding year:

One Hundred and Forty Thousand Dollars Expended.—In making up our annual record for 1875 of the new buildings erected in Sycamore during the year, we have been surprised to find that both in number and in value the list has rarely, if ever, been exceeded during any previous year of the existence of the town. The work has been done so quietly, and to such a large extent in the suburbs and outskirts of the city, that it has not attracted so much attention as in years previous, when the center and all parts of the city seemed alive with new structures, but the new buildings are nevertheless both numerous and valuable; and considering that it has been a time when money was scarce and hard to be obtained: that all over the country business has been depressed, and here especially the farmers (on whose prosperity we all depend) had been impoverished by the loss of their usual grain crop, it is really remarkable that so much has been done. The vitality of the place is really wonderful.

Prominent among the new public buildings of the city is Winn's elegant new hotel of pressed brick, with elegant stone trimmings. It is a structure of which any of the minor cities of the country might be proud, and one that few or none of them can surpass.

A little further west on State Street will be seen the graceful spire of the new Universalist Church, a brick building of elegant design and substantial construction, which is an ornament to the city. Its interior is beautifully finished in Gothic style, with stained glass windows and frescoed walls. Its cost will exceed that of any other church in DeKalb County.

Among the useful new industrial works in the city is the spacious brick factory buildings of the R. Ellwood Manufacturing Company. They are a fine looking group of buildings, and furnish a valuable addition to the business of the city, giving employment to over fifty workmen now, a number that will soon be considerably increased.

Another new factory, completed early in the Spring, is the sash and blind factory of Mr. F. Schroeder & Son. It is a spacious and well-planned wooden structure, two stories in height, and its machinery is of the best and most elaborate kind. It has been full of work ever since it was put in operation, and has drawn a large amount of business to the city.

Mr. Charles T. Stuart's new dwelling house, erected on the site of the old Erasmus Barnes place, fronting on the public square, is one of the most complete and well-finished buildings in our city. In design, taste and construction it is a model.

The site of the old Universalist Church on Main Street, is now occupied by a large brick dwelling house built this season by Mr. A. M. Stark, the able secretary of the Sycamore Marsh Harvester Manufacturing Company. It is of peculiar and very pleasing style, having the general appearance of an old English mansion or villa.

In the southern part of the city is the new dwelling house of Mr. David DeGraff, a large and beautiful building costing about $5,000. It is designed and finished in excellent taste and its beauty is enhanced by its commanding position on the summit of a knoll from which a spacious lawn, bordered with fine old trees, slopes gracefully an hundred feet to the road.

The following list, furnished by one of the contractors of this city, comprises the greater part of the buildings and their approximate value:

Winn's Hotel,	$18,000	J. Fulkerson, house and barn,	$ 700
Universalist Church,	12,000	H. H. Mason, house and barn,	800
R. Ellwood & Co., factory,	20,000	G. Russell, house and barn,	600
J. M. Southworth, store,	2,000	S. Mathews, house and barn,	600
A. M. Stark, house,	3,000	S. Lackey, house,	600
S. Loomis, house,	2,000	E. Tifft, house,	1,200
J. C. Waterman, house,	1,500	Wm. Phelps, house,	500
D. DeGraff, house,	4,500	J. Hopkins, house,	500
A. Johnson, house,	1,000	J. Welch, house,	600
A. Ingmanson, house,	1,500	Haley, repairs,	600
Spafford Smith, house,	1,600	Mrs. Jarvis, addition to house,	600
J. J. Bell, house,	1,000	A. R. Cameron, addition to house,	800
Geo. Knipp's six houses,	8,000	M. Painter, house,	1,200
J. Ronen's house and barn,	1,100	L. Petrie, two houses,	800
H. M. Dodge, house,	1,000	G. Fox, house,	400
G. Harrington, house,	1,200	T. Arnold, house,	1,000
T. Carr, house,	1,200	Rowe, house,	600
A. S. Miller, house,	1,800	John Stevenson, house,	400
Wm. Tifft, house,	1,600	Smith, house,	1,000
Taylor, house,	800	Wm. Underdown, repairs,	400
Mr. Henry Olin, house,	1,000	D. Marsh, addition,	300
C. T. Stuart, house,	4,000	W. H. Stokes, house,	800
H. Briggs, store,	800	Thos. Mumford, house,	800
A. Sell, store,	1,000	H. L. Boies, repairs and addition,	800
Deacon Worcester, house,	1,600	H. Paine, house,	2,000
F. Shroeder, factory,	12,000	Wm. Cox, house,	800
Mr. Wm. Graham, house,	1,500	Mrs. M. Quinn, house,	800
R. B. Tewksberry, house and barn,	1,000		
C. Tewksberry, house,	600		
F. M. Robinson, house and barn,	500		
H. Laverty, two houses and barns,	1,800		

The contractor further says :

Besides the above, there are six or eight houses in the vicinity of Charles Street, the owners of which I do not know, also four or five in the north part of town, they are worth in the aggregate about $10,000 or $12,000, and some I presume I overlooked. There has also been much building done in the vicinity outside of the city. Capt. Luther is now building himself a fine residence. Mr. Fogg is building another large house on his lot. The Harvester Factory has also made large additions to their buildings.

MANUFACTURES.

Besides the minor manufacturing interests, such as planing mills, cheese-box factory, etc., the two most important branches are the Cultivator Manufactory of R. Ellwood & Co., and the Marsh Harvester Works —both of which add largely to the business of the place.

The R. Ellwood Manufacturing Company—Was established in 1875. The company manufacture the Ellwood Sulky Cultivator, Barn-Door Hangers and Tracks, Stay-Rolls, Wire-Stretchers, Dog and Horse Powers, Pivot Castors, Rolling Colters, etc., and do general repairing, having foundry and machine shops. Their building is three stories, including basement, and cost about $20,000. Their business per annum amounts to $125,000. This year they expect to turn out and put upon the market 3,000 of their new and popular cultivators. As yet they have not been able to manufacture enough to supply the demand.

The business is controlled by R. Ellwood, who also carries on hardware business to the amount of $70,000 per annum.

The Marsh Harvester Manufacturing Company.—This now extensive manufacturing interest was established as a joint stock company in 1869. Its officers are: C. W. Marsh, President ; A. M. Stark, Secretary ; and W. W. Marsh, Superintendent. The brothers Marsh are old settlers of the county, having resided in it twenty-seven years. They first established their shops in Plano, Kendall County, in 1863, whence they removed to their present locality in 1869. Their shops here are extensive, being of brick, 640 feet in length, and in the main two stories high. They cost, including ground and machinery, $50,000. The capital stock of the company is $90,000, and about $300,000 invested in the business. In 1875 they manufactured 4,000 harvesters. Last year they built and sold 3,500, besides a large number of wind-mills, mowers and corn-plows.

Mr. C. W. Marsh represented the district composed of DeKalb, Kane and DuPage Counties in the State Senate in 1870.

MASONIC.

Sycamore Commandery, Knights Templars.
Royal Arch Chapter.
Sycamore Lodge, No. 134.

ODD-FELLOWS.

Ellwood Encampment.
Sycamore Lodge, No. 105.

DeKalb.

The township of DeKalb is situated near the center of the county, and is second to no other in its natural advantages and in its development and growth in wealth. The surface, like the remainder of the county, is mostly handsome rolling prairie; but is favored with one fine stream, a branch of the Kishwaukee, and is liberally supplied with timber from an extensive grove bordering on this stream, formerly known far and wide as Huntley's Grove.

There was, prior to the first settlement, a large Indian village at Coltonville, on the northern border of this township, but in the Fall of 1835 the Indians were removed beyond the Mississippi. It is said that a company of United States troops, engaged in assembling these Indians at Paw Paw Grove, preparatory to their removal, encamped for a night on the site of the present city of DeKalb. While here one of their number attempted to desert. He paid McClellan, a settler at the grove, a sum of money to secrete him, but McClellan, being threatened by the officer in command, gave him up, and he was tied to the rear of an army wagon and dragged on foot through the remainder of the route. The neighbors, indignant at McClellan's treachery, threatened to lynch him, and he was obliged to fly the country for safety.

FIRST SETTLERS OF DEKALB TOWNSHIP.

The first settlers of this township were John B. Collins and Norman C. Moore. Mr. Collins settled on the farm now owned by the heirs of the late Captain Burpee; Mr. Moore made a claim a mile or two north of him. They came in the Spring of 1835. During that Summer all the timbered land in the township was claimed. McClellan claimed the south end of the grove afterwards held by Mr. Huntley. James Cox claimed a farm now owned by C. W. Marsh, and James Paisley the place on which some of his family now reside.

In the Autumn of 1835, Messrs. Jenks & Co. claimed the land now occupied by Albert Schrever, dammed the creek, built a mill, and projected a town in the vicinity. The streams were much larger then than now, and it was thought that the water would be of permanent value; but a dry Summer or two convinced them of their mistake, and they never completed their proposed village.

In the Autumn of 1836 the first election in the county was held. It was held in Captain Eli Barnes' house, in the township of DeKalb, and the voters came from all parts of the county. It was an election for Justice of the Peace. Mr. Samuel Miller, of Squaw Grove, relates that ten dollars were sent down to him by one of the candidates to pay him for bringing up ten voters, and that these ten voters carried the election.

In February, 1837, Mr. Russell Huntley, representing a company of capitalists, who designed to build mills and carry on farming, moved to the south end of the grove, and bought the claim of James Root, who had succeeded McClellan. Wild-cat money was plenty then, and claims sold at higher prices than they would bring ten years after. Mr. Huntley bought all of the south part of the grove, paying $5,300 to the several claimants. His purchase embraced about 500 acres of wood land, and as much of the prairie as he chose to call his own. As it seemed desirable, however, that each should know where his line was, he made an agreement with the Brodies, of Brodies' Grove, about ten miles west of him, that the division line between them should be half way between the two groves; and he made a similar verbal arrangement with the inhabitants of Shabbona Grove on the south.

After the first two years, settlers came in very rarely. Hard times came on, money became very scarce, the people grew poor; and in 1843, when the land, for the claims to which they had paid such liberal prices, came in market, most of them found great difficulty in raising the money to enter it. As late as 1850, Mr. Huntley was offering half of the land upon which DeKalb Village now stands to any man who would furnish $1.25 per acre to enter it.

VILLAGE AND CITY OF DEKALB.

For nearly twenty years Mr. Huntley kept an excellent tavern at this place, and in the busy season it was constantly crowded by teamsters from the west, as far as the Mississippi River, who were on their way to Chicago with grain. The proceeds of the load, oftentimes, did not pay the expenses of drawing to market. For this reason, thousands of bushels of excellent wheat raised in this town were fed to cattle without threshing. This poverty among the people continued until the railroad was built through, in 1853.

In 1850 the township was organized, with the name of Orange, and Thomas M. Hopkins was chosen its first Supervisor. In that year the first store in the place was opened by J. M. Goodell, in one end of the dwelling now owned by the widow of Rufus Hopkins. In 1852, J. S. Waterman and Alvah Cartwright started another, and they, with Goodell and Ruby's store, Huntley's tavern, and a blacksmith's shop, constituted the village in 1853, when the railroad was built, revolutionizing the business affairs of the county. After this, a large and flourishing village was speedily built up at this place. Its progress was remarkable. Houses sprang up as by magic. The neighboring farmers who visited it one month would hardly recognize the place when they visited it the next. Mr. Huntley sold part of his land to three directors of the railroad company,—Holland, Robinson, and Van Nortwick,—and they together laid out the village, and speedily sold the lots at good prices. Stores, shops, warehouses, hotels, and dwellings, filled up the village plat, and the evidences of taste and refinement were to be seen in its streets and dwellings. For several years it went by the name of Buena Vista.

In 1855 its population was 557. It was confidently expected that, owing to its central location and its being upon a railroad, it would soon be made the seat of justice for the county.

The financial crash of 1857 impeded the progress of the thriving little village. Money scarce, trade dull, credit gone, prices low. Like all new towns, it was settled by a population full of enterprise, but of small capital, and the destruction of confidence and depression of trade was a serious injury to its progress. But its people were full of enterprise, courage and enthusiasm for the prosperity of their town. They taxed themselves heavily for all needed improvements, and worked with a will for the good of their town.

In 1860, a County Society for the promotion of agriculture and the mechanical arts was established, beautiful grounds selected and handsomely furnished, and flourishing annual fairs have ever since been held.

In 1861, the elegant brick building was erected for a Graded School, —for many years the finest common-school building in any town of its size in the state. It was designed to cost $8000, but its total expense has been over $25,000. The first school house in the town was a small structure built of basswood logs, and roofed with shakes, which stood near the grove, and near the line of the railroad, and for many years served both as school house and church.

In 1854, churches were built by both the Baptist and Methodist societies ; in 1860 the Catholics constructed a spacious church, and in 1864 the Swedish population, a large number of whom had gathered around this place, built a small church, in which worship is conducted in the Swedish form and language. A number of the most reputable citizens have embraced the Mormon faith, and the services of that sect have frequently been held in the place.

NEWSPAPERS.

In 1858 a newspaper under the name of the *Western World and DeKalb Review* was published in DeKalb by Mr. Andrews. This was succeeded in 1860 by the *DeKalb Leader*, edited by E. B. Gilbert ; and this in 1861 by the *DeKalb Times*, edited by G. D. R. Boyd. In 1867 the *DeKalb County News* was started. It is still published, and is an influential weekly Republican journal, L. H. Post, editor and proprietor. Mr. Post is also Postmaster of the city.

PROMINENT CITIZENS.

The first lawyer in the place was Marcus White, who commenced practice in 1855. The first resident physician was Dr. Hyslop. In 1859 Dr. Rufus Hopkins, of Sycamore, who had always had a considerable practice in that town, removed to DeKalb, and as a physician, banker and active man of business, has been a prominent actor in the affairs of the town. The first bank was established in 1859 by J. R. Hamlin and E. T. Hunt.

The four brothers, Glidden, who first settled here in 1841, have been among its most worthy and active citizens.

E. B. Gilbert, Esq., who came to Sycamore in 1847, and to DeKalb in 1852, was elected Justice in 1853, and by successive elections has ever since held the office.

Harvey Thompson, J. F. Glidden, and Jabez L. Cheasbro, have long been among the most popular and reliable grain dealers in the county.

Hon. Lewis L. McEwen served the county one term in the State Legislature, and has been an influential citizen for more than twenty years. He is a prominent man in the grain, coal and lumber business, in the firm of McEwen & Terwillegar.

Robert Roberts, the present County Treasurer, of the firm of Roberts & Tyler, is one of the old and worthy citizens.

In this connection may also be mentioned J. F. Glidden, the inventor of the Glidden patents for barb wire fences, and Jacob Haish, the no less enterprising inventor and manufacturer of the "S" barb wire fencing. These men have been great benefactors of the town and the

8

farming community at large, in the want which they have met by their ingenuity and, enterprise and the large number of men and amount of capital employed in the branches of business which they have established.

The brothers Isaac L. and Hiram Ellwood, have been among its most active business men.

Isaac L. Ellwood, of the firm of I. L. Ellwood & Co., has for many years been a leading citizen. He is the proprietor of the Glidden Barb Wire Factory, having purchased the extensive business, and is also largely engaged in manufacture.

It is such enterprising men as these, with R. K. Chandler, the Vaughns, Smulls, Roberts, Millers, and many others that might be mentioned, that have given tone and character to the town.

SUPERVISORS.

The supervisors of the town of DeKalb have been the following named persons: For 1850, Thomas M. Hopkins; 1851, Joseph F. Glidden; 1852, Thomas M. Hopkins; 1853, Alonzo Converse; 1854, Luman Huntley: 1855, Alonzo Converse; 1856, Marcus White; 1857, E. P. Young; 1858-59, Hiram Ellwood; 1860, Cyrus Tappan; 1861-62, J. F. Glidden; 1863, Harvey Thompson; 1864-5, Thomas M. Hopkins; 1866, J. F. Glidden; 1867, Harvey Thompson; 1868, W. C. Tappan; 1869-70-71-72, J. F. Glidden; 1873-74-75, L. M. McEwen; 1876, J. F. Glidden.

PRESIDENTS OF THE COUNCIL.

The village was incorporated under a general act in 1856, and in 1860 by a special charter, which made the President of the Board of Trustees a member of the Board of Supervisors. This position has been filled by W. H. Allen, in 1861-62; Silas Tappan in 1863; Leonard Morse in 1864; S. O. Vaughn in 1865; E. B. Gilbert in 1866; W. H. Allen in 1867-68; William H. Miller in 1869; L. M. McEwen in 1870; W. H. Record in 1871; J. S. Russell in 1872; Horace Hunt in 1873; L. M. McEwen in 1874-75-76.

WAR RECORD.

DeKalb furnished 223 men for the suppression of the rebellion. The history of their patriotism, losses, sufferings and triumphs, is too long to be recorded here, but it has been well preserved in the History of DeKalb County prepared by Mr. Boies, to which the reader is referred.

POPULATION.

The population of DeKalb (township and village) in 1855 was 1,588; in 1860, 1,900; in 1865, 1,978; in 1870, 2,164. The increase since 1870 has been in a larger ratio, as the city alone now contains 2,500 people.

BARBED WIRE MANUFACTURE.

DeKalb, through the introduction of barbed wire, has done much for the farmers, added largely to the growth of the place, and made for its manufacturers more money in the short space of two years than could have been realized in an ordinary life-time by the slow but sure process of accumulating wealth through the old established channels of trade.

There are two extensive establishments of this sort of manufacture in DeKalb, the works of I. L. Ellwood & Co., and the factory of Jacob Haish. The former manufactures

THE GLIDDEN BARB WIRE FENCE.

This was invented and established by Mr. J. F. Glidden, who first conceived the idea in the Fall of 1873, and began experimenting upon it on his own farm. The idea of a thorny or barbed wire fence, so constructed as to guard by its sharp spines or points against the pushing of stock, was not then entirely new. Michael Kelly had patented a barbed wire for fencing Nov. 17, 1868, which was re-issued April 4, 1876. But it consisted of a *flat* wire, with the barbs inserted in *holes* made through it. Mr. Glidden's first invention, patented May 12, 1874, was a decided improvement on this, consisting of a *round* fence wire and a barb formed of two short pointed pieces of wire, secured in place upon the fence wire by *coiling* between their ends, which were extended to present four points in different directions. Nov. 24, 1874, Mr. Glidden patented still another improvement, substituting for a single wire a double twisted wire, upon which was fixed a piece of pointed wire coiled in the center, forming two transverse points, in the words following: " A twisted fence wire having the transverse spur-wire bent at its middle portion about one of the wire strands of said fence wire, and clamped in position and place by the other wire strand twisted upon its fellow."

This latter is the kind manufactured at DeKalb by the Ellwood Company, and is a very desirable and popular wire fence. From manufacturing a few of these by hand on his farm, Mr. J. F. Glidden got to making the material in the city by horse-power, using at first a single horse to propel his imperfect machinery, which has been from time to time improved, till now its perfection is a matter of astonishment to all beholders. This machinery, together with the extensive establishment, has all been created out of the raw material within the incredibly short period of two years, during which time the large sums of money expended have been made in the business itself; so that it has been self-developing and self-supporting, and has created in addition a large surplus. The secret of its financial success is the fact that it has met a want everywhere urgently felt all over the great prairie country of the West; and the vast territory being of such varied climate that the demand is as great in Winter as in Summer. At no time, during any of the seasons, is there not fencing going on in some portion of the great field in which this fence is demanded—in Illinois or Iowa, in Texas or California.

Mr. Glidden first convinced his neighbors of the practicability of the invention by making with his own hands and setting about his farm portions of the fence. As these experiments were gradually improved and exhibited, the demand for the fence became urgent, and he was forced into its manufacture. As we have seen, he began on a small scale— working off a few pounds by hand, then by horse-power. In July, 1874, he entered into partnership with I. L. Ellwood, and commenced the manufacture in the city of DeKalb. The business soon outgrew their facilities. In the winter of 1874–5, they erected a portion of their present shops—a brick building 70x130 feet. The following year they doubled its capacity, increasing the machinery in the same proportion.

At present they have capacity for turning out a ton per hour of the manufactured steel wire, and have standing orders for a car-load a day. These goods are shipped to all parts of the West, Northwest and South-west—Illinois, Iowa, Minnesota, Kansas, Nebraska, Texas, Colorado, and California.

J. HAISH'S "S" BARB WIRE FENCE FACTORY.

This is the second establishment of the kind in DeKalb. It was established in 1874, and employs from eighty to ninety hands. About $80,000 capital are invested in the business. The products of this factory differ somewhat from those of the Ellwood works, being the "S" barb, so called from its likeness to the letter S before being clinched upon the wire. The results of this enterprise show the advantages of healthy competition, and demonstrate the fact that such is the demand for fences of both kinds that a dozen such establishments could not fully supply it. The field is large and constantly increasing. Mr. Haish is now shipping his "double-twisted, double-coated, fire-proof, weather-proof, stock-proof, iron-clad, steelwire" fencing to Iowa, Kansas, Nebraska, Illinois, Michigan, Indiana, New York, and Ohio, and to Texas, California, and nearly all the western states and territories.

PROGRESS IN BUILDING.

A great deal of building has been done in the town within two years, and particularly since the fire. The city seems to be passing through that phase incident to all places which attain to a solid and substantial growth, when ephemeral wooden structures give place to those of brick, stone and iron, and the main street presents a busy appearance. It is literally crowded with building materials.

Peter Wagner has nearly completed on Main Street a fine brick and stone, iron column, three-story building. It is designed for printing office, post-office and furniture store. It is one hundred feet in depth, with fine airy basement, plate-glass windows, and will cost not less than $8,000 or $10,000.

Tyler and Shea have nearly finished a sightly brick building designed for a clothing store and restaurant.

Jacob Haish is erecting a fine building, to contain a Masonic Hall, city hall and offices, with stores in the ground story, and fine large basement. It will cost $20,000.

Lott & Baird have in process of erection a new brick bank building, just west of their present bank, which will be soon completed, and be an ornament to the town.

J. F. Glidden's new building was commenced in August, and will be enclosed this fall. It will be the finest and most costly building out of Chicago or the larger cities of the state. The ground floor will be occupied for mercantile purposes; the upper stories for a hotel. It will cost about $30,000.

Love & Carter have during the year erected a new and commodious store for agricultural implements.

Hon. L. M. McEwen is erecting a large and handsome dwelling house.

W. B. King is also making arrangements for the erection of a dwelling.

Jacob Haish has erected a building for his factory 26x67, in which he has placed new machinery.

Stores in DeKalb rent anywhere from $200 to $600 per year, and in spite of hard times, rents have an upward tendency.

BANKS.

One—Private Bank ; Messrs. Lott & Baird.

HOTELS.

Two—The Eagle and the Central House, kept respectively by Frank Scripter and George Shakleton.

CHURCHES.

Catholic—Rev. Father Dun, pastor.
Swedish Lutheran—Rev. N. Nordgren, pastor.
Adventist—Rev. H. G. McCullough, pastor.
Methodist Episcopal—Rev. G. R. Van Horne, pastor.
Wesleyan Methodist—No pastor at present.
Congregationalist—No pastor at present.

PUBLIC SCHOOLS.

Graded on the Chicago plan—ten departments. High School unorganized at present. It is the intention to organize it and complete all the grades, so that pupils may pass up the inclined plane through the whole twelve years' course of instruction, and in the high school prepare for college. The building is a fine brick structure. It was built in 1861. Cost, $25,000. It is well furnished and the school is under a competent corps of teachers.

T. S. DENNISON, *Principal.*

BOARD OF EDUCATION.

JABEZ CHEASBRO, *President.*
G. W. LYON, *Clerk.*
C. C. HINMAN.

CITY OFFICERS FOR 1876.

L. M. McEWEN, *President.*
JABEZ CHEASBRO.
ALEXANDER RAY.
HIRAM EDDY.
CLARK CARTER,
P. G. YOUNG.
S. C. VAUGHAN, *Clerk.*

SOMONAUK.

In 1834, a mail route was established between Chicago and John Dixon's residence on Rock River. This route crossed the southern part of DeKalb County, running through what is now known as Freeland Corners. Near this place, in 1834, a log house was built, and to this station was given the name of Somonauk.

In 1853, the railroad was constructed through the county, and Mr. Alvarus Gage, the owner of the land on which the present town of Somonauk stands, gave to the railroad company five acres of land on which to erect their buildings, and laid out the town. A mail route was in operation through this place, running north and south, and, as it came but once a week, some delay was occasioned in the delivery of the letters. The postmaster at Somonauk was induced to remove to the station, and through the aid of the citizens near the station the office was removed, hence the name "Somonauk" at this place. After a time the office was again established at the old place, and the name "Freeland Corners" given it. During the years immediately succeeding the advent of the railroad, the town grew with extraordinary rapidity. Many came who were compelled to live in tents until they could erect a home. A man by name of Franklin Dall built the first store and warehouse here, and a Mr. Hess erected the second one.

After the advent of the manufacturing company in Sandwich, and owing to the strenuous efforts put forth by the citizens of this latter place to induce all such persons to settle there, and to the farmers to bring their produce to this market, the growth of Somonauk became slow. No manufactories were started, and the chief business of the town was trade with the surrounding populace. The growth of the town has been moderate, but healthy, and the village contains now some fifteen hundred inhabitants.

A few years since a pickle factory was established, which also cans corn. It has been doing a good trade, and, properly sustained, will be a help to the town. A cheese factory is in operation here and doing a good business. The California Windmill Company, under the control of Clark & Co., are working up an extensive trade; but as their mills are all made at Sandwich, the mechanics of that town get the benefit of the work. Somonauk should aid these gentlemen and all others in such works, and as much as possible get all the work done at home.

There are now in town enjoying a good trade, four dry goods stores, one hardware store, one grocery, two harness and saddle shops, one of whose proprietors manufactures a fine harness oil, which finds a good sale, three shoemakers, three blacksmiths, two wagon and carriage makers, two lumber yards, and three warehouses.

There are three or four physicians and two attorneys.

Somonauk contains seven churches. The Protestant Methodists, were the earliest organized. Some twenty-three years ago they effected their organization under the labors of a Mr. Watson. For some time services were held in private houses, afterwards in the school houses, until a church could be built. This congregation has now some twenty or thirty members. The pastor is the Rev. S. B. Guiberson. Two or three years after the organization of this church, the Presbyterians established a church at Northville. After being there two years they removed to Somonauk, and have remained ever since. They have a membership of fifty or sixty, under the pastoral charge of the Rev. Edward Scofield. The Baptists have a small organization here, of some fifteen or twenty members, having maintained this for some fifteen or sixteen years. Their minister is Rev. W. H. Card. The German Baptists organized some six years since. The Rev. H. Wernick is their minister. About the same time the Episcopal Methodists were constituted. They have now about thirty members in town, but have a goodly number in the country. Their pastor is Rev. R. Burns.

The Catholic Church is the largest in town. It has been organized about sixteen years, and numbers near two hundred members, embracing a large extent of territory. The priest is Father C. J. Huth.

The German Lutherans were organized about ten years since. The church, in common with the others, save the Catholic, is small, but supports an organization presided over by the Rev. G. Weiser.

THE SCHOOLS.

Prior to the foundation of the town, a school was held about a mile and a half north of town in what was known as the Poplin neighborhood. As soon as the settlement justified it, a school was formed about eighty rods south of the present town school building, and was a joint affair between the two townships. A school had also been held in a small building southeast of town, but, owing to a want of support, was in operation but a few months in the year. For the second or third term held in it, Mr. Alvarus Gage went around to all his neighbors with a subscription paper, each one agreeing to give a certain amount, irrespective of the number of scholars sent. By this means enough money was raised to continue the school four months. This gave way to the South School referred to, which was commenced about the year 1850. School was held here some three or four years, when this house (built by subscription) became too small for the number of scholars, and the present edifice was built, in which a good school has since been regularly maintained. The attendance now is 257, requiring a force of three teachers, the school being divided into primary, intermediate and high school departments. Mr. S. H. Towne is the present superintendent, having been here seven years. He has the schools in good condition, and he and his teachers are ornaments to the profession.

THE PRESS.

In December, 1875, Mr. C. A. West, an enterprising young man, with only two or three weeks' experience as a printer, came here and established the *Reveille*. The weekly circulation is now four hundred, and steadily increasing.

In Somonauk are three societies: the Masonic, Odd Fellows and Grand Army Republic. A Musical Union is also well supported, and a good dramatic company sustained. These two latter organizations furnish amusement for the citizens of the town, and from the attendance at their entertainments from the country they enjoy a good reputation.

SANDWICH.

Prior to the advent of the railroad, a post-office had been established near the present town, and was for the accommodation of the settlers midway between Newark on the south and Somonauk, now Freeland Corners, on the north. This office was named "Sandwich," by Hon. John Wentworth, familiarly known as "Long John," then United States Representative from this district, Sandwich being the name of his native New England town.

The railroad was surveyed through DeKalb County in the year 1851. The land on which Sandwich is situated, was owned by Mr. Almon Gage, still living in town, and his house was the mark used by the surveyors in their approach to this locality. His house thereby became the first building in town. Mr. Gage gave the railroad company five acres of land, on the condition that they would erect the necessary depot buildings within five years. He also laid off the town site into lots, and offered one of these lots to any one who would come and erect a building thereon. Mr. James Clark was the first to avail himself of this offer, and built a large, rambling, one-story dwelling house, afterwards known as the " Donegana " House.

Some two years after the completion of the railroad, through the influence of the citizens, a depot was established here, and was known as Newark Station. A mass-meeting had been held at Newark, and William Patten, Washington Walker and Lindsay H. Carr were appointed a committee to go to Chicago and induce the railroad company to build a depot for passengers and a warehouse. Mr. J. H. Furman had made a canvass of the surrounding country, and ascertained that some 400 persons would make this their railroad point for business or travel. On the representation of this and other facts presented by the delegates, the officers agreed to stop their trains when flagged. But the people were not to be defeated. A carriage was run from Newark, eight miles south, and all who could were induced to make as frequent trips as possible.

Such determined efforts had their effect. The railroad officers erected the necessary buildings, and Newark Station was a reality.

Mr. Gage had built a medium-sized granary, which he sold to the Carr brothers, who at once fitted it up for a store and dwelling, and in it opened the pioneer store of Sandwich. A post-office was established here known as Newark Station P.O., but the letters would often be sent on down to the town, only to be returned. Many would direct their letters to their friends here and omit the " Station " on the address. These things of course caused some delay and considerable vexation, and trouble, and the propriety of changing the name of the village was discussed. Every one wanted this, and a petition was sent to " Long John," whose influence prevailed, and the old office of *Sandwich* was revived and the name bestowed on the rising village. From the advent of the railroad, and more especially from the erection of the depot buildings, the growth of the town was rapid and vigorous. Surrounded by a fine farming country, rapidly filling up with an enterprising and intelligent people, men of liberal hearts and large purses were attracted here, and an excellent trade was soon established.

Through the influence of the Pattens, Hon. Augustus Adams, who had been a member of the Constitutional Convention of 1848, and a State Senator and Representative when residing at Elgin, Illinois, was induced to come here in 1856. He was at this time still a Senator, and was by trade a foundryman and machinist.

The residents of Sandwich well knew the importance of a manufactory to their town, and by liberal offers of aid induced him to settle among them.

The following year he removed his family here, and building his shops, laid the foundation of the immense establishment now known as the Sandwich Manufacturing Company. In 1864 he suffered a loss by fire, but at once rebuilt. In 1867 the establishment was enlarged, and a Stock Company organized with a capital of $75,000, afterwards increased to $125,000, and again to $250,000. These works employ from 50 to 250 hands, whose weekly pay-roll will average $1,500. The company manufacture the Adams Corn Sheller, which has had a large sale in this and foreign countries; the Adams and French Harvester, of which they made some 2,000 last year; also farming machinery, and when not too busily engaged on their own machinery, make a great many castings for other companies. W. L. Simmons, a prominent grain merchant here, is President of the company; and J. P. Adams, Secretary and Treasurer.

Across the street from this company's works, stand the buildings of the "Sandwich Enterprise Company." The main buildings of this and the "Sandwich Manufacturing Company," are of Batavia stone, a most durable building material. The "Enterprise Company" was organized in the Winter of 1868–9, and was originally owned and worked by the Kennedy Brothers. In 1872 the present building was erected, and the manufacture of the Enterprise Windmills actively commenced. The capital stock was $50,000, since increased to double that amount. In addition to the windmills, this company manufacture all kinds of farming machinery, and also the castings and woodwork for the Windmill Company at Somonauk. New machinery is now being placed in these works, and the facilities for more work are being rapidly augmented. They employ from twenty to thirty-five hands, whose weekly pay-roll will average $300. E. Banta is President; H. Packer, Superintendent; and B. F. Latham, Secretary.

These manufacturing companies give to Sandwich its solidity and wealth, and furnish steady employment to many of its best citizens. The town has always been an important grain market. In former years, when wheat was the main article produced by the farming community, the shipments have been enormous. During the year 1865, over 300,000 bushels of grain were sold here, one grain dealer paying out over $400,000.

In 1856, a bank was opened by Mr. M. B. Castle, which from an exchange business, that year, of $50, has grown to many times that amount, and is now a paying institution. In 1875 the Culver brothers, long merchants here, opened another bank, which is doing a good business. Mr. G. W. Culver and Robert Patten opened the first lumber yard; this is still in successful operation, and is owned by M. W. Abel. An additional one is owned by M. B. Castle & Co.

The business of the city is represented by these two lumber yards, the two banks, one large grain warehouse, the two manufacturing companies, two carriage and wagon makers, one agricultural implement store, eight groceries, five dry goods stores, two clothing stores, three hardware stores, four restaurants and saloons, one steam flouring mill, two livery stables, one cheese factory, three butchers, two coal dealers, two harness and saddlery shops, three blacksmiths, three shoe shops, one builder, a large number of carpenters and masons, two drug stores, two merchant tailors, one book and news dealer, one cigar factory, two bakeries, two photographers, one music store, six milliners, and three hotels. The professions are represented by three lawyers and seven physicians.

From the above it will be seen that the town is well represented in all trades and professions.

Sandwich supports two good papers ; the elder of these is the *Gazette*, started in 1857 by William L. Dempster, under the title of the *People's Press*. It survived only six months. In 1859 it was revived under the name of the *Prairie Home*, and again met the same fate. After a while it was again issued by James Higbee with the name of *Sandwich Gazette ;* as such it was issued bi-monthly. In a short time, however, it was made a weekly, and Mr. J. H. Furman, before mentioned, assumed control. In 1874 he sold to Mr. G. H. Robertson, the present owner and editor. It is an excellent county paper, and according to the bills returned from the company from whom the paper is purchased, the present *bona-fide* circulation is 768 weekly copies.

The *Free Press* was started in 1873 by its present owner and editor, Mr. H. F. Bloodgood, a former attache of the *Gazette* office. It is a sprightly sheet, and according to the same authority has a weekly circulation of 981 copies.

Mr. Bloodgood also publishes the *Shabbona Express*, which circulates largely in that township.

RELIGIOUS AND EDUCATIONAL INTERESTS.

The city contains six churches, all well patronized. The Baptists were the first to occupy the field. Their house of worship was erected in 1853. The Methodist Episcopal next, in 1854, and the following year the Presbyterians built their house. The Congregationalists had organized a church at Little Rock, seven miles distant, as early as 1853. In June of 1856, they removed their church here, using the Methodist whenever they had services, until July, 1857, when they erected a small house. This they sold to the German Lutherans in 1864, and built their present beautiful church edifice. In the year 1866 they built their parsonage. They organized with sixteen members, and now number nearly two hundred. Their pastor is the Rev. J. L. Granger. The minister in charge of the Baptist Church is Rev. A. L. Farr, and that of the Presbyterians is Rev. George B. Black. The German Methodists maintain a church, organized some ten or twelve years, whose pastor is Rev. C. T. Morf. Shortly after their organization that of the German Lutherans was effected. The pastor of this church is the Rev. R. Menk.

The city maintains exellent schools. The earliest efforts in this direction were made in a small, red frame house, which stood near the intersection of Main and Center Streets. School was held here from about the year 1851 or '52 until the year 1857. During the year 1855 an incorporated company was established who built an academy on the ground now occupied by the South Side School. This academy did not prove a success, and the small school house becoming too small, the district purchased the academy building and employed the principal, Professor Hendrick, to conduct school in it. As the town grew, this was found too small and at an inconvenient distance for many, and a similar building was erected on the north side of the railroad. Additions have been made to these, and three small additional buildings constructed in different parts of the city for the use of the smaller pupils. During this last year, 1875, there were enrolled 689 pupils, which required the services of eleven teachers. Mr. A. E. Bourne, a graduate of the Wisconsin State University, who has been connected with the schools some three or four years, is the superintendent.

Sandwich was incorporated as a town in 1860, with the following persons as trustees: Augustus Adams, President; Almon Gage, George W. Culver, Washington Walker, and William G. Morris; S. B. Stinson, Clerk. On the 19th day of November, 1872, the question of adopting a city organization under the general laws of the state, was submitted to the citizens, and decided in the affirmative.

The first City Council was constituted as follows:

Mayor—W. W. Sedgwick.

Aldermen—H. A. Adams, M. R. Jones, A. A. Marcy, John Woodward, Henry Jones, O. S. Hendee.

City Clerk—T. E. Hills.

The present City Council is as follows:

R. M. Brigham, *Mayor.*

Aldermen.

First Ward—J. H. Culver, Enos Doan.
Second Ward—John Woodward, Harvey Packer.
Third Ward—H. F. Winchester, Geo. Kleinsmid.

J. A. Tolman, *City Clerk.*
S. B. Stinson, *City Attorney.*

There are two Masonic lodges, two Odd Fellows, and one of the Grand Army Republic. A good Musical Union is sustained, which furnishes many evenings of profit and pleasure to the members and entertainments to the citizens. A lecture course is regularly kept up, which adds very materially in developing a correct social taste. This is well patronized by the citizens of town and the surrounding country.

MALTA.

This was one of the later townships in being settled, owing to its situation on the open prairie, at considerable distance from groves of timber. Ezekiel Whitehead became its first settler in 1851. At this time a large proportion of the land in the township was in the hands of the government, but was entered during this and the following years by C. C. Shepard, H. A. Mix, Mark Howard, and other speculators, who subsequently became rich by the rise in the value of the land.

In 1854, by a petition of the citizens of South Grove, a station was established on the railroad, then completed to Dixon, and this gave such an impulse to settlement that the township rapidly filled up. It had been a part of the town of DeKalb, but, acquiring a sufficient population, was set off by act of the supervisors, upon a petition of the inhabitants, in 1855, under the name of Milton, which was changed to Etna, and a few years after, to Malta, its present name.

The village at the station was named Malta, and a thriving town rapidly grew up at this point. The financial crisis of 1857 gave it a blow from which it was many years in recovering. In 1857 a large steam mill was built, but owing to the stringency of the times, was not profitable, and was burned down in 1861. In 1867 another large and substantial steam grist mill was erected by Mr. Abraham Peters, by the aid of liberal subscriptions on the part of the citizens. This mill has continued to do good business.

Towards the close of the war the place took a fresh start. The high prices of grain attracted settlers and gave increased value to the new prairie lands. Money became plenty, business increased, new buildings were erected, real estate doubled in value, and sales which for many years were impossible became active and frequent. Malta has since been prosperous. It is the natural center for a large extent of rich country, which, filled, as it is, with a substantial farming population, will support a town of three or four times the present population.

The first census of the town was taken in 1860; it then contained 620 souls. In 1865, the population was 849; in 1868, 1,200. The present population of the village is about 1,500. Malta furnished ninety-four soldiers for the War of the Rebellion.

The Congregationalists and Baptists have fine churches, erected in 1867.

The town contains three elevators—two of a capacity of 7,000 bushels each, and one of 2,500. It has a large flouring mill and cheese factory, eight stores, one hotel, and the usual variety of artisans' and mechanics' shops.

VILLAGE OF CORTLAND.

Prior to the opening of the Chicago & North-Western Railroad through this part of the county, the site of the Village of Cortland was composed of portions of the farms of Mr. Hall and Mr. Ezra Croof.

The latter of these two laid out the original plat, comprising all the south-western part of town, and including the grounds now occupied by the railroad buildings, and some of the western portion of the village.

The railroad was built through in 1853, and the following year the company purchased the farm of Mr. Hall, comprising the south-eastern part of town and extending across the railroad, including some of the eastern portions. Mr. Hall erected the first house in the new village, using it as a boarding-house. It stood a short distance south of the railroad tracks, on the east side of Main Street.

The first store in town was built and occupied by Mr. Marcus Washburn. As the village was not of rapid growth, it is probable this satisfied the demands of trade for a year or two.

The liberality of the railroad company in disposing of their land purchased from Mr. Hall, induced many to come to the place and engage in the various kinds of trades and business demanded by a country town. Before the building of the Cortland and Sycamore Railroad, business was exceedingly good at this point, as the merchants and tradespeople from the latter town made this their shipping and receiving point. But no sooner had this road been completed, than all this was stopped, nearly all the travel from the northern portions of the county going to the county seat.

Mr. Lovell built a large steam flouring mill, and engages extensively in buying grain from the surrounding country. This, and the buying of stock, the supplying of the farmers with groceries, drugs, dry goods and farm merchandise, and the shipping of their produce, comprise the chief business of Cortland. It now contains three dry goods stores, one drug store, one agricultural implement store, one hotel and one livery stable.

The trades are represented by one butcher, three blacksmith shops, one wagonmaker, two shoemakers and two harnessmakers. The town supports one church and a good graded school, and contains a population of near 500 hundred persons.

The earliest church organization was that of the Methodist, the only denomination who have an organized congregation.

In the Fall of 1858, some sixteen persons met at the house of Mr. Peter Moore, then occupying the ground of Prof. Curtis' dwelling, and proceeded to organize a class. Before this time, in connection with a few resident Baptists, they had conducted services occasionally at different houses ; but now the need of an organization was realized, and this handful of Christians banded together for mutual encouragement and aid. Rev. C. T. Wright was the officiating minister, and organized the congregation.

Until the year 1863 services were held in the North Side School House. That year the present church building was erected. The congregation now numbers about sixty-five members, and support their pastor, the Rev. A. C. Frick, two-thirds of the time.

The first school house was built of split bass-wood logs, and stood near the south corporation line, on Main Street. This house was 16x18 feet in size, and was used until it became too small, when a frame one was erected on the north side of town, on the lot now occupied by the house of Mr. John Woodley. This building is now used as an agricultural store, and stands adjoining the store of Moore & Sheldon on the south. It was used until the year 1868, when the present graded school building was finished. The log school house now does service as a barn for Mr. D. Joselyn.

The school is now divided into three grades—Primary, Intermediate and High School. The enrollment is 135, and the attendance 110.

The Principal is Prof. C. W. Curtis, who has had charge some four or five years.

In 1868 the Legislature changed the name of the township from Richland to correspond with that of the town, viz. to Cortland.

VILLAGE OF GENOA.

The first white inhabitant of this village was Mr. Thomas Madison, who came to this locality in the year 1836, and erected a spacious log cabin on the spot where, for thirty years after, a hotel was kept by H. N. Perkins and Luke Nichols.

Mr. Madison came from Genoa, New York, and finding a Batavia and Geneva here, as well as there, concluded to carry out the parallel, and named the place in honor of his native home.

A post-office was established here by him at that time, of which he was first postmaster.

Mr. Perkins came in the Autumn of 1837, and he, Samuel Corey,

Thomas Munnahan. and Henry Durham, bought the claim of Mr. Madison, who removed to Texas. This claim was said to occupy two sections of land, for which $2,800 was paid.

Mr. Durham came in the Spring of 1837, and opened in Madison's cabin a small stock of goods—the first in the village—for sale to the few settlers who were now rapidly filling up this portion of DeKalb,—then part of LaSalle County.

Mr. Perkins remained here until his death, some thirty years after, and by his energy and industry accumulated a very handsome competence. Henry Preston and Daniel T. Whittemore were also among the early settlers.

In the Spring of 1838, Mr. Perkins' house was entered by a party of thieves, and some $300 worth of goods carried off. Whittemore was suspected of being in league with a gang of thieves, among whom were the Brodies of Brodie's Grove, who, Mr. Perkins had good evidence to suppose, were concerned in this robbery; but no prosecution was made, nor was any of the money or goods ever recovered.

During the year 1838, the immigration of settlers was rapid, and Genoa became quite a lively little village. Dr. H. F. Page commenced the practice of medicine there; James S. Waterman opened a stock of goods, and one E. P. Gleason, who afterwards figured as a leader of the banditti, came in and bought the claim of Whittemore and Corey. He had the reputation of being a man of wealth, and began to talk about building mills, starting stores, and otherwise contributing to the growth of the business of the village. During the spring of 1838, he set out the fine row of maples now constituting a conspicuous ornament of the place. In his subsequent career he acquired an unenviable notoriety. He was accused of passing counterfeit money, and was arrested by the United States officers for that offense. Taking the officers out to see his fine crop of corn, while detaining them for dinner, he suddenly disappeared in its luxuriant growth, and for several years was not seen in the county. Returning when the evidence against him was unattainable, he started a store and saw mill, married a respectable young woman in the neighborhood, and seemed contented to lead a correct life. A few years after, he became ill, and a traveling doctor, named Smith, a boarder in his family, and reported to be attached to his wife, attended him. After eating one day of some porridge, he suddenly became violently ill, and soon died in great agony. Not long after the doctor and Mrs. Gleason were arrested on a charge of murdering him, but the evidence being insufficient, they were discharged. They were soon after married, and removed to LaSalle County, where the doctor died under very suspicious circumstances. His wife soon after died quite suddenly.

In 1848, on July 4, a great celebration was held at Genoa, at which George H. Hill delivered an oration to an audience of over a thousand people. gathered from Rockport, St. Charles, Aurora and all the surrounding country. Genoa was as large and promising a town as any of these places. Belvidere contained then only two houses. The trade of Genoa supported four large dry goods stores, each doing a large trade. There were also kept two large, well-built taverns, at which a line of stages from Elgin to Galena made a stopping-place. The road received in work, annually, parallel furrows, plowed on each side of the road, by which travelers were enabled to keep the highway across the country. Elgin being the market place of all this region of country.

But by and by other towns began to spring up, and the prosperity of Genoa began to wane. The county seat was made at Sycamore, in 1839, and trade commenced to go there. Settlements were made in other parts of the county, and other trading points came correspondingly into notice. The village life ran on in the style of all Western towns which have lost their vitality and mainsprings of action, and not until the completion of the Chicago and Pacific Railroad, in January, 1875, twenty-seven years after, did this vitality return and a revival of business commence.

During all this time the village had simply supplied the immediate necessities of the surrounding community, and had hard work to maintain an existence. But now times changed. From that time until now, one year and nine months, the population has increased from a little over one hundred to more than four times that number. Then the trade was represented by two stores, two or three shops, and one hotel. There were but little more than twenty dwellings. Now the trade is represented by three dry goods stores, three groceries, one hardware store, four blacksmith shops, one wagon shop, one harness shop, one shoe store, one jewelry store, two provision stores, two lumber yards, two grain elevators, two meat markets, two coal yards, one flax mill, one billiard hall, one tailor, and two millinery shops. Three good hotels are supported.

On September 21, 1875, the *Genoa News* was started by S. S. Tucker, Esq. It has already a very creditable subscription list, and bids fair to rank with any paper in the county. Mr. Tucker is also proprietor of the News Depot here.

About 100 dwellings have been built since June 1, 1875.

RELIGIOUS AND EDUCATIONAL INTERESTS.

The Methodist Church was organized in the year 1841, with about twenty-five members. Meetings were held in barns, dwellings and the school-house until the erection of a church in 1854. This was re-built in a commodious manner in 1870, and is now one of the best houses of worship in the township. The membership is only about fifteen, presided over by the Rev. Joseph Coldwell.

The Adventist Church was organized in 1868, with near fifteen members. The following Spring the present church edifice was built. The membership was about doubled. The pastor is the Rev. E. H. Burrington.

The present school-house was erected nearly twenty years ago. It is now entirely too small for the number of pupils in the district—some 170 —and an additional room is rented. The principal is Prof. M. McCarty.

THE GENOA HORSE-THIEF DETECTIVE CLUB.

This club was organized about the year 1854. Prior to its organization the citizens had repeatedly been made the victims of theft, particularly that of good horses, and finding the process of law generally too slow for practical purposes, banded together for aid in detecting the criminals. Since then but one horse has been stolen from a member of the club. It was found in Indiana, at a cost of more than $200. The expense was not considered, the idea being to catch the thief and show to all, the society was a reality. The club is composed of the leading men of Genoa and surrounding towns, and numbers about 150 members.

Its object is fully set forth in the following preamble:

"WHEREAS, We, the citizens of Genoa, Ill., and vicinity, under the existing state of things consider it incumbent, as heretofore, upon us, as a community who have mutual rights, to protect ourselves and property, to re-organize this society for the better protection thereof, and in case of theft mutually assist in a recovery, and use all diligence in capturing and bringing all thieves and robbers to justice that in any manner molest a member of this society. We therefore pledge ourselves and each for himself a strict obedience and conformity to the following Constitution and By-Laws."

Articles I. and II. of the Constitution read as follows:

" ARTICLE I.

" The name of this society shall continue to be the Genoa Horse-Thief Detective Club.

" ARTICLE II.

" The officers of this club shall consist of, and rank as follows: President, vice-president, secretary, treasurer, captain, a finance committee of three members, and a sentinel. All of whom shall be elected by ballot at the regular meeting of the club in September of each year, and shall continue in office for one year and until their successors are elected or appointed in their places and are qualified."

The duties of the president, vice-president, secretary, treasurer and finance committee, are similar to those in all organizations. Those of the captain and sentinel are defined in Articles VII. and IX. which read thus:

" ARTICLE VII.

" It shall be the duty of the captain in case of larceny or robbery, when properly notified, to take such action as he may deem necessary to capture any party supposed to be implicated or connected with such felony, or for the recovery of the stolen property, and for such purpose he shall have power to order out any member or members hereof (who are not exempt from such duties) and direct what course he or they shall pursue.

" He shall have power to draw money from the treasurer to defray necessary expenses therefor, provided he shall draw an order and receipt for such amount only as the circumstances may demand, and if any member or members refuse or neglect to obey such orders when so called upon, he or they shall pay one dollar each for each offense to the funds of the club, or forfeit his membership, or both, or render a satisfactory reason to the club.

" ARTICLE IX.

" It shall be the duty of the sentinel to see that none but members hereof and that are entitled to protection by the rules of this club, are present at any meeting during the proceedings of the club."

Section eleven of the By-Laws fully defines the object of the club. It is as follows:

" SEC. 11. This club shall be at the expense of searching for any

THOS. M. HOPKINS Esq.
DE KALB

stolen property and thief, when the same has been taken from any member hereof, or if there is probable cause to suspect the commission of such crime, provided such members' rights are not impaired for any cause under the rules hereof provided; also, it shall be the duty of such member, as soon as there is probable cause to suspect that a larceny has been committed, forthwith to notify the captain or president hereof, or in their absence the officer next in rank, and provided further, that all such bills and items of expense shall be investigated by the finance committee, and if the same are allowed and paid, it shall be by vote of the club.

" The widows and minor children of deceased members of this club shall be protected by this club and shall be subject to like assessments as other members."

The present rules and regulations were adopted at a meeting held at the Genoa school-house on the 20th day of February, 1875. The meetings are held monthly, are open to the members only, and all members are forbidden to divulge any proceedings or plans of the organization. The officers are elected annually, the president, secretary and treasurer being excused from any active work while in office. The president is now Mr. B. P. Brown, and thieves are generally careful to let the property of any member of this club alone.

SHABBONA — CORNTON.

In November, 1871, Messrs. John Palm, John Ray, and Charles Stevens, entered into covenants with F. E. Hinckley, Esq., President and General Manager of the Chicago & Iowa Rail Road, for the purpose of locating the depot and suitable side tracts, and for which the said named gentlemen agreed to convey to the said F. E. Hinckley the undivided one-half of eighty acres of land, to wit: the north half of the northwest quarter of the southeast quarter of section fifteen, in township thirty-eight, north range three east of the principal meridian, in the County of DeKalb. Accordingly, in the Spring of 1872, the said eighty acres were platted and surveyed by the county surveyor into lots and blocks, and the work of laying side tracks, and the depot commenced.

In the month of May, Mr. J. A. Nutall moved the first dwelling house and barn into the village, and in July, Capt. A. B. Pollock made arrangements for the grain and lumber business. William Husk and Thomas Padgett soon followed with their stocks of dry goods, groceries, and hardware, Samuel Bouslough in buying grain and selling coal. M. V. Allen erected a fine dwelling house prior to entering the drug business. Not long after S. H. Bounscomb erected a blacksmith shop, and William Heeg a fine building for the furniture business.

Death soon marked its victim, and the enterprising young man, Captain Pollock, was called, and F. W. Smith of DeKalb, took the business and ran it until recently.

Since 1872 the village has been gradually increasing in population and in business, until Shabbona has the accommodations of the much larger towns.

A beautiful church was erected in 1874, and in February, 1875, the village became known as the corporate Village of Shabbona, with over 300 inhabitants. During this year a grist mill has been erected by R.

9

Langford, and in this Centennial year of 1876, this village can boast of a large increase of population and of business, and last, but not least, of an elegant school house, which is highly ornamental to the place, and a credit to the directors of district number three.

There are three religious denominations that worship in the church. The Baptist have a settled pastor, Rev. D. L. Clouse, who built a tasty residence in 1875. The Congregational Society have no settled pastor at present. The Methodist have preaching once in two weeks by Rev. F. Pomeroy.

KINGSTON

is a new and very promising place, situated in the center of Kingston Tp., on the Chicago and Pacific railroad, and is delightfully situated, on the south of a grove of timber. It has several business places which do a good local trade.

KIRKLAND

is situated on Sec. 26, Franklin Township, on the Chicago and Pacific Railroad. Kirkland is a growing town, situated in the midst of a fine farming country, and promises to have a rapid growth.

WATERMAN

is a live prosperous town on the Chicago and Iowa Railroad, situated on Section 16, Clinton Township. It is surrounded by a very fine agricultural region, and does a very fine business. Waterman is a new town, but growing rapidly, and promises to have a steady and healthy growth.

CORTLAND

was laid out on a claim made in an early day by James and Joseph Roberts, a couple of old bachelors. In 1852 a number of buildings were erected, and among them a Baptist Church. About this time Luce's Corners was commenced half mile south. When the railroad was built in 1853 through Cortland, it absorbed Luce's Corners.

The town was first called Richland, after that Pampus, and in 1864 Legislature changed it to Cortland. A railroad has been built from Cortland to Sycamore, a distance of four miles. Cortland has a population of about 1,400.

THE VILLAGE OF HINCKLEY.

Prior to the opening of the Chicago & Iowa Railroad in 1871, the land on which the village now stands was owned and used as farm land by Mr. Samuel Miller, J. C. Coster, and C. H. Taylor. Mr. F. E. Merrill, of the firm of Merrill & Wagner, had, in 1867, built the pioneer store of this locality. It was situated in the grove about one-half mile west of town, and here he kept store and post-office until the spring of 1872.

The railroad company had, at this time, just completed their present depot, and Mr. Merrill saw that the town would of necessity grow up around that. He associated Mr. H. D. Wagner with himself, and they erected their present store, the first in the village.

The name Hinckley was given this station in honor of Hon. F. E. Hinckley, the President and builder of the railroad passing through the town. Prior to the advent of this road, the post-office was known as Squaw Grove, the name of the township. No sooner had the station been established, than lots began to be laid out, and buildings to be erected.

J. O. Curry & Co. shortly after built the elevator now owned by Maltbie & Co. Next the store of Thomas Evans was added to those mentioned, and butcher shops, shoe shops, and various like commodities appeared.

The town is of four years' growth, and at present contains three general stores, one drug store, one hardware store, one furniture store, three millinery shops, one butcher's stall, one shoemaker's shop, one lumber yard, one coal office, a bank, one hotel, one tailor, one jeweler, the Hinckley House, and a blacksmith and wagon shop. One of the best cheese factories in the county is located here.

The trade of town, outside of grain and lumber, will average fifteen thousand dollars per month annually.

The pioneer church was that of the Methodists. An organization had been in force as early as 1869. Divine worship was held in a church standing in the grove near Mr. Merrill's store. When Hinckley became in reality a village, the house was moved, and they still continue to hold services there. The actual membership is over thirty, under the pastoral care of the Rev. William Goodfellow.

The Baptists were organized in 1874. The same year they constructed their house of worship, and continued to regularly hold divine service therein. Their members number about the same as the Methodists, and are ministered to by the Rev. D. L. Richards.

Prior to the opening of the railroad, a school had been maintained many years. The country was rather thickly settled, and the early inhabitants of Hinckley soon perceived that a school house was needed which provided more room and better accommodations. In 1872 the present building was erected, sufficiently large to provide for these wants. It is divided into two departments, and will accommodate 100 pupils. The attendance is now about seventy. The Principal is Miss M. O. Severince.

An election was held on Saturday, October 21, 1876, to determine the question of incorporating the village. It was decided in the negative by a majority of seven votes. The population is now a little over three hundred.

A Few of the Pioneers

OF DEKALB COUNTY.

Arnold Stephen, 1837. minister and doctor, deceased.

Bliss Otis, 1840, farmer, living.
Butterfield Edward, 1834, farmer.
Brooks Thomas, 1835, far. deceased.
Beveridge George, 1840. far. dec.
Barnes Captain, 1837, farmer, dec.
Brown E. P. 1840. farmer, living.
Brown John S. 1844, farmer, living.
Brown J. P. 1837. farmer, living.
Brown J. W. 1846, farmer. living.
Brown J. L. 1837, farmer, living.
Brown D. P. 1837. farmer, living.
Brown William, 1855, farmer, liv.
Barber Capt. L. C. 1837, far. dec.
Barber Harry, 1837, farmer, dec.
Byres James, 1842, farmer, dec.
Bovie James, 1845, farmer, living.
Broughton C. W. 1855, farmer, liv.
Banfield Benj. 1855, farmer, living.
Beard H. C. 1846, farmer, living.

Clark John, 1841, farmer, living.
Camfield William R. 1852, farmer, living in Nebraska.
Champlin H. S. 1836, farmer, liv.
Champlin Harrison. 1836, farmer, died in California.
Colton Rufus. 1837. farmer, prominent man, deceased.
Churchill David, 1838. farmer, dec.
Crawford Alexander, 1839, far. liv.

Dobbin David, 1842, farmer, liv.
Douglass Ira, 1838, farmer, living.
Durham Henry, 1838, merchant, died in 1850.
Darling Lysander, 1835, farmer, was first County Treasurer, dec.

Davis William, 1835, farmer, liv.
Dennis Major, 1835, farmer, living.
Driscoll William, 1837, farmer, dec.

Easterbrooks John, 1836, far. dec.
Easterbrooks James, 1836, far. liv.

French William, 1842, farmer, liv.
Fay Horace, 1837, farmer, living.
Fay Wells A. 1837, farmer, dec.
Furman James. first teacher in county, lives in Chicago.
Fairelo Isaiah, 1837, farmer, living.

Gilchrist Daniel M. 1837, far. dec.
Gage Alvarus, 1840, farmer, liv.
Gage Almon, 1840, farmer, living.
Green James, 1848, farmer, living.
Graham Robert, 1844, farmer, liv.
Gregory E. S. 1837. farmer, living.
Gault William, 1836, farmer, dec.
Gandy Harris, 1838, farmer and importer Norman horses, living.
Gleason E. P. 1840, merchant, dec.

Hough George, 1840, farmer, liv.
Harris Benj. 1834, farmer.
Hodge J. A. 1856, farmer, living.
Hayden John A. 1852, farmer, liv.
Hough Burrage, 1838, farmer, dec.
Harman Amos, 1835, farmer, dec.
Hill Moses, 1838, farmer, living.
Hallaron Thos. 1850. farmer, liv.
Hanson Ezra, 1838. farmer, living.
Huntley Russell, 1837. farmer, removed to California.
Hix Henry, 1837, proprietor of saw mill, deceased.
Heath John, 1846, farmer, living.

Hamlin John R. 1838, one of the first Recorders, deceased.
Hollemsbeak A. N. 1840. far. liv.

Johnson O. P. 1834, farmer, living.
Joles Harry P. 1837, farmer, dec.
Jackman A. 1838, lumber and coal dealer, living.
Jewell Eli J. 1837, farmer, one of the first Supervisors, removed to Kansas, and there died.

Kirk William T. 1837. farmer, liv.
Keyes James, 1855, farmer, dec.
Keyes Samuel, 1855, farmer, dec.
Kirkpatrick Isaac, 1844, farmer, liv.
Kirkpatrick Hezekiah, 1844. far. liv.

Lord R. D. 1842, butcher, living.
Lee Jacob, 1836, farmer, deceased.
Latham Joseph, 1838, farmer. liv.
Lay S. H. 1841, farmer, dec.
Lee Levi, 1836, prominent minister. deceased.
Lovell James, Sr. 1838. farmer, liv.
Lyman William, 1838, farmer.

Malone David, 1850, farmer, liv.
Mackey Father, 1838, prominent minister, deceased.
McCollum James, 1839, far. dec.
Madden Henry, 1838, farmer, first member Assembly from this county, deceased.
Miller William A. 1837, far. liv.
Mack Martin M. 1838, carp. dec.
Merriman James, 1849, farmer and real estate, living.
Miller Frank, 1840, farmer, dec.
Miller Samuel, 1835, farmer.

Noble Ezekiel. 1854, farmer, liv.

Olmsted A. H. 1845, farmer, liv.
Olmsted Coleman, 1838, far. dec.
Orput John, 1827, farmer, living.

Price Simon, 1838, farmer, dec.
Prescott W. R. 1848, farmer, liv.
Pearson Geo. S. 1837. farmer, went to California, deceased.

Price Owen, 1837, farmer, removed to Iowa,
Poplin William, 1835. farmer, liv.

Pratt Almos, 1838, farmer, living.
Pastley James, 1837, farmer, dec.
Page H. D. 1839, one of the first physicians, deceased.
Perkins Henry N. 1837, far. liv.
Perkins Horatio N. 1837, far. liv.
Preston Charles, 1837, far. liv.

Rhodes Conrad B. 1836, farmer, removed to Iowa.
Robb Robert, 1837, farmer, liv.
Riddle John, 1837, farmer, dec.

Strong William, 1840, lumber and grain, living.
Stephens Samuel, 1837, farmer, liv.
Stratton, Geo. M. 1846, far. liv.
Suydam Simon, farmer, living.
Sebree William, 1834, far. dec.
Sly Joseph, 1835, first settler on Somonauk Creek in Somonauk Tp.
Stearns Newton, 1848, farmer, liv.
Starat Robert, 1837, farmer, dec.
Smith David, 1836, farmer.
Snow John, 1842, farmer, dec.
Saum Nicholas, 1842, farmer, liv.
Stark Marshall, 1837, farmer, Sheriff two terms. lumber dealer, liv.

Townsend Joshua, 1839, far. dec.
Townsend Avery, 1839, far. dec.
Town David A. 1839, farmer, dec.
Town Edmond, 1836, farmer.
Tower David, 1838. farmer, dec.

Whitmore, Daniel, 1840, far. liv.
Whitmore J. C. 1854, speculator, removed to California.
Whitmore Ezekiel, 1852, farmer, first settler in Malta.
Whitmore Clark, 1840, farmer, liv.
Whitmore James, 1840, far. liv.
Whitmore Benj. 1836, farmer, liv.
Ward William, 1835, farmer, dec.
Watson James, 1856, farmer, liv.

Wharrey Evans, 1837, farmer, one of New York company, living.

Wright Clark, 1837, farmer, one of New York company, removed to Kansas.

Waterman John C. 1837, merchant, one of the first, living.

Waterman Charles, 1838, mer. liv.

Waterman James S. 1838, farmer and merchant, first banker in county, living.

Walrod Morris, 1837, farmer, one of the first Sheriffs, now in California.

Walker Ora A. 1837, miller, dec.

Wells Solomon, 1838, farmer, removed to Wisconsin.

Wells Timothy, 1838, merchant, removed to California.

Wilcox Nathan, 1840, Bapt. minister and farmer, living.

Young E. P. 1840, merchant, dec.

POPULATION OF DeKALB COUNTY.

TOWNSHIPS.	1870.					1860.		1850.	
	Total.	Native.	For'ign.	White.	Color'd.	White.	Color'd.	White.	Color'd.
Afton	873	649	224	873		516			
Clinton	1004	863	141	1003	1	1006		350	
Cortland*	1293	1108	185	1292	1				
DeKalb	2164	1653	511	2145	19	1708		486	
Franklin	1004	813	191	1004		936		716	
Genoa	993	859	134	992	1	985		605	
Kingston	975	848	127	975		1052	1	601	
Malta	1157	840	317	1153	4	620			
Mayfield	941	786	155	941		998		564	
Milan	857	573	284	855	2	262			
Pampas*						1298		1038	
Paw-Paw	978	849	129	977	1	1107		653	
Pierce	1003	744	259	1003		945			
Shabbona	1205	909	296	1205		963		360	
Somonauk	3359	2845	514	3339	20	2227		704	
Sandwich	1844	1615	229	1829	15	952			
South Grove	795	602	193	795		662		147	
Squaw Grove	886	706	180	886		795	1	341	
Sycamore	2852	2328	524	2848	4	2253	5	974	1
Sycamore	1967	1624	343	1967		1266	5	337	1
1st Ward	292	254	38	292					
2d Ward	364	298	66	364					
3d Ward	723	597	126	723					
4th Ward	588	475	113	588					
Victor	926	696	230	926		746			

* In 1865 name changed from Pampas to Cortland.

Township Officers, 1876.

Paw Paw Township—Henry M. Boardman, Supervisor; Jesse Corney, Town Clerk; Lineman E. Hyde, Assessor; Robert Borton, Collector. James Marsden, Commissioner of Highways.

Shabbona Township—Giles M. Alexander, Supervisor; W. H. Ray, Town Clerk; Peter V. Quillot, Assessor; Ebon Stolp, Collector; James Cameron, Commissioner of Highways.

Milan Township — Edwin R. Colby, Supervisor; Wm. E. Chandler, Town Clerk: Nathan Applebee, Assessor; John Conlin, Collector; Andrew Arent, Commissioner of Highways.

Malta Township—Martin C. Dedrick, Supervisor; Alfred Ball, Corporation Supervisor; R. F. Lintleman. Town Clerk; George Chapel, Assessor; George Spickerman, Collector; Albert Banfield, James Welch, and Smith Morey, Commissioners of Highways.

Sycamore Township—Nathan Lattin, Supervisor; S. Halcomb, Town Clerk; George Walker, Assessor; Edwin Waite, Collector, Thomas Marshall, Commissioner of Highways.

Genoa Township — John Heath, Supervisor: J. B. Stephens, Town Clerk; Isaac Q. Burrough, Assessor; E. N. Burrington, Collector; Thos. St. John, Commissioner of Highways.

Afton Township — Henry Kingsley, Supervisor; Charles F. Pearle, Town Clerk; William D. Earle, Assessor; John A. Ryan, Collector; William Potter, Commissioner of Highways.

DeKalb Township—Joseph F. Glidden, Supervisor; L. O. Vaughn, Town Clerk; Hiram Eddy, Assessor; F. M. Blackman, Collector; Robt. Duffey, Commissioner of Highways.

Mayfield Township — Edwin P. Safford, Supervisor; B. F. Bacon, Town Clerk; James Sivwright, Assessor; D. W. Carpenter, Collector; Samuel Knight, Commissioner of Highways.

Kingston Township—Leroy Benson, Supervisor; A. H. Clark, Town Clerk; John W. Foster, Assessor; Marcus M. Cole, Collector; H. H. Little, Commissioner of Highways.

Somonauk Township — W. W. Sedgwick, Supervisor; John Clark, Assistant Supervisor; E. S. Johnson, Town Clerk; Amos Shepherd, Assessor; Solon Woodward, Collector; William Frazer, Commissioner of Highways.

Squaw Grove Township—John M. Curry, Supervisor; C. T. Slater, Town Clerk : James T. Glann, Assessor; Alvin Cheney, Collector; A. Cone. Jr., Commissioner of Highways.

Pierce Township—Charles A. Hubbard, Supervisor; Leonard Wehr, Town Clerk; James Gormly, Assessor : Henry Butler, Collector ; M. Ziegler, Commissioner of Highways.

Cortland Township — William Raymond, Supervisor; John King, Corporation Supervisor; C. A. Talbot, Town Clerk; Reuben O. Joselyn, Assessor*; John T. Woodley, Collector; Harlan Crossett, Commissioner of Highways.

South Grove Township—James Gibson, Supervisor; Thomas Adee, Town Clerk; Richard Becker, Assessor; Walter Barnes, Collector; Robt. Hutcheson, Commissioner of Highways.

Franklin Township — Banfield Dean, Supervisor; Frank L. Bowen, Town Clerk; Isaac R. Drake, Assessor; Nelson Delevargne, Collector; Chas. H. Gilchrist, Commissioner of Highways.

Victor Township—Hiram Loucks, Supervisor; C. A. Dewey, Town Clerk; Alvin P. Burnam, Assessor; J. W. Dale, Collector; Matthew Parker, Commissioner of Highways.

Clinton Township — Edwin Fraser, Supervisor; J. W. Giles, Town Clerk; George Greenwood, Assessor; George G. Congdon, Collector; C. F. Greenwood, Commissioner of Highways.

Town Government.

CITY OF SYCAMORE CORPORATION.

Officers—R. L. Divine, Mayor; P. K. Jones, Clerk; Hosea Atwood, Marshal.

Aldermen — John S. Brown, Milo Dayton, First Ward; Norman C. Warren, William C. Black, Second Ward; Moses Dean, James Fulkerson, Third Ward.

Council meetings first Tuesday evening of each month.

SANDWICH.

Mayor, R. M. Brigham; Clerk, I. A. Tolman; Treasurer, F. S. Mosher; Attorney, S. B. Stinson.

Aldermen — E. Doane, H. F. Winchester, H. Packer, I. H. Culver, I. A. Armstrong, I. A. Woodward.

Village Corporation.

BOARD OF TRUSTEES FOR 1876.

DE KALB.

Lewis M. McEwin, Pres.; Jabez Cheesebro, Alex. Ray, P. G. Young, Hiram Eddy, Clark Carter; Clerk, S. O. Vaughan; Harrison Whitmore, Police Magistrate.

Town Officers — J. F. Glidden, Sup.; S. O. Vaughan, Town Clerk; Justices of the Peace, E. B. Gilbert, C. C. Hinman, W. H. Day; Assessor, Hiram Eddy; Collector, F. M. Blackman; Commissioners of Highways, Clark Carter, Thomas Wright, Robert Duffey.

MALTA.

A. Ball, Pres.; R. F. Lintleman, E. A. Watkins, J. C. Pierce, S. S. Wright; C. W. Haish, Treas.; A. S. Kinsloe, Clerk.

SHABBONA.

John Palm, Stephen Branscomb, Danforth Hinkston, Hiram D. Morey, Walter Spears, Thos. Padgett, Trustees; Chas. Stevens, Clerk; C. W. Hubbell, Police Justice; Capt. T. B. Lucas, Police Constable; Henry Husk, Constable.

[U. S. Census, 1870.]

Acres of Improved Land	334,502	Bushels of Spring Wheat	398,059
Acres of Woodland	17,722	Bushels of Winter Wheat	190
Other Unimproved Land	6,551	Bushels of Rye	21,018
Value of Farms	$13,988,325	Bushels of Indian Corn	1,023,849
Value of Farming Implements and		Bushels of Oats	1,087,074
Machinery	$547,052	Bushels of Barley	289,447
Total amount of wages paid during		Bushels of Buckwheat	6,902
the year, including board	$392,889	Pounds of Wool	104,974
Value of Farm Productions, includ-		Bushels of Peas and Beans	705
ing betterments and additions		Bushels of Irish Potatoes	199,478
to stock	$2,903,726	Bushels of Sweet Potatoes	16
Value of Orchard Products	10,352	Gallons of Wine	152
Value of Garden Products	2,293	Pounds of Butter	915,804
Value of Forest Products	8,056	Pounds of Cheese	199,532
Value of Home Manufactures	6,376	Gallons of Milk sold	131,322
Value of Animals Slaughtered or		Tons of Hay	68,665
sold for slaughter	817,497	Bushels of Clover Seed	73
Value of all Live Stock	2,230,356	Bushels of Grass Seed	13,367
Number of Horses	13,044	Pounds of Hops	15,580
Number of Mules and Asses	302	Pounds of Flax	304,342
Number of Milch Cows	14,619	Bushels of Flax Seed	14,036
Number of Working Oxen	22	Pounds of Maple Sugar	62
Number of Other Cattle	18,560	Gallons of Sorghum	1,113
Number of Sheep	24,993	Pounds of Wax	468
Number of Swine	26,795	Pounds of Honey	16,054

AGRICULTURAL STATISTICS.—BY TOWNSHIPS.

TOWNSHIPS.	Improved Lands.	Value of Farms and Farming Implements.	Value of Live Stock.	Value of all Productions.	Indian Corn.
	Acres.	Dollars.	Dollars.	Dollars.	Bushels.
Afton	20,685	725,514	107,014	168,251	58,555
Clinton	21,780	891,785	148,093	201,865	74,130
Courtland	18,237	883,086	128,734	141,993	48,890
De Kalb	17,004	778,626	115,816	169,934	53,075
Franklin	17,618	709,345	134,534	169,681	49,250
Genoa	19,541	861,358	125,988	186,404	54,367
Kingston	14,837	678,035	114,745	152,146	42,185
Malta	17,516	645,952	98,602	145,187	50,301
Mayfield	15,260	648,311	117,231	155,237	43,930
Milan	18,672	657,455	98,032	111,774	57,080
Paw-Paw	21,669	1,016,990	163,211	149,539	59,580
Pierce	20,955	789,794	119,820	170,372	55,790
Shabbona	20,522	839,100	137,633	136,840	59,050
Somonauk	17,176	1,091,212	122,693	182,785	74,175
South Grove	20,390	794,713	129,315	208,549	69,895
Squaw Grove	19,265	871,491	123,733	138,125	65,236
Sycamore	15,337	839,670	130,727	173,996	44,130
Victor	18,038	812,940	114,435	141,084	64,230

LODGES AND ASSOCIATIONS.

Sycamore Chapter, No. 49, *R. A. M.*—Officers: George S. Robinson, H. P.; John Syme, King; A. N. Wheeler, Scribe; A. M. Stark, C. H.; Daniel Dustin, P. S.; A. J. Driver, R. A. C.; John Shuld, Treas.; Frank Smith, Secy.; J. M. Bourey, M. 3d V.; M. J. Johnson, M. 2d V.; E. W. Robinson, M. 1st V.; A. S. Babcock, Chaplain; G. B. Wiseman, Charles Miller, K. Wallum, Stewards; Hiram Buel, Tyler. Meets second and fourth Monday evenings of each month.

Sycamore Lodge, No. 134, *A. F. and A. M.* — Officers: J. L. Pratt. W. M.; A. N. Wheeler, S. W.; W. E. Sivwright. J. W.; Daniel Dustin, Treas.; H. T. Lawrence, Secy.; G. B. Wiseman, S. D.; J. M. Bourey, J. D.; Hiram Buel, Tyler; Levi Winn, O. S. Holcomb, Stewards. Meets monthly, at Sycamore.

Sycamore Commandery, No. 15, *K. T.* — Officers: A. W. Sawyer, E. C.; A. S. Babcock, G.; H. M. Stevens, C. G.; D. Dustin, P.; G. B. Wiseman, S. W.; F. H. Smith, J. W.; C. T. Stewart, Treas.; C. W. Miller, Rec. Meets second Wednesday in each month.

Genoa Lodge, No. 288, *A. F. and A. M.*—Officers: A. L. Hollenbeak, W. M.; Thos. Force, S. W.; Clark Baley, J. W.; S. Mead, Treas.; M. Cole, Secy.; John McClean, S. D.; S. S. Russell, J. D. Meets Wednesday evening on or before the full of the moon, each month.

DeKalb Lodge, No. 144, chartered Oct. 2, 1854, with T. C. Wetmore, W. M.; E. B. Gilbert, S. W.; J. H. Burghardt, J. W. Present officers for 1876: Daniel D. Hunt, W. M.; Martin V. Wilder, S. W.; Thomas Corkings, J. W.; P. M. Vaughan, S. D.; William Toop, J. D.; John A. White, Treas.; E. B. Gilbert, Secy.; S. O. Vaughan, Tyler. Meets first and third Wednesday of each and every month, in Jacob Haish Block.

DeKalb Chapter, No. 52, was organized Oct. 3, 1859. Present officers for 1876: S. O. Vaughan, H. P.; D. D. Hunt, E. King; J. E. Atwood, E. Scribe; Jacob Fowler, Chaplain; P. W. T. Vaughan, Captain of the Host; W. Pierce, Principal Sojourner; T. Corking, R. A. Captain; Wm. H. Allen, Master 3d Vail: P. J. Rickard, Master 2d Vail; W. B. Barber, Master 1st Vail; E. B. Gilbert, Secy.; Wm. Toop, Treas.; J. A.

White, P. G. Young, Stewards; G. N. Wadsworth, Tyler. Meets the first and third Fridays of each and every month. in Haish's Block.

Kishwaukee Lodge, No. 402. *A. F. and A. M.*—Officers: A. D. Gibbs, W. M.; B. F. Wilber, S. W.; A. N. Willis, J. W.: Robt Shannon, Treas.; H. L. Fuller, Secy.; O. Perry, S. D.; H. F. Raymond, J. D.; Parker Shannon, Tyler. Meets at Kingston.

Waterman Lodge, No. 728, *A. F. and A. M.*, located at Waterman, DeKalb Co. Ill. Dispensation granted Oct. 9, 1874. charter granted Oct. 10, 1875. Officers: I. W. Pichard, S. W.; R. P. Rowley, J. W.; E. P. Rowley, S. D.; C. F. Greenwood, J. D.; Geo. Greenwood, Secy.; O. F. Mattison, Treas.; Robt. Telford, Tyler. N. S. Greenwood, W. M., died Oct. 11, 1876. Meets first and third Saturdays of each month. Lodge numbers about forty members.

Malta Lodge, No. 320, *A. F. and A. M.*— Officers: Caleb Peters, W. M.; George Chapel, S. W.; R. M. Hevenor, J. W.; C. W. Haish, Treas.; J. C. Pierce, Secy.; H. Claxton, S. D.; D. Claxton, J. D.; R. F. Lintleman, Tyler. Meets first Thursday in each month.

Shabbona Lodge, No. 374—Dispensation in Spring of 1862, charter granted Oct. 1862. Officers: M. V. Allen, W. M.; J. W. Middleton, S. W.; I. H. Branscombe, J. W.; P. V. Quilhot, Treas.; Wm. V. Husk, Secy.; F. Ball, S. D., F. A. Frost, J. D.; I. E. Stevens, Tyler. Meets Tuesday on or before full moon in each month, and two weeks thereafter.

Cortland Lodge No. 301, *A. F. and A. M.*—Officers: S. Crossett, W. M.; G. L. C. Wheadon, S. W.; A. Cone, J. W.; James Jackson, S. D.; C. W. West, J. D.; H. D. Wagner, Secy.; Geo. Hobbs, Treas.; Christ Baie, Tyler. Meets at Hinckley, first and third Saturdays of each month.

Sandwich Chapter, No. 107.—Officers: G. W. Culver, H. P.; W. S. Simmons, K.; J. Poplin, S.; E. S. Johnson, C. H., G. Devoll, P. S.; M. Carpenter, T.; W. Marks, S. Meets first and third Tuesdays of each month.

L. H. Carr Post, No. 39, *G. A. R., Sandwich*—Officers: Fred S. Mosher, P. C.; J. N. Culver, S. V. C.; Geo. A. Frizzell, Jr. V. C.; Frank E. Mills, Adjt.; Fred. W. Sly, Qr. mr.; L. M. Shrewsbury, Surgeon; J. Tramblie, O. D.; A. H. Hill, O. G.; I. Cannan, Chap.; H. M. Barnett, Qr. Sergt.; George Leonard, Sergt. Major.

Somonauk Lodge, No. 646, *A. F. and A. M.*—Officers: C. E. Wright, W. M.; H. W. Burchin, S. W.; R. C. Thompson, J. W., T. J. Wright, T.; P. H. Evans, Secy.; L. S. Seaman, S. D.; Charles Banzet, J. D.; E. J. Carr, Tyler. Meets first and third Mondays of each month at Somonauk.

Meteor Lodge. No. 283, Sandwich—Officers: Washington L. Simmons, W. M.; Myrlin Carpenter, S. W.; Geo. H. Frizzell, J. W.; George W. Culver, Treas.; A. E. Bourne, Secy.; Van R. David, S. D.; Gustave Goodman, J. D.; Jacob Burkhart, Jr., S. S.; Wm. T. Shiland, J. S,; Wm. Delano, Tyler. Meets second and fourth Fridays of each month.

Siddons Literary Association, Sycamore, Ill, — Organized June 1, 1876, for the purpose of giving popular entertainments. Officers: Dr. Frank Allport, Pres.; George H. Francis, Treas.; A. S. Barrows, Secy.; John B. Whalen, Manager.

Ellwood Encampment, No. 173. — Officers: Alonzo Ellwood, C. P.; Geo. M. Bell, S. W.: G. M. Sivwright, H. P.; S. Buchholz. Scribe; S. Robinson, Treas.; W. W. Sivwright. J. W. Meets at Sycamore first and third Wednesdays of each month.

Sycamore Lodge, No. 105, *I. O. O. F.*—Officers: Geo. M. Sivwright, N. G. J. C. Boyle, V. G.; H. Bucholz, Secy.; H. H. Fogg, Per. Secy.: A. P. Stone. Treas.; Willis Case, Warden; S. T. Armstrong, P. G.

Cortland Lodge, No. 209, *I. O. O. F.* — Officers: D. W. Rathbun, N. G.; Wm. Raymond, V. G.; T. R. Ricker. Secy.; L. Holdridge, Treas. Meets at Cortland every Thursday evening.

Kishwaukee Encampment, No. 30, *I. O. O. F.*—Officers: T. W. Rathbun, C. P.; N. H. Peck, H. P.; T. R. Ricker, Scribe; L. Holdridge, Treas.; C. S. Staarks, S. W.; H. N. Rose, J. W. Meets at Cortland second and fourth Wednesdays.

Malta Lodge, No. 606, *I. O. O. F.*—Officers: R. Pendergrass, N. G.; J. V. Cornish, V. G.; C. M. Babcock, Secy.; Phineas Barnes, Treas.; Joseph Lamb, Conductor; D. Holderness, W.; J. V. Willett, Dep. G. M. Meets evening Tuesday evenig. Hall over J. C. Pierce's Dry Goods Store.

DeKalb Lodge, I. O. O. F. organized in 1854. Charter members were as follows: C. L. Barber, S. D. Baldwin, P. W. Vaughan, John A. White, Wm. R. Thompson, G. E. Wolcott. Present officers for 1876 are: W. R. Thompson. N. G.; P. I. Cromwell, V. G.; Charles Hiland, R. S.; W. Cheney, T.; John Dunn, P. S.

Sandwich Lodge, No. 212, *I. O. O. F.*—Officers: J. A. Tolman, N. G.; Wm. Jones, V. G.; H. F. Bloodgood. R. S.; Chas. Schnider, F. S.; Paul W. Wallace, Treasurer.

South Somonauk Lodge, No. 181, *I. O. O. F.*—Officers: Wm. Miller, N. G.; J. Rief, V. G.; T. Boos, Secy.; Ph. Thomas, Treas.; T. Boos, D. G. M. Meets every Saturday evening.

Good Templar Lodge. No. 320.— Officers: E. J. Rathbun, W. C.; Mrs. A. C. Smith. W. V.: Francis Riddle, G. D.: G. W. Savery, P. W.; C. Joselyn. W. C.; E. Ford, Secy.; Mrs. Eliza Fowler, Treas.; Daniel Rathbun. W. M.; Miss Allie Rathbun, A. W. M. Meets at Cortland every Saturday evening.

Sons of Temperance—organized April, 1875. Present officers are: Cass Davis, W. P.; Sarah Salisbury, W. A.; Fred. Phillips, R. S.; Lon Anthony, A. R. S.; Frank Wright, F. S.; Oliver Helmer, T.; Mrs. E. A. Porter, Chap.; Clara Atwood, P. W. P.; John Mead, C.: Allie Boardman, A. C.; Sarah Combs, I. S.; John Cheesebro, O. S.

Ellwood Manufacturing Company, Sycamore.—Organized Sep. 7, 1875. Capital Stock $25,000; 250 shares, $100 each. Officers: Jas Waterman, Pres.; Alonzo Ellwood, Vice-Pres.; R. Ellwood. Treas and Manager; George S. Robinson, Secy.

Beers Gang Plow Manufacturing Co.— Capital Stock at organization, March 10, 1875, was $26,000, divided into 100 shares, at $100 per share. Not in operation.

Sycamore Driving Park Association — Organized March, 24, 1874. Capital Stock $10,000. number of shares 100. Officers: Charles Kellum, Pres.; G. W. Nesbit, M.D., Secy.; H. M. Stephens, Treas. Meetings for speed trials are held annually, are most liberally patronized, and most successfully conducted. The Driving Park is immediately south of Sycamore.

Sycamore and Cortland R.R. Co.—Capital Stock $100,000. Officers: James S. Waterman, Pres.; Chauncey Ellwood, Vice-Pres. and Gen. Manager; R. Ellwood, Treas.; R. L. Divine, Secy.; R. E. Hunt, Agent.

Sycamore Marsh Harvester Manufacturing Co. — Incorporated March 31, 1869. Capital Stock $90,000. Capacity, 6,000 machines annually. Officers: C. W.Marsh, Pres.; W. W. Marsh, Supt.; A. M. Stark, Secy.

Working Men's Benevolent Association of Sycamore—Organized Jan. 22, 1875. Managed by a board of seven directors, elected annually. Directors: J. M. Bourcey, Wm. Graham, A. E. Sivwright, A. E. Hicks, D. J. Denmark, W. H. Allen, W. Crosby. The object of the Association is, mutual aid in case of sickness, disability or death.

Sons of Temperance, Sycamore Division—Officers: H. P. Hall, W. P.; H. H. Rowe, P. W. P.; G. W. Mack. R. S.; John Conyer, F. S.; S. P. Kinyon, C.: Miss Goldburg, T.; D. J. Carnes, O. S.; Mrs. H. P. Hall, I. S. Meets at Sycamore every Tuesday evening.

Woman's Christian Temperance Union — Officers: Mrs. E. M. Hall, Pres.; Mrs. V. N. Ells, Vice-Pres.; Miss Pauline Lloyd, Secy.; Miss Mary Dowe, Treas. Meets at Sycamore every Wednesday afternoon.

Excelsior Lodge Good Templars, No. 589 — Officers: S. O. Pike, L. D.; Mrs. S. M. Bell, W. C.; Miss Mary Spring, W. V.; Edward Colton, P. W.; G. L. Saywer, Chaplain; Charles Mack, F. S.; Miss Kittie Hason, Treas.; S. O. Lundgren, R. S.; Miss Helena Burdett, I. G.; Perry Watkins, O. S.; N. J. Johnson, R. H. S.; Winfield Divine, L. H. S. Meets at Sycamore every Saturday evening.

Starlight Chapter, No. 93, *O. E. S.* — A. E. Bourne, W. P.; Mrs. J. H. Fonda, W. M.; Miss Dora David, A. M.; Mrs. Helen Delano, Treas.; Mrs. Mattie G. Pratt, Secy.

Biographies.

REUBEN ELLWOOD.

The subject of this sketch was born in Montgomery County, N. Y., Town of Winden, February 17, 1821. His parents were Abraham and Sarah Ellwood. His father followed the trade of a cooper.

Reuben, after receiving his education at an Academy in Cherry Valley, Otsego County, N. Y., engaged extensively in raising broom-corn, and in the manufacture of brooms, at Glenville, Schenectady County, N. Y., where he remained some eight years.

In 1857 Mr. Ellwood removed to Sycamore, DeKalb County, Ill. He opened a hardware store, and joined with that business dealing in real estate. Belonging to that class of citizens who believe thoroughly in developing the resources of the country, and who are ready to invest their capital to this end — a class to whom this country owes largely its prosperity and independence of other nations — he has always retained his inclination for manufacturing, and for the past five years has been engaged in the making of Agricultural Implements. In 1875 he began the erection of a new manufactory, in which he proposed to invest fifty thousand dollars.

Notwithstanding his business engagements, Mr. Ellwood has found time to serve the public when it has been demanded of him. He became a Republican at the inception of that party; while a resident of Glenville was a member of the Board of Supervisors; in 1850 was sent to the State Legislature at Albany, N. Y.; in 1856, was one of the Fremont Presidential Electors in New York; in 1868, he was the unanimous choice of DeKalb County, for Representative in Congress; was subsequently chosen the first Mayor of Sycamore; and served as United States Assessor till that office was abolished.

Mr. Ellwood is a man of great enterprise, of positive traits of character, indomitable energy, strict integrity, and liberal views, thoroughly identified in feelings and acts with the growth and prosperity of the town, county, and state in which he resides.

He was married August 8, 1850, to Miss Eleanor Vedder, of Schenectady Co. N. Y., by whom he has had three sons and three daughters.

WILLIAM A. MILLER,

one of the pioneers of this county, was born in Trenton, Oneida County, N. Y., May 4. 1810. When two years old his father moved to Schagticoke, Rensselaer County, N. Y., where he was brought up till sixteen years old, when he entered as an apprentice to the plow and foundry business, at Lansingburg, N. Y. In 1830 he removed to Penn Yan, N. Y., where he remained, together with one year spent at Bath, Steuben County, till 1835, being in the meantime married. And in 1835, came with his wife to DeKalb County, and settled on a farm in Section 36, Town of Kingston. This location was then in LaSalle County, neither the Counties of Kane nor DeKalb being then laid out. Mr. Miller settled here among the Indians prior to their removal in the Fall of 1835, and was on friendly terms with those whom he knew. He has passed through all the vicissitudes of pioneer life. He has been twice over land with horses to California. His appearance on his return is well shown in the likeness on another page.

He has followed farming chiefly for a living, and has served his county several times on the Board of Supervisors. He has always been in politics an unswerving Democrat, and cast his first Presidential vote for General Jackson.

Mr. Miller was married at Penn Yan, N. Y., May 14, 1835, to Patience Allen, and has two children living. In 1873 he sold his land and retired from business. He resides in DeKalb.

JOSEPH F. GLIDDEN,

DeKalb, farmer and capitalist, son of David and Polly (Hurd) Glidden; born in Charleston, Cheshire County, New Hampshire. He is descended from the Welsh stock. There were three brothers and three sisters in the family, of whom Joseph F. was the oldest, the other brothers being Josiah W. and Stephen H. Glidden.

Joseph was brought up on a farm and educated at the common schools.

In November, 1842, he came to DeKalb County, and the following Spring purchased the claim of Russell Huntly, where he now resides, having in one body 400 acres of land.

The land came into market in January, 1843, at which time Mr. Glidden began to purchase of the government, and continued to add to it from time to time. For several years he and his brothers were in company working their farms together. Josiah W. still resides here. Stephen H. died in Minneapolis in 1875.

Mr. Glidden served on the Board of Supervisors of the County in

1851, 1861, 1862, 1866, 1869, 1870, 1871, 1872 and 1876. He is at present a Democratic nominee for State Senator, with good prospect of election. In 1852–54, he was Sheriff of the County.

He has been a great friend and benefactor of the public schools. He aided in the erection of the first log school house in the county, and was also active in planning and building the present fine public school building in the City of DeKalb, which cost $25,000. He has paid for twenty years the largest school tax of any citizen of the county, served as a member of the Board of School Directors from 1861 till 1874, during which time he was President of the Board.

Mr. Glidden has been twice married. First, he married in New York, in 1839, Miss Clarissa Foster, by whom he had three children, both deceased. Mrs. G. died in June, 1844. In October, 1851, he married his present wife, Miss Lucy Warne, by whom he has one daughter, Miss Elva F. Glidden.

Chiefly as the inventor of the "Glidden Patent" for Barb Fence Wire, has Mr. Glidden become a benefactor of the farming community of the West generally, and made himself extensively known throughout the country. We refer the reader for a particular description of this useful invention to the subject of "Barbed Wire Manufacture," in the proper history of DeKalb, on another page of this work.

DR. C. WINNE-

was born at Leesville, Schoharie County, New York, February 22d, 1832. At the age of two years, with his father's family, moved to Town of Root, Montgomery County, N. Y., where he lived till eleven years of age, when his father died, and he struck out upon the sea of life for himself. For four years after the death of his father, he worked out by the month upon farms during the summer, and worked for his board and attended district school during the winter; remaining during these four years in the neighborhood of the old homestead. When in his fifteenth year he went to live with a brother-in-law in Chautauqua County, N. Y., and commenced to learn the wagon-making trade; after two years and a half in the shop, he came to the conclusion to do something better than make wagons, and started for school at Westfield Academy, remained only one term, then taught a term of district school, and for the next five years went to school and taught alternately. In 1854, he went to the State of Mississippi, impelled mainly by a desire to see the practical working of slavery, and while there taught school, and pursued the study of medicine, graduating at the University of Michigan, Medical Department, in the Spring of 1856. Practiced one year at Williamston, Michigan, when he came to Illinois and taught one year in the Public School at Newark, Kendall County. Here he became acquainted with Rachael E. P. Misner, eldest daughter of Hon. Johnson Misner, to whom he was married, Dec. 15, 1858. He then removed to Somonauk, and again entered upon the practice of his profession. When the war broke out, he entered the service as Assistant Surgeon of the 55th Ills. Vols. and served one year, when he was promoted to be Surgeon of the 77th Ills. Vol. Infantry, in which capacity he served till the end of the war. After the close of the war he settled in Sandwich, engaging in the drug trade in connection with the practice of medicine and surgery, and by economy and industry he has accumulated a comfortable little property. He has never held any considerable office, although taking a deep interest in politics. He is a Republican; belongs to no church. He is a public spirited and valuable citizen, and is held in very general esteem by his neighbors. He has three interesting girls, and believes that life is what we make it, and, although a member of no church, he believes in one God and the Christian religion. He is an ardent supporter of free schools, and free institutions generally, and is an enthusiastic Republican, having cast but one democratic vote, and heartily repented of that.

HENRY LAWSON BOIES

was born July 5th, 1830, at South Hadley, Mass., being the son of Artemas Boies, a distinguished clergyman. Mr. Boies is of Huguenot and Scotch-Irish stock. His father removed to Boston in 1835; thence to New London, Conn., in 1840, where he died in 1845. The widow thereupon removed to Keene, N. H., her maiden home.

In 1850, Mr. Boies, being of a consumptive family, was attacked with bleeding at the lungs, and spent a winter in the Azores, returning home by the way of Liverpool and London. The next winter he went to Charleston, S. C., where he taught school a year or two. Returning north, apparently recovered, in 1852 he purchased an interest in a manufactory of gunpowder at Catskill, N. Y. After three months' residence there, his old complaint again attacked him, and he resolved that he must die or seek a change of climate for life in the open air. With this view he came to Illinois, and after looking through the northern portion of the state, bought a farm in DeKalb County, where he has ever since resided. Fighting with never-flagging determination the insidious disease which threatened his life, he at last overcame it, and now gives promise of a long life of usefulness.

In February, 1858, Mr. Boies married Harriet S. Holmes, a lady of refinement and culture, by whom he has had several children. The same year, in connection with John R. Hamlin, an old resident, he started the project of building a branch railroad to connect Sycamore with the C. & N. W. R. R. at Cortland. In 1863, Mr. Boies became connected with the *True Republican*, of which he is now the editor. It is the paper containing the largest circulation in DeKalb County, and is the organ of the Republican party of the county, and a journal of wide influence in Northern Illinois.

In 1865, Mr. Boies laid out Boies' First Addition to Sycamore; in 1871 a second addition; and in 1876 a third.

He is the author of Boies's History of DeKalb County, which is a reliable and most valuable contribution to the historical thesaurus of Illinois. In 1870, he was chosen a Secretary of the Illinois State Senate. He is now Postmaster at Sycamore. He is a gentleman of strict probity of character; a public-spirited member of society; a consistent christian, and a genial companion. In transplanting thus to the new social element of the West the minds which have been nurtured in the best life of New England enlightenment, the social tone has been elevated, and the average degree of intelligence enhanced.

CAMPBELL W. WAITE

was born in Victory, Cayuga County, New York, on July 12, 1832. His father removed to Illinois in 1840, and settled first near Chicago, and afterwards in St. Charles, Kane County.

In early life, Campbell had to hoe his own row to a great extent. From the age of twelve, he earned his own living. He learned the trade of a printer, and worked at the case till he was eighteen years of age, when he began to write for the newspapers, which was his constant occupation until 1869, when he entered upon the abstract business in Chicago, and devoted seven years close application thereto.

In 1852, Mr. Waite became associated with Thomas J. Pickett in the editorial control of the Peoria *Republican*, in which position he continued until 1857, when he established the *True Republican* of Sycamore. In 1860 he was elected chief secretary of the Illinois State Senate.

At the outbreak of the war, he enlisted in the 8th Illinois Cavalry, and was chosen adjutant. He resigned this position for that of war correspondent of the Chicago *Tribune*, which position, in connection with the same position on the St. Louis *Democrat*, he occupied until 1864, when he acted as Washington correspondent of the latter paper. In 1865 he was chosen private secretary of Governor Thomas C. Fletcher, of Missouri, which position he occupied till 1867, when he made the tour of Europe on behalf of railroad enterprises in that state.

In September, 1876, Mr. Waite, in connection with O. P. Bassett, former proprietor of the *True Republican*, started the *DeKalb County Democrat* in Sycamore, the organ of the Democracy of DeKalb County —a bright, spicy, creditable sheet.

Mr. Waite is a man who thinks his own thoughts, who wields a facile pen and who, while inimitable in the genial sketches of social life, can, when occasion requires, hurl the missives of sarcasm which go to the heart of his adversaries.

He is an old bachelor; is a hearty good fellow; is Episcopal in sentiment; and one of those men who asks little odds of the world, so that he be permitted to go his way unmolested.

L. H. POST,

proprietor of the DeKalb County *News*, at DeKalb, Illinois, was born in Rochester, New York, Oct. 19, 1839. He commenced the printing business when but little more than thirteen years of age. Entered the army as a private in the first company which left Warsaw, N. Y., at the commencement of the War of the Rebellion. Served in the army of the Potomac, being wounded in the second Bull Run battle, soon after which he was commissioned lieutenant, but owing to disability, was discharged in 1863. In May, 1869, he purchased the office of the DeKalb County *News*, a paper of large circulation, which he has since edited and published. The *News* is recognized as the leading paper of the county. In politics it is Independent Republican. The office is complete in every respect, being supplied with all the late styles of type and material, with three presses, run by steam power.

Mr. Post has filled numerous positions of trust, and is now serving his third year as Postmaster, having been re-appointed in May, 1876, to serve four years.

THOS. M. HOPKINS

was born April 23d, 1818, in the town of Salem, Washington County, New York, of comparatively poor but industrious parents. By industry and teaching school he succeeded in obtaining a common-school and academic education, and was finally licensed and admitted to the practice of law by the Supreme Court of his native state in January, 1841. In June afterwards he emigrated to the State of Illinois, and was re-admitted and licensed to practice law in the last-mentioned state in the year 1842, and thereafter resided in Illinois and Missouri engaged in his profession and teaching school the greater portion of the time until the Spring of 1846, when he was married to Miss Julia A. Hawkins, of the city of St. Louis, and immediately settled in DeKalb, DeKalb County, Illinois, where he has since resided, dividing his time alternately between the cultivation and improvement of his farm and the practice of his profession, and has consequently passed through many of the trials and tribulations incident to the settlement, improvement, and development of the Northwest. He has five children (one daughter and four sons), and three of the last-mentioned, as also himself, will probably vote for Samuel J. Tilden for President of the United States this present Fall.

GILBERT H. ROBERTSON,

editor and proprietor of the Sandwich *Gazette*, was born in Washington County, Pennsylvania, November 28, 1837. The *Gazette* was started in 1857 by William L. Dempster, and at that time called the *People's Press*. It lived six months. In 1859 it was revived and name changed to *Prairie Home*, but its life was also short. Soon thereafter James Higbee took the management and issued a bi-monthly, calling it the Sandwich *Gazette*, and it assumed a more healthy look than its predecessors. It was then changed to a weekly, and placed under the management of J. H. Furman. In 1874 Mr. Robertson purchased the *Gazette*, and ever since its circulation has been on the increase and is now one of the best sheets in the country, espousing the Republican cause with a will and power equaled by few. M. R. wields a powerful pen, and on the stump is one of the best speakers in the party.

Mr. Robertson was married to Mary L. Beveredge, May 31, 1859. She was born in Washington County, Pennsylvania, April, 1836. Three children have blessed their union.

CHAS. A. WEST,

of the Somonauk *Reveille*, was born in LaSalle County, Illinois, Sept. 24, 1850. In 1875 he started the *Reveille*, and has built up a spicy and popular paper which has now a good healthy circulation. Mr. W. is a staunch Republican, and one of the most promising young editors in the party. He was married to Miss Ella M. Winne, Aug. 30, 1876.

HENRY F. BLOODGOOD,

editor and proprietor of the Sandwich *Free Press*, was born in Rochester, New York, February 6, 1852. Mr. Bloodgood came to DeKalb County in June, 1862, and has ever since resided in the county. Mr. B. is a practical printer and an able writer, and at the advice of many citizens in July,

1873, started the *Free Press.* Notwithstanding the many troubles and discouragments incident to the building up of a newspaper, and which would have caused most men to have abandoned it, he has now the satisfaction of knowing that he is the sole owner of a healthy, prosperous and influential Republican newspaper, with a circulation second to none in the county. Mr. B. makes job printing a specialty, and will be happy to see the public at his establishment over Sandwich Bank.

THE MESSRS. C. W. & W. W. MARSH,

of Sycamore, whose portraits we present our readers in another part of this volume, have built for themselves a reputation equaled by few, the product of an idea put into a practical and remunerative form. In 1858 they invented and patented the machine since known as the Marsh Harvester, but only made experimental machines from year to year till 1863, when, having sufficiently developed and perfected their machine, they resolved to make a venture.

Locating at Plano, they began manufacturing on a more extensive scale, and soon established a reputation for their Harvesters which created a demand requiring them to enlarge their facilities for production. After ten years they sold out the Plano business, and removing to Sycamore, organized their present stock company, under the name of the Sycamore Marsh Harvester Manufacturing Co., with C. W. Marsh, Prest; and W. W. Marsh, Supt.

C. W. Marsh was born March 22, 1834, and W. W. Marsh April 15, 1836, at Ontario. Can., and their parents, Samuel and Tamar Marsh, being in comfortable circumstances, gave them good school advantages. They followed their studies at Victoria College, Coburg, Can., until the Fall of 1849, when they came to DeKalb Co. with their parents, and assisted their father in farming till 1863, in the meantime developing the idea which has made them their fortune. Hon. C. W. Marsh was elected Assemblyman in 1868, and in 1870 member of State Senate, and has since been made Prest. of the Northern Insane Asylum, and Prest. of the First Nat. Bank, Sycamore. He was married in 1860 to Miss S. Frances Waite, of N. Y., who died in 1869, leaving one son and two daughters. In 1870 Mr. Marsh went abroad, spending some time traveling over the European continent.

Too-Lates and Changes.

PIERCE TOWNSHIP.

MALONE DAVID, Farmer and Stock Raiser, Sec. 18; born in Ireland, 1810; came to this Co. 1854; Dem; owns 702 acres of land, value $31,000; value of personal property, $3,000; has six children.

PALMER JAMES, Farmer, Sec. 4; Town of Pierceville; P.O. Cortland; born in Town of Pierceville, this Co. June 5, 1854; lived here ten years, and went to Aurora in 1864, then went to Galesburg, this State, and lived there one year in store; returned to Aurora and lived there four years; Rep; Meth; personal prop. $500; married Lettie Vaughan, of Big Rock, Kane Co. July 2, 1876.

RAMER H. E. Farmer, Sec. 4; P.O. Lodi; born in Ohio, 1840; came to this Co. 1846; Rep; Meth; owns 113 acres of land, value $5,600; value of personal prop. $500; was in the army in the 13th Reg. Illinois Volunteer Infantry; married Mary Jane Filmer, who was born in Ohio; has six children.

WALTERS JACOB Jr. Sec. 27; P.O. Pierceville; lives with his father; Dem; from Ohio.

WALL WM. Sec 9; P.O. Cortland; lives with his father; Dem; Cath; from N. Y.

WALL THOS. Sec. 9; P.O. Cortland; farm 120 acres, value $6,000; Dem; Cath; from Ireland.

WALDER JOSEPH, Sec. 13; P.O. Lodi; works for Chris. Hummel; Rep; from Ohio.

WARE L Sec. 23; P.O. Lodi; farm 120 acres, value $6,000; Dem; Germany.

WILTSE WM. A. Sec. 26; P.O. Pierceville; works C. Myers' farm; Dem; from N. Y.

WILTSE S. W. Sec. 26; P.O. Pierceville; works C. Myers' farm; Dem; from N. Y.

WILTSE RODA, Sec. 3; P.O. Cortland; farm 160 acres, value $8,000; Meth; from N. Y.

WELCH BRIDGET, Sec. 7; P.O. Cortland; farm 50 acres, value $2,000; Cath; from Ireland.

WELLS LEVI, Sec. 28; P.O. Pierceville; lives with Adam Kesler; Rep; from Illinois.

WEDDIGER AUGUST, Sec. 32; P.O. Hinkley; farm 160 acres, value $8,000; Rep; Germany.

ZEIGLER J. W. Sec. 22; P.O. Lodi; works G. Zeigler's place; Dem; from Illinois.

ZEIGLER G. Sec. 15; P.O. Lodi; farm 180 acres, value $9,000; Dem; from Germany.

ZEIGLER L. Sec. 15; P.O. Lodi; farm 240 acres, value $12,000; Dem; from Germany.

ZEIGLER C. Sec. 15; P.O. Lodi; farm 159 acres, value $7,950; Dem; Luth; from Germany.

ZEIGLER L. E. Sec. 22; P.O. Lodi; works G. Zeigler's farm; Dem; from Illinois.

MALTA TOWNSHIP.

BRUNDAGE F. H. Postal Clerk and Farmer, Malta, Ill.; born in Ulster County, N. Y., 1835; came to this county in 1856; Rep.

SYCAMORE TOWNSHIP.

MACK G. W. Architect, Contractor and Builder, Sycamore; born Chenango Co. N. Y., 1828; came to this county 1856; Rep; value of real estate, $3,000; has six children.

HON. C. W. MARSH
SYCAMORE

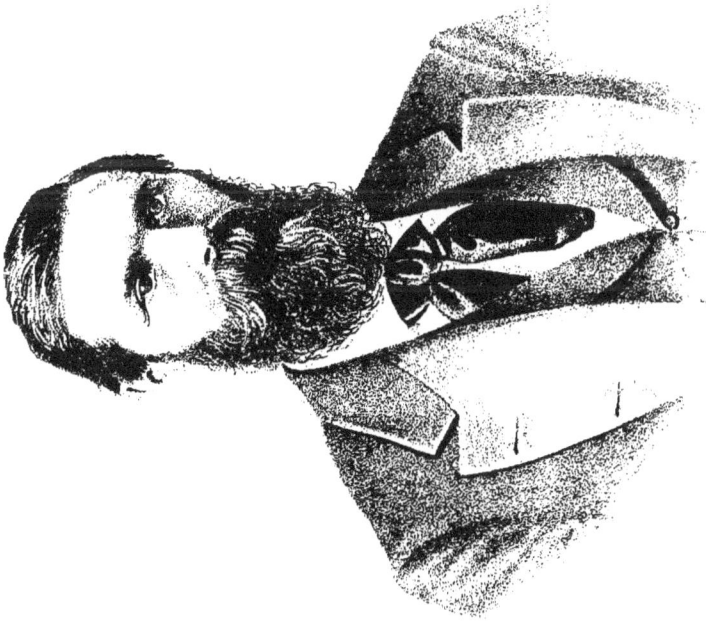

W. W. MARSH
SYCAMORE

Biographical Directory.

ABBREVIATIONS.

SYCAMORE TOWNSHIP.

A DEE STEPHEN, Retired Farmer, Sycamore; Rep; from N.Y.

AHERN DANIEL, Tailor, Sycamore; Dem; from Ireland.

ALLPORT FRANK, Physician and Surgeon; Res. and P.O. Sycamore; born in Watertown, N.Y.; came to state 1855 and county 1876; Rep; Prot.

ALEXANDER STEPHEN, Laborer, Sycamore; Rep; from Ill.

ALDEN ARTHUR S. Farmer, Sec. 34; P.O. Sycamore; Rep; Cong; N. H.; $10,000.

ALDEN E. H. Clerk Sycamore Nat. Bank, Sycamore; Rep; from Ill.

ALTHEN J. Saloon, Sycamore; Dem; from Germany.

ALDEN JESSE, Sec. 31, Sycamore; born N. H.; $7,500; Rep; Cong.

ALDEN SAMUEL, Retired Farmer, Sycamore; Rep; from N. H.

ALDEN P. M. Cashier Sycamore Nat. Bank, Sycamore; Rep; from N. H.

ALLEN WILLIAM H. Employee Harvester Works, Sycamore; Rep; from England.

ALLEN A. C. Attorney, Sycamore, Rep; from Penn.

ALLEN JOHN E. Barber, Sycamore; Rep; from Kentucky.

ALLEN JOHN, works for Wyman, Sec. 36; P.O. Sycamore; Ill; Rep; Bapt.

ALBEE T. J. Carpenter, Sycamore; Dem; from N.Y.

ALVA ASHCRAFT, Tenant Farmer, Sec. 16; P.O. Sycamore; Rep; Lib.

ATWOOD HOSEA W. City Marshal; Res. and P.O. Sycamore; born in Susquehanna Co. Pa. July 2, 1837; came to county 1851; Dem; Lib; val. real estate $1,500; was 1st Lieut. and Capt. Company F, 65th Ill. Inf; wife was Martha Stark, born in Sycamore, DeKalb Co. Ill; married Nov. 1865; three children.

ARNOLD I. R. B. & G. L. Book and Job Printers, Sycamore; I. R. B. married Adelia Nichols eight years since; born Erie Co. N.Y.; came to this state and DeKalb Co. in 1849, and have lived here twenty-seven years; Rep; Prohibitionist; Wes. Meth. G. L. married Adeline Nichols nine years since. They commenced business five years since with a small Novelty hand press, and now are running three steam presses, and are printing seven different papers beside general jobbing and book work.

ARNOLD T. B. Rev. Sycamore; born in New York 1849, came to this state in childhood, and prepared himself for the ministry when twenty-two years of age; he married Miss Helen L. Smith in 1872; she was from Wheaton, DuPage Co. Ill; she died in 1873; in 1874 he became associate editor of the *Free Methodist*, the organ of the Free Methodist Church; he is also associated with Rev. D. P. Baker, in editing and publishing the *Christian Pilgrim*, an undenominational monthly, also two Sabbath-school papers: *The Pearl* and *The Lily*. The publishing house of Baker & Arnold in Sycamore furnishes facilities for supplying Sabbath-school papers equal to any house in the West.

ARNOLD WILLIAM H. Farmer, Sycamore; Rep; from Ill.

ARNOLD IRWIN, Job Printer, Sycamore; Rep; from N.Y.

ARNOLD WILLIAM, Farmer, Sycamore; Rep; from N.Y.

ARMSTRONG GEO. O. Publisher *True Republican*. Sycamore; Rep; from Maine.

ARMSTRONG S. T. Co. Surveyor, Sycamore; Rep; from N.Y.

ARMSTED RICHARD, Farmer, tenant of Russell; P.O. Sycamore; Rep; Adv. Ill.

ANMERSON EVAN, Carpenter, Sycamore; Rep; from Norway.

ANDERSON A. Tailor, Sycamore; Rep; from Sweden.

ANDERSON AUGUST, Blacksmith, Harvester Works, Sycamore; Rep; from Sweden.

ANDERSON ANNA Mrs. widow; from Sweden.

ANDERSON OTTO, Laborer, Sycamore; Rep; from Sweden.

ANDERSON CHARLES, Molder, Ellwood's Factory, Sycamore; Rep; from Sweden.

ANDERSON NELS, employee Harvester Works, Sycamore; Rep; from Denmark.

ANDERSON D. P. Mechanic, Sycamore; Rep; from N.Y.

ANDERSON WILLARD, Blacksmith, Sycamore; Rep; from N.Y.

ANDERSON AUG. Tenant of Chatfield, Sec. 22; P.O. Sycamore; Sweden; Rep; Luth.

ANDERSON S. Laborer for Campbell, Sec. 21; P.O. Sycamore; Rep; Luth; Sweden.

ANDREWS S. Laborer, H. Benson; P.O. Sycamore; Dem; Lib; N.Y.

ANDERSON OLIVER, Farmer, Sec. 11; P.O. Sycamore; Rep; Luth; Sweden; $600.

ANDERSON PETER, Farmer, Sec. 11; P.O. Sycamore; Rep; Luth; Sweden; $600.

ASHTON P. L. T. Traveling Agt. Marsh Harvester Co; Rep; from N.Y.

AUSTIN WILLARD, Painter, Sycamore; Rep; from N.Y.

AUSTIN WILLIAM, Painter, Sycamore; Rep; from Ill.

AVERY H. M. Reuben Ellwood & Co. Sycamore; Rep; from N.Y.

BAKER D. P. Rev. Editor *Free Methodist*, Sycamore; Rep; from Ohio.

BARQUIST CHARLES, Blacksmith, Harvester Works, Sycamore; Rep; from Sweden.

BAKER JOHN, Farmer, Sec. 11; P.O. Sycamore; born in Harby, Nottinghamshire, June 24, 1822, lived there thirty years, came to this country in 1852, came to St. Charles same year, and lived in Kane Co. two years; came over the sea with the father and mother of Thomas Marshall; has lived in DeKalb Co. twenty years; Rep; Meth; 140 acres of land, val. $7,000; married Elizabeth Fothergill in May, 1867; she was from Kendall, Westmoreland, England; his wife has four children; he has two children by this wife.

BARROWS A. S. Mrs. Millinery, Sycamore; from Ill.

BANNAHAN PATRICK, Laborer, Sycamore; Rep; from Ireland.

BARNARD WILLIAM, employee Harvester Works, Sycamore; Rep; from Vt.

BARRETT GEORGE, Prop. Green House, Sycamore; Ind; from England.

BARROWS A. S. with Jno. B. Whalen, Abstract Office, Sycamore; Rep; from Ill.

BALCOM WILLIAM A. Carpenter, Sycamore; Dem; from Canada.

BABCOCK A. S. Lawyer, Sycamore; Rep; from N. Y.

BABCOCK AMOS S. Carpenter, Sycamore; Rep; from N. Y.

BABCOCK JOHN, Glove Maker; val. prop. $500; Rep; Meth; born N. Y.

BARNARD FREDRICK, Retired Farmer, Sycamore; Rep; from Vt.

BALLARD J. S. Mason, Sycamore; Rep; from N. Y.

BALLARD GEORGE, employee Marsh Harvester, Sycamore; Rep; from Ohio.

BALL J. Miss, Millinery, Sycamore; from Ill.

BALL JAMES, Tanner, Sycamore; Rep; from N. J.

BENSON H. Farmer, Sec. 19; Rep; Luth; val. prop. $500; born Sweden.

BENSON HEMAN H. Farmer, Sec. 22; P.O. Sycamore; born in Bennington Co. Vt. March 11, 1825; lived there 13 years, then came to Chicago in 1839; carried on the wagon business in Chicago for 13 years, and was burned out there in 1852; came to this town in November, 1852, and has lived here 24 years; was burned out here 1869, only few settlers here then; owns 320 acres of land, value $16,000; Rep; Lib; married Rosella Wood in June, 1847, she was from Queensburg, Warren Co. N. Y.; has nine children, five boys and four girs; has lost one boy and two girls.

BENSON HENRY, P.O. Sycamore; Rep.

BENSON JAMES H. lives with father, Sec. 22; Sycamore; Rep; Lib.

BENSON BEN. Laborer with Jackman, Sec. 17; Luth; Sweden.

BELLES M. E. Mrs. Millinery, Sycamore; from Ohio.

BELLES CHARLES W. Mason, Sycamore; Dem; from Penn.

BELLES MATT. Mason, Sycamore; Dem; from Penn.

BELLES JACOB, Carpenter, Sycamore; Dem; from Penn.

BECKLER JOHN, Cigar Manufacturer, Sycamore; Dem; from N. Y.

BEAVERS W. H. Undertaker, Sycamore; Rep; from N. J.

BEAVERS THEODORE, Undertaker, Sycamore; Rep; from N. J.

BENTLY R. H. lives on Jas. S. Waterman's farm; P.O. Sycamore.

BEAN G. F. Carpenter, Sycamore; Rep; from Vt.

BEHNER EPHRAIM employee Marsh Harvester, Sycamore; Rep; from Ohio.

BEBEE HENRY, Painter, Sycamore; from Ill.

BEAVERS W. H. S. Deputy County Clerk, Sycamore; Rep; from N. J.

BECKWITH M. A. Mrs. Boarding House, Sycamore; from Ohio.

BECKLEY LOUISA Mrs. widow, Sycamore; from N. Y.

BERRY JAMES T. Traveling Agent, Ellwood & Co. Sycamore; Rep; from N. Y.

BELLENDORF PETER, Laborer, Sycamore; from Germany; Rep.

BELL GEORGE M. Carpenter, Sycamore; Rep; from Penn.

BELL HENRY G. Farmer, Sec. 9; P.O. Sycamore; Rep; Meth; Canada.

BIERNSTIEN HORACE, Laborer, Sycamore; Dem; from Ill.

BISHOP ALBERT, Farm Laborer, Sycamore; Rep; from England.

BLANCHFIELD JOHN Mrs. Sec. 12; P.O. Sycamore; Cath; 200 acres, val. $10,000; Ireland.

BLANCHFIELD S. Farmer, Sec. 12; P.O. Sycamore; Dem; Cath; Ill.

BLANCHFIELD RICHARD, Farmer, Sec. 12; P.O. Sycamore; Dem; Cath; Ill.

BLAKE WILLIAM, Prop. Green House, Sycamore; Ind; from England.

BLACK JOHN, Farmer, Sycamore; 255 acres, val. $12,750; Rep; from Ireland.

BLACK JOHN R. Laborer, Sycamore; Dem; from N. Y.

BLACK N. Tenant Farmer, Sec. 17; P.O. Sycamore; Rep; Lib; born N. Y.

BLACK WILLIAM C. Prop. Citizen's Mills, Sycamore; Rep; from Ireland.

BOIES HENRY L. Editor, Postmaster, and Farmer; born in South Hadley, Mass. July 5, 1830; came to this county in 1854; Rep; Cong; has held the offices of Secretary of Illinois Senate, and Postmaster, Sycamore; wife was Harriet Holmes, born in Sherburne, Chenango Co. N. Y; married Feb. 19, 1858; three children.

BOLIN S. M. Laborer R.R., Sycamore; Rep; from Sweden.

BOUCK JACOB, Tenant Farmer, Sec. 31; Rep; Luth; born in Germany.

BOYLE J. C. Cooper Shop, Sycamore; Rep; from Ireland.

BOWMAN ALONZO, works in R. Ellwood's Factory; Dem; from N. Y.

BOYNTON C. O. Broker, Sycamore; Dem; from N. Y.

BOOM T. A. Mrs. Millinery, Sycamore; from N. Y.

BOURCY J. M. Foreman Foundry, Harvester Works, Sycamore; Dem; from N. Y.

BOLANGER VEIRGEL, Wagon Maker, Sycamore; Dem; from Germany.

BOLLENGER AMIEL, Barber, Sycamore; Dem; from Germany.

BRYAN O. M. Physician and Surgeon, Residence and P.O. Sycamore; born in Fairfield, Herkimer Co. N. Y. July 6, 1823; came to county in 1846; Rep; Prot; was a member of the Illinois Board of Medical Examiners U. S. V; was Brigade Surgeon and Medical Director of the Department of New Mexico; wife was Jane Leslie Voorhees, born N.Y.; four children.

BROWN OBADIAH, Farmer, Sec. 14; P.O. Sycamore; born in Loraine Co. Ohio, in 1834; came to Ottawa, Illinois, about 1836; lived there eighteen months, came to Town of Sycamore, DeKalb Co. about 1838, and has lived here thirty-eight years; is one of the oldest settlers, only three or four families were here when he came, the Indians had just left; Rep; Meth; owns 155 acres of land, value $7,750; has been Road-master; his sister, Sally Ann Brown, lives with him.

BROWN H. D. Merchant, Sycamore; born Herkimer Co. N.Y. March 19, 1839; came to state and county March 1, 1857; Dem; Prot; real estate $3,000; personal property $500; was Major 105th I.V.I.; wife was Sarah A. Hood, born Saugerties, N.Y.; married Oct. 22. 1872.

BROWN ISAAC, Farmer, Sec. 13; P.O. Sycamore; Rep; Meth; val. of prop. $4,500; N. Y.

BROWN C. M. Mrs. from Vermont.

BROWN PETER W. Retired Farmer, Sycamore; Dem; from N. Y.

BROWN THANKFUL Mrs. Sycamore; from Vermont.

BROWN FRED C. Clerk for J. H. Rodgers & Co. Sycamore; Rep; from Illinois.

BROWN W. H. Painter, Sycamore; Rep; from Ohio.

BROWN J. S. Hotel Proprietor, Sycamore; Dem; from N. Y.

BROWN GEORGE, Attorney, Sycamore; Rep; from Illinois.

BROWN CHARLES, Merchant, Sycamore; Rep; from N. Y.

BROWN AUGUSTUS, Barber,Sycamore; Rep; from Washington City.

BROWN W. T. Traveling Agent for H. S. Parish, Chicago; Sycamore; Rep; from Illinois.

BROWN JOHN, Laborer, Sycamore; Rep; from Ireland.

BROWN PETER W. Retired Farmer, Sycamore; Dem; from N. Y.

BRIGGS JOHN, works for Ellwood & Co. Sycamore; Rep; from Virginia.

BRIGGS HENRY, Shoemaker, Sycamore; Ind; from England.

BRUNDAGE MARY A. Mrs. widow of Jas. Brundage, Sycamore; from N. Y.

BRAMBLE HENRY C. works in Harvester Works, Sycamore; Rep; from Maryland.

BRAGA MATTHIAS, Moulder, Sycamore; Rep; from N. Y.

BRISBIN JAMES, Retired, Sycamore; Rep; from Canada.

BROOKS GILMAN E. Farmer, Sec. 6; P.O. Sycamore; Rep; Latter Day Saint; from Ohio.

BRUCE WILLIAM, Carpenter, Sycamore; Ind; from N. Y.,

BRENAN JAMES, Lightning Rod Agent; Dem; from N. Y.

BRENAN WILLIAM, Lightning Rod Agent; Dem; from N. Y.

BRADY WM. Laborer for Redmond, Sec. 28; Dem; Cath; Illinois.

BROWER ADOLPHUS. Stock Dealer, Sycamore; Dem; from N. Y

BRYANT W. W. Physician, Sycamore; Dem; from Mass.

BRUNSON J. N. Clerk for J. H. Rodgers & Co. Sycamore; Rep; from Mich.

BRIGGS WELLS, Tinner, Sycamore; Rep; from N. Y.

BRAND PHILANDER, Farmer, lives in Sycamore.

BUZZELL NATHANIEL, Farmer, Sec. 25; P.O. Sycamore; born in Shaumburgh, Illinois, Jan. 18, 1850; lived there two and a half years; came to town of Sycamore, DeKalb Co. Aug. 1852, and has lived here over twenty-four years, and is among the oldest settlers; only few here when he came; Rep; United Brethren; owns 50 acres of land, value $2,500. Married Miss Nettie A. Lawrence, Oct. 4, 1871; she was from this State; they have three children—all girls.

BUZZELL H. lives with brother, Sec. 24; P. O. Sycamore; Rep; Meth.

BUZZELL GEORGE, lives with father, Sec. 12; P. O. Sycamore; Rep. Lib.

BUZZELL DANIEL P. Farmer, Sec. 12; P. O. Sycamore; Rep; Spiritualist; from Vermont.

BURDETT AMOS, Drayman, Sycamore; Dem; from England.

BURDETT WILLIAM, Drayman, Sycamore; Dem; from Illinois.

BURDETT EDWARD, Laborer, Sycamore; Dem; from N. Y.

BURTON WILLIAM, Farmer, Sec. 31; P. O. Sycamore; Ind. Lib; from New Brunswick.

BURTON GEO. lives with brother, Sec. 31; P.O. Sycamore; Ind. Lib; born New Hampshire·

BURST JOHN W. Clerk R. W. M. S.; residence Sycamore; born Meredith, N. Y. July 29, 1843; came to county 1860; Rep; Lib; value personal property $3,000; held the offices of P. M. and U. S. R. W. P. O. Clerk; was First Lieutenant Co. C. 105th Ills.. Vol. In. Wife was Lettice A. Mayo, born Sycamore, Ills; married April 28th, 1871; has three children.

BURBANK ARTHUR, Clerk J. E. Southworth, Sycamore; Rep; from Vermont.

BURBANK WALTER H. Carpenter, Sycamore; Rep; from New Hampshire.

BUELL HIRAM, Butcher, Sycamore; Dem; from Mass.

BUELL CHARLES, Teacher, Sycamore; Rep; from Illinois.

BURGLEN OSCAR, Mason, Sycamore; Rep; from Sweden.

BURKE MICHAEL, Farmer, Sycamore; Dem; from Mass.

BUCHHOLZ S. Tailor, Sycamore; Dem; from Germany.

BUTTS PETER, Laborer, Sec. 29; P.O. Sycamore; Lib; no religion; born Wisconsin.

BULL M. Miss, Millinery, Sycamore; from Illinois.

BUTSON JOHN, Farmer; P.O. Sycamore; Rep; United Brethren; prop. $6,000; from Eng.

BYERS JOHN, Druggist, Sycamore; Dem; from Illinois.

CANEDY EMRA, Farmer, Sycamore; Rep; from Mass.

    CAMERON A. R. Harness Maker, Sycamore; Dem; from England.

CARLEY CHARLES H. Dealer in Butter, Eggs, Poultry, Wool, etc.; residence and P. O. Sycamore; born in Randolph, Orange Co. Vt. Jan. 23, 1844; came to county 1874; value real estate $3,000; was private, Co. G. 10th Vt. Inf. Wife was Nancy J. Huntington, born in Randolph, Orange Co. Vt. April 3, 1846; married Nov. 20, 1867; has one child.

CALAHAN MICHAEL, Blacksmith, Sycamore; Dem; from Germany.

CARLSON S. Farmer, Sec. 23; P.O. Sycamore ; Rep; Luth; val. prop. $2,000; from Sweden.

CARLSEN C. Farmer, Sec. 18; Rep; Luth; val. prop. $2,000; from Sweden.

CARLSON CHAS. employee Citizens' Mills, Sycamore; Rep; from Sweden.

CARLSON ANNA Mrs. (widow) Sycamore; from Sweden.

CARLSON PETER, Laborer, Sycamore; Rep; from Sweden.

CARLSON ANDREW, Laborer, Sycamore; Rep; from Sweden.

CASE GEO. Mechanic, Sycamore; Rep; from Penn.

CASE WILLIS, Auctioneer, Sycamore; Dem; from Illinois.

CASS W. D. Carpenter, Sycamore; Dem; from N. Y.

CAMPBELL JOHN R. Farmer, Sec. 21; P.O. Sycamore; born in Delaware Co. N. Y. Nov. 2, 1810; lived there about 25 years; lived in Chenango Co. 18 years; came to this State, DeKalb Co. 1853, and has lived here 23 years; Rep; Meth; owns 80 acres land, value $5,000. Married Clarinda Marvin in 1830; she was from Conn; has six children living and lost three.

CAMPBELL JOHN, Farmer, Sec. 21; P.O. Sycamore; Rep; Meth; prop. $4,000; from N. Y.

CAMPBELL JABEZ, Farmer, Sec. 21; P.O. Sycamore; Rep. Lib; prop. $4,000; from N. Y.

CAMPBELL SILAS, Farmer, Sec. 10; P.O. Sycamore; Rep; Meth; prop. $8,000; from N. Y.

CAMPBELL JAMES, Farmer, Sec. 36; P.O. Sycamore; Ind; Episcopal; from Dublin.

CARNES DUANE J. Lawyer; resides Sycamore; born May 27, 1848, Windsor Co. Vt.; came to state 1868, and to county 1873; Rep.

CARR BYRON T. Printer, Sycamore; Rep; from Illinois.

CARR ROBERT E. Printer, Sycamore; Rep; from Illinois.

CARR SPENCER, Carpenter, Sycamore; Rep ; from Ohio.

CARR ALONZO, Carpenter, Harvester Works, Sycamore; Rep; from Ohio.

CARR THURSTON, Carpenter, Harvester Works, Sycamore; Rep; from Ohio.

CHRISTOPHENSON JOHN, tenant Sec. 21; P.O. Sycamore; Rep; Luth; from Sweden.

CHEEK OMER, Conductor, Sycamore; Dem; from Indiana.

CHAVEL E. Machinist, Sycamore; Rep; from France.

CHAVEL LOUIS, Machinist, Sycamore; Rep; from N. Y.

CHAIMBERLIN W. G. Clerk, Sycamore; Rep; from N. Y.

CHURCHILL GEORGE, Millwright, Sycamore; Rep; from N. Y.

CHURCHILL C. J. Book Store, Sycamore; Rep; from Illinois.

CHRISMAN A. G. Butcher, Sycamore; Rep; from Denmark.

CHATFIELD JOHN, Farmer, Sec. 21; P.O. Sycamore; born in the County of Surrey, England, about 1811, lived there about thirty years, came to this country in 1841, came to this state and county the same year, and has lived here thirty-five years, is one of the oldest settlers, no houses around here when he came; Rep; Unitarian; owns 320 acres of land, val. $16,000; married Julia A. Holmes, in 1847; she was from DuPage Co; has two children, one daughter, Susan, and one son, John R. Holmes Chatfield.

CHATFIELD JOHN R. lives on father's farm, Sec. 21; P O. Sycamore; Rep; Unitarian; Ill.

CHATFIELD A. B. Hardware, Stoves, and Tinware, Sycamore; Rep; from Illinois.

CLIFFE THOMAS, Shoemaker, Sycamore; Dem; from England.

CLARK J. L. Pastor W. M. E. Church, Sycamore; Rep; from Ireland.

CLARK WATSON Rev. Pastor Baptist Church, Sycamore; Rep; from N. Y.

CONRAD CASSIUS M. County Clerk, residence Sycamore; born in North East, Erie Co. Pa. March 27, 1845; came to county in 1863; Rep; Cong; wife was Anna H. Beavers, born in Chester, N. J; married Dec. 27, 1870.

COTTRELL NORMAN L. Farmer. Sec. 28; P.O. Sycamore; Rep; Bapt; 250 acres; N. Y.

CORO C. Laborer for Westgarth, Sec. 24; P.O. Sycamore; Rep; Cath; Illinois.

CONDEE J. J. Agent Milwaukee Beer, Sycamore; Rep; from N. Y.

CONDE C. K. Laborer, Sycamore; Rep; from N. Y.

CONANT P. L. Mrs. Widow; from Mass.

CONNUART LOUIS, Merchant Tailor and Furnishing Goods, Sycamore; Dem; Germany.

COLTON A. C. Cashier for Divine & Co. Sycamore; Rep.

COLTON A. Harness, Whips, Trunks, etc., Sycamore; Rep; from N. Y.

COTES ELIZA Mrs. Millinery, Sycamore; from N. Y.

COTES W. C. Printer, Sycamore; Dem; from Ohio.

COVELL WALTER, Pattern Maker, Sycamore; Rep; from N. Y.

COVELL MERRITT, Molder, Sycamore; Rep; from Ohio.

COVELL NELSON, Machinist, Sycamore; Rep; from Illinois.

COLEMAN E. Carpenter, Sycamore; Dem; from Illinois.

CONYERS JOHN, Clerk for H. H. Rowe, Sycamore; Rep; from Illinois.

COLBART WILLIAM, Builder, Sycamore; Dem; from Ireland.

COLLIER JAMES, Farmer, Sec. 7; P.O. Sycamore; Rep; Luth; value of property $3,000.

COLLINS MICHAEL, Teamster, Sycamore; Dem; from Ireland.

CONDON DAVID, Laborer, Sycamore; Dem; from Ireland.

COOK CATHARINE Mrs. Sec. 12; P.O. Sycamore; Meth; 80 acres, value $3,000.

COOK ABRAHAM, Farmer, Sec. 12; P.O. Sycamore; Dem; Meth; from England.

COOK J. L. Mrs. Widow; from Vermont.

COOK DANIEL M. works for Harvester Works, Sycamore; Rep; from N. Y.

COMMAN JAMES, Laborer, Sycamore; Dem; from Ireland.

COX W. T. Foreman *Free Methodist* Office, Sycamore; Rep; from Mass.

COX A. S. owns Grist Mill in Rochelle, lives in Sycamore; Rep; from Mass.

COX J. Carpenter, Sycamore; Rep; from N. Y.

CRONK STEPHEN, Laborer, Sycamore; Rep; from N. Y.

CRONK J. M. Auction and Commission, Sycamore; Dem; from N. Y.

CROSBY Q. H. Clothing and Furnishing Goods, Sycamore; Rep; Illinois.

CROSBY PATRICK, Laborer, Sycamore; Dem; from Ireland.

CRESS HENRY, Painter, Sycamore; Rep; from Canada.

CRETZLER S. Shoemaker, Sycamore; Rep; from Penn.

CRIST EDWARD, Clerk for N. C. Warner, Sycamore; Rep; from N. Y.

CURREN HUGH, Laborer, Sycamore; Dem; from Ireland.

CURRIER L. M. Homœopathic Physician and Surgeon; residence and P.O. Sycamore; born in St. Lawrence Co. N. Y. January 14, 1847; came to state 1864, to county 1873; Rep; wife was Rose Beaumont, born in Freeport, Stephenson Co. Ill; married Nov. 23, 1869; one child.

CURRIER WM. B. Sycamore; Rep; born St. Lawrence Co. N. Y.

CUTLAR S. Carpenter, Sycamore; Rep; from N. Y.

CULEHEN MICHAEL, Blacksmith; Dem; from Ireland.

DAVIS R. S. M.D. Magnetic Healer, Sycamore; Rep; from Mass.

DAVIS CORNELIUS, Mason, Sycamore; Rep; from Ill.

DAVIS CAZNEAU, Editor *Helping Hand*, Sycamore; Rep; from Mass.

DAVIS G. C. Plasterer, Sycamore; Rep; from Penn.

DARNELL ENOCH, Farmer, Sec. 25; P.O. Sycamore; born in North Carolina, May 17, 1828; came to this state near Ottawa, 1830; came to Afton, DeKalb Co. 1858, lived there about 10 years; came to this town 1868, and has lived here 8 years; has lived in this state 46 years, one of the oldest settlers; Rep; United Brethren; owns 141 acres land, val. $7.000; has been School Director a number of years, also Road-master; married Cynthia A. Woods, Jan. 1, 1855, she was from Penn; has two children living; has lost two girls.

DAYTON LEWIS M. Farmer, Sec. 36; P.O. Sycamore; born October 14, 1844, in Town of Cortland, DeKalb Co. Ill; lived there about 25 years, then moved to Town of Sycamore for one year, lived in Marengo two years; came to Town of Sycamore in 1872, where they now live; Rep; Meth; owns 125 acres of land, $6,250; was in the army in the 132d Reg. Ill. Volunteers, 100 days' service in Kentucky; married Miss Helen White, on Christmas Day, 1865; she was born in Town of Sycamore this county, Sept. 13, 1848; has three children, one girl and two boys.

DAVINSON PETER, Laborer, Sec. 19; Sycamore; Rep; Luth; born Sweden.

DAWSON SIMON, Engineer Harvester Works, Sycamore; Rep; from N. Y.

DAYTON M. Restaurant, Sycamore; Rep; from Ill.

DAFOE W. Z. Night-watch Harvester Works, Sycamore; Dem; from Canada

DAVY JAMES, Butcher; Sycamore; Dem; from England.

DAWSON CHAS. E. Laborer, Sec. 28; P.O. Sycamore; Rep; Meth; N. Y.

DAVENPORT T. R. Painter, Sycamore; Dem; from Canada.

DEVEREAUX BYRON. Farmer, Sycamore; Rep; from N. Y.

DENMARK L. C. Painter, Sycamore; Rep; from Penn.

DENMARK D. J. Moulder Harvester Works, Sycamore; Rep; from Penn.

DENMARK F. S. Laborer, Sycamore; Rep; from Penn.

DEILY JACOB, Carpenter, Sycamore; Rep; from Penn.

DEAN MOSES, Banker, Sycamore; Dem; from N. Y.

DEAN GEORGE, Laborer, Sycamore; Dem; from N. Y.

DEAN C. A. Clerk for Harkness & Whittemore, Sycamore; Dem; from N. Y.

DEAN MOSES, Farmer, Sec. 1; P.O. Sycamore; Univ; prop. $12,000; N. Y

DEITZ WM. works for Lowell, Sec. 25; P.O. Sycamore; Rep; Lib.

DENNIS N. Foreman Ellwood's Boot and Shoe Store, Sycamore; Rep; from Del.

DILLER S. W. Traveler for Williams' Paint House, Chicago; Sycamore; Rep; from N. Y.

DILLER G. W. Employee Harvester Works, Sycamore; Rep; from Penn.

DICKSON LOUIS Employee Winn's Hotel; Dem; from Ill.

DICKSON N. W. Clerk Warren & Lott, Sycamore; Rep; from Wis.

DIVINE ELEZAR, Farmer, Sec. 14; P.O. Sycamore; born in Sullivan Co. N. Y. March 1, 1820; lived there 32 years; came to this town, county and state in 1852, and has lived here 24 years; Dem; Lib; owns 600 acres land, $30,000; has been School Director and Road-master; married Miss Sallie Ann Sheley, March 12, 1840; she was born in Sullivan Co. N. Y.; has seven children, four boys and three girls.

DIVINE FRANK, Farmer, Sec. 12; P.O. Sycamore; born Sullivan Co. N. Y. March 26, 1849; lived there four years; came to Sycamore, DeKalb Co. Ill. 1853, and has lived here since, 23 years; Dem; Lib; owns 220 acres land, $10,000; has held office of Road-master; married Miss Mary Bell Barron, Feb. 18, 1874, she was from Kane Co. Ill.

DIVINE DAVID, Farmer, Sec. 13; P.O. Sycamore; Dem; Lib; prop. $5,000; N. Y.

DIVINE FRANK, Farmer, Sec. 13; P.O, Sycamore; Dem; Lib; 220 acres; N. Y.

DIVINE E. Farmer, Sec. 14; P.O. Sycamore; Dem; Lib; prop. $30,000; N. Y.

DIVINE R. L. Banker, Sycamore; Rep; from N. Y.

DOW ROSWELL, Farmer, Sec. 29, Tp. 41, R. 5; P.O. Sycamore; born Hanover, Grafton Co. N. H. Jan. 14, 1824; came to county 1846; Rep; Cong; owns 235 acres; value of real estate $18,000; held the office of Supervisor three years, and County Treasurer from 1855 to 1859; wife was Theresa E. Richards, born in Madison Co. N. Y.; married Sept. 6, 1851; has five children.

DOWE AGGRIPA, retired, Sycamore; Rep; from N. H.

DODGE HIRAM, Carpenter Harvester Works, Sycamore; Rep; from N. Y.

DONNELLY P. Traveling Salesman, Sycamore; Dem; from Canada.

DOYLE EDWARD, Blacksmith, Sycamore; Dem; from Ireland.

DOYLE PHILIP, Laborer; born Ireland; Dem; Cath.

DOOLEY THOS. works for Van Duzen, Sec. 21; Dem; Cath; Ill.
DRIVER A. J. Clerk, Reuben Ellwood, Sycamore; Rep; from England.
DREW JOHN, Laborer for Mr. Dean, Sec. 1; P.O. Sycamore; Lio; Lib; N.Y.
DUNNING D. D. Carpenter, Sycamore; Rep; from N.Y.
DUNSBACK M. M. Mrs. Seamstress, Sycamore; from N.Y.
DUTTON HENRY T. Teamster, Sycamore; Rep; from N. H.
DUTTON E. F. Circuit Clerk and Recorder, Sycamore; Rep; from Vermont.
DUCK JOHN. Laborer, Sec. 17; P.O. Sycamore.
DUPAW RICHARD, Laborer. Sec. 29; born Ill; Dem; Lib.
DUNCAN C. A. Expressman, Sycamore; Rep; from Ill.
DUSKE JULIUS, Employee Harvester Works, Sycamore; Rep; from Russia.
DUNHAM E. H. Tailor, Sycamore; Rep; from N.Y.
DUGAN JOHN, Laborer, Sycamore; from Ireland.
DUSTIN DANIEL, Physician, res. and P.O. Sycamore; born in Orange Co. Topsham,
Vt; came to county 1858; Rep; Cong; val. real estate $3.500; has held the offices of County
Clerk and County Treasurer; was Col. of 105th Ill. Vol. and Breveted Brigadier General;
wife was Elmira E. Pauly, born in Warren Co. Ohio; married Oct 15, 1854; four children.

E LLWOOD ABRAM, res. and P.O. Sycamore; born in N.Y.; is Postal Clerk U. S. M; Rep.
ELLWOOD ABRAM Mrs. widow, from N.Y.
ELLWOOD ALONZO, was dealer in hardware for eighteen years, now in drugs and
groceries; Res and P.O. Sycamore; born in Montgomery Co. N.Y. June 17, 1823; came to
county May 5, 1853; Rep; Univ; 800 acres; val. real estate $20,000; held the office of Asst.
U. S. Assessor; wife was Mary M. Baker, born in Center Co. Penn; married Dec. 27, 1865;
one child.
ELLWOOD CHAUNCEY, Dealer in Boots, Shoes and Leather; res. and P.O. Syca-
more; Vice-President and General Manager of Sycamore, Courtland and Chicago R. R; born
in Montgomery Co. N.Y. Dec. 24, 1816; came to county April, 1858; Rep; Spiritualist; value
real estate $17,000; held the offices of Sec. of Ill. Senate and P. M. of Sycamore.
ELLWOOD REUBEN, Manufacturer of Agricultural Implements and Heavy Hardware;
Dealer in Hardware for twenty years; res. and P.O. Sycamore; born in Montgomery Co.
N.Y. Feb. 17, 1821; came to county 1857; Rep; val. real estate $30,000; was member of the
Legislature of N.Y. in 1850, also U. S. Assessor of 4th Congressional Dist. of Ill. and Mayor
of Sycamore; wife was Eleanor Vedder, born in Schenectady Co. N.Y; married Aug. 8, 1849;
has six children.
ELLWOOD ALBERT, res. and P.O. Sycamore; born in N.Y.; Rep.
ELLWOOD FRANK, res. and P.O. Sycamore; born in N.Y.; Rep.
ELLWOOD J. E. Drugs and Groceries, Sycamore; Rep; from N.Y.
ENGQIVESTRON FRANK, Employee Harvester Works, Sycamore; Rep; from Sweden.
ENGMANSON ANDREW, Laborer, Sycamore; Rep; from Sweden.
ELTEN ADOLPH, Foreman Sash Factory, Sycamore; Rep; from Germany.
EDDY E. Tanner, Sycamore; Rep; from N.Y.
ELLS BENJ. Painter, Sycamore; Rep; from N.Y.
ENGQUIST ANNA Mrs. widow, from Sweden.
EAMES E. B. Mrs. widow, Sycamore; from New Jersey.
EVANS IRA, Farmer, Sec. 3; P.O. Sycamore; Rep; Lib; $6,000; Ill.
EVANS OLE, Farmer, works for Ira Evans, Sec. 3; Rep; Luth.
EVANS LORENZO DOW, Farmer, Sec. 2; P.O. Sycamore; born in North Carolina,
Feb. 9, 1834; came to Kendall Co. Ill. near where Plano now stands same year, lived there
for three years and came to DeKalb Co. and has lived here since; has been in state forty-two
years; recollects when Kendall Co. was organized; was one of the oldest here; only recollects
seven or eight families here then; was not a house on prairie near here when he came; owns
168 acres land, val. $5,500; Rep; Lib; has been School Director in his district; married Miss
Mary Jewell, 1857; she was from Ohio; has four children—two boys and two girls,
ERICKSON FRANK, Laborer, Sycamore; Rep; from Sweden.
ERICKSON E. Carpenter, Sycamore; Ind; from Denmark.
EMMERSON RICHARD, Machinist, Sycamore; Dem; from Canada.
EMERSON JOHN, Laborer, Sycamore; Rep; from Sweden.

FANT AUG. Farmer, Sec. 7; P.O. Sycamore; born Sweden; Rep; Luth; val. prop. $1,000.

FARNSWORTH D. Mrs. widow, Sycamore; from Vermont.

FAIRCLO ARIAL, Drayman, Sycamore; Rep; from Ill.

FAIRCLO T. G. Mason, Sycamore; Rep; from New Jersey.

FERES ELLEN Mrs. widow, from Ireland.

FINNEGAN JOHN, Laborer, Sycamore; Dem; from Ireland.

FISHER J. P. Flouring Mill, Sec. 7; born Ohio; Dem; Lib.

FIELDSET PAUL, Painter, Harvester Works, Sycamore; Rep; from Norway.

FISHER WILLIAM, Clerk Jones & Willson, Sycamore; Rep; from N.Y.

FINLEY J. C. Book Store, Sycamore; Rep; from Ohio.

FLITCRAFT A. M. Laborer, Sycamore; Rep; from Ohio.

FLOWER CHARLES, Employee Lumber Yards, Sycamore; Rep.

FLINN JOHN G. Merchant Tailor; residence and P. O. Sycamore; born in Wicklow Co. Ireland, May 8, 1827; came to county 1857; Rep; Episcopal. Wife was Catherine Judd, born in Herkimer Co. N. Y.; married Feb. 15, 1852; has four children.

FLINN GEO. W. Clerk, Sycamore; born Herkimer Co. N. Y.; Rep; Episcopal.

FLANNERY JOHN J. Attorney and Counselor at Law; residence and P. O. Sycamore; born in St. Charles, Kane Co. Ills. Feb. 24, 1850; came to county 1873; Dem; religion liberal.

FOSTER COLONEL, tenant Sec. 28; P.O. Sycamore; Rep; Lib; from Illinois.

FOSTER WESLEY, lives with father, Sec. 33; P.O. Sycamore; Rep; Lib.

FOSTER WM. H. tenant Sec. 28; P.O. Sycamore; Rep; Lib; Illinois.

FOSTER WM. Farmer, Sec. 33; P.O. Sycamore; Rep; Bapt; val. prop. $5,000; from Vt.

FOSTER FRED. C. tenant Sec. 28; P.O. Sycamore; Rep; Lib; from Illinois.

FOGG H. H. Painter and Carpenter, Sycamore ; Rep ; from Vermont.

FOX GEO. Laborer, Sycamore; Rep; from N. Y.

FRIEDMAN A. Clothing Merchant, Sycamore; Dem; from Germany.

FRANCIS G. H. Boots and Shoes, Sycamore; Rep; from Wisconsin.

FRANZEN H. Wagonmaker and Blacksmith, Sycamore; Dem; from Germany.

FRENCH EDWARD, tenant Sec. 11; P.O. Sycamore ; Rep; Meth; from England.

FURNESS GEO. Harnessmaker, Sycamore; Ind; from N. Y.

FUNK A. M. Confectioner, Sycamore; Rep; from Penn.

FURGESON JAMES C. Lumber Dealer, Sycamore ; Rep ; from N. Y.

FURGESON ELSY, Teamster, Sycamore; Rep ; from Illinois.

GARMAN JOHN, Blacksmith, Sec. 10; P.O. Sycamore; born in Clinton Co. Penn. Jan. 1, 1843; lived there seven years; lived in Dauphin Co. about seventeen years, and learned his trade; served apprenticeship three years in Lancaster Co; came to this State in 1870; Ind; Meth; owns two houses, and twelve acres of land, value $1,000; did blacksmithing for Government on the Potomac during the war. Married Miss Mary E. Holmes, April 12, 1871; she was from Broome Co. N. Y.; has three children, one boy and two girls.

GARDNER JERRED, Laborer, Sycamore; Dem; from Conn.

GARDNER HENRY T. Laborer, Sycamore; Dem; from Conn.

GARRETSON T. DeWITT, Painter, Sycamore; Rep; from N. Y. city.

GALLAGHER WM. Rev. Pastor Cong. Church, Sycamore; Rep; from Mass.

GAULT JOHN M. Furniture Dealer, Sycamore; Dem; from N. Y.

GARVIN I. W. Physician, Sycamore; Rep; from N. Y.

GARVIN WM. tenant Sec. 13; P.O. Sycamore; Rep; Meth; from Vermont.

GARBUTT JOHN, Tenant Farmer, Sec. 35; P.O. Sycamore; Rep; Meth; from Canada.

GARMAN JOHN, Blacksmith, Sec. 10; P. O. Sycamore; Rep; Meth; from Penn.

GETSCH ANTHON, Wagonmaker, Sycamore; Dem; from France.

GILSON EDWIN. Farmer, Sycamore; Rep; from Vermont.

GILBERT V. Butcher, Sycamore; Rep; from Penn.

GILBERT WM. H. Clerk Winn's Hotel, Sycamore; Rep; from Ohio.

GILES D. A. prop. Big Grove Mills, Sycamore; Rep; from N. Y.

GREENE D. F. Laborer, Sec. 28; P.O. Sycamore; Rep; Lib; from New York.

GREENBERG PETER, Farmer, Sec. 18; P.O. Sycamore; Rep; Luth; born Sweden.

GREENBERG N. Farmer, Sec. 19; P.O. Sycamore; Rep; Luth; born Sweden.
GREEN D. C. Restaurant, Sycamore; Rep; from Penn.
GREEN ANDREW, Laborer, Flax Mill, Sycamore.
GREEN A. B. Retired; Sycamore; Rep; from Penn.
GATHERCOAL JOHN, Carpenter, Sycamore; Dem; from England.
GROVES GEO. works for Thompson, Sec. 1; P.O. Sycamore; Rep; Lib.
GRISWOLD T. M. Mechanic; Rep; from N. Y.
GRAVES CHARLES P. Physician and Surgeon; born in Keene, Essex Co. N. Y. Dec.
    29, 1831; came to county 1876; Rep; Meth; property $500. Wife Lucretia Osborn, born
    in Chautauqua Co. N. Y.; married Sept. 10, 1857; has four children.
GRAHAM WILLIAM, Foreman Marsh Harvester Works, Sycamore; Rep; from N. Y.
GROVER L. N. prop. Boarding House, Sycamore; Rep; from N. Y.
GROVER E. L. Farmer, Sycamore; Rep; from Illinois.
GRAHN HINS, Tailor, Sycamore; Dem; from Sweden.
GRAHN CHARLES, Tailor, Sycamore; Dem; from Sweden.
GUSTAVENSON BENA Mrs. Widow; from Sweden.
GUSTAFENSON S. Farmer, Sec. 27; P.O. Sycamore; Rep; Luth; property $3,000; Sweden.
GUSTAFSON GUS, Farmer, Sec. 10; P.O. Sycamore; Rep; Luth; property $4,000; Sweden.

HARRINGTON W. S. Rev. Pres. Elder Dixon Dis. Rock River Conference; Rep; N. Y.
    HALL H. P. Supt. County Schools, Sycamore; Rep; from New Hampshire.
HARROUN JNO. S. Dep. Co. Treas. Sycamore; Rep; Cong; from N.Y.
HARRINGTON JAMES, Lumber Dealer; residence and P.O. Sycamore; born in On-
    tario, Sep. 20, 1806; came to county in May, 1843; Rep; Meth; value of real estate $3,500;
    has been a member of the Legislature, and Supervisor; wife was Susan Wyman, born in
    Rutland Co. Vermont; married Oct. 22, 1872; has had nine children, seven are living.
HARRINGTON GEORGE L. Laborer; residence and P.O. Sycamore; born in Che-
    nango Co. N. Y. Aug. 20, 1839; came to county in 1843; Rep; Meth; value of real estate
    $1,500; was a private in Co. E, 1st Reg. Cal. Cavalry; wife was Mary M. Oakley, born in
    DeKalb Co. Ill; married July 11, 1866.
HALL FRANKLIN, Farmer, Sec. 5; P.O. Sycamore; born in Town of Sycamore, on the
    farm where he now lives and owns, June 10, 1844, and has lived here thirty-two years; owns
    540 acres of land, value $27,000; Rep; Universalist; married Miss Elizabeth E. Dennison,
    Feb. 7, 1872; she was born in Town of Clark, Canada West; they have two children, boys;
    has been Road-master; his father, Ephraim Hall, came to this town and county in the Fall
    of 1836, and has lived here forty years, on this farm, helped raise the first house in Sycamore,
    and is one of the few earliest settlers now living; he was born in Conn. March 15, 1803, and
    is now sixty-eight years old; his mother, Caroline Hall, was from Conn., she was born March
    22, 1810, and died March 22, 1849; had three children, lost two.
HALL EPHRAIM, Farmer, Sec. 5; P.O. Sycamore; lives with son; Rep; Lib; Conn.
HALL MARCENUS, Tenant Farmer, Sec. 24; P.O. Sycamore; Rep; U. Brethren; Illinois.
HAMILTON H. H. Clerk for J. F. Ellwood & Bro., Sycamore; Rep; from Wisconsin.
HAMMOND FOREST, Farmer, Sec. 22; P.O. Sycamore; Ind; Lib; property $5,000; Ill.
HAMMOND FRANK, lives with Hammond, Sec. 22; P.O. Sycamore; Dem; Pres; Ill.
HARMS W. M. Shoemaker, Sycamore; Rep; from N. Y.
HARMS IRA, Teamster, Sycamore; Rep; from Illinois.
HARMS JOHN, Farmer, Sec. 14; P.O. Sycamore; Lib; Lib; 400 acres, value $2,500; N. Y.
HARMES WILLIAM, Shoemaker, Sycamore; Rep; from N. Y.
HARMS JOHN J. Laborer, Sec. 14; P.O. Sycamore; Rep; Lib; from N. Y.
HANSON OLE, works for West, Sec. 34; P.O. Sycamore; Rep; Luth; Denmark.
HANSEN ANDREW, works in Harvester Works, Sycamore; Rep; from Denmark.
HANSON HANS P. Wagon Maker, Sycamore; Dem; from Germany.
HARKINS JOHN, Tenant Farmer, Sec. 24; P.O. Sycamore; Lib; Lib.
HAMILTON O. F. Farmer, Sec. 21; P.O. Sycamore; Rep; Lib; property $7,000; N. Y.
HARNED E. B. Farmer, Sec. 8; P.O. Sycamore; Rep; Christian; property $7,500; N. Y.
HALLORAN EDWARD, Laborer, Sec. 8; P.O. Sycamore; Dem; Cath.
HART PETER, Laborer, Sycamore; Ind; from Ireland.

HARBACH C. W. Medical Student, Sycamore; Rep; from Vermont.

HANCOCK JOHN, Clerk for, Reuben Ellwood, Sycamore; Rep; from Wisconsin.

HARKNESS JOHN B. Hardware, Sycamore; Dem; from N. Y,

HALGREN CHARLEY, Laborer, Sycamore; Rep; from Sweden.

HAPBENGER JOHN, Baker, Sycamore; Dem; from Germany.

HANLEY JOHN, Teamster, Sycamore; Rep; from England.

HALEY MARY Mrs. Widow; from Ireland.

HALEY JOHN Jr. Laborer, Sycamore; Dem; from Ireland.

HALEY WILLIAM, Laborer, Sycamore; Dem; from Ohio.

HALEY JOHN, Laborer, Sycamore; Dem; from Ireland.

HEWES WILLIAM, Farmer, Sec. 34; P.O. Sycamore; Pres; Rep; property $6,000; from Vt.

HEWES MIKE, works for Redmond, Sec. 28; P.O. Sycamore; Dem; Cath; from Ireland.

HEWITT JAMES, Farmer, Sec. 17; P.O. Sycamore; Rep; Meth; property $2,000; England.

HENIGAN JOSEPH, Laborer, Sycamore; Dem; from Canada.

HENIGAN CHARLES, Moulder, Ellwood's Factory, Sycamore; Ind; Illinois.

HENIGAN THOS. Laborer, Sycamore; Dem; from Canada.

HEBBARD G. K. Dry Goods, Carpets, Boots, and Shoes, Sycamore; Dem; from N. Y.

HEATH L. Teamster, Sycamore; Rep; Illinois.

HEATH LYMAN, works for Shefneer Bros. Sycamore; Rep; Illinois.

HENRIE M. Mrs. Widow, Sycamore; from Ohio.

HEWITT A. T. Laborer, Sycamore; Rep; from England.

HELSON JOHN, Farmer, Sycamore; Rep; from England.

HELSON GEORGE, Farmer, Sec. 26; P.O. Sycamore; prop. $4,000; Rep; U. Breth; Eng.

HEMENWAY H. B. Retired Farmer, Sycamore; Rep; from Mass.

HERREN WILLIAM, Tenant Farmer, Sec. 9; P.O. Sycamore; Rep; Meth; from Ohio.

HIX EUGENE, Foreman Storehouse, Harvester Co. Sycamore; Rep; from N. Y.

HIX VOLASKI, Editor *City Weekly*, Sycamore; Rep; from N. Y.

HINKLE GEORGE W. Farmer, Sec. 8; P.O. Sycamore; born in Town Eckford, Calhoun Co. Mich. Feb. 22, 1846; lived there about 27 years; came to Town of Sycamore, DeKalb Co. Ill. and has lived here since; Rep; Meth; value personal prop. $1,500; married Miss Mary E. Hill in 1868, she was from New York State; has one boy and one girl.

HOLCOMB HIRAM, Farmer, Sec. 34; P.O. Sycamore; was born in Erie Co. N. Y. Oct. 30, 1838; lived there 13 years; came to Sycamore, DeKalb Co., Ill. in 1851, and has lived here 25 years; Dem; Lib; he and his brother own 227 acres of land, value $13,620; married Miss Clara B. Dow, Feb. 4, 1863; she was born in New Hampshire, Jan. 2, 1844; he has four children, all boys.

HOLCOMB ORATOR F. Farmer, Sec. 27; P.O. Sycamore; born in Erie Co. N. Y. May 18, 1843; lived there 8 years, came to Sycamore, DeKalb Co. Ill. in 1851, and has lived here 25 years; Dem; Lib; married Harriet E. Stowe in 1865, Nov. 1; she was born in Sycamore, DeKalb Co. Dec. 26, 1845; has one boy, seven years old; the two brothers own 227 acres of land, value $13,620.

HOLCOMB REUBEN J. Sheriff of DeKalb Co; res. and P.O. Sycamore; born in Cattaraugus. Co. N. Y. Sept. 27, 1839; came to county 1842; Rep; has held the office of Constable, Collector and Sheriff; was Sergeant Co. A, 105th Ill. Vol. In; wife was Corena E. Boardman, born in St. Charles, Kane Co. Ill; married Aug. 27, 1862; has had four children, only two living.

HOLCOMB SYLVANUS, Justice of the Peace and Town Clerk; res. and P.O. Sycamore; born in Sangerfield, Oneida Co. N. Y. March 23, 1803; came to county June 7, 1839; Rep; Univ; val. real estate $2,500; was elected County Commissioner in 1842; wife was Betsy C. Chittenden, born in Cayuga Co. N. Y. Aug. 10, 1812; married Jan. 1, 1866; seven children.

HOLCOMB ORATOR S. Deputy Sheriff, Sycamore; Rep; from Ill.

HOLCOMB G. Farmer, Sec. 27; P.O. Sycamore; Dem; Lib; prop. $2,000; N. Y.

HOLMES CHAS. F. Tenant Sec. 10; P.O. Sycamore; Meth; U. Breth; prop. $800; N. Y

HOLMGREW AUG. works for Divine, Sec. 12; P.O. Sycamore; Rep; Luth; Sweden.

HODGE LEVI, Provision Market, Sycamore; Rep; from Mich.

HODGE L. S. Provision Market, Sycamore; Rep; from N. Y.

HOWE R. E. Foreman Paint Shop, Harvester Works, Sycamore; Rep; from N. Y.

HOWE D. F. Foreman Ellwood's Paint Shop, Sycamore; Rep; from N. Y.
HOLCUSSON NELSON, Laborer, Sycamore; Rep; from Sweden.
HOLLIDAY EMORY, Laborer for Story, Sec. 9; P.O. Sycamore; Rep; Meth; Vt.
HOLDRIGE EUGENE, Employee Harvester Works, Sycamore, Rep; from Ill.
HOLLAND THOMAS, Laborer, Sycamore; Dem; from Ireland.
HOPKINS JAMES, Laborer, Sycamore; Ind; from Ireland.
HOFFMAN WM. works for Bouck, Sec. 31; Rep; Luth.
HOYT R. C. Constable, Sycamore; Dem; from N. H.
HORN MICHAEL, Retired Farmer, Sycamore; Dem; Ireland.
HUNT R. E. Station Agent S. & C. R. R. Sycamore; Rep; from N. J.
HUNT WM. R. Teamster, Sycamore; Ind; from N. J.
HUBBARD NELSON, Mason, Sycamore; Rep; from Vt.
HUNDLEY J. W. Tenant Sec. 14; P.O. Sycamore; Dem; Lib; Va.
HUNTLEY CHAS. works for Leavitt, Sec. 21; P.O. Sycamore; Rep; Luth.
HYDE CHAS. E. Clerk Brown & Son, Sycamore; Dem; from N. Y.

ISAACSON CHARLES, Employee Harvester Co. Sycamore; Rep; from Sweden.

JARVIS E. Mrs. widow; from Ill.
JAMES DANIEL B. Lawyer, Sycamore; Rep; from Vt.
JAMES ADELIA Mrs. widow; from Maine.
JACKMAN F. H. Farmer, Sec. 4; P.O. Sycamore; Rep; Meth; prop. $10,000; Ill.
JACKMAN CHAS. D. Farmer, Sec. 5; P.O. Sycamore; Rep; Meth; prop. $7,500; Ill.
JESSUP JOHN, Laborer for Story, Sec. 9; P.O. Sycamore; Dem; Lib; England.
JONES HARVEY A. Attorney at Law; res. and P.O. Sycamore; born in Tippecanoe Co. Ind. Oct. 17, 1837; came to state 1856, to county 1865; Rep; Spiritualist; value of real estate $2,000; wife was Sarah D. Perkins, born in St. Charles, Kane Co. Ill; married Feb. 22, 1861; four children.
JONES ELSIE Mrs. lives on Sec. 35; P.O. Sycamore; Meth; prop. $3,000; N. Y.
JONES H. A. Lawyer; Sycamore; Rep; from Indiana.
JONES F. A. Dry Goods, Sycamore; Rep; from N. Y.
JONES H. R. Drugs, Sycamore; Dem; from N. Y.
JOHNSON K. Shoemaker, Sycamore; Rep; from Norway.
JOHNSON I. W. Manufacturer and Dealer in Furniture; res. and P.O. Sycamore; born in Brutus, Cayuga Co. N. Y. May 24, 1824; came to county Nov. 1846; Rep; Prot; wife was Hannah Boots, born in New Berlin, Chenango Co. N.Y.; married Aug. 1, 1851; two children.
JOHNSON FRANK W. Manufacturer and Dealer in Furniture. Sycamore; Rep; born Ill.
JOHNSON PETER, Carpet Weaver, Sycamore; Dem; from Denmark.
JOHNSON SONNE, Farmer, Sec. 10; P.O. Sycamore; value $700; Rep; Luth; Sweden.
JOHNSON PETER, Farmer, Sec. 15; P.O. Sycamore; prop. $5,000; Rep; Luth; Sweden.
JOHNSON JOHN, lives with father, Sec. 15; P.O. Sycamore; Rep; Luth; Sweden.
JOHNSON BENJ. lives with father, Sec. 15; P.O. Sycamore; Rep; Luth; Sweden.
JOHNSON CHARLEY, Laborer, Sycamore; Rep; from Sweden.
JOHNSON A. C. Bookkeeper, Sycamore; Rep; from Vermont.
JOHNSON P. works for I. W. Johnson. Sycamore; Rep; from Prussia.
JOHNSON C. S. Restaurant, Sycamore; Rep; from Vermont.
JOHNSON SWAN, Teamster, Sycamore; Rep; from Sweden.
JOHNSON A. works for Dow, Sec. 29; P.O. Sycamore; Rep; Luth; from Sweden.
JOHNSON PETER, Tenant, Sec. 19; P.O. Sycamore; Luth; from Sweden.
JOURES FRANK J. Tailor, Sycamore; Ind; from Austria.
JUDD JOHN, Tailor for J. C. Flinn, Sycamore; Dem; from N.Y.
JURY THOMAS. Farmer, Sycamore; Dem; from Germany.

KAIZER AUGUSTUS, employee, Ellwood's Factory, Sycamore; Rep; Germany.
KANE MICHAEL, Laborer, Sycamore; Dem; from Ireland.

KELLUM CHARLES, Lawyer; residence Sycamore; born in Susquehanna Co. Penn. March 16, 1821; came to Co. in 1855; owns 230 acres land, value $10,000; personal prop. $10,000; has held the office of State's Attorney; wife was Chloe Clement, born in LaPorte, Indiana; married March 15, 1855; has two children; Rep; Prot.

KENYON DAVID, Student, Sycamore; Rep; from Illinois.

KENYON JOHN, Student, Sycamore; Rep; from Illinois.

KENYON STACY, Retired Farmer, Sycamore; Rep; from N.Y.

KEYES GEO. W. Deputy Sheriff, Sycamore; Rep; from N.Y.

KELLY WILLIAM, Laborer, Sycamore; Dem; from Ireland.

KELLEY HUGH, Farmer, Sycamore; Dem; from Ireland.

KEMMELY FRANK, Cooper, Sycamore; Rep; from Germany.

KERNAN JAMES, Shoemaker, Sycamore; Rep; from Illinois.

KEEFE PATRICK, Laborer, Sycamore; Dem; from N.Y;

KEEFE DANIEL, Laborer. Sycamore; Dem; from Ireland.

KELLOGG H. W. Clerk for Brown & Son; Rep; from Illinois.

KELLOGG H. J. Clerk P.O. Sycamore; Rep; from Vermont.

KINGSBURY W. W. Teamster, Sycamore; Rep; from Conn.

KINGSBURY O. Painter, Sycamore; Rep; from Conn.

KINYON ALMIRA Mrs. widow; from N.Y.

KING ALFRED, Farmer, Sec. 3; P.O. Sycamore; prop. $6,000; Rep; Lib; Ohio.

KNIGHT CHARLES, Meat Market, Sycamore; Rep; from Vermont.

KNIPP GEO. F. Painter, Sycamore; Rep; from N.Y.

KNIPP GEORGE, Groceries and Provisions, Sycamore; Rep; from Germany.

KNUDSON GEORGE, Cooper, Sycamore; Dem; from Denmark.

KNAPP A. H. Furniture Dealer, Sycamore; Rep; from N.Y.

KNOX H. Jr. Cashier Pierce & Dean's Bank; Dem; from Mass.

KOHLBURNER MATT, Puddler, Sycamore; Dem; from N.Y.

KRYL CHRISTIAN, Retired, Sycamore; Dem; from Germany.

KREGR GUST, employee Harvester Works, Sycamore; Dem; Germany.

L ATTIN N. C. Mrs. Widow, Sycamore; from N.Y.

LATTIN C. A. with Nathan Lattin, Sycamore; Rep; from Illinois.

LANDFORS P. M. Tailor for J. G. Flinn, Sycamore; Rep; Sweden.

LAVERTY H. Farmer, Sycamore; Rep; from Ohio.

LAWRENCE H. T. Clerk, Sycamore; Rep; from N.Y.

LAWRENCE JOHN, Carpenter, Sycamore; Rep. from Illinois.

LAWSON JOHN, Laborer, Sycamore; Rep; from Sweden.

LATTIN NATHAN, Dealer in Grain, Stock and Seeds; residence and P.O. Sycamore; born in Chemung Co. N.Y. May 2, 1834; came to Co. in 1857; value real estate $5,000; has held the office of Supervisor; wife was Mary H. Bemis, born in Fitchburg, Mass. Dec. 21, 1830; married Dec. 24, 1857; has three children; Rep.

LATTEMORE WILLIAM, Farmer, Sec. 9; P.O. Sycamore; born in Dutchess Co. N.Y. Dec. 25, 1805; lived there twenty-one years, went to Penn. lived there six years, lived in Ohio one year and nine months, came to Union Grove, DeKalb Co. Ill. Aug. 1, 1837, lived there three years, came to this town 1840, and has lived in this county thirty-nine years; not a house in City of Sycamore when they came here; one of earliest settlers; only few here when they came; Rep; Meth; owns 40 acres farm, $2,000; has been Road-master in his district; married Miss Lydia Cook, Aug. 18, 1831; she was born Penn. Aug. 2, 1812; had one child, born July 5, 1832, and died Dec. 16, 1833.

LANGHORN WILLIAM, Painter, Sycamore; Rep; from England.

LANGHORN ROBERT, Painter, Sycamore; Rep; from England.

LAWSON ANDREW, Farmer, Sec. 7; born Sweden; Rep; Luth; val. prop. $500.

LAWSON AUGUSTUS, Laborer, Sycamore; Rep; from Sweden.

LAWTON CLARK, Carpenter, Sycamore; Rep; from N.Y.

LAWTON PERRY, Carpenter, Sycamore; Rep; from N.Y.

LAKINS JOHN, Laborer, Sycamore; Rep; from Penn.

LAKINS ALBERT, Laborer, Sycamore; Ind; from Canada.

LAWYER PETER H. Retired Farmer, Sycamore; Dem; from N.Y.

LARSON JOHN, Employee Harvester Works, Sycamore; Rep; from Sweden.

LACKEY SAMUEL, Employee Harvester Works, Sycamore; Rep; from Ohio.

LANGLOIS FRANK, Boots, Shoes, Clothing, etc., Sycamore; Dem; from N.Y.

LANDER W. A. Farmer; born Sweden; Rep; Luth; val. prop. $1,000.

LANE TIMOTHY, works on R. R; P.O. Sycamore; born Ireland; Dem; Cath.

LEE CHARLES, Employee Harvester Works, Sycamore; Rep; from New Jersey.

LEUERCTIU NICHOLS Mrs. widow, Sycamore; from N.Y.

LENDEN MAGNUS, Laborer for Wood, Sec. 8; P.O. Sycamore; Rep; Luth.

LEAVITT NATHANIEL, Farmer, Sec. 21; P.O. Sycamore; Dem; Meth; $5,000; N. H.

LEAVITT ISAAC, lives with brother, Sec. 21; P.O. Sycamore; no politics; Meth.

LISTY CHAS. Farmer, Sec. 11; P.O. Sycamore; $4,000; Germany.

LISTY CHAS. Farmer, Sec. 14; P.O. Sycamore; Rep; Meth; $4,000; Sweden.

LISHMAN R. M. Teacher, Sycamore; Rep; from Canada.

LISHMAN JAMES, Machinist, Sycamore; Rep; from Ill.

LISHMAN DAVID, Machinist, Sycamore; Rep; from Ill.

LISHMAN JAMES, Clerk Reuben Ellwood, Sycamore; Rep; from Scotland.

LISTY MARY, Sec. 11; P.O. Sycamore; born in Germany in 1811, lived there thirty years, came to this country 1842, lived in New York State three years, came to Town Sycamore, DeKalb Co. Ill. about twenty-two years ago; Luth; 40 acres land, value $1,200; her husband, Joseph Listy, died 1862; has 5 children, one died; Philip Listy lives at home with his mother; he was born in Germany, came to United States in 1842, has lived here since; he owns 66 acres land, value $2,000; Rep; Luth.

LENN NELSON, Farmer, Sec. 19; P.O. Sycamore; born Sweden; Rep; Luth; prop. $1,200.

LIEDHOLM P. Grain Dealer, Sycamore; Rep; from Sweden.

LITTLE HARRIS, Teamster, Sycamore; Rep; from N.Y.

LINSTROM A. Farmer, Sec. 7; born Sweden; Rep; Luth; val. prop. $3,000.

LINDSAY W. G. Carpenter, Sycamore; Dem; from Ill.

LINDSAY W. A. Grocery and Provision, Sycamore; Rep; from Canada.

LIENDE JOSEPH, Employee Harvester Works, Sycamore; Rep; from Sweden.

LINGENON ANDREW, Employee Ellwood's Factory, Sycamore; Rep; from Sweden.

LINDGREN ANDERSON, Employee on R. R. Sycamore; Rep; from Sweden.

LILLIER GUSTA Mrs. widow; from Sweden.

LINGSTROM JOHN, Employee Harvester Works, Sycamore; Rep; from Sweden.

LOWELL LUTHER, Lawyer and County Judge; res. and P.O. Sycamore; born in Orange Co. Vt. May 14, 1827; came to county 1856; Rep; 120 acres land, value $4,000; holds office of County Judge; wife Ann P. James, born in Orange Co. Vt. and married Feb. 20. 1859.

LOOMIS WILLIAM, Lumber Merchant; Rep; from Vermont.

LOOMIS RUBY C. Mrs. widow; from Vermont.

LOOMIS WILLIAM H. Lumber Merchant; Rep; from Vermont.

LOOMIS WALTER, Lumber Dealer; Rep; from Vermont.

LONDON WILLIAM, Farmer, Sycamore; Dem; from Penn.

LONDON RICHARD, Farmer, Sycamore; Dem; from Penn.

LOVELL ANDREW, Farmer, Sec. 25; P.O. Sycamore; Lib; $15,000; N.Y.

LOFTIEN CLOUS, Wagonmaker, Sycamore; Dem; from Germany.

LOFTIEN HANS, Blacksmith, Sycamore; Dem; from Germany.

LOTT F. W. Jeweler, Sycamore; Rep; from Ill.

LUGRIN GUST, Teacher, Sycamore; from Sweden.

LUTHER JOHN H. Capt. Proprietor Flax Mill, Sycamore; Rep; from Mass.

L'HOMMEDIEU HENRY, Farmer, Sec. 25; P.O. Sycamore; Rep; Lib; $4,000; N.Y.

MARTIN HARRY, Tanner, Sycamore; Rep; from Vermont.

MARTIN A. H. Retired, Sycamore; Rep; from Vermont.

MARTIN JOHN, Retired, Sycamore; Rep; from Vermont.

MARTIN HENRY, Produce Merchant, Sycamore; Rep; from Vermont.

MARSHALL THOS. Farmer, Sec. 14; P.O. Sycamore; born Town North Clifton, Nottinghamshire, England, Oct. 16, 1832, lived there eighteen years, came to U. S. 1850 without a cent, lived in Kane Co. short time and came to this town, county and state 1853, and has lived here twenty-three years in District No. 3; owns 369 acres land, value $18,450; Rep; Meth; has held office Road Commissioner for past six years; also been School Director number of years; married Miss Rachael Siglin in 1857; she was from Penn; has had nine children —Jacob William, Hannah Jane, George Milton, Edwin O., John Wesley, Taylor Zachary, Mary Amelia, Wilbur F. and Leslie Marshall.

MARTIN HARRY, Retired, Sycamore; born in Chelsea, Orange Co. Vt. August 19, 1807; came to county in July, 1838; Rep; Cong; real estate $2,000; wife was Jane Ann Slack, born in Plainfield, N. H.; married Jan. 11, 1836; five children, three living.

MARTIN C. F. Clerk in Post-office, Sycamore; Rep; Illinois.

MORRISON JOHN, Farmer, Sec. 17; P.O. Sycamore; Rep; Meth; from Canada.

MAYO EDWARD, Lawyer, Sycamore; Dem; from N. Y.

MASON H. H. Broker, Sycamore; Rep; from N. Y.

MAXFIELD G. A. Farmer; residence and P.O. Sycamore; born in Crawford Co. Ohio, May 17, 1828; came to county July 3, 1837; Rep; Meth; owns 270 acres of land, also the undivided ¾ of 323 acres; value of real estate $31,000; wife was S. Alvira Crocker, born in Bethany, Genesee Co. N. Y; married Dec. 14, 1852; five children, three living.

MAXFIELD FRED. G. Farmer; P.O. Sycamore; born in Sycamore, DeKalb Co. Ill; Rep.

MAXFIELD C. M. Physician, Sycamore; Rep; from Illinois.

MAXFIELD F. A. Carpenter, Sycamore; Rep; from Illinois.

MOORE JOHN, Laborer for Baker, Sec. 2; P.O. Sycamore; Rep; Lib; Illinois.

MACK G. W. Contractor and Builder, Sycamore; Rep; from N. Y.

MACK C. N. Carpenter and Painter, Sycamore; Rep; from N. Y.

MILLER JOHN, Farmer, Sec. 10; P.O. Sycamore; val. of property $500; Rep; Luth; Sweden.

MARSHALL JOHN, Farmer, Sec. 11; P.O. Sycamore; born in Nottinghamshire, England, Sep. 21, 1825, lived there twenty-six years, came to this country in 1851, came to Kane Co. Ill. same year, lived there five years, came to Sycamore, this county in 1856, and has lived here twenty years, except three years in Kane Co. adjoining; Rep; U. Brethren; 132 acres of land, value $8,000; holds the office of School Director, and has been Road-master; married Miss Eliza Baker in 1848; she was from Harby, Nottinghamshire, England; has had seven children, has lost five—Charles E. Marshall, and Emma A. Marshall, living.

MARSH C. W. Manufacturer of Marsh Harvesters, etc; residence DeKalb; P.O. Sycamore; born in Ontario, March 22, 1834; came to county in the Fall of 1849; Rep; owns 206 acres of land; value of real estate $20,000; was a member of the Legislature in 1868-9, and of the Senate in 1870-1; wife was S. Frances Waite, born in Orange Co. N. Y; died May 16, 1869; married Jan. 1, 1860; has three children.

MARSH W. W. Manufacturer of Marsh Harvesters, etc: residence and P.O. Sycamore; born in Ontario, April 15, 1836; came to this county in the Fall of 1849; Rep; value of real estate $15,000; wife was Mary J. Brown, born in Chicago, Ill; married Jan. 5, 1871; has one child.

MARSH ORLANDO, Farmer, Sycamore; Rep; from Wisconsin.

MARSH WILLIAM, Farmer, Sycamore; Rep; from Mass.

MARSH DANIEL, Farmer, Sycamore; Rep; from N. Y.

MATSON OLE, Laborer, Sec. 18; P.O. Sycamore; Luth; from Sweden.

MALLERY J. T. Restaurant, Sycamore; Rep; from Vermont.

MANDLER GEO. Saloon, Sycamore; Dem; from Germany.

MAYO Z. B. Justice of the Peace, and Attorney, Sycamore; Dem; from Vermont.

MATTHEWS S. A. Carpenter, Sycamore; Rep; from N. Y.

MATHIS GREGORY, Wagon-maker, Sycamore; Dem; from France.

MAITLAND WALTER, Tenant Farmer, Sec. 21; P.O. Sycamore; Rep; Pres; Canada.

McCAFFRY MARTIN, Laborer, Sycamore; Dem; Ireland.

McDONOUGH WILLIAM, Teacher, Sycamore; Rep; Illinois.

McDONOUGH JOHN, Farmer, Sycamore; Rep; from Ireland.

McCARVILL PETER, Laborer, Sycamore; Dem; from Ireland.

McNAUGHTON WILLIAM, Stock Dealer, Sycamore; Rep; from N. Y.

McINTYRE R. C. works in Harvester Works, Sycamore; Rep; from N. Y.

McINTYRE NEWTON, works in Harvester Works, Sycamore; Rep; from N. Y.

McFADEN MARY A. Mrs. widow; from Ireland.

McCALPIN WILLIAM, Carpenter, Sycamore; Rep; Illinois.
McVELEY RICHARD, Laborer, Sycamore; Dem; from Ireland.
McMILLAN C. W. works in Harvester Works, Sycamore; Rep; Illinois.
McCARTHY J. H. Restaurant and Grocery, Sycamore; Ind; from Newfoundland.
MEAD E. D. Carpenter, Sycamore; Rep; from N. Y.
MEAD E. B. Painter, Sycamore; Rep; from Illinois.
MEAD B. C. Horse Dealer, Sycamore; Rep; from N. Y.
MEYER LOUIS, Cabinet-maker, Sycamore; Rep; from Germany.
MENTER R. Farmer, Sec. 29; P.O. Sycamore; Dem; Lib.   •
MILEY MARGARET Mrs. widow; from Ireland.
MITCHELL RICHARD, employee Harvester Works, Sycamore; Rep; from Ill.
MITCHELL RICHARD, employee Harvester Works, Sycamore; Rep; Scotland.
MITCHELL ANDREW, Building Mover, Sycamore; Rep; from Scotland.
MILLER ANDREW, Mason, Sycamore; Rep; from Denmark.
MIDDLETON S. B. Tailor, Sycamore; Dem; from N. J.
MILLEDGE MAHLON, Building Mover, Sycamore; Rep; from Indiana.
MORRISON JOSEPH, Farmer, Sec. 28; P.O. Sycamore; born in Co. of North-
    umberland, Canada, Jan. 23, 1844; lived there twenty-four years; came to U. S. in 1868;
    came to Sycamore, DeKalb Co. the same year, and has lived here eight years; owns 100
    acres, value $5,500; personal prop. $500; married Miss Mary E. McCarthy, April 7, 1869;
    she was from Co. Northumberland, Canada; has three children, all girls; Rep; Meth.
MORGAN WILLIAM A. Carpenter, Sycamore; Rep; from Conn.
MORE J. H. Rev. Pastor M. E. Church, Sycamore; Rep; from N.Y.
MORRIS GEORGE B. Clerk Brown & Son, Sycamore; Dem; from N.Y.
MOSES JACOB, Farmer, Sycamore; Rep; from Penn.
MOYER R. B. Clerk S. & C. R. R. Depot; Rep; from N.Y.
MOE EMOND, Shoemaker, Sycamore; Ind; from Norway.
MONROE CHARLES, Painter, Sycamore; Rep; from Illinois.   •
MONCKTON GEORGE, Shoemaker, Sycamore; Dem; from Ireland.
MONCKTON GEORGE J. Painter, Sycamore; Dem; from Illinois.
MOORE ANN Mrs. widow; from N.Y.
MOSHER C. W. Clerk Marsh Harvester Co. Sycamore; Rep; from Illinois.
MURPHY JERRY, Laborer, Sycamore; Dem; from Ireland.
MURPHY ANN Mrs. widow; from Ireland.
MUNSON JOHN, Farmer, Sec. 17; P.O. Sycamore; val. prop. $500; Rep; Luth; Sweden.

NELSON CHAS. works for Alden, Sec. 34; P.O. Sycamore; Rep; Luth; Sweden.
    NELSON PERRY, Laborer, Sycamore; Rep; Sweden.
NELSON BENJ. Clerk H. H. Rowe & Co. Sycamore; Rep; from Sweden.
NELSON N. Farmer, Sec. 7; P.O. Sycamore; val. prop. $1,200; Rep; Luth; Sweden.
NELSON BENJ. Laborer. Sycamore; Rep; from Sweden.
NICHOLS IRA, Farmer, Sycamore; Rep; from N.Y.
NEPHEW BARTA, Laborer, Sycamore; Rep; from Illinois.
NEPHEW ELI, Laborer, Sycamore; Rep; from N.Y.
NORRIS WHEELER, Clerk, Sycamore; Rep; from N.Y.
NORDEN JOHN, works for Lovell, Sec. 25; P.O. Sycamore; Rep, Luth; Sweden.
NESBITT GEORGE W. Physician and Surgeon, residence and P.O. Sycamore; born
    in Attica, Wyoming Co. N.Y.; came to Co. in 1866; wife was Mary H. Davis, born in Chip-
    pawa C. W.; married June 23, 1864; has three children; Rep; Prot.
NICHOLS JOSEPH, Carpenter, Sycamore; Rep; from Illinois.
NICHOLS E. B. Farmer, Sycamore; Rep; from N.Y.
NICHOLS JOHN W. Carpenter, Sycamore; Dem; from Illinois.
NICHOLS JANE Mrs. widow, Sycamore; from N.Y.
NICOLS JOSEPH, Cooper. Sycamore; Rep; from Illinois.
NICHOLS OREN B. Printer Arnold Brothers, Sycamore; Rep; Illinois.

OSTRANDER HIRAM, Farmer, tenant of Hewes, Sec. 33; P.O. Sycamore; Rep; Bapt.

OTT JACOB, Foreman Molding Room Ellwood's Factory; Ind; Germany.

O'CONNOR JOHN, works for Lovell, Sec. 25; P.O. Sycamore; Dem; Cath.

OHLEMACHER CHRIST, Tinner, Sycamore; Dem; from Ohio.

OLIN HENRY, Retired, Sycamore; Rep; from N.Y.

O'BRIEN THOS. Laborer, Sycamore; Dem; from Ireland.

OWEN W. W. Clerk J. E. Ellwood & Bro. Sycamore; Rep; from N.Y.

ORFLO CHARLEY, Engineer Planing Mill, Sycamore; Dem; from Germany.

ORTON MILTON, Building Mover, Sycamore; Dem; from N.Y.

OAKLEY I. W. Express Agent, Sycamore; Rep; from Illinois.

O'DONNELL CHAS. Prop. Marble Works, Sycamore; Ind; from Ireland.

O'DONNELL JAMES I. Employee O'Donnell & Sheffield, Sycamore; Ind; from N. Y.

OLESON JOHN P. lives with M. S. Timmerman, Sec. 17; P.O. Sycamore; Rep; Luth; Sweden.

OLESON H. Farmer, Sec. 18; P.O. Sycamore; Rep; Luth; val. prop. $500; born Sweden.

OSBORN JAS. H. works for L. D. Evans; Lib; Christian.

PARKE L. Z. lives with son, Sec. 8; P.O. Sycamore; Rep; Spiritualist; Conn.

PABST MARIA Mrs. widow, owner of Pabst House, Sycamore; from Germany.

PARKE ALMON F. Farmer, Sec. 8; Sycamore; born in Town of Evans, Erie Co. N. Y. Jan. 25, 1837; lived there 18 years, went to DeKalb, DeKalb Co. Ill. in 1855, lived there 18 years, then came to Town Sycamore and has lived here since; Rep; Univ; owns 180 acres land, val. $9,000; has been Path-master in his district; was in the army, went as Second Lieutenant in 105th Reg. Ill. Volunteers, under Gen. Sherman, and was with him, then served as First Lieutenant and promoted to Captaincy, and commanded the company; married Ruth Hall, Sept. 1, 1870, she was born in this state; daughter of Ephraim Hall; has two children, boys.

PABST FRANK, Clerk Pabst House, Sycamore; Dem; from Ill.

PARKINSON WILLIAM, Farmer, Sycamore; Ind; from England.

PARKER J. E. Merchant, Sycamore; Dem; from Indiana.

PAPILINE H. Employee Harvester Works, Sycamore; Rep; from Sweden.

PAGE JUSTIN, Blacksmith, Sycamore; Rep.

PAGE BENJ. Retired Farmer, Sycamore; Rep; from Rhode Island.

PAINE W. BURT. Dealer in Butter, Poultry, Eggs, Wool, etc; res. and P.O. Sycamore; born in Orleans, Jefferson Co. N. Y. Aug. 29, 1847; Rep; wife was Sadie E. Ellwood, born in Herkimer Co. N. Y.; married Oct. 1, 1873; one child.

PAINE H. retired, Sycamore; Rep; from N. Y.

PAINE ELIZA Mrs. widow; from N. Y.

PERSONS EDWARD S. Farmer, Sec. 21; Sycamore; born Ontario Co. N. Y. Jan. 14, 1836; lived there 21 years; came to Moline and Rock Island, Ill. 1857; lived there one year; lived in Henry Co. 8 years, came to this county in 1866, has lived here 10 years; Rep; Meth; owns 136 acres land, val. $7,000; personal prop. $1,000; was in the army three years, was First Sergeant 112th Reg. Ill. Volunteers, 23d Army Corps, Western Army, was wounded in battle at Eutaw Creek, Georgia; holds office of School Director; married Charlotte Westlake in 1865, she was from Orange Co. N. Y.; has one daughter living and lost one.

PETERS W. F. Clerk Walter Watterman, Sycamore; Rep; from Ill.

PETERS GUSTAV, Sycamore; Rep; from Sweden.

PETERSON JOHN, Laborer, Sycamore; Rep; from Sweden.

PETERSON CHARLEY, Laborer, Sycamore; Rep; from Sweden.

PETERSON CHARLES, Employee Central Mills, Sycamore; Rep; from Sweden.

PETERSON A. Laborer, Sycamore; Rep; from Sweden.

PETERSON FRANK, Laborer, Sycamore; Rep; from Sweden.

PETERSON O. H. Printer, Sycamore; Rep; from Sweden.

PETERSON CHAS. Miller Citizens Mill, Sycamore; Rep; from Sweden.

PETERSON N. Farmer, Sec. 17; P.O. Sycamore; Rep; Luth; val. prop. $2,000; Sweden.

PETERSON GUST. Laborer, Sycamore; Rep; from Sweden.

PETERSON JOHN, Blacksmith, Sycamore; Rep; from Sweden.

PEIL ISAAC, Tenant Farmer, Sec. 2; P.O. Sycamore; Rep; Epis; England.

11

PEELE HOLGAN, Laborer, Sycamore; Rep; from Sweden.

PEELE E. A. Laborer, Sycamore; Rep; from Sweden.

PERRY ENOS J. Dentist; res. and P.O. Sycamore; born in Chester Co. Penn. Oct. 24, 1849; came to state 1871, and to county 1873; Dem; Cong; wife was Sarah E. Gerrish, born in Whiteside Co. Ill; married April 25, 1876.

PERRY ZACH. works for King, Sec. 3; P.O. Sycamore; Lib.

PETRIE SAMUEL, Brick-making Business, Sec. 29; Sycamore; born Van Buren, N. Y. June 16, 1848; lived there one and one-half years, came to Chicago in 1850, then to Charter Grove, Town of Sycamore; has lived in this county 26 years; Dem; Lib; val. prop. $2,500; has been in brick-making business 13 years, and makes from 400,000 to 600,000 yearly, and has a good and increasing business; married Mary Ann Van Dresser in 1865, she was from Lake Co. Ind. and brought up in this state; has six children, two boys and four girls; lost one little girl two years old.

PETRIE J. R. Well Digger and Borer, Sycamore; Dem; from N. Y.

PETRIE CHAS. Farmer, Sec. 19; P.O. Sycamore; Rep; Luth; val. prop. $1,500; Sweden.

PETRIE NOBLES, Teamster, Sycamore; Ind; from N. Y.

PERDUE JOHN, Molder, Sycamore; Dem; from N. J.

PERDUE THOS. Laborer, Sycamore; Dem; from Ireland.

PEAVY HORATIO, Teamster, Sycamore; Dem; from N. Y.

PECK E. A. Machinist, Sycamore; Rep; from Conn.

PEANTER M. Harness Maker, Sycamore; Dem; from Ill.

PERCY D. W. Farmer, Sec. 13; P.O. Sycamore; Rep; U. Breth; prop. $6,000; Canada.

PHELPS EDGAR M. Painter, Sycamore; Rep; from Ill.

PHELPS OSCAR, Painter, Sycamore; Dem; from Indiana.

PHELPS WILLIAM, Retired Carpenter, Sycamore; Ind; from N. Y.

PHELPS SAMUEL, Farmer, Sec. 23; P.O. Sycamore; Rep; Meth; prop. $2,000; N. Y.

PHELPS U. L. Brick Molder, Sycamore; Rep; from N. Y.

PHILLIPS P. F. Janitor, School-house, Sycamore; Rep; from N. Y.

PHERSON BENJ. tenant on Jas. S. Waterman's farm; P.O. Sycamore.

PIERCE RICHARD, Tenant Farmer, Sec. 5; P.O. Sycamore; Rep; Meth; Canada.

PLOPPER NANCY Mrs. widow, Sycamore; from N. Y.

POSTLE ISAAC, Teamster, Sycamore; Dem; from Ohio.

POWERS MARTIN, Farmer; Sycamore; Dem; from N. Y.

PRATT A. C. Mrs. Sec. 36; P.O. Sycamore; 50 acres, value $3,000; Meth; Penn.

PRATT JOHN L. Lawyer, Sycamore; Rep; from N. Y.

PRESTON GEORGE, Groceries and Provisions, Sycamore; Rep; from Conn.

PRESCOTT J. R. Painter, Sycamore; Rep; Illinois.

PITCHER R. L. Repair Shop, Sycamore; Rep; from Mass.

PITCHER CHAS. Cooper, Sycamore; Rep.

PITCHER PERRY P. Student, Sycamore; Rep; from Mass.

PIERCE DANIEL, Banker, Sycamore; Dem; from N. Y.

PIERCE RICHARD, Farmer, tenant of Holliday, Sec. 5; P.O. Sycamore; Rep; Meth; Canada.

PIKE S. O. Jr. Engineer Ellwood's Factory, Sycamore; Rep; Illinois.

PIKE S. O. Sen. Carriage Maker, Sycamore; Rep; from New Jersey.

PURCELL JAMES, Tenant; P.O. Sycamore; Cath; Lib.

PUTNAM VICTOR, Retired, Sycamore; Dem; from Vermont.

QUINN MIRANDA Mrs. widow; P.O. Sycamore; from Ireland.
    QUINN JAMES, Molder, Harvester Works, Sycamore; Dem; from Ireland.

QVARNSTRON CHAS. Laborer, Sycamore; Rep; from Sweden.

RASMUS PETER, works in Harvester Works, Sycamore; Rep; from Denmark.
    RATHBURN CHAS. J. Laborer, Sycamore; Dem; from N. Y.

REESE ADAM, Retired Farmer, Sycamore; Rep; from N. Y.

REYNOLDS W. S. Music Dealer, Sycamore; Rep; Illinois.

REYNOLDS WARD, Music Dealer, Sycamore; Rep; Illinois.

READ GEORGE HENRY, Farmer, Sec. 34; P.O. Sycamore; Manufacturer of Dutton's Cement Air-tight Burial Vaults, for DeKalb Co; born in the Province of New Brunswick, April 12, 1826; lived there about twelve years, came to this country, to Town of Virgil, Kane Co. Ill. in 1838, lived in Kane Co. thirty-six years, came to the City of Sycamore in 1874; Rep; Bapt; owns 1,000 acres of land elsewhere, valued at $15,000; owns 20 acres of land here, value $3,000; was School Director and Road-master in Kane Co. a number of years; married Miss Adeline M. Worcester, in 1856; she was from West Windsor, Vermont.

REYNOLDS JAMES S. Dealer in Coal and Stone; residence and P.O. Sycamore; born in Chenango Co. N. Y. March 27, 1826; came to county Sept. 1865; Rep; Protestant; value of real estate $2,000; has held the office of Sheriff; was Lieut. Co. H, 10th N. Y. Cavalry; wife was J. Matilda Jones, born in Cameron, Steuben Co. N. Y; has one child.

RELYEA M. Produce Dealer, Sycamore; Rep; from N. Y.

REDMOND MIKE, Tenant Farmer, Sec. 28; P.O. Sycamore; Dem; Cath; Ireland.

REDMOND JULIUS, Carpenter, Sycamore; Dem; from N. Y.

RILEY PETER, Laborer, Sycamore; Dem; Ireland.

RICHARDS NATHANIEL, Blacksmith, Sycamore; Rep; from N. Y.

RICHARDSON WILLETT, Tenant Farmer, Sec. 3; P.O. Sycamore; Rep; Meth; Illinois.

ROBINSON E. A. Laborer, Sycamore; Rep; from N. Y.

ROBINSON F. M. Clerk for Lindsay & Preston, Sycamore; Rep; from N. Y.

ROBINSON E. W. Clerk for A. Friedman, Sycamore; Rep; from N. Y.

ROBINSON W. H. Lightning Rod Agent, Sycamore; Rep; from Canada.

ROBINSON SAMUEL, Retired Farmer, Sycamore; Rep; from Canada.

ROBINSON GEO. S. Attorney, Sycamore; Rep; from Vermont.

ROBINSON F. T. Saloon, Sycamore; Dem; from N. Y.

ROWE H. H. Groceries, Boots, Shoes, and Notions; born in Windsor, Vt. March 28, 1817; came to county in July, 1846; Rep; Methodist Episcopal; value of real estate $8,000; wife was Caroline Harrington, born in Dudley, Mass. June 29, 1816; married March 20, 1863; has had nine children, only three living.

ROWE M. W. Clerk, Sycamore; born in Waukesha Co. Wis; Rep; Bapt.

ROWE HENRY, Painter, Sycamore; Rep; from Vermont.

ROSE EDWIN, Coal Merchant, Sycamore; Rep; from N. Y.

ROSE ELLSWORTH Retired Physician, Sycamore; Rep; Cong.

ROSE O. D. Stock Dealer, Sycamore; Rep; Illinois.

ROSE N. P. Painter, Harvester Works, Sycamore; Rep; from Sweden.

ROSE MONTIE, Telegraph Operator, Sycamore; Rep; Illinois.

ROGERS L. Clerk Waterman & Hoyt, Sycamore; Rep; from N.Y.

ROGERS JAMES, Employee Harvester Works, Sycamore; Dem; from N.Y.

ROGERS J. H. Dry Goods, Carpets, Boots and Shoes, Sycamore; Dem; from N.Y.

ROGERS JAMES, Painter, Sycamore; Dem; from Ireland.

ROACH JOHN, Blacksmith, Sycamore; Dem; from N.Y.

RONAN PATRICK, Employee Harvester Works, Sycamore; Dem; from Ireland.

RONAN JOSEPH, Shoemaker, Sycamore; Dem; from Ireland.

ROCKWELL F. Laborer for Whipple, Sec. 4; P.O. Sycamore.

ROWELL WILLIAM, Farmer, tenant of C. Winans, Sec. 28; P.O. Sycamore; Rep; Meth; Vt.

ROWLEY F. L. Carpenter, Sycamore; Dem; from Ill.

ROWLEY J. W. Carpenter, Sycamore; Dem; from N.Y.

ROWLEY E. J. Carpenter, Sycamore; Dem; from Ill.

ROTHENGAST MICHAEL, Barber, Sycamore; Rep; from Germany.

ROBERTS LEANDER, Retired Farmer, Sycamore; Rep; from N.Y.

ROBERTS R. H. County Treasurer, Sycamore; Rep; from N.Y.

ROSE ELLSWORTH Dr. P.O. Sycamore; retired; Rep; Cong; born N. Y.

RUSSELL OSCAR, Painter, Sycamore; Rep; from Norway.

RUSSELL GEORGE, Laborer, Sycamore; Rep; from Ill.

RUSSELL T. D. Retired, Sycamore; Rep; from N.Y.

RUSSELL C. Carpenter, Sycamore; Dem; from Vt.

RUTLEDGE JOHN, Employee Harvester Works, Sycamore; Dem; from Ireland.

RYAN THOS. Laborer, Sycamore; Dem; from Canada.

RYAN JOHN, Painter, Sycamore; Dem; from Ill.

RYAN JOHN, Farmer; P.O. Sycamore; born Ireland; Dem; Cath; val. prop. $6,000.

RYAN JAMES, Laborer, Sycamore; Dem; from Ireland.

SANFORD W. B. Confectioner, Sycamore; Dem; from Ill.

SAWYER GEO. L. Tinner, Chatfield & Smith, Sycamore; Rep; from Iowa.

SAWYER L. H. Brakeman R. R. Sycamore; Rep; from N. H.

SAWYER A. W. (G. P. Wild & Co.) Merchant, Sycamore; Rep; from Mass.

SAWYER ALFRED, Mechanic, Sycamore; Rep; from Mass.

SANDERSON F. Tailor, Sycamore; Rep; from Mass.

SAMPLE THOMAS, Employee Harvester Works, Sycamore; Dem; from Penn.

SANDBERG F. Shoemaker, Sycamore; Rep; from Sweden.

SABIN CHARLEY, Farmer, Sycamore; Rep; from Vt.

SABIN ALBERT, Farmer, Sycamore; Rep; from Vt.

SABIN WILLIAM, Farmer, Sycamore; Rep; from Vt.

SABIN B. F. Farmer, Sycamore; Rep; from Vt.

SCHUNEMANN FREDRICK, Blacksmith; Sycamore; Rep; from Germany.

SCHUNEMANN FRED W. Barber, Sycamore; Dem; from Germany.

SCHOONOVER JOHN, Painter, Sycamore; Dem; from Penn.

SCHMIDT JOHN, Laborer, Sycamore; Dem; from Germany.

SEBERG C. A. Laborer, Sycamore; Rep; from Sweden.

SELL ANDREW, Butcher, Sycamore; Dem; from Germany.

SEAMAN W. H. Farmer, tenant of Driver, Sec. 9; P.O. Sycamore; Rep; Bapt.

SINGER JACOB, Laborer, Sycamore; Dem; from Penn.

SINGER JEREMIAH, Bricklayer, Sycamore; Dem; from Penn.

SIVWRIGHT CAMPBELL, Employee Harvester Works, Sycamore; Rep; from Nova Scotia.

SIVWRIGHT G. M. Conductor S. & C. R. R. Sycamore; Rep; from Nova Scotia.

SIVWRIGHT W. E. Laborer, Sycamore; Rep; from Nova Scotia.

SILBURN WILLIAM, Farmer, Sec. 26; P.O. Sycamore; born Cambridgeshire, England, March 8, 1818, lived there thirty-two years, came to this country in 1850, and has lived here twenty-six years; Rep; Lib; owns 80 acres of land, value $5,000; has been Path-master; married Jeannette Thompson in 1849; she was from same town in England; has eight children and has lost three.

SILBURN SAMUEL, lives with father, Sec. 26; P.O. Sycamore; Rep; Lib.

SIXBURY CHAUNCEY E. Farmer, Sec. 15; P.O. Sycamore; father owns farm; born in town of Sycamore, on farm now owned by H. H. Mason, May 30, 1838; lived there about fourteen years, lived on David West's place seventeen years; was the second child born in the town of Sycamore; value personal property $1,000; served three years in the army, in 105th Ill. Vols. Co. A, 20th Army Corps, Army of the Tennessee, under Gen. Hooker; regiment was in thirty engagements; was honorably discharged; received honorable promotion to Second Lieutenant from Gov. Oglesby after returning home in 1865; married Jane Ainley April 11, 1866; she was from Canada; has four children, one boy and three girls; Rep; Meth.

SIGLIN JACOB, Farmer, Sec. 15; P.O. Sycamore; born in Chestnut Hill Township, North Hampton Co. Penn. July 19, 1810; lived there forty-three years; came to this town, county and state in 1853, and has lived here twenty-three years; is one of the oldest settlers; owns 213 acres, value $10,650; has held the offices of School Director and Road-master; married Hannah Jane Setzer in 1833; she was from North Hampton Co. Penn.; they have ten children, all living; has two sons in Oregon, one a lawyer and one keeps a large hotel, and is Postmaster; has one son and one daughter in Iowa; the other children are all well situated in this state and county; the youngest daughter, Helen, lives at home; Rep; Meth.

SHEFNEER CHARLES A. Teamster, Sycamore; Rep; from Illinois.

SHEFNEER LOUIS, Stock Buyer, Sycamore; Rep; from Ohio.

SHEFNEER LOUIS, Stock Trader, Sycamore; Rep; from Ohio.

SHEFNEER ALBERT, Stock Trader, Sycamore; Rep; from Illinois.

SHEFFIELD L. M. Retired, Sycamore; Rep; from Ohio.

SHEFFIELD H. A. Prop. Marble Works, Sycamore; Rep; from Ohio.

SHEFFIELD A. A. employee O'Donnell & Sheffield, Sycamore; Ind; from Ohio.

SHROEDER WM. Sash, Door, Blinds and Planing Mill; residence and P.O. Sycamore; born in Germany, March 18, 1847; came to state in 1854, to county in 1875; value real estate $5,000; wife was Annie Pabst, born in Kane Co. Ill; married Feb. 24, 1876; Rep; Prot.

SHULD JOHN, Blacksmith, Sycamore; Rep; from Germany.

SHEW JACOB, Laborer for Van Galder, Sec. 29; P.O. Sycamore; Rep; Lib.

SHIELDS W. H. Carpenter Harvester Works, Sycamore; Rep; from N.Y.

SHIRTLIFF WILLARD, Butter and Eggs Dealer, Sycamore; Rep; from Canada.

SHURTLEFF E. B. Lumber Dealer, Harrington & Co. Sycamore; Rep; from Mass.

SHIPPEE E. C. Dealer in Grain, Coal, and Live Stock; residence and P.O. Sycamore; born in Franklin Co. Mass. Jan. 24, 1835; came to Co. in 1854; value real estate $3,000; wife was Louisa L. Rose, born in Evans, Erie Co. N.Y.; married Sept. 15, 1855; had three children, only one living, Rep; Meth.

SKELLY WILLIAM, Painter, Sycamore; Rep; from Illinois.

SKELLY JAMES L. Painter, Sycamore; Rep; from Illinois.

SLATER JNO. Laborer, Sycamore; Dem; from Germany.

SMITH SPAFFORD, Farmer; residence and P.O. Sycamore; born in Windsor, Windsor Co. Vermont, May 18, 1809, came to Co. Sept. 20, 1839; owns 300 acres, value $20,000; has held the office of Assessor; wife was Eliza Sholes, born in Claremont, Sullivan Co. N. H.; married June 9, 1834; three children, two living; Rep; Bapt.

SMITH FRANK H. residence and P.O. Sycamore; born in Lower Canada, Jan. 1, 1838; came to state in 1844, and county in 1866; has held the offices of Alderman and Collector; wife was Annie L. Baker, born in Chautauqua Co. N.Y.; married Sept. 20, 1861; has had three children, two living; Dem; Epis.

SMITH WILLIAM, Laborer, Sycamore; Ind; from England.

SMITH CHAUNCEY, Laborer, Sycamore; Rep; from N.Y.

SMITH H. E. Printer DeKalb Co. *Democrat*, Sycamore; Dem; from Vermont.

SMITH J. G. Butcher, Sycamore; Rep; from Canada.

SMITH JOHN, Carpenter, Sycamore; Dem; from New Jersey.

SMITH A. Mrs. widow, Sycamore; from N.Y.

SMITH REUBEN A. Lightning Rod Peddler, Sycamore; Dem; from N.Y.

SMITH FRANK, Central Restaurant, Sycamore; Dem; from Canada.

SMITH JNO. G. Jr. Prop. Central Billiard Parlor, Sycamore; born in Clarenceville, Province Quebec, June 7, 1854; came to county in 1874; Rep; Prot.

SMITH M. M. Central Billiard Parlors, Sycamore; Rep; from Canada.

SMITH JAMES M. Saw Mill, Princeton, Ill.; lives in Sycamore; Rep; from N. H.

SMITH CHARLES, Hardware, etc. Sycamore; Rep; from N.Y.

SMITH SPAFFORD, Retired farmer, Sycamore; Rep; from Vermont.

SMITH F. P. employee Marsh Harvester Co. Sycamore; Rep; from Illinois.

SMITH WM. H. Farmer, Sec. 1, father's farm; P.O. Sycamore; Rep; Luth; Illinois.

SMIDT CHARLES, Plow Maker, Sycamore; Rep; from France.

SNOW BENJ. Laborer, Sycamore; Rep; from Vermont.

SNELL JAMES, Farmer, Sycamore; Rep; from Vermont.

SNELL SAMUEL, Farmer, Sycamore; Rep; from Vermont.

SOUTHWORTH J. E. Bazaar and Jewelry store; residence Sycamore; born in Windham, Portage Co. Ohio, July 18, 1831; came to Co. in 1848; value real estate $3,600; wife was Mary L. Warren, born in Allegany Co. N.Y.; married May 4, 1865; Rep; Cong.

SPENCER E. C. Clerk Finley & Churchill, Sycamore; Rep; from Vermont.

SPIER FREDERICK, Carpenter, Sycamore; Ind; from England.

SPRING H. A. Painter, Sycamore; Ind; from Illinois.

STARK MARSHAL, Farmer and Lumber Dealer; residence Sec. 21, Tp. 41, R. 5; P O. Sycamore; born in Luzerne Co. Penn. August 12, 1813; came to Co. Sept. 14, 1835; owns 778 acres land, value $40,000; has held the offices of County Assessor, School Commissioner, Sheriff, and Collector *ex-officio;* wife was Louisa Tyler, born in Susquehanna Co. Penn; married Oct. 5, 1840; has ten children; Rep; Meth.

STARK THERON, Farmer; residence and P.O. Sycamore; born Sycamore, DeKalb Co; Rep.

STARK JEFFERSON, Stock Dealer; residence and P.O. Sycamore; born in Sycamore, DeKalb Co. Ill. April 4, 1847; value real estate $2,800; was private in Co. F, 147th Regt. I. V. I.; wife was Lydia Carver, born in Wyoming Co. Penn; married Nov. 13, 1875; Rep.

STARK HENRY J. Stock Dealer, residence and P.O. Sycamore; Rep; from Illinois.

STARK ARTHUR M. Secretary of Marsh Harvester Co; res. and P.O. Sycamore; born in London, England, January 31, 1849; came to county Dec. 1870; Rep; Epis; val. real estate $3,500; wife was Ellen Holcomb, born in Sycamore, DeKalb Co. Ill; married May 20, 1873; one child.

STORY AMOS, Farmer, Sec. 9; P.O Sycamore; born Washington Co. Vt. Dec. 8, 1813; lived there about 22 years, lived in New York one winter, came to Ottawa, Ill. 1836, came to DeKalb Co. 1838, and has lived here 38 years, and 40 years in the state; only three or four houses here when he came, one of the earliest settlers; Rep; Univ; owns 200 acres land, val. $12,000; held office of Deputy Sheriff six years, and was Acting Sheriff some years; has held office of County Tax Collector, when the taxes of the whole county did not exceed $1,000; married Abby J. Hunt, 1859; she was from N. Y; has five children; she had six children.

STROBERG AUGUST, Laborer, Sycamore; Rep; from Sweden.

STUART C. T. Meat Market, Sycamore; Dem; from Mass.

STEWART CHARLES T. Butcher, Sycamore; Dem; from Mass.

STEVENS HORACE M. Farmer, Sec. 31; P.O. Sycamore; Rep; Univ; prop. $30,000; Vt.

STEVENS FRANK E. Deputy County Clerk and Recorder, Sycamore; Rep; from Ill.

STONE A. P. Butter and Eggs Dealer, Sycamore; Rep; from Vt.

STONE H. F. Employee Harvester Works, Sycamore; Rep; from Wis.

STOWE CYRUS, Tenant Farmer, Sec. 36; P.O. Sycamore; Rep; Meth; Ill.

STOCKWELL JOHN, Laborer, Sycamore; Dem; from N. Y.

STODDARD W. E. Carpenter, Sycamore; Rep; from N. Y.

STUTENROTH EDWARD, Shoemaker; Ind; from Penn.

STRINGFELLOW BENJ. Teamster, Sec. 29; Dem; Lib; prop. $500; born Penn.

STOKES WILLIAM H. Molder Harvester Works, Sycamore; Dem; from Ill.

STEPHENSON CHAS. Laborer, Sycamore; Rep; from Sweden.

STEPHENSON PETER, Tanner, Sycamore; Rep; from Canada.

STRIBERT M. Employee Harvester Works, Sycamore; Rep; from Sweden.

STOLE AUGUST, Operator Hay Press, Sycamore; Rep; from Sweden.

STANFORD CHARLES, Expressman Harvester Co. Sycamore; Rep; from Ill.

STAUGAURD HANS, Pattern Maker, Sycamore; Rep; from Denmark.

SUMNERSON A. P. Shoemaker, Sec. 7; P.O. Sycamore; Rep; Luth; born Sweden.

SULLIVAN PATRICK, Gardener, Sycamore; Dem; from Ireland.

SULLIVAN JERRY, Laborer, Sycamore; Dem; from Ireland.

SULLIVAN JOHN, Laborer, Sycamore; Dem; from Ireland.

SULLIVAN WILLIAM, Employee Ellwood's Factory, Sycamore; Rep; from Canada.

SULLIVAN EDMOND, Engineer Citizen's Mills, Sycamore; Dem; from Ireland.

SWANSON JOHN, Laborer, Sycamore; Rep; from Sweden.

SWANSON JOHN, Laborer, Sec. 8; P.O. Sycamore; Rep; Luth.

SWANSON JOHN, works for Garbert, Sec. 35; P.O. Sycamore; Rep; Luth; Sweden.

SWANSON A. Laborer, Sycamore; Rep; from Sweden.

SWANSON JOHN. Farmer,P.O. Sycamore; Rep; Luth; prop. $1,500; born Sweden.

SWANSON CHAS. Farmer, Sec. 19; P.O. Sycamore; Rep; Luth; prop. $500; born Sweden.

SWINSON CHAS. works for Varty, Sec. 25; P.O. Sycamore; Rep; Lib; Sweden.

SWAN PETER, Employee Ellwood's Factory, Sycamore; Rep; from Sweden.

SWETLAND WILLIAM E., V.D. Farmer, Sec. 35; P.O. Sycamore; born Delaware Co. Ohio, Feb. 19, 1825; lived there about seven years, lived in Wyoming, Luzerne Co. Penn. lived there about 19 years, came to this state in 1851, lived here 6 years, lived in State of Wisconsin about 19 years; practiced his profession in Wisconsin and Iowa for a number of years; Dem; Lib; val. personal prop. $500; married Mary Jones in 1852, she was born in Penn; has two children, one boy and one girl.

SWETLAND HENRY J. lives with father, Sec. 35; P.O. Sycamore; Dem; Lib; Ill.

SWEBERG A. Laborer, Sec. 18; P.O. Sycamore; Rep; Luth; Sweden.

SWIGARD H. P. Mrs. widow; P.O. Sycamore; from Ohio.

SYME DAVID A. Grain Dealer; res. and P.O. Sycamore; born in Ballymena, Antrim Co. Ireland, Sept. 15, 1841; came to county March, 1868; Rep; Cong; wife was M. E. Morton, born in Montreal, Canada; married Feb. 3, 1873.

SYME JOHN, Agl. Implement Dealer; res. and P.O. Sycamore; born in Musselborough, Scotland; came to county August, 1863; Rep; Pres; val. of real estate $4,000; has held the office of Alderman and Trustee; is Captain Co. A, 3d Batt. Ill. State Guards.

TAYLOR B. F. Harness Maker A. Colton & Son, Sycamore; Rep; from Penn.

TAYLOR S. P. Laborer, Sycamore; Dem; from N. Y.

TAYLOR GEORGE W. Photographer; res. and P.O. Sycamore; born in Hunterdon Co. N. J. Nov. 2, 1845; came to state in 1858, and county 1868; Independent in politics and religion; val. of prop. $1,500; wife was Flora H. Griswold, born in DuPage Co. Ill. and married May 9, 1871; two children.

TAYLOR RICHARD, Laborer, Sec. 29; P.O. Sycamore; Lib; Lib.

TAYLOR LOUIS Mrs. widow; P.O. Sycamore; from N..Y.

TAYLOR WILLIAM Jr. Painter; P.O. Sycamore; Rep; from Ill.

TAYLOR JOHN, Tenant Farmer, Sec. 16; P.O. Sycamore; Dem; Ireland.

TEWKSBURY R. B. Carpenter, Sycamore; Dem; from Penn.

TEUWKSBURY CHARLES, Carpenter, Sycamore; Dem; from Ill.

TEPSEN A. C. Mrs. widow, from Germany.

TENNEY JOHN C. Farmer, Sec. 34; P.O. Sycamore; Rep; United Brethren; N. H.

THURSTON DANIEL, Farmer, Sec. 29, Sycamore; born Delaware Co. Ohio, May 25, 1817, lived there twenty-one years, went to Western Pennsylvania in 1838, and lived there twenty-five years, came to this county and state Oct. 1, 1863, and has lived here thirteen years; val. personal property $1,000; married Mary Ann McCurdy in 1840; she was from Beaver Co. Penn; has four children living, lost four.

THURSTON JAMES, Teamster, Sycamore; Rep; from Ohio.

THURSTON JOHN, Brickmolder, Sycamore; Rep; from Mass.

THOMPSON THOS. Farmer; P.O. Sycamore; Rep; United Brethren; England.

THOMPSON EDWIN A. Farmer, Sec. 1; P.O. Sycamore; born in Norway, Dec. 12, 1833, lived there about twenty years, came to this country 1854, came to Walworth Co. Wis. same year, came to this county and lived in Town Mayfield four, years, lived in Wis. two years, came to this town and county and has lived here since; Rep; Luth; owns 108 acres land, $4,320; was in the army three years in Co. C, 105th Reg. Ill. Vol. 20th Army Corps, was with Gen. Sherman's march to the sea, was in several hard battles; married Esther Merrill, Sept. 23, 1858; she was from N.Y.; has one child, boy; has lost one boy and one girl.

THOMPSON A. J. Dentist; res. and P.O. Sycamore; born in Oneida Co. N.Y. April 24, 1848; came to state 1856 and county 1875; Dem; Epis; wife was Elsie M. Hunter, born in Delaware Co. N.Y.; married March 25, 1875; one child.

TIMMERMAN MARVIN S. Farmer, Sec. 17; P.O. Sycamore; born in Mindon, Montgomery Co. N.Y. June 6, 1841, lived there twenty.four years, then came to this town, county and state in 1866, and has lived here ten years; Rep; Univ; owns 310 acres land, value $18,000; is School Director in his District; married Miss Ione L. Bowen, Sept. 6, 1865; she was from Newport, Herkimer Co. N.Y. and was born Aug. 6, 1843; has two children—one boy and one girl; have lost one little girl.

TIFFT WILLIAM R. Carpenter and Builder, Sycamore; Rep; from Vt.

TIFFT E. D. Carpenter and Builder, Sycamore; Rep; from Ill.

TIFFT ELON, Carpenter, Sycamore; Rep; from Ill.

TOLL W. E. Rev. Pastor Epis. Church, Sycamore; Rep; from England.

TOMLINSON GEORGE, works for Dr. G. W. Nesbitt, Sycamore; Rep; from Conn.

TRAFFORD WILLIAM, Basketmaker, Sycamore; Rep; from England.

TRAFFORD JOHN, Machinist, Sycamore; Rep; from England.

TRACY THOMAS, Laborer, Sycamore; Dem; from N.Y.

TURK FRANK, Mason, Sycamore; Ind; from France.

TURPIN JOHN, Painter, Sycamore; Dem; from England.

TUCKER JOHN, Engineer S. & C. R. R. Sycamore; Rep; from Maine.

TUDOR JOHN F. lives with Aldan, Sec. 31; born England; Rep; Lib.

TYNDALL JESSE, Retired, Sycamore; Rep; from New Jersey.

TYSON LAWRENCE, Laborer on Sec. 21; P.O. Sycamore; Denmark; Luth.

ULLRICH AUGUST, Laborer, Sycamore; Dem; from Germany.

UNDERDOWN WILLIAM, works at Harvester Works, Sycamore; Rep; England.

UNDERDOWN EDWARD, Laborer, Sycamore; Rep; from England.

URIS FRANK, Tailor, Louis Conant's, Sycamore; Dem; from Germany.

UTTER HENRY, Teamster, Sycamore; Dem; from N.Y.

VANALSTON THOMAS, Butcher, Sycamore; Dem; from N.Y.

VAN DUNSEN ABRAM, Teamster, Sycamore; Dem; from Ill.

VAN DUSEN SIMEON, Farmer, Sec. 21; P.O. Sycamore; born in Lake Co. Ohio, April 11, 1832, lived there six years, lived in Crawford Co. about seven years, came to this state and county in 1844, and has lived here thirty-two years; one of the oldest settlers; only one house between Sycamore and Marengo when he came; only few log houses in Sycamore; has been School Director and Path-master; owns 151 acres of land, value $9,000; Rep; Meth. pref; married Miss Maria Jane Sibley, March 19, 1858; she was from New York state; has three children—two boys and one girl; lost one boy.

VAN DUZEN GILBERT, Teamster, Sec. 29; P.O. Sycamore; born Ohio; Dem; U. Brethren.

VAN DUSEN S. Farmer, Sec. 21; P.O. Sycamore; Rep; Lib. Meth; Ohio.

VARTY ISABELL Mrs. Sec. 25; P.O. Sycamore, born Westmoreland, England, Nov. 4, 1819, lived there about thirty-two years, lived in Cumberland about four years, came to U. S. in 1855, came to Town Sycamore, DeKalb Co. same year, and has lived here twenty-one years; United Brethren; 134 acres land, val. $5,500; married Thomas Varty in October, 1854; he was from Westmoreland, England; he died Oct. 20, 1871; has three children—two daughters, Maggie and Mary, and one son, Albert, now living.

VARTY ROBERT, Farmer, Sec. 25; P.O. Sycamore; Rep; Meth; $10,000; England.

VARTY MARGARET, Farmer, Sec. 25; P.O. Sycamore; United Brethren; $2,000; England.

VANGALDER TRUMAN W. Brickmaking Business, Sec. 29; Sycamore; born in Niagara Co. N.Y. July 3, 1822, lived there nine years, lived in Wyoming Co. seven years, came to Ohio in 1838, lived there one year, lived in Michigan one year, lived in Wisconsin twenty-four years, came to this state 1868, has lived here since; he makes from 700,000 to 800,000 brick yearly; has large business; Rep; Univ; value property $3,000; married Mary Phelps in 1843; she was from New York state; has eight children—four boys and four girls; lost one girl.

VANGALDER FRANK, Printer, Sycamore; Rep; from Wis.

VANGALDER WILLIAM, Teamster, Sycamore; Rep; from N.Y.

VANLONE HARRISON, Farmer, Sycamore; Rep.

WARREN M. F. Jeweler, Sycamore; Rep; from N.Y.

WAITE ETTA E. Mrs. Widow; P.O. Sycamore; from N. Y.

WARREN N. C. Dealer in Butter, Eggs and Poultry; res. and P.O. Sycamore; born in Herkimer Co. N.Y. June 9, 1835; came to county 1855; Rep; Epis; value of real estate $5.000; wife was Addie B. Brown, born in Herkimer Co. N.Y.; married May 8, 1862; one child.

WARREN GEO. O. Jeweler; res. and P.O. Sycamore; born in Allegany Co. N.Y. July 2, 1853, came to state 1864, to county 1872; Rep; Bapt; wife was Jennie C. Smith, born in Detroit, Mich.; married Jan. 13, 1874.

WAITE CAMPBELL W. Editor DeKalb Co. *Democrat;* residence and P.O. Sycamore; born in Cayuga Co. N. Y. July 12, 1832; came to state in 1840, to county in 1857; Democrat; Episcopalian; held the office of Secretary of State Senate in 1861; was Adjutant of 8th Ill. Vol. Cavalry.

WAITE ORLANDO, lives with brother, Sec. 34; P.O. Sycamore; Rep; Epis.

WAITE DANIEL, Farmer, lives with son, Sec. 34; P.O. Sycamore; Rep; Epis; Vermont.

WAITE EDWIN, Farmer, Sec. 34; P.O. Sycamore; property $4,000; Rep; Epis.

WAITE JOHN E. Farmer, Sec. 34; P.O. Sycamore; property $4,000; Rep; Epis; Vermont.

WATERMAN JOHN C. General Merchandise; residence and P.O. Sycamore; born in Herkimer Co. N.Y. Sep. 9, 1814; came to state in 1838, to county in 1839; Rep; Cong; value of real estate $10,000; has held the offices of Postmaster and Township Trustee; wife was Caroline Rogers, born in Auburn, N.Y.

WATERMAN JAMES S. Banker and Real Estate; residence and P.O. Sycamore; from Herkimer Co. N. Y. May 29, 1826; came to state in 1838, to county in 1839; Dem; Epis; 4,000 acres of land; value of real estate $175,000; wife was Abbie L. S. Cushman, born in Otsego Co. N. Y; married Jan. 30, 1853.

WATERMAN ELIZA Mrs. widow; P.O. Sycamore; from N. Y.

WATERMAN A. H. Clerk for Waterman & Hoyt, Sycamore; Rep; Illinois.

WATERMAN H. Farmer and Gunsmith, Sycamore; Dem; from N. Y.
WATERMAN JOHN, Broker, Sycamore; Dem; from Rhode Island.
WATERMAN JNO. Laborer, Sec. 3; P.O. Sycamore; Rep; Univ.
WATTERMAN WALTER, Grocery, Sycamore; Dem; Illinois.
WATERMAN LYMAN Mrs. widow; P.O. Sycamore; from N. Y.
WATERMAN JOSEPH, Stock Dealer, Sycamore; Rep; from N. Y.
WATERMAN WM. L. Farmer, Sec. 4; P.O. Sycamore; Ind; Meth; property $5,000; N. Y.
WATERMAN CLARENCE, Machinist, Sycamore; Ind; Illinois.
WALROD ERASMUS D. Farmer; residence and P.O. Sycamore; born in Montgomery Co. N. Y. June 13, 1816; came to county in June, 1835; Rep; owns 160 acres of land; value of real estate $16,000; wife was Malintha Powel, born in Monroe Co. N. Y; married Aug. 1, 1839, at Union Grove, DeKalb Co; has had six children, only one now living.
WALROD JOSEPH, Carpenter, Sycamore; Rep; from N. Y.
WALROD WALTER D. Farmer; P.O. Sycamore, born in Sycamore, DeKalb Co; Rep; Meth.
WALLEN F. works in Harvester works, Sycamore; from Sweden.
WATKINS VOLNEY, Student, Sycamore; Rep; Illinois.
WATKINS H. Grafting Fruit Trees, Sycamore; Rep; from N. Y.
WATKINS H. B. Engrafter, Sycamore; Rep; from Ohio.
WATKINS WM. C. Pattern Maker, Harvester Works, Sycamore; Rep; from N. H.
WASHBURN C. C. Mrs. Dressmaker, Sycamore; from Mass.
WALKER GEORGE, Farmer, Sycamore; Ind; from Canada.
WALKER JOHN N. Retired Farmer, Sycamore; Ind; from Canada.
WATSON PIKE, Carpenter, Sycamore; Rep; from Vermont.
WALDRON G. M. works in Marsh Harvester Works, Sycamore; Rep; from Sweden.
WALDO EDWARD, Laborer, Sec. 29; P.O. Sycamore; Dem; Lib.
WALDO NEWTON, Laborer; P.O. Sycamore; Dem; Lib; N. Y.
WALLUM K. Painter, Sycamore; Rep; from Denmark.
WEBER PHILIP, Blacksmith, Sycamore; Dem; from Germany.
WEEDEN A. G. Mason, Sycamore; Rep; from Vermont.
WEEDEN S. Mrs. widow, Sycamore; from Vermont.
WELLS HALSEY, Farmer, Sec. 27; P.O. Sycamore; Rep; Bapt; property $3,000; R. I.
WELLS EDGAR A. lives with Geo. Wells, Sec. 35; P.O. Sycamore; Rep; Bapt; N. Y.
WELLS GEO. Farmer, Sec. 35; P.O. Sycamore; Rep; U. Brethren; N. Y.
WEEDEN LUCIAN, lives with G. W. Hinkle, Sec. 8, Sycamore; born in the Town of Quechee, Windsor Co. Vermont, Jan. 15, 1856, lived there five years, then came with uncle to Sycamore, DeKalb Co. Ill. in 1861, has lived here fifteen years; his father is living in Vermont, and his mother died when he was five years old; has one brother living in Vermont; Rep; Meth; value personal property, money at interest $125.
WELANDER JOHN, Farmer, Sec. 18; P.O. Sycamore; Rep; Luth; property $1,200; Sweden.
WELKER WM. works for Gault & Knapp, Sycamore; Dem; from Germany.
WELKER WM. Cabinet Maker, Sycamore; Ind; from Germany.
WELCH BARNEY, Laborer, Sycamore; Dem; from Ireland.
WELCH COLUMBUS, lives with Divine, Sec. 13; P.O. Sycamore; U. Brethren; Ill.
WELCH DAVID A. lives with father, Sec. 12; P.O. Sycamore; Rep; Meth; Virginia.
WELCH DAVID J. Printer, *DeKalb County Democrat*, Sycamore; Dem; from N.Y.
WELCH JAMES, Laborer, Sycamore; Dem; from Ireland.
WELCH LAWRENCE, retired, Sycamore; Dem; from Ireland.
WELCH MICHAEL, Grain Dealer, Sycamore; Dem; from N.Y.
WELSH PATRICK, Laborer, Sycamore; Dem; from Ireland.
WELSH JOHN, Laborer, Sycamore; Dem; from Ireland.
WELCH W. Tenant Farmer, Sec. 12; P.O. Sycamore; Rep; Meth; Va.
WESTLAKE DAVID B. Farmer, Sec. 13; P.O. Sycamore; Lib; U. Breth; $4,000; N. Y.
WESTLAKE JOHN O. Farmer, Sec. 15; P.O. Sycamore; Univ; prop. $3,500; N.Y.
WESTGARTH ROBERT, Tenant Farmer, Sec. 24; P.O. Sycamore; Dem; Lib; England.
WEST F. works for Lovell, Sec. 25; P.O. Sycamore; Rep; Lib.

WEST ELIAS C. Farmer, Sec. 34; P.O. Sycamore; born in Erie Co. N.Y. Nov. 25, 1839; lived there about 4 years, then came to Town of Sycamore in this county, Oct. 28, 1843, and has lived here 33 years on this farm; was in the army three years, in the 105'h Reg. Ill. Vol. in Co. A, was in the Army of the Tennessee, 20th Army Corps, was in a number of battles, and was slightly wounded at Kenesaw Mountain and at Atlanta, was with Sherman in his march to the sea; holds office of School Director in his district; owns 96¼ acres land, value $7,500; Rep; Cong; married Miss Ella A. Reese, June 17, 1872, she was born in Wis and lived in this state 8 years; has two children, one boy and one girl.

WEST DAVID, Farmer, Sec. 34; P O. Sycamore; born in Sangerfield, Oneida Co. N. Y. July 16, 1806, lived there 2 years, went to Madison Co. 1808, lived there 18 years, went to Erie Co in 1826, lived there 17 years, came to Town of Sycamore, DeKalb Co. Oct. 28, 1843, and has lived here 33 years on this farm, one of the oldest settlers; snow fell 15 days during the month of October, while on their journey when they came; Rep; Cong; 107 acres of land, value $7,500; was Assessor for 8 years, also Highway Commissioner and Town Trustee, also Town Treasurer, Board Commissioners, School Director; married Sarah Chapin, April 29, 1829, she was from Connecticut, she died Jan. 23, 1849; married Lucinda Wells, May 28, 1849, she was from Sherburn, Chenango Co. N.Y.; has six children, three sons and three daughters, and has lost two.

WHARRY EVANS, Farmer; res. and P.O. Sycamore; born in Herkimer Co. N.Y. Aug. 23, 1801; came to county May, 1836; Rep; owns 120 acres of land, valued at $12,000; has held the office of Coroner; wife was Martha M. Smith, born in Washington Co. N.Y.; married Sept. 2; 1843; three children, two living.

WHARRY WALTER W. Lawyer, Sycamore; born in Ill; Rep.

WHALEN JOHN B. Proprietor of DeKalb Co. Abstract Office; res. and P.O. Sycamore; born in Penfield, Monroe Co. N.Y. Aug 5, 1850; came to state in 1870 and to county in 1872; Rep; 120 acres land; value real estate $2,000; personal prop. $8,000; held office of Deputy Circuit Clerk; wife was Nellie Farndon, born in Troy, N.Y.; married April 25, 1876.

WHEELER ALFRED W. employee Harvester Works, Sycamore; Rep.

WHEELER E. S. Rev. Resident Minister, Sycamore; Rep.

WHEELER SHEPHARD, Carpenter, Sycamore; Rep; from N.Y.

WHITNEY WALTER J. Manager of Livery and Boarding Stable, Sycamore; born in Livingston Co. N.Y. Oct. 6, 1830; came to this state 1854; Rep; Cong. pref; married Margaret E. Dow, Oct. 5, 1855, she was from Livingston Co. N.Y.; has three children, all boys.

WHITTEMORE HENRY C. Hardware Merchant; res. and P.O. Sycamore; born in Auburn, N.Y. Oct. 31, 1841; came to county 1849; Rep; was Private, Lieutenant and Captain 2d Ill. Artillery; wife was Amelia E. Martin, born in Sycamore, DeKalb Co. Ill; married March 14, 1864; four children.

WHITTEMORE LORENZO, P.O. Sycamore; Rep; Cong; from Mass.

WHITE E. F. Mrs. widow; P.O. Sycamore; from Vt.

WHIPPLE JAMES, Farmer, Sec. 4; P.O. Sycamore; Rep; Lib; Penn.

WHITTLESEY S. C. Meat Market, Sycamore; Rep; from Ohio.

WHITESIDE WILLIAM, Supt. City Schools, Sycamore; Rep; from England.

WIGGENS CHAS. lives with Stark, Sec. 21; P.O. Sycamore; Rep; Meth; Penn.

WILLIAMS GEO. W. Farmer, Sec. 29; P.O. Sycamore; Dem; Meth; prop. $2,000; born Vt.

WILLIAMS THEODORE, works for Charles T. Stewart, Sycamore; Rep; from Ill.

WILLARD H. W. Carpenter, Sycamore; Rep; from Vt.

WILLS GEORGE L. Farm Laborer, Sycamore; Rep; from Vt.

WILLIS D. W. Retired Farmer, Sycamore; Rep; from Vt.

WILD G. P. Merchant, Sycamore; Rep; from N.Y.

WILKINSON ROBERT Mrs. widow; P.O. Sycamore; from England.

WILSON THOS. lives with D. Thurston; Rep; Meth; from Scotland.

WIKE MARTIN, Retired Farmer, Sycamore; Rep; from Germany.

WINN LEVI, Hotel and Livery; res. Sycamore; born in Jefferson Co. N.Y. March 9, 1837; came to county 1869; Rep; value real estate $20,000; personal prop. $5,000; was Sutler in the army; wife was Laura Blackmer, born in Wayne Co. Mich; married July 19, 1865; one child.

WINNANS JAMES, Farmer, Sec. 17, Maxfield's farm; P.O. Sycamore; Dem; Lib.

W NANS W. I. Laborer, Sec. 10; P.O. Sycamore; Rep; Lib; Ill.

WING T. T. Retired Farmer, Sycamore; Dem; from Canada.

WING F. E. Farmer, Sycamore, Dem. from Ill.

WISE WM. H. Farmer, Sec. 9; P.O. Sycamore; born in West Prussia, Feb. 2, 1827; lived there about 21 years, came to United States 1848, lived in Wisconsin 3 or 4 years, and in Massachusetts 2 years, and in New York 1 year, lived in Wisconsin again 2 years, lived in this state about 3 years, went to California and lived there 5½ years, farmed there, came to this town, county and state February, 1864; Rep; Meth; owns 427 acres land, val. $21,350; married Caroline M. Colkins, March 12, 1864, she was from Chenango Co. N.Y. and born April 14, 1829, lived there 13 years, came to Sycamore 1842; her father kept the old hotel on corner; she has lived in Boone Co; has two boys, Willie and Charlie.

WISEMAN G. B. Foreman Ellwood & Co.'s Store; Sycamore; Dem; from N.Y.

WISEMAN G. W. Clerk Reuben Ellwood, Sycamore; Dem; from Mich.

WITHROW G. S. Woodsawyer, Sycamore; Rep; from N.Y.

WOOD HENRY, Farmer, Sec. 8; P.O. Sycamore; born in Randolph, Orange Co. Vt. Nov. 10, 1824; came to this state and county in 1836, and has lived here 40 years; helped raise the first house in Sycamore; Rep; Cong; owns 307 acres land, val. $18,000; has held office of Supervisor, Town Trustee, School Director; married Miss Elizabeth Richards; she was from Hamilton, Madison Co. N. Y.

WOOD THOS. H. Farmer; residence and P.O. Sycamore; born in Randolph, Orange Co. Vermont, Sept. 3, 1822; came to Co. in November, 1836; owns 240 acres land, value $19,000; wife was Catharine H. Allen, born in Berne, Albany Co. N.Y.; married March 10, 1864; four children, three living; Rep; Cong.

WOOD CHARLIE N. lives with father, Sec. 8; P.O. Sycamore; Rep; Cong; Illinois.

WOODARD S. Retired Farmer, Sycamore; Dem; from Vermont.

WOODARD J. D. Carpenter, Sycamore; Dem; from Illinois.

WOODRUFF ANNA Mrs. Music Teacher; from Mass.

WOODEN HARRY, Mechanic, Sycamore; Rep; from N.Y.

WOOLSEY JONATHAN D. Farmer, Sec. 27; P.O. Sycamore; born in Ashtabula Co. Ohio, Nov. 17, 1831; lived there ten years; came to Sycamore, DeKalb Co. in 1841, and has lived here thirty-five years; one of the oldest settlers; worked his trade in Sycamore fifteen years, wagon maker; owns 100 acres, value $7,500; has held the offices of School Director and Path-master; married Sarah A. Parker August 8, 1861; she was from Kentucky; has three children, all boys; Rep; Meth.

WOOLSEY JOHN, Farmer, Sec. 27; P.O. Sycamore; born in Perry, Ashtabula Co. Ohio, April 23, 1821; lived there about twenty years; came to this county in September, 1839, and has lived here thirty-seven years; one of the oldest settlers, and at that time there was only a few little old houses in Sycamore; 160 acres land, value $8,000; he married Miss Mary Warren about the year 1848; she was from Ohio, and died July 14, 1873; has had nine children, all girls; has lost two; his mother, Perthenia Woolsey, lives with him; she was born in the year 1800, and is 76 years old; his father was born in the same year, and died March 2, 1865; Rep; Meth.

WORCESTER H. W. Mason, Sycamore; Rep; from N.Y.

WORCESTER M. J. Mrs. Variety store, Sycamore; from N.Y.

WORCESTER S. W. Farmer, Sycamore; Rep; from Vermont.

WRIGHT MARY Mrs. Sec. 4; P.O. Sycamore; born in Monroe Co. Penn. August 3, 1837; lived there about seventeen years; came to this town, county and state in April, 1854; she has lived here twenty-three years, and was one of the early settlers; 200 acres land belonging to the estate, value $12,000; she married Royal Wright April 20, 1853; he was from N.Y., and was born Oct. 20, 1827; he died March 1, 1873; has eight children, six boys and two girls; Meth.

WRIGLEY CHARLES, works at Harvester Works, Sycamore; Rep; from England.

WRIGHT EBENEZER, Retired, Sycamore; Rep; from N.Y.

WRIGHT GEO. W. Farmer, Sycamore; Rep; from Mass.

WRIGHT WARREN, Retired Farmer, Sycamore; Rep; from Mass.

WYMAN ADELBERT, lives with father, Sec. 35; P.O. Sycamore; Rep; U. Breth.

WYMAN B. F. Farmer, Sec. 36; P O. Sycamore; prop. $4,000; Rep; Meth; Illinois.

WYMAN FERNANDO, lives with father, Sec. 35; P.O. Sycamore; Rep; U. Breth.

WYMAN HENRY, Laborer, Sycamore; Rep; from Illinois.

WYMAN J. Farmer, Sec. 35; P.O. Sycamore; prop. $10,000; Rep; U. Breth; Mass.

WYLDE JOHN, Auctioneer, Sycamore; Dem; from England.

DEKALB TOWNSHIP.

ABEL WM. Laborer, DeKalb; Rep; from Kentucky.

　　ADDAMS THOMAS, Sec. 7; P.O. DeKalb; 236 acres, value $12,000; from Ireland.

ALLEN W. H. with Baldwin Bros. Hardware, DeKalb; Rep; located 1856; from R. I.

ALLEN H. E. Retired Merchant, DeKalb; from New York.

ALLEN BENJ. Painter, DeKalb.

ALMY J H. Sec. 11; P.O. DeKalb; 120 acres, value $6,000; Rep; from New York.

AMOS GEO. Butcher, DeKalb; born England, 1819; came to Co. 1868; Dem; Ind; present wife was Mary Yates, born England, 1821; married 1871; three children by first wife; names, John. George, and Eliza, now living in N.Y.

ANDERSON A. P. Laborer in DeKalb; born Sweden, December 25, 1830; came to this county in 1868; value real estate $500; personal property $200; wife, Mary Andersen, born Sweden, 1834; married 1854; four children, Josephine, Selma, Ida and Julia; Ind; Luth.

ANDERSON G. Shoemaker, DeKalb; Rep; Luth; from Sweden.

ANDERSON C. J. Shoemaker, DeKalb; Rep; Luth; from Sweden.

ANDERSON JNO. works for Barbed Wire Co. DeKalb; Rep; Luth; from Sweden.

ANDERSON ANDREW, works for Barbed Wire Fence Co. DeKalb; Rep; from Sweden.

ANDERSON O. P. Laborer, DeKalb; from Sweden.

ANDERSON JNO. Laborer, DeKalb; Rep; from Sweden.

ANGEL PERRY, lives on Sec. 27; P.O. DeKalb; Rep; from Indiana.

ANDREWS ED. Baker, DeKalb; Rep; Luth.

ARNOLD WM. Section Boss R.R. DeKalb; Dem; from England.

ATWOOD J. E. Dealer in Dry Goods, Hats, Caps, Boots and Shoes, Carpets and Oil Cloths, DeKalb, Ill; born in Massachusetts in August, 1828; came to DeKalb in 1857.

ATWOOD H. Merchant, DeKalb; from Mass.

AUBLE AUGUST, works at Fence Factory, DeKalb; Rep; from Sweden.

AURNER JNO. Carpenter, DeKalb; from Penn.

BAKER CHAS. Trader, DeKalb; Dem; from N. Y.

　　BALDWIN E. B. of firm Baldwin Bros., Hardware, DeKalb; Rep; from New York.

BAKER JOHN, Farmer, DeKalb; came to county in 1861; Rep; 160 acres of land, value $7,200; has two children.

BALDWIN A. V. of firm Baldwin Bros., Hardware, DeKalb; Rep; located in 1868; from N. Y.

BAKER JNO. Engineer Flouring Mills; from England; Dem.

BANKS THOS., R.R. Laborer, DeKalb; Dem; from England.

BANKS JAMES, Farmer, Sec 18, P.O. DeKalb; 166 acres, value $6,600; from Ireland.

BARR WM. J. Sec. 31; 215 acres, value $8,600; P.O. DeKalb; Rep; from New York.

BARR L. Sec. 35; P.O. DeKalb; 80 acres, value $5,000; Rep; from New York.

BARBER C. L. Farmer, Sec. 14; P.O. DeKalb; 225 acres, value $10,000; born in town of Pike, Allegany Co. N.Y. June 29, 1814; has lived in county forty years; Rep; Spiritualist; wife, Mary M. Spring, born May 5th, 1823; married May 12, 1839; three children, Louisa, Florence and Harriet.

BARBER M. D. lives on Sec. 15; P.O. DeKalb; Rep; from Illinois.

BARBER W. B. Sec. 15; P.O. DeKalb; 257 acres, value $13,000; Rep; New York.

BADGER E. Sec. 6 and 7; P.O. DeKalb; 174 acres, value $6,000; Dem; from Canada.

BARLOW D. J. Sec. 31; P.O. DeKalb; 215 acres, value $8,600; Rep; from New York.

BARLOW C. C. lives on Sec. 31; P.O. DeKalb; Rep; from New York.

BANKE CHAS. Sec. 3; P.O. Sycamore; 160 acres, value $6,000; Rep; from Germany.

BANISTER H. lives on Sec. 29; P.O. DeKalb; Rep; from New York.

BARQUIST FRED, works for Barbed Wire Co. DeKalb; from Sweden.

BATHRICK LEVI, Engineer, Barbed Wire Co. DeKalb; Dem; from New York.

BARTLETT A. W. Sec. 19; P.O. DeKalb; 80 acres, value $4.800; Rep.

BALJQUIST G. F. Laborer, DeKalb; Rep; Luth; from Sweden.

BATHRICK NATHAN, Retired Farmer, DeKalb; Dem; from New York.

BULL HENRY, Stock Broker, DeKalb; from New York.

BARR DAVID, works at Lumber Yard, DeKalb; Rep: from Canada.

BUSBY GEORGE, R.R. Laborer, DeKalb; Rep; from England.

BALCH G. P. Jeweler, DeKalb; from Massachusetts.

BENSON JNO. works for Wire Fence Co. DeKalb; Rep; from Sweden.

BEERS JNO. S. DeKalb; from Connecticut.

BEERS E. A. Plow Manufacturer, DeKalb; from Canada.

BENTON JNO. works for Barbed Wire Co. DeKalb; Rep; from Sweden.

BERRY J. M. Rev. Baptist Minister, DeKalb; Rep; from Kentucky.

BENTLEY GEO. Clerk for F. N. Smith, DeKalb; Rep; from New York.

BENNETT J. C. Policeman, DeKalb; located 1854; Rep; from Ireland

BEAUPRE C. E. Clerk for I. L. Glidden, DeKalb; Dem; from Illinois.

BELKNAP P. W. Sec. 25; P.O. DeKalb; 72 acres, value $3,200; Rep; Freewill Bapt; Vt.

BEMIS B. P. Sec. 33; P.O. DeKalb; 160 acres, value $8,000; Rep; from N. H.

BEARD C. A. Sec. 29; P.O. DeKalb; 100 acres, value $6,000; Dem; Ind; from New York.

BIEVER JACOB, Cigar Manufacturer, DeKalb; located 1875; from Holland.

BLOUNT A. A. works at Fence Factory, DeKalb; Dem; from England.

BLANCHARD C. W. Caapenter, DeKalb; from Vermont.

BLACKMAN F. M. Clerk, DeKalb; Rep; from New York.

BLACKMAN A. B.; Rep; from N.Y.

BLAKE ALBERT, lives on Sec. 10; P.O. DeKalb; Dem; from Illinois.

BLAKE JAS. Sec. 10; P.O. DeKalb; 400 acres, value $24,000; Dem; from England.

BLAIR GEO. C. lives on Sec. 34; P O. DeKalb; Dem; from Scotland.

BOLM L. Laborer, DeKalb; Luth; from Sweden.

BOASEN RASMUS, Merchant Tailor, DeKalb; located in 1871; Rep; Luth; Denmark.

BOARDMAN CYRUS, Carpenter, DeKalb; Rep; Bapt; from New York.

BOMEGARDNER S. Sec. 16; P.O. DeKalb; 320 acres, value $11,200; Dem.

BOYES W. G. lives on Sec. 10; P.O. DeKalb; Rep; from New York.

BOYES M. Sec. 10; P.O. DeKalb; 40 acres, value $2,000; Rep; from New York.

BRUNDAGE F. H. Postal Clerk and Farmer, Malta, Ill; nativity, Ulster County, N. Y., 1835; came to county in 1856; Rep.

BRISTOW JOSEPH, Butcher, DeKalb, Ill; born Oxfordshire, Eng. 1823; came to DeKalb 1853; Rep; Calvinistic; three children.

BROWN D. D. (Tindall & Brown) Dry Goods, etc., DeKalb; born New Jersey.

BROWN JAS. H. Barber, DeKalb; born Canada; located 1875; Rep.

BROWN WARRING, Shoemaker; DeKalb; born,Conn.

BROWN A. lives on Sec. 36; P.O. DeKalb; Rep; Denmark.

BROWN ——, lives on Sec. 1; P.O. Sycamore; Dem; Conn.

BROWN BRAMER, Drug Clerk, DeKalb, born N.Y.

BRODIN WM. Teamster, DeKalb; born Sweden; located 1873; Rep; Luth.

BRADT A. Farmer, DeKalb; born N.Y.

BRADT DILLON, Butcher, DeKalb; born Fulton Co. N.Y. February 24, 1842; came to DeKalb 1875; married 1866, to Lena Cool, born December 25, 1846; Rep; Universalist.

BRADT C. E. (Bradt & Shipman) wholesale glovers, DeKalb; born N.Y.

BUNNELL O. M. Farmer, Sec. 36; P.O. DeKalb; born Cayuga Co. N.Y. Aug. 4, 1823; came to state 1855; Rep; 160 acres; val. real estate $8,800; val. per. prop. $3,000; Commissary and Q. M. of 6th Ohio Cav; wife Nancy Palmer, born Trumbull Co. Ohio; married Nov. 1861; two children.

BUNNELL JOHN, Farmer; lives Sec. 36; P.O. DeKalb; Rep; N.Y.

BURGAN ANDREW, works for wire fence factory, DeKalb; born Sweden; Rep.

BURT CHAS. Laborer, DeKalb; born Ill; Dem.

BURK JNO. Retired Farmer, DeKalb; born Can; Dem.
BUCK WM. lives on Peasley farm, Sec. 2; P.O. DeKalb; Rep; Vermont.
BURGERSON CHARLES, lives on Sec. 21; P.O. DeKalb; Bapt; Sweden.
BUCKLING E. G. Mrs. widow, DeKalb; born N.Y.
BURROUGHS GEO. J. lives on Sec. 35; P.O. DeKalb; Rep; N.Y.

CASSIDY JOS. Blacksmith, DeKalb; born Ireland; Dem.
   CARL MIKE, lives on Sec. 16; P.O. DeKalb; Dem; Ireland.
CARLSON WM. lives on Sec. 12; P.O. DeKalb; Rep; Sweden.
CARLEY C. (Paine & Carley) Produce and Commission, DeKalb.
CARTER C. (Carter & Roberts) Agricultural Implements, DeKalb; born N.Y.; Dem.
CARTER ORLANDO, Farmer, DeKalb, Ill; born Chenango Co. N.Y. 1830; came to DeKalb Co. 1847; Dem; 524 acres, value $24,000; per. prop. $5,000; seven children.
CARTER CLARK, Agricultural Implements and Farmer, DeKalb, Ill; born in Chenango Co. N.Y. 1831; came to county in 1844; Rep; 160 acres land, val. $8,000; Road Com. in 1876; five children.
CAMPBELL ALONZO, Blacksmith, DeKalb, Ill; born Wyoming Co. N.Y. 1832; came to county in 1855; Rep; four children.
CALSON JNO. works for Barbed Wire Fence Co. DeKalb; born Sweden; Rep.
CAATSE JNO. Clerk, DeKalb; born England.
CHANDLER R. K. Mrs. widow, DeKalb; born Conn.
CHEASEBRO J. Farmer, DeKalb; born N.Y.; Rep.
CHEENY R. lives on Sec. 7; P.O. DeKalb; Rep; Can.
CHENEY WESTERN, Blacksmith, DeKalb; born Can; Rep.
CHENEY O. Retired Farmer, DeKalb; born Vt.
CHEESEBRO O. B. Postal Route Agt. DeKalb; born N.Y.; Rep.
CHURCH WM. works for Barbed Fence Wire Co. DeKalb; born Eng; Rep.
CLARK JAMES, lives on Sec. 30; P.O. DeKalb; Can.
CLARK GEO. Sec. 10 and 11; 170 acres, val. $7,000; P.O. DeKalb; Rep; Vermont.
CLARK C. Sec. 11; 90 acres, val. $5,000; P.O. DeKalb; Rep; Vermont.
CLARK H. E. lives on Sec. 11; P.O. DeKalb; Rep; Ill.
CLIFFORD WM. Tinner, DeKalb; born Ohio.
COMSTOCK HEZEKIAH, Laborer, DeKalb; born N.Y.; Rep.
COLTON H. E. Sec. 16; P.O. DeKalb; 120 acres; val. prop. $4,000; Vermont.
CONLEY F. on Poor Farm; P.O. DeKalb; Dem; Ireland.
CONANT T. N., R.R. Postal Clerk, DeKalb; born Ill.
COOK R. Sec. 12; P.O. DeKalb; 130 acres, val. $5,000; Rep; Penn.
COOK M. L. Telegraph Operator, DeKalb; born Ohio; Cong; Rep.
COOK J. W. Carpenter and Builder; from Mass; Cong; Rep.
CORNWELL THOMAS, lives on Sec. 8; P.O. DeKalb; Can; Rep.
CORNFORTH JNO. Laborer, DeKalb; born Ireland; Dem.
CORKINGS THOS. Prop. DeKalb Brewery, DeKalb; born Eng; Dem.
COTTON J. H. Sec. 23; P.O. DeKalb; 4 acres, val. $1,000; Rep; Conn.
COTTON J. HUBBARD, Gardener, DeKalb; born Conn.
CROSS WM. lives on Sec. 22; P.O. DeKalb; Dem; Ill.
CRAWFORD J. Machinist, DeKalb; born Penn; Dem.
CRETZLER JOHN, lives on Sec. 30; P.O. DeKalb; Rep; Ger.
CRETZLER JOSEPH, lives on Sec. 30; P.O. DeKalb; Rep; Penn.
CREGO D. S. Sec. 35; P.O. DeKalb; 160 acres, val. $8,000; Dem; N.Y.
CREGO LEWIS, lives on Sec. 35; P.O. DeKalb; Dem; N.Y.
CROMWELL PHILIP I. Homeœpathic Physician, DeKalb, Ill; born Warren Co. N.Y. July 12, 1848; wife was Kate Hallagan, Oswego Co. N.Y.; one child.
CROMWELL J. J. Laborer, DeKalb; born N.Y.
CRONK I. lives on Sec. 1; P.O. Sycamore; Dem; born N.Y.
CRONK O. W. lives on Sec. 1; P.O. Sycamore; Dem; N.Y.

CRONK E. W. lives on Sec. 1; P.O. Sycamore; Dem; from N. Y.
CUSSON J. S. Harness Maker; DeKalb; born in Canada; located 1875.

DAY WM. H. Cooper, DeKalb; from Ohio; Dem.
DAVY R. C. works Barbed Wire Company, DeKalb; born in Ill.
DAVY M. A. Mrs. DeKalb; Widow; born England.
DAVIS J. G. Gunsmith, DeKalb; born Wales; located 1873.
DAVENPORT WM. H. Carpenter, DeKalb; born N. Y.
DAVENPORT WM. Carpenter, DeKalb; born N. Y.
DEE RICHARD, Butcher, DeKalb; born England; Dem.
DONAHUE ANN Mrs. Widow, DeKalb; born Ireland.
DOLT B. M. Retired Farmer, P.O. DeKalb; born Sweden; Rep.
DOWNEY R. Chairmaker, DeKalb; born Vermont; located 1857.
DOWDLE P. lives on Sec. 15; P.O. DeKalb; Dem; Ireland.
DODGE MARTIN, Farmer, DeKalb; born Vermont; Rep.
DODGE L. lives on Sec. 27; P.O. DeKalb; Rep; Vermont.
DODGE THOMAS, Sec. 27; 520 acres, value $31,200; P.O. DeKalb; Rep; Vermont.
DONALD HENRY, Laborer, DeKalb; born Tenn.
DORWIN N. S. Miller, DeKalb, Ill; born Franklin Co. Vt. 1820; came to county in
——; Rep; Bapt; three children; wife Annie Sabin, born Georgia, Vt.; offices held, Justice
of the Peace; Railroad Clerk, Alderman and Town Clerk.
DRESSER W. J. Sec. 10; 88 acres, value $5,000; P.O. DeKalb; Rep; N. Y.
DRESSER JAMES, lives on Sec. 9; P.O. DeKalb; Rep; N. Y.
DRAKE L. Laborer, DeKalb; born Illinois.
DUNN LAWRENCE J. Catholic Clergyman, DeKalb, Ill.
DUNN JNO. Tinner, DeKalb; born Illinois; Dem.
DUFFY GEORGE, lives on Sec 28; Rep; P.O. DeKalb; Ind.
DUFFEY MARTHY M. Mrs. Sec. 33; 110 acres, value $5,500; P.O. DeKalb; N.H.
DUFFEY ROBERT, Sec. 15; 80 acres, value $5,000; P.O. DeKalb; Dem; Ohio.
DUFFY S. Sec 9; P.O. DeKalb; 80 acres, value $3,000; Rep.
DUNHAM E. J. lives on Sec. 14; P.O. DeKalb; Rep; Illinois.
DURHAM L. Trader, DeKalb; Dem; from Penn.
DURANT L. Harness Maker, DeKalb, Ill; born in Windsor County, Vermont, in 1832;
came to county in Sep. 1874; Rep.
DURANT L. of firm Durant & Blaisdell, Harness Manufacturers, DeKalb; located in 1874; Vt.

EARL M. E. Mrs. Widow, DeKalb; from New York.
EASTERBROOK S. Sec. 36; P.O. DeKalb; 160 ac; val. $8,000; Rep; New Brunswick.
ECKER R. Sec. 1; P.O. Sycamore; 10 acres, value $3,000; from New York.
ECKMAN P. lives on Sections 2 and 3; P.O. DeKalb; Rep; from Sweden.
EDDY HIRAM, Farmer and Assessor, DeKalb; Dem; from Canada.
ELBRG ANDREW, Photographer, DeKalb; Rep; Luth; from Sweden.
ELSWORTH WM. Retired Farmer, DeKalb; from Canada.
ELLSWORTH JNO. Carpenter, DeKalb.
ELLWOOD HIRAM, Druggist and Grocer; born in Osego County, N. Y; came to county
in 1856; Rep; Universalist.
ENNIS JEROME, Teamster, DeKalb; Rep; from New York.
ENNIS PETER, Retired Farmer, DeKalb; located in 1863; Rep; from New York.
ERICKSON CHAS. works for Barbed Wire Co. DeKalb; Rep; from Sweden.
EVERETT HENRY P. Farmer, DeKalb; from Michigan.
EVES J. M. of firm of Eves & Smith, Grocers, DeKalb; located in 1874; from Penn.

FISH HOSEA, Retired Farmer, DeKalb; Rep; from Conn.
FINIAN THOMAS, Laborer, DeKalb; Dem; from Ireland.
FIGERT H. W. lives on Sec. 9; P.O. DeKalb; Dem; from Penn.

FLINN E. C. lives on Sections 4 and 5; P.O. DeKalb; Rep; from Illinois.

FLINN G. J. Sections 4 and 5; P.O. DeKalb; Rep; 160 acres, value $8,000; from Vermont.

FLINN D. E. lives on Sections 2 and 3; P.O. DeKalb; Rep; Illinois.

FLINN J. W. Postal Clerk R.R., DeKalb; Rep; from Vermont.

FOSTER MARIA, Sec 28; P.O. DeKalb; 160 acres, value $9,700; Meth; from New York.

FOWLER JAY, lives on Sec. 24; P.O. DeKalb; Rep; from New York.

FOWLER JACOB Rev. Minister M. E. Church, DeKalb; from N. H.

FOX P. L. Retired Attorney, DeKalb; from Mass.

FOREMAN CHAS. works for Barbed Wire Co., DeKalb; Dem; from New York.

FULLER THOMAS H. Restaurant, Bakery, and Fancy Groceries; born in Canada East in 1846; came to DeKalb in 1859; Rep; two years in the army; wife was Esther S. Gregory, born in New York; married Feb. 5, 1865; has one child.

FULLER THOS. of firm Fuller & Hard, Grocery and Restaurant, DeKalb; Rep; Canada.

FULLER WM. Sec. 26; P.O. DeKalb; 400 acres, value $16,000; Rep.

FULLER A. S. Ticket Agent, DeKalb; from Conn.

FRENCH O. M. Carpenter, DeKalb; from Vermont.

FRIGERT HENRY, Retired Farmer, DeKalb; from Germany.

GALLOP E. Sec. 2; P.O. Sycamore; 55 acres, value $3 000; Dem; from New York.

GANNON JNO. N. Tailor, DeKalb; from England.

GANDY MARK, Laborer, DeKalb; Dem; from Illinois.

GARNER JNO C. Clerk, DeKalb; from England.

GARBOTT HENRY, lives on Sec. 1; P.O. Sycamore; Rep; from Canada.

GARBOTT J. lives on Sec. 1; P.O. Sycamore; Dem; Indiana.

GEORGE CHAS. Furniture, with H. H. Wagner; born in Illinois.

GEORGESON E. D. Carpenter, DeKalb; Rep; from Denmark.

GILBERT WM. works for Barb Wire Co. DeKalb; from Ohio.

GILBERT E. B. Justice, DeKalb; Rep; from N.Y.

GILSON LEWIS, lives on Sec. 32; P.O. DeKalb; Dem; Penn.

GLIDDEN J. F. nativity, Charleston, N. H., 1814; came to DeKalb Co. Nov. 14, 1842; 400 acres, value $24,000; was Sheriff two years, and is now Supervisor; Dem.

GLIDDEN J. B. Sec. 10, Afton Township; born in Clarendon, Orleans Co. N.Y. in 1819; came to Ill. in 1860; 160 acres, value $7,000; personal prop. $2,000; wife was Juliet Beard, born in Clarendon, Orleans Co. N.Y. April 21, 1841; has four children; Rep.

GLIDDEN J. W. Sec. 21; P.O. DeKalb; 70 acres, value $3,500; Dem; N.Y.

GLIDDEN V. A. Tailor, DeKalb; Rep; from Ky.

GLIDDEN I. L. Glidden Barb Wire Co., DeKalb; from N.Y.

GLIDDEN O. F. works for Glidden Barb Wire Co. DeKalb.

GONANT F. Laborer, DeKalb; Sweden.

GOODRICH E. Sec. 34. P.O. DeKalb; 160 acres, value $8,000; Dem; N.Y.

GOODELL J. M. Farmer and Grain Merchant, DeKalb; from N.Y.

GOODISON JNO. Coal Dealer, DeKalb; from England.

GORDEN JAMES, lives on Sec. 26; P.O. DeKalb; Rep; Scotland.

GRIFFIN DAVID, P.O. DeKalb; from N.Y.

GROUT D. D. Sec. 31 and 32; P.O. DeKalb; 160 acres, value $8,000; Dem; Vermont.

GROUT J. W. lives on Sec. 31 and 32; P.O. DeKalb; Dem; N.Y.

GURLER G. H. Merchant, DeKalb; Rep; from N. H.

GURLER BENJ. Sec. 32; P.O. DeKalb; 168 acres, value $10,000; Rep; N.H.

HATCH A. R. Janitor, DeKalb; Rep; from N.Y.

HALL I. Retired Farmer, DeKalb; born Vermont.

HARRIS THOMAS, Farmer and Stock Raiser, Sec. 17; came to DeKalb Co. in 1858; 160 acres, value $7,000; personal prop. $2,000; Dem; Ireland.

HATCH JOHN, Sec. 21; P.O. DeKalb; 90 acres, value $6,000; Rep; Bapt; N.Y.

HAWLEY GEORGE, Carpenter, DeKalb; located in 1876; Rep; N.Y.

HAWLEY H. C. Carpenter, DeKalb; Rep; N.Y.

J. F. GLIDDEN
DE KALB

HAMN GUSTAVUS, Sexton Church, DeKalb; Rep; Luth; Sweden.

HAMILTON WILLIAM L. Farmer and Stock Raiser, Sec. 9; born in Cambria Co. Penn. in 1825; came to Ill. in 1835; came to DeKalb Co. in 1851; 200 acres, value $10,000; personal prop. $2,000; wife was Helen Andrews, of Washington Co. N.Y.; married in 1856; has eight children; Dem.

HODSON WM. Sec. 30; P.O. DeKalb; 137 acres, value $7,000; Rep; N.Y.

HARRIS JOHN, lives on Sec. 16; P.O. DeKalb; Dem; Ireland.

HARTWELL H. Poor Farm; P.O. DeKalb; Rep; N.Y.

HALLARON JNO. works for Barb Wire Co. DeKalb; Illinois.

HAYS T. lives on Sec. 6; P.O. Sycamore; Dem; Ireland.

HARD WILBUR, Grocery and Restaurant, DeKalb; located in 1875; Illinois.

HARD M. G. Restaurant, Baker and Fancy Groceries, DeKalb, Ill.; born in Kane Co. Ill. in 1850; came to DeKalb Co. in 1876; wife was Jennie Morse, born in Kane Co. Ill. in 1852; married Aug. 30, 1871; one child; Rep.

HATHAWAY FRANK, Laborer, DeKalb; Dem; N.Y.

HATHAWAY WM. Poor Farm; P.O. DeKalb; Rep; N.Y.

HANDS A. lives on Sec. 18; P.O. DeKalb; Dem; England.

HATFIELD ALBERT, Farmer, Sec. 25; P.O. DeKalb; 80 acres, value $4,000; Rep.

HAISH JACOB, Barb Fence Patentee and Manufacturer, DeKalb, Ill.; born in Carlsruhe, Germany, in 1826; came to Co. in 1851; Dem.

HELMER P. H. Sec. 12; P.O. DeKalb; 160 acres, value $9,000; Rep; N.Y.

HELMER H. K. Agent Batavia Wind Mill Co. DeKalb; Rep; N.Y.

HELMER FRANK, Student Chicago University; P.O. DeKalb; Rep; N.Y.

HEATH C. H. Laborer, DeKalb; born N.Y.

HENNESSY J. Mrs. Grocer, DeKalb; born Ireland.

HICKEY PATRICK, Laborer, DeKalb; Dem; Cath; Ireland.

HINNEGAN THOS. Laborer, DeKalb; Dem; Ireland.

HIGHLAND CHAS. Painter, DeKalb; Dem.

HILAND JNO. works for Barb Wire Fence Co. DeKalb; Dem; Penn.

HILAND JACKSON, Farmer, Sec. 24; P.O. DeKalb; born in Licking Co. Ohio, Sept. 23, 1832; came to this state in 1848; 40 acres, value $1,600; personal prop. $1,500; was musician in the 42d Reg. Douglas Brigade; wife was Juliet Price, born in Otsego Co. N.Y.; married June 8, 1856; one child; Dem.

HINMAN CHAS. C. Dentist, DeKalb; born Oneida Co. N.Y. July 24, 1827; came to county 1863; Rep; Free Thinker; wife, Sophronia H. Barnard, born Oneida Co. N.Y. July 20, 1828; married April 11, 1855; seven children, five living, Fred., Frank, James, Clara and Claude.

HOGAN DAN. Sec. 2; P.O. Sycamore; 35 acres, value $1,500; Dem; Ireland.

HOLDERNESS HORACE, Importer of Horses, DeKalb; born in Canada.

HOLDERNESS WM. Carpenter, DeKalb; born in Canada.

HOLDERNESS J. B. Carpenter, DeKalb; born in Canada.

HOYT WM. Sec. 6; P.O. Sycamore; 174 acres, value $8,000; Dem; N.Y.

HOYT LEWIS, Sec. 5; P.O. Sycamore; 227 acres, value $10,000; Dem; N.Y.

HOYT L. S. lives on Sec. 5; P.O. Sycamore; Dem; Conn.

HOYT E. M. Sec. 5; P.O. Sycamore; 210 acres, value $10,000; Dem; Penn.

HOYT M. Sec. 4; P.O. DeKalb; 160 acres, val. $6,400; Dem; N. Y.

HOWARD J. M. Blacksmith, DeKalb; born Ohio.

HOWARD JNO. Blacksmith, DeKalb; born Ohio.

HOWARD JAMES, lives on Sec. 14; P.O. DeKalb; Rep; Ohio.

HOUGHTON GEO. Watchman R.R. DeKalb; born Canada; Rep.

HOLMBOLD JOHN, lives on Sec. 9; P.O. DeKalb; Sweden.

HOLLISTER H. B. Sec. 14; P.O. DeKalb; 29 acres, val. $2,000; Rep; Ill.

HOYER J. Sec. 1; P.O. Sycamore; 100 acres, val. $5,000; Dem; N. Y.

HOYER PETER, lives Sec. 1; P.O. Sycamore; Dem; N. Y.

HOPKINS J. R. lives on Sec. 24; P.O. DeKalb; Dem; Ill.

HOPKINS S. F. Manufacturer Woodenware, DeKalb; born N. H.

12

HOPKINS HENRY, Farmer, Sec. 24; P.O. DeKalb Centre; born Washington Co. N. Y. May 19, 1829; came to state, July, 1539, to Co. 1848; Dem; 160 acres; val. real estate $6,400; pers'al p'y. $2,000; was Assessor; wife was Eveline Hamlin, born Ohio; married Sept. 1847; six children.

HOPKINS THOMAS M. Attorney and Counselor at Law, Notary Public, DeKalb; born in Montgomery Co. N.Y. in 1818; came to DeKalb Co. Ill. in 1841; Dem; he is Calvinistic in religion; baptized in infancy, believing in the 39 articles, and that he will consequently be saved, and probably die poor; has been Supervisor of the town four terms; five children; 400 acres; v l $20,000

HUGHES MICHAEL, works for Barb Wire Co. DeKalb; Dem; born Ireland.
HUDSON RICHARD B. works for Barb Wire Co. DeKalb; born N. Y.
HUDSON RICHARD, Sec. 30; P.O. DeKalb; 137 acres, val. $7,000; Rep; England.
HUDSON THOS. H. Teamster, D Kalb; born Canada.
HELSEL J. Painter, DeKalb; born N. Y.
HELSER LAWRENCE works Barb Wire Co. DeKalb; born N. Y.
HURD A. Carpenter, DeKalb; Dem; born N. Y.
HULETT E. B. Carpenter, DeKalb; born N. Y.
HUMES WM. lives on Sec. 36; P.O. DeKalb; Rep; England.
HUNGERFORD N. H. Carpenter, DeKalb; born Mich.
HUBBARD WM. Sec. 2; P O. D Kalb; 96 acres, val. $6,000; Dem; N. Y.
HUBBARD E. lives on Sec. 2; P.O. DeKalb; born Ill.
HUBBARD M. lives on Sec. 2; P.O. DeKalb; Dem; Ill.
HUNT HORACE D. Farmer and Stock Raiser, Sec. 23; P.O. DeKalb; Ind; val. prop. $500.
HUNT C. S. Sec. 19; P.O. DeKalb; 160 acres, val. $8,000; Dem; N. Y.
HUNT D. J. lives on Sec. 19; P.O. DeKalb; Dem; born DeKalb, Ill.
HUNT D. D. Sec. 35; P.O. D Kalb; 160 acres, val. $9,600; Rep; N. Y.
HUNT THEODORE, Clerk, DeKalb; born N. Y.
HUNT CHAS. M. Farmer; P.O. DeKalb; from Fulton Co. Ill.
HYSLOP Mrs. widow, DeKalb; from N. Y.

ISAAC JNO. Retired Farmer, DeKalb; from Sweden; Rep.
 ISUTH JNO. Laborer, DeKalb; born Sweden; located 1860.

JACKMAN GEO. lives on Sec. 21; P.O. DeKalb; Dem; Ill.
 JACKSON JNO. works for Barb Wire Fence Co. DeKalb; Rep; Luth; born Sweden.
JACKMAN RICHARD, Farmer, Sec. 20; born England; 230 acres, value $10,000; came to DeKalb Co. 1853; wife, Maria Jackman, born England; married 1850; eight children; Dem.
JACKSON A. S. Hardware, DeKalb; Rep; born N. Y.
JACOX ISAAC, Sec. 7; P.O. DeKalb; 120 acres, val. $5,000; Dem; Mich.
JACOX C. M. lives on Sec. 7; P.O. DeKalb; Dem; Ill.
JACOX ISAAC Jr. lives on Sec. 7; P.O. DeKalb; Dem; Ill.
JACOX WM. lives on Sec. 7; P.O. DeKalb; Dem; Ill.
JOHNSON J. P. lives on Sec. 28; P.O. DeKalb; Rep; Sweden.
JOHNSON C. O. lives on Sec. 8; P.O. DeKalb; Rep; Sweden.
JOHNSON ALFRED, lives on Sec. 14; P.O. DeKalb; Rep; Sweden.
JOHNSON L. Sec. 14; P.O. DeKalb; Rep; Sweden.
JOHNSON NELSON, Sec. 7; P.O. DeKalb; 140 acres, val. $5,000; Rep; Sweden.
JOHNSON G. M. works at Wire Fence Factory, DeKalb; Rep; Sweden.
JOHNSON HENRY, works at Barb Wire Fence Factory, DeKalb; Rep; Sweden.
JOHNSON JOSEPH, Laborer, DeKalb; Rep; Sweden.
JOHNSON PETER, works for Barb Wire Fence Co. DeKalb; Rep; Luth; Sweden.
JOHNSON J. works for Barb Wire Co. DeKalb; Rep; Sweden.
JOHNSON FRANK, Retired Farmer, DeKalb; Sweden.
JOHNSON JNO. Laborer, DeKalb; Sweden.
JOHNSON CHAS. works for Barb Wire Co. DeKalb; Rep; Sweden.

JOHNSTON S. M. works for Barb Wire Co. DeKalb; N. Y.

JONES R. M. Farmer, Sec. 24; P.O. DeKalb; 80 acres, val. $4,000; Rep; N. Y.

JORDAN THOS. clerk for C. A. Talbot; Dem; from Ill.

KELLEY J. lives on Secs. 6 and 7; P.O. DeKalb; Dem.

KENEDY JAMES, Sec. 22; P.O. DeKalb; 40 acres, val. $2,000; Rep; Epis; N. Y.

KENNEDY JAS. Laborer, DeKalb; Ireland; Dem.

KENNEDY THOMAS, Retired Farmer, DeKalb; Ireland; Dem.

KING W. B. Books, Notions, etc. DeKalb; Rep; Bapt; born N. Y.

KING L. B. Rev. Retired Baptist Minister, DeKalb; Rep; born N. Y.

KINE J. Sec. 3; P.O. Sycamore; 93 acres, val. $3,000; Dem; Ireland.

KING LYDA A. Miss, DeKalb; born N.Y.

KING GEO. works for Barb Wire Co. DeKalb; from N. Y.

KIRK GEO. Farmer, Sec. 13; born Cayuga Co. N.Y. April 26, 1824; came to this county March 28, 1868; lives on farm of Mrs. M. C. Burpee; wife, Jenny Gibson, born April 16, 1844 married May 2, 1872; two children.

KLOCK AARON, Mechanic, DeKalb; Dem; born N. Y.

KLOCK DANFORD, Carpenter, DeKalb; Dem; born N. Y.

KTARLN JNO. works for Barb Wire Fence Co. DeKalb; Sweden;

LACY WM. Sec. 19; P.O. DeKalb; 170 acres, val. $6,800; Dem; Ireland.

LACY MOSES, lives on Sec 19; P.O. DeKalb; Dem; born Ill.

LATTIN D. B. Retired Farmer, DeKalb; Rep; Meth; from N. Y.

LARSON ANNA Mrs. widow, DeKalb; born Norway.

LARSON PETER, Tailor, DeKalb; Rep; Luth; born Denmark.

LARSON AUGUST, Shoemaker, DeKalb; located 1865; Rep; Luth; born Sweden.

LAKE ANSON, lives on Sec. 30; P.O. DeKalb; Rep; N.Y.

LAWTON Lewis, lives on Poor Farm; P.O. DeKalb; Rep; born N.Y.

LAWSON CHAS. lives on Sec. 26; P.O. DeKalb; Rep; Sweden.

LAURITSEN PETER, Tailor, DeKalb; born Sweden; located 1876; Rep; Luth.

LENOX GEO. DeKalb; born N.Y.; Rep.

LENOX WALTER, Carpenter; Rep; Meth; from N.Y.

LEND ANDREW, works for Barb Wire Fence Co. DeKalb; born Sweden; Rep; Luth.

LINDSAY D. H. Barber, DeKalb, Ill; born Canada West, 1838; came to county in 1848; Dem; five children.

LIVERMORE W. A. lives on Sec. 10; P.O. DeKalb; Rep; N.Y.

LINDBERG Peter, Carpenter, DeKalb; born Sweden; Rep; Luth.

LOVE WILSON, Livery and Farmer, DeKalb, Ill; born in Chautauqua Co. N.Y. 1827; came to county 1844; Dem; 81 acres land, value $4,000; personal property $3,500; three children.

LOVE A. C. Mrs. Sec. 12; 250 acres, val. $12,500; P.O. DeKalb; born N.Y.

LOVE LEWIS D. lives on Sec. 12; P.O. DeKalb; Rep; Ill.

LOVE CHRISTOPHER, Carpenter, DeKalb.

LOVELAND HARRY, Carpenter, DeKalb; Ill.

LOWRY JOHN, Dry Goods etc., DeKalb; born Ireland; came to state 1860; Rep; Meth.

LONG JOHN, lives on Sec. 34; P.O. DeKalb; Rep; Sweden.

LOOMIS EBENEZER W. Painter, DeKalb; born Vt.

LOUIS PETER, Brickmaker, DeKalb; born Denmark.

LOTT J. D. (Lott & Baird) Banker, DeKalb; born Penn; Dem.

LUNEY EDWARD, Retired Farmer; born Ireland; Dem.

LUNEY T. A. Bank Clerk, DeKalb; born Ill.

LUNDBERG JOHN, Farmer; P.O. DeKalb; born Sweden, 1854; Rep; Luth.

LUNDAEN L. works for Barb Wire Fence Co. DeKalb; born Sweden.

LUNDSTROM JNO. Clerk C. Shirtliff, DeKalb; born Sweden; Rep; Luth.

LYON A. D. Mrs. widow, DeKalb; born N.Y.

LYON F. W. lives on Secs. 14 and 15; P.O. DeKalb; Rep; Ill.

LYON GEO. W. Farmer, Secs. 14 and 15; P.O. DeKalb; 155 acres, value $11,600; born Ontario Co. N.Y. June 5, 1819; Road Commissioner three years, Assessor four years; Rep; wife, Sophia Richardson, born February 27, 1827; married 1848; five children.

MARSH C. W. Secs. 13 and 14; P. O. DeKalb; 200 acres, val. $16 000; Rep; Can.

MAHON FRANCIS, works for Barb Wi e Fence Co. DeKalb; born Ireland; Dem; Cath.

MALONE DAVID, Farmer and Stock Raiser, Sec. 18, Pierce Tp. DeKalb Co; born Ireland, 1810; came to county 1854; Dem; 702 acres land, value $31,000; per. prop. $3,000; six children.

MATTESON JAS. Physician, DeKalb; born R. I.

MADDEN JAS. Teamster, DeKalb; born Ireland.

MARRIOTT JNO. Brewer, DeKalb; born Eng; Dem.

MACK G. W. Contractor, Builder and Architect, Sycamore, DeKalb Co. Ill; Chenango Co. N.Y. 1823; came to county in 1856; Rep; real estate $3,000; six children.

MATHER J. N. Sec. 30; P.O. DeKalb; 160 acres, val. $9,600; Rep; Vermont.

MATHEWSON OTIS, Sec. 14; P.O. DeKalb; N.Y.

MARSH SAMUEL, lives on Sec. 13; P.O. DeKalb; Rep; Canada.

MAYO E. L. M.D. Physician, DeKalb, Ill; born in Sycamore, Ill. June 16, 1843; graduated at Rush Med. College, Chicago, in 1863; real estate $6,000; personal property $3,500; wife, Alice L. Ballou; Erie Co. N.Y. Oct. 1852; married Jan. 1, 1872.

McCULLOCK H. G. Sec. 21; P.O. DeKalb; 18 acres, val. $1,600; Rep; Mass.

McDOLE JAS. A. Clerk, DeKalb; born N.Y.; located 1864.

McEVOY JNO. works Barb Wire Co. DeKalb; born Ireland; Dem; Cath.

McEWEN L. M. Dealer in Grain, Lumber, Coal, Live Stock and Stone, DeKalb, Ill; born Orang Co. N.Y. Sept. 23, 1827; came to DeKalb Co. in May, 1852; Rep; 400 acres land, value $15,00); been Supervisor fourteen years, Pres. Board of Trustees three years, two years State Legislature in 1870-71; six children.

McLOUGHLIN E. Poor farm; P.O. DeKalb; Dem; Ireland.

McMAHON GRACE Mrs. widow, DeKalb; born Ireland.

MEAD JOSEPH. Secs. 26 and 27; P.O. DeKalb; 82 acres, val. $5,200; Rep; England.

MENNIS SIDNEY, works for Barb Wire Co. DeKalb; born N.Y.

MENDELSON L. Clothing, DeKalb; born Prussia; came to state 1846; Dem.

MENDELSON A. Clerk, DeKalb; born Penn; came to state 1846; Dem.

MILLER W. H. Billiard Hall, DeKalb, Ill; born in Genoa, DeKalb Co. 1843; two children; Dem.

MILLER W. A. Retired Farmer, DeKalb; born N.Y.

MILLER M. L. lives on Sec. 20; P.O. DeKalb; Rep; Adv; Penn.

MOLANDER PETER, Laborer, DeKalb; born Sweden; Luth.

MOLANDER JNO. foreman "S" Wire Fence Factory, DeKalb; born Sweden; Luth.

MOLANDER CHAS. Mason, DeKalb; born Sweden.

MORRIS JONATHAN, Retired Farmer. DeKalb; born N.Y.

MOWERS A. Laborer, DeKalb; born N.Y.

MORRELL ENOS, Sec. 23; P.O. DeKalb; 10 acres, val. $1,000; Rep; Mass.

MOORE JACKSON, Peddler, DeKalb; born Ohio.

MORSE J. N. Physician, DeKalb; born N.Y.

MOORE A. J. Laborer, DeKalb; born Ohio; came to state 1860.

MOTT ROBERT, Sec. 20; P.O. DeKalb; 67 acres, val. $3 300; Rep; England.

MURRY MILES, works Wire Fence Factory, DeKalb; born Ill.

MUNSON PETER, Laborer, DeKalb; born Sweden; Rep; Luth.

MUZZEY IRA, Farmer and Thresher, Sec. 22; P.O. DeKalb; born in this state 1845; have always resided here; was in the 17th Ill. Cavalry. Beveridge Col; val. of prop. $1,000; wife was Sarah E. DePugh, born in Kane Co. 1854; married 1872; has two children.

MUZZEY BENJ. Constable, DeKalb; Rep; Vermont.

MUZZEY IRA C. Teamster, DeKalb; Rep; Illinois.

MUZZEY W. H Teamster, DeKalb; Rep; Illinois.

MUZZAY EDWIN A. Shoemaker, DeKalb; located in 1862; Rep; Ill.

MUDGETT IRVING, Sec. 28; P.O. DeKalb; 140 acres, value $7,700; Rep; Meth.

MUDGET SOLON, Sec. 29; P.O. DeKalb; 160 acres, value $8,000; Rep; Meth; N.Y.

NEWBERG GUS, works for Barb Wire Fence Co. DeKalb; Rep; Luth; Sweden.
NEWITT ROBERT, Shoemaker, DeKalb; located in 1854; England.

NEEDHAM D. C. Trav. Ins. Agt. DeKalb; Rep; Vermont.

NEEDHAM CHAS. Retired Farmer, DeKalb; Rep; born in Vermont.

NELSON B. C. Wagon Maker, DeKalb; Rep; Sweden.

NELSON A. Sec. 1; P.O. Sycamore; 35 acres, value $1,600; Rep; Sweden.

NELSON CHAS. lives on Sec. 1; P.O. Sycamore; Rep; Sweden.

NEWHALL FRANK, lives on Sec. 32; P.O. DeKalb; Rep; N.H.

NORDSTRON JNO. Painter, DeKalb; located in 1876; Rep; Luth; Sweden.

NORDGRAN NELSON Rev. Minister Swedish Luth., DeKalb; Rep; Sweden.

NOLAN JOHN, lives on Sec. 16; P.O. DeKalb; Ireland.

NORTON J. R. Wood Dealer, DeKalb; Rep; born N. H.

OLSEN ANDREW, works at Wire Fence Factory, DeKalb; Sweden.
ORENDORF EVA Mrs. Sec. 2; P.O. Sycamore; 200 acres, value $3,000.

ORENDORF CHAS. lives on Sec. 2; P.O. Sycamore; Rep; Ill.

OSBORN WM. lives on Sec. 10; P.O. DeKalb; Rep; Penn.

PARKER T. Secs. 5 and 8; P.O. Sycamore; 200 acres, value $8,000; Rep; Vermont.
PATTEN O. D. Carpenter, DeKalb; Rep; N.Y.

PAGE N. S. Engineer, DeKalb; born in N.Y.

PARKS SMITH, Traveling Agent, DeKalb; Rep; Meth; N.Y.

PAINE B. W. (Paine & Carley) Produce and Commission, DeKalb.

PATTERSON R. G. Laborer, DeKalb; born in Ill.

PASLEY WM. lives on Sec. 14; P.O. DeKalb; Dem; Ill.

PASLEY S. Farmer, Sec. 13; P.O. DeKalb; born in DeKalb, Ill. Aug. 25, 1842; owns farm of 80 acres, value $4,000; Dem; was in the army four years, was Sergeant.

PERRY E. S. Auctioneer, DeKalb, Ill.; born in Oneida Co. N.Y. in 1835; came to DeKalb in 1862; has two children; Rep.

PEASLY S. Sec. 2; P.O. DeKalb; 60 acres, value $3,000; Rep; N. H.

PETERSON J. Sec. 1; P.O. Sycamore; 6 acres, value $1,000; Rep; Sweden.

PETTERSON JNO. works for Barb Wire Fence Co. DeKalb; Rep; Luth; Sweden.

PETERSON CHAS. works for Barb Wire Fence Co. DeKalb; Rep; Sweden.

PETERSON AUGUST, works for Barb Wire Fence Co. DeKalb; Rep; Sweden.

PHARO WM. Sec. 22; P.O. DeKalb; 10 acres, value $2,500; Dem; England.

PIERCE W. F. lives on Sec. 35; P.O. DeKalb; Dem; Vermont.

PIERCE B. Sec. 35; P.O. DeKalb; 80 acres, value $8,000; Dem; Vermont.

PIERCE RICHARD, Retired Farmer, DeKalb; England.

PIERSON JNO. Blacksmith, DeKalb; Rep; Luth; Sweden.

PIERSON C. works for Barb Wire Fence Co. DeKalb; Rep; Luth; Ill.

PIERSON P. Farm Laborer, DeKalb; Rep; Luth; Sweden.

PRICE ADELBERT, works at Wire Fence Factory, DeKalb; Ill.

PRICE L. Mason, DeKalb; born in N.Y.

PRICE DAVID. Retired Farmer, DeKalb; Dem; N.Y.

PLANK DEWITT, lives on Sec. 34; P.O. DeKalb; Dem; Ill.

PLANK MARCUS, lives on Sec. 34; P.O. DeKalb; Dem; N.Y.

PLANK WM. W. Sec. 34; P.O. DeKalb; 320 acres, value $24,000; Dem; N.Y.

PLOWMAN THOS. lives on Sec. 15; P.O. DeKalb; Dem; England.

PLESTER WM. lives on Sec. 35; P.O. DeKalb; Rep; England.

POST L. H. Publisher of the DeKalb *News*, and Postmaster; born in Rochester, N.Y. in 1839; settled in DeKalb Co. in 1869; Rep.

POTTER S. Sec. 34; P.O. DeKalb; 94 acres, value $6,000; Dem; N.Y.

PORTER E. A. Dry Goods and Millinery, DeKalb; Rep; Conn.

RATHAPT G. Stone Mason, DeKalb; Germany.

RAY ALEX. Farmer, DeKalb; Dem; Scotland.

RANDALL IRA V. Attorney at Law and Notary Public, DeKalb, Ill.; born at Mount Holly, Rutland Co. Vt. in 1820; came to Co. in 1856; real estate $3 000; personal prop. $2,000; was a member of the House of Representatives in 1864-5; was Postmaster in Vermont and DeKalb; wife was Mrs. M. D. Randall, nativity, N.Y.; married in 1868; has one child; Rep; Meth.

REDMOND JNO. works at McEwen's lumber yard, DeKalb; Dem; Ireland.

RITTIG F. Barber, DeKalb; born in Germany.

REDMOND T. Laborer on R. R., DeKalb; Dem; Ireland.

REID ARTHUR, Laborer, DeKalb; Ireland.

RHODES WM. Saloon, DeKalb; England.

RICKARDS PETER J. Sec. 22; P.O. DeKalb; 190 acres, value $11,400; Rep; N.Y.

RICHARDSON T. Sec. 3; P.O. DeKalb; 100 acres, value $5,000; Rep; Vermont.

ROBERTS R. H. Groceries and Live Stock, DeKalb; born in Oneida Co. N.Y. in 1836; came to DeKalb Co. in Dec. 1855; is County Treasurer; Rep.

ROBERTS RICHARD, Agricultural Implements, DeKalb; Dem; N.Y.

ROBERTS W. L. Railroad Contractor, DeKalb; born Penn.

ROOT E. S. Sec. 25; P.O. DeKalb; 160 acres, value $8,000; Dem; N Y.

ROOT T. O. Sec. 12; P.O. DeKalb; 98 acres, value $5,000; Rep; Ohio.

ROOT J. Traveling Insurance Agent, DeKalb; Rep; from New York.

RONAN T. Sec. 14; P.O. DeKalb; Dem; 11 acres, value $1,200; from Ireland.

ROWE J. V. Teamster, DeKalb; from Vermont.

ROLF GEORGE, Mason, DeKalb; Rep; from England.

RUSSELL J. S. Livery, DeKalb; born in Warren County, Indiana, Sep. 25, 1834; came to DeKalb County in 1848; has three children.

RUBY B. Physician, DeKalb; Rep; from Penn.

RYON J. Poor Farm; P.O. DeKalb; Dem; from Ireland.

SALLS J. H. Drug Clerk, DeKalb; located in 1875; from Illinois.

SALISBURY C. H. Book keeper for I. Haish, DeKalb; from Vermont.

SALISBURY C. H. Clerking; nativity, Barton, Vt., 1841; came to county in 1856; Rep.

SALISBURY F. Produce Dealer, DeKalb; from Mass.

SCRIPTER FRANK. Eagle House, DeKalb; born in Wyoming Co. N. Y. Feb. 13, 1825; Rep.

SCOTT OSCAR, Waiter, DeKalb; from Illinois.

SCOTT O. T. Carpenter and Builder, DeKalb; from Vermont.

SCHERMERHORN C. Carpenter, DeKalb; from New York.

SCHRYVER C. lives on Sec. 11; P.O. DeKalb; Rep; from Illinois.

SCHRYVER A. Sec. 11; P.O. DeKalb; 230 acres, value $10,000; Rep; from N. Y.

SIMONDS JOEL H. Farmer, Sec. 23; P.O. DeKalb; born in Rutland Co. Vt. June 27, 1814; came to state June 22, 1846; Rep; Meth; 247 acres; value of real estate $15,000; value of personal property $250; has held the office of Trustee; wife was Almira Hollister, born in Courtland Co. N. Y; married Feb. 15, 1850; died Nov. 27, 1874; three children, two living.

SICKLES M. Mrs. Post-mistress, DeKalb.

SICKLES W. Carpenter, DeKalb; Rep; from New York.

SIMPSON H. B. Farmer, DeKalb; from New York.

SIMSON ASA, Teamster, DeKalb; Dem; from New York.

SIMPSON R. W. Teacher; P.O. DeKalb; Rep; Advent; from New York.

SIMMONS C. M. Com. Traveler, DeKalb; Dem; Penn.

SHRIMPTON GEORGE, Milling twenty-one years; residence, DeKalb, DeKalb Co. Ill; born in Oxfordshire, England, in 1839; came to this county in 1872; Dem; Meth; has five children; married Ann Freeman, born in Warwickshire, England, in 1841; date of marriage 1862; came to this county in 1862.

SHIER J. J. lives on Sec. 8; P.O. DeKalb; Rep.

SHAW PALMER H. lives on Sec. 29; P.O. DeKalb; Dem; Advent; from New York.

SHRIVER A. Dry Goods, etc., DeKalb; Rep; from New York.

SHIRTLIFF CALVIN, Drugs, Groceries, etc. DeKalb; Rep; Meth; from Illinois.

SHEA PATRICK, Liquor Dealer, DeKalb, Ill; born in Ireland in 1832; came to state in 1856; Dem.

SHACKLETON ISAAC, DeKalb; from N. J.

SHACKELTON M. G. Central House, DeKalb; from Northampton Co. Penn; came to this county in 1852; Dem; has one child.

SLADE JOSEPH, Sec. 19; P.O. DeKalb; 80 acres, value $4,800; Rep; from England.

SLADE JOHN, lives on Sec. 29; P.O DeKalb; Rep; from New York.

SMITH WM. lives on Sec. 16; P.O. DeKalb; Rep; born in France.

SMITH E. Sr. Sec. 16; P.O. DeKalb; 40 acres, value $1,800; Rep; from England.

SMITH E. Sec. 16; P.O. DeKalb; 270 acres, value $12,000; Rep; from England.

SMITH G. D. of firm of Eves & Smith Grocers, DeKalb; located in 1870; Rep; Illinois.

SMITH F. N. Lumber Dealer, DeKalb; Rep; from New York.

SMITH E. R. Physician, DeKalb; from Vermont.

SMITH E. N. Mrs. widow, DeKalb; from New York.

SMITH Ira H. Insurance Agent, DeKalb; from New York.

SNOW B. of firm Snow & Hatch, Druggists, DeKalb; located in 1869; Rep; from N. H.

SPANGENBERG JNO. Laborer, DeKalb; from Germany.

SPAFFORD ROOT, Sec. 12; P.O. DeKalb; 83 acres, value $4,500; Rep; from Vermont.

STRIBLING JOHN, Painter, DeKalb; Rep; from England.

STARK CHAS. Shoemaker, DeKalb; Rep; Luth; from Sweden.

STEWART I. M. works for Wire Fence Co. DeKalb; born in Illinois.

STONE GEO. Printer, DeKalb; Rep; from Illinois.

STARK CHAS. Shoemaker. DeKalb; Rep; Luth; came to state in 1868; from Sweden.

STEVENS ISAAC, Farmer and Dairyman, Sec. 24; P.O. DeKalb; born in New York, Aug. 18, 1832; came to state in 1860; Rep; 220 acres; value of real estate $8,800; value of personal property $1 000; wife was Elizabeth Steele, born in Wayne Co. N. Y; married April 27, 1858; has six children.

SWEET HIRAM, DeKalb; Rep; Meth; from New York.

SWEET ROUSE. DeKalb; Rep; Meth; from New York.

SWEET N. Cider and Vinegar Manufacturer, DeKalb; Rep; from New York.

SWANBORN JOS. works for Barb Wire Fence Co. DeKalb; from Sweden.

SWAN AUGUST, lives on Sec. 6; P.O. DeKalb; Rep; from Sweden.

SWANSON A. Physician, DeKalb; Rep; Luth; from Sweden.

SWANSON J. H. Shoemaker, DeKalb; Rep; Luth; Sweden.

SWANSON GUSTAVUS, Laborer, DeKalb; Rep; Luth; from Sweden.

SWANSON A. J. lives on Sec. 30; P.O. DeKalb; Rep; from Sweden.

STEPHENS CHARLOTTE Mrs. widow, DeKalb; from New York.

TAYLOR E. lives on Sec. 20; P.O. DeKalb; from England.

TAYLOR OTIS, Retired Farmer, DeKalb; Dem; from New York.

TADD SAML. Laborer, DeKalb; born England; Rep.

TERRY WILLIAM W. DeKalb, Ill; Farm Machinery of all kids, Wagons and Buggies; born DeKalb Co. Ill. Aug. 22, 1849; Rep; wife Millie Cooper; married Nov. 23, 1875.

TERWILLIGER GEO. Clerk L. M. McEwen, DeKalb; Rep; born N. Y.

TERWILLIGER ROBT. Laborer depot, DeKalb; born Ill.

TERWILLIGER LEANDER, Farmer, DeKalb; born N. Y.

THACKHAM WM. Laborer, DeKalb; Dem; born England.

THOMPSON JNO, Teamster, DeKalb; born Ireland.

THOMPSON JOS. R. Teamster, DeKalb; born Canada.

THOMPSON WM. R. Veterinary Surgeon, DeKalb; born Ohio.

THOMPSON N. W. Farmer, DeKalb; born N. Y.

TILTON WM. lives on Sec. 32; P.O. DeKalb; Mass.

TILL JOHN, Butcher, DeKalb; born England; located 1874; Dem.

TINDALL C. A. of firm Tindall & Brown, Dry Goods, etc. DeKalb; born Ill.

TOOP WM. Sees. 15 and 16; P.O. DeKalb; 180 acres, val. $8,000; Dem; England.
TOOP JOHN, Sec. 16, P.O. DeKalb; 60 acres, val. $3,000; Dem; England.
TRAVLAND LEWIS P. Sec. 31; P.O. Malta; 189 acres, val. $7,500; Dem; Norway.
TRUDE A. B. Drayman, DeKalb; born N. Y.
TREMBLIN CHAS. lives on Sec. 15; P.O. DeKalb; Dem; England.
TRIGG G. works for Barb Wire Co. DeKalb; Rep; Sweden.
TRIMBLE R. Laborer DeKalb; born Tenn; located 1874; Rep,
TULEY A. lives on Sec. 27; P.O. DeKalb; Rep; Indiana.
TUDOR J. Sec. 10; P.O. DeKalb; 120 acres, val. $6,000; Rep; England.
TUDOR E. lives on Sec. 10; P.O. DeKalb; Rep; England.
TUDOR G. lives on Sec. 10; P.O. DeKalb; Rep; England.
TUDOR H. lives on Sec. 10; P.O. DeKalb; Rep; England.
TYLER SANFORD A. Clerk, DeKalb; Dem; born N. Y.
TYRELL D. W. Printer, DeKalb; born Michigan.

UPSHIRE N. D. Mrs. Millinery, DeKalb; born Va.
    UPSHIRE G. S. Photographer, DeKalb; born Va.
UPSON A. M. Constable, Collector and Auctioneer; P.O. DeKalb; born Hornellsville, Steuben Co. N.Y. Sept. 24, 1827; came to Co. 1868; Dem; Cong; married Sarah A. Brown, Jan. 17, 1855, who was born March 27, 1836, in Yates Co. N.Y.; had nine children, six now living—F. B., Myron E., M. Nellie, Minnie A., Sarah J. and Charles H.

VANORTWICK A. B. Sawyer, DeKalb; born N. Y.
    VAN HORN G. Rev. Minister M. E. Church, DeKalb; born N. J.
VAN HORN O. Sec. 14; P.O. DeKalb; 27 acres, val. $3,000; Rep.
VAUGHARN P. W. Carpenter, DeKalb; born N. H.
VAUGAN S. O. Town Clerk, DeKalb; Dem; born N. H.

WADSWORTH G. N. Carpenter, DeKalb; Dem; born N. Y.
    WALSH R. lives on Sec. 14; P.O. DeKalb; Rep; Ireland.
WADSWORTH JOHN W. Wagonmaker, DeKalb, Ill; born Oneida Co. N. Y. 1801; came to Co. 1854; Rep; Cong; six children.
WAGNER P. C. Furniture, DeKalb; Rep; born Germany.
WADDELL L. A. Mrs. DeKalb; born N. Y.
WADDELL F. M. Speculator, DeKalb; born Ohio.
WADDLE M. F. Commission Merchant, DeKalb; born Ohio; located 1867; Rep.
WATSON THOS. Ret. Merchant, DeKalb; born England; Rep.
WARD FRED. W. Farmer, DeKalb; born N. J.
WARD JNO. Retired Farmer, DeKalb; born N. J.
WALDRON RICHARD, Carpenter, DeKalb; born Conn.
WAGNER H. H. Dry Goods and Notions, DeKalb; born Ill; Rep; Bapt.
WELANDER O. M. Clerk, DeKalb; born Sweden, Feb. 26, 1851; came to this county 1868; Rep; Luth.
WEAVER JNO. G. works for Barb Wire Co. DeKalb; born N.Y.
WESTERBERG A. Engineer " S" Barb Fence Co. DeKalb; from Sweden.
WHEELER LEVI, Butcher, DeKalb; born Sterling Mass. 1821; came to DeKalb Sept. 5, 1876; married 1845 to Persis L. Howe, born 1823, in Northboro, Mass; three children—Jenny and Frank L. dead, and Mary E. being the only one left; Rep; Epis.
WHITMORE J. B. Sign, Ornamental and Carriage Painter and Carriage Trimmer, Main Street, DeKalb; born Dec. 16, 1833, in Devonshire, Eng; was in the army four years; married Oct. 1868 to Hattie Carpenter, who was born Feb. 12, 1834, at Ithaca, N.Y.; Dem; 1 child.
WHITMORE CHAS. Drayman, DeKalb ; born Vt.
WHITTEMORE WM. H. Sec. 20; P.O. DeKalb; 130 acres, val. $5,000; Rep; Mass.
WHITAKER R. lives on Sec. 12; P.O. DeKalb; England.
WHITEMAN I. R. Sec. 24; P.O. DeKalb; 2 acres, val. $1,000; Dem; Ohio.
WHEAT J. lives on Sec. 1; P.O. Sycamore; Dem; Germany.

WHITMORE H. Attorney and Justice of the Peace, DeKalb, Ill; nativity, Windsor Co. Vt; came to DeKalb Co. in 1848; Rep; Meth; in the army three years; wife was Jane Lenox, from Chautauqua Co. N. Y.; four children.

WHEELER HARRY, Blacksmith, DeKalb; born N. Y.

WHITE B. S. Foreman Glidden Barb Wire Co. DeKalb; born N. Y.

WHITE BENJ. works for Barb Wire Co. DeKalb; born N. Y.

WHITE J. A. Carpenter, DeKalb; Rep; born N. Y.

WHITE E. D. Farmer, DeKalb; born N.Y.

WHITE WALTER, Bricklayer, DeKalb; born England; Dem.

WHITE HENRY, Baggagemaster, DeKalb; born England; Dem.

WHITE E. Poor Farm; P.O. DeKalb; Rep; Vt.

WHITE A. T. Sec. 20; P.O. DeKalb; 80 acres, val. $4,000; Rep; Ind; N. Y.

WHITE S. R. lives on Sec. 29; P.O. DeKalb; Dem; N.Y.

WILEY ROBERT E. Sec. 28; P.O. DeKalb; 80 acres, val. $4,000; Rep; Meth; Ireland.

WILLEY MORRIS, Farmer. Sec. 33; P.O. DeKalb; 329 acres, value $16,450; born in N.Y.; Rep; Meth; wife, Mary Willey, born N.Y.; seven children living, one dead.

WINTHER C. H. lives on Sec. 5 and 8; P.O. DeKalb; Dem.

WIDGER R. D. lives on Sec. 10 and 11; P.O. DeKalb; Rep; N.Y.

WILSON N. G. lives on Sec. 8; P.O. DeKalb; Rep; Sweden.

WILSON A. B. Retired Farmer, DeKalb; born in N.Y.

WILCOX B. M. Carriage Manufacturer, DeKalb; Rep; Cong; N.Y.

WILTBERGER J. S. Carpenter, DeKalb; Rep; Ky.

WINSHIP HELEN Mrs. widow, DeKalb; born in N.Y.

WILDER M. V. Traveling Agent Barb Wire Fence Co. DeKalb; Vermont.

WOOD GEORGE, Blacksmith, DeKalb, Ill.; born in Scotland in 1818; came to DeKalb Co. in 1855; has four children; Rep; Cong.

WOOD G. H. Carpenter, DeKalb; Rep; Bapt; Penn.

WOLCOTT E. W. Farmer, Sec. 15; P.O. DeKalb; born in this county February 11, 1854, has lived in county ever since; Rep; wife, Jennie Barber, born December 5, 1853; married December 1, 1875; one child, Bessie.

WOLCOTT M. R. Jeweler, DeKalb; Rep; Ill.

WOLCOTT G. E. Sec. 4; P.O. DeKalb; 160 acres, value $10,000; Rep; Canada.

WORMELEY HENRY, Cooper, DeKalb; Rep; Penn.

WRIGHT C. C. Sec. 14; P.O. DeKalb; 120 acres, value $3,000; Rep; Ohio.

WRIGHT F. P., Physician, DeKalb; Dem; N.Y.

WRIGHT THOMAS, Sec. 34 and 35; P.O. DeKalb; 226 acres, value $15,800; Rep.

WYMAN H. B. Sec. 1; P O. Sycamore; 170 acres, value $9,000; Dem; Ill.

WYMAN F. W. Sec. 2; P.O. Sycamore; 55 acres, value $3,000; Rep; Ill.

YATES WM. works at Fence Factory, DeKalb; England.

YOCAM J. Sec. 9; P.O. DeKalb; 40 acres, value $1,600; Rep; Penn.

ZELLER J. lives on Sec. 6; P.O. DeKalb; Rep; N.Y.

ZELLER E. R. Sec. 6; P.O. DeKalb; 116 acres, value $4,000; Rep; N.Y.

ZELLER GEO. lives on Sec. 5; P.O. DeKalb; Rep; N.Y.

SOMONAUK TOWNSHIP.

ABBEY SAMUEL, Traveling Salesman; P.O. Sandwich; Rep; Ind; from Conn.

ABEL A. W. Lumber Dealer, Sandwich; Rep; Cong; from N.Y.

ADAMS PHELPS J. Sec'y and Treasurer Sandwich Manufacturing Co ; residence Third street; P.O. Sandwich; born in Chemung Co. N.Y. in 1835; came to Illinois in 1840, and to DeKalb Co. in 1860; Rep; Cong; real estate $8,000; personal prop. $3,500; married Mary B. Phillips in June, 1861, who was born in Oneida Co. N.Y. in 1840; two children.

ADAMS AUG. Retired, Sandwich; value prop. $6,000; Rep; Cong; from N.Y.

ADAMS CHAS. H. Physician and Surgeon, Sandwich; Rep; Cong; from Illinois.

ADAMS FREDERICK, Farmer; P.O. Somonauk; Rep; Luth; from Germany.

ADAMS HENRY A. Supt. Manufg. Co. Sandwich; val. prop. $34,000; Rep; Cong; NY.

ADAMS WALTER G. Mechanic. Sandwich; val. prop. $12,500; Rep; Cong; Illinois.

ADO v JACOB, Saloon, Somonauk; val. prop. $6,000; Ind; Cath; from Prussia.

AHRANS WILLIAM, Farmer; 6 acres, value $600; Dem; Ind; from Germany.

AINSWORTH ORAMAL, Retired Carpt. Sandwich; Rep; Ind; born Vermont.

ALFORD THOMAS, Carpenter, Somonauk; prop. $800; Rep; Bapt; England.

ALLEN HIRAM P. Retired Capitalist, Sandwich; prop. $2,500; Rep; Ind; from N.Y.

ALLISON JNO. W. works in lumber yard. Sandwich; Rep; Pres; from N.Y.

AMES ASHAEL E. Laborer, Somonauk; Rep; Ind; from Vermont.

ANDERS CARL, Laborer. Sandwich; Dem; Cath; Germany.

ANTOINE J. N. General Store, Somonauk; Ind; Cath; from Illinois.

APPLE MARGARET, P.O. Sandwich; val. prop. $5 0; Meth; from Germany.

ARMSTRONG DAVID, Building Mover; P.O. Sandwich; prop. $25,000; Lib; U. Pres; N.Y.

ARMSTRONG JNO. Farmer, Secs. 13 and 14; P.O. Sandwich; Rep; Pres; from N.Y.

ARMSTRONG J. A. Furniture Dealer, Sandwich; prop. $5,000; Dem; Meth; from N.Y.

ARMSTRONG JNO. J. Farmer, Secs. 13 and 14; P.O. Sandwich; Rep; Ind; from N.Y.

ARMSTRONG WILLIAM, Farmer. Sec. 21; P.O. Somonauk; born in Washington Co. N.Y. June 20, 1805; came to Illinois in May, 1867; Rep; U. Pres; owns 250 acres, value $20,000; married Phoebe McClellan in May, 1832, born in Washington Co. N.Y. August 14, 1808; has three sons: David J. and John A. reside on homestead with father, Wm. T. resides in California.

ARNOLD EDWARD, Retired Farmer and Mechanic; resides on Church street, Sandwich; born Wayne Co. N. Y. Aug. 1811; came to Illinois in 1855; Rep; Bapt; owns house and four lots and 200 acres, value $4,000; son. Wm. H. Arnold, entered the army in Co. A, 111th Regt. N.Y. Vols ; was taken prisoner at the battle of Harper's Ferry; was paroled to Chicago and was sick three months from exposure and privation while a prisoner; was detailed as Quartermaster, stationed at Arlington Heights, Virginia; was honorably discharged at the close of the war; Mr. A. Sen. married Nancy Richey, of Orleans Co. N.Y., born in December, 1817, and died Sept. 15, 1849; married for his second wife Clarissa Mann, of Rutland, Vermont, born Feb. 20, 1831, and died April 29, 1854; married for his third wife Nancy D. Burrell, of Washington Co. N.Y., born in January, 1829; four children, one son and three daughters.

ARNOLD ELIAS C. Farmer, resides on Sec. 26; P.O. Sandwich; born in DeKalb Co. Ill. Feb. 26, 1838; Liberal in politics and religion; owns house and 3 acres, value $2,000; personal prop. $1,500; married Mary E. Van Olinda April 4, 1861, who was born in Montgomery Co. N.Y. April 17, 1845.

ARNOLD IRA M. Farmer. Sec. 21; P.O. Sandwich; born in DeKalb Co. Ill. May 10, 1843; Ind. in politics and Lib. in religion; owns 112 acres, value $10,000; married Harriet E. Ryan Sept. 9, 1863, who was born in Kendall Co. Ill. July 11, 1841; one child, a son, John W., aged 9 years.

ARNOLD ROBT. T. Farmer, Sec. 34; P.O. Somonauk; Rep; Bapt; from England.

ARNOLD Wm. Laborer, Somonauk; real estate $500; Rep; Bapt; from England.

ATHERTON DAN'L F. Farmer, Somonauk; personal prop. $800; Rep; Pres; Illinois.

ATHERTON ROLLIN C. Laborer, Somonauk; Rep; Pres; from Illinois.
ATKINS REUBEN, Blacksmith; P.O. Sandwich; Ind; from England.
AVERY DENISON H. Farmer, Sec. 7; P.O. Sandwich; Rep; Ind; from N.Y.

BABCOCK JAS. lives with Mr. Palmer, Sandwich; Rep; from N.Y.
BACON CHAS. A. General store, Somonauk; Rep; from N.Y.
BACON LAWRENCE, P.O. Freeland; Rep; Ind; from Illinois.
BACON LAWRENCE P. Farmer, P.O. Somonauk; Dem; Ind; from N.Y.
BAILEY LUTHER, Gardener; P.O. Sandwich; Rep; Ind; from N.Y.
BALDWIN FRANKLIN, Retired Farmer; resides in Hendee's Block, Sandwich; born
in Onondaga Co. N.Y. Oct. 25, 1825; came to Northville, LaSalle Co. Ill. in June, 1846; removed to Sandwich, DeKalb Co. Sept. 12, 1876; Rep; Cong; owns house and six lots, value
$3,000; has a farm of 172 acres in LaSalle Co. value $15,480; personal prop. $3,000; Treas-
urer and Director of Farmers' Insurance Co. of Northville, LaSalle Co. Ill.; married Mary
E. Johnson in May, 1845, who was born in Onondaga Co. N.Y. in 1826, and died in May,
1870, leaving three children; married for his second wife Mary J. Carpenter, in November,
1871, who was born in Luzerne Co. Penn. in November, 1838.
BALLAU N. E. Physician and Surgeon; P O. Sandwich; Rep; Ind; from N.Y.
BANTA ELIJAH, Clergyman, Sandwich; Dem; Latter Day Saints; from Kentucky.
BARK C. E. Livery and Feed Stable, Sandwich; Dem; Ind; from N.Y.
BARK GEO. Farmer, Sandwich; Dem; from N.Y.; 400 acres.
BARK WM. H. Farmer; P.O. Freeland; Dem; Ind; from N.Y.
BARKER ANSON L. Drayman; P.O. Sandwich; Rep; Ind; from N.Y.
BARKER ERASTUS I. General Merchandise, Sandwich; Rep; Ind; from N.Y.
BARNETT H. M. Laborer, Sandwich; Ind; Ind; from N.Y.
BARNES ELA, Farmer, Sandwich; Dem; Meth; from N Y.
BARROWS GEORGE B. Teacher; P.O. Sandwich; Rep: Cong; from Maine.
BASS CHAS. Teamster, Sandwich; Rep; Ind; from Illinois.
BEAL ELLERY H. Rev. Clergyman; P.O. Sandwich; Rep; Meth; from Maine.
BEAL LUTHER, Carriage Salesman; P.O. Sandwich; Rep; Meth; from Maine.
BEAL T. W. Pattern maker, Sandwich; Rep; Ind; from Maryland.
BEAL THOMAS W. Carpenter; Rep; from Illinois.
BEEBE WM. N. Retired, Sandwich; Rep; Ind; from N.Y.; value prop. $3,000.
BENNETT FRANK, works for Clark; P.O. Freeland; from N.Y.
BENOIT JOHN, Farmer, Sec. 31; Dem; Cath; 220 acres, value $1,500; pers. prop. $100.
BERRY ERASTUS, Teamster, Somonauk; Rep; Bapt; from N.Y.; prop. $500.
BERRY WM. E. Pumpmaker, Sandwich; Dem; Latter Day Saints; from Indiana.
BETZ JOHN, Lumberman, Somonauk; Rep; Luth; from Germany.
BEUGLIN HENRY, Laborer, Sandwich; Rep; Ind; from Sweden.
BEVERIDGE ANDREW, Sen. Farmer; resides on Sec. 3; P.O. Freeland; born in
Hebron, Washington Co. N.Y. in 1802; came to Illinois in 1852; settled on the farm on
which he now resides; Rep. and United Pres; married Jane Martin, May 7, 1841, who was
born in Argyle, Washington Co. N.Y. March 16, 1821; family of one son and three daughters; son only, living; Andrew Beveridge, Jr. was born in Washington Co. N.Y. Dec. 2, 1849;
resides on homestead with father; graduated at Monmouth College, Ill. in 1865; was admitted to the Bar as Attorney at Law in Chicago; was in the army, Co. A, 138th Regt.
formed of college students; honorably discharged at close of enlistment; married Mira E.
Dewey Nov. 7, 1872, who was born in Mass. in 1849; family of two daughters.
BEVERIDGE ANDREW, Jr. Farmer and Attorney at Law; P.O. Freeland; Rep; U. Pres,
BEVERIDGE ELIZABETH A. Mrs. Sec. 5; P.O. Freeland; U. Pres; from N.Y.
BEVERIDGE WM. G. Farmer, lives with mother; P.O. Freeland; Rep; Ind; from Ill.
BIBBS JAMES, Laborer, Sandwich; Rep; Meth; from Africa.
BIGELOW CHARLES, Laborer, Somonauk; Rep; Ind; from Mass.
BLAGG MARY M. Mrs. Tailoress, Sandwich; Meth; from Tenn; value $1,600.
BLAGG THOS. I. Laborer, Sandwich; Rep; Ind; from Miss.
BLANCHARD T. B. Drugs and Stationery, Somonauk; Rep; Ind; from N.Y.
BLEITC JACOB, Farmer, Sec. 2; P.O. Freeland; Rep; Bapt; from Germany.

BLISS FRANKLIN, Farmer, Sec. 32; P.O. Somonauk; Dem; Ind; from Mass.

BLISS M. O. Farmer, Sec. 33; P.O. Somonauk; Rep; Bapt; from Mass.

BLISS JNO. Dairyman, Somonauk; Rep; Luth; from France.

BLONN GEO. Clerk, Sandwich; Rep; Ind; from Germany.

BLOODGOOD HENRY F. Editor and Prop. of the *Free Press*, Sandwich, established in 1873; resides on Fourth street; born in Rochester, N.Y. Feb. 6, 1852; came to DeKalb Co in June, 1862; Rep; Lib. in religious views; owns house and lot, value $2,000; personal prop. $3,000; married Eva M. Smith May 7, 1873, who was born in Little Rock, Ill. June 29, 1854.

BLOOM JAMES W. Landlord and Prop. of Transit House, Sandwich, situated on Railroad street; born in Livingston Co. N.Y.; came to state in October, 1857; Rep; Ind. in religious views; was in the U. S. service three years, a member of the Chicago Board of Trade Battery; was honorably discharged July 3, 1865.

BOCHTLER JOSEPH, Harness-maker, Somonauk; Rep; Cath; from Germany.

BOHCLER JOSEPH. Harness-maker, Somonauk; Rep; Ind; from Germany.

BOND WILLIAM, Street Commissioner, residence Maple street, Somonauk; born in Lima, N.Y. Sept. 10, 1807; came to Illinois in 1832; assisted in erecting the second frame building in Chicago; came to DeKalb Co. in 1855; Rep; Bapt; owns house and lot; assisted in burying fourteen victims of the Indian massacre of 1332, in what is now LaSalle Co.; married Fannie Hunt August 24, 1846, born in Crawford Co. Penn. Dec. 25, 1817; his son Charles was member of the 8th Ill. Cavalry; died in the service.

BOSS THEODORE, Boot and Shoemaker, Somonauk; Ind; Ind; from Germany.

BOTHELL JAMES, Farmer, Somonauk; Pres; from Canada.

BOURNE ALBERT E. Principal of Public Schools of Sandwich, Ill. which position he has held for the last three years; residence Centre Street, Sandwich; born in Bristol, Kenosha, Wis. Feb. 11, 1849; Graduate of the State University, Madison, Wis; came to DeKalb Co. Ill. August, 1872; Rep; Ind. in religious views; married Mary L. Craig, August 7, 1871, who was born Palmyra, Wis. Aug. 7, 1849; two children.

BOYLE ROBT. H. Mason, Somonauk; Dem; Ind; came from Penn.

BRADWELL CHAS. A. Machinist; P.O. Sandwich; $1,000; Rep; Ind.

BRANDENBURG AUG. Shoemaker, Sandwich; born Ger; Rep; Luth.

BRAYTON JOHN. Laborer, Sandwich; born New York; Ind; Ind.

BRIGHAM C. H. Laborer, Somonauk; Dem; Ind; born N.Y.

BRIGHAM JEROME, Lumber Dealer, Somonauk; born N.Y.; came to Ill. 1865; Rep; Ind.

BRIGHAM ROBT. M. Farmer and Mayor of Sandwich City; born N.Y.; Rep; Bapt.

BRITT ALONZO D. Farmer; P.O. Sandwich; born N. H.; Rep; Bapt.

BROWER GARRETT W. Retired Farmer, Sandwich; born N.Y.; Rep; Ind; value $5,000.

BROWN JAS. D. Laborer, Sandwich; born N.Y.; Rep; Ind.

BROWN ANDREW M. Farmer; rents Geo. Bark's farm; P.O. Freeland; born N.Y.; Lib; Ind.

BROWN SAMUEL, Laborer; P.O. Sandwich; Canada; Rep; Lib.

BROWN THOMAS, Farmer, Sec. 33; born Scotland; came 1850; 140 ac. $10,000; per. $8 000.

BUCKINGHAM ALMUS W. Farmer; res. Sec. 32; P.O. Somonauk; born in Essex, Conn. May 8, 1832, came to DeKalb Co. Ill, 1842; Rep; Bapt; owns 200 acres, value $14,000; personal property $3,000; is Prest. of the Farmers' Insurance Co. of Somonauk; married Zerlina M. Cheever, Nov. 22, 1854, who was born New York, June 15, 1836; has had three children—two living, son and daughter.

BUCKINGHAM ADALINE Mrs. Sandwich; Conn; $2,000; Bapt.

BURBANK Mrs. Somonauk; born France; per. prop. $500; Luth.

BURCHUM WESLEY, Farmer, Sec. 8; P.O. Somonauk; born N.Y; Rep; Ind; 220 acres.

BURDICK CHAS. Horse Dealer, Somonauk; born N.Y.; came to Ill. 1853; Rep; Meth.

BURGE GEO. Broom Manufacturer, Somonauk; born Scotland; came to Ill. 1865; Rep; Ind.

BURDGE WASHINGTON, Carpenter; resides on Center St. Sandwich; born in Juniata Co. Penn. Nov. 22, 1833, removed to Huntington Co. Penn. where he remained until he was twenty-one years of age, came to DeKalb Co. Ill. in 1858; Rep; Lib. in religion: owns house and 1¼ acres, value $2,500; personal property $1,700; has been Overseer of Highways and School Director.

BURGIN ALBERT A. lives with father; P.O. Freeland; Rep.

BURGIN PETER, Farmer, Sec. 6; P.O. Freeland; born Vt; Rep; 75 acres, $5,000.

BURK JEFFRY, Laborer; P.O. Sandwich; born Ireland; Rep; Cath; $1,000.

BURK MICHAEL, Laborer; P.O. Sandwich; born Ireland; Rep; Cath.

BURKHARDT JACOB Sr. Cabinetmaker; P.O. Sandwich; born Ger; $5,000; Dem; Prot pref.

BURKHARDT JACOB Jr. Cabinetmaker; P.O. Sandwich; born Ger; $600; Rep; Luth.

BURNS JOHN R. Rev. Pastor of M.E. Cqurch, Somonauk; Ohio; Rep; was in army.

BUSCHNER W. H. Carpenter, Somonauk; born Ill; Rep; Ind.

BUTCHER JNO. LEWIS, Sandwich; born Eng; Epis.

BUTLER GEO. W. House Mover; P.O. Sandwich; born N.Y.; $2,500; Dem.

CAIN SAMUEL, Farmer, Sec. 35; P.O. Sandwich; born Ireland; Rep; Pres: 12 ac. $2,000.

CAMPBELL ALEX. Laborer, Sandwich; born Ire; Ind; Cath; $2,500.

CAMPBELL H. A. Harnessmaker, Somonauk; born N.Y.; came to Ill. 1860; Rep; Ind.

CAMPBELL JAS. Laborer, Sandwich; born Ire; Dem; Cath.

CAMPBELL JNO. Section Boss, Sandwich; born Ire; Rep; Cath; $4,000.

CANUM SARAH F. Sandwich; N.Y.; $300; Meth.

CARD WM. H. Rev. Somonauk; born Lewis Co. N.Y. Aug. 26, 1812; Bapt. Clergyman for forty years; pastor several years in New York City; the last pastorate in the East, Essex, Conn; removed to Fond du Lac, Wis. 1847, where he was pastor four years, went to LaCrosse, Wis. and labored as pastor and missionary about ten years, came to Ill. 1865, to DeKalb Co. 1869; pastor at Sandwich four years; present pastor of the Baptist Church, Somonauk; owns 150 acres land in Grundy Co. all underlaid with coal, a block with good house on it at Sandwich, which, with personal property, is valued at $10,000; married Cornelia A. Cairns, June 30, 1837, who was in New York City Dec. 15, 1817; two sons—Wm. L. traveling auditor for St. L. & R. C. N. R. R. Moberly P.O. Mo.; and Jno. C. chief clerk Auditor's office, St. Louis.

CARMAN ERVINE, Machinist; Sandwich House; 1st Lieut. in Army; Rep; Cong.

CARMEN SILAS, Mechanic, Sandwich; born Penn; Rep; Ind.

CARR CAROLINE Mrs. P.O. Sandwich; N.Y.; value $2,000; Pres.

CARR CHAS. W. Carpenter, Somonauk; born N.Y.; real estate $2,000; Meth; Rep.

CARR EUGENE J. Druggist, Somonauk; born Ill; real estate $1,000; Rep; Meth.

CARR OSCAR N. Trav. Agt; P.O. Sandwich; N.Y.; Rep; Ind.

CARPENTER M. Farmer; P.O. Sandwich; born N.Y.; Rep; Ind; 107 acres, $10,000.

CASS CLARENCE W. Machinist; P.O. Sandwich; Il; Rep; Cong.

CASS J. W. Mrs. P.O. Sandwich; born N.Y.; $1,800; Cong.

CASTLE MILES BEACH, Banker and Lumber and Coal Dealer, Sandwich; Senator Castle was born Albany, N.Y. August, 1828; his father was a commissioned officer of cavalry, war of 1812; he is cousin of Wm. A. Beach, the noted criminal lawyer of New York City; Mr. C.'s education was a two years, course at Jonesville Academy, so that he is emphatically a self-made man; he came to Ill. in 1858, and settled in Sandwich in 1864, where he has since resided; he is one of the principal owners of a bank in Sandwich, and one in Kendall Co; he has always been a Republican, and is now serving his second term in the State Senate; he is an easy, pleasant speaker, though not obtrusive; married Freelove Kinney in 1857, who was born Homer Co. N.Y. 1834; three children living.

CHAMBERLIN BENJ. Laborer, Sandwich; from Ohio; Dem; Ind.

CHAMBERLAIN SANDFORD, Laborer, Manf. Co. Sandwich; born N.Y.; Rep; Ind.

CHAMPLIN ORLANDO C. Painter, Sandwich; born N.Y.; Rep; Ind.

CHAPMAN W. N. Clerk Drug Store, Sandwich; born N.Y.; Rep; Ind.

CHARLESWORTH DAVID, Laborer, Sandwich; born England; Ind.

CHEEVER EZRA, Somonauk; from N.Y.; came to Ill. 1846; Rep; Pres.

CHIFFER LOUIS, Farmer, Somonauk; born France; Rep; Luth.

COMINERLIN FREDERICK, Laborer, Sandwich; from Germany; Ind Pres; value $1,000.

CLAPPER SUMNER, Blacksmith, Sandwich; born Penn; Rep; Luth.

CLARK ISRAEL S. Farmer; resides on Sec. 10; P.O. Somonauk; born in Conn. Sept. 1819, came to DeKalb Co. in Sept. 1842; Rep; Ind. in religion; owns 157 acres, value $9,500; personal property $2,000; has held offices of Assessor and Collector; collected the first tax levied after organization of Somonauk Township, by Town Collector; entered the army. August, 1862, in Co. H, 105th Regt. Ill. Vol. Inf; was in the series of battles commencing with Resaca, May 15, 1864 to the arrival of Sherman at Richmond by way of the sea. Some of the most noted were Kenesaw Mountain, Snake Creek Gap, Peach Tree Creek, continuing three days, and the taking of Atlanta; was honorably discharged June 7, 1865; married Cornelia E. Potter, Dec. 25, 1849, who was born in Lewis Co. N.Y. July 4, 1825; has had seven children, four living.

CLARK H. S. Retired Farmer, Sandwich; from Conn; Rep; Pres; value $2,500.

CLARK JNO. Farmer and Trader, res. Gage Street, Somonauk; born Middlesex Co. Conn. Feb. 3, 1821; removed to Ill. DeKalb Co. Sept. 1842; Dem; Independent in his religious views; 400 acres, Sec. 10 and 14, with other real estate, value $34,000; personal property $10,000; has acted Supervisor several terms; married Amelia B. Shailer, Feb. 29, 1858, who was born in Middlesex Co. Conn. Aug. 10, 1819; Mr. Clark had three dollars in money, which was the extent of his worldly wealth when he landed in DeKalb Co; his present handsome property is another illustration of what energy and attention to business will accomplish in the State of Illinois.

CLARKE M. G. Rev. Resides in Sandwich; born in Woodstock, Conn. Dec. 1809; lived on farm with parents till over twenty years of age, occasionally teaching district school winters in his native town; in early youth became interested in religion, and united with the Baptist Church in Woodstock, entered the Theological Seminary of Newton, Mass. in 1832; graduated in 1837; in the Autumn of that year was ordained Pastor of the Second Baptist Church at Suffield, Conn; after a few months he returned to the old farm life, on account of ill health; he was called to Massachusetts, to take up work that was commenced while a student at Newton, where, under his direction, a fine meeting house was erected; after a severe illness, in which his life was despaired of, he removed to Norwich, Conn. and organized the Central Baptist Church; in 1846, he was called to the pastorate of the First Baptist Church of Springfield, Mass; after six years of prosperous work in Springfield, he accepted for a time the secretaryship of the American Foreign Bible Society; he purchased the *Mother's Journal*, and committed its editorial work to his wife, Mrs. Mary G. Clarke; he was now called to the charge of the Tabernacle Baptist Church, Philadelphia; here again his health failed, a partial sunstroke produced congestion of the brain, of which he never fully recovered; removed to Indianapolis, Ind. where he started the *Witness*, a religious paper, and continued to edit and publish it until driven away by congestive chills; he was elected financial secretary of the University of Chicago, which office he held for three years, during which time the main building of the university was erected and the Dearborn Tower and the great tele-cope was placed in it; the net assets of the university were increased largely during his administration; he and his sons issued a number of valuable books, such as the "Patriotism of Illinois," "Wisconsin in the War," and the "Life of Mr. Lincoln;" he preached for a time for the church at Evanston, when he left to accept the Corresponding Secretaryship of the Baptist State Convention of New York; the result of an injury again compelled him to give up all active ministerial labor, and by the most eminent medical advice he has taken charge of a farm; he has rented for a term of years Mr. Hubbard Latham's farm, where he now resides with his family; he has two sons in Chicago in business.

CLARK MATTHEW T. Renter, Sec. 10; P.O. Sandwich; born Conn; Rep; Bapt.

CLARK NATHANIEL, Farmer, Somonauk; Ireland; Rep; Meth; $1,400.

CLOSE WM. Carpenter and Joiner; res. Green Street, Sandwich; born Union Co. Penn. Aug. 11. 1828; came to Ill. 1851, and DeKalb Co. 1865; Rep; Meth; owns house and lot worth $1,000; entered army Aug. 8, 1862, Co. G, 104th Reg. I. V. I. was in engagement at Hartsville, Tenn. where he was captured with his brigade, and taken to Murfreesboro, paroled ten days later and sent north, reorganized and left Chicago for the front Feb. 12, 1863, with rank of Sergeant, promoted for bravery, honorably discharged in July 5, 1865; married Caroline Munson, Dec. 19, 1849, was born in Green Co. N.Y. Nov. 23, 1829; five children.

COE ELI G. Former Secretary of the Sandwich Enterprise Co. which place he resigned on account of ill health; resides on North Main Street, Sandwich; born Ontario Co. N.Y. in 1834; came to Illinois in 1854, and to DeKalb Co. in 1871; Rep; Cong; owns house and lot, value $2,000; was in the army as Commissary of the 8th N. Y. Cav. two and one-half years, honorably discharged Feb. 1864; married Anna L. Whitman, June. 1871, who was born in Ontario Co. N.Y. in 1838; the following are some of the principal battles: Ball's Bluff, Winchester, Antietam, Harper's Ferry, South Mountain, Fredericksburg, Chancellorsville and Gettysburg.

COLE EDWARD, Laborer, Somonauk; Rep; Meth.

COLE EDWARD, Carpenter, Sandwich; Rep; Ind; N.Y.

COLE RUFUS A. Tailor, Sandwich; Rep; Ind; born Canada.

COLE R.C. Nursery, Somonauk; Rep; Meth; prop. $1,200; born N.Y.

COLLIER JNO. Laborer, Sandwich; Rep; Ind; born Ill.

COLEMAN STEPHEN D. Farmer, resides on Sec. 21; P.O. Sandwich; born Rutland Co. Vt. 1826; came to Ill. 1856; Rep; Ind; owns 300 acres of land; val. $18,000; personal prop. $5,000; married Margaret L. Fraser, Sept. 11, 1855, who was born Rutland Co. Vt. 1837; has had six children, five living.

COLYER ELLIOTT. Laborer, Sandwich; Dem; born Ill.

COMSTOCK BENJ. Carpenter and Joiner; P.O. Sandwich; Rep; Lib; $2,000; born Conn.

COMSTOCK W. A. Prop. Somonauk Exchange, Somonauk; Rep; Epis; born N Y.

CONE AVERY E. Machinist, Sandwich; Rep; Ind; Wis.

CONVERSE I. C. Mechanic, Sandwich; from Penn; Ind; Pres.

CONKLIN WM. Teamster, P.O. Sandwich; Rep; Ind; from N.Y.

CONNOLLY JAMES, Railroadman, Somonauk; $500; Dem; Cath; born Ireland.

COOK DANIEL G. Pump Manufacturer, Sandwich; Meth; Dem; $1,000; born N. J.

COOK JOHN Mrs. P.O. Sandwich; born Penn; $2,500; Meth.

COOPER CHAS. Butcher, Sandwich; born Penn; Rep; Meth.

CORLINSKY CHARLES, Merchant; P.O. Sandwich; born Poland; Israelite.

COTTON H. C. Farmer, Sec. 21 and 22; P.O. Somonauk; born Ohio; Dem; Bapt.

COTTON RICHARD, Farmer, lives with brother, Sec. 21; born Ohio; Dem; Ind.

COTTON R. D. Farmer, Secs. 21 and 22; P.O. Somonauk; born Ohio; Dem; Ind.

COX ELIZA C. Mrs. Dressmaker, Sandwich; Ohio; $600; Latter Day Saint.

COY CHAS. P. Farmer, Sandwich; born Vt; Rep; Ind; 160 acres, val. $11,000.

COY HORACE, Farmer, Sandwich; from Vt. Rep; Ind; $700.

CRAPSER A. P. Grocer; P.O. Sandwich; Ill; real est. $1.500; per. prop. $500; Rep; Cong.

CRAPSER G. W. Traveling Agent; P.O. Sandwich; born Ill; Rep; Ind.

CRAPSER WM. H. Farmer; P.O. Sandwick; $6,000; Rep; Ind; born N. Y.

CRAWFORD DAVID W. Grocer; P.O. Sandwich; born Saratoga Co. N.Y. Sept. 16, 1843; came to Ill. March, 1858; Rep; of the firm of Thompson & Crawford.

CRAWFORD PERRY, Painter; Sandwich; born Penn; Rep; Ind.

CROFOOT D. K. Dry Goods, Boots and Shoes, Sandwich; Ind; Ind; $6,000 stock; N.Y.

CROFOOT RUSSELL D. Retired Merchant, Sandwich; born Conn; Dem; Ind.

CULLEN THOMAS, Farmer, Somonauk; real est. $6,000; Ind; Meth; Ireland.

CULVER AMASA J. Cheese Maker; P.O. Sandwich; born in Rutland Co. Vt. May, 1849; moved to DeKalb Co. Ill. Nov. 6, 1873; Rep. and Bapt; owns house and 2½ lots on Main Street, Sandwich, valued at $1,000; married Alice Pels e, July 13. 1869, who was born in Rutland Co. Vt. March 19, 1852.

CULVER JNO. L. General Merchandise, Sandwich; Rep; Ind; val. $2,500; born N.Y.

CULVER THOS. E. Merchant, Sandwich; Rep; Ind; $2,000; born N.Y.

CULVER SENECA, Mechanic; P.O. Sandwich; born Vt; Rep; Bapt; 28 acres, $700.

CULVER BROS., G. W. & J. H. Bankers, Sandwich; Rep; real estate $50,000; N.Y.

CURRY HUGH S. Carpenter, Sandwich; born Canada; Ind; Ind.

CURRY ROBEKT, Carpenter, Sandwich; born Ireland; Rep; Ind.

CURTISE HENRY, Postmaster, Somonauk; Rep; Pres; born N.Y.

CUSHMAN SAMUEL R. Bakery and Restaurant; P.O. Sandwich; born Mass; Ind.

DANNEWITZ PHILIP, Farmer, Sec. 20; Somonauk; Dem; Pres; 160 acres; Germany.

DARNELL BENJ. Retired Grocer, Sandwich; Rep; Cong; $1.500; born N. C.

DARROW HENRY, Farmer, Sec. 24; P.O. Sandwich; 14 acres; Rep; Bapt; born Conn.

DAVID CAROLINE Mrs. born Penn; P.O. Sandwich; $1,000; Meth.

DAVID JOHN C. Physician; P.O. Sandwich; Rep; Cong; from Penn.

DAVID V. R. Dentist, Sandwich; Rep; Ind; born Penn.

DAVIDSON ALBERT, Tinner, Sandwich; Rep; Ind; born Ill.

DAVIS GEORGE W. retired; resides on Church Street, Sandwich; born DeKalb Co. Ill. July 29, 1838; Rep; Lib; owns house and lot, valued $4,000; married Eliza M. Gage, March, 1862, who was born Allegheny Co. N.Y. Nov. 15, 1831; one child.

DAVIS WILLIAM, Farmer; residence on West Church St., Sandwich; born in Bristol Co. Mass. Jan. 1, 1802; followed a seafaring life for sixteen years, trading at Brazil, West Indies, and Europe; was master of vessel for eight years; during the time had command of the following brigs: Agenora, Louisiana, Phoebe, Pandora, and the ship Fame; came to DeKalb Co. Ill. in 1835; and settled on the farm on which he now resides over forty years ago; Rep; Meth; owns 114 acres, valued at $17,000; personal property $6,000; married Eliza Dennis, Providence, R. I. in April, 1826, who was born at Tiverton, R. I. in 1801; has four children living.

DAVIS WM. Laborer, Sandwich; Rep; Bapt; from Kentucky.

DEAN S. H. Blacksmith, Somonauk; Rep; Meth; value of house and lot $800; Vt.

DEAN THOS. A. Harness, Sandwich; Rep; property $800; N. H.

DEE FRED H. Painter, Sandwich; property $600; Rep; Ind; England.

DELANO WM. Miller; P.O. Sandwich; Rep; Bapt; from Vt.

DENNIS W. A. Farmer, Sec. —; P.O. Somonauk; Ill; Rep.

DILLINGER SAML., Moulder; P.O. Sandwich; Rep; Ind; from Penn.

DEVINE EDW. Farmer; P.O. Freeland; Dem; Cath; value of property $12,000; New York.

DEVOLL G. B. Mechanic, Sandwich; Rep; Ind; from R. I.

DEWEY OLIVER, Farmer, Sec. 4; P.O. Freeland; Rep; Cong; 270 acres val. $13,500; Mass.

DEWEY O. BURDETTE, rents father's farm; P.O. Freeland; Rep; Cong; Mass.

DICKINSON MARMADUKE, Merchant Tailor, Sandwich; Ind; Ind; England.

DICKSON WM. H. Farmer, Sandwich; Ind; Ind; Penn.

DIDIO JOHN, Saloon, Somonauk; Dem; Cath; from France.

DIETRICH FREDERICK, Laborer, Sandwich; Rep; Ind; from Germany.

DIETRICH LEWIS, Farmer and Brick Maker, located about one mile from the City of Sandwich; only Brick Yard in vicinity; born in Germany, Dec. 26, 1841; came to Illinois in 1854, to DeKalb in 1857; Rep; Bapt; owns 110 acres, Sec. 27, value $9,300; brick yard $1,000; personal property $4,000; married Phoebe Haibach, Jan, 1, 1866, who was born in Germany, Nov. 14, 1846; five children, all living.

DIETRICH NICHOLAS, Laborer, Sandwich; Rep; Meth; Germany.

DIMOND WM. H. Farmer, Sec. 2; P.O. Freeland; Rep; Pres; 130 ac; val. $10,000; N. Y.

DOANE ENOS, Contractor and Builder, and Dealer in Building Materials of all kinds, office, West Railroad St., near Castle's Lumber Yard; residence LaFayette St., between Second and Third, Sandwich; born in Chester Co. Penn. Sep. 16, 1834; came to Illinois in 1856, and to DeKalb Co. in 1867; Rep; Ind. in religion; 320 acres in Iowa, two houses and lots in Sandwich, value $4,500; personal property $1,500; is a member of the Common Council of the City of Sandwich; married Carrie A. Wilson, Aug. 7, 1857, born in Belfast, Me. in 1840; five children living.

DOAN HENRY H. Carpenter and Joiner, Sandwich; Rep; Ind; from Penn.

DOAN ISRAEL, Carpenter and Joiner, Sandwich; Rep; Ind; from Penn.

DOANE JOS. B. Carpenter and Joiner, Sandwich; Rep; Ind; from Penn.

DOBBIN J. BLAIR, Farmer, Sec. 6; P.O. Freeland; Rep; U. P.; from Illinois.

DORE JAS. Moulder; P.O. Sandwich; Dem; Ind; from Canada.

DOUGLASS JOHN F. Millinery and Ladies' Furnishing; P.O. Sandwich; Rep; Pres; N. Y.

DOYT JONATHAN L. Moulder; P.O. Sandwich; Rep; Ind; Conn.

DRAIN LUMAN S. Painter, Sandwich; Rep; Ind; value of property $500; Ill.

DUBROCK G. W. Dry Goods, Somonauk; Rep; Luth; property $3,000; Germany.

DRILLON AUGUST, Tailor, Sandwich; Rep; Cath; from France.

DUNHAM C. Dealer in Musical Instruments, Sandwich; Rep; Meth; from N. J.

DUNN GEO. Laborer, Sandwich; Dem; Cath; property $1,000; Illinois.

DURELL WM. H. Sandwich; Rep; Ind; from Wisconsin.

DURLEY DANIEL E. Moulder, Sandwich; Dem; Ind; from Mass.

DURBIN J. A. Merchant Tailor, Sandwich; Rep; Ind; from Ohio.

DUTCHMAN JOHN, Laborer, Somonauk; prop. $300; Cath; Dem; from Switzerland.

DYAS JOSEPH, Landlord and Proprietor of the "Sandwich House;" born in Albany, N. Y. Jan. 1, 1825; came to state in Oct. 1863; Rep; Freewill Bapt; owns hotel and four lots, valued at $5,000; has been Superintendent of Schools, Town Treasurer and Clerk; married Mary A. Miner, May 9, 1847, who was born at Peru, Berkshire Co. Mass. May 24, 1827; has a family of three boys and one girl; has kept the Sandwich House for the past eleven years.

DYAS JOSEPH, Theological Student; P.O. Sandwich; Rep; Cong; from Mass.

DYAS WEBSTER, Drug Clerk; P.O. Sandwich; Rep; from Mass.

E AMES M. V. Foreman, Machine Shop, Sandwich; Rep; Ind; property $1,700; Alabama.

EARNSHAW JNO. Stone-cutter, Sandwich; Ind; Latter Day Saint; England.

EASTMAN CALVIN, Retired Farmer, Sandwich; Rep; Christian; N. H.

EBERLY GEO. Laborer, Sandwich; Rep; Ind; Illinois.

EBERLY JOHN W. Drayman; P.O. Sandwich; Rep; Illinois.

EBENINGER VALENTINE, Laborer, Sandwich; Rep; Meth; from Germany.

EHLER WM. Shoemaker, Sandwich; Dem; Prot; from Germany.

ELDRIDGE LUTHER, Retired Farmer, Sandwich; Rep; value of property $1,200.

ENGEL CHAS. Laborer, Somonauk; Rep; Luth; from Germany.

ESTABROOK EDW. A. Laborer; Rep; Ind; from N. Y.

ESTABROOKS MARY Mrs., Sec. 28; N. C.; P.O. Somonauk; Bapt.

EVANS P. H. Cheese Maker; resides on Ann St. Somonauk; born in Oneida Co. N. Y. May 5, 1847; came to Ill. in 1868, and to DeKalb Co. 1872; Rep; Lib; personal property $1,000; enlisted in Co. B, U. S. Regulars, in Sept. 1861; served eighteen months and re-enlisted in the 24th N.Y. Cavalry; served till close of the war; was wounded in left knee in battle of Antietam; honorably discharged in 1865; married Marrietta Eldrid, Nov. 9, 1869, who was born in Jefferson Co. N.Y. August, 1850.

EVERTS R. P. Mrs. P.O. Sandwich; property $1,000; Bapt; from N. Y.

EWINGS GEO. Retired Farmer, Sandwich; Rep; Latter Day Saint; property $10,000; Ohio.

FALGER CHAS. Blacksmith; Ind; Ind; from N. Y.

FALZ ADOLPH, Carpenter, Somonauk; Dem; Luth; from Germany.

FAIRBANKS REUBEN G. House, Carriage, and Sign Painter, shop and residence on Fourth St., head of Washington, Sandwich; born in Kendall Co. Ill. July 10, 1849; came to DeKalb Co. in 1854; Rep; Liberal; owns house and four lots, value $1,500; married Mrs. Lydia A. Haish, Jan. 24, 1872, born in Burlington, Kane Co. Ill., May 9, 1852.

FALZ FRED, Carpenter, Somonauk; Dem; Luth; from N. Y.

FANNING JOHN, Iron Moulder; P.O. Sandwich; Dem; Cath; from Ireland.

FARLEY WM. Farmer, Sec. 34; P.O. Somonauk; Rep; Ind; 209 acres; Illinois.

FARR ARCHIBALD L. Rev. Pastor Baptist Church; P.O. Sandwich; Rep; from N. Y.

FAY MARGARET A. Mrs. P.O. Freeland; property $2,000; U. P.; from Ohio.

FERGUSON ROBT. Clerk, Sandwich; Rep; Pres; property $3,500; from N. Y.

FERGUSON WM. C. Farmer, Sec. 6; P.O. Freeland; Rep; U. P.; property $3,500. Ohio.

FINCH FRANKLIN, Painter, P.O Sandwich; Rep; Ind; Illinois.

FINCH CALEB B. Carpenter; P.O. Sandwich; Rep; Meth; from N. Y.

FISH CHAS D. Farmer, Sandwich; Dem; Ind; born in N. Y.

FISH GEORGE J. Carpenter; Sandwich; from Penn; Rep; Ind.

FISHER ELEAZER, Farmer, residence on Second Street, Sandwich; born in Northfield, Vt. Oct. 17, 1810; came to Illinois in 1857, and to DeKalb Co. in 1864; Rep. and Meth; owns house and three lots; (son, Henry H. entered the army, served 100 days, then re-enlisted in the 7th Vermont for three years, served his full time and re-enlisted, and was transferred to 1st New York Batt. went into an engagement and never heard from since, supposed to have been killed); married Chloe C. Knight, April 16, 1837, who was born in Williston, Vt. Dec. 3, 1814; has had ten children, four living.

FISHER HENRY, Molder; P.O. Sandwich; val. $1,000; Eng; Rep; Ind.

FISHER W. Laborer; P.O. Sandwich; born Vt; Rep; Bapt.

FITCH CLARK, Carpenter and Painter; P.O. Sandwich; born Vt; $1,000; Rep; Cong.

FLETCHER JNO. Molder, Sandwich; from Eng; Rep; Ind.

FOLTZ EDWARD, Railroadman, Somonauk; Rep; Luth; born N.Y.

FOREMAN GEO. Tenant Farmer; P.O. Somonauk; born Eng; Ind.

FOREMAN HENRY, Retired, Somonauk; Rep; Luth; born Germany.

FORSYTH ANNA Mrs. relict of Jno. Forsyth, who died Nov. 15, 1864; res. Fourth Street, Sandwich; born Allegheny Co. Penn. July 21, 1801; came to Ohio 1820, Illinois 1867; Pres; owns house and four lots, $3,000; had three sons in the army—Capt. Jas. S. Forsyth, Co. H, 105th Reg. late of Chicago, who died Oct. 1875, A. G., of same company, R. W. Forsyth was in Ohio Reg; was married June 7, 1827; had nine children, five living, three sons and two daughters.

FORSYTH WM. T. Farmer, Secs. 3 and 4; P.O. Freeland; 130 acres; Rep; Ind; born Ohio.

FOSGATE JOSIAH, Farmer, Sec. 4; P.O. Freeland; 166 acres, $7,000; Rep; born N.Y.

FOX LESTER S. Baker, Somonauk; Dem; Cath; born N.Y.

FRANK H. J. Peddler, Sandwich; Rep; Prot; val. $1,000; born Germany.

FRANCES JOSEPH, Switchman, Sandwich; Rep; Cath; born Mass.

13

FRANCIS JOSEPH, Laborer, Sandwich; Ind; Ind; $500; France.

FRANK HENRY, Carpenter, Somonauk; Rep; Luth; born Germany.

FRASER CHARLES H. Farmer, Sec. 23; P.O. Sandwich; born Illinois, Aug. 15. 1850 Rep; Ind; property $1,200; married Miss Fanny Dudley, March 25, 1872, who was born at Guilford, Conn; one child.

FRASER LYMAN, Retired Farmer, Sec. 21; P.O. Sandwich; Ind; Ind; $8,000.

FRASER WILLIAM, Farmer, Sec. 14; P.O. Sandwich; born Washington Co. N.Y. April 29, 1816; came to Kendall Co. Ill. 1843, remained 12 years, had only $34 when he came to DeKalb Co. 1855 ;Independent in politics and religion; owns 517 acres, val. $30,000; personal property $4,000; married Mary Faxon, April 12. 1842, who was born in Washington Co. N.Y. Oct. 31, 1819; nine children.

FRASER WM. Jr. lives with father; P.O. Sandwich; Rep; Ind; born Ill.

FREINE EUGENE. Farmer; P.O. Somonauk; Ind; Cath; born France.

FREELAND E. K. Laborer, Sandwich; Rep; Ind; born N. J.

FRENCH ANDREW L. lives with father; P.O. Freeland; Rep; born Ill.

FRENCH E. C. Farmer, Sec. 24; P.O. Sandwich; Rep; Bapt; 160 acres, $6,500; born Vt.

FRENCH GEO. B. lives with father; P.O. Freeland; Rep; born Ill.

FRENCH WM. Farmer, Sec. 9; P.O. Freeland; born Washington Co. N.Y. 1811; came to Ill. June, 1842; Rep; Ind. in religious views; owns 285 acres in homestead and 162 acres in Squaw Grove Tp; married Belle Beveridge, Oct. 29, 1833, born Washington Co. N.Y. Nov. 17, 1815; had seven children, five living, two sons and three daughters; Mrs. B. is a member of the U. P. Church.

FRICK A. C. Mrs. Sandwich; $750; Meth; born N.Y.

FRIZZELL GEO. H. Machinist, Sandwich; Rep; Ind; born Me.

FULLER EUGENE M. Stock Dealer, Sandwich; Rep; Ind; from N.Y.

FULLER JOS. S. Retired Farmer, Sandwich; Rep; Bapt; val. $3,000; born Mass.

FULLER STEPHEN, Stock Dealer; P.O. Sandwich; Rep; Meth; prop. $700; born N.Y.

GAGE A. Stock Dealer, P.O. Sandwich; real est. $28,000; Rep; Spir; born N.Y.

GARDINER E. P. Mechanic, Sandwich; Rep; Cong; $1,500; born Conn.

GAGE ALMON, Retired; resides cor. Church and Main Streets, Sandwich; born in Sudbury, Rutland Co. Vt. June 1, 1804; came to Ill in DeKalb Co. in 1844; Mr. Gage was original proprietor and starter of the City of Sandwich, and identified with its growth and prosperity; Rep. and Ind. in his religious views; owns house and lot, 21 acres of timber, val. at $5,000; personal prop. $30,000; married Alvira Carpenter, May 13, 1832, born in Conn. Feb. 24, 1812; has had three children, two living; son, Jesse L. Gage, enlisted in Co. H, 105th Reg. I. V. I. Sept. 2, 1862, was with his regiment in the battles from Nashville to the taking of Atlanta, which engagement he was killed, Aug. 12, 1864; Mr. Gage was a soldier, always prompt in the discharge of duty and universally beloved by his comrades; his remains were brought to Sandwich for interment.

GAGE ALVARUS, Retired; resides on Gage Street, Somonauk; born in Rutland Co. Vt. June 1, 1804; came to Illinois in 1843; Rep; Meth; owns house and 23 acres, value $5,000; has held the office of Justice of the Peace and Assessor; married Eucla Brigham, March 30, 1831, who was born in Worcester Co. Mass. June 6, 1806; has had four children, one son and three daughters, only one living, the wife of Thomas Wright.

GARDNER HENRY C. Farmer; Sec. 24; P.O. Sandwich; Rep; Ind.

GATES JNO. M. Engineer, Sandwich; born Germany; Lib; Pres.

GAYLORD WILLIAM L. Retired Farmer, Sandwich; Rep; Cong; prop. $4,000; from N.Y.

GEORGE FRANK, Farmer, Sec. 19; P.O. Somonauk; Dem; Cath; 60 acres; born France.

GEORGE HENRY, Farmer, Sandwich; Rep; Ind; val. $500; from Germany.

GIFFORD VINCENT, House Builder, Somonauk; Rep; Ind; val. $100; from N.Y.

GILLETT S. B. Mrs. Millinery Furnishing Goods, Sandwich; Cong; val. prop. $2,000.

GILLESPIE JOHN, Farmer, Somonauk; Rep; Ind; born N.Y.

GILLISPIE JNO. L. Tenant Farmer; P.O. Somonauk; Rep; from N.Y.

GLETTY HENRY, Farmer, lives with father, Sandwich; Rep; Pres; Ill.

GLETTY JACOB, Farmer. Sec. 34; P.O. Sandwich; 182 acres, $11,000; Rep; Pres; France.

GLETTY LEWIS, lives with father; Rep; Ind; France.

GOODELL J. M. Retired; Rep; Ind; val. $700; born N.Y.

GOODELL THOS. Laborer, Sandwich; Dem; Ind; born N.Y.

GOODFELLOW WM. Presiding Elder Mendota Dist; P.O. Sandwich; Rep; $3,000; Ohio.

GGODMAN GUSTAV, Merchant, Sandwich; Ind; born Germany.

GOOR DANL. Laborer; P.O. Sandwich; from Switzerland.

GOULD H. Miss, Retired Teacher, Somonauk; val. per. prop. $200; Pres; born Mass.

GRAHAM ISAAC, Farmer, Sec. 6; P.O. Freeland; born in Washington Co. N.Y. May 6, 1817; removed with his parents to Franklin Co. Ohio, 1817, where he resided until 1853, when he removed to DeKalb Co. where he has ever since resided; on the 12th Sept. 1839, was married to Nancy Livingston, in Franklin Co. Ohio; the issue of this marriage is five children, three sons and two daughters, all living except the oldest daughter, who died Nov. 1869; his sons, Edward, Alexander and Wm. John, all reside in Kansas; Alexander was a soldier in Co. H, 2d Iowa Inf; honorably discharged June, 1865; receives a pension for wounds received before Atlanta.

GRAND GEO. Laborer; P.O. Sandwich; Rep; Bapt; from Alabama.

GRANDDANDAN PROSPER, Farmer; P.O. Somonauk; Dem; Cath; from France.

GRANGER JNO. L. Rev. Pastor Cong. Church, Sandwich; Rep.

GRAVES HENRY, Retired Farmer; P.O. Sandwich; Rep; Meth; from N.Y.

GRAVES HENRY C. Nurseryman, residence and office head of North LaFayette street, Sandwich, Ill.; born in Rutland Co. Vt. in 1827; came to Illinois in 1845, and to DeKalb Co. in 1857; Ind. in politics and religion; owns 33 acres, and other real estate, value $4,500; val. personal prop. and investment in nursery business, $11,000; married Jane Perkins in 1856, who was born in Columbia Co. N.Y. in 1830; Mrs. Graves died July 6, 1874; family of five children.

GREENFIELD SAMUEL Sen. Retired Farmer, P.O. Sandwich; Rep; Meth; England.

GREENFIELD SAMUEL, Farmer, Sandwich; prop. $1,000; Rep; Ind; from Mich.

GREENMAN ALONZO G. Dealer in Stock and Wool; residence N. Main street, Sandwich; born in Orleans Co. N.Y. Dec. 28, 1822; came to Illinois in 1854, and DeKalb Co. in 1856; Rep; Ind. in his religious views; owns house and lot and four acres, value $5,000, and brick store on Railroad street, value $7,000; personal prop. $4,000; married Jemima Allen at Monroe Co. N.Y. June 8, 1852, who was born in Tompkins Co. N.Y. Dec. 15, 1823; Mr. G. has been Marshal of Sandwich two terms.

GREENWOOD DAVIS, Moulder; P.O. Sandwich; Rep; Ind; from Mass.

GRIESE JOHN, Painter, Somonauk; Rep; Luth; from Germany.

GRIFFITH F. E. Millwright; P.O. Sandwich; Rep; Ind; from N.Y.

GROVER JAMES, Mechanic; P.O. Sandwich; Rep; Ind; from N.Y.

GROVER LYMAN, Mechanic; P.O. Sandwich; Rep; Ind; from N.Y.

GUIDOT T. J. Boot and Shoemaker, Somonauk; Rep; Ind; Switzerland.

GURLEY GEO. W. Mcht. Sandwich; Dem; Cong; from Illinois.

H AAS G. Harness-maker, Sandwich; Dem; Ind; from Illinois.

HAIN WILLIAM, Laborer, Somonauk; Rep; Luth; from Germany.

HALABETER CLIA Mrs. widow; Saloon, Somonauk; val. prop. $300.

HALL CHAS. W. Painter, Sandwich; Rep; from Penn.

HALL DAVID A. Laborer; P.O. Sandwich; Rep; Meth.

HALL JOHN H. Machinist; P.O. Sandwich; Rep; Cong; from N.Y.

HALL JACOB M. Farmer; residence corner Church and Greeen streets, Sandwich; born in Ontario Co. N.Y. Dec. 2, 1815; came to Illinois in 1838; Rep; Meth; 150 acres and house and lot in Sandwich; total value $12,000; married Lurana, daughter of Major Dennis, Sen., Nov. 7, 1842, who was born in Providence, R. I. June 29, 1815; two sons and two daughters; sons married and settled about two miles from Sandwich; one daughter settled in Mo. and one lives with parents.

HALL JNO. W. Farmer, Sec. 36; P.O. Sandwich; Rep; from Illinois.

HALL O. L. Retired Farmer, Sandwich; Rep; Meth; from N.Y.

HALL WM. C. Carpenter, Sandwich; Rep; Meth; from Penn.

HALL WM. T. Laborer; P.O. Sandwich; Rep; Meth; from N.Y.

HALTON PAT. K. Laborer, Sandwich; Rep; Cath; from Ireland.

ALMOND HAMLIN, Farmer, Sec. 8; P.O. Somonauk; Rep; Ind.

HAMLIN JOSEPH, Assistant P. M. at Freeland; Rep; Ind; from Conn.

HAMMER FRANK, Farmer, Sandwich; Rep; Luth; from Germany.

HANSON WM. works Buckingham's farm; P.O. Sandwich; Rep; Bapt; Germany.

HARDELL PERMELIA C. Boarding House, Sandwich; from N.Y.

HARDY JOSIAH E. Teacher; P.O. Somonauk; Rep; Ind; from Ohio.

HARMON ANTHONY, Farmer, Sec. 21; P.O. Somonauk; Rep; Ind; from N. C.

HARMON AMOS W. Farmer, Sec. 16; P.O. Somonauk; Rep; Ind.

HARMON DAVID E. Farmer, Sec. 28; P.O. Somonauk; Rep; Ind; from N. C.

HARMON GEO. Farmer; P.O. Somonauk; Rep; Ind; from Illinois.

HARMON JAS. H. Farmer, Sec. 32; P.O. Somonauk; Rep; Ind; from Illinois.

HARRINGTON BUEL S. Clerk; P.O. Sandwich; Rep; Ind; from Illinois.

HARRIS DANIEL, Farmer; Rep; Canada.

HART THOS. Farmer, Secs. 14 and 15; P.O. Sandwich; Dem; Bapt; from Conn.

HARTMAN JOSEPH, Clerk, Sandwich; Dem; Cath; Germany.

HARVEY E. W. Artist, Sandwich; Rep; Meth; N.Y.

HARVEY JOHNSON, Lumber Dealer; residence on N. Main street, Sandwich; born in Madison Co. N.Y. in August, 1805; came to DeKalb Co. Ill. in 1864; Rep; Cong; house and two lots, value $5.000; personal prop. $1,000; married Polina Walker Jan. 1831, who was born in Berkshire Co. Mass. in 1808; family of one son and daughter; son, J. Barton Harvey, died, as near as can be learned, some time in October, 1864, at Millen, Ga., the result of brutal treatment at Andersonville, at the hands of his rebel jailors, where he was confined as a prisoner; entered the U. S. service in 8th N.Y. Cav., Co. D, at the age of 20; fought in twenty-five battles and several skirmishes, his regiment being in advance of the army of the Potomac; taken prisoner June 30, 1864, at Stony Creek Station, Va., and sent to Andersonville; for years his friends could get no trace of him, until his brother, T. W. Harvey, of Chicago, after untiring exertion, discovered his remains at Beaufort, S. C., in the Spring of 1869.

HARVEY ROSHER P. Cigar-maker, Sandwich; Ind; Ind; New Jersey.

HASS JNO. Tailor, Sandwich; Rep; Ind; Germany.

HATCH CHAS. O. Laborer, Sandwich; Dem; Ind; Illinois.

HAUPT CHAS. Shoemaker; P.O. Sandwich; Rep; Luth; Germany.

HAUPT FRED. Shoemaker; P.O. Sandwich; Rep; Luth; Germany.

HAWTHORN W. W. Nurseryman, Somonauk; Rep; Ind; Vermont.

HAY GEO. P. Retired Merchant; P.O. Sandwich; Rep; Ind; N.Y.

HAY ISAAC M. Farmer, Sec. 19; P.O. Sandwich; Ind; Ind; from N.Y. City.

HAYMOND JOHN, Farmer, Sandwich; Rep; Ind; Illinois.

HAYMOND RACHEL Mrs Sandwich; from Ohio; prop. $9,000.

HEFFRON EDWARD, Laborer, Sandwich; Rep; Cath; Mich.

HENDEE OLIVER S. Farmer; residence corner Castle and Fourth streets, Sandwich; born in Sudbury, Rutland Co. Vt. Feb. 18, 1812; removed to Essex Co. N.Y. in 1815; came to Kendall Co. Ill. in 1851, and to DeKalb Co. in 1857; Rep; Bapt; owns 60 acres in Ill. and 360 in Iowa; value $13,600; personal prop. $4,000; has held the office of Alderman of the city of Sandwich two terms; married Eleanor Y. Smith Sept. 11, 1844, who was born in Essex Co. N.Y. Oct. 20, 1823, and died Sept. 5, 1856; married for his second wife Elizabeth Sedgwick, March 11, 1858, who was born in N.Y. April 3, 1830; three children living.

HENGESBACH HENRY, Farmer, Sec. 30; P.O. Somonauk; Dem; Germany.

HENN AUGUST, Shoemaker, Somonauk; Rep; Prot; Germany.

HENN WILLIAM, Undertaker, Somonauk; Dem; Prot; Germany.

HENNIS HENRY, Saloon, Sandwich; Dem; Luth; Germany.

HENRICH JOSEPH H. Laborer, Somonauk; born Ger; Dem; Luth.

HENRY CHESTER, Farmer, Sec. 16; born Washington Co. N.Y. Sept. 3, 1829, came to DeKalb Co. Ill. 1854; Rep; United Pres; owns 160 acres, value, $10,400; married Ellen A. French, Oct. 11, 1860, who was born Washington Co. N.Y. Dec. 20, 1840; has five children living.

HENRY GEORGE B. Farmer; P.O. Somonauk; lives with father; Rep; Ind.

HENRY JOHN, Laborer, Somonauk; Georgia; Rep.

HENRY JAMES, Farmer, Sec. 28; P.O. Somonauk; born Washington Co. N.Y. Jan. 22, 1512, came to Ill. April, 1854; Rep; Pres; 220 acres land, val. $20,000; son John V.; entered the army Aug. 16, 1862, eighteen years of age, in Co. H, 105th Regt. I. V. I., served two years as aid to Col. Dustin, a part of the time transferred to 17th Ill. Cav. Col. Jno. Beveridge, now Gov. as Q. M; honorably discharged June, 1865; is now at Quincy, Ill. Asst. Supt. of Mail Agencies; James Henry married Jennette. sister of Gov. Beveridge, Oct. 29, 1837, who was born in Washington Co. N.Y. 1813; nine children.

HENTH CASPER, Catholic Priest; P.O. Somonauk; born Prussia; came to Ill. 1870.

HENWOOD HARRIETT Mrs. P.O. Sandwich; born N.Y.; $1,000; non-professor.

HENWOOD W. H. Laborer; P.O. Sandwich; born N.Y.; Rep; Ind.

HEPNER AUGUST, Farmer, Sandwich; Ind; Luth.

HERMIS JOHN, Stone mason, Sandwich; Germany; $800; Dem; Cath.

HEROLD HERMAN, Laborer, Sandwich; Germany; Ind; Ind.

HESS G. Merchant, Somonauk; born France; real estate and per. prop. $17.000; Dem; Ind.

HESS HENRY, Clerk for father, Somonauk; born Ill; Dem; Ind.

HESS PAUL, Clerk, Somonauk; born France; Dem; Ind.

HICK B. Clergyman, Sec. 24; P.O. Sandwich; born Conn. 1797; 55 acres, $3,000; Ind; Bapt.

HICKEY THOS. Drayman and Express; P.O. Sandwich; born Ireland; Dem; Cath.

HICKOCK CULLEN C. Moulder, res. head of Eddy St; born Rutland Co. Vt. 1826, came to Ill. 1862, DeKalb Co. 1871; Rep; Ind; owns house and 1½ acres, value $1,500; married Susan Dougherty, Feb. 1851, who was born in Ireland, 1827; nine children.

HILLS FRANK E. Asst. Sec. of the Enterprise Co. Sandwich; Rep; Lib; Conn.

HILLS JOHN, Mechanic, Sandwich; Rep; Meth; N.Y.

HINDRECKS NANCY Mrs. Sandwich; born N.Y; Cong.

HINKELL PETER, Laborer; P.O. Sandwich; born Penn; Rep; Ind.

HINSDALE EBENEZER, Sandwich; born Mass; Rep.

HINTON JAS. A. Moulder; P.O. Sandwich; born New York; Rep; Ind; value $1,500.

HINTON JAS. A. Mechanic, Sandwich; born N.Y.; Rep; Ind; $2,000.

HILL ABRAM H. keeps Boarding House and is Deputy Marshal of City of Sandwich; res. on Second St; born Mich. Sept. 1842; came to Ill. 1852, DeKalb Co. 1858; Rep; Lib; entered army in 127th Regt. I. V. I. Co. F.; was with the regiment in seventeen battles, among the most severely contested in the history of the war; the following are some of the principal: Assault on Vicksburg, Mission Ridge, Kenesaw Mountain, Taking of Atlanta; was honorably discharged June 5, 1865; married Persis Seeber, Sept. 29, 1866, who was born Jefferson Co. N.Y. Dec. 1843; two children.

HILLS HUBERT S. Traveling Agt. Sandwich; born N.Y.; Rep; Cong.

HILLS LORENZO R. Carpenter, Sandwich; born N.Y.; Rep; Meth; value $4,000.

HILYARD HENRY, Laborer, Sandwich; Tenn; $800; Rep; Bapt.

HOAG MARY M. Mrs. res. First St. Sandwich; born Dutchess Co. N.Y. March 10, 1813, came to Ill. 1843; Cong; son Edward, born Genesee Co. N.Y. July 25, 1839, enlisted in first call for three months men, re-enlisted Fall 1861 in Co. H, 10th Regt. I. V. I. went to Cairo with his regiment, died Feb. 5, 1862, at Mound City, Ill. where his remains still are. Mrs. H. was married at Putnam Co. N.Y. May 31, 1831, to Daniel Hoag, of Columbia Co. N.Y.; had seven children, five living.

HOBERLIN FRED. Farmer; P.O. Somonauk; born Germany; Dem; Luth; 80 acres.

HOEPNER HENRY C. Farmer, Sec. 10; P.O. Sandwich; born Germany; Rep; Luth.

HOFF DAVID P. Photographer; P.O. Sandwich; born Ill; Rep; Bapt.

HODES CHAS. H. Moulder; P.O. Sandwich; born N.Y.; Dem; Lib.

HOFF JACOB, Shoemaker; P.O. Sandwich; born N. J.; $1,000; Rep; Meth.

HOFFMAN EDWARD, Farmer, Sandwich; Germany; Luth.

HOFFMAN J. Blacksmith, Somonauk; Germany; came to Ill. 1863; prop. $2,500; Ind; Cath.

HOGLE JOEL, Farmer, Sandwich; born Ohio; Rep; Ind.

HOHEN CHARLES, Stonemason; P.O. Sandwich; born Germany; Dem; Cath.

HOLBROOK C. H. Mechanic, Sandwich; born N.Y.; Dem; Ind.

HOLMAN HENRY, Farmer; P.O. Somonauk; Germany; Dem; Luth.

HOLMES FAYETTE, Farmer, Sec. 16; P.O. Sandwich; born N.Y.; Rep; Ind; 170 ac. $10,700

HOWE FRANCIS A. Painter; P.O. Sandwich; born N.Y.; Rep; Meth.

HOWE LEANDER O. Laborer; P.O. Sandwich; born N.Y.; $1,200; Rep; Meth.

HOWE PHINEAS, Retired Farmer; P.O. Sandwich; Luzerne Co. Penn; Rep; Meth; $7,000.

HOUGH JOHN, Painter, Sandwich; born N.Y.; Dem; Ind.

HOXSEY N. L. Mrs. Somonauk; born N.Y.; per. prop. $5,000; Christian.

HOXSEY EDWARD, Grain Dealer, Somonauk; born Mass; $10,000; Ind; Ind.

HUESKA WM. Harnessmaker; P.O. Sandwich; born Germany; Ind; Prot. Ref.

HUGHES DAVID, Baker; P.O. Sandwich; born Scotland; Ind; Pres.

HUHN MARCUS, Farmer, Sec. 39; 268 ac. value $15,000; personal $1,000; Ger; Dem; Cath.
HUMMELL BATHSHEBA A. Mrs. Sec. 1; Conn; Ill. 1839; 80 acres, val. $3,500; Ind.
HUMMEL JULIUS M. Agricultural Implements, Sandwich; Rep: Ind; value $3,000.
HUSTON JAMES C. rents farm of I. Graham; P.O. Freeland; born Penn; Rep; Meth.
HUSTON WILLIAM, Farmer; P.O. Freeland; born Penn; Rep; Luth.
HYOTT JOHN. Barber, Sandwich; Canada; Rep; Ind.

ISMON GEO. L. Laborer, Sandwich; N.Y.; Rep: Ind; $85,000.

IVES JULIUS, Retired Farmer; res. Church St; P.O. Sandwich; born Conn. 1820; came to state 1849, to DeKalb Co. 1873; Rep; Bapt; has been Supervisor of Goshen; married Sarah L. Carothers, Nov. 1873, born N.Y. 1830; had four children, one son living.

JACOBS HENRY, Cigarmaker; P.O. Sandwich; born Columbus, Ohio; Ind; Ind.
JACOBS WM. T. Cigarmaker; P.O. Sandwich; born Columbus, Ohio; Ind; Ind.
JACKSON ROBERT B. Mechanic, Sandwich; Conn; Rep; Bapt; $2,000.
JAMES BENJ. Moulder, Sandwich; born Penn; Rep; Ind; $700.
JOHNSON FREEBORN, Physician, Sandwich; born Vt; Rep; Ind; $1,600.
JOHNSON RICHARD F. Carriage Trimmer, Sandwich; Ireland; Rep; Bapt.
JOHNSON WM. Farmer, P.O. Somonauk; lives on Jno. Clark's farm; born Eng.
JOLES WM. Blacksmith and Carriage Maker; residence Church Street; P.O. Sandwich; born in DeKalb Co. Nov. 4, 1840 (his father, H. P. Joles, was a pioneer in DeKalb Co. and died July 25, 1876, aged 61); Rep; Bapt; was among the first to respond to the call for volunteers as a member of Co. E, 13th Reg. Ill. Vols. with which he served 3 years; honorably discharged; re-enlisted in Co. H, 156th Reg. in which he served till the close of the war in the rank of First Lieutenant; honorably discharged; married Mary J. Muzzy, Aug. 6, 1864; born Washington Co. N. Y. 1848; four children.
JONES ALFRED W. Barber, Sandwich; R.R. Street; born Ills; Ind; Meth.
JONES MRS. H. Widow of H. P. Jones, P.O. Sandwich; Pres; $2,000; born N. Y.
JONES HENRY C. Retired Farmer; P.O. Sandwich; Meth; Rep; val. $15,000; born Pa.
JONES WM. A. Moulder, Sandwich; Rep; Pres; Penn.
JUDSON O. E. Retired Farmer, Sandwich; Rep; Ind; prop. $12,000; born Mass.

KAIN MILTON, Farmer, Sec. 24; Sandwich; Ind; Ind; 125 acres, val. $14,000; born N.Y.
KELLEY DAVID, works for D. H. Avery; Rep; Ind; born N. Y.
KELLOGG BENJAMIN F. Machinist, residence cor. Eddy and 3d Streets, P.O. Sandwich; born Herkimer Co. N. Y. March 22, 1842; came to Illinois 1855; to DeKalb in 1871; Rep. and Meth; entered the army Nov. 2, 1861, Co. A, Yates' Sharpshooters; was in Battle of New Madrid, Mo. in skirmish line in advance on Corinth, also in its defense; assisted in organizing the 1st Alabama Cavalry, rank of 1st Lieutenant and Regimental Commissary; sent by Sherman with his brigade to destroy railroads and bridges in rear of Hood's Army; succeeded and returned by cutting their way through the enemy with a loss of two hundred and sixty out of eight hundred; was wounded in the leg in this fight; went with Sherman to the sea; honorably discharged Feby. 1865; married Sarah F. Rollins Oct. 10, 1871; born Concord. N. H. Oct. 1848; one daughter.
KELLOGG GEO. Retired Farmer, Somonauk; came Ill. 1856; Rep; Ind.
KENNEDY BURR A. Blacksmith, Sandwich; Ind.
KENNEDY CHAS. F. Farmer, Sec. 36; P.O. Sandwich; 120 acres; Rep. Bapt. born N. Y.
KENNEDY E. A. Hardware, Sandwich; val. $4,000; Rep; Meth; born N. Y.
KENNEDY H. W. Carpenter, Sandwich; val. prop. $3,000; Ind; Ind; born N. Y.
KERN JOSEPH D. Jr. Agent for Warder, Mitchel & Co., manufacturers of Champion Reaper and Mower, Springfield, Ohio; resides cor. of Church and Wells Sts. Sandwich; born Canada, Aug. 3d, 1832; came to Kendall Co. Ill. 1839; came to DeKalb Co. May 1st. 1876; Rep; Lib; owns house and lot val. $1,500; enlisted Aug. 9, 1862, in Co.H, 89th Regt. I.V. I; some of the most noted engagements he was in were, Stone River, Liberty Gap, Chickamauga, Missionary Ridge, Dalton, Buzzards' Roost, Resaca, and New Hope Church; in the last he lost his left arm; was honorably discharged March 20, 1865; has been Sheriff of Kendall Co. two terms; collector of Town of Bristol three terms; married Mary E. Lewis, Sept. 20, 1860, who was born Kendall Co. Ill. 1842; have three children living.
KENT HENRY F. Mechanic; P.O. Sandwich; Rep. Bapt; born Conn.

KENT LUTHER, Grocer, Sandwich; Rep; Bapt; val. prop. $5.000; born Conn.
KENYON WM. H. Carpenter, Sandwich; Rep; Bapt; val. prop. $850; born N. Y.
KESLER CHRISTIAN, Laborer; P.O. Sandwich; Rep; Ind; born Germany.
KESSLAR WM. Farmer; P.O. Sandwich; Rep; Ind; born Germany 1847.
KINDRED JACOB, Laborer, Somonauk; Rep; Ind; born N. C.
KINDRED LEWIS, Tailor, Somonauk; Rep; Ind; born Ohio.
KINGSBURY MRS. E. B. owns Steam Grist Mill, Sandwich; born Maine.
KINGSBURY ROBT. W. Manager of Steam Grist Mill; P.O. Sandwich; born Cal.
KINNEY REV. D. N. Farmer, Sec. 4; Sandwich; Rep; Bapt; 90 acres; val. prop. $10,000.
KIRKLAND RICHARD G. Laborer, Sandwich; Rep; Ind; born Ills.
KIRKBRIDE WINFIELD S. Grocer, Sandwich; Rep; Ind; born N. Y.
KLEINSMID GEO. Hardware, Sandwich; Rep; Pres; val. prop. $32 000; born Prussia.
KOALZOW ERNEST, Laborer, Somonauk; Rep; Luth; born Germany.
KOLP H. Farmer, Sec. 28; P.O. Somonauk; Rep; Luth; 80 acres; born Germany.
KUHN CHARLES, Laborer, Somonauk; Rep; Ind; born Germany.
KUHN MARCUS, Farmer; Sec. 29; Dem; Cath; 268 acres; val. prop. $15,000; Germany.

L A BRANT JACOB A. Harnessmaker, Sandwich; Rep; born Ills.
  LA BRANT LEVI, Harness and Saddlery, Sandwich; Rep; Ind; Ohio.
LACOCK ANDREW, Retired Farmer; P.O. Freeland; Rep; U. P.; prop. $800; born Ireland.
LACOCK THOS. Laborer, Sandwich; Rep; Pres; val. prop. $600; born Ireland.
LACOCK WM. Laborer, Sandwich; Rep; Cath; born Ireland.
LAMBERSON JNO. T. Painter, Sandwich; Rep; Bapt. val. prop. $2,000; born N. Y.
LATHAM BENJ. F. Secretary Enterprise Co; P.O. Sandwich; Rep; Ind.
LATHAM JOSEPH F. Retired Farmer; resides on 3d St. Block 11, Eddy's Addition, Sandwich; born New London Co. Conn. Aug. 11, 1817, moved with parents to Brooklyn, N. Y. 1829, remained till 1838, when he came to DeKalb Co. Ill; at that time there were but few white families residing in what is now the township of Somonauk; Rep; Independent in his religious views; owns 298 acres in one farm and 26 acres in another, and house and 3 lots, val. $26,000; per. property $2,500; married Charlotte Estabrooks, March 20th, 1845, who was born Tioga Co. N. Y. Dec. 1821; have had eight children, five living.
LATHAM HUBBARD, Farmer; P.O. Willamette; Rep.
LATHAM THOMAS F. Farmer, resides Sec. 26; P.O. Sandwich; born Conn. 1812. came to Ill. 1838; Independent in politics and religion; owns 215 acres, val. $20,000; per. prop. $4,000; married Jane Ayers, 1837, who was born Ohio 1820; four children.
LATHROP MARCUS, Dealer in Eggs and Poultry; P.O. Sandwich; Rep; Ind. born Vt.
LE BRANT HENRY K. Painter; resides on Main St. Sandwich; born DeKalb Co. Ills. Oct. 19, 1851; Rep; Bapt; married Maggie Hanson April 25, 1863, who was born in Germany, February, 1851, and came to U. S. 1853; two children.
LeDOYT MONROE, Farmer, P.O. Sandwich; Rep; Ind; born Conn. 1829; val. prop $2,000.
LEE RICHARD, Laborer for E. Devine; P.O. Freeland; Dem; Cath; born Ireland.
LEHMANN CHRIS, Meat Market, Sandwich; Dem; Luth; real est. $3,000; born Prussia.
LEHMANN WM. works for father, Sandwich; Dem; Luth.
LEONARD GEORGE F. Laborer, Sandwich; Rep; Ind; N. Y.
LEWIS CHAS. S. Agricultural Implement Dealer, Somonauk; Rep; Ind; born Ill.
LEWIS DAN'L W. Gunsmith, Sandwich House; Rep; Lib; born N. Y.
LEWIS EDW. Night Watchman at Man'f'g Co. Sandwich; Rep; Ind; owns 1-10 stock Co; N.Y.
LEWIS ED. W. Attorney at Law and Magistrate, Somonauk; Rep; Ind; prop. $2,000; N. Y.
LEWIS N. B. lives with father, Sandwich; born Ill.
LEWIS ROBERT H. Laborer, Sandwich; Ind; Ind; Germany.
LEWIS WM. H. Mcht. Sandwich; Rep; Ind; val. prop. $5,000; born N. Y.
LINCOLN S. C. Laborer, Sandwich; Rep; Bapt; born Ill.
LOOMIS LYMAN, Farmer, Sec. 18; P.O. Somonauk; Rep; 84 acres; born N. Y.
LOOMIS RILEY, Laborer, Sandwich; Ind; Ind; born N. Y. 1808; came to Ill. 1855.
LOSEE FRANK, Carpenter, Sandwich; Rep; Ind.
LOSEE GEORGE, Laborer, Sandwich; Ind; Pres; Penn.

LOSEE MILTON H. Clerk; Rep; born Ill.

LOSEE GILBERT, Retired Merchant; P.O. Somonauk; $6,000. Rep; Pres; N.Y.

LOUGHLIN HENRY, works for Ryther; P.O. Somonauk; Rep; Ind; born N.Y.

LOUMAN JOHN, Tinner; P.O. Somonauk; Rep; Ind; born in Penn.

LOW WM. R. Police Magistrate; resides South Main St. Sandwich; born Prince Edward Co. Canada, Jan. 30, 1827; came to DeKalb Co. June 30, 1856; Rep; Lib; 5 acres, value $4,000; personal property $20,000; entered army 1862; honorably discharged March 15, 1863, on account of poor health; inventor of Adams & French Harvester, so justly popular everywhere; married Lydia Christy, Nov. 9, 1852, born Prince Edward Co. Canada, Sept. 25, 1834; five children.

LOWE CHARLES H. Clerk; P.O. Sandwich; Rep; Lib; born Canada.

LOWE ELIZA Mrs. Boarding House; P.O. Sandwich; Meth; value $3,000; born Indiana.

LOWE R. J. Dr. Physician; P.O. Sandwich; Dem; Ohio.

LUDWIG CHAS. Clerk; P.O. Sandwich; Dem; Ind; born Ill.

LUDWIG GUSTAVUS, Retired Merchant; P.O. Sandwich; Rep; Evang; born Germany.

LUKINS A. J. Foreman *Free Press;* P.O. Sandwich; Rep; Ind; born Penn.

LUKINS GEORGE W. Farmer and Business Agent; residence East Church St. Sandwich; born in Harrison Co. Ohio, Dec. 11, 1829; came to Illinois in 1846, to DeKalb Co. in 1867; Rep; Cong; owns house and 10 acres in Sandwich, value $5,500; married Mary Wood, April 20. 1854, who was born in Cattaraugus Co. N.Y. March 19, 1834; came with her father, Uriah D. Wood, to Illinois, when she was only 5 years of age, 1839, and settled on Rock River, Whiteside Co; the Indians were being removed west during this year.

LUMBERMAN THOMAS, P.O. Somonauk; value $900, personal $600; Rep; Ind; Germany.

LYND ELIZABETH Mrs. value $600; born England.

LYONS STEPHEN DANIEL, Laborer; P.O. Sandwich; Rep; Ind; born N.Y.

MACK JOHN, Physician; P.O. Freeland; Rep; Ind; born N.Y.

MACK JOHN, Laborer; value $900; Rep; Bapt; Germany.

MACK PATRICK, Laborer, Somonauk; Dem; Cath; born Ireland.

MACOMBER JOSEPH B. Broom Manufacturer, Sandwich; Rep; Ind; from N.Y.

MACOMBER W. B. Machinist, Sandwich; $3,200; Rep; Ind; born N.Y.

MAGINNIS NICHOLAS, Laborer, Sandwich; $2,000; Rep; Cath; Ireland.

MANAHER EUGENE, Merchant; P.O. Sandwich; Rep; Ind; Ill.

MANLEY HENRY H. Farmer, residence on P. McClellan's farm, Somonauk; born Cattaraugus Co. N.Y. Aug. 28, 1840; came to Ill. 1846, and to DeKalb Co. March, 1872; Rep; Ind. in religion; entered the army as a member of 4th Wis. Battery, 1861, raised at Beloit; served 3 years; was in the series of battles around Richmond, Va; honorably discharged in fall 1864; married Lucy Hogle, Feb. 8, 1866, who was born in Seneca, N.Y. May 3, 1845; family of three boys.

MARCY ABRAM A. Mechanic; residence 3d and LaFayette Sts. Sandwich; born Luzerne Co. Pa. Feb. 27, 1832; came to Ill. 1844, and to DeKalb Co. 1854; Rep; Ind. in his religion; owns several buildings and city lots, valued at $10,000; has been Alderman in the City of Sandwich two terms; married Amanda Ryon, Dec. 29, 1858, who was born Wayne Co. Pa. Aug. 7, 1834, daughter of Wm. Ryon, who came to Ill. 1836; 3 children.

MARKS WM. Retired Merchant; P.O. Sandwich; Rep; Ind; born N.Y.

MARLIN C. Mrs. Sandwich; value prop. $1,200; Cath; born Germany.

MARSELLUS DAVID, Farmer, Sec. 24; P.O. Sandwich; Rep; Ind; 196 acres, $15,000; N.Y.

MARSH DEXTER M. Retired Farmer; P.O. Sandwich; Rep; Ind; born Mass.

MARSH ROBERT, Stone Mason; P.O. Sandwich; Rep; Pres; born England.

MARTIN EDWARD, Laborer, Somonauk; Rep; Bapt; born Canada.

McBRIDE ALVIN S. lives with father; P.O. Freeland; Rep; U. Pres; born Ill.

McBRIDE SAMUEL, Farmer, resides on Secs. 5 and 8; P.O. Freeland; born Washington Co. Ohio, April, 1825, came to DeKalb Co. Ill. 1852; Rep; U. Pres; owns 137 acres, value $8,000; was private in the army; married Rebecca Stewart, Oct. 1, 1851, who was born in Ohio, April, 1831; two children.

McCAN JOHN, Farmer, Sandwich; Ind; Ind; from Ireland.

McCANDLESS JOHN L. Carpenter and Builder, Sandwich; Rep; Cong; born N.Y.

McCANDLESS MATHEW, Cabinetmaker, Sandwich; Rep; Bapt; N.Y.

McCANDLESS M. Mrs. Millinery Furnishing Goods, Sandwich; born Ohio.

McCARTHY DENNIS, Railroadman, Somonauk; $1,000; Ind; Cath; born Ireland.

McCARTHY WM. Blacksmith, Sandwich; Rep; Epis; born England.

McCHWHORTE JOHN A. Blacksmith; P.O. Sandwich; Rep; Lib; born N.Y.

McCLELLAN PETER C. Farmer, Sec. 29; P.O. Somonauk; born in Hebron, Washington Co. N.Y. Oct. 26, 1829; came to DeKalb Co. Feb. 1867; Rep; Pres; 160 acres, value $10,000; married Isabelle Beveridge, Sept. 7, 1864, who was born Hebron, Washington Co. N.Y. Oct. 5, 1830; one daughter.

McELWAIN EDWARD, works for Whittle; P.O. Somonauk; Rep; Lib; born Ill.

McFARLAND MARGARET Mrs. Sandwich; $1,200; U. Pres; Penn.

McGINNIS HUGH, Yard Boss Manufacturing Co. Sandwich; Dem; Cath; born Ireland.

McGUIRE JOS. Retired Farmer, Sandwich; $3,000; Rep; Ind; born Penn.

McGUIRE JOS. Butcher, Sandwich; value $2,000; Rep; born Penn.

McINTYRE JNO. J. Cooper; P.O. Sandwich; Rep; Pres; born N.Y.

McKINDLY H. N. Grocer, Sandwich; value prop. $7,000; Ind; Ind; born N.Y.

McLEAN ROBERT, Moulder; P.O. Sandwich; Dem; Ind; born N.Y.

McLEAN T. H. Moulder, Sandwich; Rep; Ind; from N.Y.

McMAHN RICHARD, Laborer, Sandwich; Rep; Cath; Ireland.

McNEVIN JOSEPH, Telegraph Operator at Somonauk; Dem; Cath; from Ireland.

McNEVIN JOSEPH, boards with Goodell, Somonauk; Dem.

McNORTON JOHN, Retired Farmer; P.O. Sandwich; $3,000; Rep; Bapt; born N. H.

MEAD JONATHAN, Iron Moulder, residence cor. 1st and Castle Sts. Sandwich; born Chenango Co. N.Y. May 26, 1824; moved to Western N.Y; remained two years; came to Ohio in 1837, to Ill. Feb. 1856; Rep; Bapt; owns house and two lots, value $1,000; enlisted Aug. 1862, in Co. H, 105th Regt. I. V. I; remained in the service to the close of the war; was on detached duty in Commissary Dept. most of the time; honorably discharged June, 1865; married Jane C. Connal, March 18, 1851; she was born Salem, Washington Co. N.Y. June 10, 1827; seven children, five living.

MENK RODOLPH, Pastor Evang. Luth. Sandwich; Germany.

MERWIN CHAS. General Store, Somonauk; $8,000; Rep; Pres; born N.Y.

METCALF GEORGE, Windmill and Plow Property, Tools, etc..

MEYERS WM. E. Farmer, Sandwich; Rep; Ind; born Ill.

MICHAEL MARY Mrs. P.O. Sandwich; $1,200; Cong; born Germany.

MILLER ARTEMUS, Livery on Eddy St. residence 5th St. Sandwich; born Oswego Co. N.Y. July 8, 1825; came to Ill. 1855, and to DeKalb Co. in 1865; Rep; Ind; owns 320 acres in Whiteside Co. house and lot in Sandwich, total value $10.000; per. prop. $2,000; married Adelia Washburn, Oct. 1846, who was born in Westchester Co. N.Y. 1829; one child.

MILLER C. Laborer; P.O. Sandwich; born Germany; Rep; Pres.

MILLER CHRIS. Laborer, Sandwich; Ireland; Dem; Cath.

MILLER DANIEL O. Farmer; renter; P.O. Freeland; born Pa; Rep; Ind.

MILLER LEWIS, Farmer, Sec. 1, Sandwich; Germany; came Ill. 1854; Ind; Pres; $8,000.

MILLER STEPHEN, Retired Farmer; resides on 3d Street, Jole's addition; P.O. Sandwich; born Saratoga Co. N. Y. Sept. 18, 1820; came to Ill. in 1846; came to DeKalb 1873; Rep; Meth; owns 267 acres, value $20,000; personal property $2,000; (Mrs. M. owns house and two lots, value $2,000); married Mrs. Maria Finch, relict of the late Darius Finch, June 12, 1873, who was born Columbia Co. N. Y. Feb. 10, 1818. Mrs. Miller has six children by her former marriage; Mr. Miller has three children.

MILLER WM. Mason, Somonauk; born Germany; Rep; Luth.

MINER DENNON, P.O. Sandwich; born Mass; resides Sandwich House; Rep; Cong.

MINK AUGUST, Laborer, Sandwich; Germany; Rep; Pres.

MISICK CHARLES L. Dr. Physician and Surgeon; res. Railroad Street, Sandwich; born East Troy, Rensselaer Co. N. Y. Nov. 2, 1823; came to Ill. in 1855; Rep; Bapt; graduated at the Ohio Medical College 1859, and at the Hahnemann Medical College, Chicago, 1869; also attended a course of lectures at the Eclectic Medical College Cincinnati; practiced two years in Steuben Co. N. Y; three years in McHenry Co. Ill; eight years in Ogle Co. Ill; one year at Rockford; settled in Sandwich, DeKalb Co. in 1870; married Susan Collier, Sept. 1848; born in Howard, Steuben Co. N. Y. in 1831 ; family of four children.

MITTEN SAML. Sandwich; born Ireland; val. $1,600; Rep; Ind.

MISNER PETER A. Farmer; res. S. Eddy St. Sandwich; born Hamilton Co. Ohio, July 11, 1819; came to Kendall Co. Ill. Nov. 18, 1833; removed to DeKalb 1865; Rep; Cong; owns house and lot in Sandwich, val. $2,000 ; 130 acres in Kendall Co. val. $9,750; per. prop. $3,000 ; married Fannie Brainard Oct. 4, 1840, who was born in Bradford Co. Pa. 1812, died Sept. 17, 1853: three children by this marriage ; married for his second wife Louise Russell, Feb 19, 1856, who was born in Bradford Co. Pa. Feb. 23, 1827; two children by the last marriage.

MITCHELL JOHN, Farmer, Sandwich; Sec. 34; 130 acres; val. $10,000; N. Y; Rep; Meth.

MITCHEL NELSON R. Trav. Agent, Sandwich; N. H; Rep.

MOFFET WM. T. Rev. res. Sec. 5, lot 12, near church edifice; P.O. Freeland; born in Monroe Co. Ind. July 27, 1837; graduated at the Indiana State University at Bloomington 1858, and the Theological Seminary of the Northwest, at Monmouth, Ills. 1861; ordained and installed Pastor of the U. P. Church, April, 1861, which pastorate he still fills. This Church was organized in 1846, with a membership of twenty-one. Its first pastor for nine years, Rev. R. H. French, is now located at Peotone, Ill. Present membership 200. Mr. Moffet is a Republican; owns two acres with house valued at $2,500; married Jennie M. Robb, April, 1861, who was born in Pittsburgh, Penn. Oct. 1841; died Feb. 1869, leaving five children; married for his second wife Elizabeth Shepherd, Feb. 1872, who was born in Xenia, Ohio, May 12, 1841.

MOELLER E. Mrs. P.O. Sandwich; born Germany; $1,000; Meth.

MOLITAR NICHOLAS, M. D. Physician and Surgeon, Somonauk; born Germany; came to Ill. 1852. Asthma; Catarrh, Lung and Female Diseases a specialty, having had twenty-four years' practice.

MONROE JOHN, works for Manchester; P.O. Sandwich; born Ga; Rep; Ind.

MONTGOMERY J. IVOR, Lawyer and Collecting Agent; res. Church St. Sandwich; born LaSalle Co. Ill. March 13, 1847; came to DeKalb Co. Dec. 1875; Ind. in politics ; Liberal in religion; 240 acres in Iowa, improved; 20 in Ill; total value $8,000; per. prop. $10,000; was Deputy County Superintendent of Schools in LaSalle Co. four years; has been teacher in public schools eight years; was admitted to the bar Ottawa, Ill. Oct. 28, 1869; has held several township offices; married Mary A. daughter of Thomas Lett, Esq. May 21, 1871, who was born in LaSalle Co. Ill. Dec. 1853; wife owns in her own right farm valued at $10,000; one daughter, Miss Jessie.

MOORE BYRD M. Farmer; P.O. Sandwich; born Wis; Rep; Meth.

MOORE CALISTA Mrs. Farmer, Sandwich; born N. Y; Cong; val. $6,000.

MOREY R. E. Merchant, Sandwich; born Ill; Rep; Ind; val. per. prop. $1,500.

MORRILL W. H. Machinist, Sandwich; born N. Y; Rep; Bapt.

MORRIS FRANK H. Laborer; P.O. Sandwich, born N. Y; Rep; Meth.

MORRIS GEO. Carpenter and Joiner, Sandwich; born England; Ind; Ind.

MORRIS WM. Laborer, Sandwich; born N. Y; Rep.

MORRIS WM. H. Laborer; P.O. Sandwich; born N. Y; Rep; Ind.

MORSE GEORGE, Carriage Maker; P.O. Sandwich; born England; Rep; Ind.

MORSE J. G. Carriage and Wagon Maker, Somonauk; German; per. prop. $600; Rep; Bapt.

MORTENTHLEN FRED. born Switzerland; came here 1865; Rep; Ind.

MOSHER CHAS. (Manager for H. C); Sandwich; born Ill; Rep; Ind.

MOSHER D. T. Farmer, Sandwich; born N. Y; Rep; Ind; val. prop. $2,200.

MOSHER FRED. S. Banker, Sandwich; born N. Y; Rep; Pres; val. real estate $7,000.

MOSHER HENRY C. General Merchandise, Sandwich; born Ill; Rep; Meth.

MOSS DEXTER M. Laborer; Sandwich; N. Y; Rep; Cong.

MUNSON ALVAH, formerly Teacher and Mechanic; res. on Washington St. Sandwich; born Southington, Hartford Co. Conn. June 9, 1795; parents came to Greene Co. N. Y. when he was six years of age; came to DeKalb Co. Ill. 1857; Rep; Methodist in belief; owns house and two lots, value $2,500 ; married Lucy W. White, Hamilton Co. N. Y. Jan. 18, 1829, who was born West Haven, Rutland Co. Vt. April 7, 1806; have had six children, five living. Mr. Munson was in the war of 1812, and assisted in guarding the City of New York against the enemy, and is in receipt of a monthly pension of eight dollars per month.

MUNSON FRANK A. Postmaster at Sandwich; born Crawford Co. Penn. March 9, 1838; came to Ill. April 1854; entered the army as private, April 19, 1861, in Co. H, 10th Reg. Ill. Vol. Inft ; was made Capt. Co. H in 1863; lost his left arm in battle of Peach Tree Creek, Ga. July 18, 1864; was honorably discharged July 4, 1865; Rep; Ind. in religious views; owns house and lot, val. $2,500; married Mary E. Woodward Nov. 9, 1868, who was born at Cherry Ridge, Wayne Co. Penn. 1848.

MUNGER JAS. Laborer, Sandwich; born N. Y. City; Rep; Cong.

MUNGER WM. H. Landlord and Proprietor Emmons House; born N. Y; Rep; Ind.

MUNCH JOHN G. Saloon; P.O. Sandwich; Ger; Dem; Luth.

MYAT JOHN works for Mr. Paine; P.O. Freeland; born Ill; Rep; Ind.

MYOTT JOHN, Laborer; P.O. Sandwich; Canada; Rep; Cath.

MYRES ADELBERT, General Store; Somonauk; born Ger; came Ill. 1855; Rep; Ind.

MYRES C. Drayman; P.O. Sandwich; born Pa; Rep; Ind.

MYRES JOSIAH C. Drayman, Sandwich; born Ohio; Rep; Ind; $1,500.

NATHAN MICHAEL, Clothing Merchant, Sandwich; $15,000; born Prussia; Ind; Ind.

NATZEL CHRISTINA Mrs. Washerwoman, Sandwich; from Germany; Meth.

NEEDHAM ARNOLD T. Rev. Pastor M. E. Church, Sandwich ; born Isle of Guernsey; Rep.

NEGUS MYRON H. Rev. Retired Clergyman; P.O. Sandwich; born N. Y; Rep; Bapt.

NICHOLSON ARTHUR H. Merchant and Mnfr. Cider and Vinegar; born N. Y; Rep; Lib.

NICHOLSON CHARLES, Farmer and Book Agent, Sec 28, Somonauk; P.O. Sandwich; born Putnam Co. N. Y. June 30, 1819; came to Ill. 1870; is liberal in political and religious views; owns 44 acres, val, $4,000; was Revenue Assessor of the 26th Coll. Dist. of State of N. Y; married Fannie S. Cady Aug. 13, 1850, who was born in Florence, Oneida Co. N. Y. May 15, 1828; has five children.

NOLAN JOHN, Lives on Devine farm; P.O. Freeland; born Ireland; Dem; Cath.

NYE S. D. Janitor, Sandwich; born N. Y; Rep; Ind.

OBRECHT JOHN, Farmer, rents Sec. 30; France; Ill. 1869; per. prop. $1,000; Ind; Cath.

OLDRIDGE DANIEL, Laborer, Sandwich; Ill; Rep; Ind.

ORMSBY WM. A. Telegraph Operator, Sandwich; born Ill; Rep; Ind.

ORMISTON MARGARET Mrs. P.O. Sandwich; $2,500; born Eng; Meth.

ORR C. E. Photographer, Sandwich; born N. Y; Dem; Ind.

ORR SAML. Sandwich; been confined to his bed for 20 years; Penn; Rep; Pres; prop. $25,000.

OSBORN GEO. Farmer, Sec. 35; P.O. Sandwich; born in Oswego Co. N. Y. June 15, 1825; came to Illinois in 1849, to DeKalb in 1873; Rep; Bapt; owns 94 21-100 acres, value $8,000; married Frederica Newman, Jan. 14, 1862, who was born in Edinburgh, Scotland, Aug 22, 1827; Mrs Osborn came from Scotland to Wisconsin some forty years ago, to Illinois in 1857; Mrs. Osborn had four children by a former marriage; son David J. Newman, was in the army in Co. A, 22d Reg. Wis. Vols.; lost his left leg in battle of Kenesaw Mountain, June, 1864; was honorably discharged, and lives in Bay City, Mich.

PACKER HARVEY, Supt. of Enterprise Co., Sandwich; Rep; Vt.

PACKER JNO. F. Carpenter, Sandwich; Rep; Ind; from N. Y.

PAINE JOHN K. Livery; P.O. Sandwich; property $8,000; Rep; Ind; from N. H.

PARK HARBERSEN, works for Coleman, Sandwich; Ind; Ind; from Scotland.

PARKER RAYMOND P. owns Mail and Stage Line between Sandwich and Cortland which makes a round trip every Tuesday, Thursday and Saturday; residence and office on Railroad Street; born in Whiting, Vt. July 27, 1844; came to Illinois in 1869, and to DeKalb Co. in 1874; Liberal in Politics; Independent in Religion; owns house and lot valued at $1,000; personal property $500; married Mary Underwood, Nov. 19, 1874, who was born in Sandwich DeKalb Co., Ill. Dec. 29, 1839. Mrs. Parker has a daughter by a former marriage.

PALM JEREMIAH, Mechanic, Sandwich; Rep; Ind; property $1,000; from Ohio.

PALMER A. B. Blacksmith; P.O. Sandwich; Rep; Ind; from N. Y.

PALMER ALEX. H. Druggist, Sandwich; Rep; Pres; property $25.200; from N. Y.

PARRIS HIRAM, Carpenter and Joiner; P.O. Sandwich; Rep; Ind; from N. Y.

PATTEN WILLIAM, Farmer; residence on Sec. 13; P.O. Sandwich; born in Greenwich; Washington Co. N. Y., Jan. 21, 1817; came to Illinois in May. 1843, and is now living on the place on which he first settled; Republican; United Presbyterian; owns 470 acres in homestead, with over three miles of tile drain on it, and 320 acres in Iowa. valued at $32,000; personal property $6,000; has been Supervisor seven or eight terms, Chairman one year, which he resigned to join the army, member of the Legislature in 1854-5 and in 1858-9, State Senator from 1866 to 1870; entered the army as Captain of Co. II, 156th Reg. I V.I., in 1864, served to the close of the war, honorably discharged; married Elizabeth Pratt, Oct. 1843, born in Washington Co. N. Y. in 1819, died Jan. 8. 1856; had five children by this marriage, three living; married for his second wife Jane Somes, in 1856, who was born in Washington, N. Y., in April, 1829; five children.

PATTEN AGNES Mrs. Sandwich; U. P.; 236 acres; from N. Y.

PATTEN EDW. M. Farmer, Sandwich; Rep; Meth; from Illinois.

PATTEN GEO. Teacher, Sandwich; Rep; Ind; from Illinois.

PEIRCE GERTRUDE Mrs. Sandwich; Epis; N.Y.; $1,400.

PELLING WM. Laborer, Somonauk; Rep; Meth; came to Ill. in 1845; from England.

PETREE JOHN, Tailor, Somonauk; value of property $450; Rep; Bapt; Germany.

PFEFIR NICHOLAS, Blacksmith, Somonauk; Dem; Cath; from Germany.

PHELPS ALONZO E. Retired Physician; P.O. Sandwich; Rep; Cong; from N. Y.

PHILPS JOS. E. Merchant, Sandwich; property $2,000; Rep; Pres; from N. Y.

PHELPS JOS. E. Clerk, Sandwich; Rep; Cong; Illinois.

PHELPS LESTER, Blacksmith, Sandwich; Ind; Ind; from N. Y.

PHELPS T. B. Machinist, Sandwi h; Rep; Ind; from N. Y.

PHELPS WM. C. Book-keeper, Mfg. Co; P.O. Sandwich; Rep; from N. Y.

PHILPOT GEO. Farmer, Sec. 32; P.O. Somonauk; Dem; Cath; from Germany.

POINTBOAN ANTOINE, Laborer, Sandwich; Rep; Cath.

POLLING C. D. Shirt Cutter, Sandwich; Rep; Ind; from N. Y.

POLMAN CHRIST, Blacksmith, Sandwich; Ind; Luth; from Germany.

POMLARE ANTOINE, Laborer, Sandwich; Ind. Cath.

POMEROY DAVID R. Dentist; res. Plano, Ill; P.O. Plano or Sandwich; office No. 9, South R. R. St. Sandwich; has had an experience of practice in his profession of twelve years; born Canada, May 7, 1841; came to state March, 1856; Rep; married Loretta McDonald, July 3, 1867, who was born Aug. 6, 1848.

POOR JERRY, Farmer, Somonauk; Rep; Lib.

POPP GEO. Saloon, Sandwich; Ind; Ind; from Germany.

POPLIN JESSE F. Farmer, Sec. 27; P.O. Somonauk; born in DeKalb Co. Ill. Feby. 5, 1845; Rep; Ind. in Religious views; entered the army Aug. 16, 1862, in Co. H, 105th Reg. I.V.I., served to the close of the war, was with Sherman in his march to the sea, wounded at battle of Lawtonville, S. C., and honorably discharged June 7, 1865; married Carrie Carr April 11, 1866, who was born in LaSalle Co. June 10, 1843; two children.

POPLIN WM. B. Farmer, Sec. 27; P.O. Somonauk; property $12,000; Rep; Ind; from N. C.

POTTER HART, Farmer, Sandwich; property $4,000; Rep; Ind; from N. Y.

POTTER HENRY, Farmer, Somonauk; property $3,500; Rep; Pres; from N. Y.

POTTER L. D. Mechanic; P.O. Sandwich; property $2,000; Rep; from N. Y.

POTTER T. Druggist, Sandwich; Rep; Ind; property $1,500; from N. Y.

POWELL JAMES T. Retired; Rep; value of property $1,500; from Mass.

PRATT ALMUS, Farmer, Sec. 27; born in Middlesex Co. Conn., Nov. 22, 1806; came to Illinois in 1839; Rep; Bapt; 137 acres, value $15,000; personal property $4,500; married Sallie A. Collins Oct. 11, 1829, who was born in Conn. in Feb. 1810, and died June 16, 1858, leaving eight children; married for his second wife Elizabeth J. Bartlett, Feb. 16, 1859, who was born in Granville, Nova Scotia, Feb. 5, 1821; children now living five. Son, Gilbert E., was born in Conn. April 21, 1832; Attorney at Law, member of Michigan Legislature in 1860; joined the 8th Reg. of M.V.I., as Captain of Co. A. landed in Port Royal, S. C., Sept. 1861, was wounded in the foot at the battle of Coosaw River, wounded and taken prisoner at the battle of James Island, and lay in Charleston prison five months, exchanged, was chosen Lieut. Col. 23d Mich., and killed at Bowling Green, April 6, 1863.

PRATT CHAS. H. Merchant, Sandwich; Rep; Cong; property $10,000; from Conn.

PRATT FRED A. works father's farm; P.O. Sandwich; Rep; Ind; from Illinois.

PRATT HENRY H. Farmer; P.O. Sandwich; Rep; Cong; property $4,000; from Conn.

PRESTON CHAS, Carpenter, Somonauk; property $600; Rep; Luth; from Germery.

PRENTICE W. J. Tailor, Sandwich; Rep; Ind; from Canada.

PRICE LAFAYETTE, Laborer, Somonauk; Rep; Ind; from N. Y.

PRICE T. Laborer, Somonauk; Rep; Ind; from N. Y.

PRICE WM. works for T. J. Skinner; P.O. Somonauk; Rep; Ind; from N. Y.

QUITT WALTER S. Carriage Painter, Sandwich; property $600; Dem; from N. Y.

RAFF JOSEPH, Blacksmith, Somonauk; Rep; Luth; from Germany.

RALPH J. W. Engineer; P.O. Sandwich; Rep; Ind; from N. Y.

RANGER ALFRED, Carpenter and Joiner; residence on Fourth Street, Sandwich; born in St. Lawrence Co., N. Y. May 9, 1829; came to Illinois in 1870, to DeKalb Co. in 1871: Rep; Independent in religious views; owns house and four lots, valued at $2,000; married Melissa D. Farmer, Sep. 29, 1853, who was born in St. Lawrence Co. N. Y. Oct. 4, 1831; family of three boys.

RARICK R. W. Well Borer; P.O. Sandwich; Rep; Meth; Illinois.

RAY JAS. T. Cariage Maker, Sandwich; Ind; Cath; property $9,000; from Mass.

REED CHAS. D. Furniture Dealer, Sandwich; Rep; Meth; from Mass.

REDING JNO. Farmer, Sec. 18; P.O. Somonauk; Dem; Luth; 80 acres; from Germany.

REIFF JOSEPH, Blacksmith, Somonauk; Ind; Luth; from Germany.

REYNOLDS T. B. Sandwich; Ind; Pres; from England.

RICE JESSE B. Farmer; P.O. Sandwich; Rep; Ind; from N. Y.

RICE MARSHALL, Farmer on 11. Latham's farm; P.O. Sandwich; Rep; Ind; N. Y.

RICHEY J. K. Clairvoyant and Botanic Physician; residence, East Railroad Street; office at residence; born in Saratoga Co. N. Y; came to Illinois in 1856, to DeKalb Co. 1875; Independent in political and religious views; wife was Elvira F. Cheever of Lima, Allen Co., Ohio; married in Dayton, Nov. 11, 1874.

ROBBINS GEO. S. Station Agent, Somonauk; Rep; Ind; born N. C.

ROBERTSON GILBERT H. Editor and Prop. Sandwich *Gazette;* res. Fourth and Cedar Streets, Sandwich; born Washington Co. N.Y. Nov. 28, 1837; came to Illinois 1874: Rep; Pres; val. personal property $4,000; married Mary L. Beveridge, May 31, 1859. who was born in Washington Co. Penn. April, 1836; three children.

ROBINSON JAS. Laborer, Sandwich; Dem; born Ireland.

ROBERTSON JNO. Laborer, Sandwich; Rep; Ind; born Va.

ROBERTSON WM. Gardener on Armstrong's farm; Rep; U. Pres; born N.Y.

ROBINSON FRANK W. Barber, Sandwich; Rep; Lib; born Ill.

RODEBAUGH ABRAM J. Laborer; P.O. Sandwich; Rep; Ind; born Ohio.

ROGERS GEO. W. Agricultural Implement Dealer, P.O. Sandwich; $2,000; Rep; Ind.

ROGERS STEPHEN S. Farmer, Sandwich; Rep; Ind; val. $2,000; from N.Y.

ROMPF AUGUST, Broom Maker, Somonauk; Luth; born Germany.

ROOD, HARTEY A. Farmer, Somonauk; Rep; Lib.

ROOD RUFUS Hardware Clerk; P.O. Sandwich; Dem; Ind; born Ill.

ROOD RUFUS B. Clerk, Sandwich; born Ill; Dem; Ind; val. prop. $3,000.

ROSE JNO. G. Farmer, Sec. 8; P.O. Somonauk; Dem; Bapt; 160 acres, $8,000; born R. I.

ROSENTRETER EDWARD and AUGUST, Owners of the Wind Grist Mill, Somonauk, located at head of Market Street; born in Germany—Edward, May 8, 1851; August in January, 1839; both came to Illinois in 1869, and to DeKalb Co. 1874; both Rep. and Luth; each owning house and lot and the mill jointly; val. $9,000; Edward married Anna Graves, 1872; August married Hannah Henneman, 1876; each has two children.

ROWE JOHN, boards with Goodell, Somonauk; Rep.

RUPP H. Clerk, Sandwich; Rep; born Penn.

RYTHER DANIEL, Farmer and Bridge Builder, and has a new Cider Mill; resides on Sec. 20; P.O. Somonauk; born Erie Co. N.Y. March 6, 1830; came to Ill, 1867; Rep; Ind. in religious views; owns 82 acres. val. $6,000; married Ann Bolor, Oct. 19, 1851. who was born in England, March 6, 1830; seven children.

RYTHER WM. H. Building Mover; P.O. Somonauk; $1,500; Rep; Ind; born N.Y.

SACHTER JNO. Laborer; from Switzerland; Rep; Cath.

SAMPSON EZRA, Retired Farmer; P.O. Sandwich; $2,000; Rep; Meth; born Vt.

SAILSBERY KELSEY, retired; resides on South Main Street, Sandwich; born in Chenango Co. N.Y. April 9, 1820; came to DeKalb Co. May 18, 1846; Rep; Meth; house and five acres. value $4,000; personal $4,000; married Lydia A. Burlingame, April 26, 1846, who was born in Chenango Co. N.Y. Nov. 3, 1818.

SAMPSON LYMAN P. Switchman, Sandwich; Rep; Ind; $700; born N.Y.

SANDWICH ENTERPRISE CO. Manufacturers of Wind Mills, Feed Mills, Cultivators, Pumps, and Hedge Trimmers, located on east side of Main Street, Sandwich; business formerly carried on by Kennedy Bros; was established under its present management in Winter of 1868-69; capital stock $84,500; President, E. Banta; Vice President, E. A. Kennedy; Secretary, B. F. Latham; Superintendent, Harvey Packer.

SANER FREDRICK, Harness Maker, Somonauk; Rep; Bapt; Germany.

SANDWICH MANUFACTURING CO. started by A. Adams in 1856, and carried on by A. Adams & Sons till 1867, when it was enlarged and incorporated under the name of Sandwich Manufacturing Co; capital stock $250,000; employs from 150 to 200 men; engaged principally in the manufacture of power and hand corn shellers and Adams & French Harvesters; President, W. L. Simmons; Vice President, G. W. Culver; Secretary and Treasurer, J. P. Adams; Assistant Secretary, W. C. Phelps; Superintendent Mechanical Department, H. A. Adams; Directors: W. L. Simmons, A. Adams, E. Lewis, G. W. Culver, E. Banta, H. Latham, H. A. Adams.

SANFORD GEO. T. Laborer; P.O. Sandwich; Rep; Ind; born N.Y.

SATTERLEE ALBERT, Photographer, Sandwich; Dem; Bapt; born N.Y.

SAUNDERS MARIA Mrs. widow; P.O. Sandwich; $700; three children; born N.Y.

SCHAFMAN AUGUST, Meat Market, Somonauk; Dem; Luth; born Germany.

SCHAFMAN GEORGE, Lightning Rods, Somonauk; Dem; Luth; Germany.

SCHAFMAN JOHN, Meat Market, Somonauk; $6,000; Dem; Luth; born Germany.

SCHARDT WM. Switchman, Somonauk; real est. $1,000; Rep; Luth; born Germany.

SCHEIDECKER JULIUS, Carpenter, Somonauk; Rep; Ind; born France.

SCHEIFER WILLIAM, Retired Farmer, Sandwich; Rep; Univ; N.Y.

SCHEFFERLE HERMAN, Shoemaker, Somonauk; Ind; Cath; born Switzerland.

SCHMIDT FRANK, Laborer, Sandwich; Rep; Ind; born Germany.

SCHOENENBERGER EMILE, works on A. Harmon's farm, Somonauk; Rep; Luth; France.

SCHOENENBERGER JACQUES, Farmer, Somonauk; per. prop. $300; Dem; from France.

SCOFIELD E. Rev. Pastor Pres. Church, Somonauk; born Vt; Rep.

SCOFIELD NATHANIEL W. City Marshal, Sandwich; Dem; Ind.

SCOTT ALEX. C. Blacksmith, Somonauk; Rep; Meth; born Penn.

SCOTT JOHN, Farmer, Secs. 13 and 14; P.O. Sandwich; Dem; Ind; 115 acres, $7,000; N.Y.

SEAMAN ALFRED W, Restaurant, Sandwich; Rep; Ind; val. $2,000; from N.Y.

SEAMAN L. S. Teacher Public School, Somonauk; Lib; Univ; born Ill.

SEAMAN MARY, widow, Somonauk; val. $600; from N.Y.

SEARS ARCHIBALD, Retired Farmer; resides head of Wolf Street, Sandwich; born Putnam Co. N.Y. Feb. 23, 1802; came to Illinois 1836, and to DeKalb Co. 1865; Rep; Ind. in religious views; owns 3½ acres in corporation, valued at $6,000; val. of personal prop. $130,000; has been Justice of the Peace, Supervisor and County Surveyor of Kendall Co. Ill; married Susan Hadden, June, 1833, who was born in N.Y. Dec. 25, 1815, and died June 10, 1845. leaving two children; married for his second wife Rachel M. Smith, Aug. 23, 1850, born at Hebron, Conn. Oct. 26, 1818; six children by last marriage, all living.

SEEBER JOSEPH, Farmer, Sandwich; $3,000; Ind; Ind; N.Y.

SEDGWICK WESTEL W. Attorney at Law; resides cor. Fourth and LaFayette Streets, Sandwich; born Oneida Co. N.Y. June, 1827; came to Ill. 1844, and to DeKalb Co. 1857; Rep; Pres; has several houses and lots in city, 380 acres in Iowa; value real estate $18,000; personal prop. $15,000; Justice of the Peace 16 years; Trustee and President of Board of Trustees several years; Mayor of City of Sandwich two terms; Supervisor 7 years; Chairman of Board of Supervisors 4 years; member of Legislature of 1862–63; member of Constitutional Convention, 1869–70; Trustee of Insane Asylum, Jacksonville, Ill; married Sarah A. Toombs, June 7, 1848, who was born in Erie Co. N.Y. Nov. 1827; six children living.

SEIUS JNO. Butcher, Sandwich; Ind; Ind; born England.

SEVERY HENRY A. Farmer; P.O. Sandwich; Rep; Ind; 120 acres; born Me.

SEVRY JOHN M. Farmer, Sec. 28; P.O. Somonauk; born Oxford, Me. Nov. 4, 1829; came to state 1853; Rep; Ind; 133 acres, $12,000; married Sarah Hubbard, Jan. 14, 1854, born Wells, Me. Oct. 23, 1829; two children.

SHAFMANN JOHN P. Farmer, Sec. 27; P.O. Somonauk; Dem; Pres; Germany.

SHALES DENSMORE, Laborer; Sandwich; from Penn; Dem; Ind.

SHELHON JOSEPH, Laborer; Somonauk; born in Germany; Rep; Cath.

SHEPARD AMOS, Dealer in Stock and Wool; resides on Main Street Sandwich; born in Fairfield Co. Conn. Dec. 10, 1831; came to DeKalb Co. Ill. 1857; has been Assessor of Town of Somonauk 16 successive years; married Anna E. Hall, Feb. 1858, who was born in Fairfield Co. Conn. 1848; has family of four children, three sons and one daughter.

SHILAND DAVID, Mechanic; P.O. Sandwich; born N.Y.; Rep; Ind.

SHILAND WM. T. Manf. Boots and Shoes, Sandwich; born N.Y; Presb; Rep; prop. $3,000.

SHRENSBURG L. M. Barber; Sandwich; born Ill; Rep.

SHUELER JOHN, Retired Farmer, Somonauk; born Conn; Rep; Bapt.

SHULTZ FERDINAND, Farmer, P.O. Sandwich; born Prussia; Meth; Ind; owns 200 ac.

SIEGLINGER JOHN, Farmer, Sec. 20; P.O. Somonauk; Germany; Dem; Luth; prop. $5,000.

SIMMONS CALVIN, Laborer, Sandwich; Rep; Ind; from N. Y.; prop. $800.

SIMMONS WM. works for C. D. Fish; Sandwich; born N.Y; Dem; Ind.

SIMMONS W. L. Produce Dealer, Sandwich; born Ohio; prop. $2,000.

SIMPSON ROBERT J. Iron Moulder, Sandwich; Canada; Ind; Ind; prop. $800.

SKEEL O. M. Machinist and Engraver, Sandwich; Rep; Cong; born Ill; prop. $1,500.

SKINNER E. Laborer, Sandwich; born Penn; Rep; prop. $1,200.

SKINNER HARVEY S. Painter, P.O. Sandwich; born Mich; Dem; Bapt.

SKINNER JNO. Retired Farmer, Sandwich; born Penn; Rep; Ind.

SKINNER THOS. J. Farmer, Sec. 16; P.O. Sandwich; born Penn; Rep; prop. $6,500.

SLACK FREDERICK A. Blacksmith, Sandwich; from Penn; Ind; Cong.

SLY FREDERICK W. Merchant, P.O. Sandwich; born Ill; Rep; Meth.

SLY FRED W. Salesman, P.O. Sandwich; born Ill; Rep; Meth.

SMITH CHAS. G. Farmer, Sec. 22; P.O. Sandwich; born in Utica, N. Y., June 2, 1820, came to Illinois in May, 1853; Rep; Independent in religious views; owns 16 acres, value $1,000; entered the army as private in Company F, 127th Regiment Illinois Volunteer Infantry, August, 1862; was in the battles of Vicksburg, Kansasport, and Yazoo River; was honorably discharged September, 1864; suffers from poor health on account of exposure in the army; married H. M. Odell, Dec. 17th, 1842, who was born in Grafton, N. Y., February, 1826; has eight children.

SMITH ED. F. Street Commissioner, Sandwich; born New Jersey; Rep; Meth; prop. $8,000.

SMITH ELIJAH, Retired Farmer, Sandwich; born Mass; Rep; Cong; prop. $4,500.

SMITH FRANK, Carpenter, Somonauk; born Germany; Rep; Luth.

SMITH GEO. A. Painter, Sandwich; born N. Y; Rep; Ind; val. of prop. $1,500.

SMITH JOHN G. Jeweler, P.O. Sandwich; born Col; Ohio.

SMITH JULIUS H. Retired Farmer, Sandwich; from N. Y; Rep; Ind; prop. $1,000.

SMITH JULIUS H. Peddler, Sandwich; from N. Y; Rep; Ind; prop. $800.

SMITH LUCY B. Mrs. P.O. Sandwich; from N. H; Cong; prop. $4,000.

SMITH LORENZO D. Mechanic, P.O. Sandwich; army two yrs; born N. Y; Rep; Ind.

SMITH M. Laborer, P.O. Sandwich; born N. Y; Dem; Ind; prop. $1,000.

SMITH NATHANIEL, Photographer and General Insurance Agent, resides 4th Street, Sandwich, also in Chicago; born in Saratoga Co. New York, Dec. 2, 1822; came to Illinois 1850; Rep; Liberal in religious views; owns 17 acres in DeKalb County; 310 acres in Iowa; house and two acres and 20 city lots, value, $12,000; personal prop. $12,000, consisting of photograph galleries and stock in incorporated Co's; married Elizabeth Fisk, August 31, 1854, who was born Nov. 21, 1826, in N. Y; has four children.

SMITH ORRIN T. Laborer, Sandwich; Rep; Ind.

SMITH RENSSELAER, Retired Farmer, resides South Main Street, Sandwich; born Otsego Co. New York, March 12, 1801; came to LaSalle Co. June 15, 1844; remained till 1866, when he removed to DeKalb Co; Rep; Meth; owns 240 acres, value $15,000; has been Justice of Peace; married Lovina Bardwell, Jan. 3. 1830; born in Bradford County, Penn., February 23. 1805; has fifteen children; son Stephen entered the army in 1862, Company H, 105th Regiment; was with Sherman in his march to the sea; honorably discharged at close of the war; died about three years after of disease contracted from exposure in the army.

SMITH THOMAS, Retired Farmer, Sandwich; from England; Rep; Bapt.

SMITHSON THOS. Mrs. Sandwich; born England; Bapt; val. of prop. $10,000.

SNOW CHARLES A. Traveling Agent, Sandwich; from Vermont; Dem; Ind; prop. $2,000.

SNYDER J. Laborer, Sec. 33; P.O. Somonauk; Germany; Rep; Luth.

SPACH GEORGE, Tailor, Somonauk; France; Rep; Luth; val. of prop. $300.

SPRINGER DAVIS, Retired Farmer, Somonauk; born N. Y; Rep; Christian; prop. $600.

SPRINGER WM. Painter, Somonauk; born Penn; Rep; Ind.

STAFFORD JOSEPH, Blacksmith, Sandwich; born France; Dem; Cath.

STAHL ADOLPH, Farmer, Sec. 1; Sandwich; Germany; Rep; Pres; prop. $11,800.

STALP LUDWIG, Farmer, Sec. 1; Sandwich; Germany; Rep; Pres; 160 ac; val. $6,000.

STEBBINS EDWARD, Mechanic, P.O. Sandwich; born Mass; Rep; Ind.

STUBBINS RODERICK, lives with son, P.O. Sandwich; born Mass; Meth; Rep.

STEELE JOHN M. Station Agent, P. O. Sandwich; born Ill; Rep; Ind.

STEPHENSON CHAS. N. Blacksmith, P.O. Sandwich; born Penn; Rep; Ind.

STEPHENSON PAUL, Butcher, P.O. Sandwich; born Penn; Rep; Meth; prop. $1,500.

STEVENS CHAS. V. General Agent Cal. Wind Mill, Somonauk; Rep; Bapt; prop. $1,200.

STEVENS JAS. C. lives with son, Chas. V., Somonauk; from N. H; Dem; Ind.

STEWART ELIJAH, Farmer and Justice of the Peace, resides Sec. 3; P.O. Freeland; born in Washington Co. Pennsylvania. 1802; moved with parents while quite a child to Ohio and settled in what is known as the Western Reserve, Youngstown; came to Illinois in 1840, and to DeKalb Co. in 1853; Rep; U. Presb; owns 165 acres, value $10,000; has held the office of Justice of the Peace eight terms; married Agnes McGeahy, June 8th, 1825, who was born in Adams Co. Pennsylvania, in 1803; Mrs. S. died December 19th, 1874; had eight children, seven living; three sons; one is a farmer, one a clergyman; son William is a physician; moved South, and was assassinated in his own house, Carroll County, Miss., on account of his political opinions.

STILES FRED P. Machinist, P.O. Sandwich; born Ill; Rep.

STILES CORNELIUS C. Carpenter and Builder, P.O. Sandwich; born N.Y; Rep; Cong.

STILES LUTHER H. Clerk, P.O. Sandwich; born Ill; Rep; Cong.

STILES WM. H. Physician, P.O. Sandwich; born Ill; Rep; Cong.

STINSON STEPHEN B. Attorney and Ins. Agent, Sandwich; Rep; Cong; prop. $3,000.

STINSON WM. T. Teacher and Student, P.O. Freeland; born Ohio; Rep; U. Pres.

STOCKHOLM ALFRED, Meat Market, Sandwich; born N. Y; Rep; Ind; prop. $3,000.

STOCKHOLM JOHANNA, Sewing, Sandwich; from N. Y; Ind; prop. $1,200.

STONE HOLLIS L. Carpenter, Sandwich; from Wis; Dem; Ind.

STONE WM. F. Tinner, Sandwich; born Connecticut; Rep; Ind.

STRAIT JOSEPH, Farmer, Somonauk; Rep; from N.Y.

STRATTON JOHN C. Retired Farmer, Sandwich; Rep; Pres; N.Y.

STRONG JOHANNA Mrs. Sandwich; Cong; from Conn.

STRASLOT EUGENE, Mechanic, Sandwich; Ind; Rep; France.

SUMNER I. Drugs and Stationery, Somonauk; Rep; Ind; N.Y.

SWARTZ PHILLIP, Laborer, Somonauk; Dem; Luth; Germany.

SWEENEY DANIEL M. Iron Moulder, Sandwich; Dem; Cath; Conn.

TAYLOR C. R. Dentist, Sandwich; Rep; Cong; England.

TAYLOR GEORGE, Farmer, Somonauk; Rep; England.

TAYLOR GEO. W. Laborer; P.O. Sandwich; Rep; Ind; Ohio.

TAYLOR JOHN C. Furniture Dealer and Undertaker; place of business corner of Main and Center streets, Sandwich; residence on N. Main street; born in Chautauqua Co. N.Y. August 16, 1836; removed to Illinois in 1856; Rep; Cong; owns house and lot, value $2,500; personal prop. $6,000; has held the office of County Treasurer in Kendall Co. two terms; has been a member of the Common Council of Sandwich two terms; enlisted in Co. D, 36th Reg. I. V. I. in August, 1861; was wounded in the battle of Stone River and Kenesaw Mountain in right arm; re-enlisted in January, 1864, as veteran in the 36th Reg.; was wounded again in the right arm, disabling it, June 19, 1864; was honorably discharged in October, 1864; married Emma J. Wright Dec. 25, 1865, who was born in Lisbon, Kendall Co. Ill. in 1845.

TAYLOR MILO, Clerk, Sandwich; Rep; Meth.

TEMPLETON WILEY, works for C. D. Fish; P.O. Sandwich; Dem; Ind; Indiana.

TIMBERLY F. O. Mechanic Mnfg. Co.; P.O. Sandwich; Rep; Bapt; Maine.

TIMBERLY HIRAM, Harnessmaker; P.O. Sandwich; Rep; Bapt; Maine.

THOMAS AMOS, Clerk, Sandwich; Rep; Ind; Canada.

THOMAS EDWARD, Physician, Somonauk; Ind; Lib; England.

THOMAS FRED. Painter, Somonauk; Rep; Luth; Germany.

THOMAS G. W. Shipper for Enterprise Co. Sandwich; Lib; Dem; Canada.

THOMAS PHILLIP H. Coal and Lumber, Somonauk; Rep; Ind; Germany.

THOMPSON R. C. Photographer; P.O. Somonauk; Dem; Ind; Illinois.

THOMPSON & CRAWFORD, Groceries, Sandwich, on N. Railroad street; Edward N. Thompson was born in N.Y. City, March 14, 1836; came to Illinois in his infancy, in 1836; Dem; Ind; married Julia Crawford in January, 1868, who was born Feb. 19, 1844, in N.Y.; one child. David W. Crawford was born at Charlton, Saratoga Co. N.Y. Sept. 16, 1848; came to Illinois in March, 1858; Rep; Ind. in his religious views.

THORPE HENRY M. Farmer, Sec. 21; P.O. Somonauk; Rep; Ind; N.Y.

TALMAN JUDSON A. Hardware and Tinware, Sandwich; Rep; Bapt; Carrollton, Ill.

TOWNSEND OTIS A. Farmer, Sec. 34, Somonauk; Rep; Lib; Mass.

TOWNSEND SILAS, Farmer, Sec. 34; P.O. Somonauk; Rep; Mass.

TOWN SAMUEL H. Principal of Somonauk Graded School; taught in this school three years previous to 1870; assumed the Principalship of the Geneva Graded School for two years; returned and took charge of the Somonauk School in the Fall of 1873, which position he still fills; residence on Sycamore street, Somonauk; born in Keene, N. H. August 24, 1843; graduate of Kimball Union Academy, Meriden, N. H.; came to Illinois in the Fall of 1866; Rep; Meth. Epis; owns house and lot, value $2,000; married Julia Lowe, May 13, 1869, who was born in LaSalle Co. Ill. in November, 1852.

TRAMBLIE JULIUS, Shoe Dealer; P.O. Sandwich; Rep; Ind; from Vermont.

TRAUT PETER, Machinist, Sandwich; Ind; Cath; Wisconsin.

TRIMBLE LEWIS, Laborer; P.O. Sandwich; Rep; Cath; N.Y.

TROEGER EDWARD F. Mechanic; P.O. Sandwich; Rep; Ind; Illinois.

TROEGER HENRY A. Mechanic; P.O. Sandwich; Rep; Ind; Penn.

TROUT GEO. W. Carriage Maker; P.O. Sandwich; Dem; Latter Day Saints; Ohio.

TURNER HOPE, Laborer, Sandwich; Rep; Meth; Virginia.

VAN OLINDA C. Mrs. Sec. 15; P.O. Sandwich; Cong; N.Y.

VAN OLINDA DANIEL J. Retired Farmer; P.O. Sandwich; Dem; Christian.

VAN SCOY ABRAHAM T. Teacher, Sandwich; Rep; non-sect.

VAN WINKLE JOHN H. Moulder; P.O. Sandwich; Rep; Ind; Germany.

VERMILYE LARAY, Painter, Sandwich; Rep; Pres; N.Y.

VERMILYE VALENTINE M. Physician and Surgeon, Sandwich; Rep; Ind; N.Y.

VERNON J. B. Machinist, Sandwich; Rep; Meth; N.Y.

VORIS WILLIAM, Farmer, Sec. 12; 80 acres, val. $5,000; Rep; from N.Y.

WALKER THEODORE J. Mechanic, Sandwich; Rep; Ind; Illinois.

WALLACE AMBROSE, Laborer, Somonauk; Dem; England.

WALLACE C. W. Blacksmith; P.O. Sandwich; Rep; Lib; Illinois.

WALLACE GEO. R. Hardware, Sandwich; Rep; Ind; Penn.

WALLACE PAUL W. Victualer and Meat Market, situated on Railroad street, Sandwich, Ill.; born in Philadelphia, Penn. Dec. 20, 1832; came to DeKalb Co. in March, 1854; Rep; Meth; owns house and lot, value $3,000; personal prop. $2,500; has been Alderman of City of Sandwich; married Sallie M. Erwin June 19, 1853, who was born at Bucks Co. Penn. June 27, 1834; has seven children.

WALLACE W. H. Clerk, Sandwich; Rep; Meth; Penn.

WALTER GUSTAV, Carriage-maker, Sandwich; Ind; Prot; France.

WALTER JOHN, Wagon-maker, Somonauk; Dem; Cath; Germany.

WALTER VOLTEN, Wagon-maker, Somonauk; Dem; Cath; Illinois.

WALTERS WM. Carpenter, Sandwich; Dem; Pres; Illinois

WARD PATRICK, Laborer, Sandwich; Rep; Cath; Ireland.

WARD WM. Painter, Sandwich; Rep; Ind; N. J.

WARNER JAS. Clothing, Sandwich; Ind; N.Y.

WATERBURY LOUISA Mrs. Sandwich; Bapt; N.Y.

WATKINS GEO. F. Broom Mnfr.; P.O. Sandwich; Rep; Meth; Mass.

WATKINS THEODORE A. Carpenter, Sandwich; Rep; Bapt; Mass.

WEBER F. Stone Mason, Sandwich; Rep; Cong; Germany.

WEBBER JOHN G. Farmer; P.O. Freeland; Luth; Germany.

WEIR THOS. A. Clerk for Jno. L. Culver, Sandwich; born N.Y.; Ind; Ind.

WELCH JAS. Farmer, Sec. 21; P.O. Sandwich; born N.Y.; Rep; Ind; 70 acres, $5,500.

14

WEEKS JOSEPH, Retired Farmer, and is now engaged in the Hardware business; resides on East Railroad Street, Sandwich; born in Gallatin Co. Ill. July 26, 1808, went to Kentucky in 1812 with his parents on account of Indians and Fever and Ague; came to DeKalb Co. in 1857; Rep; Bapt; owns house and seven acres in City of Sandwich, valued at $5,000; personal property $3,700; married Maria Tolman, April 18, 1844, who was born in Seneca Co. N. Y. Oct. 8, 1817. Mrs. W. is daughter of the late Rev. J. F. Tolman and brother of Rev. C. F. Tolman, Foreign Missionary to Assam three years, and now Secretary of Baptist Foreign Missions, located 61 Washington Street, Chicago.

WEEKS JOS. H. Telegraph Operator and Asst. Agent, Sandwich; Canada East; Rep; Ind.

WELLS DAVID A. Millwright; Rep; born Mass; Ind; $1,500.

WELLS EUGENE, Broommaker, Somonauk; N.Y.; came here 1854; Rep.

WELLS JAMES J. Manufacturer of "The Centennial Animal Trap;" born in the town of Eusopus, Ulster Co. N.Y. June 25, 1817; lived in that county and Oneida County thirty-seven years; came to LaSalle Co. this state, in 1854; came to this town and county in 1856; he is the patentee and sole owner of "The Centennial Animal Trap," which is acknowledged as the best ever offered to the community; value personal prop. $1,000; married Miss Eliza Brinckerhoff in 1839; she was from Dutchess Co. N.Y.; they have three children, two girls and one boy.

WELLS MERCY W. Mrs. Boarding House; P.O. Sandwich; born N.Y.; Meth.

WERNIC HENRY, Pastor German Church, Somonauk; born Ohio; Rep; Bapt.

WEST AUGUST, Butcher; P.O. Sandwich; born Ill; Rep.

WEST CHARLES A. Ed. and Prop. of the *Somonauk Reveille*, born LaSalle Co. Ill. Sept. 24, 1850, came to DeKalb Co. 1870; Rep. and Lib. in his religious views; per. property $1,200; married Ella M. Winne, Aug. 30, 1876, who was born in Troy, N.Y. in 1856. The *Reveille* is issued every Saturday morning.

WEST H. Mrs. P.O. Sandwich; born Germany; $2,000; Bapt.

WEST MOSES, Retired Farmer, Sandwich; from Mass; Rep; Ind.

WESTFALL HEMAN, Retired Farmer; P.O. Freeland; born N.Y.; Dem; Meth.

WEVER HENRY, Farmer, Sandwich; Germany; Ind; Pres.

WHIEL NOEL, Shomaker, Somonauk; born France; Rep; Cath.

WHITCOMB GEO. H. Coal Dealer, Sandwich; born N. H.; Rep; Cong.

WHITCOMB W. A. Clerk, Sandwich; born N. H.; Rep; Ind.

WHITE ALANSON A. Mechanic; P.O. Sandwich; born Tioga Co. N.Y.; Rep; Cong.

WHITE ALEX. G. Farmer, Sec. 9; born Washington Co. N.Y. Jan. 19, 1817, came to Ill. 1848, to DeKalb Co. 1851; Rep; United Pres; owns 160 acres, val. $11,200; married Mary J. Robertson, N.Y. May 5, 1849, born Washington Co. N.Y. May 25, 1825, died Sept. 26, 1850; married his second wife, Eliza Howison, Sept. 18, 1858, who was born Scotland, Aug. 1825; have one son, Jno. R. who resided at home with parents; born Sept. 18, 1850, Wheatland, Ill; Rep; United Pres.

WHITE EDWARD A. Painter, Sandwich; from N.Y.; Rep.

WHITE FRED L. Carpenter and Joiner, Sandwich; born N.Y.; Ind; Bapt.

WHITE JOHN, Carpenter and Joiner; P.O. Sandwich; born N.Y.; Dem; Pres.

WHITE JOHN, Laborer, Sandwich; Ireland; Ind.

WHITE JOHN, Carpenter, Sandwich; N.Y.; $8,000; Dem; Ind.

WHITE MOSES, Retired Farmer, Sandwich; N.Y.; $12,000; Rep; Meth.

WHITE SETH M. Farmer, Sec. 36; P.O. Sandwich; born Tioga Co. N.Y. Feb. 3, 1810; came to Ill. 1861; Rep; Cong; 13 acres, value $7,000; married Sarah Roy, Aug. 1833, born Orange Co. N.Y. Aug. 12, 1815; two children; foster father of M. M. Pomeroy; Mr. White is of English descent, and Mrs. W. is Scotch; son, A. G. White, entered the army Aug. 1862, in 105th Ill. Regt; was with Sherman in his march to the sea, and was honorably discharged at close of the war; son is a Rep.

WHITE THOMAS, Farmer, Sec. 32; P.O. Somonauk; born Washington Co. N.Y. Feb. 15, 1815, came to Ill. 1857; Dem; Ind; 167 acres, $10,000; married A. Eliza Tucker, Feb. 1837, born Greenwich, N.Y. June, 1815; five children.

WHITE VALENTINE, Carpenter, Sandwich; Rep; Latter Day Saint.

WHITMORE DANIEL, Retired Farmer, Sandwich; born N.Y.; Rep; Meth.

WHITMORE JAS. Retired Farmer, Sandwich; N.Y.; Rep; Ind.

WHITMORE WM. M. Farmer, Sandwich; born Ill; Ind; Ind.

WHITNEY EDWARD D. Farmer; P.O. Freeland; born N.Y.; Rep; Ind; $1,000.

WHITTLE ALEXANDER, Farmer, Sec. 18; P.O. Somonauk; born Canada, Feb. 14, 1834, came to Ill. 1852, DeKalb Co. 1864; Rep; Univ; 160 acres, value $10,00(; married Elizabeth Early, Feb. 28, 1849, who was born Canada, March 5, 1838; two children.

WIESER GEO. Rev. Pastor of St. John's Evangelical Church, Somonauk; born Switzerland, June, 1839; entered the Theological Seminary at St. Chrishone, 1860, and graduated Sept. 1865, came to New Buffalo, Mich. Oct. 1865; Pastor of St. John's Church two years; then removed to Casco, St. Clair Co. in 1867; Pastor of St. Peter's Church five years, came to DeKalb Co. 1872; entered pastorate of St. John's Church, which he now fills; church has membership of thirty-five families at about four each; married Louise Artus, June 12, 1866, born Saxony, 1849; five children living.

WILCOX ASA, Stonemason; P.O. Sandwich; born N.Y.; $1,200; Rep; Meth.

WILCOX FRANK, Blacksmith; P.O. Sandwich; born Ill; Rep; Ind; Sergeant in ar.n.y.

WILKINS MARY Mrs. relict of Rev. Wilkins, Somonauk; born England; Bapt; $800.

WILLIS JOHN E. Carpenter and Joiner and House Mover, Sandwich; born in Cayuga Co. N.Y. Feb. 6, 1833, came to DeKalb Co. Ill. 1874; Rep; Meth; personal property in Wis. $1,500; entered the army as Sergeant, in Co. G. 50th Wis. Nov. 1862, · ent with his regiment from St. Paul, Minn. in command of Gen. Sibley, across the plains to the mountains to regulate Indian troubles; honorably discharged Sept. 23, 1865; married Mary W. Clark, Jan. 1, 1858, who was born in Scott Co. N.Y. March 22, 1833; two children.

WILLIAMS JOHN, Railroader, Somonauk; born Va; Rep; Ind.

WILLIAMS JOHN A. Farmer, Sandwich; lives with father; Rep; Ind.

WILLIAMS SAMUEL, Farmer, Sec 1; Sandwich; Penn; came to Ill. 1836; Rep; 100 a. $4.500.

WILMARTH LEONARD, Farmer, Sec. 12; Sandwich; $5,000; N.Y.; Rep; Ind; came Ill. 1845.

WILSER GEORGE Rev. Pastor Evan. Church, Somonauk; born Switzerland; came here 1865.

WILSEY ANDREW J. Ice Cream and Confectionery, Sandwich; born N.Y.; Dem; Ind; $3,000.

WILSEY BENJ. Jeweler, Sandwich; born N.Y.; Rep; Ind.

WILSEY HARRIETT Mrs. Dressmaker, Sandwich; born Penn; Ind; $6,000.

WILSON ALEXANDER, Farmer; res. Sec. 2; P.O. Freeland; born N.Y.; came to Ill. 1843; Rep; Ind; was in the army, Co. V, 113th Regt. I. V. I.

WILSON CHARLES E. Farmer; resides on Sec. 2; P.O. Freeland; born Onondaga Co· N.Y. July 19, 1841, came to DeKalb Co. Ill. 1848; Rep; Ind; owns 140 acres, value $7 000; per. property $2,000; married Alice M. Fay, Oct. 21, 1868, who was born DeKalb Co. Ill. 1849; one daughter.

WILSON HARISON, Farmer, Sec. 2; P.O. Freeland; 83 acres, value $4.500; Ill; Rep; Ind.

WILSON JAMES M. Farmer, Sec. 2; P.O. Freeland; val. $7.000; N.Y.; came Ill.1842; Rep; Ind.

WILTGON D. G. Tailor, Somonauk; value real estate $1,700; personal $900; Rep; Ind.

WINCHESTER EDWARD A. Farmer, Sec. 19; P.O. Sandwich; born N.Y.; Rep; Ind.

WINCHESTER HENRY F. Farmer, Sandwich; 295 acres; Ind; born Vt.

WINTER MATHEW C. Farmer, Secs. 5 and 8; P.O. Freeland; 150 acres; Rep; U. Pres; Ohio.

WINTER M. H. Farmer, Sec. 5; P.O. Freeland; prop. $9,000; Rep; U. Pres; born Ohio.

WIRTZ GEORGE, Farmer; P.O. Sandwich; Rep; Bapt; born Ill.

WITKOWSKY M. D. Clerk, Sandwich; Dem; Ind; born Ill.

WOLFORD FRANK, Laborer; P.O. Sandwich; Rep; Ind; born Penn.

WOHLFERT PETER, Laborer, Sandwich; Dem; Ind; born Germany.

WOLFE SCOTT H. Machinist, Sandwich; Rep; Luth; born Penn.

WONDER JACOB, Butcher, Sandwich; $1,000; Ind; Bapt; from Penn.

WOOD W. H., D.D., Clergyman, Somonauk; Meth; born England.

WOODRUFF HORACE, Carriage Maker; P.O. Sandwich; $1,000; Rep; Ind; born N.Y.

WOODWARD JOHN E. Mechanic, Sandwich; Rep; Pres; Penn.

WOODWARD ROBERT K. Books, Stationery and News Depot, res. cor. Elm and 3d Sts. Sandwich; born in Wayne Co. Penn. Nov. 13, 1843; came to DeKalb, Ill. 1859; Rep; Pres; owns house and lot, val. $1,200. $500 in business; married I. Vermilye, Dec. 29, 1868; who was born in Poughkeepsie, N.Y. Dec. 29, 1846; Mr. W. entered U. S. service, Co. H, 105th Regt. I. V. I. Aug. 1862; was with his Regt. in the series of battle, some of the most severely contested, with Sherman, from Resaca to his arrival at Richmond, among which were the taking of Atlanta and battle of Kenesaw Mt; honorably discharged Jan. 16, 1866.

WOODWARD SOLON, Groceries and Glassware; P.O. Sandwich; $2,500; Rep; Pres; born Pa.

WRIGHT ELISHA B. Gardener; P.O. Sandwich; Rep; Cong; born N.Y.

WRIGHT C. E. Druggist and Optician; resides on Green street, Somonauk; born in Genessee Co. N.Y. in March, 1842; came to DeKalb Co. Ill. in 1861; Rep; Lib; owns house and lots, valued at $800; personal prop. $6,000; entered the army in September, 1862, in Co. H, 105th Reg. I. V. I.; was with his regiment three years; was honorably discharged in May, 1865; married Altha Wright, in May, 1867; she was born in LaSalle Co. Ill. in October, 1848.

WRIGHT GEO. Hardware, Somonauk; $5,000; Dem; Ind; born Ill.

WRIGHT HARRISON. Hardware, Somonauk; $5,000; Dem; Ind; born N.Y.

WRIGHT HENRY, Stock Buyer, Somonauk; Rep; born Ill.

WRIGHT ISAAC, Cooper and Gardener, Sandwich; house and lot; born N.Y.

WRIGHT JAMES E. Clerk Drug Store, Somonauk; Dem; Ind; born Ill.

WRIGHT JOHN, boards with Goodell. Somonauk; Rep; N.Y.

WRIGHT STEPHEN D. Farmer, resides Secs. 27 and 28; P.O. Somonauk; born Genesee Co. N.Y. May, 1823; came to Ill. 1844, and to DeKalb Co. 1855; Dem; Lib; owns 134 acres, val. $10,000; per. prop. $2,000; married Ruby M. Johnston, Nov. 23, 1855; who was born Monroe Co. N.Y. May, 1833; one son.

WRIGHT THOS. Mechanic, Sandwich; Rep; Cong; born N.Y.

WRIGHT T. J. Farmer, Sec. 33, Somonauk; 104 acres, val. $10,000; Dem; Ind; N.Y.

YOUNG FRANK, Mechanic. Sandwich; Rep; Cong; N.Y.

YOUNG GEO. Shoemaker, Sandwich; Luth; Ind; born Baden, Germany.

YOUNG PHILIP, Mason, Somonauk; Luth; Germany.

ZIMMERMAN CONRAD, Retired Farmer, Sandwich; $400; Rep; Meth; from Germany.

CORTLAND TOWNSHIP.

ADAMS JOSEPH, Carpenter and Postmaster, Cortland; Rep; from N. Y.
 ADAMS MRS. E. Postmistress, Cortland; from N. Y.
ADAMS CHARLES, Assistant Postmaster, Cortland; Rep; from N.Y.
ALDIS JAMES, Farmer, Sec. 33; P.O. Cortland; Meth; Ind; from England.
ALDIS ROBERT, Laborer on James Aldis' farm, Sec. 33; P.O. Cortland; from England.
ALDIS WILLIAM, employee Hartman House, Cortland; Rep.
ALLEN BENJAMIN, Farmer, Sec. 1; P.O. Sycamore; born in Washington Co. N. Y.,
 April 20, 1829; lived there seventeen years; came to DeKalb County, in Town of Sycamore,
 in 1846; lived there eighteen years, and came to the Town of Cortland in 1864, and has lived
 there twelve years; Rep; Bapt; was school director in Sycamore, and is now Town Commis-
 sioner; owns 156 acres of land, valued $11,000; married Abigail L'hommedieu, of New York
 state, Oct. 10, 1852; has a girl and two boys adopted.
ANDERSON CHAS. works in cheese factory; P.O. Sycamore; he was born Feb. 17, 1850,
 in Smo'and, Sweden; came to United States May, 1873; came to this county same year;
 Luth; his father's family live in DeKalb.
ARTLIP E. Trader, Cortland; Dem; from Illinois.
AVERILL JAMES, Farmer, Sec. 11; 40 acres, $1,600; P.O. Sycamore; Dem; Penn.

BARNEY S. M. lives on farm of D. London, Sec. 16; P.O. Sycamore; Dem; from N. Y.
 BALIS R. P. Farmer; lives in Cortland; owns 300 acres joining town; Rep; Vermont.
BATES WILLIAM J. Agent Agricultural Machinery, Cortland; born in Chenango Co.
 N. Y. Oct 15, 1830; lived in that state 14 years; came to this state in 1845, and has lived in
 this county 31 years; he was the first officer in the Town of Pierce, after it was organized;
 has taught school 20 winters in one district in the Town of Pierce; was Assessor in this town
 for six years; Rep; Lib; owns farm of 160 acres, value $8,000; married Miss Sarah Hunt
 in 1851, she was from Kane Co; has one child, a boy; has lost five children.
BAXTER ELISHA M. Rev. Farmer, Sec. 21; Minister; P.O. Cortland; born July
 20, 1831, in Cornwall, Vermont; lived there ten years; came to N. Y. 1841; lived in Horicon,
 Warren Co. N. Y. thirty years; came to this county 1871, and assumed pastorate of Free Will
 Baptist Church in Cortland; Rep; owns house and lot, $600; personal, $500; married twice;
 first to Caroline Middleton, of Warren Co. N. Y., and had five children; second wife Sarah
 Townsend, of Cortland, and has two children.
BALIS THEODORE, son of R. P. Balis, Cortland; Rep; from Vermont.
BANNISTER D. P. Produce and Commission, Cortland; Rep; from N. Y.
BANNISTER DANIEL P. Coal merchant, Cortland; Rep; from N. Y.
BADGER EDMOND. Farmer, Sec. 29; P.O. Cortland; Epis; Dem; from Lower Can.
BADGER EDGAR, lives on Peter Moore's farm, Sec. 29; P.O. Cortland; Dem.
BADGER EDGAR, lives with Edmond Badger, Sec. 29; P.O. Cortland; Dem.
BALIS JOHN H. Farmer, Sec. 30; P.O. Cortland; 37 acres; Cong; Rep; from N.Y.
BALIS JOHN, Farmer, Sec. 29; P.O. Cortland; 87 acres, val. $4,000; Rep; Cong; from Vt.
BARRITT JAMES, Laborer William Postle's farm, Sec. 25; P.O. Lodi; Dem; from England.
BENSON JAMES, Tenant on James Lovell's Jr. farm, Sec. 2; P.O Sycamore.
BEALER JOHN, lives on James Postle's farm, Sec. 26; P.O. Lodi, Kane Co.; Dem; Germany.
BINGHAM JOHN, Farmer, Sec. 19; P.O. Cortland; 50 acres, val. $2,500; Meth; Rep; Eng.
BOYCE JAMES D. Laborer, Cortland; Dem; from N. J.
BOYCE J. lives on Geo. Bucklin's farm, Sec. 36; P.O. Lodi.
BOYLE RICHARD, lives on Dennis Kelly's farm, Sec. 25; P.O. Lodi; Dem; from Ireland.
BROOKS WILLIAM, Laborer; P.O. Lodi; Rep; from N.Y.
BRAND C. Farmer, Sec. 1; P.O. Sycamore; Rep.
BROWN EBEN, Farmer. Sec. 10; P.O. Sycamore; born Sept. 18, 1801, Hillsboro, N. H.;
 lived there fourteen years; came to this county in 1849, and has lived here twenty-seven years.
 Rep; Bapt; owns 62½ acres land, value $3,750; value personal property, $1,000; married
 Lepha Nichols; she was born in New York State; have one daughter.

BLANK CHARLES, lives on James Waterman's farm, Sec. 10; P.O. Sycamore; Rep; Sweden.
BUTLER THOS. Farmer, Sec. 36; 90½ acres, value $3,600; P.O. Lodi, Kane Co.; Dem; Ill.
BURBANK GEORGE W. Farmer, lives with father. Sec. 8; P.O. Sycamore; Rep; from Vt.
BLACKBURN JAMES, Carpenter, Sec. 11; P.O. Sycamore; Ind; from Canada.
BURDICK J. J. Carpenter, Cortland; Rep; from N. Y.

CLARK JAMES, lives on the G. W. Gandy est. farm, Sec. 15, P.O. Sycamore; 148 acres, value $6,400; Dem; from N. Y.
CARLSOM PETER C. lives with Mr. Lawyer. Sec. 8; P.O. Sycamore; born South of Sweden, Oct. 25, 1845; lived there twenty-four years; Rep; Luth; value personal property, $200; his family are in Sweden.
CARLSON ANDREW J. works for G. W. Savery, Cortland; Rep; from Sweden.
CALHOUN ANDREW, retired, Cortland; Rep.
CALHOUN W. R. Carpenter, Cortland; Rep.
CAMPBELL A. S. Farmer, Sec. 1; P.O. Sycamore; 94 acres, val. $3,760; Ind; from N.Y.
CAMPBELL ROBT. retired; P.O. Sycamore; Dem.
CHEASEBRO J. E Farmer, Sec. 17; P.O. Cortland; 43 acres; Disciple; Rep; from N.Y.
CHEASEBRO JOHN L. Farmer, Sec. 8; P O. Sycamore; born in Madison Co. N. Y., June 11, 1817; was raised in Erie Co.; lived there until twenty-four years old; came to this state, DuPage Co. and lived there two years; came to this county 1844, and has lived here thirty-two years; Rep; Meth; owns 80 acres land, value $8 000; personal, $200; has been Commissioner; married Patience P. Wheeler, of Hebron, N.Y. 1841; has one child, daughter; his son was Prof. in Iron City Commercial College, Pittsburgh, died three years ago, twenty-nine years old.
CHAMPLIN BENJ. Tenant Farmer, Sec. 29; P.O. Cortland; born in Genesee Co. N Y. Feb. 5, 1820; lived there fourteen years; came to this state in 1834, and has lived here forty-two years; was at the raising of the first house built in Sycamore, this county; Rep; Univ; value personal property, $600; has held office of Commissioner; married Miss Amanda M. Russell, of Erie Co. N. Y. and has four children.
CHAMPLIN C. V. Engineer Lovell's Mills, Cortland; from Ill.
CHRISTMAN PHILANY Mrs. Sec. 18; P.O. Cortland; born German Flats, Herkimer Co. N Y., July 19, 1835, and lived there twenty years; came to this town and county in 1857, and has lived here nineteen years; Lib. religion; owns 190 acres land, value $4,500; personal property $1,000; married John Christman, Oct. 19, 1857; he was born in Herkimer Co. N Y.; has two children, one girl and one boy.
CLARK HENRY. Farmer, Sec. 26; 120 acres, value $6,000; P.O. Lodi, Kane Co.; Rep; Penn.
CLARK LORENZO M. Farmer, Sec. 24, Lodi; born Stratford, Fairfield Co. Conn. in year 1800, November 27; lived there twenty-one years; went to Wayne Co. N. Y. 1826; lived there thirteen years; came to this state, in Kane Co. in 1839; lived there two years; came to DeKalb Co. in 1841, and has lived here thirty-five years; no land in market at that time; owns 400 acres, value $25,000; Dem; Lib; married Miss Rachel P. Moody, of Amherst, Mass. Feb. 9, 1825; have lived together over fifty-one years; have had five children, and have three children living.
COURT HENRY, lives on Mrs. C. A. Ludwigsen's farm, Sec. 16; P.O. Cortland; Dem; England.
CONDON JOHN, Farm Laborer.
COOLIDGE P. S. Farmer, Sec. 9; P.O. Sycamore; Dem.
CRANDELL J. D. Carpenter, Cortland.
CRANE F. S. Farmer, Sec. 15; P.O. Sycamore; Rep.
CROSSETT DWIGHT, Farmer, Sec. 28; P.O. Cortland; 155 acres; Pres; Dem; from N.Y.
CROSSETT HARLAN, Farmer, Sec. 28; P.O. Cortland; 120 acres; Pres; Dem; from N. Y.
CRAWFORD E. Mrs. Sec. 34; 86 acres, val. $4,300; P.O. Cortland; from N.Y.
CRANDALL JOHN, Carpenter, Cortland; Rep; from N. Y.
CURTIS C. W. Prof. Principal School, Cortland; Rep; from Conn.

DALY P. J. Merchant, Cortland; Dem; from Ireland.
DAVIS JOHN W. Retired Farmer; lives in Cortland; Rep; from Ohio.
DALY MICHAEL, Liquor Dealer; P.O. Cortland; born in County Mayo, Ireland, 1839; came to this county Sept. 1869; has family of one boy and two girls; wife was Miss Barbara E. Daley, Co. Mayo, Ireland, born 1854; married March, 1869; Dem; Cath.
DAYTON ALVON, Farmer, Sec. 1; P.O. Sycamore; 360 acres; Meth; Rep; from Conn.

DAYTON O. M. Farmer, Sec. 1; P.O. Sycamore; Rep; from Ill.

DEGRAFF DAVID, Farmer, Sec. 5; P.O. Sycamore; 160 acres; Cong; Dem; from N.Y.

DOBSON LAVINA Mrs. widow, Sec. 29; P.O. Cortland.

DORATHY E. B. Night Watchman Depot, Cortland; Rep; from Wisconsin.

DOWD PATRICK, Railroad Laborer, Cortland; Dem; from Ireland.

DUNN JOHN, works in Lovell's mill, Cortland; Dem; from New Jersey.

ELLIOTT MORRIS, Farmer, Sec. 2; 78 acres, value $3,900; P.O. Sycamore; Rep; Ill.

ELLIOTT JAMES, Farmer, Sec. 1; P.O. Sycamore; Rep.

ELLIOTT CLARENCE, Farmer, Sec. 1; P.O. Sycamore; Rep; from Ill.

ENNIS HARRIET Mrs. (widow), Cortland; from N. Y.

ELY C. F. Farmer, Sec. 17; P.O. Sycamore; born in Wyoming Co. N.Y. Nov. 1823; lived there 35 years; came to this county 1858, and has lived here 18 years; Dem; Meth; value personal property $8,000; his wife owns 93 acres, value $6,000; he is justice of the peace; married Miss Lydia M. Jordan, in 1850; she was born in Town Moriah, Essex Co. N. Y.; have three children.

ESPEY GEORGE W. Drug and Grocery Business, Village of Courtland; born in Georgetown, Ohio, Sept. 5, 1842; lived in that state twenty-two years, came to this state Nov. 1868; was traveling for mercantile house in Chicago about three years; was in the army four years and two months; was 1st Lieut. in the 59th Ohio Regt. Western Army; was wounded slightly three times; was in a number of battles; has been in the Drug and Grocery business here since 1874, and doing a good and increasing business; married Carrie E. Sacket in 1873; she was from this town; has one child, Effie M. Espey.

EWING HIRAM, Farmer, Sec. 34; P.O. Cortland; 80 acres; Latter Day Saint; Rep; Ohio.

EWING LYMAN, Laborer, with M. B. Ewing; P.O. Cortland; Rep; from Ill.

EWING MILO B. Farmer, Sec. 34; P.O. Cortland; Ind; from DeKalb Co.

FINCH MORRIS, son of Solomon Finch, Sec. 15; P.O. Sycamore; Rep.

FINCH S. M. Farmer, Sec. 15; P.O. Sycamore.

FINCH SOLOMON, Farmer; P.O. Sycamore; 71 acres, val. $3,550; Bapt; Rep; from N.Y.

FORD A. J. Stock Dealer, Cortland; Rep; from Ill.

FORD H. Stock Dealer, Cortland; owns 3 acres; Rep; from N. Y.

FORD EDSON A. Stock Dealer, Cortland; Rep; from Ill.

FRICK A. C. Rev. Pastor M. E. Church, Cortland; Rep; from Ill.

FARGESON ROBERT, lives on John Pooler's farm, Sec. 19; P.O. Cortland; Rep; Scotland.

FOWLER O. T. Farmer, lives in Cortland; Ind; from Ill.

FULCHER THOS. works for James C. Wright, Sec. 30; P.O. Cortland.

GARBURT HENRY, lives on W. D. Bush's farm, Sec. 6; P.O. Sycamore; Rep; from Canada.

GARBURT JOHN, lives with Henry Garburt, Sec. 6; P.O. Sycamore; Rep; Can.

GANDY FRANCIS M. Farmer, Sec. 9; P.O. Sycamore; born June 27, 1845, in this county, and has lived here ever since; Dem; Bapt; owns 90 acres, $4,000; personal, $1,000; married Miss Sarah L'hommedieu, Oct. 31, 1870; she was born in this state; has had two children and lost them.

GAHAGAN EDWARD, Farmer; owns 35 acres; lives in Cortland; Dem; from Ireland.

GANDY J. L. Laborer, Sec. 9; P.O. Sycamore; Dem.

GANDY H. H. Farmer, Secs. 9 and 10; P.O. Sycamore; 173 acres; Dem; Ohio.

GANDY A. J. lives on H. H. Gandy's farm, Sec. 9; P.O. Sycamore; Dem; Ill.

GALE GEORGE H. Farmer, Sec. 35; P.O. Lodi; born March 24, 1849, in DuPage Co. Ill; came to this county in 1856; Rep; Meth; father owns farm; value personal property $500; married Miss Jane Ella Combs, of McHenry Co. May 2, 1875; she owns prop. val. $1,000.

GESTLAR AUGUST, Shoemaker, Cortland; Dem; from Germany.

GODING J. Mason, Cortland; Rep; from England.

GOODRICH C. H. Teamster, Cortland; Rep; from N. Y.

GOULD JOHN, works for Joseph H. Snyder, Sec. 22; P.O. Cortland; Bapt; Rep.

GREEN THOS. lives on Daniel Pierce's farm, Sec. 6; P.O. Sycamore; from England.

GROVER CHARLES, Farmer, Sec. 2; P.O. Sycamore; Rep; from N.Y.

GREEN ROYAL, lives on James Waterman's farm, Sec. 5; P.O. Sycamore; Dem; from Ill.

GUSTAFSAN FRANK, Farmer, Sec. 14; P.O. Sycamore; born Oct. 27, 1845, in Sweden; lived there 25 years; came to this country 1870; came to Wayne Station this state and lived there four years; came to this county 1874; Rep; Luth; owns 40 acres, $800; married Emily Victoria in December, 1874; she was born in Sweden; has two nice children.

HAVENS ALBERT, Blacksmith, Cortland; Rep; from N. Y.

HATHAWAY JAMES, Horse Trainer, Cortland; Ind; from N. Y.

HAWLEY SAMUEL, Farmer, Sec. 25; P.O. Lodi; born in Fairfield Co. Conn. March 10, 1794; lived there 58 years, then came to Kane Co. Ill. and lived there about three years; then came to Town of Cortland, DeKalb Co. and has lived here 20 years in May, 1876; he is 82 years of age; Rep; Cong; he has been one of the Selectmen of the town, and has held other town offices; owns 35 acres, $5,000; he married Miss Betsy Smith, of Fairfield Co. Conn. Sept. 30, 1818; she was born Oct. 23, 1799; they have lived together 56 years; have had three children, two now living—one son and one daughter.

HARTWELL CYRUS W. Farmer, Sec. 29; P.O. Cortland; born Feb. 20, 1823, in Chatauqua Co. N. Y.; lived there 27 years; came to Kane Co. in 1850, and lived there 20 years; came to this county in 1869; Rep; Cong; owns 7¼ acres, value $500; married Miss Elizabeth Wells, of Berkshire Co. Mass. in 1846; has two children.

HEALEY MICHAEL, Grocer, Cortland; Dem; Ireland.

HILDRETH TRUMAN, Retired Farmer, Cortland; Ind; from N. Y.

HITCHCOCK O. retired, Cortland; Rep.

HOLDREDGE WAYNE, Farmer, Sec. 28; P.O. Cortland; born in Chenango Co. N.Y. and came to this state in 1854; Rep; Meth; owns 68 acres, value $5,000; personal $1,000; married Miss Clara Densmore, of New York State; has one child.

HOLDRIDGE L. works for Henry Townsend, Sec. 18; P.O. Cortland; Rep; N.Y.

HOLDRIDGE GERSHON, Farmer, Sec. 2; P.O. Cortland; Rep; from N.Y.

HOLDRIDGE G. Farmer, Sec. 20; P.O. Cortland; 80 acres; Freewill Bapt; Rep; from N.Y.

HOLDRIDGE LESTER, Farmer; P.O. Cortland; 80 acres in Iowa, value $600; Univ; Rep; N.Y.

HODGE EDSON, Farmer, Sec. 21; P.O. Cortland; born 1811, in Otsego Co. N. Y. lived there 47 years; came to this state and county in 1858, and has lived here 19 years; Rep; Freewill Bapt; owns 76 acres, value $4,000; personal $600; married Jerusha King, of this state, and has six children.

HOUSE ALFRED, Farmer, Sec. 20; 140 acres, value $7,000; Rep; from N. Y.

HOLLAND HENRY, Miller, Cortland; Rep; from England.

HOLLAND GEORGE, son of Robt. Hollend, Sec. 32; P.O. Cortland; Meth; Rep.

HOLLAND ROBERT, Farmer, Sec. 32; P.O. Cortland; 210 acres, value $12,000; Rep; Ireland.

HORN TIMOTHY, works for Jonathan Matteson, Sec. 17; P.O. Sycamore; Dem.

HORAN JOHN, Farmer, Sec. 12; P.O. Sycamore; Dem; from Ireland.

HOPKINS THOMAS, Farmer, Sec. 12; P.O. Sycamore; Dem; from Ireland.

HOPKINS CYRUS B. Farmer, Sec. 27; P.O. Cortland; born in Clarence, Erie Co. N.Y. Aug. 7, 1812; came to this state in 1838, and has lived here 38 years; Rep; Meth; owns 177 acres, value $9,000; personal $1,000; has been commissioner and held other offices; married Miss Fanny Larkin, of Greene Co. N. Y. Dec. 6. 1836, and has eight children.

HUBBEL. M. R. Retired Farmer, Cortland; Rep; from N. Y.

HUFTAILEN DAVID, Farmer, Sec. 33; 80 acres, $4,000; P.O. Cortland; Meth; Rep; N.Y.

INGHAM N. T. Carpenter, Cortland; Rep; from Ill.

INGHAM ASHAEL, Farm Laborer, Cortland; Rep; Ill.

INGHAM ELLIS E. Farmer, Sec. 29; P.O. Cortland; born in Delaware Co Ohio, Nov. 27. 1845; came to Illinois, in DeKalb Co. 1846, and has lived here 30 years; Rep. Liberal; value personal prop. $600; was in the army in the 17th I. V. C., commanded by Gov. Beveridge; was in hospital at Alton, Ill., St. Joe, Mo. and Ft. Leavenworth, Kan. and was honorably discharged; married Ella M. DeForest. from N. Y. 1868; has one child, boy.

JORDAN THOMAS, Clerk for C. A. Talbot; Dem; from Ill.

JONES MOSES, Retired, Cortland; Dem; from N. Y.

JOHNSON ALFRED L. Farmer, Sec. 31; P.O. DeKalb; born in Auburn, N. Y. April 17, 1845; lived there two years; came to Sycamore in 1847; came to Town of Cortland in this county 1849, and has lived here 27 years; Rep; Epis; owns 102 acres, value $5,100; married Miss Carrie M. Root, from New Jersey, near New York City, Dec. 1872; has one child, a little girl.

JOHNSON AARON, lives in Ohio Grove; P.O. Sycamore; Rep; from Sweden.

JOHNSON ALFRED, son of Isaac Johnson, Sec. 31; P.O. Cortland; Rep; from N.Y.

JOHNSON A. P. lives on Mrs. Alice Love's farm, Sec. 18; P.O. Sycamore; Rep; from Sweden.

JOHNSON ISAAC, Farmer, Sec. 31; P.O. Cortland; Rep; from N.Y.

JOHNSON JOHN, lives in Ohio Grove; P.O. Sycamore; Rep; from Sweden.

JOHNSON R. Farm Laborer, Sec. 36; P.O. Lodi.

JOSLYN ALBERT, Farmer, Sec. 16; P.O. Sycamore; Rep; from N Y.

JOSLYN ALVIRUS, Farmer, Sec. 32; P.O. Cortland; Rep; from N.Y.

JOSLYN DEWITT C. Farmer, Sec. 29; P.O. Cortland; 58½ acres, $7,500; Meth; Rep; N.Y.

JOSLYN JOHN, son of Harry A. Joslyn, Sec. 16; P.O. Sycamore; Rep; from Ill.

JOSLYN PHINEAS, son of Albert Joslyn Sec. 16; P.O. Sycamore; Rep; from Ill.

JOSLYN P. V. Farmer, Sec. 33; P.O. Cortland; Rep; from N.Y.

JOSLYN REUBEN O. Farmer, Sec. 17; P.O. Cortland; 170 acres, value $8,500; Ind; N.Y.

JOSLYN HARRY A. Farmer, Sec. 16; P.O. Sycamore; born Dec. 10, 1816, in Genesee Co. N. Y.; lived there 21 years; came to this county in 1838, and has lived here 38 years; Rep; Univ; owns 93 acres, value $6,000; was sheriff of this county two years, and deputy sheriff eight years; has taught school; was school director, and helped organize graded schools in Sycamore; was one of fifteen who voted the old Abolition ticket; married Miss Lucy Ann Waterman, of Genesee Co. N. Y. in 1841; has five children.

JORDAN EDWARD F. Farmer, Sec. 16; P.O. Cortland; prop. $1,000; Meth; Rep; N.Y.

JORDAN JOHN. Farm Laborer; P.O. Cortland.

JORDAN WILLIAM, Sec. 16; P.O. Sycamore; Rep; from Ill.

JORDAN MOSES W. Farmer, Sec. 16; P.O. Cortland; born in Moriah, Essex Co. N.Y. Dec. 5, 1819; lived there 10 years; lived in Genesee Co. 22 years; came to this state and county in 1852; Rep; Meth; owns 67 acres, value $5,000; personal, $6,000; was ordained minister in M. E. Church, and preached about 18 years; practiced medicine 10 years; has been school director; married Miss Betsy Perkins, of Hampton, Washington Co. N. Y.; has one son, Edward F. Jordan, is married and lives with father.

JOHNSON G. Laborer, Sec. 14; P.O. Sycamore; born in Tioga Co. Penn. June 23, 1841; lived there eight years, then went to Ohio and lived there seven years; has lived in Indiana and Michigan; Rep; no religion; unmarried; owns lots value $200.

KANDALL N. Retired Farmer, Cortland; Rep; from Penn.

KENNEDY MARTIN, Blacksmith, Cortland; Dem; from Ireland.

KELSEY ALBION H. Farmer, Sec. 30; P.O. Cortland; born Genesee Co. N. Y. Aug. 9, 1851; lived there two years; came to this state 1853; Rep; Meth; value property $500.

KELSEY H. S. Farmer, Sec. 30; P.O. Lodi; Meth; Rep; from N.Y.

KELSEY WILLIAM A. Farmer, Sec. 30; 54 acres, value $2,700; P.O. Lodi; Meth; Rep; N.Y.

KENNEDY MICHAEL, Laborer, Cortland; Dem; from Ireland.

KENNEDY PATRICK, Blacksmith, Cortland; Dem; from Ireland.

KENNEDY WILLIAM, Laborer, Cortland; Dem; from Ireland.

KENAN ANN Mrs. (widow), Cortland; from Ireland.

KING JOHN, Depot Agent, Cortland; Dem; from New Jersey.

KING NATHAN, Farmer; owns 2 acres; Cortland; Rep; from N. Y.

KING BURNARD, Farmer, Sec. 25; P.O. Lodi; value property $600; Bapt; Rep; from Penn.

KING L. H. lives on Davis Rogers' farm, Sec. 15; P.O. Sycamore; Rep; from Penn.

KINGSTON GEO. M. Farmer, Sec. 8; 144 acres, $10,000; P.O. Sycamore; Meth; Rep; N.Y.

KINYON DEXTER, son of Geo. W. Kinyon, Sec. 8; P.O. Sycamore; Rep; from Ill.

KINYON GEO. M. Farmer, Sec. 8; P.O. Sycamore; 130 acres, value $9,100; Rep; from N.Y.

KINYON J. W. son of Geo. W. Kinyon, Sec. 8; P.O. Sycamore; Rep; from Ill.

KLEMM JOHN, Farmer, Sec. 3; P.O. Lodi; born in Baden on the Rhine, Germany, in June, 1836; lived there 12 years; came to this country June, 1848; came to DuPage Co. and lived there 7 years; came to this county in 1855; Dem; Cath; owns 200 acres, value $9,000; personal, $1,000; married Miss Mary Guinter, of Penn. in 1864; has six children.

KUGLER CHRIS. Farmer, Sec. 21; P.O. Cortland; 80 acres, value $4,000; Rep; Cong; Ger.

LANGAN C. J. Clerk for P. J. Daly, Cortland; Ind; from N. Y.

LEWIS G. W. Physician, Cortland; Rep; from N. Y.

LAWTON O. J. Farmer, Sec. 17; P.O. Cortland; born in Rhode Island, about 1798; went to Chenango Co. N. Y. about 1812, lived there 35 years, then came to DeKalb Co. Ill. and has lived here 29 years; Dem; Lib; owns 60 acres; $3,500; personal, $500; married Sallie Meeker, who was born in New Jersey; has six children.

LAWTON C. A. son of O. J. Lawton, Farmer, Sec. 17; P.O. Sycamore; Rep; Bapt; N.Y.

LAWTON LEWIS, Farmer, Sec. 20; P.O. Cortland; 57 ac. $2,850; Freewill Bapt; Rep; N.Y.

LANE DANIEL T. Farmer, Sec. 21; P.O. Cortland; 40 acres, value $2,000; Bapt; Rep; N. H.

LAWYER JOHN S. son of David S. Lawyer, Sec. 8; P.O. Sycamore; Meth; Dem.

LEWIS MIROM, Farmer, Sec. 31; 80 acres, value $3 200; P.O. DeKalb; Rep; from N. Y.

LEWIS J. B. Farmer, S c. 31; 80 acres, val. $3,200; P.O. DeKalb; Rep; N. Y.

LEFLER GEO. W. Dr. Proprietor of Hartman House, Cortland, and Veterinary Surgeon; born in Lodi, Seneca Co. N. Y. Aug. 6, 1833; lived in that state 13 years, then lived and studied with Dr. Geo. W. Dadd, veterinary surgeon of Boston seven years; then went to London, England, and studied in the Royal Veterinary College two years, and graduated there; returned to U. S., lived in New York till the breaking out of the war; enlisted as veterinary surgeon in the army, and was discharged by special order No. 515 of Gen. Halleck, to receive appointment of veterinary surgeon of cavalry, depot at Washington, D. C., and he served in that capacity until close of the war, and has since practiced his profession in Toledo, Detroit and Chicago. The citizens of DeKalb, Kane, and adjoining counties, can avail themselves of his professional services.

L'HOMMEDIEU CHARLES, Farmer, Sec. 11; P O. Sycamore; Rep; N. Y.

LITTLE O. F. Farmer, Sec. 5; P.O. Sycamore; Rep; from Ill.

LITTLE WILLIAM H. Farmer, Sec. 14; P.O. Cortland; Rep; from Ill.

LONDON DOW, Farmer, Sec. 17; lies on Richard London's farm; P.O. Sycamore; Dem; Penn.

LOVELL JAMES Sr. Farmer, Sec. 1; P.O. Sycamore; Rep; from N.Y.

LONDON JUSTICE, Farmer, Sec. 3; P.O. Sycamore; born in Clearfield Co. Penn. May 30, 1850; lived there five years; came to this state and county in 1855, and has lived here 21 years; Dem. Lib; value personal property $1,000; married Adelia Remington, in Town of Cortland, Dec. 3, 1874.

LORING THEODORE, Justice, Cortland; Rep; from N. Y.

LOVELL ALONZO L. Flouring Mill and Grain Business, Cortland; P.O. Cortland; born in Tompkins Co. N. Y. Nov. 5, 1826; lived there 11 years; came to St. Charles, Kane Co. June 1837, came to Town Cortland 1839, has lived in this county 37 years; has been in business 20 years in this village, 14 years in lumber, and 6 years in milling business; Rep. Lib; owns 185 acres, $7,500; owns flouring mill here; has been supervisor and held other offices; married Miss Ellen F. Jarvis, in 1858, who was born Joliet; has two children, girls.

LOVELL JOHN, Farmer, Sec. 2; 175 acres, value $10,500; P.O. Sycamore; Ind; from N. Y.

LOVELL JAMES, Jr. Farmer, Sec. 2; 270 acres, val. $16,200; P.O. Sycamore; Rep; from N.Y.

LUDWIGSEN C A. Mrs. (widow) Cortland; from N. Y.

LYONS CALEB, Retired Farmer; P.O. Cortland; Ind; from N.Y.

MATTESON W. H. lives on farm of Mrs. D. Matteson, Sec. 17; P.O. Cortland; Rep; N.Y.

MATTICE ADAM, Carpenter, Cortland; Rep; from N.Y.

MARRIOTT JOSEPH, Tenant Farmer, Sec. 6; P.O. DeKalb; born July 21, 1836, in Nottingham, England; lived there twenty-nine years; came to U.S. in 1865; came to DeKalb Co. and has lived here eleven years; Lib; Meth; value of prop. $1,000; married Miss Alice Lane July 18, 1858; she was born in England; has six children.

MATTESON D, Mrs., Sec. 17; P.O. Cortland; 40 acres, value $2,400; from N.Y.

MACKER C. J. Farmer, Sec. 9; P.O. Sycamore; 40 acres, val. $2,400; Rep; Ill.

MATTESON U. B. Produce and Commission, Cortland; Rep; from N.Y.

MALONE DANIEL, Railroad Section Foreman, Cortland; Rep; from Ireland.

MATTESON JOHN, Farmer, Sec. 35; 120 acres, val. $4,800; P.O. Cortland; Rep; Sweden.

McMAHAN JAMES, Farmer, Sec. 33; 80 acres, val. $3,200; P.O. Cortland; Dem; Ireland.

MALONE PATRICK, Railroad Hand, Cortland; Dem; from Ireland.

MATTESON A. B. Clerk for Moore & Sheldon, Cortland; Ind; from N.Y.

MATTESON JONATHAN, Farmer, Sec. 17; P.O. Cortland; 60 ac. $3,600; Ind; Spiritualist.

MARVIN WILLIAM, Harnessmaker, Sec. 20; P.O. Cortland.

McALPINE THOMAS, Farmer, Sec. 35; P.O. Lodi; 193 acres, value $9,650; Rep; Ohio.

McCALL DANIEL, Farmer, Sec. 1; P.O. Sycamore; Rep; from N.Y.

McLAGAN MRS. A. E. Cortland; owns 27 acres joining town, value $1,620; from N.Y.
McLAGAN ALEXANDER, Carpenter, Cortland; Rep; from N.Y.
MERRITT JOSEPH, Lives H. M. Stephen's farm, Sec. 6; Dem; P.O. Sycamore.
MEEKER MARTIN, Teacher, Cortland; Rep; from N.Y.
MEEKER JOHN, Retired Farmer, Cortland; Rep; from N.Y.
MEEKER C. G. Farmer, Sec. 9; P.O. Sycamore; Rep; from Ill.
MEEKER C. J. Farmer, Sec. 9; P O. Sycamore; Rep; from Ill.
MEEKER WILLIAM, Farmer, Sec. 9; P.O. Sycamore; val. $15,000; Bapt; Rep; from N.Y.
MILNAMOW BERNARD, Merchant, Cortland; 160 acres in Pierce Tp; Cath; Dem; Ireland.
MITTERMICK HENRY, lives on Thos. Butler's farm, Sec. 36; P.O. Lodi; from Germany.
MILLER CLARENCE, son of W. F. Miller, Sec. 27; P.O. Cortland; Rep.
MILLER CYRUS, lives with P. H. Lawyer, Sec. 17; P.O. Cortland; Dem; from N.Y.
MILLER W. F. Farmer, Sec. 28; P.O. Cortland; 225 acres, val. $9,000; Bapt; Rep.
MILLER HORACE, Lives on Joseph Adams' lot, Cortland; Rep.
MORDOFF GEORGE, Lives on farm of M. Mordoff, Sec. 22; P.O. Cortland; Rep; from Ill.
MOORE PETER, Merchant, Cortland; Dem; from N.Y.
MURPHY JAMES, Clerk for P. J. Daly, Cortland; Dem; from Ireland.
MURDOFF MYRON, Farmer, Sec. 22; P.O. Cortland; 102 acres; Rep; Meth; from N.Y.
MYRES J. W. Horse Trader, Cortland; Rep; from Canada.

NEWMAN THOS. H. G. Farmer, Sec. 32; P.O. Cortland; 60 acres; Dem; from England.
  NORRIS GEORGE, Gardener, Sec. 5; P.O. Sycamore.
NORTRIP GEORGE, Laborer, Sec. 36; P.O. Lodi; Rep; Meth.

OLESON ANDREW, works for G. W. Savery, Sec. 29; P.O. Cortland; Rep; from Sweden.
  O'MAILEN PATRICK, Farmer, Sec. 13; P.O. Lodi; Dem; from Ireland.

PARKHURST B. B. Music Dealer, Cortland; Rep; from Penn.
  PALMER AZARIAH, Carpenter, Cortland; Rep; from N.Y.
PALMER J. L. Retired; Cortland; Rep; from N.Y.
PALMER AZARIAH, Carpenter, Cortland; Rep; from N.Y.
PALMER HIRAM, Farmer, Sec. 35; P.O. Lodi; 95 acres, val. $6,000; Rep; from Vt.
PALMER SHELDON C. Sec. 26; P.O. Lodi; 90 acres, val. $4,500; Rep; from N.Y.
PARKER SILAS S. Farmer, Sec. 8; P.O. Sycamore; 45 acres; Freewill Bapt; Rep; N.Y.
PALMER SIDNEY, Farmer, Sec. 35; P.O. Lodi; 80 acres; Rep; from N.Y.
PARKE NELSON R. Mason; P.O. Cortland; 115 acres, val. $6,900; Rep; from N.Y.
PAGE AUSTIN, Farmer, Sec. 5; P.O. Sycamore; 80 ac; val. $5,600; Rep; Mass.
PETERSON AUGUSTUS, works for Henry Pooler, Sec. 19; P.O. Cortland; Rep; Sweden.
PETERSON JOHN, works Henry Pooler, Sec. 19, P.O. Cortland; Rep; Sweden.
PETERSON ALFRED, works for Henry Pooler, Sec. 19; P.O. Cortland; Rep; Sweden.
PECK W. H. Mason, Cortland; Dem; from Conn.
PECK TIMOTHY, Fruit Dealer, Cortland; Dem; from Conn.
PECK T. S. employee Marsh Harvester Works, Sycamore.
PECK D. L. Lawyer, Sycamore; Dem; from Miss.
PELTON LYSANDER, Farm Laborer; P.O. Cortland; Rep.
PELTON LEANDER, works for R. P. Balis, Sec. 20; P.O. Cortland.
PHILPOT THOS. Farmer, Sec. 35; P.O. Lodi; 80 acres, $4,000; Rep; Meth; Ireland.
PIERCE DANIEL, Banker, Sycamore, lives on Sec. 6; P.O. Sycamore.
PIERCE J. Stock Buyer, Cortland; Ind; from N.Y.
PLESTER RICHARD, Farm Laborer.
PORTER COOLIDGE, Farmer, Sec. 9, P.O. Sycamore; 400 acres, $16,000; Univ; Rep; N.Y.
POSTLE DAVID, son of James Postle, Sec. 29; P.O. Cortland; Dem; from Ohio.
POSTLE SHEDRICK, son of James Postle, Sec. 29; P.O. Cortland; Dem; from Ohio.
POSTLE WEBB, son of James Postle, Sec. 29; P.O. Cortland; Dem; from Ohio.
POSTLE WILLIAM Jr. son William Postle, Sec. 22; P.O. Lodi; Dem; from Ohio.

POSTLE WILLIAM, Farmer, Sec. 25; P.O. Lodi; born in Madison Co. Ohio, Oct. 24, 1819; lived there twenty-two years; came to DeKalb Co. in 1842, and has lived here thirty-three years; Dem; Meth; owns 287 acres of land, value $15,000; personal prop. $1,500; is justice of the peace; married Miss Elizabeth R. Blackman, of N.Y; has seven children.

POOLER HENRY, Farmer, Sec. 19; P.O. Cortland; 325 ac. val. $17,875; Rep; N.Y.

POWERS NED, Farmer, Sec. 31; 160 acres, value $6,400; Dem; from Ireland.

POSTLE JAMES, Farmer, Sec. 26; 100 acres, value $5,000; P.O. Cortland; Dem; from Ohio.

R AYMOND WILLIAM, Retired Farmer, Cortland; Rep; from N.Y.
RATHBUN MILLARD, son of E. J. Rathbun, Sec. 32; P.O. Cortland; Rep; from Ill.

RATHBUN D. W. son of E. J. Rathbun, Sec. 32; Rep.

RATHBUN E. J. Farmer, Sec. 32; 80 acres, val. $3,600; Rep; from N.Y.

RAPLEE MILES W. lives with Jesse Raplee, Sec. 16; P.O. Cortland; Dem; from N.Y.

REMINGTON AMOS, Mason; Rep; from N.Y.

REED A. M. Farm Laborer.

REED COLUMBUS, Lumber and Coal, Cortland; Rep; from Conn.

REED ROBERT, Farmer, Sec. 29; P.O. Cortland; born in British North America, April 6, 1844; lived there ten years, went to Boston, Mass. in 1854, and lived there about twelve years; sailed on a merchant vessel for five years; came to this county in 1867, and has lived here nine years; Rep; Bapt; owns 73 acres land, value $3,600; personal prop. $500; married Amy E. Peck, from British North America in 1870; has one son.

RICKER T. R. Shoemaker, Cortland; Rep; from New Hampshire.

RIDDELL FRANCIS, Farmer, lives in Cortland; Rep; from Canada.

ROBERTS LAVANDA, Farmer, Sec. 21; P.O. Cortland; was born in DeKalb Co. Ill. Aug. 6, 1851; lived in Sycamore twelve years, then went to McHenry Co., lived there three years, then returned to this county, and has lived here since; Rep; Freewill Bapt; owns 105 acres of land, value $4,160; personal $1,000; married Miss Emma Hodge, of this county, in November, 1874.

ROSE A. B. Farm laborer; P.O. Cortland; Rep; from New York.

ROSE GEORGE W. Farm laborer; P.O. Cortland; Rep; from New York.

ROSE H. N. Carpenter and Mason; P.O. Cortland; Dem; from Conn.

ROSE C. D. Telegraph Operator, Cortland; Rep; from Ill.

ROSE ORVILLA, Laborer, Cortland; Rep.

ROGERS DAVIS, Farmer, Sec. 15; P.O. Sycamore; 90 acres, $7,000; Bapt; Rep; from N.Y.

ROGERS AMOS, Farmer, Sec. 15; P.O. Sycamore; 71 acres, $3,550; Bapt; Rep; from N.Y.

RAPLEE JESSE, Farmer, Sec. 18; P.O. Cortland; 107 acres, $6,420; Dem; Bapt; from N.Y.

RUSSELL JOHN S. Farmer, Sec. 35; P.O. Lodi; 160 acres, $8,000; Pres; Rep; Ireland.

RUSSELL J. HARVEY, son of John S. Russell, Sec. 35; P.O. Lodi; Meth; Rep; from Ill.

RUSSELL W. J. Farmer, Sec. 34; P.O. Lodi; born June 26, 1843, in Erie Co. Pa; lived there one year, came to Kane Co. Ill. in 1844, and lived there ten years, came to this county in 1854 and has lived here twenty-two years; Rep; Bapt; was in the army in the 88th (2nd Board of Trade) I. V. I; was in fifteen engagements, and was honorably discharged from the service; was one of three men who did not leave his company during the war; married Sarah J. Hopkins, of DeKalb Co. July 4, 1869; has one child.

S EAMAN J. P. Farmer, Sec. 15; P.O. Sycamore; 120 acres, value $6,600; Rep; from N. Y.
SACKETT D. B. Retired Farmer; P.O. Cortland; Dem; from New York.

SAWYER SAMUEL W. lives in the Village of Cortland; P.O. Cortland; born March 29, 1827, near Zanesville, Ohio; went to Delaware Co. N. Y. in 1830, and lived there eleven years, lived in Steuben and Tioga Counties, New York, and also in Tioga, Penn., has lived in this state eleven years; Rep; Meth; married Louise Carey, Chenango Co. N. Y. in 1857; has two children, one son and one daughter.

SAVERY G. W. Farmer and Gardener; P.O. Cortland; born in Oxford, Grafton Co. New Hampshire, Aug. 20, 1818; lived there twenty-four years, came to Chicago in 1844, lived there thirteen years, and manufactured shingles, came to Cortland, this county, in 1857, and has lived here nineteen years; was in the Mexican war, in the battles of Contraris and Churubusco, was wounded in last-named place, he now draws pension; has been town collector; owns 20 acres of land, value $2,000; Rep; Universalist; married Miss J. C. Wood, in 1856; she was born in Chicago; has three children.

SAWYER CHARLES, Farm Laborer; P.O. Cortland.

SAWYER DAVID S. Farmer, Sec. 8; P.O. Sycamore; 129 acres, $12,000; Meth; Dem; N.Y.

SAWYER E. H. Farmer, Sec. 17; P.O. Sycamore; 25 acres, $1,850; Meth; Rep; from Conn.

SELL ANDREW, Butcher, Sycamore; Dem; from Germany.

SEELEY HARRISON, Laborer, Sec. 15; P.O. Sycamore; Rep; from Illinois.

SEXTON C. A. Farm Laborer; P.O. Cortland.

SCOTT CHRISTOPHER, Farmer, Sec. 2; P.O. Sycamore; born in Franklin Co. Mass. June 5, 1801; lived there eleven years, then went to Chautaqua Co. N. Y., lived there thirty-one years, then came to DuPage Co. Ill. and lived there twenty-five years, came to this town and county in 1868, and has lived here eight years; is seventy-five years old; Rep; Christian Church; owns 143 acres of land, valued at $8,580; personal property $3,000; has been School Director and held other offices; married Marinda Metcalf, of Vermont, in 1826; she died in 1866; has five children.

SHAW HARVEY, Farmer, Sec. 20; P.O. Cortland; 4 acres, value $2,000; from New York.

SHELDON N. B. Merchant, Cortland; Rep; from New York.

SHERMAN SOLOMON, Farmer, Sec. 26; P.O. Cortland; 95 acres; Freewill Bapt; Rep; N.Y.

SHAW JOSEPH, Carpenter, Sec. 5; P.O. Sycamore.

SIMONS JOHN, Farmer, Sec. 14; P.O. Cortland; Rep; from Ill.

SMITH J. P. Farmer, Sec. 36; P.O. Lodi; 220 acres, $10,000; Bapt; Rep; from N.Y.

SMITH WILLIAM H. Tenant Farmer, Sec. 2; P.O. Sycamore; Rep; from Wis.

SMITH EBEN O. Farmer, Sec. 3; P.O. Sycamore; born Sept. 9, 1852, in Town of Cort-land, DeKalb Co; lived here two years, then went to Grundy Co. Iowa, lived there thirteen years, then came to this county in 1867, and has lived here nine years; Rep; Bapt; he farms G. G. Spring's farm, 110 acres; value personal property $500; has been assistant sheriff at the county fair; his mother, sister, and three brothers live with him.

SMITH LUCY Mrs. Sec. 20; P.O. Cortland; 80 acres, value $4,500; from New York.

SMITH C. O. Baggage Master, Depot; Cortland; Rep; from New York.

SMITH WILLIAM G. lives on Alvi Joslyn's farm; P.O. Cortland; Ind; from New York.

SMITH CHRISTIAN, Farmer, Sec. 21; P.O. Cortland; born in Darmstadt, Germany, in March, 1850; came to the United States in June, 1868; Dem; Luth; owns 76 acres of land, value $3,000; personal $400; married Miss Caroline Kugler, Jan. 1872, who was born in Oswego; has two children.

SNOW CHARLES, Blacksmith, Cortland; Rep; from New York.

SNOW GEORGE, Invalid; Cortland; from Prince Edward's Island.

SNOW FRED J. Farmer, Sec. 22; P.O. Cortland; born in Wayne Co. N. Y. and came to this state and county in 1841, and has lived here thirty-five years; was among the earliest settlers here; Rep; Lib; owns 117 acres of land, value $6,000; married Mary M. Dixon; she was born in Ohio; has four children.

SNOW WILLIAM, Farmer, Sec. 22; P.O. Cortland; Rep; 160 acres, value $6,700; from N. Y.

SWANBURG PETER, Farmer, Sec. 11; P.O. Sycamore; born in Sweden, Feb. 1, 1828; lived there forty-one years; came to the United States in 1869; came to Chicago the same year; was carpenter for C. & N. W. R.R.; came to this county two years ago; Rep; Luth; 80 acres of land, worth $2,000; value of personal property $800; married Engre Nelson in 1853; she was born in Sweden, in 1825; has seven children.

SNOW MARLOW, Farmer, Sec. 22; P.O. Cortland; 40 acres; $2,000; Rep; from DeKalb Co.

SNYDER JOSEPH, Farmer, Sec. 22; P.O. Cortland; Rep.

SNYDER JOSEPH H. Farmer, Sec. 22; P.O. Cortland; 131 acres; Meth; Rep; from Penn.

SPRING GEO. G. Farmer, Sec. 3; P.O. Sycamore; Rep.

SPOHN D. A. Farmer, Sec. 2; P.O. Sycamore; 90 acres, value $7,200; Rep; from New York.

SPOHN WILLIAM, son of D. A. Spohn; Sec. 2; P.O. Sycamore; Rep; from New York.

STEDMAN WILLIAM E. Painter; P.O. Cortland; born in Grand Rapids, Michigan, May 29, 1851; lived there seven years, then came to Chicago, lived there three years, then went to Paw Paw, Mich. and lived there about thirteen years, then came to DeKalb, Ill; Rep; Freewill Bapt; his father was in the army, 13th Reg. Michigan Infantry; died at Bridgeport, Ala.; his mother, who is fifty-four years of age, lives with him; she was born in New York State; owns his house and lot, valued at $500; he is a practical taxidermist and naturalist.

STRACK HENRY, Laborer, Cortland; Dem; from Germany.

STARK CHARLES, lives on A. Joslyn's farm, Sec. 32; P.O. Cortland; from N.Y.

STAFFORD ISAAC, Farmer, P.O. Cortland; 25 acres, $1,250; Bapt; Ind; from Vt.

STAFFORD GEO. E. lives on Isaac Stafford's farm, Sec. 15; P.O. Sycamore; Dem; N.Y.

SULLIVAN JOHN, Farmer. Sec. 36; P.O. Lodi; 100 acres, value $4,000; Dem; Ireland.
SWANBERG AUGUST, Farmer in Ohio Grove; P.O. Sycamore; Rep; from Sweden.
SWANBERG PETER, Tenant-Farmer, Sec. 2; P.O. Sycamore; Rep; from Sweden.

TALBOT JOSEPH, Harness Maker, Cortland; Rep; from England.
  TALBOT C. A. Harness Maker, Cortland; Rep; from England.
TAYLOR LEMUEL, Farm Laborer.
TOWNSEND HENRY A. Farmer, Sec. 18; P.O. Cortland; real est. $500; Meth; Rep; Eng.
TOWNSEND AMOS, Farmer. Sec. 19; P.O. Cortland; born Jan. 24, 1811, in Rutland
  Co. Vt; lived there forty-two years, came to the United States in 1853, came to DeKalb Co.
  same year, and has lived here twenty-three years; Rep; Wesleyan Meth; owns 230 acres of
  land, value $12,000; personal $1,000; married Miss Ann Sharp, of England, July 5, 1847;
  has six children.
TOWNSEND WILLIAM J. lives on A. Townsend's farm; Sec. 16; P.O. Cortland; England.
TOWNSEND HENRY, Farmer, Sec. 18; P.O. Cortland; 100 ac; val. $5,000; Rep; England.
TUCKER JOHN, Shoemaker, Cortland; Rep; from England.
TUPPER OLIVER, Farmer, Sec. 28; P.O. Cortland; 200 acres; Meth; Rep; from Canada.
TYLER A. W. son of Freeman Tyler, Sec. 3; P.O. Sycamore.
TYLER FRANK, son of Freeman Tyler, Sec. 3; P.O. Sycamore.
TYLER DeWITT, son of Freeman Tyler, Sec. 3; P.O. Sycamore.
TYLER ROUELLE, son of Freeman Tyler, Sec. 3; P.O. Sycamore.
TYLER FREEMAN, Farmer, Sec. 3; P.O. Sycamore; born in St. Lawrence Co. N.Y.
  March 13, 1819; lived there thirteen years; moved to Ashtabula Co. Ohio, in 1833, lived there
  seven years; came to Winnebago Co. this state, in 1843; lived in Beloit nine years; lived in
  Og'e Co. Ill. five years, then came to DeKalb Co. and has lived here seven years; Ind; Lib-
  eral; owns 210 acres land, value $13,650; personal prop. $1,000; married Miss Harriet N.
  Sexton in Ohio in 1843; she was born in N.Y. State; has six children.

UPDIKE WILLIAM C. lives on the Crawford farm, Sec. 34; P.O. Cortland; Rep; Iowa.

VAN AMBURG MATTHEW, lives in Ohio Grove; P.O. Sycamore.
  VAN AMBURG JOSEPH, lives in Ohio Grove; P.O. Sycamore.
VAN AMBURG MARCENUS, lives in Ohio Grove; P.O. Sycamore.
VINER V. Farmer, Sec. 26; P.O. Cortland; 86 acres, $4,300; Bapt; Dem; from N.Y.
VINER CHARLES, Farmer, Sec. 27; P.O. Cortland; Bapt; Dem; from Ill.

WATKINS ARTHUR S. Teamster, Cortland; Rep; from N.Y.
  WALKER WM. Farmer, Sec. 10, P.O. Sycamore; 88 ac; $4,400; Rep; from Ireland.
WARD JOHN, Farmer, Sec. 34; P.O. Cortland; 160 acres, $8,000; Rep; from Ohio.
WATSON ASA, Farm Laborer; P.O. Lodi.
WATSON JAMES, Farm Laborer; P.O. Lodi; Dem; from Ireland.
WATSON LAWRENCE, Capitalist, Sec. 36; P.O. Lodi; Dem; from Ireland.
WATERBURY JOHN, Farmer, Sec. 8; P.O. Sycamore; 160 acres; Meth; Dem; from N.Y.
WARREN LUKE A. Farmer, Sec. 18; P.O. Sycamore; born Dec. 9, 1819, in Delaware
  Co. N.Y; lived there thirteen years, went to Alleghany Co. in 1832 and lived there thirty-two
  years; came to Whiteside Co. this state, in 1864; lived in Ogle Co. five years; came to this
  Co. in 1871; Ind. Rep; Bapt; owns 23½ acres land, value $2,000; personal prop. $500; has
  taught school winters for some years; married Miss Ursula Foster, of Orleans Co. N.Y. in
  1841; has seven children.
WALKER WILLIAM, Sen. lives with Wm. Walker, Sec. 10; P.O. Sycamore; Rep; Ireland.
WALKER JOHN, lives with Wm. Walker, Sec. 10; P.O. Sycamore; Rep; from Ireland.
WALKER JAMES, lives with Wm. Walker, Sec. 10; P.O. Sycamore; Rep; from Ireland.
WADSWORTH E. D. Farmer, Sec. 27; P.O. Cortland; 100 acres, value $5,000; Rep; from N.Y.
WADSWORTH HENRY, lives with E. D. Wadsworth, Sec. 27; P.O. Cortland; Rep; N.Y.
WESTGATE JONATHAN, Peddler, Cortland; Rep; from Penn.
WHITSON J. M. Traveling Salesman for Notions and Fancy Goods, Cortland; Rep; Maryland
WHEELER A. Farmer, Sec. 16; P.O. Sycamore; Rep.
WHEELER LUTHER, Farmer. Sec. 16; P.O. Sycamore; 106 acres; Bapt; Rep; from Penn.

WHEELER LUTHER, Farmer, Sec. 17; P.O. Sycamore; Rep; from Ill.

WHEELER L. Farmer, Sec. 3; 56 acres, val. $4,200; Meth; Rep.

WHEELER LYSANDER, Farmer, Sec. 3; P.O. Sycamore; 68 acres; Rep.

WHITE COLLINS, Farmer, Sec. 33; P.O. Cortland; 80 acres; Meth; Rep; from Canada.

WHITE IRA, son of Collins White, Sec. 33; P.O. Cortland. Rep; from Ill.

WILTZE FREEDOM, lives with Richard Wiltze. Sec. 34; P.O. Cortland; Rep; from N.Y.

WILLSON T. H. Farm Laborer.

WILLMARTH E. F. lives on Sec. 15; P.O. Sycamore; Rep; from N.Y.

WILCOX JAMES O. Farmer, Sec. 30; P.O. Cortland; prop. $800; Rep; from N.Y.

WILLIAMS B. S. Rev. Farmer, Sec. 9; P.O. Sycamore; born in Canterbury, Windham Co. Conn. Feb. 22, 1812, lived there twenty-two years; came to Hamilton Theological Institution, N.Y. now Madison University; was ordained and entered the ministry in 1838; first pastorate was Smithville, Chenango Co. N.Y; preached in N.Y. twenty-five years; pastor of three churches during that time; came to this state and Co. in 1863; preached in DeKalb one year; married Miss E. M. Wood, of Windham Co. Conn. Oct. 18, 1838, and has two children; owns 75 acres, value $4,500; personal prop. $1,000.

WILLMARTH EMERY, Farmer, Sec. 15; P.O. Sycamore; 58 acres; Rep; from N.Y.

WILLIAMS BYRON, lives on Austin Page's farm, Sec. 5; P.O. Sycamore; Rep; from N.Y.

WILTZE RICHARD, lives on Mrs. Rhoda Wiltze's farm, Sec. 35; P.O. Cortland; 40 acres, value $1,400; Rep; from N.Y.

WILLMARTH EMMET, Farmer, Sec. 2; P.O. Sycamore; born August 1, 1847, near Willett, N.Y; lived there several years, then moved to Chenango Co. about six years; moved to Will Co. Ill. in 1856, and came to DeKalb Co. and was there three years; lived in Kendall Co. three years; was in the army; was Corporal in the 147th I.V.I.; was honorably discharged; lived in LaSalle Co. one year; came to DeKalb and has lived here since; married Miss Mary L. Scott, of Cortland, May 28, 1873; she was born in Bloomingdale, DuPage Co.; has one child; Rep; Bapt.

WOODLEY J. T. Carpenter, Cortland; Rep; from England.

WOODLEY T. T. Shoemaker, Cortland; Rep; from England.

WORMSLEY JNO. W. Farm Laborer.

WOOD JOHN, Farmer, Sec. 1; P.O. Sycamore; 140 acres; Rep; from Ill.

WRIGHT C. W. lives on R. P. Balis' farm, Sec. 20; P.O. Cortland; Rep; from Ill.

WRIGHT CHARLES, son of John Wright, Sec. 31; P.O. Cortland; Rep; from Ill.

WRIGHT JOHN, Farmer, Sec. 30; P.O. Cortland; born in Lincolnshire, England, Sept. 19, 1824; came to U.S. in 1829; came to N.Y. and lived in Oneida Co. nine years; came to this State in 1838, to Charleston, now St. Charles; came with family from N.Y. State in one-horse wagon, five children, and was nine weeks on the journey; they did not sleep in a house but two nights during the entire journey; he and his brother James walked all the way; lived at Union Grove; was here when they took the first vote to establish the county seat of DeKalb Co. and has lived here thirty-eight years; one of the earliest settlers; Rep; Meth; owns 70 acres land, $5,000; personal prop. $5,000; has held office of Supervisor two years and Commissioner three years; married Jane Ingersoll in 1845; she died Jan. 25, 1868; married Ellen Clark in March, 1869; has had four children, two sons by first wife, and two by second wife.

WRIGHT JAMES C. Farmer, Sec. 30; P.O. DeKalb; born in Manchester, England, July 2, 1826; came to this country in 1828; came to Oneida Co. N.Y. and lived there eight years; came to St. Charles, this State, in 1836, and lived there four years; then came to this Co. in 1840, and has lived here thirty-six years; Rep; Meth; owns 170 acres land, value $10,000; lived in California four years; was Justice of the Peace; married Miss Elizabeth Wilbur, of Genoa, Feb. 26, 1854.

WYMAN GEO. lives in Ohio Grove; P.O. Sycamore.

YOUNG W. N. Laborer, Sec. 9; P.O. Sycamore; Rep.

YOUNG PETER, Farmer, Sec. 23; P.O. Lodi; born in Perthshire, ten miles northwest of Perth, Scotland, on old Hansel, Monday, Jan. 12, 1812; lived there twenty years; came to U. S. in 1832; lived in town of Salem, N.Y. six years; came to DeKalb Co. in 1836, and has lived here forty years; Dem; Pres; owns 700 acres land, value $35,000; married Barbara Robertson in 1862; she was born in Scotland; has five children, three boys and two girls.

PAW PAW TOWNSHIP.

ADAMS R. A. Farmer, Sec. 8, P.O. East Paw Paw; val. $4,500; Dem; Prot; from Shabbona.

ANDERSON A. Laborer on P. B. Oleson's farm, Sec. 24; P.O. Leland; Luth; Norway.

ADAMS J. L. Farmer and Stock Raiser, Sec. 7, T. 37, R. 3 E.; P.O. East Paw Paw; born Boston, Mass. June 15, 1814; came to State and Co. Sept. 1849; Dem; Univ; owns 120 acres land, val. real estate $6,000, val. per. prop. $2,000; was Road Commissioner six years, School Trustee three years; first wife was Martha J. Barnes, from Oneida Co. N.Y. Sept. 23, 1817; second wife was Mrs. Harriet Firkins (wid. of Ashel), born Monroe Co. Mich. Jan. 25, 1823; married to first wife March, 1839; to second wife March 3, 1864; has had nine children by first wife, eight living and one dead; one child by second.

ALEXANDER H. T. Farmer and Stock Raiser, Sec. 33, T. 37, R. 3 E.; P.O. Earl; born Louistown, Mifflin Co. Penn. Sept. 4, 1824; came to Co. May 1, 1850; Dem; Pres; owns 330 acres land, val. real estate $16,500, val. per. prop. $4,000; wife was Martha J. Sharp, born Westmoreland Co. Penn. Dec. 14, 1826; married May 14, 1851; has seven children, all living, four girls and three boys.

ANDERSON JNO. Laborer on P. Peterson's farm, Sec. 25; Luth; from Norway.

ARMSTRONG JAS. W. Laborer, Sec. 17; P.O. East Paw Paw; Rep; Meth; from N.Y.

ATHERTON JAS. Farmer, Sec. 20; P.O. East Paw Paw; val. $2,000 Rep; Prot.

ATHERTON JNO. B. lives with father, Sec. 19; P.O. LaClair; Rep; Prot.

ATHERTON R. Farmer, Sec. 19; P.O. LaClair; $10,000; Rep; Prot; from Mass.

ATHERTON WM. Farmer, Sec. 19; P.O. LaClair; Rep; Prot; from Penn.

AVERY CHAS. Rents of C. Pierce, Sec. 18; Dem; Prot; N.Y.

AVERY ISAAC H. Farmer and Stock Raiser, Sec. 29, T. 37, R. 3 E.; P.O. Earl; born in Westerlow, Albany Co. N.Y. March 3, 1807; came to Co. June 11, 1850; Rep; Meth; owns 165 acres land, val. real estate $9,900, val. per. prop. $3,500; was School Director three years; Path-master eight years; wife was Elizabeth L. Osterander, born Clarkson, Monroe Co. N.Y. Jan. 27, 1810; married June 15, 1833; has had nine children, five living and four dead, two girls and seven boys.

AVERY ISAAC R. lives with father, Sec. 29; P.O. Earl; val. prop. $500; Rep; Prot.

BAHNEY L. Laborer, works J. Teyrening's farm, Sec. 13; P.O. Victor Centre; Prot; Rep.

BAKER ANDREW, Laborer, works H. M. Boardman's farm, Sec. 4; P.O. Cornton; Cong.

BAKER EDWARD, lives with father on Sec. 9; P.O. Shabbona Grove; Rep; Prot; N. Y.

BARTLETT A. F. lives with father on Sec. 8; P.O. E. Paw Paw; Rep; Meth.

BARTLETT ELI O. Farmer and Stock Raiser, Sec. 16, Tp. 37, R. 3 E.; P.O. East Paw Paw; born Thompson, Geauga County, Ohio, March 17th, 1830; came to this state and county April, 1844; Rep; Cong; owns 277½ acres of land; value of real estate, $13,850; value of personal property, $4,000; first wife was Lydia L. Bartlett, born Thompson, Geauga County, Ohio, July 18, 1830; died Oct. 21, 1860, aged 31 years; second wife was Harriet A. Wales, born in Blenhen, Schoharie County, New York, Sept. 29, 1836; married to first wife, June 21, 1849; to second wife April 10, 1861; has had six children—two dead and four living—two by first, and four by second wife.

BARTLETT MOSES, Farmer and Stock Raiser, Sec. 9, Tp. 37, R. 3 E.; P.O. East Paw Paw; born Clarendon, Geauga County, Ohio, Oct. 11, 1824; came to this state, Dec. 8, 1840; came to this county April, 1844; Rep; Pres; owns 247 acres of land; value of real estate, $14,820; value of personal property, $5,000; was School Director three years; Overseer of Highways five years; Deacon in Presbyterian Church twenty years; first wife was Martha R. Harper, born in Argyle, Washington Co. N. Y., March 19, 1823; died Oct. 2, 1872, age 52 years, 6 months, and 13 days; second wife was Mary Christy (wid. of John), born Greenwich, Washington Co. N. Y., Feb. 7, 1826; married to first wife June 10, 1848; to second wife Oct. 2, 1873; has one son by first wife.

BARTLETT M. A. Farmer and Stock Raiser, Sec. 8, Tp. 37, R. 3 E; P.O. East Paw Paw; born Thompson, Geauga Co. Ohio. Dec. 25, 1816; came to this state Dec. 8, 1840; came to this county April, 1844; Rep; Meth; owns 170 acres of land; value of real estate, $9,350; value of personal prop. $5,000; was School Commissioner one year, 1845; Highway Commissioner two years; Overseer of Highways eight years; School Director ten years; wife was Mary Ann Fowler, born in Westfield, Mass., Oct. 10, 1811; married January 1, 1839; has had five children, four living and one dead—four girls and one boy.

BAKER OLE C. Farmer and Stock Raiser, Sec. 26, Tp. 37, R. 3 E.; P.O. Leland; born in east part of Norway, April 14, 1847; came to U. S. July, 1850; came to this county March 1, 1869; Dem; Prot; owns 160 acres of land; value of real estate, $8,000; value of personal prop. $1,500; wife was Julia Knudson, from Mission Township, LaSalle Co. Ill., April 14, 1844; married May 15, 1867; has four children—three boys and one girl.

BEALE W. L. Laborer, works Wm. R. Mann's farm, Sec. 32; P.O. Earl; Dem; from Pa.

BECKMANN WM. Farmer, Sec. 33; P.O. Earl; Luth; prop. $5,000; from Germany.

BENSON S. Farmer, Sec. 26; P.O. Leland; Meth; prop. $20,000; from Norway.

BERG FRED, Farmer, Sec. 28; P.O. E. Paw Paw; rents farm of H. E. Powers; Luth.

BERGISON H. Laborer on S. Benson's farm, Sec. 26; Leland; Luth; from Norway.

BLAIR JNO. Farmer, Sec. 23; P O. Leland; Epis; val. of prop. $800; from Ireland.

BOARDMAN H. M. Farmer, Sec. 4; P.O. Cornton; Rep; Cong; from Vermont.

BOSTON ROBERT, Farmer and Stock Raiser, Sec. 10, Tp. 37, R. 3 E; P.O. Ross Grove; born Lobo Township, Upper Canada, Feb. 13, 1840; came to this state and county April, 1844; Rep; Prot; owns 219½ acres of land; value of real estate, $17,000; value of personal property, $2,000; was School Director eight years; Township Collector one year; was fourth Sergeant of 4th Illinois Cavalry, Company I; wife was Lucy S. Place, born in Shazy, Clinton Co., N. Y., Oct. 18, 1847; married Oct. 17, 1867; has two children—one boy and one girl.

BREESE VINCENT E. Laborer on Rob't. Hampton's farm, Sec. 7; P.O. E. Paw Paw; Rep.

BREESE VINCENT, Farmer and Stock Raiser, Sec. 7; P.O. East Paw Paw; born in Amboy, N. J., Jan. 14, 1814; came to this state and county June 2, 1841; Dem; Prot; owns 110 acres of land; value of real estate, $6,050; value of personal property, $1,200; first wife was Sarah L. Hyatt, born in N. Y. State; second wife was Mrs. Caroline Santee (wid. of Samuel), born Bergen Co., N. J., Nov. 4, 1832; married to first wife June 28, 1853; to second wife Nov. 28, 1868, has had four children by first wife—one dead and three living—and one child by second.

BURCH A. P. Broommaker, Sec. 19; P.O. LaClair; Rep; Prot; from Ohio.

BURCH A. W. Broommaker, Sec. 19; P.O LaClair; Rep; Bapt; from Ohio.

BURCH HENRY, Farmer, Sec. 19; P.O. LaClair; Rep; Prot; prop. $500; from Mich.

BUTTERFIELD SOLOMON, Farmer, Sec. 20; P. O. Earl; Ind; Prot; from N. Y.

BUTTERFIELD W. H. Farmer and Breeder of Holstein Cattle, and Proprietor of Paw Paw Cheese Factory and Creamery, Sec. 19; P.O. LaClair; born in Winnebago Co., Ill., July 22, 1839; came to this county in 1843; Rep; Atheist; owns 175 acres of land; val. of real estate, $8,750; val. of personal prop. $3,500; wife was Frances E. Shoudy, born Rock Island, Rock Island Co., Ill., January 11, 1843; married April 25, 1861; has had four children—two dead and two living.

CAIN RUFUS, Farmer, Sec. 31; P.O. Earl; property $9,000; Rep; Bapt; from Mass.

CAIN ZIPPORAH Mrs. widow Wm., lives with son on Sec. 31; P.O. Earl; Mass.

CARD S. L. Farmer; rents of Jas. Wolcott, Sec. 32; P.O. Earl; Rep; Bapt; from Mass.

CARTER H. A. Farmer, rents of S. Hyde, Sec 6; P.O. E. Paw Paw; Rep; Meth; Illinois.

CHAPMAN WM. J. Farmer and Stock Raiser, Sec 9. Tp. 37, R. 3 E; P.O. E. Paw Paw born in Paw Paw Township, DeKalb Co. Ill., Dec. 17, 1854; Rep; Prot; owns 80 acres of land; value of real estate $4,000; value of personal property $1,000; wife was Alpha Firkins, born in Paw Paw Township, DeKalb Co. Ill. Feb. 20, 1856; married Dec. 25, 1873; has one child, girl, aged eight months.

CHESLEY MARY A. Mrs. widow of Lorenzo D; lives on Sec. 29; P.O. Earl; Prot; Illinois.

CLAPSADDLE A. Farmer, Sec. 24; P.O. Leland; Prot; property $16,000; from N. Y.

CLAPSADDLE FRED. Farmer, Sec. 24; P.O. Leland; Prot; property $9,500; from N. Y.

CLAPSADDLE G. H. Farmer, Sec. 24; P.O. Leland; Prot; Dem; property $9,500; from N. Y.

CLARK F. E. Farmer, rents of C. B. Clark, Sec. 31. P.O. Earlville; property $500; Mass.

CONNELL. D. C. Farmer, Sec. 12; P.O. Leland, LaSalle Co; Dem; property $20,500; Ca.

CONNELL LOUIS, lives with father, Sec. 12; P.O. Leland, LaSalle Co; Prot; prop. $3,000; Ill.

CONNELL WM. lives with father, Sec. 12; P.O. Leland, LaSalle Co; Prot; prop. $3,000; Ill.

COOK M. L. Mason, E. Paw Paw; Meth; property $1,000; Vermont.

COOPER ELIZABETH H. Mrs. widow of Geo. C; Sec. 23; P.O. Leland,; from N. Y.

COOPER JNO. laborer on A. W. Lake's farm, Sec. 25; P.O. Leland; Rep; Prot; from N. Y.

COOPER MARGARET E. Mrs. widow of Jas., lives on Sec. 23; P.O. Leland; Prot; Wis.

15

COOPER TRACY, Farmer, rents of Mrs. Mulford, Sec. 12; P.O. Ross Grove; Rep; Prot; Mich.

COREY DAVID, lives with father, Sec. 10; P.O. Shabbona Grove; Rep; Prot; from Tp.

COREY JESSE, Farmer and Stock Raiser, Sec. 10, Tp. 37, R. 3 E; P.O. Cornton; born in Wantage, Sussex County, N. J., Sept. 6, 1818; came to this state and county Oct. 1, 1845; Rep; Cong; owns 120 acres of land; value of real estate $7,200; value of personal property $2,000; was Town Clerk twenty years, Justice of the Peace four years, Township School Treasurer twenty years, Deacon in Congregational Church ten years; wife was Catharine Nicholson, born in Fishkill, Dutchess Co. N. Y. Sep. 23, 1816; married Aug. 27, 1840; has had eight children, four living and four dead.

CUMMINGS SILAS, laborer on J. P. Hampton's farm, Sec. 6; P.O. E. Paw Paw; Dem; Mass.

CUMMIN WM. Farmer, Sec. 28; P.O. Earlville; 160 acres; Rep; Meth; from N. Y.

DAVIS D. C. Mrs. lives on Sec. 10; P.O. Ross Grove.

DAVIS G. N. Farmer, Sec. 12; P.O. Ross Grove; Prot; property $8,000; from Co.

DAVIS LEVI H. Farmer and Stock Raiser, Sec. 30, Tp. 37, R. 3 E; P.O. Earlville; born in Providence, Saratoga Co. N. Y., Aug. 2, 1837; came to county in December, 1846; Rep; Second Adventist; owns 80 acres of land, val. of real estate $4,400; val. of personal property $1,500; has been a Preacher of the Gospel twelve years; wife was Mary J. Sawyer, born in Glenville, Schenectady Co. N. Y., Sep. 20; 1824; married Oct. 7, 1869; has one child—boy, born Jan. 16, 1872.

DAVIS R. C. Farmer, Sec. 30; P.O. Earlville; Second Adventist; property $2,500; from N. Y.

DEMING ASA, Postmaster, Ross Grove; and farm, Sec. 11; Dem; Prot; from N. Y.

DEMING CLARK E. lives with father, Sec. 11; P.O. Ross Grove; Dem; Prot; N. Y.

DEMING C. J. Farmer, rents of J. W. Stevens, Sec. 4; P.O. Ross Grove; Dem; Prot; N. Y.

DEMING E. Farmer, Sec. 13; P.O. Ross Grove; Prot; from county.

DEMING O. R. Farmer, rents of J. W. Stephens, Sec. 4; P.O. Ross Grove; Dem; Prot; N. Y.

DENERARY MARY Mrs. widow of Jno; lives on Sec. 11; P.O. Ross Grove; Cath; Ireland.

DENNERY MICHAEL, laborer, Sec. 1; P.O. Ross Grove; Rep; Prot; Illinois.

DeWOLF WALTER W. Farmer, Sec. 30; P.O. Earlville; Rep; Prot; from Co.

DICKINSON H. S. Wheelwright, E. Paw Paw; Rep; Prot; N.Y.

DIETZ PHILLIP, Laborer, E. Paw Paw; Luth; Germany.

DOLE ALONZO, Farmer and Stock Raiser, Sec. 31, Tp. 37, R. 3 E.; P.O. Earlville; born in Greenfield, Franklin Co. Mass. Oct. 25, 1805; came to state and county June 17, 1848; Rep; Meth; owns 165 acres land, value $8,250; personal prop. $2,000; was School Director six years; Township Trustee six years; Supervisor three years; also Contractor on the Chenango Canal, N.Y. two years, 1835; also Contractor on the North Branch Canal four years, 1839 and Contractor on the Croton Water Works two years, 1837-38; also Assessor, School Director, and Auditor of Asylum, Bradford Co. Penn.; wife was Jane Griffin, born in Athens, Bradford Co. Penn. Dec. 1, 1819; married Jan. 17, 1839; has had six children, five living and one dead, two girls and four boys; eldest son, Jno. D. Dole, was killed in the battle of Stone River, Dec. 31, 1862; was private in Co. D, 34th Ill. Infantry.

DOLE T. A. lives with father on Sec. 31; P.O. Earlville; Cong; Penn.

DONAHY JNO. Laborer on Jno. Sterns' farm, Sec. 1; P.O. Ross Grove; Ireland.

DUGAN B. Farmer, rents of Mrs. Julia Heaton, Sec. 1; P.O. Shabbona Grove; Cath; Ireland.

DUNN J. Laborer on R. Cain's farm, Sec. 31; Epis; England.

DUNTON S. Farmer, Sec. 7; P.O. E. Paw Paw; Rep; Prot; N.Y.

EATON CLARK, lives with father on Sec. 20; P.O. LaClair; Rep; Prot; Ohio.

EATON GEO. lives with father on Sec. 20; P.O. LaClair; Rep; Prot; Mich.

EATON DYER, Farmer, Sec. 20, Tp. 37, R. 3 E.; P.O. LaClair; born in Derighter, Chenango Co. N.Y. June 29, 1802; came to state and county Dec. 30, 1851; Rep; Bapt; owns 80 acres land, value $4,000; personal prop. $1,000; wife was Emeline Clark, born in Wooster, Ohio, Sept. 18, 1812; died Jan. 21, 1875, aged 63 years and three months; married April 4, 1832; has had twelve children, nine living and three dead; seven boys and five girls.

EDWARDS O. D. Farmer, Sec. 17; P.O. E. Paw Paw; Rep; Pres; from N.Y.

ELLING E. Sen. Laborer on E. O. Bartlett's farm, Sec. 16; P.O. E. Paw Paw; Luth; Norway.

ELLING E. Jr. lives with father on Sec. 16; P.O. E. Paw Paw; Norway.

FAUST CATHARINE Mrs. widow of Jacob; E. Paw Paw; Meth; from N.Y.

FIRKINS L. Farmer, Sec. 5; P.O. E. Paw Paw; Dem; Meth; N.Y.

FIRKINS JUDSON W. Farmer and Stock Raiser, Sec. 9, Tp. 37, R. 3 E.; P.O. East Paw Paw; born in Paw Paw Township, DeKalb Co. Ill. June 6, 1852; Rep; Prot; owns 120 acres land, value $6,000; personal prop. $1,200; was Path-master three years; wife was Jerusha A. Soper, born in Upper Canada, Dec. 12, 1851; married Dec. 31, 1871; has had two children, one dead, and one living, a boy, aged four years.

FIRKINS L. A. lives with father on Sec. 5; P.O. E. Paw Paw; Meth; Illinois.

FIRKINS ROXANA P. Mrs. widow of A. T. Hyde, who was born in N.Y. State Sept. 3, 1817; married Jan. 1, 1839; died.Sept. 2, 1849; Mrs. Firkins was married to her second husband, Calvin Porter, who was from N.Y. State; married July 8, 1850; married to third husband, Chas. E. Firkins, Oct. 6, 1851; who was born in Cayuga Co. N.Y., Dec. 19, 1824; died Oct. 7, 1871; Mrs. F. was born in Thompson, Geauga Co. Ohio. April 22, 1818; lives on Sec. 9; P.O. East Paw Paw; owns 120 acres land, value $6,000; personal property $2,000; Cong.

FIRKINS WM. Farmer, Sec. 7; P.O. E. Paw Paw; Rep; Meth; from Tp.

FISH S. N. Physician and Surgeon, E. Paw Paw; Rep; Prot; Vermont.

FITZGERALD P. H. Farmer, Sec. 16; P.O. E. Paw Paw; Rep; Cath; Lower Canada.

FLETCHER S. lives with sister on Sec. 22; P.O. Earlville; Rep; N.Y.

FLEWELLIN EDWIN, Farmer and Stock Raiser, Sec. 27, Tp. 37, R. 3 E.; P.O. Earlville; born in Yorktown, Westchester Co. N.Y. April 4, 1835; came to state and county Oct. 20, 1861; Rep; Cong; owns 243 acres land, value $12,150; personal prop. $3,000; wife was Jane Creswell, born in Glasgow, Scotland, Dec. 15, 1834; married June 4, 1856; has seven children, all living, four boys and three girls; youngest child, a girl, was born June 16, 1876.

FOARD FIDELIA A. Mrs. widow of B. G. Valentine, who was born in Canaan, Columbia Co. N.Y. May 27, 1831; died Sept. 6, 1868, aged 38 years and four months; married Oct. 27, 1858; Mrs. Foard was born in Tioga Co. N.Y. June 18, 1828; married to W. J. Foard, who was born in Middlefield, Geauga Co. Ohio, Sept. 7, 1837; married August 25, 1870; had three children by first husband, two living and one dead; and one child by second husband; Mrs. Foard lives on Sec. 6, Tp. 37, R. 3 E.; P.O. East Paw Paw; owns 90½ acres land, value $3,600; personal prop. $1,200.

FOILES HENRY C. Farmer and Stock Raiser, Sec. 9, Tp. 37, R. 3 E.; P.O. Shabbona Grove; born in Northampton, N.Y. August 4, 1824; came to county March 1, 1851; Rep; Prot; owns 200 acres land, value $10,000; personal prop. $2,500; wife was Marietta Burdick, born in Caledonia Co. N.Y. May 15, 1831; died Sept. 4, 1870, aged 39 years, three months and twenty days; married August 3, 1850; has five children, four boys and one girl.

FORD W. J. Farmer; Sec. 6; P.O. East Paw Paw; Rep; Prot. val. prop. $1,000; from Mich.

FRANTZ A. J. Farmer, P.O. East Paw Paw; born Alleghany Co. Md. Jan. 23, 1847; came to state and Co. March 28, 1872; Rep; Meth; owns 160 acres land in Iowa; val. real estate $1,600; val. per prop. $1,000; was private Co. I, 3d Md. Infantry, enlisted March 22, 1864, discharged June 28, 1865; wife was Lucy Thompson, born Warren Co. Virginia Aug. 19, 1849, has one child, girl, Gracie D. Frantz, born Manlius, Bureau Co. Ill. Dec. 4, 1871; married in Leavenworth, Kansas, Jan. 30, 1869.

FRANTZ B. F. Rev. Student, East Paw Paw; Rep; Meth; from Penn.

FRANTZ JOS. Farmer, East Paw Paw; Rep; Meth; val. prop. $8,000; from Md.

FULLER HENRY, lives with father, Sec. 16; P.O. LaClair; Ind; Bapt; prop. $350; N.Y.

FULLER IRA E. Farmer, Sec. 16; P.O. LaClair; Rep; Bapt; val. prop. $5,500; from N.Y.

FULLER M. W. Blacksmith, East Paw Paw; Rep; Prot; from Ohio.

GARDNER H. S. Carpenter, Sec. 11; P.O. Ross Grove; Meth; val. prop. $400; from N.Y.

GOBLE T. Farmer, Sec. 19; P.O. LaClair; Rep; Bapt; val. prop. $4,000; Penn.

GODFREY HARRIET Mrs. widow of Caleb, lives Sec. 11; P.O. Ross Grove; Bapt. N.Y.

GOODYEAR MARY Mrs. widow of Lloyd, East Paw Paw; Meth; val. prop. $500; N.Y.

GORTON THOS. J. Farmer and Stock Raiser, Sec. 8, T. 37, R. 3 E.; P.O. East Paw Paw; born Oswego, Kendall Co. Ill. Nov. 4, 1842; came to Co. March 17, 1868; Ind; Prot; owns 125 acres land, val. real estate $6,845; val. per. prop. $1,200; wife was Ann E. Shibley, born Oneida Co. N.Y. July 3 1843; married March 2, 1865; has two children, boys.

GRIFFETH RHODY Mr. widow of Ariel E. East Paw Paw; Bapt; from N.Y.

GROVER WM. Farmer, Sec. 6; P.O. East Paw Paw; Rep; Meth; val. prop. $1,800; N.Y.

GUNDERSON A. Farmer, Sec. 5; P.O. East Paw Paw; Luth; from Norway.

GUNDERSON C. Laborer L. Firkin's farm, Sec. 5; P.O. East Paw Paw; Luth; from Norway.

GUNDERSON T. A. Farmer, Sec. 9, P.O. East Paw Paw; Luth; from Norway.

HAMPTON, J. RILEY, lives with father. Sec. 7; P.O. East Paw Paw; Rep; Meth; $4,000.

HAMPTON ROBT. F. Farmer. Sec. 7; P.O. East Paw Paw; Rep; Meth; $2,700; Co.

HAMPTON J. P. Farmer and Stock Raiser, Sec. 6, Tp. 37, R. 3 E; P.O. East Paw Paw; born Paw Paw, Tp. DeKalb Co. Ill. Feby. 28, 1848; Rep; owns 154 acres land; val. real est. $6,900; val. per. prop. $1,500; wife was Kate Nicholson, born Paw Paw Tp. DeKalb Co. Ill. Sept. 20, 1847, married Dec. 23, 1869, has one child living, boy, and one dead, boy.

HAMPTON ROBERT, Farmer and Stock Raiser, Sec. 7, Tp. 37, R. 3 E; P.O. East Paw Paw; born East Gwillimbury, Upper Canada, March 27, 1821; came to State and Co. June 1st, 1846; Rep; Meth; owns 289 acres land; val. real estate $15,900, val. per. prop. $5,000; was Road Com. three years, Tp. Trustee sixteen years, Supervisor eleven years, Assessor one year, State Representative two years, Co. Treas. two years; wife was Lydia Zemmer, born Fairfield Co. Ohio, July 16, 1818; married Jan. 1st, 1843; has had eight children, seven living and one dead; five boys and three girls.

HAIM W. H. Farmer, Sec. 32; P.O. Earlville; Rep; Cong; val. prop. $9,250; Kane Co. Ill.

HARDY WM. Laborer Robt. Harper's farm; Sec. 14; P.O. Ross Grove.

HARPER A. G. lives with father. Sec. 35; P.O. Leland; Rep; Prot; val. prop. $1,000; N.Y.

HARPER D. C. Carpenter, lives with father, Sec. 35; Rep; Prot; val. prop. $500; from N.Y.

HARPER JAS. Farmer, Sec. 15; P.O. Ross Grove; Rep; Pres; from N.Y.

HARPER JAMES, Farmer and Stock Raiser, Sec. 35, Tp. 37, R. 3 E; P.O. Leland corn Argyle, Washington Co. N. Y. June 19, 1820; came to Co. Dec. 3d, 1854; Rep; United Pres; owns 400 acres land; val. real estate $20,000; val. per. prop. $2,000; first wife was Elizabeth Smiley, born Lyons, Wayne Co. N. Y. Nov. 20, 1826, died Oct. 15, 1851, married Oct. 18, 1845; second wife was Elizabeth Comins, born Steuben, Oneida Co. N. Y. Nov. 15, 1833, married March 18th, 1854; has had twelve children, nine living and three dead, eight boys and four girls.

HARPER JAS. Jr. lives with father, Sec. 14; P.O. Ross Grove; Rep; Prot; from Tp.

HARPER JAS. Jr. lives with father, Sec. 35; P.O. Leland; Rep; from N.Y.

HARPER ROBERT, Farmer and Stock Raiser, Sec. 14, Tp. 37, R. 3 E.; P.O. Ross Grove; born Argyle, Washington Co. N.Y. June 11, 1813; came to state and county July 20, 1848; Rep; U. Pres; owns 245 acres land; value real estate $12,250; value personal property $3.00 ; first wife was Ann Oswald, born Hannibal, Oswego Co. N.Y. 1817; married March 20, 1840, died May 30, 1848, age 29 years; second wife was Ann Brown, born Brockville, Can., Oct. 2, 1821; married Oct. 9, 1852; has had seven children, three dead and four living; three by first wife and four by second wife.

HARPER THOS. Farmer, Sec. 14; P.O. Ross Grove; Rep; Prot; from Tp.

HARPER THOS. lives with father, Sec. 35; P.O. Leland; Rep; Prot; from N.Y.

HARPER WM. Farmer and Stock Raiser, Sec. 14, Tp. 37, R. 3 E.; P.O. Ross Grove; born Argyle, Washington Co. N.Y. June 18, 1815; came to state and county Oct. 20, 1844; Rep; U. Pres; owns 700 acres land; value real estate $35,000; value personal prop. $6,000; wife was Sarah Kirk, born Argyle, Washington Co. N.Y. Aug. 16, 1814; married April 28, 1848; has had five children, four living and one dead, four boys and one girl.

HELDEBRANT HENRY, Farmer. East Paw Paw; Pres; from N.Y.

HELDERBRANT JACOB, P.O. East Paw Paw; Prot; from N.Y.

HESLET CORA Mrs. widow of Jos. lives with father, Sec. 8; P.O. East Paw Paw; Meth; Ohio.

HILL S. G. lives with son, Sec. 3; P.O. Leland; Rep; Cong; from N.Y.

HOAG D. C. Farmer, Sec. 20; P.O. LaClair; Ind; Prot; prop. $7,000; from N.Y.

HOAG F. A. lives with father, Sec. 20; P.O. LaClair; Ind; Prot; prop. $1,000; from Co.

HOGE R. Farmer, Sec. 32; P.O. Earlville; Rep; Cong; prop. $5,000; from Iowa.

HOLMES C. S. Farmer, Sec. 2; P.O. Leland; Rep; Cong; prop. $5,000; from N.Y.

HOLMES GEO. R. Farmer, Sec. 25; P.O. Leland; Dem; Prot; prop. $1,500; from N.Y.

HOLMES JOS. L. Farmer, Sec. 26; P.O. Leland; Rep; Cong; prop. $12,200; from N.Y.

HUBBELL CHAS. Farmer, rents of J. McFarland, Sec. 23; P.O. Leland; Rep; Prot; N.Y.

HUNTER C. Laborer, Sec. 12; P.O. Ross Grove; Rep; Meth; from Mo.

HURLBUT E. S. Farmer, Sec. 15; P.O. East Paw Paw; Rep; Meth; prop. $3,500; Ohio.

HYDE J. B. Farmer and Stock Raiser, Sec. 6, Tp. 37, R. 3 E.; P.O. East Paw Paw; born Chazy, Clinton Co. N.Y. March 5, 1822; came to state and county Aug. 1848; Rep; Meth; owns 177 acres land; value real estate $10,600; value personal prop. $4,000; was Justice of the Peace five years, Commissioner of Highways four years; wife was Catherine Shaw, born in Lansing, N.Y. Feb. 14, 1833; married April 30, 1855; has three children living, two boys and one girl, and one boy dead.

HYDE EUNICE Mrs. widow of Jonathan, lives Sec. 22; P.O. Earlville; Univ; $8,500; N.Y.

HYDE SIMEON E. Farmer and Stock Raiser, Sec. 27, Tp. 37, R. 3 E.; P.O. Earlville; born Grand Isle Tp. Grand Isle Co. Vt. Sept. 24, 1821; came to county Oct. 20, 1848; Rep; Cong; owns 577 acres land; value real estate $28,850; value personal property $5,000; was Township Assessor six years, School Director twenty-four years; wife was Marion L. Thomas, born Swanton Tp. Franklin Co. Vt. July 14, 1827; married Oct. 13, 1847; has had six children, three dead and three living, four boys and two girls.

J ORSTED A. Laborer on Jno. H. Larson's farm, Sec. 9; P.O. Shabbona Grove; Luth; from Norway.

K ELLY MARTIN, Farmer, Sec. 20; P.O. LaClair; Dem; Cath; prop. $300; from Ireland.

KETCHUM E. D. Laborer, Sec. 30; Rep; Prot; from Aurora.

KETCHUM J. Farmer, Sec. 19; P.O. LaClair; Pres; prop $7,000; from N.Y.

KETCHUM J. E. Farmer, Sec. 19; P.O. LaClair; Rep; Prot; from N.Y.

KIDNEY FRANCIS, Farmer, Sec. 20; P.O. LaClair; Rep; Prop; prop; $4,000; from Ohio.

KIRK JOHN, Farmer, Sec. 14; P.O. Ross Grove; Rep; Prot; prop. $600; from N.Y.

L ARSON JNO. H. Farmer, Sec. 9, P.O. Shabbona Grove; Rep; Luth; from Ill.

LACLAIR ANN Mrs. widow of Johnson, lives in East Paw Paw; Meth; from N.Y.

LAKE A. W. Farmer, Sec. 25; P.O. Leland; Rep; Cong; prop. $10,000; from N.Y.

LAMBERT C. Farmer, Sec. 32; P.O. Earlville; Dem; Prot; prop. $1,000; from N. Y.

LAMBERT F. Laborer, Sec. 8; P.O. East Paw Paw; Rep; Meth; from N.Y.

LAPORT ALONZO, Farmer, Sec. 14; P.O. Ross Grove; Rep; Prot; from N.Y.

·LAPORT NARCIS, Sec. 14; P.O. Ross Grove; Cath; Dem; prop. $500.

LAWSON FRANCIS Rev. Minister Union Ind. Church, Sec. 21; P.O. Earlville; Rep; N.Y.

LYNCH JAS. lives with father, Sec. 35; P.O. Leland; Dem; Cath; Mass.

LYNCH THOS. Farmer and Stock Raiser, Sec. 35, Tp. 37, R. 3 E.; P.O. Leland; born Co. Longford, Ireland, Feb. 1816; came to U. S. June 15, 1843; came to county March 1, 1865; Dem; Cath; owns 160 acres land; value real estate $12,000; value personal property $3,000; wife was Margaret Feeney, born Co. Longford, Ireland, Jan. 16. 1825; married April 5, 1846; has seven children, four boys and three girls.

LYMAN CHAS. Laborer, East Paw Paw; Rep; Prot; from N.Y.

LYONS J. B. Farmer and Stock Raiser, Sec. 14, Tp. 37, R. 3 E.; P.O. Leland; born in Co. Tyrone, Ireland, Nov. 12, 1836; came to U. S. May 28, 1856; came to county June 5, 1856; Ind; Pres; owns 200 acres land; value real estate $6,300; value personal prop. $2,000; wife was Elizabeth McFadden, born Sterling, Cayuga Co. N.Y. Aug. 17, 1841; married March 2, 1866; had one child, Benjamin Lyons, born June 18, 1868, died Sept. 18, 1868, age three months.

M ANN W. R. Farmer, Sec. 32; P.O. Earlville; Rep; Cong; prop. $9,250; from N. H.

MARSHALL GEO. Laborer, Sec. 33; P.O. Earlville; Rep; Epis; from England.

MARSDEN JAMES, Farmer and Stock Raiser, Sec. 4, Tp. 37, R. 3 E.; P.O. East Paw Paw; born Lancashire, England, Dec. 22, 1830; came to state and county Dec. 11, 1856; Rep; Pres; owns 188 acres land; value real estate $9,000; value personal property $2,000; was Road Commissioner one year, Path-master eight years; wife was Mary Cunningham, born Lancashire, Eng. Jan. 3, 1830; married March 11, 1853; have no children.

MARVYNE J. C. Agent; lives with father, Sec. 26; P.O. Leland; from Penn; Rep; Prot.

McCLYMONDS CHAS. Farmer, rents of M. C. Lake, Sec. 23. P.O. Leland; Rep; Prot.

McFADDEN WM. Laborer on Robt. Harper's farm, Sec. 14; P.O. Ross Grove; Rep; U. Pres.

McFARLAND JAS. Farmer, Sec. 23; P.O. Leland; from N. Y; Rep; Pres; val. prop. $5,000.

McGIBENY D D. Prof. Rev. Agent, Paw Paw; Rep; from N. Y; Bapt; val. prop. $3,000.

McKAY THEODORE, Laborer on E. Flewellin farm, Sec. 28; P.O. Earl; farm N.Y; Prot.

McMAN JAS. Laborer on G. R. Holmes' Sec. 25; P.O. Leland; from Ireland; Dem; Cath.

MERRITT J. H. Farmer, rents of W. J. Merritt, Sec. 13; P.O. Ross Grove; Rep; Prot.

MERRITT N. Farmer, Sec. 1; P.O. Ross Grove; from N. Y; Rep; Prot.

MINARD SAMUEL, Farmer and Stock Raiser, Sec. 35, T. 37, R. 3, E; P.O. Leland; born Esopus, Ulster Co. N. Y. Sept. 15, 1828; came to County June 15, 1855; Rep; Meth; owns 360 acres land; val. real estate $18,000; val. per. prop. $1,000; wife was Juliet F. Baxter, born Meadville, Crawford Co. Penn. Feb. 13, 1844; married Oct. 27, 1867.

MILLER J. B. Farmer and Stock Raiser, Sec. 2, T. 37, R. 3, E; P.O. Shabbona Grove; born Long Island, Suffolk Co. N. Y. Jan. 1, 1833; came to State and County March 16, 1868; Rep; Prot; owns 140 acres land; val. real estate $7,000: val. per. prop. $2,000; was School Director three years; wife was Eliza J. Leek, born Long Island, Suffolk Co, N. Y. March 15, 1846; married April 11, 1864; has had four children—one dead and three living—one boy and two girls living, and one girl dead.

MOORE WM. Farmer, Sec. 36; P.O. Leland; from N. Y; Rep; Prot.

MOREY P. A. Farmer, Sec. 30; P.O. Earl; from N. Y; Prot; val. prop. $9,500.

MORRSION WM. Farmer, Sec. 11; P.O. Ross Grove; from Ireland; Dem; Cath.

MOSHER A. W. Farmer, rents of Lin H. Davis, Sec. 31; P.O. Earl; from Me; Rep; Prot.

MOSS JAS. E. Farmer, rents of Wm. Shepardson, Sec. 1; P.O. Ross Grove; from N. Y. Rep.

MURRY JOHN, Farmer, Sec. 32, T. 37,R.3, E; P.O. Earl; born Rahainy, Westmeath Co. Ireland, Dec. 25, 1814; came to U. S. March 1846; came to Ill. Aug. 1849; came to county March 1, 1874: Dem; Cath; owns 160 acres land; val. real estate $7,200; val. per. prop. $800; first wife was Mary Duncan, from Co. Tipperary, Ireland, died March 16, 1858; second wife was Margaret McCue, born Co. Longford, Ireland, died March 28, 1862; third wife was Jane Campbell, widow of Edward, born in Ireland; has had three children—two by first and one by second wife.

MURRY MICHAEL lives with father on Sec. 32; P.O. Earl; from Ill; Dem; Cath.

NESBET AGNES Mrs. widow of Matthew, lives on Sec. 22; P.O. Leland; from N. Y; Pres.

NESBIT JAS. Farmer, Sec. 28; P.O. Earl; from Tp; Rep; Cong.

NISBET WM. Farmer, Sec. 22; P.O. Leland; from Tp; Rep; Cong; val. prop. $14,000.

NICHOLSON D. Farmer, Sec. 16; P.O. Ross Grove; from N. Y; Prot.

NICHOLSON J. Farmer, Sec. 15; P.O. E. Paw Paw; from N. Y; Prot.

NICHOLSON T. Farmer, Sec. 15; P.O. E. Paw Paw; from N. Y; Ind; Prot.

OLESON C. S. Farmer, Sec. 25; P.O. Leland; from Norway; Rep; Prot; val. prop. $14,000.

OLESON H. Farmer, rents of S. Hyde, Sec. 21; P.O. Ross Grove; from Norway; Luth.

OLESON M. Farmer, rents of Mrs. Eliza H. Cooper, Sec. 23; from Norway; Luth.

OLESON P. B. Farmer, Sec. 24; P.O. Leland; from Norway; Meth; val. prop. $7,000.

OLESON S. E. Laborer on Sec. 16; P.O. E. Paw Paw; from Norway; Luth.

PAINE F. W. Farmer, Sec. 29; P.O. Earl; from Me; Rep; Bapt; val. prop. $9,000.

PETERSON LOUIS, Farmer, Sec. 25, rents N. Hill; P.O. Leland; from Norway; Luth.

PATRICK WILLIAM, Farmer and Stock Raiser, Sec. 18, Tp. 37, R. 3 E.; P.O. East Paw Paw; born in West Walton, Lincolnshire, England, Sept. 18, 1826; came to U. S. Aug. 18, 1846; came to county in November, 1868; Prot; owns 347 acres land, value $17,350; personal prop. $1,500; wife was Mary Congrave, born in Leicestershire, England, August 16, 1826; married March 4, 1849; has had nine children, seven living and two dead; three boys and six girls.

PETERSON PETER, Farmer, Sec. 25; P.O. Leland; Rep; Luth; Norway.

PLACE CLAUDIUS, Farmer, Sec. 15, Tp. 37, R. 3 E.; P.O. Ross Grove; born in Shazy, Clinton Co. N.Y. July 31. 1845; came to state and county June 1, 1849; Rep; Meth; was private in Co. H, 88th Ill. Infantry; was wounded in the should.r in the battle of Dallas, Georgia, May 27, 1864; wife was Elizabeth A. Smith, born in N.Y. State, Nov. 27, 1850; married Sept. 13, 1876,

PLUNKETT JOHN, Farmer, Sec. 2; P.O. Ross Grove; Dem; Cath; Ireland.

PLUMMER S. A. Butter Dealer, E. Paw Paw; Rep; Meth; N.Y.

POWERS E. B. Farmer and Stock Raiser, Sec. 33, Tp. 37, R. 3 E.; P.O. Earlville; born in Earlville, LaSalle Co. Ill. Sept. 16, 1842; came to county in August, 1847; Rep; Cong; owns 280 acres land, value $14,000; personal prop. $5,000; was School Trustee three years, Path-master seven years; wife was Nancy A. Weddell, born in Paw Paw Tp. DeKalb Co. Ill. March 22, 1851; married Dec. 1, 1867; has two children, both girls, one eight and the other four years of age.

PRATT DEXTER B. Farmer and Stock Raiser, Sec. 17; rents of J. W. Nicholson; P. O. East Paw Paw; born in Potsdam, St. Lawrence Co. N.Y. May 10, 1829; came to state and county in November, 1857; Rep; Prot; wife was Susan R. Nicholson, born in Enfield Tp. Tompkins Co. N.Y. May 26, 1843; married March 19, 1862.

PRICE WM. Carpenter; lives on Sec. 8, East Paw Paw; Rep; Prot; Prince Edward's Island.

PROUD A. Laborer on Wm. Nesbit's farm, Sec. 22; P.O. Earlville; Rep; Cong; N.Y.

PUTMAN W. Laborer on Mrs. M. H. Whitman's farm, Sec. 33; P.O. Earlville; Prot; Wis.

QUILHOT C. W. Farmer, Sec. 4; P.O. E. Paw Paw; Rep; Cong; N.Y.

QUINN EDWARD, Farmer, Sec. 4; P.O. Shabbona Station; Dem; Cath; Ireland.

QUILHOT M. V. Farmer and Stock Raiser, Sec. 4; P.O. Shabbona Grove; born in Kinderhook, Columbia Co. N.Y. Feb. 2, 1811; came to state and county Nov. 3, 1853; Rep; Pres; owns 104 acres land, value $6,760; personal prop. $1,000; wife was Elizabeth Tarner, born in Amsterdam, Holland, Dec. 27, 1814; married Sept. 5, 1853; has two children, one boy and one girl.

RADLEY J. Farmer, Sec. 31; P.O. Earlville; Dem; Bapt; N.Y.

RADLEY J. P. Farmer, Sec. 31; P.O. Earlville; Dem; Prot; N.Y.

RANGE WM. Farmer, rents of Eunice Hyde, Sec. 22; Rep; Prot; N.Y.

ROHRABACHER J. W. Farmer, rents of Wm. Nisbet, Sec. 22; P.O. Earlville; Rep; Prot; N.Y.

ROCKABRAND WILLIAM, Farmer, Sec. 33; P.O. Earlville; born in Keierde, Grayne, Germany, July 24, 1833; came to U.S Sept. 20, 1861; came to this county Feb. 16, 1869; Rep; Luth; owns 120 acres land, value $6,000; personal prop. $1,000; wife was Caroline Beckman, born in Essershausen, Germany, March 30, 1832; married Jan. 8, 1862; has one child, aged ten years and four months.

RYAN THOS. Laborer on M. V. Quilhot's farm, Sec. 4; P.O. Shabbona Grove; Cath.

SCOTT B. S. Lab. on Jas. Harper's farm, Sec. 15; P.O. Ross Grove; Prot; N.Y.

SCULLY O. Lab. on Jas E. Moss' farm, Sec. 1; P.O. Ross Grove; Prot; Rep, Mich.

SHIELD JAS. Laborer on Wm. Watson's farm, Sec. 26; P.O. Leland; Rep; Pres; N. Y.

SLOCUM W. Farmer, Sec. 8; P.O. E. Paw Paw; Rep; Bapt; N.Y.

SMITH ANNA Mrs. widow of George, Sec. 18, E. Paw Paw; Prot; from County.

SMITH V. lives with daughter on Sec. 18; P.O. E. Paw Paw; Rep; Prot; from N. Y.

SNYDER JNO. laborer on G. R. Holmes' farm, Sec. 25; P.O. Leland; Prot.

SPEARS HARRISON, Farmer, Sec. 10, Tp. 37, R. 3 E; P.O. Ross Grove; born in Coos Co., N. H. July 7, 1813; came to county in 1846; Rep; Seventh Adventist; owns 80 acres of land; value of real estate $4,000; value of personal property $500; wife was Mrs. Sallie Spears (widow of Benjamin), born in Seneca Co. N. Y., Sep. 25, 1806; married Nov. 1841, has had three children, one dead and two living, one boy and two girls.

SPEARS Z. lives with father on Sec. 10; P.O. Ross Grove; Rep; Prot; prop. $1,500; Kane Co.

STAHL W. F. Farmer, Sec. 4; P.O. Shabbona Grove; Rep; Bapt; from Germany.

STERN JOHN, Farmer, Sec. 1; P.O. Ross Grove; Rep; Meth; from Penn.

STEVENS JOHN, Farmer, Sec. 34. Tp. 37, R. 3 E; P.O. Earlville; born in Bainbridge, Chenango Co. N. Y., Sep. 20, 1799; came to state in May 1845; came to county June 13, 1849; Rep; Cong; owns 120 acres of land; value of real estate $6,600; value of personal property $800; was Road Commissioner four years, School Director sixteen years; wife was Mariam Benedict, born in Coventry, Chenango Co. N. Y. April 30, 1805; married Jan. 13, 1825; has had eight children, five living and three dead, three boys and five girls.

STEVENS J. W. Farmer and Stock Raiser, Sec. 4; P.O. Leland; born in Columbia, Herkirmer Co. N. Y., Dec. 18, 1836; came to state and county in Nov. 1861; Rep; Prot; owns 200 acres of land; value of real estate $12,000; value of personal property $2,000; wife was Mary L. Hill, born in Sullivan, Madison Co. N. Y., March 27, 1838; married Jan. 21, 1861; has two children, boys.

STEVENS W. R. Farmer and Stock Raiser, Sec. 34; P.O. Earlville; born in Coventry, Chenango Co. N., March 6, 1832; came to state and county June 13, 1849; Rep; Cong; 80 acres of land; value of real estate $4,400; value of personal property $800; was School Director eight years, Path-master three years; wife was Eliza E. Hyde, born Shazy, Clinton Co. N. Y. Oct. 6, 1840; married Jan. 1, 1856; has two children by adoption, one boy and one girl.

STEWERT JAS. laborer on Wm. R. Stevens' farm, Sec. 33; Rep; Cong; from N. Y.

STEWARD ROBT. laborer on Wm. Patrick's farm, Sec. 18; Meth; Illinois.

STURGEON J. D. Farmer, Sec. 30; P.O. Earlville; Rep; Prot; from Wis.

SWENSON S. laborer on S. Benson's farm, Sec. 26; P.O. Leland; Luth; from Norway.

TALBOT N. E. Farmer, rents of S. Butterfield, Sec. 20; P.O. LaClair; Rep; Prot; N. Y.

TAYLOR LUCY Mrs. widow of Thos. G; P.O. E. Paw Paw; Epis; from England.

TELEFSON P. laborer on M. Bartlett's farm, Sec. 9; P.O. E. Paw Paw; Luth; from Norway

TENNESON A. laborer on O. C. Baker's farm, Sec. 26; P.O. Leland; Prot; from Norway.

TERPENING J. Farmer and Stock Raiser, Sec. 13; P.O. Victor Centre; born in Columbia, Herkimer Co. N. Y., March 30, 1811; came to county Nov. 1, 1851; Rep; Prot; owns 320 acres of land; value of real estate $16,000; value of personal property $2,500, wife was Mary Clapsaddle, born in Frankford, Herkimer Co. N. Y., June 28, 1812; married in Dec. 1832; has two children, one son and one daughter, both living.

THOMPSON L. laborer on Wm. Moore's farm, Sec. 36; P.O. Leland; Luth; Illinois.

THOMPSON THOS. laborer, Sec. 8; P.O. E. Paw Paw; Rep; Luth; from Sweden.

THORP O. U. Farmer, rents of A. Clappsaddle, Sec. 24; P.O. Leland; Prot.

TIPPETTS STEPHEN, Farmer and Stock Raiser, Sec. 6; P.O. East Paw Paw; born in Geneva, Ontario Co. N. Y., May 1, 1817; came to state and county in May, 1852; Dem; Meth; owns 87 acres of land; value of real estate $4,350; value of personal property $1,000; wife was Mrs. Margaret Wilson, born in Trumbull Co. Ohio, July 10, 1828; married July 10, 1853; has no children.

TUNTLAND T. Farmer, Sec. 36; P.O. Leland; Luth; prop. $10,000; from Norway.

TYNE L. laborer on Jos. L. Holmes' farm, Sec. 26; P.O. Leland; Cath; Illinois.

VALENTINE D.C. Farmer, Sec. 4; P.O. E. Paw Paw; Rep; Meth; value of property $2,300; from N. Y.

VALENTINE R. M. Farmer and Stock Raiser, Sec. 5; P.O. East Paw Paw; born in Canaan, Columbia Co. N. Y., Feb. 20, 1817; came to state and county May 13, 1849; Meth; Rep; owns 168 acres of land, value of real estate $8,400; value of personal property $3,000; was Road Commissioner six years; first wife was Lydia C. Fowler, born in Courtland Co. N. Y., March 5, 1818; married Oct. 28, 1841; died Aug. 8, 1857; second wife was Margaret C. Vanriper, born in Seneca Co N. Y., Nov. 3, 1825; married Feb. 10, 1858; died Jan. 15, 1859; aged 34 years 2 months and 12 days; third wife was Mrs. Elizabeth Stewart (widow of Benjamin), born in Tompkins Co. N. Y., March 9, 1829; married April 5, 1858; has five children by first wife, and one child, dead, by second.

VANRIPER HENRY A. Postmaster and General Store, East Paw Paw; $8,000; Rep; N.Y.

VANRIPER SILAS C. Clerk, East Paw Paw; Rep; from N.Y.

WALES LORETA Mrs. wid. of Levi S., East Paw Paw; val. $1,000; Meth; from N.Y.

WALRATH M. Laborer, Sec. 6; P.O. East Paw Paw; $500; Rep; Meth; Kentucky.

WARREN B. S. J. lives with father on Sec. 19; P.O. LaClair; Prot; from N.Y.

WATERBERRY S. Laborer on S. Butterfield's farm, Sec. 20; P.O. Earl; Dem; Prot; N.Y.

WATSON WM. Farmer, Sec. 26; P.O. Leland; val. prop. $9,500; Rep; Pres; from N.Y.

WEDDELL CHAS. lives with father on Sec. 21; P.O. Earl; Rep; Prot.

WEDDELL W. B. Farmer, Sec. 21; P.O. Earl; val. prop. $30,000; Rep; Cong; from Penn.

WHITMAN J. L. Farmer, Sec. 31; P.O. Earl; val. prop. $1,000; Rep; Prot; from Ill.

WHITMAN MELISSA H. Mrs. Sec. 33; P.O. E. Paw Paw; wid. of Daniel H.,who was born Newport, R. I. Nov. 26, 1814; came to Co. Nov. 15, 1845; died Nov. 15, 1863, age 48 years, 11 months and 11 days; Mrs. Whitman was Melissa H. Hoxie, born Oswego Co. N. Y. Aug. 23, 1827; married June 2, 1844; lives on Sec. 34, T. 37, R. 3 E; P.O. Earl; owns 640 acres land in the State; val. real estate $32,000; val. per. prop. $4,000; Cong; has seven children, two girls and five boys.

WHITMAN WM. D. Farmer, lives with mother on Sec. 33; P.O. Earl; Rep; Cong; from Ill.

WHITMAN C. W. Farmer, lives with mother on Sec. 33; P.O Earl; val. $500; Rep; Prot.

WILLIAMS JNO. R. Farmer, rents of S L. Jenks, Sec. 33; P.O. Earl; $700; Rep; Prot; N.J.

WILTSIE OLIVER, Farmer and Stock Raiser, Sec. 35, T. 37, R. 3; P.O. Leland; born Hannibal, Oswego Co. N.Y. Dec. 25, 1822; came to State and Co. April 18, 1863; Rep; Meth; owns 120 acres land; val. real estate $6,000; val. per. prop. $1,000; was School Director eleven years; wife was Susan S. Comins, born Steuben, Herkimer Co. N.Y. Nov. 14, 1826; married Aug. 21, 1844; has had four children, three living and one dead, two boys and two girls.

WIRRICK GEO. Farmer, Sec. 30; P.O. LaClair; Rep; from Ohio.

WIRRICK GEO. W. lives with father on Sec. 30; P.O. LaClair; Prot.

WOODWARD A. Farmer, Sec. 19; P.O. LaClair; owns 90 acres land; Rep; Bapt; from N.Y.

WOODWARD O. B. lives with father on Sec. 19; P.O. LaClair; val. $800; Rep; Prot.

MALTA TOWNSHIP.

A DAMS THOMAS, Farmer, Sec. 28; P.O. Malta; 160 acres, value $4,800; Ind; from Canada.
 ADEE WILLIAM, Lumber and Coal Merchant, Malta; Rep; from N.Y.

ALBERDING ADAM, Farmer, Sec. 6; P.O. Malta; born in Germany in May, 1844; came to DeKalb Co. June, 1866; family of two children; wife was Miss Minnie Alberding, from Germany; farm of 120 acres, value $6,450; personal prop. $500; Rep; Meth.

ALBERLING JULIUS, Farmer, Sec. 4; P.O. Malta; 160 acres, value $8,000; Rep; Germany.

ALBERDEEN ADAM, Farmer, Sec. 6; P.O. Creston; 157 acres, value $7,850; Ind; Germany.

ANDERSON AXIEL, lives on J. A. Corey's farm, Sec. 2; P.O. Malta; Rep; from Sweden.

ANDERSON AUGUSTUS, works for J. A. Corey, Sec. 2; P.O. Malta; Rep; from Sweden.

ANDERSON JOHN, Farmer, Sec. 33; P.O. Malta; 80 acres, value $2,400; Rep; Sweden.

ASPLUND OSCAR, works for L. Farley, Sec. 12; P.O. Malta; Rep; from Sweden.

ASHCRAFT ALBERT, Farmer, Sec. 25; P.O. Malta; 80 acres, value $4,000; Rep; from N.Y.

ASKIA NILS T. Lives on Sec. 28; P.O. Malta; 80 acres, value $3,200; Rep; from Norway.

B AUM ADDISON, Son of Jacob Baum, Sec. 11; P.O. Malta; Dem; from N.Y.
 BAUM MADISON, Son of Jacob Baum, Sec. 11; P.O. Malta; Dem; from N.Y.

BAUM JACOB, Farmer, Sec. 11; P.O. Malta; born in Montgomery Co. N.Y. Nov. 30, 1817; came to DeKalb Co. in the Spring of 1865; has a family of eight children; wife was Miss Rachel Elwood, of Montgomery Co. N.Y.; farm of 160 acres, value $6,500; Dem.

BALL ALFRED, Station Agent C. & N. W. R. R.; P.O. Malta; born in the Town of Freedom, Cattaraugus Co. N. Y. July, 22, 1826; came to DeKalb Co. in the Fall of 1854, and settled in Malta; family, one child; wife was Miss Mary Walker, from Boston, Mass; value of real estate $4,000; is Supervisor, and was Postmaster twelve years; Cong; Rep.

BALL E. A. Baggage Master R.R., Malta; Rep; from Illinois.

BANDFIELD ALBERT, Sec. 33; P.O. Malta; born in Bradford Co. Penn. Sept. 4, 1844; came to DeKalb Co. Dec. 25, 1852; has family of two children; wife was Miss Ellen Veale, from England; married March 8, 1868; owns farm 120 acres; value of real estate $4,800; personal $1,000; Rep.

BANDFIELD BENJ. Retired Farmer; lives with A. Bandfield; Sec. 33; P.O. Malta; Ind; N.Y.

BAILEY SAMUEL, Farmer, Sec. 10; P.O. Malta; 140 acres, value $7,000; Rep; from N. Y.

BAILEY S. S. Farmer, Sec. 10; P.O. Malta; 100 acres, value $5,000; Rep; from New York.

BARNES PHINEAS, Laborer, Malta; Dem; from New York.

BARNES PHEBE Mrs. Widow, Malta; from New York.

BABCOCK C. M. Jeweler, Malta; Rep; from Michigan.

BAXTER ESKAT, Farmer, Sec. 20; P.O. Creston; 100 acres, value $4,000; Rep; England.

BAXTROM G. works for McCrea & Lintleman, Malta; Rep; from Sweden.

BALCOM WILLIAM, Mason, Malta; Rep; from New York.

BALCOM GEORGE W. Farmer, Sec. 2; P.O. Malta; 40 acres, value $1,600; Rep; New York.

BALCOM ALBERT J. son of Geo. W. Balcom; Sec. 2; P.O. Malta; Rep; from Illinois.

BAHR FRED, Farmer, Sec. 23; P.O. Malta; 140 acres, value $5,600; Dem; from Germany.

BAGSTER JAMES, Farmer, Sec. 17; P.O. Creston; 320 acres, value $12,800; Rep; England.

BENSON L. Farmer, Sec. 25; P.O. Malta; 80 acres, value $3,200; Rep; from Sweden.

BEATTY WILLIAM, Sec. 9; P.O. Malta; lives on H. H. Harrington's farm; Dem; Ireland.

BECK PETER, Sec. 17; P.O. Malta; works for A. Coffin; Rep; from Denmark.

BILNEY WILLIAM, Laborer; Malta; Ind; from England.

BLACKMAN IRA, Retired; Malta; Rep; from New York.

BOOLER MICHAEL, Farmer, Sec. 32; P.O. Malta; 80 acres, value $3,200; Dem; Ireland.

BOCK WILLIAM, Farmer, Sec. 5; P.O. Malta; 80 acres, value $4,000; Dem; from Germany.

BOCK HENRY, Farmer, Sec. 5; P.O. Malta; 80 acres, value $3,200; Dem; from Germany.

BOWMAN EDMOND, Laborer, Malta; Rep; from Norway.

BOWMAN EDWARD, clerk for G. W. Smiley. Malta; Rep; from Norway.

BOYLES WILLIAM H. Sec. 32; P.O. Creston; works for Alex. Southern; Rep; from England.

BRUCE WILLIAM W. Sec. 32; P.O. Creston; works for Alex. Southern; Dem; from Indiana.

BREAKY JOHN, Farmer, Sec. 19; P.O. Creston; 216 acres, value $8,640; Ind; from Canada.

BRINAN MATT. Sec. 1; P.O. Malta; works for P. Ryan; Dem; from Ireland.

BROWN D. W. Carpenter, Malta; Dem; from Pennsylvania.

BRUNDAGE F. H. Postal Clerk R.R. Malta; Rep; from New York.

BUTLER S. E. Farmer, Sec. 24; P.O. Malta; born in Bloomingdale, Ill. Aug. 5, 1845; came to DeKalb Co. March, 1872; no family; wife was Miss Sarah Payne, from Buchanan Co. Iowa; married March 11, 1874; farm 255 acres; value of real estate $14 000; value of personal $500; Rep.

BURTO. H. Farmer, Sec. 23; P.O. Malta; 120½ acres, value $65 per acre; Rep; New Jersey.

BURG O. Farmer, Sec. 32; P.O. Malta; 160 acres, value $6 400; Rep; from Norway.

CADWELL SIMON, Farmer, Sec. 14; P.O. Malta; 160 acres, value $8,000; Rep; N. Y.
CAFFERY TERRY, Railroad Laborer, Malta; Dem; from Ireland.

CLARK WILLIAM, Mason, Malta, Rep; from England.

CLAXTON HORACE, Carpenter; Rep; from England.

CLAXTON HENRY, Farmer. Sec. 23; 40 acres, value $2.000; Rep; from England.

CLAXTON DAVID, Carpenter; Rep; from England.

CLACKNER JERRY, Farmer, Sec. 8; P.O. Creston; 80 acres, value $3,200; Dem; New York.

CODY JOHN, Farmer, Sec. 33; P.O. Malta; 80 acres, value $3,200; Dem; from Ireland.

COADY PATRICK, Saloon, Malta; Dem; from Ireland.

CORNISH JAMES, clerk for D. F. Pease, Malta; Rep; from New York.

COREY J. A. Farmer, Sec. 2; P.O. Malta; 160 acres, value $6.400; Rep; from Mass.

COREY W. H. Farmer, Sec. 35; P.O. Malta; 160 acres, value $6,400; Rep; from Mass.

COLEMAN JOHN, Farmer, on Thos. Stinson's farm, Sec. 28; P.O. Malta; Dem; Ireland.

COLLAMORE HENRY Jr. Farmer, Sec. 8; P.O. Malta; 80 acres, val. $3,200; Ind; England.

COLLAMORE WILLIAM, Sec. 8; P.O. Creston; lives on H. Collamore's farm; Ind; England.

COFFIN ALONZO, Farmer, Sec. 17; P.O. Malta; 160 acres, value $8,000; Dem; from N. Y.

CRANDALL JANE Mrs. Sec. 15; 160 acres, value $8,000; from New York.

CONNERS MICHAEL, Sec. 1; P.O. Malta; works for P. Ryan; Dem; from Ireland.

COCHRANE W. G. Merchant Tailor, Malta; Rep; from Penn.

COOPER OSCAR, Sec. 8; P.O. Creston; works for E. Hooper; Ind; from Illinois.

CHERRY W. E. Peddler, Malta; Rep; from New York.

CROUCH H. B Farmer, Sec. 27, Malta; Rep; from Michigan.

CUNNINGHAM GARRET, Sec. 24. P.O. Malta; lives on T. Solon's farm; Dem; Ireland.

CUNNINGHAM THOMAS, Railroad Laborer, Malta; Dem; from Ireland.

DAHL CARL, Sec. 16; P.O. Malta; works Jas. Homan's farm; Rep; from Poland.
DEILY JACOB, Farmer, Sec. 5. P.O. Malta; 80 acres, value $3,200; Rep; Illinois.

DELBRIDGE THOMAS, Farmer, Sec. 9; P.O Malta; born in Devonsh re, England, March 25, 1831; came to DeKalb Co. in the Spring of 1858; family of nine children; wife was Miss Ellen Collonmore, from Devonshire, England; farm of 680 acres; value of real estate $30,600; value of personal estate $5,000; Rep.

DEDRICK PHILIP, Farmer; Rep; from New York.

DEDRICK F. H. Farmer, Sec. 11; P.O. Malta; Rep; from N.Y.

DEDRICK MARTIN C. Farmer, Sec. 11; born in Columbia Co. N. Y., April 26, 1824; came to this county in the Spring of 1860; family, four children; wife was Miss Elizabeth Fowler, from Columbia Co. N. Y.; married June 22, 1850; farm of 240 acres, value $12,000; personal $2,500; is supervisor; Rep.

DOAN J. W. Farmer, Sec. 14; P.O. Malta; born in St. Lawrence Co. N. Y. March 19, 1841; ca ne to DeKalb Co. Jan. 25, 1857; has family of three children; wife was Miss Elizabeth Alee, from Delaware Co. N. Y; has farm of 240 acres; value of real estate $12,000; Rep.

DOTY JOSEPH, Farmer, Sec. 35; P.O. Malta; 80 acres, value $3,200; Rep; from Illinois.

DODGE THOMAS W. Farmer, Sec. 10; P.O. Malta; 160 acres, value $8,000; Rep; Vermont.

DOANE CHARLES, son of J. E. Doane; Sec 26; P.O. Malta; Rep; from Illinois.

DODD WARD M. Carpenter, Malta; Rep; from Penn.

DOANE J. E. Farmer, Sec. 26; P.O. Malta; 255½ acres, value $15,330; Rep; from New York.

DYKEMAN JOHN S. Farmer, Sec. 18; P.O. Creston; 120 acres, value $6,000; Ind; New York.

DYKEMAN ANNA Mrs. Sec. 19; P.O. Creston; 140 acres, value $7,000; from New York.

ELENBERG ANDREW, Farmer, Sec. 36; P.O. Malta; 80 acres, val. $3,200; Rep; Sweden.

ENGSTROM A. F. Shoemaker, Malta; Rep; from Sweden.

EWINSON E. G. Farmer, Sec. 32; P.O. Malta; 80 acres, value $3,200; Rep; from Norway.

FITZGERALD THOMAS, Laborer, Malta; Dem; from Ireland.

FITZGERALD MICHAEL, Blacksmith, Malta; Dem; from New York.

FARLEY LAWRENCE, Farmer, Sec. 12; P.O. Malta; born in Mayo Co. Ireland, in the year 1834; came to DeKalb Co. in the Fall of 1860; has family of seven children; wife was Miss Catharine Downey, from Louth Co. Ireland; owns farm of 320 acres; value of real estate $12,800; Cath; Dem.

FERGUSON SAMUEL O. Farmer, Sec. 22; P.O. Malta; born in Jefferson Co. N. Y. April 19, 1836, came to Illinois, and settled in Malta Tp. March 10, 1859; has family of three children; wife was Miss Olive S. Farr, from St. Lawrence Co. N. Y; married March 8, 1859; owns farm of 115½ acres; value of real estate $5,800; personal $1,000; Meth; Rep.

FLEMMING JOHN, works for Jas. Welch; Sec. 27; P.O. Malta; from Vermont.

FLEMING MIKE, works for Thos. Mearns; Sec. 13; P.O. Malta; Dem; from Ireland.

FORBES ALEXANDER, works for J. H. Rowe; Sec. 30; P.O. Creston; from Scotland.

FOX ROBERT, Farmer, Malta; Rep; from England.

FOSTER ROBERT, lives on P. R. Pierce's farm, Sec. 6; P.O. Creston; Ind; England.

FRANCISCO JAMES, Night Watch Railroad, Malta; Rep; from New York.

GATHERCOAL S. Farmer, Sec. 12; P.O. Malta; 80 acres, value $4,000; Ind; England.

GILBLIN LARRIE, works for Jas. Hunt; Sec. 34; P.O. Malta; Ind; from Vermont.

GATHERCOAL EDMUND, Farmer, Sec. 13; P.O. Malta; born in Cambridge, England, Dec. 11, 1812; came to DeKalb Co. in the Spring of 1855; family eight children; wife was Miss Sarah Garner, from Norfolk, England; married May, 1841; farm 80 acres; value of real estate $4,000; no pol.

GIVENS FLOYD, works for J. W. Doan; Sec. 14; P.O. Malta; from Illinois.

GIVINS JACOB, Farmer. Sec. 34; P.O. Malta; real estate $4,000; personal prop. $1,000.

GRAHAM SAMUEL, Principal High School; P.O. Malta; born in Ginger Hill, Pa. Dec. 23, 1851; came to Illinois in the Spring of 1874, and settled in Malta; graduated at the Waynesburg College in the year 1873; at present reading law; single man; Rep; value of personal property $800.

GRAY NORMAN, Farmer, Sec. 35; P.O. Malta; 80 acres, value $3,200; Rep; from Conn.

GUSTUS A. Farmer, Sec. 35; P.O. Malta; 120 acres, value $4,800; Rep; from Sweden.

GUSTUS JOHN, lives with A. Gustus, Sec. 35; P.O. Malta; Rep; from Sweden.

GUSTAVUS ANDREW, lives on A. T. Engstman's farm, Sec. 10; P.O. Malta; 80 acres; val. $3,200; Rep; from Sweden.

HAISH C. W. Hardware Merchant, Malta; Dem; from Germany.

HAISH J. A. Clerk, Malta; Rep; from Illinois.

HANSEN OREN, Farm Laborer, Malta; Rep; from Denmark.

HANSON OLE, Farmer, Malta; Rep; from Denmark.

HANSON CEMAN, Laborer, Malta; Rep; from Denmark.

HANSON OLE, Laborer, Malta; Rep; from Sweden.

HATCH CAROLINE C. Mrs., Malta; from Vermont.

HALL CHARLES H. Farm Laborer, Malta; Rep; from New Hampshire.

HALL CHASE A. Cooper, Malta; Rep; from New Hampshire.

HARDER P. M. Farmer, Sec. 22; P.O. Malta; born in Columbia Co. N.Y. March 4, 1844; came to DeKalb Co. April 15, 1876; family of five children; wife was Miss Ellen Vanslyck from Columbia Co. N.Y.; married Oct. 10, 1865; farm of 127 acres, value $6,000; Dem.

HARDER J. Farmer, Sec. 26; P.O. Malta; 20 acres, value $2,000; Rep; from Penn.

HANSEN HANS, works for A. W. Townsend, Sec. 2; P.O. Malta; Rep; from Norway.

HAMILTON JAMES L. Farmer, Sec. 11; P.O. Malta; 160 acres, value $9,000; Rep; N.Y.

HARRINGTON H. H. Farmer, Sec. 16; P.O. Malta; 160 acres, val. $8,000; Rep; from N. H.

HEVENOR R. M. Blacksmith, Malta; Rep; from N.Y.

HECOX WILLIAM, Farmer, Sec. 16; P.O. Malta; 160 acres, value $6,400; Rep; from N.Y.

HOLLAND JOHN, Farmer, Sec. 7; P.O. Creston; born in Devonshire, England, March 29, 1830; came to DeKalb Co. in the Spring of 1867; settled in Malta Township; served three years in the late war in Co. F, 104th Ill. Vol.; has a family of nine children; wife was Miss Eliza J. Collmore, from Devonshire, England; married in November, 1855; value of personal property $2,000; Dem; Cong.

HOOPER EDWIN, Farmer, Sec. 7; P.O. Creston; born in Devonshire, England, July 30, 1847; came to DeKalb Co. in May, 1856; has a family of two children; wife was Miss Mary Woodard, from Wisconsin; value of personal prop. $1,000; Dem.

HOOPER WILLIAM, Farmer, Sec. 8; P.O. Creston; born in Devonshire, England; came to DeKalb Co. in May, 1856, and settled in Malta Tp; farm of 120 acres, value $6,000; personal prop. $500; family of four children; wife was Miss Betsy Smith, from Devonshire, England.

HOOPER JAMES, Jr., Grain Dealer, Malta; Rep; from N.Y.

HOOPER RICHARD, lives with W. Hooper, Sec. 8; P.O. Creston; Ind; from England.

HOOPER WILLIAM, Farmer, Sec. 8; P.O. Creston; 120 acres, value $4,800; Rep; England.

HOMAN DAVID, Proprietor Livery Stable; P.O. Malta; born in Oneida Co. N.Y. July 24, 1845; came to DeKalb Co. in the Fall of 1846; has a family of two children; wife was Miss Mary E. Cline, from Belvidere, Ill.; married Sept. 5, 1867; owns farm of 80 acres, val. $4,000; personal prop. $2,000; is constable; Rep.

HOMAN THOMAS, Retired Farmer, Malta; Dem; from N.Y.

HOLMAN M. works in Pierce's Cheese Factory, Malta; Rep; from Sweden.

HOLMAN CHARLES, works for J. W. Doan, Sec. 14; Rep; from Sweden.

HOLDERNESS JOSEPH, Sen., lives with J. Holderness, Jr. Sec. 1; P.O. Malta; Rep; Eng.

HOLDERNESS JOSEPH, Farmer, Sec. 1; P.O. Malta; 98 acres; Rep; from England.

HOLDERNESS THOMAS, Farmer, Sec. 25; P.O. Malta; 160 acres, value $8,000; Rep; Eng.

HOLDERNESS DAVID, works for Thos. Holderness, Sec. 25; P.O. Malta; Dem; Canada.

HOLDERNESS JAMES C. works for W. H. Scofield, Malta; Rep; from Canada.

HOOPER J. C. Retired, Malta; Rep; from N.Y.

HOUSE JAMES, lives on Thos. De'bridge's farm, Sec. 16; P.O. Malta; Rep; from England.

HUNT JAMES, Farmer, Sec. 34; P.O. Malta; 160 acres, value $8,000; Rep; from Ireland.

HUEBER WILLIAM M. Farmer, Sec. 15; P.O. Malta; 120 acres, value $4,800; Ind; Germany.

HURT W. H. Farmer, Sec. 24; P.O. Malta; 103 acres, value $5,150; Dem; from New Jersey.

HURT BENJAMIN, Farmer, Sec. 24; P.O. Malta; 120 acres, value $4,000; Ind; New Jersey.

HULTNAN CAROLINE Mrs. Malta; from Sweden.

HUEBER G. Farmer, Sec. 3; P.O. Malta; 240 acres, value $10,000; Dem; Germany.

JOHNSON O. lives with A. J. Johnson, Sec. 35; P.O. Malta; Rep; from Sweden.

JOHNSON JOSEPH, works for Alex. Southern, Sec. 32; P.O. Creston; Rep; Sweden.

JOHNSON A. J. Farmer, Sec. 35; P.O. Malta; born in Sweden, March 15, 1842; came to DeKalb Co. in the Summer of 1853; family, one child; wife was Miss L. Samlson, from Sweden; married May 24, 1873; farm of 160 acres, value $8,000; Rep.

JOHNSON JOHN G. Farmer, Sec. 28; P.O. Malta; 123 acres, value $3,690; Rep; Norway.

JOHNSON FRED, lives on J. F. Phelps' farm, Sec. 34; P.O. Malta; Rep; from Denmark.

JOHNSON CHARLES, works for A. W. Townsend, Sec. 2; P.O. Malta; Rep; from Sweden.

JOHNSON GUSTAVUS, works for A. Vanpatten, Sec. 26; P.O. Malta; Rep; from Sweden.

JOHNSON H. works for John H. Rowe, Sec. 30; P.O. Creston; Rep; from Denmark.

JUKLS AARON, Carpenter, Malta; Ind; from England.

KEAST SAMUEL, lives on A. Phelps' farm, Sec. 34; P.O. Malta; Rep; from England.

KENDALL LAWRENCE, Wagon Maker, Malta; Dem; from Germany.

KINSLOE A. S. Postmaster; P.O. Malta; born in Huntington Co. Penn. Dec. 15, 1840; came to DeKalb Co. in April, 1854; was tax collector one term, and served nearly four years in the late war, in Co. D, 53 1 Ills. Vol; wife was Miss Carrie Cook, from Conn; family of one child; Rep.

KELLEY MARK, Carpenter; lives with James Bagster, Sec. 17; P.O. Creston; Rep; N.Y.

KEMPSON T. Farmer, Secs. 29 and 28; P.O. Malta; 240 acres, value $9,600; Rep; England.

LANE GOWEN, Farmer, Sec. 11; P.O. Malta; 37 acres, value $1,000; Dem; from Ireland.

LANE HENRY Mrs. Sec. 11; P.O. Malta; 120 acres. value $4.800; from Ireland.

LABRANT WM. Furniture Dealer and Undertaker, Malta; born in Crawford Co. Ohio; came to this county in the Fall of 1851; has four children; wife was Mrs. Elizabeth Myers, from Crawford Co. Ohio; Rep; Meth; value of real estate $2,000.

LANE JOHN, Farmer. Sec. 11; P.O. Malta; 43 acres, value $1.500; Dem; from Ireland.

LARSON O. K. Farmer, Sec. 36; P.O. Malta; 80 acres, value $3,200; Rep; from Norway.

LATTIMER JAMES H. Farmer, Malta; Dem; from Ireland.

LADEW ALBRO, works for McCrea & Lintleman, Malta.

LEACH JAMES, Farmer, Sec. 19; P.O. Creston; 196 acres, value $11.760; Ind; Ireland.

LEACH WILLIAM, son of James Leach, Sec. 19; P.O. Creston; Ind; from Canada.

LEACH EDWARD, son of James Leach, Sec. 19; P.O. Creston; Ind; from Canada.

LEACH ROBERT, son of James Leach, Sec. 19; P.O. Creston.

LETHEBY WILLIAM, works for James Bagster, Sec. 17; P.O. Creston; Ind; England.

LEWIS EDWARD, Trader, Malta; Rep; from New York.

LINTLEMAN RICHARD E. Dealer in Lumber, Coal and Grain; P.O. Malta; born in Hanover, Germany, March 13, 1834; came to DeKalb Co. Oct. 1868, and settled in Malta; served three years in the late war, in Co. E. 113th Ills. Vol.; has been town clerk six years; value of real estate $5,000; personal prop. $5,000; wife was Miss Cornelia F. Chittenden, from Kendall Co. Ill.; family of one child; Rep.

LINCH PATRICK, lives on Mr. Fish's farm, Sec. 34; P.O. Malta; Ind; from Ireland.

LITHERBY JOHN, works for John Dykeman, Sec. 18; P.O. Creston; Ind; from England.

LIND L. M. Mrs. Millinery, Malta; from N.Y.

LLOYD E. W. Farmer, Sec. 21; P.O. Malta; 188 acres, value $9.400; Rep; from Mass.

LLOYD C. Butcher, Malta; Rep; from Illinois.

LOCK JAMES, Farmer; P.O. Malta; 240 acres, value $9,600; Rep; from England.

LOWE LORENZO D. Farmer, Sec. 1; P.O. Malta; 160 acres, value $6,400; Rep; from N. Y.

LONSTED CARL, works for W. H. Corey, Sec. 35; P.O. Malta; Rep; from Sweden.

LUNDBURG JOHN, Section Foreman R. R; Rep; from Sweden.

MAGUIRE FRANK, Farmer, Sec. 7; P.O. Creston; 40 acres, value $1,600; Dem; N.Y.

MARVIN H. H. Retired Farmer, Malta; Dem; from N.Y.

MAURER GEORGE J. Farmer, Sec 5; P.O. Malta; born in Germany Oct. 13, 1835; came to DeKalb Co. in the Spring of 1856; farm of 80 acres, value $4,000; personal prop. $1,000; wife was Miss Mary Dailey, from Ohio; married Dec. 20, 1862; family of three children; Rep; Evang.

MARTEN PETER, works for L. Farley, Sec. 12; P.O. Malta; Rep; from Sweden.

McCREA ABRAM, Dealer in Lumber, Coal and Grain; P.O. Malta; born in Orange Co. N.Y. July 15, 1821; came to Illinois in the Spring of 1860, and settled in Malta; has served two terms as supervisor; value of estate $15,000; wife was Miss Eliza Chase, from Rochester, N.Y.; family of two children; Rep.

McCABE JOHN, Farmer, Sec. 27; P.O. Malta; 160 acres, value $8,000; Dem; from Ireland.

McMARTIN MALCOLM, Farmer, Sec. 25; P.O. Malta; 160 acres, val. $6,400; Canada.

MEARNS THOMAS, Farmer, Sec. 13; P.O. Malta; born in Kildare Co. Ireland, in Dec. 1828; came to DeKalb Co. in Nov. 1858; owns farm of 160 acres, value $8,000; wife was Miss Mary Brown, from Sligo Co. Ireland; family of eight children; Cath; Dem.

MILTON WILLIAM, Farmer, Sec. 36; P.O. Malta; 40 acres, value $1,600; Ind; England.

MITCHELL THOMAS, Farmer, Sec. 28; P.O. Malta; 160 acres, value $4,800; Dem; Ireland.

MIEAR INTON, Wagon Maker, Malta; from Germany.

MOREY SMITH, Farmer, Sec. 20; P.O. Malta; born in Onondaga Co. N.Y. Sept. 29, 1812; came to DeKalb Co. in the Spring of 1853; owns farm of 264 acres, value $13,200; personal prop. $2,000; is town commissioner; wife was Miss Janette Smith, from Suffield, Conn.; married Jan. 1, 1839; family of three children; Rep.

MOREY A. S. Farmer, Sec. 22; P.O. Malta; Rep; from New York.

MOREY W. H. Farmer, Sec. 22; P.O. Malta; Rep; from New York.

MUTON JOHN, Farmer, Sec. 20; P.O. Malta; 124½ acres, value $4.980; Ind; from England.

NEWHOUSE ALLEN, Laborer, Malta; Rep; from Norway.

NELSON THOMAS, lives on David Homan's farm, Sec. 10; P.O. Malta; Rep; Denmark.

NEWSHAM CHARLES, lives on A. Van Patten's farm, Sec. 26; P.O. Malta; Ind; from Penn.

NELSON NELS, Blacksmith; P.O. Malta; Rep; from Sweden.

NILSON AUGUST, Laborer, Malta; Rep; from Sweden.

NILSON PETER, Laborer, Malta; Rep; from Sweden.

OLESON ALBERT, works for A. W. Townsend, Sec. 2; P.O. Malta; Rep; from Norway.

ORPUT WILLIAM, Retired, Malta; Rep; from Ohio.

ORPUT J. M. Machinist, Malta; Rep; from Ohio.

ORPUT JAMES, Mechanic, Malta; Rep; from Ohio.

PATTERSON R. M. Farmer, Sec. 22; P.O. Malta; 80 acres, val. $4,000; Dem; from N.Y.

PETERS CALEB, Proprietor Malta Flouring Mills; P.O. Malta; born in England, Dec. 25, 1832; came to DeKalb Co. in the Fall of 1858; value of real estate $10,000; wife was Miss Mary Graves, from London, England; married in June, 1856; has a family of six children; Rep.

PEGG J. C. Farmer, Sec. 7; P.O. Creston; born in Chatham, N. Y. Oct. 14, 1845; came to DeKalb County in the Fall of 1868, and settled in Malta Tp; has family of two children; wife was Miss Mary A. Somers, from DeKalb Co. Ills; married Nov. 9, 1872; has farm 80 acres; value of real estate $4,000; personal $1,000; Meth; Rep.

PEGG JAMES C. lives with Joseph Somers, Sec. 31; P.O. Creston; Rep; from N. Y.

PEASE D. F. Merchant, Malta; Rep; value of property $8,000.

PENDERGRASS R. Carpenter, Malta; Rep; from New York.

PETERSON A. Mason, Malta; Rep; from Sweden.

PETERSON PETER G. Farmer, Sec. 27; P.O. Malta; 53 acres, value $1,500; Rep; Norway.

PHELPS W. Farmer, Malta; Rep; from New York.

PHELPS J. F. Carpenter, Malta; Rep; from New York.

PHELPS ALBERT, Farmer, Malta; Rep; from New York.

PIERCE J. C. Merchant, Malta; Ind; Cath; from New York.

QUINN MICHAEL, works for P. Ryan, Sec. 1; P.O. Malta; Dem; from Ireland.

RADCLIFF DAVID, Drayman, Malta; Rep; from Penn.

REDMOND MURT, lives on T. Goodison's farm, Sec. 1; P.O. Malta; Dem. from Penn.

REDMOND MURT, Farmer Sec. 1; P.O. DeKalb; born in Carlow Co. Ireland, Jan. 26, 1826; came to DeKalb Co. in the Spring of 1872, and settled in Malta Tp; has family of eight children; wife was Miss Eliza Harris, from Carlow Co. Ireland; she died June 1, 1875; farm of 160 acres, value $8,000; was school director one term; Cath; Dem.

REESER J. B. lives on Thos. Delbridge's farm, Sec. 18; P.O. Malta; Rep; from Illinois.

REISER GILBERT, works for Alex. Southern, Sec. 32; P.O. Creston; Rep; from Norway.

REHRS HENRY, Farmer, Sec. 15; P.O. Malta; 80 acres, va'ue $3,200; Dem; Germany.

RIDGE JOHN, works for John Breaky, Sec. 19; P.O. Creston; from England.

RICKARD JAMES, Teamster, Malta; Rep; from New York.

RIST FREDERICK, Baker, Malta; Dem; from Germany.

ROWE JOHN H. Farmer and Stock Raiser, Sec. 30; P.O. Creston; born in Devonshire, England, March 13. 1831; came to DeKalb Co. in the Spring of 1851, and settled in Malta Tp; has a family of five children; wife was Miss Tamson H. Summers, from Canada; married Feb. 24, 1861; owns land to the amount of 1,280 acres; value of real estate $64,000; value of personal property $12,000; Rep.

ROY PETER, works for J. E. Doane, Sec. 26; P.O. Malta; Rep; from Denmark.

ROY GEORGE, works for Thos. W. Dodge, Sec. 10; P.O. Malta; Ind; from Denmark.

ROLF R. Mason, Malta; Rep; from England.

RUBY B. W. Druggist, Malta; Rep; from Ohio.

RADCLIFF JAMES, Retired; Rep; from Penn.

RYAN P. Farmer, Sec. 1; from Ireland.

STAFFORD OLIVER, Retired; lives with James Lock; Sec. 33; P.O. Malta.

SEXTON LEWIS, lives on Mr. Pegg's farm, Sec. 7; P.O. Malta.

SCOFIELD WM. H. Prop. Orient House; P.O. Malta; born in Chautauqua Co. N. Y. Oct. 19, 1838; came to Illinois in the Spring of 1860, and settled in Malta; has a family of five children; wife was Miss Jennie E. Orput, of this county; he served one year in the late war in Co. D, 29th Ill. Reg; Rep.

SHAVER HENRY, Hardware Merchant, Malta; Dem; from New York.

SHEARS FRED, Harness Maker; Dem; from Ohio.

SLYTER ALFRED, works for P. N. Harder, Sec. 22; P.O. Malta; Dem; from New York.

SMITH A. works for Mrs. Jane Crandall, Sec. 15; P.O. Malta; Rep; from England.

SMITH W. R. Carpenter, Malta; Rep; from New York.

SOLON JNO. Farmer, Sec 13; P.O. Malta; Cath; from New York.

SOLON TIMOTHY, Farmer, Sec. 13; P.O. Malta; born in Ireland, May 15, 1822; came to DeKalb Co. in the Fall of 1853; has a family of four children; wife was Miss Mary Welch, from Ireland; owns farm of 280 acres, value $11,200; Cath; Ind.

SOMERS J. Farmer and Stock Raiser, Sec. 31; P.O. Creston; born in Somersetshire, England, April 8, 1824; came to DeKalb Co. in the Spring of 1856, and settled in Malta Tp, has a family of six children; wife was Miss Jemima Dunn, from Utica, N. Y.; married Dec 12, 1845; farm of 640 acres; value of real estate $32,000; value of personal property $6,000, Meth; Rep.

SUMNER JNO., M.D., Physician and Surgeon, Malta; born in Washington Co. Penn, July 29, 1833; came to county June 15, 1865; family, three children; wife was Miss Mary Foster, from Washington Co. Penn; married Sept. 15, 1862; Rep; Pres; value of personal property $500; Rep; Pres.

SOMERS WILLIAM J. son of Jos. Somers, Sec. 31; P.O. Creston; Rep; Canada.

SPICKERMAN WILLIAM, Farmer, Sec. 21; P.O. Malta; 320 ac; value $12,800; Rep; N.Y.

SPICKERMAN GEORGE. works for J. E. Hamilton, Sec. 11; P.O. Malta; Rep; N. Y.

SPICKERMAN GEORGE, Farmer, Sec. 21; Rep; from New York.

STOLBERG ANDREW, lives on W. H. Woolston's farm, Sec. 25; P.O. Malta; Rep; Germany.

SOUTHERN ALEXANDER, Farmer, Sec. 32; P.O. Creston; born in Ashford, Kent Co. England, Feby. 28, 1826; came to DeKalb Co. in the Fall of 1856, and settled in Malta Tp; family, three children; wife was Miss Mary Jane Rowe, from Devonshire, England; married in the Summer of 1857; farm of 320 acres; value of real estate $12,800; value of personal property $4,000; Rep.

SMILEY ROBERT M. Retired, Malta; Dem; from N. Y.

SMITH LYMAN, Teamster, Malta; Dem; from New York.

SMILEY G. W. Hardware and Agricultural Implements, Malta; Dem; from New York.

SWAIN JOHN W. Farmer, Sec. 6; P.O. Creston; 160 acres, value $8,000; Ind; New York.

THOMPSON WILLIAM, works for John H. Rowe, Sec. 20; P.O. Malta; Rep; England.

TINDALL T. J. Farmer, Sec. 15; P.O. Malta; 320 acres, value $16,000; Rep; Mich.

TILL HENRY, Farmer, Sec 5; P. O. Malta; 160 acres, value $6,400. Rep; from England.

TILL GEO. W. Harness Maker, Malta; Rep; from England.

TOWNSEND A. W. Farmer, Sec. 2; P.O. Malta; 651 acres, value $32,550; Rep; New York.

TOPP ROBERT, Laborer, Malta; Dem; from Scotland.

TRAVELIN PETER, lives on J. Johnson's farm; Sec. 36; 80 ac; value $3,200; Rep; Norway.

TROSEN NILS, lives with Fred Johnson, Sec. 34; P.O. Malta; Rep; from Denmark.

UHR BERGE K. Farmer, Sec. 16; P.O. Malta; 80 acres, value $3,200; Rep; from Norway.

VARLEN ANDREW, Farmer, Sec. 25; P.O. Malta; 160 acres, value $8,000; Rep; from Norway.

VAN PATTEN ABRAM, Farmer, Sec. 26; P.O. Malta; born in Schenectaty N. Y. May 19, 1839; came to DeKalb Co. in the Spring of 1865; has a family of four children; wife was Miss Harriet A. Conde, from Schenectady, N. Y.; married Oct 19, 1866; owns farm of 320 acres; value of real estate $16,000; personal property $2,500; served three years in the late war, in Co. E. 105th Ills. Vol; Rep.

WATKINS F. M. Carpenter, Malta; Rep; from Mass.

WATKINS RILEY, Retired, Malta; Rep; from Mass.

WATKINS E. A. Butcher, Malta; Cong; Rep; value of property $3,000.

WATERMAN P. Farmer, Sec. 6; P.O. Creston; 128½ acres, value $6,437; Dem; New York.

WARREN GEORGE, lives on Thos. Brown's farm, Sec. 32; P.O. Malta; Rep; from N. Y.

WATT GEORGE, works for John H. Rowe, Sec. 30; P.O. Creston; Rep; from Scotland.

WELCH JAMES, Farmer, Sec. 27; P.O. Malta; 174 acres, value $8,700; Dem; from Ireland.

WESTMAN LUCY Mrs. Malta; from Sweden.

WILKINSON R. H. Rev. Pastor M. E. Church, Malta; Rep; from Indiana.

WILLETT J. W. Harness Maker, Malta; born in Chenango Co. N. Y. in 1832; came to DeKalb Co. in 1850; family, two children; wife was Miss Magdelane Ennis, from Tioga Co. N. Y. married in 1853; Rep; is Justice of the Peace; value of real estate $1,500.

WRIGHT S. T. Grocer, Malta; Dem; from New York.

WINTROM PETER, lives on A. W. Townsend's farm, Sec. 2; P.O. Malta; Rep; Sweden.

WILLERETT JACOB G. Farmer, Sec. 4; P.O. Malta, 557 ac; val. $27,850; Rep; Germany.

WILLIS J. R., M.D. Physician, Malta; Rep; from New York.

WOODWORTH O. C. Cheesemaker, Malta; Rep; from Illinois.

WORCESTER E. B. Farmer, Sec. 2; P.O. Malta; 120 acres, value $3,600; Ind; from Illinois.

ZELLAR EDWIN, Farmer; P.O. Malta; 100 acres, value $5,000; Rep; from New York.
ZENTMEYER B. A. Barber, Malta; Dem; from Penn.

AFTON TOWNSHIP.

ALLEN W. H. Farmer, Sec. 32; P.O. Waterman; born N.Y.; Lib; Lib.
ALFRED N. Farmer, Sec. 8; P.O. DeKalb; Rep; Lib; val. prop. $4,000.

AMOS JNO. Farmer, Sec. 14; P.O. DeKalb; born Ky; Rep; Adv; $4,000.

ANDERSON J. A. works for C. W. Broughton; born Sweden; Rep; Luth.

ANDERSON CHAS. Laborer, with Patten, Sec. 35; P.O. DeKalb; Rep; Luth.

ANDERSON N. D. Sec. 17; P.O. DeKalb; born Sweden; Rep; Luth; val. prop. $3,000.

ANDERSON A. J. Sec. 17; P.O. DeKalb; born Sweden; Rep; Luth; val. prop. $2,400.

ARNOLD JAMES, lives with Washington Lenox, Sec. 4; P.O. DeKalb; born in Maine, Nov. 16, 1830; began sea-faring life at eight years of age and sailed to India, California and up the Mediterranean Sea, and to all parts of the world, was wrecked upon South Sea Islands and held a prisoner ten months, was tattooed and escaped with sixteen others after suffering great hardships, sailed on lakes three years, came to this state and county in 1851; was in the army three and a half years, in 52d Reg. Ill. Vol. Co. C; was in thirty-two battles and was not wounded nor sick; was with Sherman in his march to the sea in 16th Army Corps, and honorably discharged at close of war; has been married three times and buried three wives, and has lost two children; never went to school a day in his life.

ARMLIN WILLIAM W. Farmer, Sec. 26; P.O. DeKalb; born in Schoharie Co. N.Y. March 27, 1841; lived there about twenty-five years, went to Broome Co. and lived there two years, came to northern part Michigan and lived there two years, came to Afton, DeKalb Co. Ill. in 1872, and has lived here since; Dem; Adv; val. per. prop. $1,000; was in the army, 134th Regt. N.Y Vol. 1st Brigade, 2d Div. 11th Army Corps, under Gen. Howard; was wounded at battle Gettysburg; honorably discharged; married Miss Nancy Morrell, June 19, 1872; she was born in Maine; has one child—girl; lost two children.

ARMLIN J. HENRY, Laborer, Sec. 26; lives with brother; Dem; Lib.

ASH THOS. W. Farmer, Sec. 6; P.O. DeKalb; born Mich; Rep; Lib; val prop. $500.

BACKMARK ISAAC, Farmer, Sec. 19; P.O. DeKalb; born Aug. 13, 1827, in Sweden; lived there about thirty-three years, came to this country 1865, and has lived here eleven years; lived in Mississippi one year; Rep; Luth; owns 98 acres land, val. $4,000; personal prop. $800; married Mary Johnson, from Sweden, in 1865; has three children, two sons and one daughter; lost two children.

BALDWIN H. H. Farmer, Sec. 3; P.O. DeKalb; born N.Y.; Rep; Univ; val. prop. $4,000.
BAIE DANIEL, Farmer, Sec. 36; P.O. Waterman; born Ger; Rep; Luth; prop. $2,000.
BAIE AUG. Laborer; works D. Baie's, Sec. 36; P.O. Waterman; Rep; Luth.

BATCHELL S. Laborer for McDole, Sec. 9; Dem; Lib.

BENSON JOHN, Farmer, Sec. 20; P.O. DeKalb; born Sweden, June 12, 1829; lived there thirty-nine years; came to this country Aug. 9, 1868; came to Chicago, went to Batavia, Kane Co. and lived there six years; came to DeKalb Co. Town of Afton, Feb. 1875; Rep; Luth; rents farm of John Baker; per. prop. $2,000; married Ann Anderson in 1857; she was from Sweden; has two children—one boy and one girl; has lost five daughters.

BEAN ALVIN C. Farmer, Sec. 34; P.O. Waterman; born Maine; Rep; Meth; prop. $3,000.

BERLIN ALFRED, lives with J. B. Glidden, Sec. 10; P.O. DeKalb; Rep; Lib.

BENT J. J. Farmer, Sec. 8; P.O. DeKalb; Dem; Lib; val. prop. $4,000.

BEARD A. C. Farmer, Sec. 16; P.O. DeKalb; born N.Y.; Dem; Adv; val. prop. $2,000.

BLOOMCHRIST S. Tenant on White's farm, Sec. 33; P.O. DeKalb; born Sweden; Rep; Luth.

BLOOMCHRIST JNO. Tenant, White's farm, Sec. 33; P.O. DeKalb; born Sweden; Rep; Luth.

BOLEND NED. lives with son, Sec. 25; P.O. DeKalb; Dem; Cath.

BOLEND JNO. Farmer, Sec. 25; P.O. DeKalb; born Ireland; Dem; Cath; val. prop. $12,000.

BOLER ANTON, Farmer, Sec. 31; P.O. Waterman; born Ger; Rep; Luth; val. prop. $3,000.

BOVEE SAML. D. Farmer, Sec. 5; born Ind; Rep; val. prop. $7,000; U. Breth.

BOVEE RICHARD, Farmer, Sec. 4; P.O. DeKalb; born N.Y.; Rep; Lib; val. prop. $4,000.

BOVEE J.

BROUGHTON C. W. Farmer, Sec. 31; P.O. DeKalb; Rep; Bapt; born Mass; prop. $25,000.

BROUGHTON C. P. lives with father, Sec. 31; Rep; Bapt.

BROWN H. N. lives with Mr. Low, Sec. 23; born Sweden; Rep; Seven Day Bapt.

BROCK LAWRENCE, lives with father, Sec. 1; P.O. DeKalb; born N.Y.; Dem; Cath.

BROCK P. Farmer, Sec. 1; P.O. DeKalb; born Ireland; Dem; Cath; val. prop. $15,000.

BURR W. Laborer; lives with A. C. Bean, Sec. 34; Lib; Lib.

BUDD ASA, Farmer, Sec. 36; P.O. Hinckley; Dem; Cath; $7,000.

BUDD ALBERT, lives with father, Sec. 36; born Ill; Dem; Cath.

BURT HARRISON L. Farmer, Sec. 22; P.O. DeKalb; born N.Y.; Rep; Adv; prop. $8,000.

BYRNE JNO. lives with Jno. McGirr, Sec. 25; Dem; Cath.

CALSON CHAS. Laborer; works for Elwood; P.O. DeKalb; born Sweden; Rep; Luth.

CARTER JAS. Farmer, Sec. 2; P.O. DeKalb; born Mass; Rep; Meth; prop. $20,000.

CANNON JNO. Laborer; lives with A. C. Bean, Sec. 34; born Ind; Lib; Lib.

CHAMBERS MOSES, Farmer, Sec. 26; P.O. DeKalb; born on the Lackawanna River, Aug. 16, 1823; lived there nine years, went to Tompkins Co. N.Y. in 1832, lived there about twenty-two years, came to Little Rock, Kendall Co. 1855, and lived there five years, then came to Afton, this county, and has lived here seventeen years; Rep; Lib; owns 294 acres land, val. $14,000; has been School Director number of years; married Miss Sarah Tyler in 1844; she was from Tompkins Co. N.Y.; has four children—two boys and two girls.

CHAFFEE M. Laborer, with J. Pooler; Ind; Adv.

CHAFFEE GEO. Tenant Farmer, Sec. 2; P.O. DeKalb; Dem; Lib; born Penn.

CLARK CHAS. Laborer for H. B. Gurler, Sec. 5; Dem; Cath.

COEN ANDREW, Laborer; works for Elwood, Sec. 11; born N.Y.; Dem; Cath.

COYNE MICHAEL, Farmer, Sec. 29; P.O. DeKalb; born Can; Dem; Cath; val. prop. $5,000.

COYNE PATRICK, Farmer, Sec. 21; P.O. DeKalb; born Ireland; Dem; Cath; prop. $6,000.

COYNE PATRICK, Farmer, Sec. 21; P.O. DeKalb; from N.Y.; Dem; Cath; prop. $2,000.

CONNELL JNO. Laborer for Z. F. Park, Sec. 33; P.O. Waterman; Dem; Cath.

COX JAS. Farmer, Sec. 1; P.O. DeKalb; Dem; Cath; born Ireland; $6,000.

COSTELLO M. Laborer, with H. B. Skeels, Sec. 3; Dem; Cath.

COOLEY S. W. Laborer; lives with Shoop, Sec. 32; Rep; Meth.

CURTIS ELIJAH, Farmer, Sec. 8; P.O. DeKalb; born in Town of Douglass, Worcester Co. Mass. Nov. 23, 1836; lived there eighteen years, came to Town Shabbona, this county and state in 1854; lived there one year; lived in Sublet, Lee Co. two years, returned to this county and lived three years; was in the army three years, two and a half months in 58th Regt. Ill. Vols. Co. C; served under Grant and Sherman, was in five heavy battles, was wounded at Shiloh, April 6, 1862, and at Corinth Oct. 4 same year, and at "Yellow Bayou," May 18, 1864, and is a pensioner; honorably discharged at close of war; owns 200 acres land, val. $10,000; personal $2,000; Rep; Adv; married Candace Bovee, July 2, 1866; she was from N.Y.; she died June 22, 1875, buried DeKalb; has one child, David Grant Curtis.

CUMMINGS JNO. Tenant Farmer, Sec. 11; P.O. DeKalb; born Ireland; Dem; Cath.

DALY M. Contractor, Waterman; Rep; Lib; from New York.

DeFOREST LANSING, Farmer, Sec. 24; P.O. DeKalb; born in Town of Stark, Herkimer Co. N. Y. May 10, 1832; lived there twenty-four years, went to Rome, Oneida Co. in 1856, lived there one year, came to Cortland, DeKalb Co. Ill. in 1857; came to Town of Afton, and has lived here nineteen years; owns 210 acres of land, value $10,000; Rep; Universalist; has been Commissioner of Highways for the past sixteen years, and also School Director; married Miss Lurena Kingsbury, Feb. 5, 1851; she was born in Booneville, Oneida Co. N. Y; has six children, one son and five daughters, lost one daughter, nine years old.

DEGNAN THOS. lives with brother Jos. Sec. 1; P.O. Cortland; val. of prop. $3,000; Ireland.

DEGNAN JOS. Farmer, Sec. 1; P.O. Cortland; val. of prop. $4,000; Dem; Cath; from Ireland.

DIEDERICH PETER, Farmer, Sec. 22; P.O. DeKalb; born eighteen miles from Luxemburg, on the line of Prussia. March 12, 1825, lived there about twenty five years; came to U. States Sep. 25, 1851, came to Fulton Co. N. Y. lived there three years, came to Chicago in 1854, lived there two years, lived in St. Louis one winter, came to DeKalb in 1856, and lived there about seven years, lived three miles west of DeKalb three years, has lived in this town eleven years; owns 160 acres of land, value $8,000; married Catharine Tyson, March 29, 1856; she was born in the Town of Battanberg, six miles from Luxemburg, it joins France; they have eleven children, four sons and seven daughters.

DOLK ALLEN, Laborer for Mr. Robbins; Rep; Luth; from Sweden.

DOLK S. P. works H. P. Robbins, Sec. 29; Rep; Luth.

DUREE JNO. Laborer, lives with Gurler; Dem; Lib.

EARL WM. D. Farmer, Sec. 8; Rep; Lib; value of property $8,000; from Vermont.

ELLIOTT WM. F. lives with father, Sec. 4; P.O. DeKalb; Rep; Lib.

ELLIOTT TAPPAN R. Farmer, Sec. 4; P.O. DeKalb; born in Thornton, New Hampshire, Nov. 18, 1809; went to Hooksett, same state, and lived there and in City of Manchester two years, and in Derry two years, came to this state and county in the Spring of 1855, and has lived here twenty-one years; Rep; Cong; owns 80 acres of land, value $6,000; value of personal property $1,000; has been Commissioner of Highways some years, also School Director nine years; married twice; first time to Elmira Carr of Thornton, N. H; she died in 1855; married Mrs. Jane Kelly, Jan. 28, 1858; she was born in N. Y; has one son by first wife.

FARRELL PAT. Farmer, Sec. 12; P.O. DeKalb; Dem; Cath; val. of prop. $4,000; Ireland.

FALEN L. Dem; Cath; P.O. DeKalb; from Ireland.

FARMER E. J. Farmer, Sec. 20; P.O. DeKalb; Rep; Advent; val. of prop. $5,000; Ireland.

FARRELL B. Farmer, Sec. 12; P.O. DeKalb; Dem; Cath; from Ireland.

FINNAN MIKE, Farmer, Sec. 12; P.O. DeKalb; Dem; Cath; val. of prop. $4,000; Ireland.

FEE JAS. Tenant Farmer, Sec. 27; Ind; Presb; from Ireland.

FINNEGAN BARNEY, Laborer for M. Hickey, Sec. 8; P.O. DeKalb; Dem; Cath.

FREEMAN WILLIAM, Farmer, Sec. 19; P.O. DeKalb; born in Town of Fairview, York Co. Penn. May 28, 1837; lived there fourteen years, lived in Carlisle two years, lived in Somerset one year, went to Greensburg and Philadelphia, lived in Cumberland Co. came to this state and county in 1867, and lived in Town of Milan seven years, then came to this town and has lived here two years; owns 145 acres of land, value $7,200; value of personal property $600; Lib; Lib; has held the office of School Director; married Elizabeth Cretzler, Aug. 25, 1858; she was born in Germany; came to the United States when two and one-half years old; has ten children, six boys and four girls.

FREEMAN LEVI, lives with brother on Sec. 19; Dem; Lib.

GIVINS N. Farmer, Sec. 7; Rep; Advent; value of property $4,000.

GLIDDEN CHAS. lives with father, Sec. 10; P.O. DeKalb; Rep.

GLIDDEN HARRIET B. Mrs. widow, lives on Sec. 4; P.O. DeKalb; born in Saratoga Co. N. Y. Aug. 5, 1824; lived there three years, lived in Orleans Co. twenty-six years, came to DeKalb Co. Ill. in 1853, and bought farm on which she now lives, has lived here twenty-three years, is one of the oldest settlers; Universalist; owns 320 acres of land, value $10,000; married Mr. Clark Glidden, Feb. 14, 1847; he was born in Orleans Co. N. Y. Feb. 8, 1823; he died Feb. 1, 1871; has had six children, lost one son and one daughter; she has four sons now living.

GLIDDEN J. B. Farmer, Sec. 10; P.O. DeKalb; Rep; Univ; val. of prop. $7,000; from N. Y.

GLIDDEN WILLIS C. lives with mother, Sec. 4; Rep; Lib; P.O. DeKalb.

GLIDDEN IRA B. lives with his mother, Sec. 4; Rep; Lib; P.O. DeKalb.

GLIDDEN BURTIS, lives with his mother, Sec. 4; Rep; Lib; P.O. DeKalb.

GLIDDEN ARTHUR J. lives with his mother, Sec. 4; Rep; Lib; P.O. DeKalb.

GASMANN GEORGE, Farmer, Sec. 11; P.O. DeKalb; born in Prussia, Dec. 12, 1834, lived there fifteen years, came to United States in 1856, came to LaSalle Co. Ill. and lived there ten or twelve years, then came here and has lived here ten years; Ind; Cath; owns 160 acres of land, value $6,000; married Barbara Klemm in June, 1868; she was from Germany; has three children, two boys and one girl.

GOODWIN A. Laborer, with McDole, Sec. 29; P.O. DeKalb; Rep; Lib.

GREENE R. A. Farmer, Sec. 15; P.O. DeKalb; Rep; Lib; val. of prop. $5,000; New York.

GREENE JOHN, lives with father, Sec. 15; P.O. DeKalb; Rep.

GURLER HENRY B. Farmer, Sec. 5; P.O. DeKalb; born in Chesterfield, New Hampshire, May 21, 1840, lived there about eight years, lived in Town of Keene about eight years, came to this county and state in 1855, and has lived here twenty years; Rep; Bapt; owns 235 acres, value $13,000; has been School Director, and now holds the office of School Trustee; was in the army during the war eighteen months, in Co. K, 42d Regiment Ills. Vols., also in Co. K, 132d Ill. Reg. served under Gens. Fremont and Halleck, and was honorably discharged; married Selenia Roth, March 27, 1867; she was born in the Town of Ickford, Buckinghamshire, England, Dec. 21, 1844; has two children, girls, Stella Francis, and Lulu Mary.

H AYES ROBT. Laborer, works for Powers; P.O. DeKalb; Dem; Cath; from Ireland.

HARD PAUL, Laborer for H. L. Burt. Sec. 22; Dem; Lib.

HANSEN PETER, lives with Watson; Rep; Luth; from Denmark.

HANSEN OLE, lives with McKarrell, Sec. 6; Luth.

HATCH DUANE, lives with father, Sec. 7; P.O. DeKalb; Rep; Lib; N. Y.

HATCH SILVESTER, Farmer, Sec. 7; P.O. DeKalb; Rep; Lib; val. of prop. $7,000; N. Y.

HATCH WALLACE W. Farmer; P.O. DeKalb; Rep; Advent; val. of prop. $1,500; N. Y.

HATHAWAY FRANK, Laborer for H. L. Burt, Sec. 22; Rep; Lib.

HICKEY MICHAEL, Farmer, Sec. 8. P.O. DeKalb; Dem; Cath; val. of prop. $4,000; Ireland.

HOBAN JNO. Laborer for Boland, Sec. 25; Dem; Cath.

HOSTETTER JOS. works for Mr. DeForest, Sec. 24; Lib. Cath; from Germany.

HORN WM. Laborer, with J. Powers, Sec. 28; P.O. DeKalb; Dem; Cath; from England.

HOARD F. Laborer, with R. Bovee, Sec. 4; Rep; Lib.

HOMAR HENRY, Tenant Farmer, Sec. 6; McKarrall owns farm; Meth; from N. Y.

I NGHAM A. works for De Forest; Rep; Lib.

J OHNSON J. Farmer, Sec. 5; P.O. DeKalb; Rep; Luth; val. of prop. $4,000; Sweden.

JOHNSON FRANK, lives with J. H. White, Sec. 7; Rep; Luth.

JOHNSON JNO. T. tenant on Monson's farm; P.O. DeKalb; Rep; Luth; Norway.

JOHNSON JOHN, Farmer, Sec. 10; P.O. DeKalb; Rep; Luth; val. of prop. $5,000; Sweden.

JOYCE P. Laborer for Mr. Broughton; Dem; Cath; from Ireland.

JONES J. D. Rep; Lib; value of property $6,000; P.O. DeKalb; from Wales.

JEFFERSON W. Laborer for M. Purcell, Sec. 16.

JOYCE MICHAEL, Dem; Cath.

K ELLEY T. A. Farmer, Sec. 4; P.O. DeKalb; $4,000; Rep; Meth; from N.Y.

KELLY J. J. Carpenter, Waterman; Dem; Cath, born in Penn.

KELLY JAS Farmer, Sec. 14; P.O. DeKalb; val. prop. $4,000; Dem; Cath; Ireland.

KINGSLEY H Sec. 28; P.O. DeKalb; val. prop. $6,000; Rep; Christian; born in Penn.

KIRWAN JNO. Tenant, Sec. 36; P.O. DeKalb; Dem; Cath; Ireland.

KLEMM NICHOLAS, Farmer, Sec. 22, DeKalb Co.; born in Baden, Germany, Oct. 10, 1830; lived there nine years, and came to the U.S. in 1848; came to Chicago, Ill. same year; lived in DuPage Co. seven years; lived in town of Pierce, this Co. seven years; came to the town of Afton and has lived here nine years; owns 240 acres, value $12,000; personal prop. $1,000; married Sophia Schimer March 13, 1860; she was born in Baden, Germany; they went to school together; has eight children, four boys and four girls; Dem; Cath.

KRETZLER W. W. Laborer for W. D. Earl, Sec. 8; Rep; Lib.

LAWRENCE WM. H. Tenant on Carter's farm, Sec. 15; Rep; Meth; England.

LAWRENCE WM. works for R. A. Greene, Sec. 15; P.O. DeKalb.

LAWTHER JAMES, Farmer, Sec. 5; P.O. DeKalb; born in Ireland, July 20, 1793; lived there thirty-one years; came to U. S. in 1824; landed in Quebec; lived in N.Y. state, Schoharie Co. two years, and in Montgomery Co. thirty-one years; came to this state and Co. in 1857; has lived here nineteen years; he was 83 years old in July, 1876; lives on farm of 80 acres, value $4,000; has held the office of School Trustee; married Jane Lowry in 1819; she was born in Co. Down, Ireland, in 1795, and is now 82 years old; they have been married fifty-seven years; has had eight children; five living, two sons and three daughters; Rep; Pres.

LALLEY EDWARD, Farmer, Sec. 24; val. of prop. $3,000; Dem; Cath; Ireland.

LALLEY FRANK, Farmer, Sec. 24; Dem; Cath; from Ireland.

LAWLER JOS. Farmer, Sec. 11; P.O. DeKalb; val. prop. $6,500; Dem; Cath; Ireland.

LENOX WASHINGTON, Farmer, Sec. 4; P.O. DeKalb; born in Kendall Co. Ill. April 23, 1835; went to Chautauqua Co. N.Y. and lived there about twenty years; came to DeKalb Co. in 1855, and has lived in the towns of DeKalb and Afton twenty-one years; owns 190 acres, value $9,500; personal prop. $2,500; has held the offices of School Director, and Trustee and Steward in the Church; married Mrs. M. J. Love in July, 1856; she was born in N.Y.; has four children, three boys and one girl; his little boy, Georgie, 4½ years old, rides his pony any where, bridles and mounts himself, without aid; Rep; Meth.

LINDEN JNO. Farmer, Sec. 18; P.O. DeKalb; $3,000; Rep; Luth; born Sweden.

LOW CHAS. A. Farmer, Sec. 23; P.O. DeKalb; born in Upper Canada April 15, 1837; lived there eighteen years, and came to U. S. and to DeKalb Co. Ill. in 1855, and has lived here twenty-one years; went to California in 1859 and lived there eight years, and returned to this Co. in 1867; went to California in 1868 as agent for the Marsh Harvester Co.; returned in 1870, and has lived here since; three years in the agricultural business, and three years farming; value personal prop. $1,500; married Miss Margaret Ellen Orr in 1861; she was from Ohio; has one little boy; Rep; Advent.

LYONS MARTIN, Farmer, Sec. 26; P.O. DeKalb; val. prop. $10,000; Dem; Cath; Ireland.

LYONS JNO. Farmer, Sec. 25; P.O. DeKalb; val. prop. $15,000; Dem; Cath; Ireland.

MAKARRALL R. Farmer; P.O. Malta; val. prop. $4,000; Pres; from Ireland.

MASON J. Farmer; tenant on Barry's farm, Sec. 5; P.O. DeKalb; Rep; Lib.

MARTIN F. Laborer; lives with Wiltberger; Dem; Cath; born in Ca.

MACK M. lives with Wiltberger; Dem; Cath; Ireland.

McANDREWS J. J. Laborer for Rollins, Sec. 34; Dem; Cath; Ireland.

McCORMICK JAMES, Farmer, Sec. 2; P.O DeKalb; born in Co. Longford, Parish Billashee, Ananghmore, Ireland; was baptized March 7, 1823; came to U. S. in 1851; lived one winter in Oswego Co. N.Y., two years in Orange Co. N.Y., and one winter in Cincinnati; lived in Tennessee and Mississippi, and in Dayton, Ohio, three years; came here in January, 1856, and has lived here eighteen years; owns 160 acres, value $6,400; married Miss Hannah Rourk Jan. 17, 1858; she was from Co. Limerick, Ireland; has six children; Ind; Cath.

McCARTIN JOHN, Carpenter; Cath.

McCARTHY DANIEL, Sec. 18; P.O. DeKalb; Dem; Ireland.

McDOLE JOHN, Farmer, Sec. 29; P.O. DeKalb; born in Chemung Co. N.Y. Aug. 29, 1823; lived there thirty-five years; came to this state and Co. in 1858, and has lived here eighteen years; owns 80 acres, value $4,000; has held the office of Town Collector two years, and School Director six years; has been married twice; first time to Catharine Swazy, in 1846; she was from Chemung Co. N.Y., and died Aug. 6, 1868; married Millie Andrews, of DeKalb, Dec. 15, 1872; had nine children by first wife; lost one; Rep; Advent.

McDOLE ASA V. Farmer, Sec. 9; P.O. DeKalb; born in Chemung Co. N.Y. June 24, 1848; lived there twelve years; came to Sugar Grove, Kane Co. in 1859, and lived there about four years; came to town of Pierce, this Co. in 1863; came to the town of Afton the same year, and has lived here thirteen years; owns 120 acres, value $4,800; personal prop. $500; married Ida Jennette Baird March 22, 1871; she was born in N.Y.; has two children, both girls; Rep; Advent.

McDERMOT MIKE, Laborer for Bolend, Sec. 25; Dem; Cath.

McDOLE DANIEL, lives with father, Sec. 29; P.O. DeKalb; Rep; Advent; N.Y.

McGIRR JNO. Farmer, Sec. 25; P.O. DeKalb; val. prop. $30,000; Dem; Cath; Ireland.

McGIRR DENNIS, lives with father, Sec. 25; Dem; Cath.

McGLINN JAS. Farmer, Sec. 20; P.O. DeKalb; val. prop. $12,000; Dem; Cath; Ireland.

McGLINN THOS. Jr., Tenant on father's farm, Sec. 20: Dem; Cath; N.Y..

McGLINN A. Tenant, Sec. 20; Dem; Cath.

McGLINN JAMES, Tenant, Sec. 20; Dem; Cath.

McGLINN A. Carpenter; Dem; Cath.

McGUIRE JNO. works for Jno. Amos, Sec. 14; Dem; Lib; England.

McKARRELL DAVID, Farmer, Sec. 6; val. prop. $2,500; Rep; Prot; Ireland.

McKARRELL JAS. Farmer, Sec. 6; val. prop. $7,500; Prot; Ireland.

McNAMARA ROBT. Farmer; P.O. DeKalb; val. prop. $6,000; Dem; Cath; Ireland.

MENTON CHAS. Laborer for Murrey; P.O. DeKalb; Dem; Cath; Michigan.

MENNIS CHAS. Farmer, Sec. 20; P.O. DeKalb; Rep; Lib; born in N.Y.

MENIHAN JAS. Farmer; P.O. DeKalb; val. prop. $5,000; Dem; Cath; Ireland.

MENEHAN JAMES, Farmer, Sec. 23; P.O. DeKalb; born in Co. Limerick, Ireland, in 1822, lived there twenty-six years, and came to the U. S. in 1850; came to Philadelphia, Penn., at Bull's Head, and lived there ten years; then came to DeKalb Co. Ill. in 1860, and has lived here sixteen years; owns 120 acres, value $5,000; married Martha Kilgore in 1859: she was from Co. Donegal; Ireland; has five children; Dem; Cath.

MENEHAN DENNIS, Farmer, Sec. 27; P.O. DeKalb; born in Co. Limerick, Ireland, about 1823; lived there twenty-four years; came to U. S. and lived in Penn. about four years; came to Cortland, DeKalb Co.; came to town of Afton and has lived here nineteen years; is a citizen of the U. S.; owns 160 acres, value $6,000; married Miss Margaret Favy in the Fall of 1857; she was from Co. Mayo, Ireland; has seven children, two sons and five daughters; Lib; Cath.

MINIGAN MICHAEL, Laborer for Mr. Robbins; P.O. DeKalb; Dem; Cath; N.Y.

MILLER JNO. Laborer for J. Bovee, Sec. 5; P.O. DeKalb; Lib; Meth; N.Y.

MOSHER EDWIN L. Farmer, Sec. 16; P.O. DeKalb; born in Saratoga Co. N.Y. Jan. 2, 1834; lived there twelve years; moved to Orleans Co. lived there eleven years; came to town of Clinton, DeKalb this state, in 1857, went to Orleans Co. N.Y. and lived three years; came to this county and state in 1862, and has lived here fourteen years; owns 160 acres, value $9,000; held offices of Town Commissioner and School Director for some years; married Miss Mercy Ann Waterbury in March, 1854; she was from Orleans Co. N.Y.; has four children, all boys; Rep; Advent.

MULROY MATTHEW, Farmer, Sec. 13; P.O. DeKalb; born County Mayo, Parish Hinady, Ireland, Dec. 11, 1833; came to U. S. in Dec. 1853; came to N. Y. and lived there 3 years; came to Chicago in 1856; worked on railroad at Sycamore; worked in DeKalb one year; worked in Mississippi, worked in St. Louis, also in Louisiana; has lived in this county 17 years; Dem; Cath; married Catharine Malone, Nov. 24, 1861; she was born in Kings Co. Ireland, in 1838, March 25; she owns farm 160 acres; has eight children.

MULLIGAN THOS. works for Shoop; P.O. DeKalb; Dem; Cath.

MURREY PATRICK C. Farmer, Sec. 26; P.O. DeKalb; Dem; Cath; prop. $8,000; Ireland.

MURREY PAT. Farmer, Sec. 11; P.O. DeKalb; Dem; Cath; prop. $6,000; born Ireland.

MURREY PETER, Laborer, works for Elwood, Sec. 11; P.O. DeKalb; Dem; Cath.

MULLEN RICHARD, Farmer, Sec. 26; P.O. DeKalb; Cath; Dem; 200 acres; born Ireland.

NEGUS GEO. rents Wilson's farm, Sec. 26; P.O. Waterman; Rep; Meth; born N. Y.

NEUDING AUG. lives with A. Peterson, Sec. 10; Rep; Luth; born Sweden.

NEWHALL JOHN P. Farmer, Sec. 6; P.O. DeKalb; born in Athol, Worcester Co. Mass. Feb. 20, 1817; lived there 11 years; lived in Phillipston four years, lived in Cheshire Co. N. H. 24 years; came to this county and state in 1856; lived in Town DeKalb 2 years, lived here 18 years; Rep; Meth; owns 50 acres land, $3,000; has held office of School Director; married Miss Emeline L. Hopkins, Nov. 7, 1841; she was born in Colerain, Mass. lived there 4 years, then lived in Cheshire Co. N. H. until 1856; has one child—son, John F. Newhall, he is married and lives in DeKalb.

NELSON JOHN, Farmer, Sec. 18; P.O. DeKalb; Sweden; Rep; Luth; val prop. $3,000.

NELSON CHAS. lives with J. H. White, Sec. 7; Rep; Luth.

NOBLE E. Farmer, Sec. 14; P.O. DeKalb; value of real estate $4,000; value of personal property $600; born in Castleton, Rutland Co. Vt. May 31, 1819; is a son of Ezekiel and Harriet Noble; served thirteen years on Co. Board of Supervisors, Justice one term; married first in 1842, to Nancy A. Tyler, of Newark Valley, Tioga Co. N. Y; second to Mary E. Ingersoll, of Owego, N. Y; has had eleven children, six living.

NOBLE EZEKIEL. Farmer, Sec. 14; P.O. DeKalb; born Vt; Rep; Meth; prop. $6,000.

NOBLE A. J. lives with father, Sec. 14; P.O. DeKalb; Rep; Meth; born N. Y.

NUGENT THOS. Tenant J. Boland. Sec. 24; P.O. DeKalb; Dem; Cath; born Ireland.

O'BRIEN M. Laborer, works for Martin Lyons; Dem; Cath.

O'BRIEN PATRICK. Farmer; P.O. DeKalb; born Ireland; Dem; Cath; prop. $12,000.

O'BRIEN JOHN, Farmer, Sec. 15; P.O. DeKalb; born in Co. Clare, Ireland, June 24, 1842; lived there 16 years; came to U. S. 1858; came to Lodi, Kane Co. same year, and lived there 12 years; came to this county in 1870, and has lived here 8 years; owns 80 acres land, val. $3,500; personal $800; Dem; Cath; married Miss Mary Butler in 1868; she was from Lodi; has four children, three sons, one daughter.

O'BOYLE JAS. Farmer, Sec. 36; born Ireland; Dem; Cath; value of property $6,000.

OLESON O. Laborer for Gurler, Sec. 5; Rep; Luth.

OLESON JNO. Farmer, Sec. 9; P.O. DeKalb; born Sweden; Rep; Luth; val. prop. $5,000.

PARK Z. F. Farmer, Sec. 33; P.O. Waterman; Dem; Meth; val. prop. $12,000; born N. Y.

PATTEN S. W. Farmer, Sec. 35; P.O. DeKalb; Rep; Meth; prop. $15,000; born N. Y.

PEARL ORSON, Farmer, Sec. 20; P.O. DeKalb; born in Wellington, Tol and Co. Conn. June 24, 1804; lived there 9 years; went to Susquehannah Co. Penn. 1813; lived there one year; lived in Dutchess Co, N. Y. 4 years; lived in Oswego, Tioga Co. N. Y. 30 years; came to this state and county, Oct. 1854; has lived in Town Afton 22 years; Rep; Meth. Adv; owns 80 acres land; $4,000; personal $1,000; held office first Justice of the Peace after this town was organized; has been Town Treasurer five years, also Town Collector; married Betsey Brainerd, June 9, 1825; she was from Bradford Co. Penn; she died March 23, 1872; she was member of Methodist Church 55 years; married Mrs. Catharine L. Hawley, May 9, 1872; she was from Oswego Co. N. Y.; has six children, two sons and four daughters.

PEARL CHAS. F. lives with father, O. Pearl, Sec. 20; Rep; Adv.

PETERSON FRANK, lives with father, Sec. 10; Rep; Luth.

PETERSON JNO. Laborer for J. Oleson; P.O. DeKalb; Rep; Luth; born Sweden.

PETERSON ANDREW, Farmer, Sec. 10; P.O. DeKalb; Rep; Luth; prop. $12,000; Sweden.

PETERSON PETER, Farmer, Sec. 17; Rep; Luth; val. prop. $6,500.

PETERSON S. son of P. Peterson, Sec. 17; P.O. DeKalb.

PETERSON SAMUEL, Sec. 20; P.O. DeKalb; born Norway; Luth; val. prop. $3,500.

POOLER JOHN, Farmer, Sec. 13; P.O. DeKalb; born Town German Flats, Herkimer Co. N. Y. Aug. 11, 1824; lived there 28 years; lived in Steuben Co. 5 years; came to this town and county Dec. 1, 1857, and has lived here 19 years; Rep; Meth. pref; owns 330 acres land, value $15,000; has been School Director; married Miss Elizabeth Roof in 1852; she was from Town Stark, Herkimer Co. N. Y.; has six children, four boys and two girls.

POTTER WILLIAM, Farmer, Sec. 34; P.O. Waterman; born Town Washington, Dutchess Co. April 3, 1825; lived there 14 years; came to Wyoming Co. Town Castile, 1839; lived there 8 years; came to Aurora, Kane Co. 1847, lived four years in Town Co; came to this county 1851, and has lived here about 25 years; Rep; Meth; owns 240 acres land, val. $13,000; has been Commissioner, also School Director for many years; married Harriet Baxter, Aug. 14, 1853; she was born in Mich; has five children, four sons and one daughter; lost one son five years old.

POWERS PATRICK, Farmer, Sec. 14; P.O. DeKalb; Dem; Cath; prop. $6,000; Ireland.

POWERS JNO. Farmer, Sec. 28; P.O. DeKalb; Dem; Cath; prop. $10,000; born Ireland.

PURCELL MARTIN, Farmer, Sec. 16; P.O. DeKalb; Rep; Lib; prop. $6,000; born Penn.

PURCELL THOS. Farmer, Sec. 19; P.O. DeKalb; Rep; Adv; val. prop. $600; born Penn.

RALEIGH WALTER, lives with A. C. Beard, Sec. 16; Dem; Lib.

ROLLINS G. W. Farmer, Sec. 34; P.O. Waterman; Rep; Meth; prop. $8,000; Maine.

ROBINSON BRIDGET Mrs. farms Sec. 36; P.O. Hinckley; born Co. Mayo, Ireland, 1834. and lived there 13 years; came to Yorkshire, England, and lived there 4 years; came to U. S. in 1851; lived in Williamsburgh, N. Y. 3 years; came to DeKalb Co. Ill. in June, 1855, and has lived here 21 years, and is one of the oldest settlers; Cath; owns 236 acres land, val. $15,000; married John Robinson, March 24, 1855; he died Feb. 17, 1868; she has three sons, and lost one daughter.

ROBBINS H. P. Farmer, Sec. 29; P.O. DeKalb; born Mass; Rep; Adv.

ROOSE JOHN, Laborer, with Patten, Sec. 35; P.O. DeKalb; Rep; Luth; born Sweden.

ROACH PATRICK, Laborer, works for Elwood, Sec. 11; P.O. DeKalb; Dem; Cath; Ireland.

RYON JOHN A. Farmer, Sec. 14; P.O. DeKalb; born in Wayne Co. Penn. April 27, 1836; lived there 2 years, came to Kendall Co. near Plano in 1838, was eight weeks coming in wagon, lived there 21 years, came to this county in 1861, lived in Missouri 3 years, came to this town in 1858, and has lived here 8 years; Rep; Univ; owns 157 acres land; $8,000; personal $1,500; was in army, 8th Ill. Cavalry, Co. K, 1st Separate Brigade, Dept. Washington; honorably discharged at close of war; holds office of Justice of Peace and Town Collector; married Miss Lizzie Dunbar, Dec. 1, 1863, she was born Owego, N. Y.; has four children, three boys and one girl; never had a doctor for children.

SANFORD FREMONT, Laborer, for Mrs. Glidden, Sec. 4.

SCHIMER B. lives with Klemm, Sec. 22; born Germany; Rep; Cath.

SIMPSON REXFORD, lives with H. Kingsley, Sec. 28; P.O. DeKalb; born Town Green, Chenango Co. N. Y. June 24, 1848, lived there six years, moved to Town Cortland this county and state, lived there until 1861, moved to DeKalb, and has lived there ever since, 15 years; Rep; Adv; owns 5 lots in DeKalb, value $300; his father, mother, brother, and one sister live in DeKalb.

SIMPSON WM. Laborer for T. Purcell, Sec. 19; Rep; Lib.

SHOOP GEORGE W. Farmer, Sec. 32; P.O DeKalb; born in Crawford Co. Ohio, March 28, 1851, lived there 2 years, came to Kane Co. Ill. 1853, lived there about 2 years, came to DeKalb in 1855, and has lived here ever since, 21 years, went to Crawford Co. for several years; Dem; Meth; val. personal prop. $1,500; married Miss Flora J. Sturtevant, June 30, 1873; born in Kane Co. Ill; she is one of the heirs of the Sturtevant estate, upon which they now live; has one child, a little boy two years old Nov. 4.

SHEFFIELD GEORGE, Farmer, Sec. 19; P.O. DeKalb; born Oneida Co. N. Y. Feb. 5. 1831, lived in Chenango Co. N. Y. at New Berlin 24 years; came to Town Shabbona, DeKalb Co. Ill. 1855, came to Town Afton, and has lived here 11 years; Rep; Lib. Prot; owns 160 acres land, val. $8,000; personal $1,500; has held office of Road Commissioner and School Director; married Miss Frances A. Wagner, 1857, she was from Chenango Co. N.Y; has four children; two sons and two daughters.

SHEFFIELD ERASTUS, lives with son, Sec. 19; P.O. DeKalb; Rep; Lib; born N. Y.

SKEELS H. B. Farmer, Sec. 3; P.O. DeKalb; born N.Y.; Dem; Lib; val. prop. $8,000.

SMITH DAVID, Farmer, Sec. 2; P.O. DeKalb; born Ohio; Dem; Lib; val. prop. $4,000.

SMITH JNO. works for W. Watson, Sec. 17; P.O. DeKalb; Rep; Luth.

SMITH CHAS. works for W. Watson, Sec. 17; P.O. DeKalb; Rep; Luth.

SIMPSON EUGENE, works for E. Sheffield, Sec. 19; Dem; Lib.

STRYKER D. B. Farmer; P.O. Waterman; born N.Y.; Dem; Pres; $6,500.

STRYKER C. J. son of D. B. Stryker; Dem; Meth.

STRYKER A. A. son of D. B. Stryker; Dem; Meth.

STREM GUS. Farmer, Sec. 18; P.O. DeKalb; born Sweden; Rep; Luth; $3 000.

STURTEVANT R. Farmer, Sec. 3; P.O. DeKalb; born N.Y.; Rep; Adv; val. prop. $6,500.

SWANSON DON, Farmer, Sec. 18; born Sweden; P.O. DeKalb; Rep; Luth; $3,500.

SWANSON PETER, Laborer for Mrs. Glidden, Sec. 4; P.O. DeKalb; Sweden; Rep; Luth.

TONAER PATRICK, Tenant, Sec. 22; P.O. Waterman; born Ireland; Dem; Cath.

WAKEFIELD WM. Farmer, Sec. 16; born Vermont; Rep; Lib; $800.

WATSON WM. Farmer, Sec. 17; P.O. DeKalb; born Mass; Rep; Adv; prop. $20,000.

WARD J. W. Farmer, Sec. 21; P.O. DeKalb; born in Town Rutland, Rutland Co. Vermont, Nov. 6, 1829; lived there twenty-five years; came to Joliet, Will Co. Ill. 1854; lived there one winter; came to Town of Afton, this county, and has lived here about twenty-one years; Rep; Cong; owns 150 acres land, $9,000; personal $1,500; has held office Justice Peace some years, also Com. Highways, School Trustee and School Director; married Miss Susan Ward, Sept. 30, 1850; she was from Highgate, Franklin Co. Vermont; has four children—two girls and two boys.

WELCH PATRICK, Farmer, Sec. 32; P.O. Waterman; Ireland; Dem; Cath; prop. $6,000.

WELCH JNO. Laborer for Z. F. Park, Sec. 33; Dem; Cath.

WHITE F. W. lives with J. J. Bent, Sec. 8; Dem; Lib.

WHITE JAS. H. Farmer, Sec. 7; P.O. DeKalb; born Mass; Rep; Adv; val. prop. $10,000.

WHITE WM. lives with R. Bovee, Sec. 4; Lib; Rep.

WHEELER ZACHARY T. Farmer, Sec. 2; P.O. DeKalb; born Town of Lee, Eden Co. Mich. Oct. 6, 1848; lived there about nine years; lived one year in Marshall, also in Olivet, then came to DeKalb Co. Ill. 1858, and has lived here eighteen years; Rep; Univ; owns 117 acres land. $6,000; personal $1,500; has held office School Director; married Miss Lizzie M. Pierce, Jan. 7, 1874; she was from Vermont.

WILCOX EUGENE H. Tenant Farmer, Lattin's farm, Sec. 10; born Royalton, Niagara Co. N.Y. Jan. 6, 1848; lived in Cambria; lived in Genesee Co. two and a half years, came to Ill. and to this county 1864; has lived here since, except going South for a while in Mississippi and Louisiana; Rep; Cong; married Mary A. Noyes, May 11, 1875; she was from Kansas; they have two children—one boy and one girl.

WILCOX NORMAN W. Laborer; lives with brother, Sec. 10; P.O. DeKalb; N.Y.. Rep; Cong.

WILTBERGER WILLIAM H. Farmer, Sec. 33; P.O. Waterman; born in Hart Co. Munfordsville, Kentucky, Dec. 8, 1836; lived there eleven years, came to Chicago and lived there thirteen years, came to Town Clinton, this county, one year, then came to Afton and lived here eleven years; Rep; Meth; owns 280 acres land, $12,000; was in the army three years in 105th Regt. Ill. Vols. 20th Army Corps, Army Cumberland and Army Tennessee; was with Sherman in march to the sea; was in hospital only four days; honorably discharged; married Antoinette Fuller, Jan. 1866; she was born Attica, Wyoming Co. N.Y.; has three children—one girl and two boys.

WILLARD WM. Laborer, Sec. 26; lives with Armlin; Dem; Meth.

WILTBERGER JOS. W. lives with son, Sec. 33; born Philadelphia; Rep; Pres.

WOODS I. S. Farmer, Sec. 34; P.O. Waterman; born Penn; Rep; Meth; $6,000.

PIERCE TOWNSHIP.

A LLEN JOHN, Sec. 4; P.O. Cortland; farm 160 acres, value $8,000; Dem; Cath; Ireland.

ALLEN JOHN, Jr., Sec 4; P.O. Cortland; lives with his father; Dem; Cath; Ireland.

AUSTIN W. E. Farmer and Stock raiser, Sec. 15; P.O. Lodi; born in Rock County, Wisconsin, Jan. 5, 1857; came to county in the Spring of 1863; no children; wife was Miss Christina Howard, of Kane County, Ill; married Oct. 24, 1875; farm 440 acres, value $22,000; personal $6,000; Rep; Bap.

ARNOLD HERMAN, Laborer, Sec 3; P.O. Pierceville; rents of Chas. Dellenbach; Rep; Ill.

ASHTON WM. Sec. 36; P.O. Hinckley; farm 120 acres, value $6,000; Rep; from Wales.

AUSPASH HENRY, Sec. 23; P.O. Pierceville; works Henry Moot's farm; Dem; Germany.

B ISER JOHN, Sec. 14; P.O. Lodi; farm 160 acres, value $8,000; Rep; from Germany.

BUERER HENRY, P.O Lodi; Sec. 26; farm 80 acres, value $4,000; Rep; from Illinois.

BUERER HENRIETTA B. Sec. 24; P.O. Lodi; farm 119¼ acres, value $6,000; Germany.

BUTLER HENRY, P.O. Lodi; Sec. 13; farm 80 acres, value $4,000; Dem; Cath.

BUTLER JAMES. Sec. 2; P.O. Lodi; works for Mrs. Eliza Renwick; from Illinois.

BUTLER THOMAS, Jr., Sec. 1; P.O. Lodi; lives with his father; Dem; Cath; from Illinois.

BUTLER THOMAS, P.O. Lodi; Sec. 1; farm 370 acres, value $14,800; Dem; Cath; Ireland.

BUTLER ANDREW, Sec. 1; P.O. Lodi; lives with his father; Dem; Cath; from Illinois.

BURNETT H. C. Sec. 10; P.O. Lodi; works M. Burnett's farm; Rep; from Michigan.

BURNETT M. Sec. 10; P.O. Lodi; farm 80 acres, value $4,000; Rep; from New York.

C ARTER DANL. Sec. 8; P.O. Cortland; works J. Watterman's place; Dem; Cath; Ireland.

CARTER PATRICK, P.O. Cortland; Sec. 8; lives with D. Carter; Cath; Dem; Ireland.

CARTER DANIEL, Farmer, Pierce Township, Sec. 8; born in Ireland, May 24, 1846; came to county, Sep'. 3, 1866; 160 acres, value $8,000; personal property $1,800; Dem.

CHAPMAN EDWARD, Sec. 2; P.O. Lodi; works for B. O. Snow; Dem; from New York.

CORCORAN THOMAS, Farmer and Stock Raiser, Sec. 18; born in Mayo County, Ireland, in 1822; came to state in 1845; family, three children; wife was Miss Ann Eliza Boyle, from Lake Co. Ill; married Nov. 29, 1870; 200 acres, value $10,000; Personal $3,000; Dem; Cath.

COX JOHN Jr., Sec. 6; P.O. Cortland; works B. Milnamow's farm; Dem; Cath; Ireland.

COX JOHN, Sec. 7; P.O. Cortland; works M. Haley's place; Dem; Cath; from Ireland.

CLINE B. Sec. 9; P.O. Cortland; farm 80 acres, value $4,000; no pol; from Germany.
COUSE PETER, P.O. Pierceville; Sec. 28; farm 80 acres, value $4,0 0; Dem; from Germany.
COUSE AUGUST, Sec. 28; P.O. Pierceville; farm 80 ac; value $4,000; Ind; Luth; Germany.
CORCORAN GEO. Sec. 18; P.O. Cortland; lives with Thos. Corcoran, Dem; Cath; Canada.
CORCORAN ANTHONY, P.O. Cortland; Sec. 18; lives with T. Corcoran; Dem; Cath; Ireland.
COMPTE GEO. Sec. 21; P.O. Pierceville; works for Geo. Schule; Ind; from Illinois.
COLTER BERNARD, P.O. Lodi; Sec. 2; works for Mark Walsh; Dem; Cath; from Ireland.

DEE PATRICK, Sec. 9; P.O. Cortland; farm 20 acres, value $1,000; Dem; Cath; Ireland.
DEGMAN T. Sec. 6; P.O. Cortland; farm 80 acres, value $4,0 0; Dem; Cath; Ireland.
DELLENBACH CHARLES, Farmer and Stock Raiser, Sec. 33; P.O. Pierceville; born in France, Nov. 27, 1831; came to county in 1854; family, one boy and two girls; wife was Miss Catharine Roth, from Germany; born Aug. 13, 1840; 200 acres, value $10,000; personal property $1,000; Rep; Luth.
DELLEBICH JAS. Sec. 17; P.O. Pierceville; farm 80 acres, value $4 000; Dem; from France.
DEMME C. Sec. 31; P.O. Hinckley; farm 120 acres, value $4,800; Dem; Luth; from Germany.
DOOLEY TIM, P.O. Cortland; Sec. 5; works W. J. Bates' farm; Dem; Cath; from Illinois.
DOUBLEDAY GEO. Sec. 4; P.O. Cortland; farm 79 acres, value $3,160; Rep; Meth; N. Y.
DENTON J. H. Sec. 14; P.O. Lodi; farm 160 acres, value $8,000; Rep; from New York.
DIENST HENRY, P.O. Pierceville; Sec. 21; 200 acres, value $10,000; Ind; Evang; Germany
DILLON JOHN, P.O. Lodi; Sec. 13; farm 80 acres, value $4,000; Dem; Cath; from Ireland.

EASTERBROOK GEO. Mrs. Widow; Sec. 15; 200 acres, value $10,000.
EBERLY JACOB, P.O. Pierceville; Sec. 26; farm 160 acres, value $8,000; Rep; Penn.
EBERLEY GEO. Sec. 36; P.O. Hinckley; farm 80 acres, value $4,000; Rep; from Penn.
ERHARDT CHRISTIAN, Farmer and Stock Raiser, Sec. 16; P.O. Pierceville; born Wurtemberg, Germany, June 20, 1821; came to county in 1856; family, three boys and three girls; wife was Miss Mary Eislan, from Wurtemberg, Germany; married in 1848; 160 acres, value $8,000; personal $1,500; Dem; Luth.
ERHARDT GEO. Sec. 16; P.O. Pierceville; lives with his father; Dem; from New York.
ELSMAN HENRY, P.O. Cortland; Sec. 31; rents farm of Mrs. B. Robinson; Dem; Germany.
ENNIS JAMES, P.O. Hinckley; Sec. 36; works F. Young's place; Dem; from Ill.

FARAL JAMES, Sec. 6; P.O. Cortland; farm 143 acres, val. $4,290; Dem; Cath; Ireland.
FINLEY THOMAS, P.O. Cortland; farm 80 acres; value $4,000; Dem; from Ireland.
FISHER JOHN, P.O. Cortland; Sec. 30; rents of Mrs. B. Robinson; Dem; from Germany.
FINLEY BRIDGET, P.O. Cortland; Sec. 18; farm 320 acres, val. $12,800; Cath; Ireland.
FURY JAMES, Sec. 9; P.O. Cortland; farm 40 acres, value $2,000; Dem; Cath; from Ireland.
FURGESON D. Sec. 27; P.O. Pierceville; Rep; from Ill.

GANNON MICHAEL, Sec. 8; P.O. Cortland; works for T. Gormley; Dem; Cath; Mich.
GALLAGHER PATRICK, P.O. Pierceville; Sec. 20; part owner 400 acres, val. $20,000; Dem; Cath; from Ireland.
GALLAGHER THOMAS, P.O. Pierceville; Sec. 20; part owner 400 ac; Ind; Cath; Ireland.
GARLOCK SAMUEL, Sec. 24; P.O. Lodi; farm 200 acres, val. $10,000; Rep; from Ill.
GARLOCK ANDREW, P.O. Lodi; Sec. 14; 160 acres, val. $8,000; Rep; from Ill.
GEORGE W. H. Sec. 32; P.O. Pierceville; farm 80 acres; val. $4,000; Rep; from Germany.
GORMLEY THOMAS E. Sec. 8; P.O. Cortland; lives with father; Ind; Cath; Mass.
GORMLEY MICHAEL, P.O. Cortland; Sec. 8; works for Thos. Gormley; Dem; Cath; Ireland.
GORMLEY THOMAS, P.O. Cortland; Sec. 8; 606 acres, val. $24,846; Dem; Cath; Ireland.
GORMLEY JAMES, P. O. Cortland; Sec. 5; works Thos. Gormley's farm; Dem; Cath; Mass.
GOCKLEY LEVI, Sec. 27; P.O. Pierceville; lives on Henry Grim's place; Rep; from Penn.
GRIM HENRY, Farmer and Stock Raiser, Sec. 27; born Dauphin Co. Pa., July, 1831; came to Illinois April, 1851; Rep; Evang; 920 acres, value $36,800; personal, $2,000; wife, Ebby Loudermilch, born Dauphin Co. Pa. Aug. 24, 1834; married March 2, 1853; 1 girl, 5 boys.
GRIM DANIEL, P.O. Pierceville; Sec. 33; farm 120 acres, val. $6,000; Rep; from Penn.

17

H AISH A. Sec. 26; P.O. Lodi; farm 160 acres, value $8,000; Rep; from Germany.

HENAUGHAN M. Sec 20; P.O. Cortland: lives with father; Dem; Cath; from Ill.

HENAUGHAN JOHN, Farmer and Stock Raiser, Sec. 20; P.O. Cortland; born Mayo Co. Ireland, 1824; came to state May, 1849; family, nine children living, two dead; wife was Miss Mary Welch, Mayo Co. Ireland; married 1854; 304 acres, value $15,200; personal $3,000; Dem; Cath.

HIEMER LEWIS, P.O. Pierceville; Sec. 16; born Hesse Darmstadt, Germany, 1830; came to county 1857; family, two boys, three girls; wife was Miss Mary Buck, from Ogleheim, Prussia; married Aug. 1863; farm 80 ac; val. $4,000; personal, $1,000; Dem; Luth.

HENEGAN M. Sec. 19; P.O. Cortland; farm 120 acre , val. $6,000; Dem; Cath; Ireland.

HILL MOSES, P.O Pierceville; Sec. 27; born Trumbull Co. Ohio, Aug. 5, 1820; came to county 1843; one of first settlers in town; family, three children; wife was Miss Martha Mattee, from Schoharie Co. N. Y. born Jan. 7, 1831; married June 5, 1855; 160 acres, val. $8,000; personal, $2,000; justice of the peace; road com; Rep; Meth; expects to make about 200 barrels of cider this Fall.

HICKEY TIMOTHY, Sec. 5; P.O. Cortland; born Tipperary, Ireland, 1844; came to state 1830; family four children; wife was Miss Bridget Allen, from DeKalb Co. Ill; 120 acres, value $4,800; personal $2,000; Dem; Cath.

HORAN MARY, Sec. 7; P.O. Cortland; farm 40 acres, value $1,600; Cath; from Ireland.

HORAN T. Sec. 7; P.O. Cortland; lives with mother; Dem; Cath; from Ireland.

HORAN PAT. Sec. 7; P.O. Cortland; farm 26 acres, val. $1,040; Dem; Cath; from Ireland.

HORAN JOHN, Sec. 7; P.O. Cortland; farm 115 acres, val. $4,600; Dem; Cath; Ireland.

HORAN P. Sec. 30; P.O. Pierceville; farm 240 acres; value $12,000; Dem; Cath; from Ireland.

HOLDRIDGE WINSLOW, P.O. Cortland; Sec. 10; works N. B. Sheldon's place; Dem; N.Y.

HOPKINS J. E. Sec. 3; P.O. Cortland; farm 120 acres, value $4,800; Rep; from Ill.

HOLLAND THOMAS, P.O. Cortland; Sec. 5; 80 acres, val. $3,500; Rep; Meth; from Iil.

HOFFMAN FRED. Sec. 25; P.O. Hinckley; lives with Fanny Lintner; Rep; from Germany.

HUMMEL C. H. Farmer and Stock Raiser, Sec. 13; P.O. Lodi; born Hesse Darmstadt, Germany, 1809; came to county 1850; family, two boys; wife was Miss Margaret Biser, from St. John, Germany, born 1813; married 1836; 400 acres; val. $20,000; personal, $2,000; Rep; Evang.

HUMMEL JOHN, P O. Lodi; Sec. 12; farm 144 acres, value $7,200; Rep; from Ill.

HUMMEL CHRISTIAN, P.O. Lodi; Sec. 13; lives with father; Rep; Evang; from Germany.

HUMMEL PETER, P.O. Lodi; Sec. 13; lives with father; Rep; Evang; from Germany.

HUMMEL P. Sec. 12; P.O. Lodi; farm 160 acres, val. $8,000; Rep; from Ill.

HUBBARD MRS. E. A. Farming and P.M. Sec. 33; born Berkshire Co. Mass. 1837; came to county March 1859; 160 acres, val. $7,200; husband Edward M. Hubbard, born in Berkshire Co. Mass. 1835, died May 4, 1874; married 1859; six children, three boys, three girls.

HUBBARD C. A. Farmer, Sec. 27; born Berkshire Co. Mass. June 2, 1827; came to Co. 1852; Ind; Meth; 280 acres, val. $10,000; personal, $2,500; supervisor three terms; wife was Miss Eunice Apthorp, born Berkshire Co. Mass. June 4, 1830; married May 1, 1850; six children, five boys, one girl.

HUBBARD JAMES A. Sec. 35; P.O. Hinckley; works W. A. Tanner's farm; Rep; from Ill.

J OHNSON LEWIS, Sec. 3; P.O. Cortland; rents Wm. Keenen's farm; no pol; from England.

JOHNSON JOHN, P.O. Lodi; Sec. 22; works on G. Zeigler's place; Dem; from Illinois.

JORDAN MICHAEL, Sec. 2; P.O. Cortland; farm 160 acres, val $6,400; Cath; Ireland.

JORDAN MICHAEL, P.O. Cortland; Sec. 30; with his father; Dem; Cath; from Illinois.

JORDAN JOHN, Farmer and Stock Raiser, Pierce Township, Sec. 30; born in Ireland, in 1822; came to county in 1854; Dem; 500 acres, value $25,000; personal $5,000; school director; wife was Margaret Henneghan, born in Ireland, 1827; married Sept. 1853; ten children, seven boys and three girls.

K ESLER M. Sec. 23; P.O. Lodi; farm 80 acres; value $4,000; Ind; Luth; from Penn.

KESLER JOHN, P.O. Lodi; Sec. 23; lives with his father; Rep; Meth; from Penn.

KESLER SIMON, P.O. Lodi; Sec. 23; lives with his father; Rep; Meth; from Penn.

KESLER ELI, Sec. 23; P.O. Lodi; lives with his father; Rep; Meth; from Penn.

KESLER ADAM, P.O. Pierceville; Sec. 28; farm 160 acres, value $8,000; Ind; from Penn.

KLEIN THEODORE, Farmer and Stock Raiser, Sec. 35; born Germany April 27. 1833; came to Illinois in 1854; Rep; Cath; 240 acres, value $12,000; personal $1,500; wife Miss Caroline Ahait, born in Wurtemburg, Germany, Oct. 17, 1845; married April 5, 1866; four children.

KLEMM JOHN, Sec. 3; P.O. Lodi; born in Baden, Europe, June, 1836; came to county in 1848; arm 200 acres, value $8,000; personal property $1,000; family, four boys and two girls; wife was Miss Mary Guinder, from Penn; married May 13, 1864; Dem.

KLOTZ WILLIAM, Farmer, Sec. 29; born in Germany, July 3. 1831; came to county in 1871; family, five boys and two girls; wife was Miss Mary Lamky, from Germany; married May, 1856; farm of 160 acres, value $8,000; personal $700; Dem; Luth.

KNAPP A. B. Sec. 13; P.O. Lodi; farm 80 acres, value $4,000; Rep; from New York.

KNAPP MILTON, P.O. Lodi; Sec. 13; lives with his father; Rep; from Vermont.

KNAR EDWARD, P.O. Pierceville; Sec. 27; works for Henry Grim; Rep; from Penn.

KUTER GEO. Sec. 35; P.O. Hinckley; farm 80 acres, value $4,000; Rep; from Penn.

KULP WM. Sec. 35; P.O. Hinckley; farm 80 acres, value $4,000; Rep; from Illinois.

KUNS JACOB, P.O. Lodi; Sec. 25; farm 80 acres, value $4,000; Rep; from Germany.

L ACEY JOHN, P.O. DeKalb; Sec. 11; works farm for T. M Hopkins; Dem; Cath; Illinois.

LALEY PATRICK, P.O. Cortland; works for Bridget Finley; Dem; Cath; Ireland.

LAULER JOHN, Sec. 8; P.O. Cortland; farm 160 acres, value $8,000; Dem; Cath; Ireland.

LEHN HENRY, P.O. Pierceville; Sec. 20; works for T. Gallhagher; Dem; Luth; Denmark.

LINTNER N. Sec. 36; P.O. Hinckley; farm 60, value $3,000; Rep; from Ohio.

LINTNER FANNY, P.O. Hinckley; Sec. 25; farm 200 acres, value $10,000; from Penn.

LINEMAN CHAS. Minister; Sec. 23; P.O. Lodi; from Germany.

LYNN CONRAD, P.O. Pierceville; Sec. 27; lives on Henry Grim's farm; Dem; Germany.

M ANGEL ADAM, Sec. 33; P.O. Pierceville; works his wife's place; Rep; from Germany.

MANGEL HARRIET, P.O. Pierceville; Sec. 33; farm 120 acres, value $4,800; N. Y.

MALONE E. J. Farmer, Sec. 7; born in Ireland, Feb. 25, 1840; came to county March 1. 1857; 220 acres, value $12,000; personal property $2,000; Dem; six children.

MAUER C. Sec. 21; P.O. Pierceville; rents farm of Geo. Schule; no pol; from Germany.

MACK CHAS. Sec. 27; P.O. Pierceville; lives on Henry Grim's farm; from Canada.

MALRONEY THOMAS, P.O. Cortland; Sec. 9; works for T. Gormley; Dem. Cath; Ireland.

MILNAMOW M. Sec. 5; P.O. Cortland; farm 270 acres, value $10,800; Dem; Cath; Ireland.

MILNAMOW THOMAS, P.O. Cortland; Sec. 5; lives with his father; Dem; Cath; Illinois.

MILLER JOHN, P.O. Lodi; Sec. 23; works for Henry Auspash; Dem; from Germany.

MOODY A. Sec. 10; P.O. Lodi; farm 80 acres, value $4 000; Dem; from New Brunswick.

MURPHY JAMES, P.O. Lodi; Sec. 12; works for Patrick Welsh; Dem; Cath; from Ireland.

MURPHY EDWARD, P.O. Cortland; Sec. 17; works farm for P. Taylor; Dem; Cath; Ireland.

MURRAY WM. Sec. 8; P.O. Cortland; works for T. Gormley; Dem; Cath; from Illinois.

MURN PETER, P.O. Cortland; Sec. 5; rents farm of Michael Haley; Dem; Cath; Ireland.

N EVINS MICHAEL, P.O. Cortland; Sec. 8; works for T. Gormley; Dem; Cath; Ireland.

NIHRENG WM. Sec. 32; P.O. Pierceville; 160 acres, val. $8,000; Dem; Pres; Germany.

O 'CONNOR M. Sec. 9; P.O. Cortland; farm 40 acres, value $2,000; Dem; Cath; Ireland.

ORGAN J. P. Sec. 16; P.O. Cortland; lives on the D. Organ place; Ind; from Illinois.

ORGAN JOHN, Farmer, Sec. 16; P.O. Cortland; born in DeKalb County Aug. 7, 1855; lived here since; has ½ interest in farm of 280 acres; value of real estate $14,000; personal property $2,000; single man; Ind; Cath.

ORGAN W. J. Sec. 16; P.O. Cortland; lives on David Organ's place; Ind; from Illinois.

ORGAN'S DAVID, Estate Sec. 16; P.O. Cortland; farm 280 acres, value $12,600; from Ireland

OVITT S. D. Sec. 4; P.O. Cortland; farm 160 ac. val. $6,400; Ind; from Kendall Co. Ill.

P ALMER JAMES, P.O. Cortland; Sec. 4; rents from S. D. Ovitt; Dem; from Illinois.

PHELPS JAMES A. Sec. 3; P.O. Cortland; lives on Mrs. Wiltse's farm; Rep; N.Y.

PABSTMAN GEORGE, Farmer and Stock Raiser, Sec. 4; P.O. Cortland; born in Bavaria, Germany, Nov. 18, 1818; came to Co. in 1868; family, four children; wife was Miss Margaret Oldrich, from Baden, Germany; married Nov. 21, 1851; owns farm of 160 acres, value $8,000; personal, $3,000; Dem; Cath.

PHILBIN JOHN, P.O. Lodi; Sec. 11; works for John Walsh; Dem; Cath; Ireland.

PHILBIN DENNIS, P.O. Lodi; Sec. 11; works for John Walsh; Dem; Cath; from Ireland.

PLEPP JACOB, Farmer, Sec. 24; P.O. Lodi; 80 acres; value $4,000; Dem; born in Germany.

POPE FREDERICK, P.O. Pierceville; Sec. 21; works for Henry Dinest; Dem; Evang; Germany.

POSSON M. L. Sec. 34; P.O. Pierceville; farm 100 acres, val. $8,000; Rep; from N.Y.

RAMER JOHN, P. O. Pierceville; Sec. 32; farm 160 acres; val. $7,000; Rep; from Ohio.

RAMER ELI, Sec. 22; P.O. Pierceville; farm 140 acres; value $7,000; Rep; from Penn.

RAMER PETER, Farmer and Stock Raiser, Sec. 29; born in Penn. in 1830; came to Co. in 1847; Rep; Meth; 160 acres, value $8,000; personal prop. $2,000; school director; wife was Miss E. Garlach, born in Germany in 1829; married in 1855; five children; two boys and three girls.

RAMER GEO. Sec. 22; P.O. Pierceville; farm 80 acres; value $4,000; Rep; from Ohio.

RAMER A. Sec. 32; P.O. Pierceville; farm 80 acres; value $4,000; Rep; from Ohio.

RAMER HENRY, P.O. Pierceville; Sec. 27; farm $160 acres; value $8,000; Ind; from Penn.

RENWICK MRS. ELIZA, Sec. 2; P.O. Lodi; widow of Herbert Renwick, who died July 29, 1876; he was born in Scotland, Oct. 12, 1825; came to Co in 1850; left family of three children; wife was Miss Eliza Burnett, from Branch Co. Mich; married March 19, 1861; farm 240 acres; value $12,000; personal prop. $3,000.

RENWICK ROBT. Sec. 3; P O. Lodi; farm 80 acres; value $3,200; Rep; from Canada.

REDELSBURGER FRANK, P.O. Cortland; Sec. 16; farm 120 ac; val. $6,000; Dem; Germany.

ROTH HENRY, Farmer and Stock Raiser; Sec. 33; born in Hesse Darmstadt, Germany, in 1813; came to Co. March 12, 1854; Dem; Luth; 120 acres, value $7,000; personal prop. $2,000; wife, Kath L. Lamar, born in Hesse Darmstadt, Germany, October 26, 1820; married June, 1841; came to America in June, 1847; four girls.

ROBERTSON JOHN, Sec. 17; P.O. Cortland; rents farm Mrs. Hart; Rep; from Scotland.

RUNKLEY FRED. Sec. 28; P.O. Pierceville; works Aug. Guisler's farm; Rep; from Ill.

RUPPREHT M. Sec. 28; P.O. Pierceville; blacksmith; Dem; from Germany.

SALEVY RANSOM, P.O. Cortland; Sec. 8; works for T. Gormley; Dem; from Ill.

SCHWEITZER JOHN, Jr. Sec. 25; P.O. Lodi; works his father's place; Rep; from Ill.

SCHMIDT H. P. farmer, Sec. 34; P.O. Hinkley; born in Hesse Darmstadt, in 1823; came to Co. in 1854; family of three boys; wife was Miss Aver Struck, born in Hesse Darmstadt, Germany, in 1829; married in 1851; 160 acres, value $8,000; personal prop. $600; Dem; Luth.

SCHULE GEORGE, Farmer and Stock Raiser, Sec. 21; Pierce Township; born in Hesse Darmstadt, Germany, in 1840; came to America in 1847, and to the Co. in 1854; Dem; 360 acres land, value $18,000; personal prop. $3,000; wife was Mary Ann Shoop, born in Crawford Co. Ohio, in 1844; married Dec. 2, 1862; five children, three boys and two girls.

SCHULE HARTMAN, P.O. Pierceville; Sec. 21; lives with Geo. Schule; Dem; Luth; Germany.

SCOTT EDWARD, P.O. Lodi; Sec. 2; works for Mark Walsh; Dem; Cath; from Ill

SCHULE H. Sec. 9; P.O. Cortland; farm 80 acres, value $4,000; Ind; from Germany.

SCHULE JOHN, P.O. Cortland; Sec. 9; lives with H. Schule; Ind; from Germany.

SHOOP SAMUEL, P.O. Pierceville; Sec. 33; rents farm of Mrs. E. N. Hubbard; Rep; from Ill.

SHOOP SAMUEL E. Farmer, Sec. 33; P.O. Pierce; born in Babcock Grove, DuPage Co. in April, 1847; came to DeKalb Co. Town of Pierce, and has lived here ever since, twenty-eight years; Rep; Meth; personal property $2,000; married Miss Lucy Axtell in February, 1874; she was from Bureau Co. this state; has one child.

SHOOP S. Sec. 28; P.O. Pierceville; farm 130 acres, value $6,500; Rep; from Germany.

SHUMAKER PETER, P.O. Lodi; Sec. 23; farm 80 acres, value $4,000; Rep; from Germany.

SHURTLEFF CHAS., P.O. Cortland; rents farm of C. O. Boyanton; Rep; from Canada.

SHAFER HENRY, P.O. Lodi; Sec. 24; rents farm of Israel Kuler; Ind; from Penn.

SIMPSON AARON, Sec. 15; works for E. J. Austin; Rep; from Sweden.

SNOW B. O. Sec. 2; P.O. Lodi; born in Wayne Co. N.Y. Sept. 22, 1852; came to Co. in 1853; family of two children; wife was Miss Estella Lyon, N.Y. City, born Feb. 8, 1854; married Dec. 9, 1872; works his father's farm; 200 acres, value $10,000; personal prop. $3,000; Rep; Meth.

SNOW J. I. Sec. 2; P.O. Lodi; farm 200 acres, value $10,000; Rep; from Mass.

SMITH H. P. Sec. 34; P.O. Pierceville; farm 160 acres, value $8,000; Dem; from Germany.

SMITH H. P. Jr. Sec. 34; P.O. Hinckley; lives with H. P. Smith; Dem; from Ill.

SMITH A. G. Contractor and Builder, Sec. 23; born in Crawford Co. Ohio, Sept. 2, 1842; came to Illinois in 1862; Ind; Evang; 80 acres land, value $4,000; wife was Mary Ann Shoop, born in Crawford Co. Ohio, April 16, 1841; married March 5, 1863; two children.

WALSH JOHN, P.O. Lodi; Sec. 11; farm 347 acres, value $17,350; Dem; Cath; Ireland.

WALSH THOMAS, P.O. Lodi; Sec. 12; lives with his father; Dem; Cath; Ireland.

WALSH MARK, Farmer and Stock Raiser, Sec. 2; P.O. Lodi; born in Mayo Co. Ireland, May 10, 1838; came to Co. in 1848; family of one boy; wife was Miss Mary A. Scott, from Illinois; married Sept. 28, 1869; died July 21, 1876; farm 240 acres; value $12,000; personal prop. $3,000; Assessor one term; Cath; Dem.

WALSH MICHAEL, P.O. Lodi; Sec. 12; lives with his father; Dem; Cath; from Ireland.

WALSH PATRICK, Jr. Sec. 12; P.O. Lodi; Dem; Cath; from Ireland.

WALSH PATRICK, Sen. Sec. 12; P.O. Lodi; farm 320 acres, value $16,000; Dem; Ireland.

WALTERS JOSEPH, P.O. Pierceville; Sec. 27; lives with his father; Dem; from Ohio.

WALTERS JACOB, P.O. Pierceville; Sec. 27; farm 25½ acres, value $1,250; Dem; Ohio.

WALTERS BARNHART, Sec. 27; P.O. Pierceville; lives with his father; Dem; from Ohio.

ZIEGLER MICHAEL, Farmer and Stock Raiser, Sec. 22; P.O. Lodi; born Wurtemburg, Germany, September 20, 1820; came to Co. 1849; family, three boys, one girl; wife was Miss Lavina Ramer, from Ohio; married November 28, 1853; farm 160 acres, value real estate $8,000; value personal property $2,000; is School Director and Road Commissioner; Dem; Luth.

SQUAW GROVE TOWNSHIP.

A GAN J. Laborer, Sec. 11; P.O. Hinckley; Ind; Lib.

AKERLY WM. Farmer, Sec. 36, P.O. Little Rock; born in N.Y.; Dem; Lib.

AHRENS HENRY, Farmer, Sec. 15; born in Brunswick, Germany, July 19, 1827; lived there twenty-nine years; came to U. S. in 1856; came to Yorkville, Kendall Co. and lived there six years, then came to this town and county, Squaw Grove. and has lived here fourteen years; Rep; Luth; farms Dr. Hopkins' place; sold his farm to Wm. Baker; has held office of Path-master; married Miss Amelia Brinckman in 1854; she was from Brunswick, Germany; they have nine children, four boys and five girls.

ALLBEE BERNARD C. Farmer, Sec. 32; P.O. Hinckley; born in Aurelis, Cayuga Co. N.Y. June 10, 1811; went to Ohio in 1815, lived there twenty-four years; then came to this state and Co. in 1838, and has lived here thirty-eight years; is one of the oldest settlers; owns 160 acres, value $10,000; personal prop. $1,000; has held the offices of School Director and Path-master; married Mary E. Jones Jan. 4, 1840; she was born in N.Y. City; has thirteen children, seven boys and six girls, all living; Rep; Lib.

ALLBEE J. son of B. Allbee, farmer, Sec. 33; P.O. Hinckley; Ind; Lib.

ALLBEE G. son of B. Allbee, farmer, Sec. 33; P.O. Hinckley; Ind; Lib.

ALLBEE C. son of B. Allbee, farmer, Sec. 33; P O. Hinckley; Ind; Lib.

ALDER G. B. Farmer, Sec. 4; P.O. Hinckley; tenant; Rep; Meth.

ANDERSON JOHN, Laborer for Mrs. Seebree; P.O. Hinckley; Luth; Lib.

ASHTON WILLIAM, Farmer, Sec. 1; P.O. Hinckley; born in Montgomeryshire, Wales, April 19, 1819; lived there about seventeen years, then lived in Radnorshire six years; came to this country and to this state in 1842, and has lived here thirty-four years; he and Thos. Evans came to this country in the same ship, Siddon's Black Ball Line; and both came together to this state; owns 296 acres, value $18,000; personal prop. $3,000; married Miss Sarah Lewis in 1846; she was from Radnorshire, Wales, born in 1829; has five children, four boys and one girl; Ind; Bapt.

ANSBATH ———, Farmer, Sec. 3; P.O. Hinckley; Rep; Luth.

ANKEL H. Farmer, Sec. 21; P.O Hinckley; value $4,000; Dem; Pres.

B ASTIAN A. Farmer, Sec. 20; P.O. Hinckley; value prop. $12,000; Dem; Lib.

BAKER B. Tenant farmer, Sec. 17; P.O. Hinckley; Rep; Lib.

BASTIAN GUSTAVUS, lives with brother on Sec. 20; P.O. Hinckley; $400; Dem; Luth.

BAKER R., P.O. Hinckley; Lib; from England.

BAKER R. Farmer, P.O. Hinckley; Rep; Meth.

BAKER WM. works at elevator; P.O. Hinckley; Rep; Bapt.

BALE AUG. Farmer, Sec. 18; value of prop. $10,000; Rep; Luth, born in Germany.

BALE C. Coal Dealer; P.O. Hinckley; Rep; Luth; born in Prussia.

BANDELL WILLIS, Blacksmith, Sec. 15; Rep; Meth; born in N.Y.

BARLOW T. W. Telegraph Operator; P.O. Hinckley; Ind; Meth.

BAUDER J. H. Dry Goods; P.O. Hinckley; Lib; Lib.

BLAKELY JOHN, Laborer, Sec. 15; P.O. Hinckley; Lib. Rep.

BEITEL MILTON Farmer, Sec. 29; P.O. Hinckley; born in Ohio August 25, 1850; lived there about two years, then came to Ottawa, Ill. in 1852, and remained there about two months, then came to this town and county in the same year, and has lived here twenty-four years; value personal prop. $600; married Miss Josephine Lane March 2, 1874; she was born in Poughkeepsie, Datchess Co N.Y.; has one child, a little girl; Rep; Meth.

BEITEL JULIUS T. Farmer, Sec. 32; P.O. Hinckley; born August 23, 1825, in Northhampton Co. Penn; lived there twenty-five years; came to Ohio in 1850, and lived there two years; came to this state and Co. in 1852, and has lived here twenty-four years; owns 294 acres, value $16,000; personal prop. $2,000; has been Supervisor of the town, and also Town Clerk and School Director; married Miss Emma Trager in 1848, she was from Bethlehem, Penn.; has twelve children; Rep; Meth.

BEITEL EUGENE F. Manager Union Cheese Factory; P.O. Waterman; born in Northhampton Co. Penn. May 19, 1849; came to Ohio in 1850; came to this state and Co. in 1852, and has lived here twenty-four years; married Miss Carrie Michel, in Sandwich, Nov. 22, 1873; she was from Ohio; has had two children; one living, a little girl; Lib; Lib.

BEVERIDGE JAMES, Farmer, Sec. 28; P.O. Hinckley; lives with R. Palmer; born in the state of Penn. March, 1853; lived there five years; came to DeKalb Co. in 1858, and has lived here ever since, except when taking a trip of several years out West, in Colorado and other states; his two sisters are living in this county, and his father is in Saline Co. Kan; Rep; Meth.

BECKER CHAS. F. Shoemaker; P.O. Hinckley; Ind; Luth.

BEACHAM HENRY, Farmer, Sec. 24; P.O. Hinckley; val. prop. $5,000; Rep; Bapt; Eng.

BEACHAM JNO. Farmer, Sec. 24; P.O. Hinckley; $4,000; Rep; Lib.

BISCH PETER, lives with father, Sec. 19; P.O. Hinckley; Rep; Meth.

BISCH N. Farmer, Sec. 19; P.O. Hinckley; val. prop. $9,000; Ind; Meth; born Germany.

BISH PETER, Farmer, Sec. 20; P.O. Hinckley; born in Luzerne Co. Penn. Feb. 2, 1839; lived there sixteen years; came to DeKalb Co. in Sept. 1854, and has lived here twenty-two years; was 80 acres, value $4,500; personal prop. $1,000; has been Assessor of the town, and Commissioner and School Director of this district; married Sarah Ann Allbee in 1857; she was born in this town and Co.; has five children, three girls and two boys; Ind; Lib.

BINDER HENRY, Mason; P.O. Hinckley; Dem; Cath; from Germany.

BOGET RODERICK, Tenant, Sec. 21; P.O. Hinckley; Rep; Lib; born in N.Y.

BOGET MARION, lives with brother on Sec. 21; P.O. Hinckley; Dem; Meth.

BORKELTS WILHELMINA Mrs. P.O. Hinckley; Luth; from Germany.

BORCHER AUG. P.O. Hinckley; Rep; Luth.

BRIMER GEO. W. Tenant; P.O. Hinckley; born in Bristol, Kendall Co. March 15, 1844; came to DeKalb Co. and has lived in this state nineteen years; lived in Wisconsin some years; was in the army three years, in the 33d Wis. Vols. under A. J. Smith, with Grant; was in twenty-seven battles, and was wounded three different times, shot with three buckshot and ball; was Policeman in Minn; married Annie Fagan in 1870; she was from Lake Co. Ill.; has two children; Dem; Cath; value of prop. $300.

BUSHBORN HERMAN, Farmer, Sec. 26; P.O. Hinckley; val. prop. $4,000; Rep; Luth.

BUSHNELL ELMER, Farmer. Sec. 36; P.O. Little Rock; $10,000; Rep; Meth.

BUSHNELL W. J. Farmer, Sec. 36; P.O. Little Rock; val. prop. $7,000; Rep; Lib; N.Y.

BUNNING WM. Barber; P.O. Hinckley; Lib; Luth.

CAIN JOHN, Farmer, Sec. 27; P.O. Hinckley; val. prop. $6,000; Rep; Pres.

CARR W. H. Farmer, Sec. 26; P.O. Hinckley; val. prop. $4,000; Rep; U. Pres; N.Y.

CHEENEY WM. Cooper; P.O. Hinckley; Rep; Meth.

CHEENEY A. works in lumber yard; P.O. Hinckley; Rep; Bapt; born in New Hampshire.

CHEENEY A. Laborer; P.O. Hinckley; Rep; Meth.

CLEVELAND SIMON, Farmer, Sec. 25; P.O. Hinckley; born in Oneida Co. N.Y. Nov. 25, 1828; lived there forty-four years; came to this state and Co. in 1872; owns 158 acres, value $9,500; personal prop. $2,000; has held the offices of Town Assessor and School Director; married Miss Cornelia Webb June 20, 1852; she was born in Oswego Co. N.Y.; has six children, five sons and one daughter.

CLINTON G. W. Butcher; P.O. Hinckley; Rep; Meth.

CLEVELAND CHAS. lives with father; P.O. Hinckley; Rep; Bapt; born in N.Y.

CONE ISABELLE Miss, Farms Sec. 2; P.O. Hinckley; born in Albany. N.Y. July 10, 1825; lived there one year, then went to Oneida Co.; lived there nineteen years; came to this town of Squaw Grove, this Co. and has lived here thirty-one years; owns 80 acres land; she has six sisters and two brothers, and all live within three miles of one another; her mother died in May, 1873; Cong.

CONE ARCHIBALD, Farmer, Sec. 2; P.O. Hinckley; lives with Miss I. Cone; born in Johnston, Paisley, Scotland, July 13. 1792; lived there 24 years; came to this country 1816; came to Albany Co. N.Y. and lived there 10 years; went to Oneida Co. and lived there 17 years; came to this county in 1843 and has lived here 33 years; he is 84 years old; Rep; Pres; owns 15 acres land, $1,000; married Sept. 26, 1816, Rosetta Cunningham, of Ayrshire, Scotland; had eleven children, two sons and seven daughters; his house was the first house between Big Rock and Squaw Grove.

CONE ARCHIBALD Jr. Farmer, Sec. 3; P.O. Hinckley; born in New Hartford, Oneida Co. N. Y. May 15, 1832; lived there and in N. Y. Mills 11 years; came to this state in 1843, and has lived here 33 years; his father's was the first house on the prairie between Big Rock and Squaw Grove, and is now standing; Ind; Meth. religion pref; owns 200 acres, val. $10,000; personal prop. $2,000; holds office of School Director and Commissioner of Highways; married Ann Bailey, July 4, 1866; she was born in England; has six children.

CONE WILLIAM, Farmer, Sec. 4; P.O. Hinckley; born in New Scotland, near Albany, in Albany Co. N. Y. Sept. 13, 1822; lived in the state 21 years; came to DeKalb Co. in this state in 1843, and has lived here 33 years; Rep; Univ; 345 acres of land, value $15,500; was in Mexican War; went across the plains and had several skirmishes with Indians; was in California 3½ years; married Miss Margaret McFarlane, she was born in Scotland; has five children, one married; his father from Scotland, lives at Squaw Grove.

COSTER J. C. Farmer, Sec. 14; P.O. Hinckley; born in Town of Nassau, Rensselaer Co. N.Y. August 18, 1815; lived there 26 years, then moved to Chenango Co. and lived there 6 years, then came to this state in Kane Co. and lived there one year, then came to Squaw Grove in DeKalb Co. and has lived here 27 years, only several here when he came; Rep; Meth; owns 418 acres land, value $30,000; 500 in Wisconsin and 120 in Iowa; val. personal property $12,000; has held office of Justice of the Peace four years; has held office of School Director a number of years; married his first wife, W. Marie Weeks, in 1838; she died 1850; married S. R. Bathwick; has four children, one son died in army.

COSTER R. L. Cheese Maker; P.O. Hinckley; Ind; Meth.

COSTER PETER, P.O. Hinckley; Ind; Meth.

COSTER ALEX. Agent Agricultural Works; P.O. Hinckley; Rep; Meth.

COULSON WM. Farmer. Sec. 22; P.O. Hinckley; born Eng; Rep; Meth; 164 acres.

CURRY J. M. Farmer, Sec. 17; P.O. Hinckley; value $10,000.

D ARNELL JAMES. Farmer, Sec. 6; P.O. Hinckley; val. $10,000; Rep; Cong.

DARNELL A. Farmer, Sec. 3; P.O. Hinckley; Rep; Lib.

DARNELL ENOCH B. Farmer, Sec. 22; P O. Hinckley; born in Marshall Co. Ill. Dec. 9, 1837; lived there 3 years; came to Kendall Co. in 1840, and lived there until 1869; came to this town and county same year, and has lived here 7 years; Rep; Meth; owns 50 acres land, value $3,000; personal prop. $800; was in the army 3 years and 45 days in the 13th Regiment Ill. Vol. Co. E, 15th Army Corps, under Gen. Sherman; was in fifteen battles, was struck twice with ball before Vicksburg, but was not off duty; was honorably discharged at close of war; married Miss Mary Mills, March 7, 1866; she was from Chatauqua Co. N. Y. born March 7, 1840; has three children, one boy and two girls.

DARNELL BENJAMIN A. Farmer, Sec. 35; P.O. Hinckley; born in Town of Evans, Marshall Co. Ill. June 12, 1833; born in a fort on Sandy Creek built for protection against Black Hawk during the Black Hawk war; came to Kendall Co. 1840, and lived there 18 years; came to DeKalb Co. 1864, and has lived here 12 years; taught school 14 winters, and has been ordained Elder 17 years; Republican; Christian Church; owns 120 acres land, $6,000; has been Path-master; married Ann C. Neer, 1858; she was from Harper's Ferry; has seven children, all boys.

DAVIS EVAN, Farmer, Sec. 12; P.O. Hinckley; born in Cardiganshire, South Wales, Nov. 3, 1831; lived there 15 years, then followed the sea about 10 years, sailing to all parts of the world; was mate of light ship " Frying Pan" Shoals off North Carolina coast about 2 years; came to this county in 1858—18 years ago; owns 82 acres land, value $4,000; personal prop. $500; holds office of School Director; married Miss Amelia Price in 1860; she was born near Hamilton, N. Y. in Dec. 1841; has two children, one boy, one girl.

DALE THOS. L. Laborer; P.O. Hinckley; Rep; Lib.

DALE THOS S. Farmer, Sec. 9; P.O. Hinckley; born Eng; Ind; Epis; val. prop. $8,000.

DALE JAMES, lives with father, Sec. 9; P.O. Hinckley; Ind; Epis.

DALE THOS. lives with father, Sec. 9; P.O. Hinckley; Ind; Epis.

DAVIS JAS. Mechanic; P.O. Hinckley; Lib; Cong.

DEVINE M. Farmer, Sec. 34; P.O. Hinckley; prop. $5,000; Dem; Cath.

DIXON J. Farmer, Sec. 7; P.O. Hinckley; Lib; Lib; val. prop. $10,000.

DOBBIN DAVID M. Farmer, Sec. 31; P.O. Freeland; born in Ireland in 1814; came to this country in 1823; came to Washington Co. N.Y.; lived in Ohio some years; came to this state and county in 1845, and has lived here 31 years; Rep; U. Pres; 120 acres land, value $7,200; has been School Director; married Miss Eliza M. Stott, Sept. 1852; she was from Washington Co. N.Y.; has had eight children.

DOMITY THOS. Laborer; P.O. Hinckley; Lib; Lib.

DUGAN PATRICK, Farmer, Sec. 34; P.O. Hinckley; Dem; Cath.

EASTERMAN JOHN, Mason; P.O. Hinckley; Dem; Bapt.

ECKHERT WM. Laborer, Sec. 18; P.O. Hinckley; Rep; Luth.

EASTABROOKS JAMES L. Farmer, Sec. 15; P.O. Hinckley; born in Tioga Co. N.Y. Dec. 9, 1818; lived in N. Y. State 5 years; lived in Penn. about 12 years, and came to DeKalb Co. Town of Squaw Grove, Sept. 1836, and has lived here 40 years, only four or five families here when he came; 160 acres land, val. $10,000; Dem; Meth; married Miss Elizabeth Cone in 1847; she was born in Oneida Co. N. Y.; has four children, two boys and two girls.

ELSENAN AUGUST, Billiard Room; P.O. Hinckley; Dem; Luth.

EVANS THOS. Farmer, Sec. 11; P.O. Hinckley; born in Radnorshire, Wales, July 26, 1818; lived there 25 years, came to U. S. in 1843; came to this town and county, and has lived here ever since, 33 years; owns 560 acres land, value $30,000; personal $3,000; Ind; Bapt; has held office of School Director; married Miss Mary Cone in 1844, June 25; she was from Oneida Co. N. Y.; has three sons and one girl.

EVANS THOS. Jr. Farmer, Sec. 11; P.O. Hinckley; Rep; Lib.

EVANS WM. Farmer, Sec. 2; P.O. Hinckley; val. $15,000; Rep; Cong.

EVANS T. Farmer, Sec. 12; P.O. Hinckley; Ind; Bapt.

EVANS ARCHIBALD, Farmer, Sec. 12; tenant on father's farm; Lib; Lib.

FAXON H. J. Farmer, Sec. 27; Rep; Meth; $12,000.

FAY E. H. Farmer, Sec. 27; P.O. Hinckley; val. $10,000; Rep; Lib.

FAY WELLS A. Farmer; P.O. Hinckley; val. prop. $15,000; Rep; 2d Adv; born N.Y.

FAY A. W. Farmer, Sec. 19; P.O. Hinckley; Rep; Lib; val. prop. $8,000; born this Co.

FAVOR B. K. Farmer, Sec. 24; P.O. Hinckley; Rep; Cong; prop. $15,000; Kendall Co. Ill.

FAHS J. Tenant Farmer, Sec. 13; P.O. Hinckley; Rep; Meth; born in Md.

FOSTER MOSELY W. Farmer, Sec. 25; P.O. Hinckley; Rep; Meth; $12,000.

FLANDERS S. Lib. Rep; P.O. Hinckley.

FRUDY GEO. Mason; P.O. Hinckley; Rep; Meth.

FRENCH A. son of J. W. French, Farmer, Sec. 31; P.O. Hinckley; Rep; U. Pres.

FRENCH J. W. Farmer, Sec. 31; P.O. Hinckley; val. $8,000; Rep; U. Pres.

FULLER JOHN T. Dry Goods and Groceries; P.O. Hinckley; Ind; Meth; born N. Y.

GARRETT W. A. Carpenter; P.O. Hinckley; Dem; Lib.

GARRETT WILLIAM, Carpenter, Hinckley; Rep; Meth.

GAMAGE A. Laborer; P.O. Hinckley; Dem; Lib.

GLANN J. F. Farmer, Sec. 9; value of property $8,000; P.O. Hinckley; Ind; Lib.

GOOD JANE Mrs. P.O. Hinckley; Meth; value of property $4,000.

GRAINART L. tenant on W. Leifheit's farm; P.O. Hinckley; Rep; Luth.

GRANART F. Farmer, Sec. 17; P.O. Hinckley; Rep; Luth; value of property $8,000.

GREENWOOD PHILIP, Farmer (Albert Watson's farm). Sec. 18; P.O. Hinckley; born June 19, 1828, in Gloucestershire, England, Cleve Parish; lived there about eighteen years; came to the U. S. in 1846; came to Westchester Co. N. Y. and lived there eighteen years; was overseer of Mrs. Dashwood's farm garden; came to Sandwich, DeKalb Co. in 1855, and has lived here eighteen years; has held the office of Overseer of Roads; Rep; Meth; value of personal property $3,000; married Margaret Leecock, of Ireland; she died in 1864; married Lisette Norton in Oct. 1872; she was from Canada; had four children by first wife and three by present wife.

HARTMAN W. Farmer, Sec. 5; P.O. Hinckley; Rep; value of property $8,000.

HARTMAN C. Farmer, Sec. 7; P.O. Hinckley; Dem; Luth; value of property $50,000.

HARTMAN AUG. Tenant Farmer, Sec. 7; P.O. Hinckley; born in Prussia, Feb. 9, 1854; came to this country in 1854; came to Yorkville, Kendall Co. lived there one year, came to this county in 1855, and has lived here twenty-one years; personal property $500; married Miss Caroline George, Dec. 31, 1875; has one daughter; his wife was born in Chicago.

HARTMAN A. Farmer, Sec. 5; P.O. Hinckley; Dem; Luth.

HARRINGTON GEORGE, Farmer, Sec. 13; P.O. Hinckley; born in New Berlin, Chenango Co. N. Y. Sept. 26, 1835; lived there thirteen years, came to Kane Co. Ill, in 1848, came to this town and county in 1849, and has lived here twenty-eight years; Rep; Bapt; owns 160 acres of land, value $8,000; personal property $2,500; was in the service during the war two years and ten months; was with Gen. Hooker in campaign from Chattanooga to Atlanta, and with Sherman in his march to the sea, was in thirteen heavy engagements, was in hospital twice for short time, was honorably discharged at the close of the war; has been Town Collector, and is School Director; married Alvira A. Ward on Thanksgiving day, 1858; she was born near Bloomington, Ill; has three children, girls.

HASTIE G. Tenant Farmer, Sec. 11; P.O. Hinckley; Rep; Cong.

HASTIE J. Laborer, Sec. 11; P.O. Hinckley; Rep; Meth.

HASTIE W. Tenant Farmer, Sec. 11; P.O. Hinckley; Rep; Meth.

HAMLIN J. Blacksmith, Hinckley; Meth; Lib; from New York.

HALL STEPHEN A. Farmer, Sec. 21; P.O. Hinckley; Rep; Bapt; prop. $8,000; England.

HENRY ISABELLA Mrs. widow of Alexander Henry; Sec. 31; P.O. Waterman; born in Washington, May 14, 1808; lived there sixty-one years, came to Squaw Grove, DeKalb Co. Ill. in 1869; lived there since; U. Presbyterian Church; she married Alexander Henry, April 23, 1840; he died Dec. 23, 1876; has one adopted child; owns 40 acres of land, value $2,400.

HEMENWAY F. L. Farmer, lives with mother, Sec. 25; P.O. Hinckley; Rep; Meth.

HEMENWAY LOUISA J. lives on Farm, Sec. 25; P.O. Hinckley; born in Turin, Lewis Co. N. Y; lived there twenty-four years, lived in Herkimer Co. six years, taught school there, came to this state in 1843, lived four years in Will Co., has lived here twenty-eight years, is one of the earliest settlers; owns 164 acres of land, value $10,000; personal property $500; married William Hemenway in 1837; he was from Herkimer Co. N. Y; he died Jan. 1870; he was Town Assessor for ten years; has five children.

HENDERSON JNO. Rep; Meth; P.O. Hinckley.

HEROLD AUG. Farmer; P.O. Hinckley; Rep; Meth; val. of property $4,000; from Germany.

HITCHCOCK C. H. Physician; P.O. Hinckley; Rep; Lib; born in Maine.

HILL GEO. Carpenter; P.O. Hinckley; Rep; Lib.

HOOK WM. Wagon Maker, Hinckley; Advent; Rep.

HOWELL STEPHEN V. Farmer, Sec. 15; P.O. Hinckley; born in Prince Edward Co. Ameliasburg, Canada, Sep. 10, 1844, lived there seventeen years, then came to the United States and joined U. S. Military Telegraph Co. following the army with Gens. Blunt, Sanborn, Curtis, and Burnside, followed Price in last raid through Mo. was in service five and a half years, at close of war was in mercantile business in Aurora one year, was on C. B. & Q. R.R., and also on Hannibal & St. Jo. R.R; came here in 1868; married Miss Ella Sebree June 28, 1868; she was born here, and is the daughter of the oldest, and one of the wealthiest settlers in this county; Ind; Meth; owns 200 acres of land, value $15,000.

HOLDENHOUSE HENRY, Blacksmith; born August 23, 1819, in Montgomery Co. N. Y; lived there nineteen years, went to Jefferson Co. and lived there twenty-five years, came to this state in 1867; learned trade in Watertown, N. Y; Rep; Liberal; value of prop. $3,000; married Miss Mary Smith of Otsego Co. N. Y; she died in 1871; has three children, all daughters, one married and lives in Wisconsin.

HOPKINS CHARLOTTE Mrs. P.O. Hinckley; Lib. Church; value of property $500.

HOBBS G. E. Farmer, Sec. 8; P.O. Hinckley; Ind; Lib; value of property $15,000.

HOWESON ALEX. Farmer, Sec. 34; P.O. Hinckley; Rep; U. Pres; value of property $10,000.

HOLBROOK J. Laborer; P.O. Hinckley; Rep; Baptist.

HUBBARD JAMES A. Farmer, Sec. 35; P.O. Hinckley; William Tanner owns farm; born in Pierceville, this county, Jan. 10, 1853, and has lived here twenty-three years; Ind; Meth; value of personal property $750; married Miss Phebe Cone, Aug. 15, 1874; she was born in Town of Squaw Grove; has two children, girls.

HUBBARD H. Mechanic; P.O. Hinckley; Rep; Meth.

IRWIN T. Farmer, tenant, Sec. 34; P.O. Hinckley; Rep; U. Pres.

JACKSON J. F. Farmer; P.O. Hinckley; Dem; Lib; value of property $7,000.

JAMES F. Sec. 27; P.O. Hinckley; Rep; Bapt.

JONES H. Farmer, Sec. 1; P.O. Hinckley; Lib; value of property $8,000.

JOHNSON OLOF. Laborer; P.O. Hinckley; Rep; Luth.

JOHNSON B. F. Clerk; P.O. Hinckley; Rep; Meth.

JOHNSON JOHN. Farmer. Sec. 26; P.O. Hinckley; Lib. Luth; value of property $400.

JUDD R. M. Groceries and Dry Goods, Hinckley; Rep; Meth; from Wisconsin.

KENNEDY O. B. Mrs. P.O. Hinckley; Lib; value of property $4,000; from Mass.

KEAHLER N. Farmer, Sec. 21; P.O. Hinckley; Dem; Cath; from Germany.

KIRKPATRICK E. son of J. Kirkpatrick; Farmer; P.O. Hinckley; Rep; U. Pres.

KIRKPATRICK J Farmer, Sec. 31; P.O. Hinckley; value of property $10,000; Rep; U. Pres.

KIRBY PAT. Laborer on R.R; P.O. Hinckley; Dem; Cath; from Ireland.

KIMMERLY CHRIS, Laborer; P.O. Hinckley.

KING FRED, Shoemaker; P.O. Hinckley; Lib. Luth.

KOHLA C. Tenant Farmer. on Sec. 23; P.O. Hinckley; Lib. Luth.

KUTER SIMON, Carpenter, Hinckley; Rep; Evangl. Meth; from Penn.

KNTER SIMON E. Carpenter, Hinckley; Meth.

KUTER JOHN, Coal Dealer, Hinckley; Rep; Meth.

LANGSTON W. Laborer, Sec. 15; P.O. Hinckley; Lib. Rep.

LANGE CHRIS. Farmer, Sec. 26; P.O. Hinckley; born Ger; Ind; val. prop. $4,000.

LEIFHEIT WM. Farmer, Sec. 18; P.O. Hinckley; born Hanover, Germany, in August, 1821; came to this country 1850; lived in Kendall Co. one year; came to this county 1856, and has lived here twenty years; owns 525 acres land, value $26,000; personal property $2,000; holds office of School Director; married Caroline Eckhart, 1850; she was born in Germany; has eleven children—six boys and five girls.

LEIFHEIT WM. Farmer, Sec. 6; from tier; Dem; Luth.

LEIFHEIT EARNEST, Farmer, Sec. 18; P.O. Hinckley; farms father's farm; born in town of Somonauk. DeKalb Co. Ill. October 21, 1850; lived there five years; came to this town 1855 and has lived here ever since, twenty-one years; value of personal property $500; his father is one of the oldest settlers and property holders.

LEIFHEIT CHRIS. works on R.R; P.O. Hinckley; Rep; born Ger; Luth.

LEE EDWARD, Laborer, Sec. 34; P.O. Hinckley; Ind; Lib.

LEE R. Laborer, Sec. 34; P.O. Hinckley; Dem; Cath.

LEE G. W. Carpenter; P.O. Hinckley; Rep; Meth.

LEONARD FRANK. Painter; P.O. Hinckley; Rep; Cong.

LEINAUER JNO. Butcher; P.O. Hinckley.

LUSCUMB JOSEPH, Tenant Farmer, Sec. 33; P.O. Hinckley; born in Cramahe, Can. Feb. 4. 1843; live there fifteen years; came to St. Clair County, Michigan, 1868; lived there eight years, and then came to Town of Squaw Grove, this county, and has lived here ten years; Rep; Meth; owns 40 acres land, value $1,200; personal property $500; married Miss Annie Ordway, October 31, 1871; she was born in State of Maine; has one child, little boy.

LOVELAND L. C. Carpenter; P.O. Hinckley; Rep; Lib.

LOVELAND FRANK, Carpenter; P.O. Hinckley; Lib.

LOCKWOOD A. Harnessmaker; P.O. Hinckley; Rep; Lib.

MAN GEO. B. Laborer, Sec. 17; P.O. Hinckley; Rep; Bapt.

MAHAFFEY J. Farmer, Sec. 21; P.O. Hinckley; Rep; Pres; val. prop. $4,000.

MALTBIE HENRY M. Elevator and Grain; P.O. Hinckley; born Mt. Morris, Livingston Co. N.Y. Oct. 27, 1836; lived there eighteen years; came to Kane Co. 1854; lived there two years, came to this county 1856, and has lived here twenty years; owns farm 40 acres, $4,000; Rep; Meth. He and E. Price own and operate two elevators here at Hinckley, and have handled the grain here since the R.R. was built; they pay from $10,000 to $15,000 per year in freights alone, and they handle from 300,000 to 400,000 bushels yearly; they own two elevators, $12,000; they also own and operate elevator and lumber yard at Blunt.

MALTBIE H. Farmer, Sec. 13; P.O. Hinckley; Rep; Bapt; val. prop. $2,000.

MASON GEO. F. Farmer, Sec. 36; P.O. Little Rock; born N.Y.; Rep; Lib; val. prop. $6,000.

MANK AUGUST, Farmer, Sec. 36; P.O. Hinckley; born Ger; Dem; Pres; val. prop. $4,000.

McCLEERY MARTIN, Farmer, Sec. 30; P.O. Waterman; born in Wayne Co. Ohio, July 22, 1847; lived there four years, then came to Town of Clinton, DeKalb Co. Ill. and lived in that town twenty-three years; came to this town 1874; Rep; Pres; owns 163 acres land, $10,000; personal property $3 000; has held office of School Director; married Miss Sarah A. French, Jan. 21, 1872; she was born in Town of Somonauk; has three children— two boys and one girl.

McCARTHY M. Farmer, Sec. 28; P.O. Hinckley; Dem; Cath; val. prop. $5 000.

McELWAIN ROBERT, Farmer, Sec. 26; P.O. Hinckley; born County Cavan, Ireland, May 12, 1820, lived there forty-six years.; came to U. S. 1866; and came to this county in 1874; Rep; Pres; owns 80 acres land, $4,000; per. prop. $500; married Miss Frances Love, of County Cavan, Ireland; she died 1872; married Susan Hutton 1874; she was from Canada; has five children, lost one.

McGINNIS NELSON, Laborer with Foster, Sec. 25; P.O. Hinckley; Rep; Meth.

McCLELLAN J. Farmer, Sec. 34; P.O. Hinckley; Rep; U. Pres; val. prop. $7,000.

McCLELLAN S. N. Farmer, Sec. 34; P.O. Hinckley; Rep; U. Pres; val. prop. $4,000.

MERRILL F. E. Merchant; P.O. Hinckley; born N.Y.; Meth.

MILLER SAMUEL Jr. Proprietor Livery Stable; P.O. Hinckley; born in Town Squaw Grove, DeKalb Co. Sept. 2, 1851, and has lived here ever since, twenty-five years; farmed three years and run threshing machine; has been in livery business since March, 1875, the only one here; Rep; Meth. preference; owns lots and barns where he is doing business, and house and lot in the village, val. $5,000; holds office of constable.

MILLER SAMUEL, Farmer, Sec. 15; P.O. Hinckley; born in Harrison Co. Indiana August 1, 1808; lived there eight years; went to Floyd Co. 1816; lived there twenty year ; came to Town of Squaw Grove, DeKalb Co. in 1835, and has lived here forty-one years in October; only few houses between here and Belvidere when he came; only two houses between here and Aurora, and one house within twelve miles north; only three made claims in the town when he came; they are dead; plenty of Indians then; owns about 270 acres land, value $16,000; personal $4,000; Ind; Meth; married twice : first Miss Gelly M. Sebree, and the second Miss Jane Cone, from Oneida Co. N.Y.; has had eight children, four living.

MILLER MARSHALL, Farmer, Sec. 16; P.O. Hinckley; born Ind; Dem; prop. $7,500.

MILLER W. Farmer, Sec. 9; P.O. Hinckley; Rep; Lib; val. prop. $10,000.

MILLER SAMUEL, Livery; P.O. Hinckley; Lib.

MIKE JENNY, Sec. 32; P.O. Hinckley; Lib; Luth; from Germany.

MORSCH JACOB, Farmer, Sec. 29; P.O. Hinckley; born in Baden, Germany, Oct. 29, 1831; came to this country in 1847; came to LaSalle Co. same year; lived there thirteen years; lived in Town of Waltham, same county, eight years; came to this town and county Spring 1869, and has lived here seven years; Rep; Meth; owns 440 acres land, $22,000; personal $2,000; has been School Director and Path-master in his district; married Miss Elizabeth Smith in 1860; she was from Baden, Germany; has seven children—four boys and three girls.

MORTON H. M. Farmer, Sec. 20; Rep; Moravian; val. $12,000.

MOZ GEO. Farmer, Sec. 3; P.O. Hinckley; born Ger; Dem; Luth; val. prop. $5,000.

MULROY JOHN, Section Boss on R.R.; P.O. Hinckley; Dem; Cath.

MULROY H. Laborer on R.R.; Dem; Cath.

NASH W. F. Laborer, Sec. 15; P.O. Hinckley; Rep.

NESBIT G. Laborer; P.O. Hinckley; Dem; Meth.

NICHOLS CLARK, Farmer; P.O. Hinckley; Sec. 13; Rep; Bapt; val. prop. $5,000.

NORTH J. Laborer; P.O. Hinckley; Rep; Meth.

NORTON CHAS. M. Farmer; resides with his father, O. M. Norton, Sec. 2; Rep; Lib.

NICHOLS PAUL H. Farmer, Sec. 22; P.O. Hinckley; born in Chenango Co. N.Y. July 12, 1834; lived there eleven years; came to Kane Co. this state May, 1845; lived there fourteen years; came to this town, DeKalb Co. in 1859, and has lived here seventeen years; owns 405 acres land, value $22,000; value personal property $3,000; Rep; Bapt; has been Town Treasurer past fourteen years; married Miss Sarah Skiff, in Kane Co. Ill. from Warren Co. N.Y. in 1858; has four children—three boys and one girl.

NORTON ORRIN M. Farmer, Sec. 2; P.O. Hinckley; born Geauga Co. Ohio, near Cleveland, Nov. 27, 1824; lived there twelve years; came to this state and county in 1836; has lived here forty years; he and his sister, Orrie Norton, were twins; Rep; Lib; owns 305 acres land, $23,000; personal $2,500; has been School Director; married Miss Jemima Drake, Christmas day, 1853; she was from N.Y.; has had two children—lost one; their only son, Charles, lives at home, is married.

NORTON H. H. Minister; Sec. 6; Lib; Luth.

OLSEN NELSON, Laborer, lives with Mr. See, Sec. 35; P.O. Hinckley; born Denmark; Rep.

OTT JOHN, Farmer, Sec. 5; P.O. Hinckley; value $8,000; Rep; Luth.

OWEN G. Farmer, Sec. 20; P.O. Hinckley; value $4,000; Rep; Lib.

PALMER O. B. Farmer, Sec. 27; value $10,000; P.O. Hinckley; Rep; Bapt.

PALMER C. S. Billiard Hall, Hinckley; Rep.

PALMER GAIL, Carpenter; Hinckley; Rep; Meth.

PALM E. Carpenter; P.O. Hinckley; Lib; Lib.

PALMER M. M. Farmer, Sec. 36; P.O. Hinckley; born Mass; Rep; Meth; val. $60 per acre.

PACKARD W. O. Laborer, Sec. 15; Hinckley; Rep; Meth.

PECK B. W. Cooper; P.O. Hinckley; Rep; Pres.

PETERSON C. Carpenter; P.O. Hinckley; Ind; Lib.

PETERSEN JOHN, Laborer for P. Slater; Denmark; P.O. Hinckley; Luth.

PETERSON CHRIS. Carpenter; Hinckley; Lib; Luth.

PERRY JACOB, farm tenant, Sec 13; P.O. Hinckley; born Wales; Dem; Bapt.

PHELAN JAS. M. Farmer, Sec. 21; P.O. Hinckley; born Canada; Dem; Meth.

PICKMAN E. Farmer, Sec. 6; P.O. Hinckley; Ind; Luth; value of property $6,000.

POTTER GEO. Farmer, Sec. 13; P.O. Hinckley; Rep; Lib; prop. $2,000.

POTTER O. Farmer, Sec. 13; Rep; Lib; $2,000.

POILE R. Carpenter; P.O. Hinckley; Ind; Bapt.

POLLICK JOSEPH, works for E. Bushnell, Sec. 36; born N. Y.; Lib.

PRINCE A. F. Tailor; P.O. Hinckley; Rep; Lib.

PRICE HARVEY, Farmer; lives with father; Ind; Bapt.

REMSNIDER A. Farmer, Sec. 16; P.O. Hinckley; Ind; Luth.

REMSNIDER GEO. Tenant Farmer, Sec. 5; P.O. Pierceville; from Germany; Rep; Luth.

REED C. A. Furniture Store; P.O. Hinckley; Rep; Cong.

RADLEY ALBERT, Tenant, Sec. 15; born in New York State 1844, lived there four years; came to DuPage Co. Ill. 1848, lived there four years; went to Vermont in 1852, lived there seven years; came to Indiana in 1859; served during the war in the army, Gen. Wood was his division commander; was in the battle of Murfreesboro and Mission Ridge; was sick three months, would not go in hospital; married Miss Mary E. Seeley, 1869; has three children, two girls and one boy.

REINGARDT CHAS. Tenant Farmer, Sec. 16; P.O. Hinckley; from Germany; Rep; Luth.

RICHARDS REV. D. T. Clergyman; Rep; Bapt.

RICHMOND H. Tenant Farmer, Sec. 30; P.O. Hinckley; Rep; Lib.

ROSANDER JOHN ALBERT, lives with John Snook, Sec. 3; P.O. Hinckley; born in Smolin, Sweden, Sept. 25, 1844, lived there twenty-two years, and came to this country in 1867; came to Indiana; went to Rockford, in this state, four years; lived in Chicago and worked on B. and Ohio R.R.; Rep; Luth; value of property $100; has one sister in Rockford, and two brothers and two sisters in the old country.

RUGGLES F. L. Farmer; P.O. Hinckley; Rep; Bapt.

RUSSELL ARTHUR, Carpenter; P.O. Hinckley; from Mass.; Rep; Bapt.

SCHRAMM ——, Mechanic; P.O. Hinckley; Rep; Luth.

SCOTT HENRY, works on railroad; P.O. Hinckley; Rep; Bapt.

SCHELLA H. Farmer, Sec. 21; P.O. Hinckley; born in Hanover, Germany, Jan. 15, 1837; lived there thirty-two years, then came to this country, 1869; lived in New York two months; came to DeKalb County; worked four years for P. C. Nichols, now rents Dr. Hopkins' farm; married Minnie Pangrlnell, 1869; she was born in Brunswick, Germany; has three children, two girls and one boy.

SEVERANCE FRANKLIN C. Farmer, Sec. 13; P.O. Hinckley; born in Greenfield, Franklin Co. Mass.; lived in that state twenty-six years, then came to Big Rock, Kane Co. this state, in 1840; owns twenty acres land, $2,500; Rep; Meth; was Commissioner in Kane Co. and School Director; married Miss Hannah Winslow, of Charlamont, Mass. 1837; she was born in Colerain, Mass.; she died in May, 1848; have four children; married Melicent Hawks, of South Deerfield, Franklin Co. Mass. in 1854; she died in 1870.

SEVERANCE HENRY, Farmer, Sec. 24; born at Charlamont, Mass. March 11, 1838; lived in Mass. two years; came to Kane Co. Ill. in 1840; Rep; Meth; 164 acres land, $8,000; personal property $2,000; married Miss C. L. Henry, April 21, 1869; born in Smyrna, Chenango Co. N. Y.; has three children, all boys.

SEVERENCE GEO. Farmer, Sec 21; P.O. Hinckley; born Hinckley; Rep; Meth; val. $8,000.

SEEBREE SARAH J. lives on farm, Sec. 15; P.O. Hinckley; born in Erie Co. Penn. Feb. 7, 1813, and came to Kentucky in 1816; lived there five years, and came to Indiana and lived there eighteen years, and came to this county, Town of Squaw Grove, 1840, and has lived here thirty-six years; for one year after she came here her nearest neighbor was fourteen miles away, on Fox River; owns 600 acres land, value $36,000; was married to her husband, John Sebree, December 11, 1834; he was born in Virginia; he died April 30, 1863; has had five children, has two living, one boy and one girl.

SEE JNO. I. lives with father, Sec. 35; P.O. Hinckley; Rep; Bapt.

SEE JNO. Farmer, P.O. Hinckley; Ind; Lib; value of property $9,000.

SEELEY L. Blacksmith; P.O. Hinckley; Dem; Lib.

SEELEY LAFAYETTE, Carpenter; P.O. Hinckley; Dem; Bapt.

SEEBREE W. M. Manager Cheese Factory; P.O. Hinckley; Ind; Lib.

SLATER C. T. Lumber Dealer; P.O. Hinckley; born in Ill.; Rep; Meth.

SLATER P. F. lives with father; P.O. Hinckley; born in Ill.; Rep; Meth.

SLATER PHILO, Farmer, Sec. 15; P.O. Hinckley; born in Slatersville, Tompkins Co. N. Y. May 20, 1824, and lived there thirteen years; emigrated with father's family to Sugar Grove, Kane Co. Ill. in 1838, and lived there sixteen years; came to this county, Town of Squaw Grove, in March, 1854, and has lived here twenty-two years, and in the state thirty-eight years; Rep; Meth. his religious preference; owns 400 acres land, value $30,000; he has held office of Supervisor, Justice Peace, and other offices of Town and County; he married Miss Sallie Nichols, November 10, 1847, she was from Chenango Co. N. Y. and daughter of Dea. C. C. Nichols; they have five children, two sons, three daughters; his father, Thos. Slater, was one of the earliest settlers in Kane Co. and the state, and has lived here thirty-eight years, and is now eighty-eight years old; his wife, Mrs. Mary Slater, died October 8, 1874, they having lived together fifty-six years; the parents of both Mr. and Mrs. Slater celebrated their Golden Wedding the same year, one in June and the other on Thanksgiving Day, in the year 1868.

SMITH HENRY, Farmer, Sec. 4; P.O. Hinckley; born in Somonauk, LaSalle Co. Jan. 5, 1846; lived there twenty-eight years; lived on father's farm; came to this town and county 1874, and has lived here two years; Dem; Luth; owns 139 acres of land, value $6,000; value personal property $1,000; has held office of School Director; married Miss Mary Yagle in 1869; she was born in Hesse Darmstadt, Germany; has two children, boy and girl.

SMITH J. Farmer, Sec. 7; P.O. Hinckley; value $6,000; Dem; Luth.

SMITH J. W. Tenant Farmer, Sec. 11; P.O. Hinckley; Ind; Lib.

SNOOK JOHN, Farmer, Sec. 3; P.O. Hinckley; Lib; Lib; val. prop. $10,000.

STREVER JOHN, Farmer, Sec. 26; P.O. Hinckley; born in Argyle, Washington Co. N. Y. Feb. 17, 1823, and lived in that state 45 years; came to Sandwich, DeKalb Co. Ill. Feb. 19, 1868, and has lived here 9 years; Rep; Meth; owns 160 acres land, $10,000; personal prop. $1,000; has been School Director; married Nancy Armstrong in 1849; she was from Argyle, Washington Co. N. Y.; she died May 7, 1863; has five children; lost four daughters.

STRONG CHAS. Laborer, Sec. 15; P.O. Hinckley; Lib. Rep.

STEWART JNO. R. Farmer, Sec. 35; P.O. Hinckley; Lib; Pres; val. prop. $4,000.

STALDER WM. Farmer, Sec. 36; P.O. Hinckley; born Germany; Ind; Lib.

SUPEMA ED. Laborer, Sec. 15; P.O. Hinckley; Dem; Cath.

SWEET ALFRED E. Farmer, tenant J. E. Coster; P.O. Hinckley; Rep; Cong;

TALLMAN J. A. Banker; P.O. Hinckley; Rep; Meth; born Penn.

TAYLOR DAVID, Carpenter; P.O. Hinckley; Rep; Meth.

TANNER OSCAR M. Farmer, Sec. 15; P.O. Hinckley; born in Jefferson Co. Town of Alexander, N. Y. Feb. 3, 1828; lived there 8 years and came to Kane Co. Ill. in 1836, and lived there 23 years; came to Town of Afton in this county and lived there 6 years, and then came to Squaw Grove and has lived here 11 years; Rep; pref. Advent; owns 185 acres land, val. $14,000; personal property $2,000; has served as School Director a number of years; married Sarah J. Spaulding in Kane Co; she was born in New York in 1851; has five children, one son and four daughters.

TAYLOR C. H. Rep; Bapt; P.O. Hinckley.

THELEN J. Farmer, Sec. 11; P.O. Hinckley; prop. $10,000; Re ; Lib.

TIBBETS CHAUNCEY, works for J. McClelland, Sec. 34; Rep; Meth.

TREOGER F. J. Farmer, Sec. 32; P.O. Hinckley; prop. $10,00 ; Rep; Meth.

TUTTLE GEO. Carpenter, Hinckley; Meth.

VANORDEN P. Tenant Farmer, Sec. 10; P.O. Hinckley; Rep; Lib.

VAN NOSTRAND EUNICE, Milliner and Dressmaking, Hinckley; born in Onondaga Co. N. Y. June 1, 1839; came to this state and county, in Town of Somonauk, in 1843, and lived there until 1876; was Postmistress at Freeland for three years; came to Town of Hinckley in Spring of 1876, and built a store and opened the Millinery and Dress Making business; has very nice stock of goods, and is doing a good and constantly increasing business; Lib. religion; value of property $1,200; married M. R. Van Nostrand in 1866; he was from Dutchess Co. N. Y.; he was in the army four years; was killed while engaged in the Enterprise Manufacturing Works at Sandwich, in 1871.

VON OHLEN WILLIAM, Farmer, Sec. 3; P.O. Hinckley; born in Brunswick, Germany, May 14, 1843 came to U. S. 1843; came to this state in Sandwich same year, lived there two years, and has lived in this county ever since; Rep; Evang; owns 157 acres land, val. $7,000; val. personal prop. $1,000; was in the army 22 months, in Co. B 36th Reg. Ill. Volunteers, was wounded at Pea Ridge and Murfreesboro; married Mary Ann Roth in 1867; she was born in Germany; has two children, one boy and one girl; was Tax Collector in Town of Victor, and School Director of Squaw Grove.

WALKER J. Laborer; P.O. Hinckley; Rep; Lib.

WALLACE M. T. Harness Maker; P.O. Hinckley; Lib; Meth; born Mich.

WAGNER Mrs. P.O. Hinckley; Meth; val. prop. $2,000.

WAGNER H. D. Dry Goods and Groceries; P.O. Hinckley; Ind; Lib.

WARD JOSEPH, works livery; P.O. Hinckley; Rep; Bapt; born N. J.

WARD JOHN, P.O. Hinckley; born in Penn; Rep; Bapt.

WARD J. M. Butcher; P.O. Hinckley; Rep; Bapt.

WEST C. W. Butcher; P.O. Hinckley; Rep; Meth.

WEAVER NORMAN; Hotel; P.O. Hinckley; Lib; Lib; born Conn.

WHEELER S. Mechanic; P.O. Hinckley; Ind; Lib.

WHITE A. G. Clerk Lumber Yard; P.O. Hinckley; Rep; Lib.

WHEELER SAMUEL, Wagonmaker; P.O. Hinckley; Dem; Meth; born N.Y.

WHEATON G. L. C. Jeweler; P.O. Hinckley; Rep; Lib.

WHITE A. Farmer; P.O. Hinckley; Rep; Meth.

WIELERT WM. Farmer, Sec. 7; P.O. Hinckley; born in Brunswick, Germany, July, 1848; came to U. S. in 1869; came to Squaw Grove, DeKalb Co. Ill; has lived here 9 years; Dem; Luth; 160 acres land, $7,200; married Sarah Hartman May 6, 1873; she was born in this county; has one child, girl.

WILCOX C. Farmer, Sec. 28; P.O. Hinckley; Rep; Meth.

WINSLOW P. S. Rep; Bapt; val. prop. $10,000; P.O. Hinckley; born Mass.

WINSLOW F. L. Railroad Agent; P.O. Hinckley; Rep; Bapt.

WINSLOW A. C. Mrs. Farmer, Sec. 13; P.O. Hinckley; 140 acres; Meth; val. $8,500.

WIRKEN FRITZ, Tenant, Sec. 4; P.O. Hinckley; Rep; Luth.

WILLIE FRANK, Laborer; P.O. Hinckley; Rep.

WIKOFF L. H. Druggist; P.O. Hinckley; Rep; Lib.

WYOTT LEGRAND, Expressman; P.O. Hinckley; Rep; Meth.

YOUNG G. R. Rep; Bapt; P.O. Hinckley; born N. Y.
 YOUNG A. E. Carpenter; P.O. Hinckley; Rep; Bapt.
YOUNG FRANK, Mechanic; P.O. Hinckley; Rep; Lib.

ZIMMER WM. Clerk; Rep; Lib.

FRANKLIN TOWNSHIP.

ADAMS G. C. Farmer, Sec. 15; P.O. Kirkland; from Maine; Ind; Prot; val. prop. $6,000.
 ALLISON JAS. Farmer, Sec. 9; P.O. Wallace; from Penn; Rep; Prop; val. prop. $7,000.
ALLEN FRED. Laborer, R. B. Proctor's farm, Sec. 7; P.O. Wallace; N.Y.; Rep; Prot.
ANDERSON HENRY, Farmer; rents of W. Rowen, Sec. 10; P.O. Kirkland; Ca; Rep; Prot.
ARMINGTON WM. Wallace P.O.; from Boston; Dem; Prot.
AUER WM. Laborer; P.O. Wallace; from Milwaukee; Luth.
AVES F. Farmer, Sec. 15; P.O. Kirkland; from Ger; Dutch Cath; val. prop. $2,500.
AXERSON J. Laborer on B. N. Dean's farm; P.O. Belvidere; from Sweden; Dem.

BANKS GEO. W. lives with father, Sec. 5; P.O. Cherry Valley; Rep; Prot.
 BALL J. H. Merchant; P.O. Wallace; from Ohio; Rep; Prot; val. prop. $1,500.
BANKS ALFRED, Farmer and Stock Raiser, Sec. 5, Tp. 42, R. 3 E.; Cherry Valley P.O.; born Hartford, Oxford Co. Me. July 14, 1806; came to state and county July 4, 1845; Rep; Univ; owns 347 acres land; value real estate $17,400; val. per. prop. $7,000; was Road Com. ten years, Collector one year; wife was Sarah Foster, born Rome, Kennebec Co. Me. April 4, 1810; married Sept. 8, 1833; has had five children—four boys living, and one girl dead.
BALL C. C. Merchant; P.O. Wallace; from Ohio; Rep; Prot; val. prop. $1,500.
BARRINGER EDWARD, Farmer, Sec. 35; P.O. Kirkland; N.Y.; Rep; Prot; prop. $14,000.
BAUM MADISON, Carpenter; P.O. Wallace; from N.Y.; Prot.
BENSON HENRY, Farmer and Stock Raiser, Sec. 13, Tp. 42, R. 3 E.; born Christenstad, Sweden, May 21, 1837; came to U. S. October, 1853; came to state and county March 17, 1868; Dem; Luth; owns 120 acres land; val. real estate $4,800; val. personal property, $1,000; was first corporal 1st Ill. Light Artillery; wife was Johanna Nelson, born Christenstad, Sweden, April 1, 1825; married Sept. 1, 1858; has four children, two boys and two girls.
BENSON P. Farmer, Sec. 13; P.O. Kirkland; Rep; Luth; prop. $1,000; from Sweden.
BECKHORN E. Laborer; P.O. Wallace; from N. J.; Rep; Prot.
BLACO B. Merchant; P.O. Wallace; Bapt; from N. Y.
BOOTH HENRY, Laborer; P.O. Kirkland; from Eng; Prot.
BROWN HARRISON, P.O. Wallace; from Ohio; Rep; Meth.
BROWN ERASTUS, Carpenter; P.O. Wallace; Rep; Meth; from N.Y.
BRIGHT WM. Laborer; P.O. Wallace; from Eng; Rep; Epis.
BROWN MARTIN, Laborer, Sec. 5; P.O. Cherry Valley; from Eng; Epis.
BUTMER JOHN, Laborer, Sec. 9; P.O. Cherry Valley; from Ireland; Dem.
BURCHFIELD S. Laborer, Sec. 13; P.O. Kirkland; from Penn; Rep; Prot; val. prop. $150.
BURKE THOS. Laborer; P.O. Wallace; from Penn; Rep; Prot.
BYERS M. Farmer, rents of D. Miller; P.O. Wallace; from Penn; Rep; Prot.

CARLTON ALICE Mrs. widow of Claude; P.O. Kirkland; from Iowa.
 CASTLE WM. Farmer, Sec. 31; P.O. Wallace; from Eng; Epis.
CASTLE JNO. Laborer; P.O. Wallace; from Eng; Epis.
CAMPBELL WM. Farmer, Sec. 29; P.O. Wallace; from Ireland; Cath.
CAMPBELL SAMUEL, Farmer, Sec. 6; P.O. Wallace; Rep; Pres; prop. $3,500; from Ireland.
CHAMBERLIN BENTON, Farmer, Sec. 7; P.O. Wallace; Dem; Prot; prop; $3,000; N. Y.
CHAMBERLIN HENRY, Farmer, Sec. 28; P.O. Kirkland; Dem; Prot; $22,500; Belvidere, Ill.
CHURCHILL RICHARD, Farmer; P.O. Kirkland; Dem; Prot; prop. $8,000; from Vt.

CHURCHILL OLIVER, Farmer, Sec. 19, Tp. 42, R. 3 E.; P.O. Wallace; born in Fairfax, Fairfax Co. Vt. Jan 28, 1804; came to state and county Nov. 25, 1843; Ind; Prot; owns 220 acres land; val. real estate $10,000; val. personal prop. $1,000; was Justice of the Peace four years, School Trustee seven years; first wife was Pantha L. Andrews, born Cattaraugus Co. N. Y. 28, 1804; second wife was Nancy Riddle, born Jefferson Co. Tenn. Aug. 22, 1818; married to first wife Feb. 12, 1829; to second wife March 1, 1855.

CHRISTOFSON PLAT, Laborer on S. A. Fager's farm, Sec. 12; P.O. Kirkland; Luth; Norw.

CLINE H. M. Farmer, Sec. 7; P.O. Wallace; from Ohio; Univ.

CLINE HENRY, Farmer, Sec. 8; P.O. Wallace; United Brethren; prop. $4,500; from Ohio.

CLINE B. lives with father, Sec. 8; P.O. Wallace; from Boone Co; United Brethren.

CONNELLY P. Blacksmith, Kirkland; Dem; Cath; val. prop. $400; from Ireland.

COLE A. Cooper, lives with Henry W. Welty, Sec. 24; P.O. Kirkland; Rep; Univ. from Ca.

COLE L. L. Farmer, Sec. 23; P.O. Kirkland; Rep; Prot; from N.Y.

COLE S. G. Farmer, Sec. 23; P.O. Kirkland; Rep; Prot; from Ca.

COLE A. from Ca; Rep; Prot; P.O. Kirkland.

COUNTRYMAN S. Painter; P.O. Wallace; Rep; Meth.

COLEMAN JOHN, Laborer; P.O. Wallace; Cath.

COLEMAN E. Laborer; P.O. Wallace; from Ogle Co.

CROSBY PORTER, Farmer, Sec. 25, Tp. 42, R. 3 E.; P O. Kirkland; born Kingston, DeKalb Co. Ill. Dec. 29, 1855; Rep; Prot; owns 104 acres land; val. real estate $4,160; val. personal prop. $600; wife was Emma J. Barringer, born Franklin Tp. DeKalb Co. Ill. Aug. 17, 1858; married March 8, 1876.

CRONKHITE D. B. Farmer, Sec. 28; P.O. Kirkland; Dem; Prot; prop. $1,500; from Co.

CRONKHITE D. Farmer, Sec. 28; P.O. Kirkland; Dem; Prot; prop. $8,000; from N.Y.

CRAVER CHAS. Laborer; P.O. Kirkland; from Me; Rep; Prot.

CRAGE ROBT. Clerk; P.O. Wallace; from Boone Co; Rep; Bapt.

CROONAN JAS. from Ireland; Dem; Cath; P.O. Kirkland.

CULLIGAN THOS. Farmer, Sec. 27; P.O. Kirkland; from Indiana; prop. $2,000; Cath.

CUMMINGS JOHN, Farmer, Sec. 6; P.O. Cherry Valley; Rep; Meth; prop. $600; Ireland.

DAVIS CHAS. Farmer, rents of Alfred Banks, Sec. 4; P.O. Cherry Valley; Cath; val. prop. $1,000; from Sweden.

DAUGHERTY MICHAEL, Laborer; P.O Kirkland; from Ireland; Dem; Cath.

DEAN B. N. Farmer and Stock Raiser, Sec. 1, Tp. 42, R. 3 E.; P.O. Belvidere; born Paris, Oxford Co. Me. June 1, 1820; came to state and county May 1, 1838; Rep; Prot; owns 640 acres land; val. real estate $28,800; val. personal prop. $8,000; was Road Commissioner three years, Justice of the Peace four years, Supervisor three years; first wife was Lydia Smith, born Canada West, Oct. 18, 1822; second wife was Mary A. Parker born Augusta, Me. Oct. 13, 1840; married to first wife Nov. 6, 1844, to second wife April 29, 1872; has one child by first wife.

DEAN JOSIAH, Farmer, Sec. 3; P.O. Kirkland; Rep; Prot; val. prop. $500; from Mass.

DEAN WM. Sec. 16; P.O. Wallace; from Iowa; Prot.

DELAVERGNE GEO. Farmer, Sec. 28; P.O. Kirkland; Rep; Prot; prop. $2,500; from N.Y.

DECKER ALBERT, Laborer on B. N. Dean's farm; Sec. 1; P.O. Belvidere; Rep.

DECKER B. Grocer; P.O. Wallace; from Germany; Rep; Cath.

DELAVERGNE WM. H. Farmer, Sec. 28; P.O. Kirkland; Rep; Prot; prop. $2,000; N.Y.

DELAVERGNE NELSON, Farmer; P.O. Wallace; Rep; Prot; from N.Y.

DICKSON H. L. Laborer, Kirkland; Prot.

DONOHUE LAWRENCE, Laborer; P O. Wallace; from Ireland.

DRAKE I. R. Farmer, Sec. 29; P.O. Wallace; Prot; from N.Y.

ELLIS GILBERT, Cabinet Maker; P.O. Wallace; Meth; from N.H.

ELLITHORP J. W. Farmer; P.O. Wallace; Rep; Prot; from Ca.

EDLER FRED. Lumber Dealer; P.O. Kirkland; from Chicago.

EMHOUSE H. Farmer, Sec. 14; P.O. Kirkland; value of prop. $3,500; Rep; from Germany.

ERNST L. Farmer, Sec. 6; P.O. Wallace; value of prop. $10,000; Dem; Luth; from Penn.

EYCHANER JACOB, Laborer; P.O. Kirkland; Meth; from N.Y.

EYCHANER JOS. Laborer; P.O. Kirkland; Meth; from N.Y.

F AGER S. A. Farmer, Sec. 12; P.O. Kirkland; val. of prop. $3,000; Dem; Luth; Sweden.
FAGAN M. Farmer, Sec. 23; P.O. Kirkland; val. of prop. $3,000; Dem; Cath; Ireland.
FOX GEO. Sen., Farmer, Sec. 6; P.O. Wallace; value of prop. $5,000; Rep; Prot; Ireland.
FOX GEO. Jr. lives with father, Sec. 6; P.O. Wallace; Prot; from N.J.
FOX SARAH A. Mrs. widow of Allen, Sec. 5; P.O. Cherry Valley; Wes. Meth; from Ohio.
FOX HENRY, Farmer, Sec. 5; P.O. Cherry Valley; Rep; Meth; from Tp.
FOX TIMOTHY, rents of Wm. Gordon, Sec. 7; P.O. Wallace; val. of prop. $500; Prot; Co.
FORCE PAT. Laborer; P.O. Wallace; Dem; Cath; from Ireland.
FOSTER WESLEY, P.O. Kirkland; Rep; Meth; from Tp.
FOSTER WALLACE, P.O. Kirkland; Rep; Prot; from Co.
FOWLER A. D. Telegraph Operator, Kirkland; value of prop. $1,200; Rep; from Wis.
FOWLER JAS. Laborer; P.O. Wallace; Dem; Cath; from N.Y.
FREE M. Laborer; P.O. Wallace; Cath; from Rockford, Ill.
FURGASON B. Blacksmith; P.O. Wallace; Rep; Prot; from Boone Co.
FURGASON WM. Laborer; P.O. Wallace; Luth; from Sweden.

G ALLERNO C. Farmer, Sec. 16; P.O. Wallace; val. of prop. $500; Rep; Prot; from Canada.
GALLERNO D. Farmer, Sec. 17; P.O. Wallace; Dem; from Canada.
GALLAHER R. Laborer; P.O. Wallace; Rep; Spiritualist; from Ogle Co.
GARLAND H. Farmer, Sec. 14; P.O. Kirkland; value of prop. $4,000; Dem; Prot; N.Y.
GARDNER E. H. Clerk, Kirkland; Rep; Prot; from Boone Co. Ill.
GATES ELIZABETH Mrs. widow of George, Kirkland; val. prop. $1,000; Pres; Rochelle.
GATES WM. Laborer, Kirkland; Dem; Pres; from Rochelle, Ill.
GATES PHILLIP, P.O. Kirkland; Dem; Pres; from Rochelle, Ill.
GIBBS C. D. Farmer and Farmer, Sec. 1, Tp. 42, R. 3 E.; P.O. Belvidere; born in Springfield, Otsego Co. N.Y. Nov. 2, 1832; came to this state and Co. May 26, 1844; owns 125 acres, value $3,750; personal prop. $500; was School Director three years, Pathmaster four years; first wife was Mila A. Lucas, born in Franklin Tp. DeKalb Co. Ill. Jan. 1, 1845, and died March 10, 1863; his second wife was Amanda M. Bacon, born in Potter Co. Penn. Jan. 31, 1845; married to first wife Jan. 1, 1861; to second wife Jan. 28, 1873; has two children, one by first wife, and one by second wife; Rep; Prot.
GIBBS A. Farmer, Sec. 1; P.O. Belvidere; value of prop. $2,700; Rep; Meth; from N.Y.
GIBBS A. S. Farmer, lives with father, Sec. 1; P.O. Belvidere; Rep; Prot; from Co.
GIBBS W. Farmer, Sec. 1; P.O. Belvidere; came to Co. in 1845; Rep; Meth; from N.Y.
GIBBS B. S. Farmer, Sec. 12; P.O. Belvidere; Rep; Meth; from N.Y.
GILCHRIST WARREN, Farmer, Sec. 20; P.O. Wallace; Rep; Prot; from Co.
GILCHRIST ELIZABETH L. Mrs. wid. Dan'l M.; val. prop. $8,000; Univ; Long Island.
GILCHRIST CHAS. Farmer, Sec. 20; P.O. Wallace; Rep; Prot; from Co.
GLEIS C. Farmer, Sec. 7; P.O. Wallace; val. of prop. $2,500; Rep; Luth; from Germany.
GORHAM E. Farmer, Sec. 23; P.O. Kirkland; val. of prop. $2,500; Prot; from N.Y.
GOFF WM. Farmer, Sec. 12; P.O. Belvidere; Ind; Prot; from Co.
GREENHOW RICHARD, Farmer and Stock Raiser, Sec. 34, Tp. 42, R. 3 E.; P.O. Kirkland; born in England, Nov. 10, 1841; owns 264 acres, value $10,560; personal prop. $2,000; bachelor; Rep; Prot.
GREENHOW MARY Mrs. widow of Jas.; P.O. Kirkland; value of prop. $14,500; Christian.
GRAVES A. D. Farmer and Breeder of Ayrshire Stock, Sec. 30, Tp. 42, R. 3 E.; P.O. Wallace; born in Guilford, Piscataquis Co. Maine, April 25, 1826; came to this state Oct. 3, 1845; came to Co. in April, 1848; owns 160 acres, value $8,000; personal prop. $2,000; was Town Clerk six years, and Tp. Treasurer eleven years; wife was Salina L. Churchill, born in Cattaraugus Co. N.Y. May 3, 1831; married April 13, 1850; has six children, one girl and five boys; Rep; Prot.
GREENHOW JOHN, Farmer, Sec. 34; P.O. Kirkland; Prot; from England.
GUNN ELIZA A. Mrs. widow of Alex.; Sec. 17; P.O. Wallace; val. of prop. $8,000; Wes. Meth; from N.Y.

H ARRINGTON S. P. Farmer, Sec. 33; P.O. Wallace; val. of prop. $9,000; Rep; Vermont.
HATCH ELSY, Painter, Kirkland; val. of prop. $2,000; Rep; Meth; South Grove.
HALLER G. Farmer, Sec. 16; P.O. Wallace; val. of prop. $1,000; Rep; Luth; Switzerland.

18

HALLER JACOB, Farmer, Sec. 15; P.O. Kirkland; val. of prop. $4,000; Rep; Prot; Switzerland.

HARLEY WM., P.O. Wallace; Dem; Cath; Ireland.

HALT EDWIN, Farmer, Sec. 25, Tp. 42, R. 3 E.; P.O. Kirkland; born in Franklin Tp. DeKalb Co. Ill. Dec. 2, 1854; owns 90 acres land, value $3,600; personal prop. $1,000; was Path-master six months; wife was Ida J. Rote, born in Franklin Tp. DeKalb Co. Ill. Dec. 9, 1858; married Dec. 28, 1875; Rep; Meth.

HALTENHOFF CHAS. Saloon, P.O. Wallace; from Germany; Dem; Luth.

HARRINGTON SAMUEL H. Farmer, lives with father, Sec. 33; P.O. Wallace; Rep. from Co.

HALLADAY J. H. Farmer, Sec 9; rents of J. Allison; P.O. Wallace; Prot; prop. $400; N.Y.

HEISER WM. Laborer; P.O. Wallace; val. prop. $500; Rep; Prot; from Ill.

HESTER JNO. Laborer; P.O. Wallace; Dem; Cath; from Ireland.

HEYWARD THOS. Farmer, Sec. 23; P.O. Kirkland; Rep; Epis; from England.

HERSCH ALBERT, P.O. Kirkland; Luth; from Germany.

HICKS JOEL H. Farmer and Stock Raiser, Sec. 24. Tp. 42, R. 3 E; P.O Kirkland; born in Shelton, Genesee Co, N. Y. Aug. 10, 1816; came to state Aug. 9, 1840, came to county March 1, 1873; Rep; Prot; owns 180 acres of land; value of property $3,000; first wife was Thankful Kingsley, born in Oneida Co. N.Y. July 11, 1832; second wife was Ann E. Andrews, born in Albany, N. Y. Feb. 3, 1827; married to first wife May 1, 1849; to second wife March 5, 1873; has four children by first wife.

HOLLINSMITH JOS., P.O. Kirkland; from Rockford.

HOLLINSMITH STEPHEN, P.O. Kirkland; from Rockford.

HOLLINGSWORTH W. S. Butcher, Kirkland; Rep; Prot; val. of prop. $1,000; Illinois.

HOLLENBACK GEO. Laborer; P.O. Kirkland; Rep; Meth; value of property $500; Illinois.

HOLMES GEO. Farmer; P.O. Kirkland; value of property $10,000; Rep; Epis; England.

HODGEKISS JNO. Laborer; P.O. Kirkland; Prot; from England.

HOUSE C. Farmer, Sec. 5; P O. Cherry Valley; Rep; Meth; value of property $500; N. Y.

HOVEY SARAH Mrs. wid. Chas P.; Sec. 8; P.O. Wallace; Meth; val. of prop. $2,000; N. Y.

HUMPHREY P. J. Mrs. wid. Col. Thos. W ; Sec. 2; P.O. Belvidere; Meth; from Michigan.

HYSER JOHN, Farmer, Sec 31, Tp. 42, R 3 E; P.O. Wallace; born in Schoharie Co. N.Y. Feb. 28, 1816; came to state and county in Oct. 1864; owns 130 acres of land; value of real estate $8,450; value of personal property $2,000; wife was Julia A. Willesey, born in Schenectady Co. N. Y. Oct. 6, 1823; married Feb. 10, 1841; has had nine children, 2 dead, 7 living.

HYSER PETER, Farmer, Sec. 31; P.O. Wallace; Dem; Prot; from New York.

JOHNSON H. Farmer; P.O. Wallace; Rep; Prot; from Maine.

JOHNSON AUGUST, P.O. Kirkland; Rep; Luth; value of property $600; Sweden.

KEITH T. lab. on J. W. Kingsbury's farm, Sec. 10; P.O. Wallace; Rep; Prot; Illinois.

KELLY E. Farmer, Sec. 13; P O. Kirkland; Rep; Prot; val. of prop. $3,500; New York.

KEENAN JAS. Farmer, Sec. 23; P.O. Kirkland; Dem; Cath; val. of prop. $1,000; Ireland.

KINGSBURY J. W. Farmer and Stock Raiser, Sec. 10, Tp. 42, R. 3 E; P.O. Wallace; born in Franklin Tp. DeKalb Co. Illinois, Nov. 20, 1851; Rep; Prot; owns 298 acres of land; value of real estate $14,900; value of personal property $4,000; was School Director six months, Path-master eighteen months; wife was Sarah A. Dean, born in Franklin Township, DeKalb Co. Ill. Jany. 11, 1855; married Jany. 15, 1873; has one child, a girl, aged two years and ten months.

KIRK W. T. Merchant, Kirkland; Rep; Quaker; from Penn.

KIRK JAS. Farmer, Sec. 25; P.O. Kirkland; Rep; Prot; born in county.

KING O. Drugs; P.O. Wallace; Ind; Univ; from Illinois.

KIRK E. A. Drugs and Groceries, Kirkland; Rep; Prot; value of prop. $9,000; from township.

KOCH JOHN, Farmer, Sec. 19; P.O. Wallace; Dem; Prot; val. of prop. $5,000; from Penn.

KOCH JACOB, Farmer, Sec. 30; P.O. Wallace; Dem; Meth; val. of prop. $10,000; Penn.

KOCH LEVI, Farmer, Sec. 30; P.O. Wallace; Dem; Prot; value of property $5,000; Penn.

KOCH HENRY, Farmer, Sec. 19, P.O. Wallace; Dem; Luth; from Penn.

LARSON S. Farmer, Sec. 3; P.O. Kirkland; Luth; from Denmark.

LARSON GEO. Farmer, Sec. 3; P.O. Kirkland; Rep; Luth; from Denmark.

LANSON S. Farmer, Sec. 12, P.O. Kirkland; Luth; value of property $1,000; from Denmark.

LASKEY P. H. Laborer; P.O. Wallace; from Ireland.

LANG CASPER, Laborer, Kirkland; Rep; Luth; value of property $3,000; Germany.

LEE J. B. Butter Dealer, Kirkland; Dem; Prot; from Penn.

LEE S. S. Mrs. Millinery and Dress Making, Kirkland; Prot.

LEE T. H. Farmer, Sec. 2; rents of father; P.O. Kirkland; Ind; Prot; val. of prop. $300; Penn.

LEE JOHN, Farmer, Sec. 2; P.O. Kirkland; Dem; Prot; val of prop. $5,000; from Penn.

LILLEY J. W. Farmer; rents of H. O. Roke, Sec. 18; P.O. Wallace; Dem; Prot; from Ohio.

LIVINGSTON A. L. Hardware, Kirkland; Rep; Bap; value of property $4,000; Scotland.

LIPKEY JNO. Laborer; P.O. Wallace; Rep; Luth; from Germany.

LOSEE MORGAN, Farmer, Sec. 19; P.O. Wallace; Rep; Christian; from New York.

LOCKETT DANL. Laborer; P.O. Wallace; Rep; Prot; from Michigan.

LUCAS EBER, Farmer, Sec. 10, P.O. Kirkland; Rep; Prot; from Indiana.

LUNBAR L. Farmer, Sec. 14; Luth; value of property $1,600; from Sweden.

LUCKETT JOHN, Farmer, Sec. 8; P.O. Wallace; Rep; Prot; val. of prop. $4,400; county.

LYMAN JOHN, Farmer and Stock Raiser, Sec. 20, Tp. 42, R. 3 E; P.O. Wallace; born in Herkimer Co. N. Y. May 24, 1827; came to state and county June 1, 1854; Rep; Prot; owns 225 acres of land; value of real estate $12,000; value of personal property $2,000; first wife was Amelia N. Andrews, born in Oneida Co. N. Y. in 1833; second wife was Mary E. Reynolds, born in London, Eng. Dec. 25, 1840; married to first wife Oct. 28, 1856; second wife July 1, 1862; has two children by first wife, and two by second.

M ADDEN JOS. Carpenter; P.O. Wallace; from Chicago; Rep; Prot.

MACK WM. H. Farmer; P.O. Wallace; from N.Y.; Univ; val. prop. $2,500.

MACK W. S. Farmer; P.O. Wallace; from N.Y.; Rep; Prot.

MESSMORE WM. C. Farmer; P.O. Wallace; from Upper Can; Rep; Meth; val. prop. $8,000.

MESSMORE JANE wid. Jno. P.O. Wallace; from Can; Meth.

MERRILL H. F. Farmer, Sec. 25; P.O. Kirkland; from N.Y.; Free Thinker.

MILLER HENRY, Farmer and Dairy, Sec. 31, Tp. 42, R. 3 E.; P.O. Wallace; born Steuben, Oneida Co. N.Y. March 9. 1830; came to state and county Spring 1845; Rep; Meth; owns 400 acres land; val. real esta e $18,000; val. per. prop. $2,000; wife was Matilda Patten, born Starkville, Herkimer Co. N.Y. July 9, 1833; married Feb. 14, 1856; has three children —two girls and one boy.

MILLER R. Farmer, Sec. 14; P.O. Kirkland; from Germany; Evang; val. prop. $1,400.

MILLER O. M. Shoemaker; P.O. Wallace; from Rockford, Ill; Rep; Meth.

MILES HENRY, Farmer, Sec. 12; P.O. Kirkland; born Boone Co; Rep; Prot; val. prop. $150.

MILES W. Farmer, Sec. 12; P.O. Kirkland; Rep; Prot; val. prop. $12,000; from county.

MILES W. L. Kirkland P.O.; from Ind; Rep; Meth; val. prop. $1,500.

MIDDLETON JNO. Farmer, Sec. 14; P.O. Kirkland; from Ind; Rep; Prot.

MINER CHAS. Billiard Hall, Kirkland; from Co; Rep; Bap; val. prop. $1,000.

MINER ELIZA J. Mrs. wid. Daniel J., Kirkland; from N.Y.; Bapt.

MILL C. Laborer; P.O. Wallace; from France.

MIDDLETON EDWARD, Farmer, Sec. 13; P.O. Kirkland; from Ind; Dem; Prot.

McCOY I. N. Farmer and Stock Raiser, Sec. 11, Tp. 42, R. 3 E.; P.O. Belvidere; born Franklin Tp. Washington Co. Ind. July 23, 1816; came to state and county Jan. 1836; Rep; Bap; owns 233½ acres land; val. real estate $10,820; val. per. prop. $1,200; was Township Trustee two years, School Director ten years, Path-master three years; wife was Cynthia A. Pennell, born Fayette Co. Ind. Nov. 20, 1822; married Nov. 28, 1838; has seven children—two boys and five girls.

McCOY J. V. Farmer and Stock Raiser, Sec. 14, Tp. 42, R. 3 E.; Kirkland P.O.; born Franklin Tp. DeKalb Co. Ill. May 13, 1842; Rep; Meth; owns 114½ acres land; value real estate $4,000; val. per. prop. $1,000; was Collector one year, Assessor one year, Path-master one year and School Director six years; wife was Ellen Karnan, born in Dublin, Ireland, June 24, 1844; married Dec. 28, 1862; has five children—four boys and one girl.

McCUE TERRY, Laborer; P.O. Kirkland; from Wis; Dem; Cath.

McCARTHY EDWIN, Kirkland P.O.; from Can; Rep; Meth; val. prop. $500.

McDOWELL WM. Law Student; P.O. Kirkland; from Tp; Dem; Prot.

McDOWELL M. Farmer; P.O. Kirkland; from Tp; Dem; Prot; val. prop. $2,000.

McDOWELL W. A. Farmer, Sec. 1; P.O. Kirkland; from Co; Dem; Prot.

McDOWELL, JOHN, Farmer and Stock Raiser, Sec. 1, Tp. 42, R. 3 E.; Kirkland P.O.; born York Co. Penn. Dec. 2 1812; came to state and county Sept. 16, 1835; Dem; Christian; owns 215 acres land; val. real estate $8,600; val. per. prop. $2,000; was School Trustee three years, Path Master twelve years; wife was Martna Riddle, born Jefferson Co. Tenn. April 22, 1822; married Jan. 31, 1839; has six children—four boys and two girls.

McGINNIS JAS. Farmer, Sec. 11; P.O. Kirkland; from Ireland; Dem; Cath; val. prop. $3,000.

McKEE EDWARD, Laborer; P.O. Wallace; from Co; Rep.

McMULLEN WM. Farmer, Sec. 29; P.O. Wallace; from N.Y.; Rep; Prot; val. prop. $8,000.

McMULLEN CHAS. W., P. O. Wallace; from Co; Rep; Prot; val. prop. $1,000.

MOON JOHN, Farmer, Sec. 28, Tp. 42, R. 3 E.; Kirkland P.O.; born in Lancaster, Eng. Aug. 10, 1846; came to U. S. June. 1851; came to State and Co. June. 1851; Rep; Epis; owns 164 acres land; value real estate $7,380; val. per. prop. $2,000; wife was Angeline E. Travler, born Lycoming Co. Penn. Aug. 23, 1853; married March 16, 1874; has one child, daughter, aged nineteen months.

MOON THOS. Wallace P.O.; from Eng; Rep; Epis.

MOON WM. Farmer; P.O. Kirkland; from Co; Rep; Epis; val. prop. $4,000.

MOODEY EDWARD, Farmer, Sec. 7; P.O. Wallace; from Mich; Prot.

MOODEY AUGUSTUS E. Laborer, Sec. 7; P.O. Wallace; from Mich; Prot.

MOORE A. B. Farmer, Sec. 14; P.O. Kirkland; from Penn; Rep; Pres; val. prop. $10,000.

MONTGOMERY WM. Farmer, Sec. 29; P.O. Wallace; from Penn; Rep; Prot; prop. $1,000.

MONTGOMERY JNO. Farmer, Sec. 11; P.O. Kirkland; Prot.

MOTT HENRY, Farmer, Sec. 2; P.O. Kirkland; from Kendall Co; Rep; Prot; val. prop. $5,000.

MURPHY CHESTER, Laborer; P.O. Wallace; from Ca.

MURPHY RICHARD, Laborer. Jane Witter's farm, Sec. 9; from Canada; Rep.

MYERS SPENCER, Farmer and Stock Raiser, Sec. 20, Tp. 42, R. 3 E.; P.O. Wallace; born Milford, Otsego Co. N.Y. Oct. 12, 1816; Rep; Univ; owns 900 acres land; value real estate $3,600; val. per. prop. $5,000; was Constable twelve years.

MYERS C. T. Farmer, Sec. 35; P.O. Kirkland; from Germany; Luth; val. prop. $12,000.

NATHANIEL A. Laborer; P.O. Wallace; Rep; from Maine.

NELSON PETER, lives with son, Sec. 13; P.O. Kirkland; Rep; Luth; from Sweden.

NISEN H., Kirkland; value of property $500; from Germany.

NORMAN E. Farmer, Sec. 1; P.O. Belvidere; value of property $500; Rep; Prot; from Ca.

OSTIN ANDREW, Laborer; P.O. Wallace; Luth; from Sweden.

OVEROCKER MARY, widow of George; P.O. Wallace; Prot.

OVEROCKER JACOB, Laborer; P.O. Wallace; Rep; Bapt; from New York.

PAULSON B Laborer, B. N. Dean's farm, Sec. 1; P.O. Belvidere; Dem; Luth; Sweden.

PAULSON PETER, Farmer, rents of Thos. Dean; P.O. Kirkland; Rep; Luth; Sweden.

PAULSON JNO. Farmer, rents of Thos. Dean; P.O. Kirkland; Rep; Luth; from Sweden.

PETERSON C. J. Farmer, Sec. 1; P.O. Belvidere; Rep; Luth; val. of prop. $1,300; Sweden.

PETERSON O. Farmer, Sec. 13; P.O. Kirkland; Rep; Luth; val. of prop. $5,000; Sweden.

PETERSON C. Farmer, Sec. 3; P.O. Kirkland; Luth; from Denmark.

PENNELL LUKE, Farmer, Sec. 13; P.O. Kirkland; Rep; Christian; prop. $4,700; Indiana.

PENNELL J. N. Farmer, Sec. 13; P.O. Kirkland; Rep; Prot; val. of prop. $4,000; Illinois.

PERRY R. W. Farmer, Sec. 12; P.O. Belvidere; Rep; Bapt; from New York.

PITAN ERNEST, Laborer; P.O. Kirkland; Dem; Luth; from Germany.

PITAN WM. Laborer; P.O. Kirkland; Luth; from Germany.

PEAKE CHAS. Boarding House; P.O. Wallace; Rep; Meth; from Illinois.

POOL LEWIS, Wagon Maker; P.O. Wallace; Rep; Prot; from Michigan.

POWERS A. Laborer, Sec. 13; P.O. Kirkland; Prot; from Boone Co. Ills.

PROCTOR R. B. Farmer and Stock Raiser, Sec. 7, Tp. 42, R. 3 E; P.O. Wallace; born in Knox Co. Ohio, Sept. 29, 1827; came to state and county in Feb. 1839; Rep; Meth; owns 365 acres of land; value of real estate $14,000; value of personal property $2,500; was School Trustee three years; wife was Sarah C. Lyon, from Steuben Co. N. Y. born Feb. 14, 1837; married March 12, 1856; has eight children, five boys and three girls.

QUINN PATRICK, Farmer; P.O. Kirkland; Cath; Dem; value of property $700; from Ireland.

RANDALL B. Laborer; P.O. Belvidere; from Genesee Co. N. Y.

RAVNER WM. Farmer, Sec. 4; P.O. Wallace; Meth; value of property $500; N. Y.

REID S. B. Laborer; P.O. Kirkland; Rep; Prot; from Kansas.

RIDDLE JAS. Farmer, Sec. 11; P.O. Kirkland; Dem; Prot; val. of prop. $300; from Penn.

RIDDELL E. Grain Buyer; P.O. Wallace; Prot; from Cherry Valley, Ills.

ROWIN STEPHEN G. Farmer and Breeder of Devon Cattle and Red-eye Stock of Horses, Sec. 26, Tp. 42. R. 3 E; P.O. Kirkland; born in Batavia, Genesee Co. N. Y. Sept. 24, 1820; came to state and county in Oct. 843; Rep; Liberal; owns 500 acres of land; value of real estate $20,000; value of personal property $3,000; was Road Commissioner two years, Supervisor two years, Assessor seven years, Post-master one year; wife was Emelife B. Baker, born in Pompey, Onondaga Co. N. Y. Jan. 31, 1821; married July 11, 1847; has five children, four boys and one girl.

ROWIN BOYD D. Farmer, Sec. 36, Tp. 42, R. 3 E; P.O. Kirkland; born in Pembrook, Genesee Co. N. Y. March 9, 1824; came to state and county in May, 1843; Rep; Atheist; owns 200 acres of land in county and 320 acres in Iowa; value of property $30,000; wife was Mary L. Thomas, born in Clarendon, Genesee Co. N. Y. May 10, 1827; married Nov. 4, 1847.

ROWIN WM. H. Farmer and Stock Raiser, Sec. 26, Tp. 42, R. 3 E; P.O. Kirkland; born in Hebron, Washington Co. N. Y. Dec. 3, 1799; came to state and county in June 1843; Rep; Prot; owns 80 acres of land; value of real estate $8,000; value of personal property $800; was Road Commissioner three years, first wife was Betsey Gorham, born in Fairfield, Rutland Co. Vermont, May 17, 1801; second wife was Maria Gabey, born in Union, Broome Co. N. Y. Janv. 7, 1822; had nine children by first wife, and two by last wife.

ROWIN FRANK S. Agent; P O. Kirkland; Rep.

ROWIN FRED B. Rep; P.O. Kirkland.

ROWIN T. B. Farmer; P.O. Kirkland; from New York.

ROTE AMOS H. Farmer and Stock Raiser, Sec. 36, Tp. 42, R. 3 E; P.O. Kirkland; born in Blooming Grove. Lycoming County. Penn. June 20, 1829; came to state in Oct. 1845; came to county in Dec. 1847; Rep; Meth; owns 120 acres of land; value of real estate $6,000; value of personal property $2,000; wife was Hannah Ault, born in Muncy, Lycoming Co. Penn. Nov. 14, 1832; married April 17, 1855; has five children, three boys and two girls.

ROACH WM. Farmer Sec. 3; P.O. Cherry Valley; Rep; Prot; val. of prop. $2,500; Ohio.

ROACH H. Farmer, Sec. 3; P.O. Cherry Valley; Rep; Prot; val. of prop. $5,000; Ohio.

ROACH S. B. Farmer, Sec. 4; P.O. Cherry Valley; Rep; Prot; val of prop. $10,000; Ohio.

ROMNEY FRANK, Agent; P.O. Wallace; Epis; from England.

RORABAUGH S. Farmer, Sec. 4; P.O. Cherry Valley; Rep; United Brethren; Penn.

ROKE HENRY O. Farmer; P.O. Wallace; Prot; from New York.

RORABAUGH S. B. Farmer, Sec. 11; P.O. Belvidere; Rep; Prot; val. of prop. $400; Penn.

ROSE U. H. Farmer, Sec. 16; P.O. Wallace; Rep; Prot; from New York.

SAAM GEO. Laborer, Jno. McNeil's farm, Sec. 5; P.O. Wallace; from Germany; Rep; Cath.

SCHERRER JNO. Laborer, Kirkland; from Ohio; Rep; Prot; val. prop. $100.

SCHERRER E. Laborer; P.O. Wallace; from Rockford, Ill; Rep; Prot.

SCHOONMAKER REBECCA Mrs. wid. Jno; P.O. Kirkland; from Iowa.

SCHOONMAKER JNO. M. Farmer, Sec. 32; P.O. Wallace; from N.Y.; Rep; Meth.

SERGENT C. Farmer; P.O. Kirkland; from N.Y.; Rep; Prot.

SEARLE R. B. Shoemaker; P.O. Wallace; from Rockford. Ill; Rep; Meth.

SERGENT ALONZO. Laborer, Sec. 11; from N.Y.; P.O. Kirkland; Rep; Prot.

SEIBERT J. Farmer, Sec. 14; P.O. Kirkland; from Germany; Rep; Luth; val. prop. $2,500.

SELEE WM. D. Wagonmaker, Sec. 3; P.O. Kirkland; from N.Y.; Rep; Prot; val. prop. $1,500.

SHOREY J. Farmer; P.O. Wallace; from N.Y.; Rep; Meth; val. prop. $1,000.

SHEPHERD FRANK, Laborer; P.O. Wallace; from N.Y.; Rep; Epis.

SHRIVER DANIEL, Lab. Wm. N. Thompson's farm; P.O. Cherry Valley; Md; Rep; Prot.

SHAUEL CHAS. Lumber; P.O. Wallace; from N.Y.; Rep; Prot.

SLAYMAKER JASPER, Farmer, Sec. 7; P.O. Wallace; from Penn; Dem; Prot; prop. $500.

SPIERS R. B. M.D. Physician and Surgeon, Kirkland; from Ca; Epis.

SPENCER M. H. Mrs. wid. A. M. Sec. 5; P.O. Cherry Valley; from Ohio; Wes. Meth.

SPANSON T. Farmer, Sec. 1c; P O. Kirkland; from Eng; Rep; Prot; val. prop $4,000.

STRONG CHAS. W. Farmer, Sec. 6; P.O. Wallace; Meth; val. prop. $3,000.

STEWERT WM. Agent; P.O. Kirkland; from Co; Dem; Prot; val. prop. $2,000.
STENNER R. Farmer; lives with brother, Sec. 2; P.O. Kirkland; from Ger.
STENNER V. Farmer, Sec. 24; P.O. Kirkland; from Ger; Ger. Cath; val. prop. $4,000.
STENNER JACOB, Farmer; P.O. Kirkland; from Ger; Rep; Luth.
STENNER JNO. Laborer; P.O. Kirkland; from Co; Ger. Cath.
STRAWN JAS. Farmer, Sec. 8; P.O. Wallace; from Can; Dem; Prot; val. prop. $500.
STRAWN GEO A. lives with father, Sec. 8; P.O. Wallace; from Co; Prot.
STRAWN JAS. A. Farmer, Sec. 16; P.O. Wallace; from Co; Prot.
STRAWN THEODORE, Farmer, Sec. 3; P.O. Kirkland; from Tp; Rep; Prot.
STRAWN BENJAMIN, Farmer, Sec. 3; P.O. Kirkland; from Can; Rep; Univ; prop. $5,000.
STRAWN GEO. lives with father, Sec. 3; P.O. Kirkland; from Tp; Rep; Prot.
SULLIVAN DENNIS, Wagonmaker, Kirkland; from Belvidere, Ill; Dem; Cath; prop. $500.
SUTER J. Farmer, Sec. 10; P.O. Belvidere; from Ger; Prot.
SMITH PAT, Farmer, Sec. 23; P.O. Kirkland; from Ireland; Dem; Cath; val. prop. $5,000.
SMITH R. Farmer, Sec. 15; P.O. Kirkland; from N.Y.; Rep; Pres; val. prop. $2,000.
SWANSON S. Laborer, B. N. Dean's farm, Sec. 1; P.O. Kirkland; from Sweden; Rep.

THOMPSON A. Farmer, Sec. 12; P.O. Kirkland; Meth.
THOMPSON JOS. Farmer, Sec. 24; P.O. Kirkland; N.Y.; Rep; Meth; prop. $2,000.
THOMPSON WM. A. rents of L. Shirley, Sec. 5; P O. Cherry Valley; from Ca; Rep; Prot.
THOMAS WALTER, Laborer; P.O. Wallace; Rep; from Penn.
TRUDE JOHN, Farmer; P.O. Kirkland; from Can; Ind; Pres; val. prop. $500.
TURPIN B. Laborer; P.O. Wallace; from Penn; Rep; Prot.
TURNER JERRY, Farmer, Sec. 17; P.O. Wallace; Prot; val. prop. $500.
TURBULL SARAH Mrs. Wallace P.O.; from Mo; Prot.

UPSTONE PHILLIP, Blacksmith; P.O. Wallace; from Eng; Prot.
UPSTONE WALTER. Blacksmith, Kirkland; from Eng; Epis; val. prop. $700.
URE WM. Laborer; P.O. Wallace; from Rochelle, Ill; Dem; Prot.

VAN WERT WM. Farmer, Sec. 9; P.O. Cherry Valley; from N.Y.; Rep; Prot; prop. $5,500.
VANDRESER GEO. G. Farmer; P.O. Wallace; from Tp; Rep; Prot.

WALTZ HENRY, Laborer; P.O. Wallace; from Wis; Dem; Prot.
WALKER W. S. Laborer; P.O. Wallace; from Ohio; Rep; Prot.
WARE HENRY, Kirkland P O.; from Eng; Rep; Prot.
WEST HENRY, Laborer; P.O. Kirkland; from N.Y.; Rep; Prot.
WEBSTER HENRY, lives with brother, on Sec. 18; P.O. Wallace; from Lee Co; Rep; Meth.
WELTY H. W. Farmer and Miller, prop. "Lacey Mills," Sec. 24, Tp. 42, R. 3 E.; P.O.
Kirkland; born Washington Co. Md. March 10, 1822; came to state and county April 1856;
Rep; Evang. Association; owns 50 acres land; val. real estate $7,000; val. personal prop.
$1,000; wife was Sarah E. Ramsey, born Clearfield Co. Penn. July, 1837; married March
29, 1857; has had three children, two living and one dead.
WEBSTER L. Farmer, rents of D. Miller, Sec. 18; P.O. Wallace; Rep; Meth; from Lee Co.
WEAVER A. B. Farmer, Sec. 14; P.O. Kirkland; Dem; Meth; prop. $800; Penn.
WEED J. R. Farmer, Sec. 2; P.O. Kirkland; Univ; val. prop. $4,000; from N.Y.
WILLIAMS GEO. Wagon Maker and Carpenter, Kirkland; Rep; Prot; prop. $350; Penn.
WILLIAMS CHAS. Laborer on A. B. Moore's farm, Sec. 14; Rep; Prot; from Penn.
WITTER JANE Mrs. widow of Wm. Sec. 9; P.O. Wallace; Prot; val. prop. $2,000; N.Y.
WING A. Laborer on J. Suter's farm, Sec. 10; P.O. Kirkland; from Germany; Luth.
WILLIS LOUIS, Laborer; P.O. Wallace; Rep; Meth; from N. J.
WITTER JOS. Farmer, Sec. 2; P.O. Kirkland; from Co; Rep; Prot; val. prop. $4,000.
WOLCOTT A. J. T., M.D. P.O. Wallace; from Mich; Dem; Pres.
WOLCOTT P. Rep; Univ; P.O. Wallace; from N. J.
WOOD G. W. Grain Dealer, Kirkland; from Quincy, Il'; Prot.

WOOD J. H. Farmer; P.O. Wallace; from Penn; Rep; Prot; val. prop. $5,500.

WRIGHT JAS. Laborer; P.O.Wallace; Rep; Prot; from N.Y.

WRIGHT I. Farmer, Sec. 15; P.O. Kirkland; Rep; val. prop. $200; from N.Y.

YAGER CHAS. C. lives with father, Sec. 18; P.O. Wallace; Dem; Prot; prop. $600; Penn.

YOUNG J. Farmer, Sec. 4; P O. Wallace; Rep; Freewill Bapt; prop. $15,000; N. H.

YOUNG J. A. lives with father, Sec. 4; P.O. Wallace; from Co; Rep; Bapt.

ZIMMERMAN JAS. Farmer, Sec. 33; P.O. Wallace; from Ca; Rep; Prot; val. prop. $2,000.

SOUTH GROVE TOWNSHIP.

ADEE THOMAS, Farmer, Sec. 27; P.O. Malta; Delaware Co. N.Y.; Rep; Prot; prop. $13,750.

ALBERDING WM. Farmer, Sec. 20; P.O. Malta; from Germany; Luth; val. prop. $3,200.

ADEE GEORGE D. Farmer, Sec. 14; P.O. South Grove; born Delaware Co. N.Y. Dec. 2, 1838; came to state and county Oct. 1843; Rep; Meth; owns 310 acres land; value real estate, $12,400; val. per. prop. $4,000; wife was Elizabeth J. Nichols, born Og'e Co. Ill. March 17, 1845; married Dec. 25, 1866; has three children—two boys and one girl.

ANDERSON JOHN, Laborer; P.O. Dustin; from Sweden; Rep; Luth.

ANDERSON JOHN, P.O. South Grove; from Sweden; Dem; Luth.

ASHELFORD A. Farmer, Sec. 36; P.O. DeKalb; born Somersetshire, Eng. Feb. 24, 1833; came to state and county Dec. 24, 1855; Rep; owns 520 acres land; value real estate, $18 200; val. per. prop. $4,000; wife was Ellen McMurchy, born Upper Canada, July 6, 1834; married Feb. 3, 1862; has four children—two boys and two girls.

ASHELFORD GEO. Farmer, Sec. 25; P.O. South Grove; Eng; Rep; Prot; val. prop. $12,600.

AXTER JOHN, P.O. Dustin; from N.Y.

AYRES C. Laborer on Robt. Hutcheson's farm; P.O. Malta; from Virginia; Dem; Meth.

BAXTER WM. Farmer, Sec. 20; P.O. Creston; from Eng; Rep; value property, $500.

BARNES WALTER, Farmer; rents of Wm. M. Byers, Sec. 11; P.O. South Grove; from N.Y.; value property, $3,560; Dem; Meth.

BECKER RICHARD, Farmer; lives with son, Sec. 16; P.O. Dustin; from Green Co. N.Y.; Rep.

BECKER EDWARD L. Farmer; P.O. Dustin; from Delaware Co. N.Y.; Rep; Meth.

BEAN JOHN, Laborer on A. B. Byers' farm, Sec. 10; P.O. South Grove; Ireland; Dem; Cath.

BEDDALL GEO. P.O. Dustin; from Eng; Prot.

BECKER JOHN T. Farmer, Sec. 16; P.O. Dustin; from Green Co. N.Y.; Rep; Meth.

BINNING WM. Farmer, Sec. 20; P.O. South Grove; from Germany; Rep; Luth; prop. $3,200.

BISHOP ALBERT, Laborer on A. Ashelford's farm, Sec. 25; P.O. DeKalb; from Eng; Rep.

BISHOP CHAS. Laborer on A. Ashelford's farm, Sec. 25; P.O. DeKalb; from Eng; Rep; Prot.

BODDEN F. Laborer on Geo. Kempson's farm; P.O. Creston; from Erg; Epis.

BOSS FRED. Farmer; P.O. Dustin; from Germany; Luth.

BRADLEY WM. Farmer; P.O. Dustin; from N.Y.; Rep; Pres.

BROWN ANDREW, Laborer on Jas. Stack's farm; Prot; P.O. South Grove.

BURGDORFF BRIDGEHAM, Farmer, Sec. 30; P.O. Creston; born Herkimer Co. N.Y. Aug. 11, 1853; came to state and county 1859; Rep; Meth; owns 160 acres land; value real estate $7,200; val. per. prop. $1,000; wife was Louella S. Irwin, born Washington Co. N.Y. Sept. 13, 1859.

BYERS A. B. Farmer and Stock Raiser, Sec. 10; P.O. South Grove; born Delaware Co. N.Y. Oct. 22, 1831; came to state and county Oct. 1842; Rep; Prot; owns 1,120 acres land; val. real estate $48,100; val. per. prop. $4,000; wife was Mary A. McCrae, born Canada West, Nov. 11, 1834; married Feb. 21, 1857; has eight children.

BYERS WILLIAM M. Farmer, Sec. 15; P.O. South Grove; born Delaware Co. N. Y. March 20, 1821; came to state and county Oct. 23,*1841; Rep; Prot; owns 967 acres land; value real estate $40,000; val. per. prop. $4,000; was School Trustee, Road Commissioner one year, Supervisor ten years, and Tp. Tre·s, eighteen years; wife was Jane Adee, born Delaware Co. N.Y.; married Sept. 1, 1859; has four children.

BYERS JOHN, lives with father, Sec. 15; P.O. South Grove; from Co; Rep; Meth.

BYERS ROBT. lives with father, Sec. 13; P.O. South Grove; from DeKalb Co.; Rep; Meth.

BYERS JAMES, Farmer, Sec. 13; P.O. South Grove; from N.Y.; Rep; Prot; val. prop. $42,500.

CASLINE A. J. Laborer, Wm. M. Byers' farm, Sec. 15; P.O. South Grove; Dem.

CASLER M. Farmer; P.O. Dustin; from N.Y.; Dem; Meth.

CHAPELL ENOCH, Farmer, Sec. 34; P.O. Malta; Berkshire, Mass; prop. $11,000; Rep; Cong.

CHAPELL WILLIAM D. Laborer, Geo. J. Dettmer's farm, Sec. 19; P.O. Deerfield Prairie; from Beloit, Wis; Rep; Bapt.

CHRISTIANSON NELSON, Laborer, E. Chapell's farm; P.O. Malta; Denmark; Rep; Luth.

CLARK WM. Farmer, Sec. 17; P.O. Deerfield Prairie; from France.

COFFEE MICHAEL, P.O. South Grove; from Ireland; Dem; Cath.

COFFEE WM. P.O. South Grove; from Ireland; Dem; Cath; val. prop. $3,500.

COYN EDWARD, Laborer; P.O. Kirkland; from Ireland; Dem; Cath.

COREY MARY E. Mrs. widow of Daniel Corey, Sec. 34; P.O. Malta; born Hampshire Co. Mass. December 17, 1827; came to state and county November, 1856; Bapt; 320 acres; value real estate $15,000; personal property $2,000; married February 4, 1851.

COREY GEO. Laborer; P.O. Malta; from Mass-; Rep; Bapt.

COX R. Farmer, Sec. 21; P.O. Malta; from Kendall Co; Rep; val. prop. $11,000.

CONNORS DENNIS, Laborer, Henry Mace's farm; P.O. Malta; from Ireland; Dem; Cath.

CORLSON JOHN, Laborer; P.O. Sycamore; from Sweden; Luth.

COOMBS JOS. P.O. South Grove; from Eng.

CORTRIGHT MARTIN, Laborer; P.O. Dustin; from Mich.

CHRISTMAN HENRY, Farmer and Stock Raiser, Sec. 8; P.O. Dustin; born in German Flats, Herkimer Co. N.Y. Feb. 1, 1831; came to state and county Feb. 13, 1855; Rep; Prot; owns 525 acres land; value real estate $23,625; val. per. prop. $4,000; has been Postmaster four years, Assessor one year, Road Com. four years; wife was Louisa C. Pooler, born German Flats, Herkimer Co. N.Y. Feb. 6, 1837; married Dec. 29, 1853; has three children, all girls.

CRUIKSHANK JAMES, Laborer, T. Renwick's farm, Sec 2; P.O. So. Grove; Pres; Ireland.

CRONAN JAS. Laborer on A. B. Byers' farm, Sec. 10; P.O. South Grove; Cath; Ireland.

CRETAN M. Laborer on A. Ashelford's farm, Sec. 36; P.O. Lodi; Dem; Cath; from Ireland.

CURRIER E. Farmer, Sec. 13; P.O. South Grove; val. of prop. $5,500; Dem; Epis; N. H.

CUPP JAS. Carpenter; P.O. Wallace; Rep; Prot; from Virginia.

DECKER CHAS. Laborer; P.O. Dustin; Dem; from New York.

DECKER MARGARET Mrs. widow of James; P.O. Dustin; Meth; from New Jersey.

DETTMER GEO. WM. Farmer, Sec. 19, Tp. 41, R. 3 E; born in Hesse, Germany, Feb. 11, 1808; came to state and county April 3, 1858; Rep; Evang; owns 80 acres of land; value of real estate $3,600; wife was Wilmina Alderding, born in Hesse, Germany, June 14, 1810; married Jany. 1836; has five children.

DETTMER CHAS. W. Farmer, Sec. 19, Tp. 41, R. 3 E; P.O. Deerfield Prairie; born in Hesse, Germany, March 3, 1839; came to state and county in 1856; Rep; Evang; owns 80 acres of land; value of real estate $3,200; value of personal property $1,000; wife was Mary Koch, born in Franklin, Penn. Jany. 17, 1838; married Jany. 1, 1866; has 3 children.

DETTMER GEORGE J. Farmer, Sec. 19, Tp. 41, R. 3 E; P.O. Deerfield Prairie; born in Hesse, Germany, Feb. 26, 1848; came to state and county April 3, 1858; Rep; owns 243 acres of land; value of real estate $10,935; value of personal property $4,000; has been assessor two years.

DECKER WARREN, Farmer; P.O. Dustin; value of property $2,000; Rep; Meth; Ohio.

DECKER WM. Farmer; P.O. Dustin; value of property $6,000; Rep; Meth; from Ohio.

DENNIS ISAAC, P.O. Malta; Meth; Dem; from New York.

DEDRICK M. L. Farmer, Sec 35; P.O. Malta; Rep; Prot; from Columbia Co. N. Y.

DIXON LAVAUNT, P.O. Kirkland; Dem; Univ; from Miss.

DOANE CHARLES, Farmer, Sec. 35, T. 41, R. 3 E; P.O. Malta; born in St. Lawrence Co. N. Y. July 13, 1835; came to state and county Feb. 28, 1860; Dem; Protestant; owns 160 acres of land; value of real estate $6,400; value of personal property $1,500; wife was Harriet M. Munroe born in Waddington, St. Lawrence Co. N. Y; married Jany. 4, 1860; has four children.

DOGAN FRANK, P.O. South Grove; Dem; from Wisconsin.

DONOHUE JOHN, Laborer; P.O. Deerfield Prairie; Dem; Cath; from Ireland.

DOLAN PHILLIP, Laborer; Sec. 15; P.O. South Grove; Dem; Cath; New York.

DONNELLY EUGENE, Laborer; Sec. 13; P.O. South Grove; Dem; Cath; from Ireland.

DRAIM HIRAM, Farmer, rents of Andrew Jackson, Sec. 6; P.O. Deerfield Prairie; value of property $500; Rep; Cong; from New York.

DRISKELL T. D., P.O. South Grove; Rep; Prot; from Tp.

EMMERSON F. laborer on A. Ashelford's farm, Sec. 36; P.O. DeKalb; Rep; Prot.

ERICKSON CHAS. Laborer; P.O. Dustin; Rep; Luth; from Sweden.

ERICKSON ALBERT, Laborer; P.O. Dustin; Luth; from Sweden.

FETTERLEY H. B. Laborer; P.O. Dustin; Rep; Meth; from New York.

FETTERLEY JACOB, P O. Dustin; Rep; from New York.

FOX CLARENCE P. Farmer, Sec. 4, Tp. 41, R. 3 E; P.O. Kirkland; born in Oneida Co. N. Y. April 14, 1853; came to state and county in Sep. 1873; Dem; Protestant; owns 140 acres of land; value of real estate $6,300; value of personal property $1,000; bachelor.

FOX CLINTON D. Farmer, P.O. Wallace; Dem; Prot; from New York.

FOLEY JAMES, P.O. Dustin; from Harrisburg, Penn; Cath.

GARLOCK WM. rents farm of M. Casler; P.O. Dustin; Rep; Meth; from New York.

GIBSON JAMES, Farmer, Sec. 23; P.O. So. Grove; Rep; Pres; prop. $16,580; Scotland.

GIBSON WM. Farmer and Stock Raiser, Sec. 26, Tp. 41, R. 3 E; P.O. South Grove; born in DeKalb Co. Ill. Oct. 23, 1851; Rep; Meth; owns 160 acres of land; value of real estate $7,000; value of personal property $1,000; wife was Alice Murphy, born in Wilmington, Del. Feb. 25. 1856; married March 2, 1876.

GIBSON JOHN, P.O. South Grove; Rep; Prot.

GILLIS GEORGE A. Farmer, Sec. 32, Tp. 41, R. 3 E; P.O. Creston; born in Washington Co. N. Y. June 7, 1824; came to state and county Aug. 9, 1851; Rep; Protestant; owns 240 acres of land; value of real estate $10 600; value of personal property $2,000; was Road Commissioner two years, Supervisor two years, Post-master four years, Township Clerk two years; wife was Amy T. Irving, born in Washington Co. N. Y; married Nov. 13, 1855; has six children.

GOODRICH F. S. Laborer; P.O. Dustin; Rep; Meth.

GREENHOW WM. C. Farmer and Stock Raiser, Sec. 3, Tp. 41, R. 3 E; P.O. Kirkland; born in Franklin Tp. DeKalb Co. Ill. Jany. 10, 1843; Rep; Christian; owns 198 acres of land; value of real estate $10.890; value of personal property $2,000; wife was Emma Hyser, born in Schenectady Co. N.Y. Dec. 18, 1856; married Sept. 2, 1873; has one boy.

GRIFFITH SAMUEL, P.O. South Grove; Dem; from Maryland.

HARMAN JOHN, Farmer; P.O. Dustin; value of property $200; Rep; Meth; from Canada.

HEMMING JAS. P.O. DeKalb; Epis; from England.

HOOKER GEORGE C. Farmer and Stock Raiser, Sec. 35, Tp. 41, R. 3 E; P.O. Malta; born in Wyoming Co. N. Y. Aug. 20, 1835; came to state and county in 1857; Dem; Protestant; wife was Sarah C. Tobias, born in Wyoming Co. N. Y. Jany. 1, 1841; married March 16, 1862.

HOYT IRA, Laborer, Geo. Adee's farm, Sec. 14; P.O. South Grove; Rep; Bapt; from N. Y.

HOLDERNESS THOS. Laborer on G. W. Worden's farm, Sec. 16; P.O. Malta; Prot; Ca.

HOXE PETER, Farmer; P.O. Dustin; Dem; Meth; from New York.

HOWE F. W. Peddler; P.O. Dustin; from Vermont; Rep; Adventist.

HOWE WM. Laborer; P.O. Dustin; from Rockford, Ill.

HOWE C. M. Blacksmith; P.O. Dustin; from Rockford, Ill; Rep; Meth.

HOWE WM. Laborer; P.O. Dustin; Rep; Meth.

HUGHES MICHAEL, Laborer on Geo. M. Tindall's farm, Sec. 10; P.O. South Grove; Dem; Meth; from New York City.

HUTCHESON ROBT. Farmer, Sec. 29; P.O. Malta; Scotland; Rep; Pres; prop. $8,200.

HUTCHESON GEO. from Scotland; P.O. South Grove; Ind; Pres.

JACKSON WM. Laborer on Wm. M. Byers' farm, Sec. 15; P.O. South Grove; Eng; Rep; Meth.

JACKSON ANDREW, Farmer, Sec. 30; P.O. Creston; Rep; Meth; prop. $8,215; N. Y.

JARVIS EDWARD, Farmer; P O. Wallace; from England; Epis.

JOHNSON S. Farmer; P.O. Malta; from Denmark; Luth.

JOHNSON PETER, Laborer on John McKenzie's farm; P.O. Malta; from Denmark; Luth.

JOHNSON FRED. Laborer on Thos. Adee's farm; P.O. Malta; from N. Y.; Rep; Meth.

JOHNSON L. lives with son, on Sec. 29; P.O. Malta; from Denmark; Luth.

JOHNSON M. C. Laborer on P. Rickard's farm; P.O. Deerfield Prairie; Rep; Luth; Denmark.

JOHNSON ROBT. Laborer on P. Rickard's farm; P.O. Deerfield Prairie; Dem; Pres; Wis.

JOHNSON A. Laborer on Walter Barnes' farm, Sec. 11; P.O. South Grove; from Germany.

JONES O. Farmer. Sec. 22, P.O. Malta; Rep; Protestant; val. prop. $4,000; from South Wales.

KENDRICK ORVIL, P.O. Dustin; Rep; Meth; from N. Y.

KENNEDY PATRICK, Laborer; P.O. South Grove; from Ireland; Dem; Cath.

KENNEDY JAMES, Farmer, Sec. 33, Tp. 41, R. 3 E.; P.O. Malta; born Co. Donegal, Ireland; came to state and county March 1861; Dem; Cath; owns 160 acres, value $5,600; personal, $300; wife was Mary Frees, born Co. Donegal, Ireland, May 16, 1829; married Sept. 17, 1858; has nine children.

KEENAN ROBERT, P.O. South Grove; from Wis; Dem; Cath.

KEMPSON GEO. Farmer, Sec. 32; P.O. Creston; from Eng; Rep; Meth; val. prop. $12,600.

KING E. C. Farmer; P.O. Dustin; Rep; Meth; val. prop. $5,000; from N. Y.

LASKEY THOS. A. Farmer; P.O. Wallace; from Eng; Dem; Epis; val. prop. $7,000.

LASKEY PETER P. Laborer; P.O. Wallace; from Eng; Dem; Epis.

LASKEY EUGENE A. Laborer; P. O. Wallace; from Belvidere, Ill; Dem; Epis.

LANE JOHN, Laborer on Geo. C. Hooker's farm, Sec. 35; P.O. Malta; Dem; Cath; Ireland.

LANDT JOHN, Painter; P.O. Creston; from Rockford, Ill.

LAKE WARREN, Laborer on J. S. Shaver's farm, Sec. 21; P.O. Malta; Rep; Meth; Ohio.

LLOYD JOHN, Farmer, Sec. 27, Tp. 41. R. 3 E.; P.O. Malta; born South Wales, May 9, 1827; came to state and county October, 1852; Rep; Protestant; owns 240 acres land, val. $10,800; val. personal prop. $2,500; wife was Catherine R. Jones, born South Wales, Oct. 31, 1830; married July 24, 1850; has five children, all girls.

LLOYD S. Farmer, Sec. 34; P.O. Malta; from Mass; Rep; Cong.

MASTERSON JOHN, lives with father, Sec. 13; P.O. South Grove; Dem; Cath; Ireland.

MASTERSON JOS. Laborer, Sec. 10; P.O. South Grove; Dem; Cath; from N. Y.

MACE MARY A. Mrs. widow of James, who was born Chalmsford, Oxfordshire, Eng. Oct. 17, 1800, died Feb. 2, 1871, age 70 yrs. and 4 mos; Mrs. Mace lives on Sec. 16, Tp. 41, R. 3 E.; P.O. Dustin; born Isle of Wight, Hampshire, Eng. Oct. 6, 1814; came to county April 23, 1859; Epis; owns 40 acres land; val. prop. $1,900; married April 3, 1862; has three children.

MACE HENRY, Farmer, Sec. 33, Tp. 41, R. 3 E.; P.O. Malta; born London, Eng. July 12, 1834; came to state and county October, 1851; Dem; Epis; owns 240 acres land; value real estate $9,600; val. personal prop. $2,500; wife was Mary E. Worden, born Pine Creek, Ill; April 7, 1839; married Jan. 2, 1867; has four children.

MASTERSON LAWRENCE, Farmer, Sec. 13, Tp. 41, R. 3 E.; P.O. South Grove; born Co. Meath, Ireland, Aug. 15, 1813; came to U. S. May 15, 1850; came to state and county May 13, 1855; Dem; Cath; owns 230 acres land; val. real estate $9,200; val. personal prop. $4,000; wife was Mary O'Brian, born Co. Meath, Ireland, Feb. 4, 1815; married Nov. 25, 1839; has eleven children.

MASTERSON P. from Ireland; Dem; Cath; P.O. South Grove.

MADDEN RICHARD, Laborer on Wm. M. Byers' farm, Sec. 15; P.O. South Grove; Cath; Ire.

MADSON S. Laborer on S. Lloyd's farm; P.O. Malta; from Denmark; Rep; Meth.

MADSEN H. Laborer on S. Johnson's farm; P.O. Malta; from Denmark; Luth.

MARTIN JOHN, Farmer; rents of Jas. Renwick, Sec. 21; P.O. Malta; from Ireland; Cath.

MACE EDWARD J. Laborer; P.O. Dustin; from England; Epis.

McCARTY PATRICK, Laborer, Sec. 24; P.O. South Grove; from Ireland; Dem; Cath.

McCRAE FRANK, Laborer on Thos. Renwick's farm, Sec. 2; P.O. South Grove; Rep; Iowa.

McKENZIE JOHN Jr. Farmer, Sec. 32; P.O. Malta; Rep; Prot; prop. $15,200; Scotland.

McKENZIE JOHN Sr. Farmer, Sec. 29; P.O. Malta; Rep; Pres; prop. $3,700; from Scotland.

McKENZIE WM. Farmer, Sec. 29; P.O. Malta; from Scotland; Rep; Pres; prop. $13,700.

McLAUGHLIN JAS. Laborer on Jas. Byers' farm, Sec. 13; P.O. South Grove; from N. Y.

McMURCHY MALCOM, Farmer, Sec. 32; P.O. Malta; from Kane Co. Ill.

McMURCHY DANIEL, Farmer; P.O. Malta; from Canada; prop. $6,400; Rep; Pres.

McQUEEN HUGH Jr. lives with father; P.O. Malta; from Scotland; Rep; Pres.

McQUEEN JOHN, lives on farm with father; P.O. Malta; from Scotland; Rep; Pres.

McCARTY THOMAS, Farmer, Sec. 1, Tp. 41, R. 3 E.; P.O. South Grove; born in Co. Dublin, Ireland, Jan. 28, 1810; came to U.S. April 17, 1848; owns 160 acres, value $5,600; personal prop. $1,000; wife was Mary Molas, born in Co. Dublin, Ireland, Aug. 15, 1812; married in April, 1848; has two children; Cath; Dem.

McMURCHY JENET Mrs. Widow of Malcolm, who was born in Argyleshire, Scotland, April 3, 1802, and died Feb. 14, 1865, aged 62 years and 10 months; Mrs. McMurchy lives on Sec. 32, Tp. 41, R. 3 E.; P.O. Malta; born in Dumfriesshire, Scotland, Dec. 23, 1813; owns 160 acres, value $6,400; personal prop. $3,000; married March 29, 1842; has six children, four boys and two girls.

McQUEEN HUGH, Sen., Farmer, Sec. 33, Tp. 41, R. 3 E.; P.O. Malta; born in Wigtonshire, Scotland, July 29, 1829; came to this state and Co. Aug. 30, 1866; owns 160 acres, value $6,400; personal prop. $1,500; wife was Jane McKenzie, born in Ayrshire, Scotland; marr ed June 7, 1847; has seven children; Pres; Rep.

MESSICK JOHN, Farmer, Sec. 2; P.O. South Grove; Rep; Meth; from Maryland.

MERPHY JAMES, Laborer; P.O. Dustin; Cath; Dem; from McHenry Co. Ill.

MINER A. Laborer on Jas. Renwick's farm; P.O. Malta; Rep;

MINARD HENRY, Laborer on Geo. C. Hooker's farm, Sec, 35; P.O. Malta; Dem; Kane Co.

MILLER ALBERT, P.O. South Grove; Luth; from Germany.

MILLER HENRY, P.O. Kirkland; Luth; from Germany.

MOWERS AARON, Farmer and Stock Raiser, Sec. 17, Tp. 41, R. 3 E.; P.O. Deerfield Prairie; born in Stark, Herkimer Co. N.Y. May 10, 1828; came to this state and Co. Sept. 31. 1853; owns 320 acres of land, value $12,800; personal prop. $2,000; was Path-master four years; wife was Margaret Rickard, born in Stark, Herkimer Co. N.Y. Feb. 2, 1831; married in March, 1851; has seven children, five boys and two girls; Rep; Luth.

MOWERS FAYETTE, P.O. Deerfield Prairie; Rep; Luth; from Winnebago Co. Ill.

MOWERS HARVEY, P.O. Deerfield Prairie; Rep; Luth; from Co.

NEILSON GUSTAV, Laborer on R. Cox's farm; P.O. Malta; Rep; Luth; from Sweden.

NELSON JOHN, P.O. South Grove; Dem; Luth; from Sweden.

NEWELL GEORGE, Farmer and Stock Raiser, Sec. 7, Tp. 41, R. 3 E.; P.O. Dustin; born Magdalen Laven, Co. Essex, England, Sept. 14, 1795; age 81 years; came to this state and Co. in May, 1851; owns 200 acres, value $8,000; personal prop. $2,500; wife was Hannah E. Shuttleworth, born in Highongar, Co. Essex, England, Feb. 27, 1803; married May 10, 1828; has had nine children, four dead and five living; Epis.

NELSON GEO. Laborer on A. Ashelford's farm, Sec. 36; P.O. DeKalb; Rep; Luth; Denmark.

NELSON CHAS. Farmer; P.O. South Grove; Luth; from Sweden.

NEWELL SAMUEL, P O. Dustin; Epis; from Canada.

NORRIS A. Laborer on Jno. Lloyd's farm; P.O. Malta; Rep; Bapt; from Missouri.

PATTEN J. H. Farmer, Sec. 6; P.O. Wallace; val. of prop. $16,000; Rep; Prot; N.Y.

PAGE B. B. Farmer; P.O. Dustin; val. of prop. $8,000; Rep; Meth; from Mass.

PATTEN M. D. Farmer and Breeder of Ayrshire Stock, Sec. 6, Tp. 41, R. 3 E.; P.O. Wallace; born in Herkimer Co. N.Y. March 10, 1848; came to this state and Co. in April, 1851; owns 200 acres, value $9,000; personal prop. $2,500; has been township clerk three years, school director seven years; wife was Evaline S. Graves, born in DeKalb Co. Jan. 7, 1852; married April 6, 1870; has two children, both boys; Rep; Prot.

PALMER ELIZABETH A. Mrs. wid. of Morris E.; Postmistress; P.O. South Grove; Cath; N.Y.

PALMER SCHUYLER, Laborer; P.O. Malta; born in Co.; value of prop. $1,200; Bapt.

PETERSON VICTOR, Laborer on Chas. Doane's farm, Sec. 35; Prot; from Sweden.

PERKINS A. H. Farmer; P.O. Dustin; Meth; from Canada.

POOLER CHAS. Farmer; P.O. Dustin; Dem; Prot; from N.Y.

PURCELL JAMES, Farmer, Sec. 22; P.O. South Grove; prop. $10,500; Dem; Cath; Ireland.
PITT JAS. Laborer; P.O Kirkland; Dem; from Chicago.

QUINN MICHAEL, P.O. South Grove; Dem; Cath; from Ireland.
QUINN PATRICK, Sen., P.O. South Grove; val. prop. $4,000; Dem; Cath; Ireland.
QUINN JAS. Farmer, Sec. 25; P.O. South Grove; val. prop. $16,000; Dem; Cath; Ireland.
QUINN M. lives with father, Sec. 25; P.O. South Grove; Dem; Cath; from Ireland.
QUINN PATRICK, Jr., P.O. South Grove; value of prop. $4,000; Dem; Cath; Ireland.

REIL PETER, Sen., Farmer; P.O. Dustin; from N Y.
REIL PETER, Jr., Laborer, Sec. 35; P.O. Malta; Dem; Prot; from Ca.

RAND W. Farmer, Sec. 31, Tp 41, R. 3 E.; P.O. Crest n; born in Genesee Co. N.Y. March 28, 1829; came to this state and Co. in July, 1845; owns 146 acres, value $6,570; personal prop. $2,000; wife was Jane Moon, born in Lancaster, England, Feb. 26, 1834; married May 6, 1855; has nine children; Rep; Meth.

RAND H. L. Farmer, Section 31, Tp. 41, R. 3 E ; P.O. Creston; born in Genesee Co. N. Y. Jan. 7, 1832; came to this state and Co in 1846; owns 160 acres, value $7,200; personal prop. $1,000; wife was Laura A. Pritchard, born in Plattsburg, N.Y. July 9, 1833; married Nov. 24, 1856; has three children; Rep; Meth.

RENWICK JAMES, Farmer, Sec. 28, Tp 41, R. 3 E.; P.O. Malta; born in Dumfries-shire, Scotland, June 3, 1832; came to this state and Co. in Oct. 1850; owns 440 acres of land, valu· $22,000; personal prop. $5,000; wife was Rosina Becker, born in Delaware Co. N.Y.; married Feb. 28, 1861; has three children; Rep.

REDDICK AUGUSTUS, Laborer, Sec. 13; P.O South Grove; from Germany.

RENWICK THOS Farmer, Sec 2; P.O. South Grove; val. of prop. $21,000; Rep; Prot.

RICHARDS JAMES, Farmer, Sec. 19, Tp. 41, R. 3 E.; P.O. Deerfield Prairie; born in Saratoga Co. N.Y. Sept. 3, 1818; came to this state and Co March 26, 1868; owns 82 acres, value $4,100; personal prop. $1,000; is Postmaster Deerfield Prairie P.O.; was also Assessor one year; wife was Lucretia Ward, born in Mass.; married Oct. 26, 1849; has three children; Rep; Cong.

RICKARD DAVID, Farmer, Sec. 19; P.O. Deerfield Prairie; Rep; Prot; prop. $9,200; N.Y.

RICKARD ALONZO, Farmer; P.O. Deerfield Prairie; Rep; from county.

ROTHWELL ROBERT, Farmer, Sec. 5, Tp. 41, R. 3 E; P.O. Dustin; born in Manchester, England, Nov. 24, 1844; came to state and county March 1, 1870; Epis; owns 61 acres of land; value of real estate $3,000; value of personal property $500; wife was Fannie Stanfield, born in Hanford, England, April 12, 1843; married June 22 1869. ✔

ROSENCRANS C. Laborer on Jas. Renwick's farm; P.O. Malta; Rep; from New York.

ROWE PATRICK, Lab. on A. B. Byers' farm, Sec. 10; P.O. So. Grove; Dem; Cath; Ireland.

RUDDOCK CHARLES, Farmer, Sec. 36, Tp. 41, R. 3 E; P.O. Sycamore; born in St. Lawrence Co. N. Y. Jany. 3, 1826; came to state and county March 1, 1852; Rep; Meth. Epis; owns 160 acres of land; value of real estate $7,280; value of personal property $1,500; wife was Mary I. Moore, born in DeKalb, St. Lawrence Co. N. Y. June 17, 1835; married April 29, 1852; has five children, two boys and three girls.

RUTLEG PAT., P.O. South Grove; Dem; Cath; value of property $6,000; from Ireland.

SAFFORD CHAS. lives with father, Sec. 13; P.O. South Grove; Rep; Prot; born in county.
STAFFORD HENRY, Farmer, Sec. 13; P.O. So. Grove; Rep; Prot; born N. H.
SATTERLEE ALONZO, laborer on Jas. Byers' farm, Sec. 13; P.O. South Grove; Wisconsin.
SCHNEE JOSEPH F. Rev. Farmer, Sec. 18, Tp. 41, R. 3 E; P.O. Deerfield Prairie; born in Union Co. Penn. June 17, 1820; came to state and county May 1, 1865; Rep; Evangelic Association; owns 240 acres of land; value of real estate $12,000; value of personal property $3,000; wife was Margaret Woodside, born in Dauphin Co. Penn. Aug. 22, 1825; married Feb. 13, 1844; had six children, one dead, five living.
SCHERMERHORN CLARK, Farmer, Sec. 20; P.O. Creston; Rep; Meth; New York.
SCHERMERHORN CHAS. Farmer, Sec. 20; P.O. Creston; Rep; from New York.
SCHERMERHORN ROSA B. Widow of Simon Schermerhorn; P.O. Creston; Meth; N. Y.
SCHNEE JOS. W. lives with father, Sec. 18; P.O. Deerfield Prairie; Rep; Evang; from Penn.
SCHNEE EDWARD N. lives with father, Sec. 18; P.O. Deerfield Prairie; Rep; Evang; Ill.
SENIK JOHN, P.O. Kirkland; Luth; from Germany.
SHAVER J. S. Farmer, Sec. 21; P.O. Malta; Dem; Meth; val. of prop. $8,700; New York.

SHADBOLT WM. Laborer; P.O. Wallace; from England.

SHADBOLT GEO. Farmer; P.O. Wallace; Rep; from England.

SPENCER E. C. School Teacher, South Grove District No. 1; P.O. Sycamore; Rep; Prot; Vt.

STACK JAS. Farmer; P.O. South Grove; val. of property $10,000; Dem; Cath; Chicago, Ill.

STEUBEN WM. Farmer; P.O. Dustin; Rep; Prot; from New York.

SULLIVAN JEREMIAH, Farmer, Sec. 33, Tp. 41, R. 3 E; P.O. Malta; born in Cork Co. Ireland, Sep. 16, 1835; came to state and county Aug. 2, 1857; Dem; Cath; owns 160 acres of land; value of real estate $6,400; value of personal property $500; wife was Catharine Sullivan, born in Cork Co. Ireland; married March 18, 1866; has five children.

SUTTON WM. Laborer, T. D. Driskell's farm, Sec. 11; P.O. So. Grove; Rep; Meth; Ireland.

SULLIVAN M. Farmer, Sec. 24; P.O. South Grove; Dem; Cath; from Ireland.

SWEET GEO. Laborer; P.O. Dustin; value of property $1,000; Rep; Meth; Mass.

THOMPSON REBECCA O. Mrs. wid. Mathew; lives with son, Sec. 11; P.O. S. Grove; Meth.

THOMPSON JOHN A. Farmer, Sec. 11; P.O. So. Grove; Rep; Meth; from county.

THOMPSON A. C. Farmer, Sec. 11; P.O. South Grove; Rep; from New York.

TINDALL GEORGE M. Farmer, Sec. 10, Tp. 41, R. 3 E; P.O. South Grove; born in DeKalb Co. Ill. Nov. 17, 1851; Rep; Meth; owns 180 acres of land; value of real estate $9,000; value of personal property $3,000.

TRUDE FRANK, Lab. on T. D. Driskell's farm, Sec. 11; P.O. So. Grove; Rep; Me h; county.

TRUDE WM. Laborer on A. B. Byers' farm, Sec. 10; P.O. South Grove; Rep; born in county.

TYLER ALBERT W. Farmer and Stock Raiser, Sec. 25, Tp. 41, R. 3 E; P.O. South Grove; born in Painesville, Ohio, Dec. 23, 1843; came to state and county in 1845; Ind; Rep; Meth; owns 162 acres of land; value of real estate $8,100; value of personal property $1,000; wife was Hattie E. Wagner, born in LeRoy, Boone Co. Ill. Feb 7, 1850; married Oct. 11, 1871; has one boy, age three years and seven months.

UPDYKE HAMPTON, Farmer and Stock Raiser, Sec. 9, Tp. 41, R. 3 E; P.O. South Grove; born in Sussex Co. N. J. Dec. 25, 1811; came to state and county April 27, 1866; Rep; Meth; owns 420 acres of land; value of real estate $14,000; value of personal property $2,000; was justice of the peace five years, also assessor one year; wife was A. E. Kellum, born in Bridgewater, Susquehanna Co. Penn. Sep. 23, 1814; married Dec. 31, 1840.

VAN HORN JAS. H. lives with father, Sec. 18; P.O. Deerfield Prairie; Rep; Meth; Illinois.

VAN HORN THOMAS C. Farmer, Sec. 18, Tp. 41, R. 3 E; P.O. Deerfield Prairie; born in Otsego Co. N. Y. May 11, 1814; came to state and county June 1, 1851; Rep; owns 200 acres of land; value of real estate $8,000; value of personal property $2,000; wife was Mary D. Johnson, born in Otsego Co. N. Y; married in Feb. 1849; has three children, two boys and one girl.

WALTZ M. Clerk; P.O. Wallace; Dem; Meth; from New York.

WELTY GEO. W. lives with father, Sec. 30; P.O. Creston; Rep; Evang. Assoc'n; Illinois.

WELTY DANIEL, Farmer, Sec. 30, Tp. 41, R. 3 E; P.O. Creston; born in Lancaster Co. Penn. March 16, 1817; came to state an l county in June, 1848; Rep; Evang; owns 320 acres; value of real estate $14,400; value of personal property $1,500; wife was Diana Ernest, born in Perry Co. Penn; married Dec. 18, 1847; has eight children, six boys and two girls.

WELTY LEVI F. lives with father, Sec. 30; P.O. Creston; born Kendall Co; Rep; Evang. Ass'n.

WELTY JEREMIAH, lives with father, Sec. 30; P.O. Creston; from Kendall Co; value prop. $1,000; Rep; Evang. Assoc'n.

WEBSTER FRED. Laborer, Jas. Stack's farm; P.O. South Grove; Dem; Prot; from Elgin, Ill.

WILTSE ELIJAH, Farmer and Stock Raiser, Sec. 18, Tp. 41, R. 3 E; P.O. Deerfield Prairie; born Schenectady Co. N.Y. April 3, 1827; came to state and county April 24, 1857; Rep; Prot; owns 320 acres land; value real estate $16,000; val. per. prop. $4,000; wife was Mary Wells, born Lorain Co. Ohio; married Dec. 18, 1849; has five children.

WILSON ROGER, Farmer, Sec. 1, Tp. 41, R 3 E; P.O. Kirkland; born Yorkshire, Eng. July 9, 1809; came to U. S. 1810; came to state and county Oct. 1, 1863; Dem; Univ; owns 193 acres land; val. real estate $10,615; val. per. prop. $4,000; first wife was Mary Burdick, born Scipio, Cayuga Co. N.Y. April 25, 1813; second wife was Elizabeth Clark, born Olive Green, Washington Co. Ohio, Aug. 27, 1826; has two children by first wife.

WILLIS ROB T. Farmer, Sec. 23; P.O. South Grove; from Eng; Prot; val. prop. $15,800.

WILLIAMS JOHN, P.O. Malta; from Eng; Rep; Epis.

WILTSE SILAS, lives with father, Sec. 18; P.O. Deerfield Prairie; Ohio; prop. $300; Rep; Prot.

WILTSE WELLS, lives with father, Sec. 18; P.O. Deerfield Prairie; Ohio; prop. $500; Rep; Prot.

WILLIS SMITH C. Blacksmith; P.O. Dustin; from N.Y.; Rep; Prot.

WILLIS LAURA A. Mrs. wid. Geo. W. P.O. Dustin; from N.Y.; val. prop. $1,000; Adv.

WILKIE WM. J. Farmer; P O. Dustin; from Clinton, Ill; Rep; Prot.

WILSON H. C. Kirkland P.O.; from Mich; Dem; Cong.

WILLIAMS S. B. Laborer; P.O. Wallace; from Washington Co. N. Y.; Rep; Prot.

WILLIAMS L. L. Laborer; P.O. Wallace; from Washington N.Y.; Rep; Bapt.

WORDEN BENJAMIN, Farmer, Sec. 14, Tp. 41, R. 3 E; P.O. South Grove; born Delaware Co. N.Y. Jan. 10, 1814; came to state and county Jan. 1, 1838; Rep; Bapt; owns 250 acres land; value real estate $12,500; val. per. prop. $3,000; wife was Martha J. Fergason; born Delaware Co. N.Y. Jan. 16, 1818; married Jan. 3, 1833; nine children: six boys, two girls.

WORDEN STEPHEN H. Lab. Jno. Lloyd's farm; P.O. Malta; DeKalb Co; prop. $1,000; Rep.

WORDEN GEO. W. Tenant Farmer, Sec. 16; P.O. Malta; Ogle Co; prop. $2,500; Rep; Pres.

WOODWORTH A. G. Laborer; P.O. South Grove; from Winnebago Co. Ill; Rep; Meth.

WORDEN BENJAMIN Jr. South Grove P.O.; Rep; Meth.

WORDEN FRANK, South Grove P.O.; Rep; Meth.

WOLCOTT JNO. Kirkland P.O.; from Chicago; Rep; Prot.

MILAN TOWNSHIP.

ABBOTT EMERY, Sec. 10; P.O. Malta; Rep; from N.Y.

ABBOTT WM. B. Farmer, Sec. 10; P.O. Malta; 160 acres; from N.Y.; Rep.

ANDERSON J. Farmer, Sec. 25; P.O DeKalb; born in Norway, Dec. 25, 1820; came to county in the Spring of '55; has family of eight children; wife was Miss Isabelle Hanson, from Norway; farm 160 acres, value $4,500; personal, $500; Rep.

APPLEBEE NATHAN, Sec. 1; P.O. DeKalb; 240 ac; Rep; from Ill; Meth.

APPLEBEE GEO. lives with father, Sec. 1; P.O. DeKalb; Rep; Meth; from Ill.

ANDERSON NELS, Sec. 1; P.O. DeKalb; 100 acres; Rep; Luth; from Sweden.

ARENT ANDREW, Sec. 26; P.O. Cornton; 240 acres; no politics; from Norway.

BLAIR ROBT. Farmer, Sec. 7; P.O. Creston; lives with Wm. Blair; Rep; Pres; Scotland.

BERG E. O. works for Wm. Browne, Sec. 11; P.O. Malta; Rep; from Norway.

BERG THEODORE O. Farmer, Sec. 19; P.O. Lee; born in Norway, Dec. 23, 1833; came to this county July 10, 1854; has family of three children; wife was Miss Mary Dannelson, from Norway; married May 26, 1858; farm 400 acres, value $16,000; personal, $1,000; Luth; Rep.

BENSON PETER, Farmer, Sec. 1; P.O. DeKalb; 80 acres; Rep; Luth; from Sweden.

BERRY RICHARD, works for A. W. Howard, Sec. 20; P.O Shabbona; Rep; from England.

BROWNE WM. Farmer and Stock Raiser, Sec. 11; P.O. Malta; born in Donegal County, Ireland, March 13, 1831; came to this county in the Spring of 1855 and settled in Milan Tp; has a family of four children; wife was Miss Sarah Seely, of Pittsford, Mich; married Dec. 18, 1859; farm 390 acres, value $15,840; personal estate $5,000; Meth; Rep.

BRAWKER DANIEL, Farmer, Sec. 31; P.O. Lee; 52½ acres; Ind; from N.Y.

BLAIR WM. Farmer and Stock Raiser, Sec. 7; P.O. Creston; born in Dunse, Berwickshire, Scotland, Feb. 28, 1824; came to this county in the Fall of 1854; family of six children; wife was Miss Mary McNeal, from Rothsay, Co. Bute, Scotland; married Sept. 24, 1856; farm 345 acres, value $17,250; personal, $2,000; Rep; Pres.

BROWN JAMES, works for A. O. Donald, Sec. 31; P.O. Lee; Dem; Cath; from Ireland.

BROWN GABRIEL, rents farm of U. Oakland, Sec. 18; P.O. Lee; Rep; from Norway.

BROWNE NATH'L, P.O. Malta; 200 acres; Rep; Meth; from North Ireland.

COSTER A. H. Farmer, Sec. 13; P.O. Malta; 120 acres; Rensselaer Co. N. Y.; Rep.

CRESTERSON C. Blacksmith; P.O. Malta; Rep; from Denmark.

CAMPBELL DAVID, Farmer, Sec. 3; P.O. Malta; rents farm of J. F. Phelps; Rep; from N.Y.

COTTON ALONZO S. Farmer, Sec. 3; P.O. Malta; born in Winnebago Co. Ill. July 4, 1846; came to this county in the Spring of 1867; has a family of three children; wife was Miss Clementine Dodge, from Ohio; married Nov. 5, 1866; farm 264 acres, value $13,200; personal, $1,000; is also school director; Rep.

CARPENTER NOAH, Farmer, Sec. 15; P.O. Malta; Dem; from Ill.

CONDON JAMES, Farmer, Sec. 5; P.O. Malta; born in Tipperary Co. Ireland, in 1829; came to this county in the Fall of 1856; family, six children; wife was Miss Catherine Welch, from Ireland; married in the year 1840; owns farm of 160 acres, value $5,600; personal, $300; Dem; Cath.

CONDON WM. Sec 5; P.O. Malta; lives with father; Dem; Cath; from Wisconsin.

CONDON MICHAEL, Sec. 5; P.O. Malta; with father; Dem; Cath; from Wisconsin.

COLSON FRED. Sec. 1; P.O. DeKalb; works for Nels Anderson; Rep; from Sweden.

CONLIN JOHN, Farmer, Sec. 22; P.O. Malta; born in Armagh Co. Ireland, March 31, 1836; came to this county in the Spring of 1866; has family of seven children; wife was Miss Frances M. Roe, from Ogle Co. Ill; married May 11, 1863; owns farm 80 acres, value $3,200; personal, $600; Dem.

CAMPBELL JAMES, School Teacher, Sec. 1; P.O. Malta; rents place of O. Tisdell; Rep; N.Y.

CODY PETER O. Farmer, Sec. 26; P.O. Cornton; farm 100 acres; from Norway.

CHALLAND F. Sec. 30; P.O. Cornton; 80 acres; Rep; from Ill.

CARROLL JOHN, Farmer, Sec. 7; P.O. Malta; 160 acres; Dem; Cath; from Ireland.

COX GEO. C. Farmer, Sec. 27; P.O. Shabbona; born in Montgomery Co. N. Y. Feb. 1, 1839; came to this county in Sept. 1870; has family of two children; wife was Miss Sarah E. Marcy, from Luzerne Co. Penn; married Feb. 20, 1861; 160 acres, value $8,800; personal, $1,500; also justice of the peace; Rep.

CHRISTOPHER C. O. Farmer, Sec. 19; P.O. Lee; 107 acres; Rep; from Norway.

CHRISTOPHER C. Sec. 19; P.O. Lee; lives with father; Rep; from Norway.

COFIELD PETER, P.O. Lee; Sec. 32; works for A. Downer; Rep; from Germany.

COLBY E. R. Farmer, Sec. 33; P.O. Lee; 160 acres; supervisor; Dem; from N. Y.

COOSE CHAS. Farmer, Sec. 9; P O. Malta; born in Germany, Aug. 6, 1822; came to this county in the Spring of 1865; has family of five children; wife was Miss Mary Ame, from Germany; married in 1854; farm 160 acres, value $6,400; personal $300; Luth; Rep.

CHANDLER W. E. Sec. 29; P.O. Lee; farm 120 acres; Rep; from N. Y.

CHANDLER A. J. Sec. 29; P.O. Lee; lives with his father; Rep; from Ill.

COLE C. B. farm 40 acres; P.O. Cornton; no politics; from England.

DODD REUBEN, Farmer, Sec. 36; P.O. Cornton; 200 acres; Rep; from N. J.

DODD ISAAC M. lives with father, Sec. 36; P.O. Cornton; Rep; from N. J.

DURYEE WM. W. Farmer, Sec. 11; P.O. Malta; born in Hillsdale Co. Mich. Oct. 29, 1851; came to county in the Fall of 1864; no family; wife was Miss Ida Gould, from this county; married Oct. 29, 1875; farm of 157 acres, value $7,850; personal, $1,000; was collector one term; Rep.

DOWNER A. Farmer, Sec. 32; P.O. Lee; 320 acres; Rep; from Canada.

DUFFEY JOHN, Farmer, Sec. 2; P.O. Malta; 160 acres; Rep; from Ohio.

DAVENPORT NILES, Laborer, lives with Henry Young, Sec. 36; P.O. Cornton; Rep; Ill.

DONALD A. O. Farmer, Sec. 31; P.O. Lee; 290 acres; Dem; Cath; from Ireland.

DONALD JOHN O. lives with father, Sec. 31; P.O. Lee; Dem; Cath; from Ohio.

EGLESTON C. A. Mrs. Sec. 14; P.O. Malta; 160 acres; from N. Y.

EGLESTON GEO. Sec. 14; P.O. Malta; lives with his mother; Rep; from Cleveland, Ohio.

EAMES SOREN, Farmer, Sec. 17; P.O. Lee; born in Norway, Sept. 8, 1835; came to county in the Spring 1868; has family of three children; wife was Miss Martha Olson, from Norway; married March 21, 1871; farm 80 acres, value $4,000; Rep; Luth.

EREKSON THOMAS, Sec. 16; P.O. Malta; farm 120 acres; Rep; from Norway.

EAMES LEWIS, Sec. 17; P.O. Lee; farm 160 acres; Rep; from Norway.

ERIKSEN ERIK, Sec. 8; P.O. Malta; born in Norway, June 6, 1847; came to this county in the Spring of 1870; no family; wife was Miss Sophia Coose, from Germany; farm 120 acres, value $3000; personal, $100; Rep; Luth.

FLORA M. Sec. 35; P.O. Cornton; rents A. V. Wormley; Dem; from Canada.

FINK WILLIAM A., Farmer, Sec. 21; P.O. Malta; born in Madison Co. N.Y., Jan. 22, 1822; came to this county July, 1854; has family of four children; wife was Miss Sophia Tuller, from Cayuga Co. N. Y.; married Sept. 22, 1853; has farm 160 acres; value $8,000; personal, $1 500; Rep.

FITZGERALD MICHAEL, Sec. 4; P.O. Malta; born in Monaghan Co. Ireland, Aug. 15, 1836; came to this county in the Spring of 1865; has family of six children; wife was Miss Margaret McCarvill, from Monaghan Co. Ireland; married Sept. 4, 1859; farm 120 acres, value $6,0 0; personal, $500; Ind; Cath.

GROVER WM. Sec. 6; P.O. Creston; farm of 156 acres, value $7,800; Ind; from Illinois.

GOULD RACHAEL Mrs. Sec. 1; P.O. Malta; widow of B. S. Gould, who died March 10, 1875; he was born in Dutchess Co. N. Y. Sept. 16, 1825; located in this county in the Spring of 1858; left a family of eight children. Mrs. Gould was Miss Rachael Hines; from Bradford Co. Penn; married Sept. 17, 1853; has farm of 144½ acres, value $7,200; personal $1,000.

GRISWOLD D. B. P.O. Malta; Sec. 21; born in Weatherfield, Conn. Nov. 26, 1832; came to this county in the Spring of 1856; has a family of nine children; wife was Miss Vilena Wescott, from Ohio; born June 7, 1836; married Aug. 13, 1854; farm 80 acres, value $4,000; personal $1,000; Rep.

HOLVERSON S. Sec. 31; P.O. Lee; farm 107 acres, value $5,350; Rep; Luth; from Norway.

HOLVERSON E. Sec. 31; P.O. Lee; lives with his father; Rep; Luth; from Illinois.

HART PATRICK M. P.O. Malta; Sec. 16; born in Sligo Co. Ireland, Aug. 1, 1833; came to this county in the Spring of 1865; family, five children; wife was Miss Margaret Burns, from Sligo Co. Ireland; married Jan. 1, 1854; farm 240 acres, value $11,500; personal $800; Meth; Rep.

HOWARD A. W. Sec. 20; P.O. Shabbona; farm 160 acres, value $8,000; Rep; from Vermont.

HENDERSON SAMUEL, P.O. Lee; Sec. 29; 160 acres, val. $8,000; Rep; from Pennsylvania.

HANCHETT H. H. Sec. 32; P.O. Lee; rents T. Hallett's farm; Rep; from Ohio.

HICKEY JOHN, P.O. Cornton; Sec. 35; farm 80 acres, value $4,000; Ind; from Ireland.

HUDSON JOHN, P.O. Malta; Sec. 11; works for Wm. Duryee; Ind; from Illinois.

HILL PETER, Farmer, Sec. 3; P.O. Malta; rents place of John Wedlake; Rep; Canada.

HART CHRISTOPHER, Farmer, Sec. 22; P.O. Malta; born in LaSalle Co. Ill. Feb. 4, 1850; came to this county in the Spring of 1861; single man; farm 100 acres, value $8,000; personal $225; Dem; Cath.

HART P. M. Mrs. Sec. 22; P.O. Malta; farm 160 acres, value $8,000; Cath; from Ireland.

HART PATRICK, Sec. 22; P.O. Malta; lives with his mother; Dem; Cath; from Ireland.

HART FRANCIS, P.O. Malta; Sec. 22; works for his mother; 80 acres; Sec. 23; Cath; Dem; from N. Y.

HART STEPHEN, P.O. Malta; Sec. 15; 80 acres, value $4,000; Dem; Cath; from Ireland.

HART JOHN, Sec. 26; P.O. Cornton; 80 acres, value $4,000; Dem; Cath; from Ireland.

HART THOMAS, Sec. 26; P.O. Cornton; farm 80 acres, value $4,000; Dem; Cath.

HUDSON RICHARD, Sec. 1; P.O. Malta; works for B. S. Gould; Rep; from Canada West.

HOWE D. E. School teacher, Sec. 14; P.O. Malta; boards with E. M. Reynolds; Rep; N. Y.

HOWARD L. A. Sec. 13; P.O. DeKalb; 100 acres, value $4,000; Rep; from New Hampshire.

HENDRICKSON G. Sec. 9; P.O. Malta; farm of 157 acres, value $7,500; Rep; from Norway.

HYER ANDREW, Sec. 6; P.O. Creston; farm of 100 41-100 acres, val. $5,000; Rep; Illinois.

HUNTER L. Sec. 36; P.O. Cornton; rents farm of L. M. McEwen; Rep; from New York.

JOHNSON K. D. Sec. 30; P.O. Lee; farm 80 acres, value $4,000; Rep; Luth; from Norway.

JOHNSON A. H. Sec. 29; P.O. Lee; farm 160 acres, value $8,000; Rep; from Norway.

JOHNSON MAGNUS, Sec. 2; P.O. Malta; born in Sweden, Nov. 16, 1833; came to DeKalb Co. Aug. 18, 1854; has family of three children; wife was Miss Christina Johnson, from Sweden; married July 16, 1863; farm 80 acres, value $3,200; personal, $1,000; Rep.

JOHNSON K. Sec. 30; P.O. Lee; farm 80 acres, value $4,000; Rep; Luth; from Norway.

JOHNSON JOHN M. Sec. 18; P.O. Lee; farm 80 acres, value $4,000; Rep; from Norway.
JOHNSON T. Sec. 6; P.O. Malta; 105 acres, value $4,200; Rep; from Norway.
JOHNSON OLE O. Sec. 32; P.O. Lee; rents Wm. Irwin's farm; Rep; from Norway.
JOHNSON IRA M. Sec. 6; P.O. Creston; farm 160 acres, value $6,400; Rep; from Norway.
JACOBSON GOODMAN, Sec. 18; P.O. Lee; farm 106 acres; no politics; from Norway.

KITTLESON HALBERT, Sec. 30; P.O. Lee; lives with his father; Rep; from Norway.
KITTLESON LAVINA, Sec. 17; P.O. Lee Station; farm of 160 acres; Luth; Norway.
KITTLESON OLE, Sec. 30; P.O. Lee; farm 80 acres, val. $4,000; Rep; Luth; from Norway.
KITTLESON AUSTIN, Sec. 17; P.O. Lee Station; lives with his mother; Rep; Luth; Ill.
KITTLESON OLIVER, Sec. 30; P.O. Lee; farm 120 ac; val. $5,500; Rep; from Norway.
KETTLESON O. O. Sec. 16; P.O. Lee Station; farm 80 acres, val. $3,200; Rep; Norway.
KETTLESON HENRY, P.O. Lee Station; Sec. 17; 80 ac; val. $4,000; Rep; Luth; Norway.
KRENTZFIELD PETER, P.O Malta; Sec. 17; 80 ac; val. $4,000; Rep; from Germany.
KENUTSON E. Sec. 23; P.O. Malta; farm 80 acres, val. $4,000; Rep; from Norway.
KEAST AMOS, P.O. Malta; Sec. 4; 183 acres; value real estate $9,150; from England.
KERWIN WM. Sec. 26; P.O. Cornton; farm 160 acres, val. $8,000; Dem; Cath; Ireland.
KENNEDY PATRICK, P.O. DeKalb; Sec. 13; farm of 100 acres, val. $4,000; Dem; Cath.
KATAN PATRICK, P.O. Malta; Sec. 9; farm of 160 acres, val. $8,000; Dem; Cath; Ireland.

LARSON LARS, P.O. Malta; Sec. 23; farm 160 acres, val. $8,000; Rep; from Norway.
LARSON OLE, Sec. 23; P.O. Malta; lives with his father; Rep; from Ill.
LARSON O. T. Sec. 23; P.O. Malta; owns 160 acres, val. real estate $6,400; Rep; from Ill.
LARSON L. Sec. 23; P.O. Malta; lives with O. T. Larson; Rep; from Norway.
LARSON DAN'L, P.O. Cornton; Sec. 36; rents farm of A. Johnson; no politics; from Norway.
LARSON LARS, P.O. Malta; Sec. 24; farm 160 acres, value $8,000; Rep; from Norway.
LANGERUD O. O. Sec. 32; P.O. Lee; farm 40 acres, value $2,000; no politics; from Norway.
LEWIS B. N. Sec. 15; P.O. Malta; works for Pat. Quinn; Dem; from France.

MOORE GEO. Sec. 33; P.O. Lee; farm 240 acres, value $12,000; Dem; from Germany.
MOORE GEO. Jr. Sec. 33; P.O. Lee; with father; Dem; from Germany.
MALLAY WILLIAM, Sec. 15; P.O. Malta; born in Ireland, Feb. 1826; came to county in Fall of 1858; family, eight children; wife was Miss Wineford Pettitt, from Galway Co. Ireland; married Dec. 1851; owns farm 240 acres, value $9,600; personal $600; Dem; Cath.
MIHM MICHAEL, Sec. 28; P.O. Lee; farm 160 acres, value $8,000; Dem; from Germany.
MURRAY JOHN, Sec. 34; P.O. Cornton; farm 200 ac. val. $3,000; Ind; Cath; from Ireland.
MURRAY EDWARD, Sec. 34; P.O. Cornton; lives with his father; Dem; Cath; from Ohio.
MURRAY PATRICK, Sec. 34; P.O. Cornton; lives with his father; Dem; Cath; from Ireland.
MURRAY DENNIS, P.O. Cornton; Sec. 34; lives with his father; Dem; Cath; from Canada.
MONSON JOHN, P.O. DeKalb; Sec. 24; works A. K. Stiles' farm; Rep; from Germany.
MAHER JAMES, Sec. 27; P.O. Lee; born in Tipperary Co. Ireland, in 1827; came to this county in the Spring of 1860; family, eight children; wife was Miss Margaret Crowley, from Kilkenny Co. Ireland; married April 19, 1858; farm of 160 acres, value $8,000; personal $1,000; Dem; Cath.
MUNSON PETER, Sec. 35; P.O. Cornton; farm 160 acres, value $7,000; Rep; from Norway.
MULROYNE THOMAS, P.O. Malta; Sec 13; works M. O'Brien's farm; Dem; Cath; Ireland.
MOORE A. F. Farmer, Sec. 15; P.O. Malta; works for Noah Carpenter; Rep; Michigan.
MARSHALL JAMES M. Sec. 14; P.O. Malta; 80 acres, value $4,000; Ind; from England.
McMAHON G. W. Farmer, Sec. 23; P.O. Malta; born in Allen Co. Indiana, Aug. 5, 1846; came to county, March, 1874; family, three children; wife was Miss Mary E. Watterman, from Kane Co. Illinois; married Oct. 1, 1868; farm of 80 acres, value $4,000; personal $1,200; Rep.
McQUAIRK PATRICK, Sec. 5; P.O. Creston; 120 acres, value $4,800; Dem; Cath; Ireland.
McNEILL JOHN, P.O. Creston; Sec. 5; farm 120 acres, value $4,800; Rep; from Scotland.
MILLER CHAS. P.O. Malta; Sec. 8; farm 80 acres, value $4,000; Rep; from Germany.
McGURMOTT JOHN, Sec. 5; P.O. Malta; rents farm of John Reed; Dem; Cath; Ireland.
MOLLENCOPF JOHN, Sec. 1; P.O. Malta; rents farm of J. Stinson; Dem; from Penn.

19

NORTON PATRICK, Sec. 5; P.O. Malta; farm 120 acres, value $4,800; Dem; Cath; Ireland.

NORTON THOMAS, Sec. 5; P.O. Malta; lives with his father; Dem; Cath; from Penn.

NOREM OLE J. Sec. 20; P.O. Lee; born in Norway. Dec. 14, 1834; came to this county in the Fall of 1865; has family of two children; wife was Miss Julia Christopher, from Norway; married Dec. 20, 1867; farm 240 acres, value $12,000; personal $1,000; Luth; Rep.

NEWSHAM JOHN F. Sec. 9; P.O. Malta; born in Erie Co. Penn. Jan. 24, 1842; came to county Feb. 1867; no family; wife was Miss Maggie A. Brown, from Erie Co. Penn; married October 1, 1868; farm 160 acres, value $8,000; Rep.

OLSON H. H. Sec. 31; P.O. Lee; farm 80 acres, value $4,000; Rep; from Norway.

OLSON H. Sec. 31; P.O. Lee; farm 80 acres, val. $4,000; Rep; from Norway.

OLSON LARS, P.O. Lee; Sec. 20; born in Norway, Jan. 12, 1835; came to this county in the Spring 1873; has family of four children; wife was Miss Annie Peterson, from Sweden; married Jan. 10, 1861; farm 160 acres, value $8,000; personal, $500; Rep; Luth.

OLESON OLE B. Sec. 7; P.O. Creston; 103¼ acres, val. $5,200; Rep; Meth; from Norway.

OLSON A. K. Farmer, P.O. Malta; Sec. 10; born in Stavanger, Norway, March 31, 1849; came to county in the Fall of 1873; has family of two children; wife was Miss Elsie Jenson, from Freedom, LaSalle Co. Ill; married March 7, 1872; farm 160 acres, value $8,000; Rep.

OLSON OLE H. Sec. 25; P.O. Cornton; farm 160 acres, value $8,000; no politics; Norway.

OLSON JOHN, P.O. Lee; Sec. 16; born in Norway, April 11, 1830; came to this county in the Spring of 1861; has family of seven children; wife was Miss Annie Halver, from Norway; married Dec. 25, 1856; owns farm 160 ac; val. $7,200; personal, $1,000; Rep; Luth.

OAKLAND IRA, Farmer, Sec. 20; P.O. Lee; born in Norway, Dec. 22, 1832; came to this county in the Spring of 1854; has family of six children; wife was Miss Isabelle Lewis, from Norway; married April 4, 1862; farm 160 acres, val. $8,000; personal, $1,000; Rep; Meth.

PREDLAU DAVID, P.O. Cornton; Sec. 35; works for Peter Shambo; Rep; from Ill.

PROCTOR HENRY, P.O. Malta; Sec. 3; works for A. S. Cotton; Rep; from Ohio.

PEARCE JOSEPH, Farmer, Sec. 33; P.O. Lee; born in Champaign Co. Ohio, Aug. 24, 1829; came to this county in the spring of 1860; has a family of five children; wife was Miss Sarah Nellis, from Montgomery Co; married Nov. 11, 1857; farm 160 acres, value $8,000; personal, $1,500; Dem.

PETERSON L. Sec. 19; P.O. Lee; farm 106 acres; value $5,000; Rep; from Norway.

PRESCOTT KENUTE, Sec. 13; P.O. Lee Station; rents farm of T. Berg; no politics; Norway.

PUFFER, A. R. Sec. 3; P.O. Malta; farm of 80 acres, value $4,000; Dem; from Mass.

PADDISON W. H. Sec. 4; P.O. Malta; rents farm of John Bowley; no politics; England.

QUINN PATRICK, P.O. Malta; Sec. 15; 160 acres, value $8,000; Dem; Cath; Ireland.

REYNOLDS E. M. Sec. 14, Tp. 39, 3, E; P.O. Malta; farm 160 acres; Rep; from Vermont.

ROLAND DAVID, P.O. Malta; Sec. 2; works for Geo. Roland; Rep; from Ohio.

ROLAND GEORGE W. Farmer, Sec. 2; P.O. Malta; born in Trumbull Co. Ohio, Jan. 1, 1839; came to county in the Spring of 1857; has family of four children; wife was Miss Sarah J. Taylor, from Pennsylvania; married Nov. 1, 1861; farm 160 acres, value $8,000; personal $3,000; Rep.

REYNOLDS PETER, P.O. Malta; Sec. 14; lives with E. M. Reynolds; Rep; from Vermont.

RANNEY RATAS, P.O. Malta; Sec. 3; lives with A. R. Puffer; Rep; from Vermont.

SATTERLEE J. L. Carpenter and Joiner, Sec. 3; P.O. Malta; Rep; from New York.

SCALLY JAMES, Farmer, Sec. 22; P.O. Malta; Ind; Cath; from Chicago.

SKELLEY THOMAS, Farmer, Sec. 22; P.O. Malta; born in Longford Co. Ireland, March 20, 1821; came to county in the Fall of 1858; has a family of six children; wife was Miss Annie Long, from Longford Co. Ireland; born July 16, 1826; married Dec. 14, 1847; farm 160 acres, value $8,000; personal $1,00; Cath; Dem.

SHERIDAN PATRICK, Sec. 33; P.O. Shabbona; 240 ac. val. $12,000; Rep; Cath; Ireland.

SHERIDAN RICHARD, Sec. 33; P.O. Shabbona; lives with his father; Dem; from Scotland.

SHAW WM. Sec. 2; P.O. Malta; lives with John Duffey; Dem; from Pennsylvania.

STONE JACOB, Farmer, Sec. 10; P.O. Malta; farm 160 acres, value $8,000; Ind; Meth; Penn.

SCHEIDECKER GEO. P.O. Malta; Sec. 25; 220 acres, value $10,000; Rep; from France.

SCOTT GEORGE, Farmer, Sec. 34; P.O. Cornton; rents farm of Mrs. J. W. Stevens; Rep; Ills.
SEVERSON OLE, Sec. 19; P.O. Lee; rents O. Lanning's farm; Rep; from Norway.
SHAMBO PETER, Sec. 35; P.O. Creston; farm 160 acres, value $8,000; Rep; from Canada.
SANDERSON S. H. Sec. 29; P.O. Lee; farm 160 acres, val. $8,000; Rep; Luth; from Norway.
SANDERSON HENRY H. Sec. 29; P.O. Lee; lives with his father; 80 ac. Sec. 20; Rep; Ill.
SCHMICK HENRY, Sec. 3; P.O. Malta, farm 80 acres, value $4,000; Rep; from Germany.

TYSDAL OSMAND O. Sec. 12; P.O. Malta; lives with L. Tysdal, Rep; from Norway.
TYSDAL KNUTE, Sec. 12; P.O. Malta; lives with L. Tyndal; Rep; from Norway.
TYSDAL LEWIS, Sec. 12; P.O. Malta; rents farm of A. J. Hodge; Rep; from Norway.
TYSDAL OSMAND, Sec. 20; P.O. Lee Station; farm 120 acres, value $6,000; no pol; Norway.
THOMAS L. C. Sec. 14; P.O. Malta; rents farm of W. N. Downing; Rep; from New York.
TRAVLIND PETER P. Sec. 18; P.O. Creston; farm 106 acres, val. $5,300; no pol; Norway.
THOMPSON O. Sec. 31; P.O. Lee; farm 80 acres, value $4,000; Rep; from Norway.
TALBOTT WM. P.O. Malta; Sec. 16; rents farm of P. A. Phelps; Rep; from Indiana.

VEAL OLIVER, P.O. Malta; Sec. 4; farm of 160 acres, value $6,400; Rep; from England.
VEAL M. Sec. 4; P.O. Malta; rents farm of Oliver Veal; Rep; from England.
VEAL SAM'L, P.O. Malta; Sec. 8; farm 200 acres, value $8,000; Rep; from England.

WELLS A. L. Sec. 28; P.O. Shabbona; farm 160 acres, value $8,000; Rep; from N. Y.
WEST ALFRED, P.O. Shabbona; Sec. 28; works for A. L. Wells; no politics; from Ohio.
WEDLAKE JOHN, Farmer, Sec. 2; P.O. Malta; born in Somersetshire, Eng. May, 1827; came to this county in the Spring of 1860; family, one child; wife was Miss Harriet Orchett, from Somersetshire, Eng; married April 5, 1851; farm 240 acres, value $12,000; Rep.
WEDLAKE HENRY, P.O. Malta; Sec. 2; lives with his father; Rep; from England.
WERTZ MARK, Farmer, Sec. 5; P.O. Malta; born in Elliswilley, Germany, May 31, 1832; came to this county June 21, 1865; has a family of two children; wife was Miss Harriet E. Hatch, from Jefferson Co. N. Y.; married June 21, 1871; farm 80 ac; val. $4,000; Rep; Cath.
WATSON JOHN, Sec. 28; P.O. Cornton; farm 320 acres, value $16,000; Dem; from Mass.
WOODS PATRICK, P.O. Malta; Sec. 24; born in Louth Co. Ireland, March 16, 1827; came to county Feb. 25, 1874; has family of six children; wife was Miss Mary Moore, from Co. Galway, Ireland; married Nov. 29, 1857; farm 80 acres; value real estate $4,000; personal, $1,400; Ind; Cath.

YOUNG HENRY, Sec. 36; P.O. Creston; farm 80 acres, value $3,000; Rep; from Ill.

KINGSTON TOWNSHIP.

ADAMS JOHN, lives on Josiah Burkey's farm, Sec. 17; P.O. North Kingston.

ARTLEY CHARLES, Farmer, Sec. 31; P.O. Kingston; Rep.

ARBUCKLE W. Farmer, Sec. 9; P.O. North Kingston; Rep; val. prop. $800; from Ill.

ARBUCKLE B. B. Farmer, Sec. 3; P.O. North Kingston; Rep; Meth; prop. $8,000; Ohio.

ARBUCKLE JOSEPH F. Farmer, Sec. 9, P.O. North Kingston; born Erie Co. Penn, 1805; came to Ill 1839; has lived in DeKalb Co. ever since; Rep; Meth; 140 acres, val. $7,000; personal prop. $500; Postmaster North Kingston; wife was Amanda Smith, born Portage Co. Ohio, 1810; married Jan. 28, 1829; five children.

ARBUCKLE D B. Farmer, Sec. 10; P.O. North Kingston; Rep; from Ill.

AURNER LEONARD, Farmer, Sec. 27; P.O. Kingston; born Armstrong Co. Ohio, 1810; came to Ill. 1838, has lived in county ever since; Rep; owns 430 acres, value $20,000; val. personal prop. $1,600; wife was Ellen Burghardt, born Vermont, 1827; married 1874; has seven children by first wife, five children by second wife.

AURNER W. R. Farmer, Sec. 19; P.O. Kingston; Rep; from Ill.

AURNER MICHAEL, Laborer, Sec. 23; P.O. Kingston; from Penn.

AURNER J. Farmer, Sec. 29; P.O. Kingston; val. prop. $4,000.

AURNER CHAS. Farmer, Sec. 8; P.O. Kingston; Rep; from Ill; val. prop. $200.

ARNOLD W. Farmer, Sec. 10; P.O. Genoa; Rep; Meth; from England.

AVERY TRUMAN, Farmer, Sec. 24; P.O. Genoa; Rep; from N.Y.

AVERY WALLACE, lives with Truman Avery, Sec. 24; P.O. Genoa; Rep; from N.Y.

BAXTER FRANK, Laborer; P.O. Genoa; Rep; from Penn.

BACON H. Farmer, Sec. 7; P.O. Belvidere; Rep; from N.Y.

BALL D. P. Farmer, Sec. 28; P.O. Kingston; Rep; from Penn; val. prop. $4,700.

BALL DELOS, lives on John Uplinger's farm; Sec. 28; P.O. Kingston; Rep; from Ill.

BALL WM. Farmer, Sec. 8; P.O. Kingston; Rep; from Canada.

BARNES ELIZABETH Mrs. widow; Kingston.

BEERS GEORGE, lives on Jno. Judd's estate, Sec. 36; P.O. Sycamore; Rep.

BENSON LEROY, Farmer, Sec. 9; P.O. North Kingston; Rep; from N.Y.

BELL JAMES B. Farmer, Sec. 11; P.O. Kingston; born Penn. 1820; came to Ill. 1843; Rep; Bapt; 80 acres, value $4,300; val. personal prop. $1,000; wife was Miss Esther Read, born Ohio, 1832; married 1855; has six children.

BEAN A. A. Farmer, Sec. 29; P.O. Kingston; born in DeKalb Co. in 1850; value of prop. $500; wife was Emily J. Vosburgh, born in Canada n 1851; married in 1870; one child; Rep.

BEAN SAMUEL, Farmer, Sec. 29; P.O. Kingston; born in Kennebec Co. Maine, in 1818; came to Illinois in 1843; owns 280 acres, value $12,100; personal property $1,000; wife was Mary E. Towns, from Augusta, Maine; has six children; Rep.

BIRD THOMAS, Farmer, Sec. 12; P.O. Genoa; born in Ireland in 1822; came to Ill. in 1860; value of prop. $1,000; wife was Miss Ellen Conly, born in Ireland; married in 1851; have three children; Dem; Cath.

BIGGSBY L. E. Farmer, Sec. 18; 40 acres; P.O. Kingston; Rep; from Mass.

BLISS L. J. Farmer, Sec. 20; P.O. Kingston; born in Vermont in 1826; came to this state in 1854; 160 acres, value $8,000; wife was Annie Hill, born in Kingston, DeKalb Co. in 1838; married in 1860; has three children; Rep.

BOWKER W. S. Farmer, Sec. 17; P.O. Kingston; born in N.Y. in 1822; came to this state in 1845; 120 acres, value $6,000; personal prop. $1,000; wife was Miss Mary V. D. Worcester, born in Canada in 1826; married July 4, 1851; has two children; Rep; Meth.

BOWKER W. J. Farmer, Sec. 17; P.O. Kingston; Rep;

BOYLE TIMOTHY O. Farmer, Sec. 24; P.O. Genoa; Dem; from Ireland.

BRAINARD L. B. Farmer, Sec. 3; P.O. Belvidere; value of prop. $11,100; Rep; N.Y.

BRANT C. Farmer, Sec 8; P.O. North Kingston; Rep; from Germany.

BRANCH H. F. Farmer, Sec. 10; P.O. Kingston; born in DeKalb Co. in 1843; owns 160 acres, value $6,000; personal prop. $1,500; has been Justice of the Peace; wife was Delia Witter, born in Boone Co. in 1852; married in May, 1876; Rep.

BRIDGE FRANK, Farm Laborer; P.O. North Kingston; Rep.

BRIDGE F. D. Farm Laborer; P.O. North Kingston; Rep.

BRIDGE GEORGE, Farm Laborer; P.O. North Kingston; Rep.

BROWN J. S. lives on E. Lucas' farm, Sec. 6; P.O. Kirkland; Rep.

BURKEY JOSIAH, Farmer, Sec. 7; 80 acres; P.O. North Kingston; Rep; from Germany.

BURTON RICHARD, Farmer, Sec. 13; P.O. Genoa; born in Canada in 1821; came to Illinois in 1842; owns 320 acres, value $16,000; personal prop. $2,000; wife was Sarah Russell, born in Kentucky; married in 1846; has seven children; Rep; Meth.

BURTON G. F. Farmer, Sec. 13; P O. Genoa; Dem.

BURTON W. R. Farmer, Sec. 13; P.O. Genoa; Dem; from Illinois.

BURCHFIELD H. Farmer, Sec. 30; P.O. Kingston; value of prop. $3,000; Rep.

BROWN V. Engineer; P.O. Kingston; value of prop. $500; Rep; from N.Y.

CAMPBELL J. R. Sec. 7; P.O. Kingston; Dem; from Penn.

, CAMPBELL HENRY, Sec. 7; P.O. Kingston; Dem; from Penn.

CAMPBELL THOS. Farmer, Sec. 7; P.O. Kingston; born in Union Co. Penn. in 1827; came to this state in 1855; 69 acres, value $3,400; personal prop. $700; was in 30th Ill. Infantry; wife was Harriet Rowles, born in Penn. in 1826; married in 1848; five children; Dem.

COLVIN IRA, Farmer, Sec. 20; P.O. Kingston; Dem.

CARLSON JOHN, Farmer, Sec. 24; P.O. Genoa; Rep; from Sweden.

CANNABAUM THOS. Farmer, Sec. 24; P.O. Genoa; Dem; from Ireland.

CHAPMAN JULIUS, Proprietor of Kingston Flouring Mills, P.O. Kingston; born in Ashtabula Co. Ohio, in 1812; came to Ill. in March, 1837; owns 1400 acres, value $90,000; is School Director and Commissioner of Highways; wife was Miss Susan Durham, born in Delaware Co. N.Y. in 1847; married in 1840; Dem.

CHASE W. B. Physician and Surgeon; residence Kingston Station; P.O. Kingston; born in Dutchess Co. N.Y. Sept. 3, 1821; came to this state March 24, 1852; wife was Abigail Carson, born in Ireland in 1830; married July 8, 1874.

CHASE WM. B. Physician, Sec. 32; P.O. Kingston; born in 1821; came to Ill. in 1852; surgeon U.S.A.; wife was Mrs. Abbie Edge, born in Ireland in 1833; married in 1874; her first husband was Geo. Edge; has nine children; Rep; Meth.

CHEASEBRO JAMES L. Farmer, Sec. 32; P.O. Sycamore; born in Madison Co. N.Y. March 13, 1815; came to Ill. in 1856; wife was Eliza Sherman, born in Oswego Co. N.Y.; married Feb. 25, 1836; has ten children; Rep.

CLARK SUSAN Mrs. Sec. 31; P.O. Kirkland; widow of Robert Clark, who died in 1864; born in England in 1818; came to U.S. in 1854; owns 80 acres land, val. $4,000; personal prop. $500; name before marriage, Susan Gathercoal; married in 1836; has seven children.

CLARKE A. H. Merchant, Kingston, Ill.; Rep; Quaker.

COLE WASHINGTON, Farmer, Sec. 4; P.O. North Kingston; born N.Y. 1810; came to this State in 1835; owns 125 acres, value $6,250; personal prop. $1,000; is School Director; wife was Harriet Stiles, born in N.Y. in 1813; married in 1834; has five children; Dem.

COLE M. N. Farmer, Sec. 3; P.O. North Kingston; val. of prop. 10,500; Rep; Bapt; N.Y.

COLE W. L. Farmer, Sec. 4; P.O. North Kingston; val. of prop. $2,300; Rep; from Ill.

COLE J. A. Farmer, Sec. 4; P.O. North Kingston; val. of prop. $4,300; Rep; from Ill.

COLE N. Sec 36; P.O. Kingston; 10 acres, val. $450; Rep; from N.Y.

COLE R. C. Sec. 36 P.O. Kingston; 10 acres, val. $450; Rep; from N.Y.

COLLIER J. Farmer, Sec. 34; 80 acres; P.O. Kingston; Rep.

CRISSINGER S. Farmer, Sec. 34; P.O. Kingston; born in Penn. in 1843; came to this state in 1874; 40 acres, value $2,000; personal prop. $700; wife was Miss Mary Uplinger, born in Penn. in 1843; married in 1866; has two children; Dem; Pres.

DANEILS JOHN, Farmer, Sec. 34; P.O. Kingston; born in England.

DIBBELE I. H. Mrs. Farmer Sec. 19; P.O. Kingston.

DIBBLE JAMES, Carpenter, Kingston Station; P.O. Kingston; Rep; from N.Y.

DIBBLE H. Farmer, Sec. 19; P.O. Kingston; Rep; from N.Y.

DIBBLE A. W. Farmer, Sec. 31; P.O. Kirkland; born in N.Y. in 1831; came to Ill. in 1833; owns 120 acres, value $6,000; personal prop. $1,500; wife was Mary May, born in Penn. in 1836; married in 1858; has four children; Rep.

DIBBLE JOHN, son of Mrs. J. H. Dibble, Sec. 19; P.O. Kingston; Rep.

DICKSON JERRY, Mason, Kingston; Rep; from Penn.

DONNAHUE PATRICK, Farmer, Sec. 24; P.O. Genoa; Dem; from Ireland.

DURHAM M. Farmer, Sec. 12; P.O. Genoa; Rep; from Ill.

DUNLEVY FRANK, Laborer; P.O. Genoa; Cath; from N.Y.

DYER JOHN D. Farmer, Sec. 24; P.O. Genoa; Rep; from N.Y.

FOSTER J. W. Capt. Farmer, Sec. 9; P.O. Kingston.

FOSTER N. C. Farmer, Sec. 16; P.O. Kingston; Rep.

FAIRCLO M. Farmer, Sec. 35; P.O. Sycamore; born DeKalb Co. 1842; Rep; rents farm of I. Fairclo; val. prop. $4,000; wife was Lula Hicks, born DeKalb Co. 1850; married 1873; has two children.

FAIRCLO ISAIAH, Farmer, Sec. 35; P.O. Sycamore; born 1802 in N. J.; came to state 1835; Rep; Pres; owns 250 acres, value $12,000; val. per. prop. $1,000; wife was Hannah Judd, born Conn; married 1825; has eight children.

FAIRCLO J. Farmer, Sec. 36; P.O. Sycamore.

FULLER H. R. Groceries, Boots and Shoes, Kingston; Rep; from Mass.

FUGSTRON A. Laborer on Sec. 35; P.O. DeKalb; Dem; from Sweden.

GARDNER JOHN O. Laborer, Sec. 22; P.O. Kingston; Rep; from N.Y.

GATHERCOAL THOMAS Kingston P.O.; from Eng; val. prop. $800.

GLEASON J. J. Mason; P.O. Kingston; Dem; from N.Y.

GIBBS A. D. Farmer, Sec. 6; P.O. North Kingston; Rep; val. prop. $3,000.

GORHAM FRANKLIN, Farmer, Sec. 8; P.O. North Kingston; Rep; N.Y.

GORHAM ALBERT, Farmer, Sec. 8; P.O. North Kingston; Rep; from N.Y.; prop. $3,000.

GOFF ALBERT, Farmer, Sec. 7; P.O. North Kingston; Rep.

GRANGER W. M. Farmer, Sec. 33; 80 acres; P.O. Kingston; Rep.

GRIGGS ELI, Farmer, Sec. 8; 300 acres; P.O. North Kingston; Rep.

GROUT H. P. Farmer, Sec. 31; P.O. Kirkland; born Windsor Co. Vt. 1836; came to Ill. 1853; Rep; owns 82½ acres, val. $5,000; per. prop. $1,000; was in Co. C. 52d Ill. Infantry; wounded at Shiloh in the abdomen, one inch above and to the right of navel, and the ball passed into the intestines, laid there twenty-one days, and then passed off through the alimentary canal; wife was Mrs. Mary A. Foster; married 1863; one child.

GREEN LEVI, Farmer, Sec. 9; P.O. North Kingston; Rep; from N.Y.; val. prop. $8,000.

HAWLEY AUSTIN, Farmer, P.O. Kingston; Dem; Luth; from Ill.

HANCOCK S. Carpenter, Sec. 21; P.O. Kingston; Rep; N. J.; val. prop. $1,000.

HAULY AUSTIN, Farmer, Sec. 14; P.O. Kingston; born Cook Co. Ill. 1839; came to county 1869; Dem; Luth; was in the 8th Ill. Cav. five years; was prisoner at Andersonville; received an honorable discharge.

HARE GEORGE, Farmer, Sec. 6; P.O. North Kingston; Rep; from state.

HARE MARTIN, Farmer, Sec. 7; 45 acres; P.O. North Kingston; Rep.

HARE HENRY, Farmer, Sec. 19; P.O. Kingston.

HARPER O. Farmer, Sec. 19; P.O. Kingston; Rep.

HARPER J. Farmer, Sec. 9; P.O. North Kingston; Rep; from N.Y.

HAWKS GEO. W. Rev. Pastor M. E. Church, Kingston; Rep.

HALLWRIGHT ALONZO, Farmer, Sec. 24; P.O. Genoa.

HAGAN P. Farmer, Sec. 5; P.O. Kingston; Rep; from Ger.

HECKMAN PHILIP, Farmer, Sec. 10; P.O. North Kingston; born Morgan Co. Ohio, 1823; came to state 1852; Rep; Freewill Bapt; owns 230 acres, val. $11,000; per. prop. $3,000; wife was Miss Sarah A. Farley, born Morgan Co. Ohio 1830; married 1849; has eight children.

HILL W. W. Farmer, Sec. 21; P.O. Kingston; Rep; from Ill.

HILL W. E. Sec. 24; P.O. Genoa.

HILL G. H. Farmer, Sec. 21; P.O. Kingston; Rep.

HILL LEONARD, rents farm of S. H. Stiles, Sec. 2; P.O. Genoa; Rep; from Ill.

HOWARD H. Farmer, Sec. 2; P.O. Genoa; Rep.

HOLROYD W. Farmer, Sec. 1; P.O. Genoa; born Leeds, Eng. 1819; came to Ill. 1843; Rep; Advent; owns 160 acres, val. $8,300; per. prop. $2,000; wife was Ann Hana, born Canada; married 1869.

HOLROYD JAMES, Farmer, Sec. 14; P.O. Genoa; val. prop. $2,500; Rep.

HOLROYD C. H. Farmer, Sec. 1; P.O. Genoa; from Ill.

HOAG ELIAS, Laborer; P.O. Genoa; Dem; from Mich.

HOUGHTON JOHN, Farmer, Sec. 26; P.O. Kingston; Rep; val. prop. $1,000.

HURD E. rents farm of I. Northrup, Sec. 34; P.O. Kingston.

IVES N. L. Farmer, Sec. 30; P.O. Kirkland; born Nov. 18, 1836, in N.Y.; came to Ill. 1846; Rep; owns 245 acres, val. $12,000; val. per. prop. $1,000; has been Road Com. and Town Coll; wife was Eliza Aurner, born DeKalb Co; married 1861; two children.

JANZEN THEODORE, Farmer, Sec. 5; P.O. Kingston; Rep; from Ger.

JOHNSON JAMES, Farmer, Sec. 27; P.O. Kingston; Rep; from N. H.; val. prop. $700.

JOHNSON AARON R. Farmer, Sec. 18; P.O. North Kingston.

KAPPEL SAMUEL, Farmer, Sec. 19; P.O. Kingston; Rep.

KENADY JAMES, lives on Samuel Tittle's estate, Sec. 28; P.O. Kingston; Rep.

KIANAN W. Farmer, Sec. 2; P.O. Genoa; Dem; from Ireland,

KINKNER JAMES, Farmer, Sec. 34; P.O. Sycamore; Rep; val. prop. $2,000; Pa.

KNOPP FERDINAND, Farmer, Sec. 8; P.O. North Kingston; from Germany.

KNOX T. G. Farmer, Sec. 24; P.O. Genoa; Rep; from Ill.

KNOX T. G. Farmer, Sec. 13; P.O. Genoa; Rep; from Ill; val. prop. $10,000.

KINKNER JOHN, Farmer, Sec. 34, P.O. Sycamore; born Penn. 1848; came to DeKalb Co. 1849; Rep; val. prop. $1,000; wife was Ella Parker, born in county 1854; married July 1, 1875.

LANCTON CHARLES, Farmer, Sec. 2; P.O. Genoa; Rep; from Ill.

LANCTON A. Mrs. widow, Sec. 2; P.O. Genoa.

LEMLEY P. Farmer, Sec. 9; P.O. North Kingston; Rep; from Ger.

LENDSTROM S. F. Farmer, Sec. 6; P.O. Kingston; born Sweden, 1837; came to state 1869; Rep; Luth; wife was Christina Johnson, born Sweden; married 1866; six children.

LEONARD PATRICK, Farmer, Sec. 1; P.O. Genoa; born Ireland 1837; came to Ill. 1856; Cath; owns 120 acres, val. $6,000; val. per. prop. $1,000; is School Director; was in 105th I. V. I. Co. A, three years, was honorably discharged; wife was Jennette Strong, born Genoa, Ill; married Dec. 2, 1866; has three children.

LITTLE H. H. Farmer, Sec. 10; P.O. Genoa; born Erie Co. N.Y. 1824; came to Ill. 1845; Ind; Meth; owns 160 acres, val. $8,000; val. per. prop. $1,400; has been School Trustee and Highway Commissioner; wife was Ester Heckman, born Morgan Co. Ohio 1831; married October 1, 1873.

LITTLE E. B. Farmer, Sec. 11; P.O. Genoa; born N.Y. 1845; came to Ill. 1846; Rep; owns 180 acres, val. $9,000; per. prop. $800; was in 9th Ill. Cav. two years, as Corporal; wife was Miss Laura Strong, born Ill. 1852; married 1875.

LITTLE JAMES, Farmer, Sec. 12; P.O. Genoa; Rep.

LOWE O. S. Farmer, Sec. 32; P.O. Kingston; born Sullivan Co. N.Y. 1850; came to Ill. 1870; Rep; Christian; val. per. prop. $500; wife was Miss Laura Knight, born DeKalb Co. 1851; married June 9, 1872; two children.

MALTBY J. Farmer, Sec. 10; P.O. Genoa; Rep; from Ill; val. prop. $4,000.

McGINNIS HENRY, Farmer, Sec. 15; P.O. Kingston; Rep; from Ireland; prop. $1,500.

MASTERSON L. Farmer, Sec. 31; P.O. Kirkland; born Brooklyn, N. Y. 1856; came to Ill. 1861; Dem; val. prop. $1,500; wife was Mary Murray, born N.Y. 1854; married 1874; two children.

MAITLAND JAMES, Farmer, Sec. 32; P.O. Kingston; Rep.

McCLELLAN JANE Mrs. wid. Sec. 33; P.O. Kingston.

McALLISTER CHAS. Farmer, Sec. 29; P.O. Kingston; Rep; from N.Y.

McCLELLAN JOHN, Farmer, Sec. 33; P.O. Kingston; Rep.

McGINNIS PATRICK, Farmer. Sec. 16; P.O. North Kingston; Dem; from Ireland.

McALLISTER J. C. M.D. Physician, Kingston; Rep; from N.Y.

McKEAGUE NORTON, Farmer. Sec. 32. S.W. ¼; P.O. Kingston; born Canada, 1830; came to Ill. 1853; Rep; owns 80 acres, value $5,000; personal prop. $2,000; School Director; has been Path-master; wife was Mary A. Ault, from Penn; married 1854; six children.

McDONOUGH JOHN, Farmer, Sec. 24; P.O. Genoa; Dem; Cath; from Ireland.

McNELLIS JOHN, Laborer; P.O. Genoa; Dem; Cath; from Ireland.

McDONALD W. W. Farmer, Sec. 10; P.O. North Kingston; born Washington Co. Ohio, 1820; came to Illinois 1852; Rep; owns 135 acres, value $6,750; val. personal prop. $900 wife was Miss Sarah Stephens, born Ohio; married 1856; has seven children.

McDONALD D. S. Laborer, Sec. 10; P.O. Kingston; Rep; from Ohio.

MEAD S, Farmer and Dealer in Stock, Sec. 23, P.O. Kingston; born Otsego Co. N.Y. Jan. 22, 1822; came to Ill. Sept. 12, 1843; Rep; owns 163 acres, value $8,000; val. personal property $3,000; wife was Rosetta E. Corwin, born Cortland, N.Y.; married Feb. 14, 1849; has four children.

MERRILLS LOUIS, Farmer, Sec. 28; 80 acres; P.O. Kingston; Rep; from N.Y.

MINER D. J. Farmer, Sec. 7; P.O. North Kingston; Rep.

MIGNAULT LOUIS, House and Carriage Painter, Sec. 32; P.O. Kingston; born Montreal, Can. 1845; came to Ill. 1860; Rep; Cath; owns prop. val. $1,200; Hospital Steward of Sycamore Guards; wife was Miss Addie Ellsdworth, born Platte City, Mo. 1850; married 1870; three children.

MILLER A. J. Farmer. Sec. 17; P.O. Kingston; born Penn. 1828; came to county 1855; Rep; 65 acres, value $3,250; personal property $600; Path-master; was in 30th I. V. I.; discharged 1865; wife was Miss Mathilda Tittle, born N.Y. 1838; married July 3, 1856; four children.

MILLIGAN JAMES, Farmer, Sec. 12; P.O. Genoa; Dem; Cath; val. prop. $1,000; Ireland.

MURRY JOHN, Laborer; Sec. 15; P.O. Kingston; Dem; from Ireland.

MULLIGAN JAMES, Farmer, Sec. 24; P.O. Genoa; Dem; from Ireland.

NORMAN THOMAS, Farmer, Sec. 4; P.O. North Kingston; from England.

NORTHRUP J. Farmer, Sec. 34; 40 acres; P.O. Kingston.

NICHOLS CHARLES, Farmer. Sec. 35; P.O. Sycamore; born Sweden, 1844; came to Ill. 1854; Rep; rents farm of Ira Douglass; was in I. V. I. four years, and received an honorable discharge; wife was Dilana Douglas, born in county 1852; married 1872; has two children.

O'BRIEN WILLIAM, Farm-Laborer, Sec. 22; P.O. Kingston; from Ireland.

OLLMAN FERDINAND, Farmer, Sec. 8; P.O. North Kingston; Rep; from Germany.

ORR JNO. P. Laborer, Kingston; Rep; from Penn.

ORR JOHN, Laborer, Kingston; Rep; from Penn.

ORR THEODORE, Laborer, Kingston; Rep; from Penn.

OSBORN W. G. Farmer, Sec. 13; P.O. Genoa.

PEARSON JOHN, Laborer, Sec. 24; P.O. Genoa; Rep; Luth; from Sweden.

PHILIPS ROBT. Farmer, Sec. 20; P.O. Kingston; Dem; from England.

PARKER H. N. Farmer, Sec. 35; P.O. Kingston; born N.Y. 1814; came to state 1854; Rep; Meth; 174 acres, value $8,700; personal prop. $500; wife was Miss Mary A. Stillwell, born Kentucky, 1812; married 1833; seven children.

PARKER ELIZA J. Mrs. resides Sec. 34; P.O. Kingston; widow of Parly Parker; born Indiana 1832; came to Ill. 1853; owns 100 acres, value $5,000; val. personal prop. $1,000; Meth; married 1848; has six children.

PETERS EDGAR A. Farmer, Sec. 34; P.O. Sycamore; rents farm of Isaac Northrop; born Sycamore, DeKalb Co. 1848; Rep; value prop. $1,000; wife was Miss Ella Roberts, born Rutland Co. Vt. 1852; married 1874; one child.

PETERSON C. I. Sec. 24; P.O. Genoa; from Sweden.

PICKART ELDER P. Min. Bapt. Ch; P.O. North Kingston; Rep.

POUST SIMON, Farmer, Sec. 23; P.O. Kingston; born Penn. 1825; came to state 1847; Ind; owns 122 acres, value $6,000; val. personal prop. $1,500; School Director; wife was Lorinda J. Amsden, born N.Y.; married 1853; has eight children.

POWERS CLINTON, Farmer, Sec. 10; P.O. Genoa; Rep; from Ill; val. prop. $1,000.

PRESTON A. Farmer. Sec. 8; P.O. Kingston; Rep; from N. J.

PULS WILLIAM, Farmer, Sec. 5; P.O. Kingston; born Germany, 1838; came to state 1856; Rep; Evang. Association; 182 acres, value $9,000; personal property $1,000; Pathmaster and School Director; wife was Hannah Stienmiller, born Germany, 1844; married 1864; four children.

PULS FREDRICK, Farmer, Sec. 5; P.O. North Kingston; born Germany, 1843; came to State 1859; Rep; Evang. Association; 40 acres; value of property $6,000; wife was Christena Seraven, born Germany, 1846; married 1870; one child.

QUIGLEY J. Farmer, Sec. 9; P.O. North Kingston; Rep; from N.Y.

QUIGLEY A. C. Farmer and Mechanic, res. on Sec. 9; P.O. North Kingston; born N.Y. 1845; Rep; was in 141st Reg. I. V. I.; discharged Oct. 11, 1864; wife was Miss Helen A. Green, born Ohio, 1843; married 1868; has one child.

REYNOLDS W. B. Farmer, Sec. 20; P.O. Kingston; Dem; from Penn.

ROSAKRANS Z. Farmer, Sec. 8; P.O. Kingston; 122 acres, val. $6,000; Rep; from N.Y.

RAIRDIN FRANK, Farmer. Sec. 31; P.O. Kirkland; born McHenry Co. Ill. 1848; has lived in DeKalb Co. 15 years; Rep; owns 80 acres, value $4,000; val. personal prop. $1,600; wife was Mary Hait, born DeKalb Co. 1851.

ROWAN THEODORE, Farmer, Sec. 31; P.O. Kirkland; Rep.

ROBERTS E. R. Farmer, Sec. 32; P.O. Sycamore; born Oswego Co. N.Y. 1842; came to Ill. 1849; Rep; Meth; 80 acres, val. $4,000; personal prop. $1,000; wife was Catharine Wike, born Germany, 1865; four children.

RUSSELL JOHN, Farmer, Sec. 26; P.O. Kingston; born in Ohio, 1813; came to Ill. 1848; Rep; Meth; owns 400 acres, val. $20,000; val. personal property $3,000; has been Assessor and School Trustee; wife was Miss Mary A. Flemming, born Ohio 1810; married Dec. 28, 1833; has five children living.

RUSSELL S. S. Farmer, Sec. 23; P.O. Kingston; born Lebanon, Ind. 1844; came to state 1849; Rep; Meth; val. prop. $1,000; wife was Eliza Newett, born England; married 1868.

SAUM S. Farmer and Dealer in Stock, Sec. 22; P.O. Kingston; prop. $3,000; Rep; Meth; Ill

SAUM J. B. Farmer, Sec. 27; P.O. Kingston; Rep.

SANTEE STEPHEN, Farmer, Sec. 26; P.O. Kingston; born Luzerne Co. Penn. 1841; came to Ill. 1867; German Reform Church; owns 135 acres, val. $6,750; val. per. prop. $600; wife was Susan Uplinger, born Luzerne Co. Penn. Sept. 25, 1846; married 1863; has seven children.

SAUM N. Farmer, Sec. 22; P.O. Kingston; value of prop. $16,000; Rep; Meth; from Va.

SEWARD W. W. Farmer, Sec. 30; P.O. Kingston; rents farm of 80 acres of Mrs. Stewart; born in N.Y. in 1843; came to Ill. in 1851; value of prop. $600; wife was Mary J. Owen, born in Kane Co. Ill. in 1848; married in 1865; has three children; Ind; Meth.

SHELLENBERGER ISAAC, Farmer, Sec. 29; P.O. Kingston; born in Penn. in 1812; came to this state in 1845; to DeKalb Co. in 1869; 202 acres, value $10,000; value personal prop. $2,000; wife was Miss M. Leiter, born in Penn; married in 1836; has nine children; Rep; Meth.

SHELLENBERGER W. E. Farmer, Sec. 29; P.O. Kingston; Rep; from Ill.

SHERMAN I. C. Blacksmith and Farmer, Kingston Station; residence Sec. 21; P.O. Kingston; born in Erie, Penn. Jan. 4, 1837; came to this state in 1860; owns 194½ acres, value $9,000; personal prop. $1,000; has been town clerk four years; wife was L. M. Stewart, born in N.Y.; married in 1860; has five children; Rep.

SHELEY DIER, Farmer, Sec. 3; P.O. Genoa; born in Erie Co. Ohio, July 16, 1829; came to Ill. in 1859; owns 129 acres, value $5,000; personal prop. $1,000; has been Assessor three years; was in 4th Iowa Cav. Co. B, seventeen months; wife was Lois M. Norton, born in Erie Co. Penn.; married in 1854; has six children; Rep; Free Bapt.

SHRADER ANCE, Farmer, Sec. 27; P.O. Kingston; val. prop. $2,500; Rep; Germany.

SHANKLEMIER MICHAEL, Farmer, Sec. 7; P.O. North Kingston; from Germany.

SMITH WILLIAM, Farmer, Sec. 24; P.O. Genoa; Dem; from Ireland.

SMITH J. W. Farmer, Sec. 1; P.O. Genoa; born in England in 1848; came to this state in 1854; owns 80 acres, value $4,000; personal prop. $800; wife was Miss B. Keney, born in Ireland; married in 1865; has three children; Dem.

SMITH F. P. Laborer on Sec. 10; P.O. North Kingston; Rep; from N.Y.

SMITH EDWARD E. Laborer, Sec. 24; P.O. Genoa; Dem; Cath; from N.Y.

SMITH WILLIAM, Section Boss on R.R.; Sec. 24; P.O. Genoa; Dem; Cath; Ireland.

SNYDER JOHN, Farmer. Sec. 7; P.O. North Kingston; Rep; from Canada.

STARK HARMON M. Farmer, Sec. 31; P.O. Kingston; born in Sycamore in 1841; works farm of Marshall Stark (who owns); 360 acres, value $18,000; was in 105th I. V. I. three years; served full time and received an honorable discharge; went through all battles with the regiment; wife was Mary J. Patent, of Wisconsin; married in 1866; has four children; Rep.

STUART LYMAN, Farmer and Dealer in Lumber, Sec. 27; P.O. Kingston.

STUART LUCY P. Sec. 21; P.O. Kingston; Meth; from Mass.

STUART JAMES, Farmer, Sec. 27; owns over 300 acres; P.O. Kingston; Rep; from N.Y.

STEWART JAS. Y., P. M. and dlr. Groceries, Boots and Shoes, Kingston; Rep; val. $10,000.

STILES S. H. Farmer, Sec. 2; P.O. Genoa; Rep; from N.Y.

STRAG CHAS. Farmer, Sec. 4; P.O. North Kingston; Rep; from Germany.

STREGE HENRY, Farmer, Sec. 4; P.O. North Kingston; 80 acres, value $4,000; Germany.

TAZWELL R. Station Agent at Kingston Station; P.O. Kingston; Rep; from Ill.

THURLBY W. Farmer, Sec. 4; P.O. Belvidere; from England.

THOMAS R. B. Farmer, Sec. 30; P.O. Kingston; value of prop. $5,000; Rep; from N.Y.

THOMAS HENRY M. Farmer, Sec. 19; P.O. Kingston; Rep.

THOMAS H. M. Farmer, Sec. 5; P.O. North Kingston; Dem; from Germany.

TITTLE JOHN, Laborer on Sec. 17; P.O. Kingston; Rep; from Penn.

TOPLIN ORVIL, Farmer, Sec. 15; P.O. Kingston; val. prop. $1,000; Rep; from N.Y.

TUTTLE W. C. Hotel Proprietor, Kingston Station; P.O. Kingston; born in Mass. in 1818; came to this state in 1843; value of prop. $2,000; was at Huntsville, Ala., in 1864 as army station agent; wife was Miss Hattie Washburn, born in Maine in 1848; married in 1868; has four children by first wife; Rep; Univ.

UPLINGER JNO. Farmer, Sec. 28; P.O. Kingston; Rep;

UPLINGER J. H. Dealer in Hardware, Tinware, Pumps, Lime, Hay, Cement, Stucco, Farm Machinery, and Building Material, Kingston, Ill.; born in Penn. in 1852; came to this state in 1867; P.O. Kingston.

VAN FLEET NATHAN; Farmer, Sec. 24; P.O. Genoa.

VANDEBURGH H. G. Farmer, Sec. 32; P.O. Kingston; born in N.Y. in 1827; came to Ill. from Ohio in 1845, and lived in this Co. ever since; owns 164½ acres, value $7,080; personal prop. $1,000; has been Assessor twice, and is now Road Commissioner; wife was Miss Mary E. Knight, born in Ill.; married March 4, 1864; three children; Rep.

WABER N. Farmer, Sec. 33; P.O. Kingston; Rep; from Germany.

WAIT C. Farmer, Sec. 12; P.O. Genoa; val. of prop. $4,800; Rep; from Ohio.

WAIT W. H. Farmer, Sec. 4; P.O. Belvidere; Rep; from Ohio.

WAIT SCOTT A. Farmer, Sec. 12; P.O. Genoa; born in Ill. in 1852; owns 120 acres, value $6,000; personal prop. $1,200; is School Director; wife was Miss A. Corson, born in Penn. in 1855; married in 1874; has one child; Rep.

WASHBURN R. W. Farmer, Sec. 3; P.O. North Kingston; Rep; Bapt; from Ill.

WHITNEY S. D. Farmer, Sec. 10; P.O. North Kingston; born in Erie Co. Ohio, in 1836; came to this state in 1848; owns 125 acres, value $6,000; personal prop. $2,000; was in 9th Ill. Cav Co. I, fourteen months; wife was Harriet Vail, born in Tompkins Co. N.Y. in 1835; married April 2, 1856; has four children; Rep.

WITTER S. Farmer, Sec. 11; P.O. North Kingston; Rep; Meth; from Ill.

WILLIAMS SARAH, Sec. 9; P.O. North Kingston; val. of prop. $4,000; Meth; N.Y.

WIFFIN M. C. Farmer. Sec. 13; P.O. Genoa.

WITTER P. Mrs. residence Sec. 11; P.O. North Kingston; born in Herkimer Co. N.Y. in 1818; came to Ill. in 1849; owns 142 acres, value $7,000; personal prop. $300; Meth.

WOOD OTIS, Farmer, Sec. 4; P.O. Kingston; born in Middlesex Co. Mass. in 1823; came to this state in 1845; 253 acres, value $12,650; personal prop. $1,000; wife was Mrs. Nancy Brown, born in Ky.; married in 1866; no children; Rep.

WOOD GEO. E. Farmer, Sec. 24; P.O. Genoa; born in Kingston, DeKalb Co. in 1844; owns 400 acres land; wife was Miss Mary Rudd, born in Coldwater, Mich. in 1844; married in 1867; has one child; Rep.

WORCESTER M. L. Farmer, Sec. 17; P.O. Kingston; Rep; from Mass.

WORNAKA E. Farmer, Sec. 28; P.O. Kingston.

WRIGHT MARK, Laborer; P.O. Genoa; Rep; from Ill.

WYLYS A. N. Blacksmith, Kingston; Rep; from N.Y.

WYLYS GEORGE, Blacksmith, Kingston; Rep; from N.Y.

ZINZSER Mrs. Sec. 6; P.O. Belvidere; value of prop. $6,000.

MAYFIELD TOWNSHIP.

ALDRICH AMANDA Mrs. wid. of W. B. Aldrich, Sec. 8; 160 acres, val. $8,000; from N.Y.
ATWOOD MORRIS, Sec. 4; P.O. Sycamore; Rep; from Penn.

ATWOOD HOLMES, Laborer, Sec. 26; P.O. Sycamore; 2 acres, val. $100; Rep; from Conn.

AULT M. Farmer, Sec. 5; P.O. Sycamore; born Pa. 1827; came to Ill. 1850; owns 202 acres, value $10,100; property $1,500; School Director three years; wife was Sarah Gross, born in Pa. 1831; married 1858; four children.

BAKER SAMUEL F. Sec. 10; P.O. Sycamore; Dem.
BERGH C. JEFF. V. D. Farmer, Sec. 4; P.O. Sycamore; Dem; from Ohio.

BAKER NATHAN, Farmer, Sec. 4; P.O. Kingston; born in Penn. Feb. 18, 1820; came to Illinois in 1869; Rep; Luth; value of property $1,000; School Director; was in the 5th Penn. Cavalry, wife was Catharine Ault; born in Penn; married in 1842; nine children.

BACON B. F. Farmer, Sec. 16; P.O. Sycamore; born in Sturgis, Mich. in 1832; came to Illinois in 1852; has lived in the state since; Wes. Meth; Rep; was in grocery and butchering line at Sycamore, seven years; owns 120 acres, value $6,000; value of personal property $1,200; is Town Clerk; wife was Chloe Fox, from Ohio; married in 1855; has five children.

BERGH A. V. D. Farmer, Sec. 4; P.O. Kingston; born in Tioga Co. N. Y. Dec. 1816; came to this county Nov. 8, 1845; has remained in county ever since; Dem; owns 141 acres, value $7,210; value of personal property $1,000; has been commissioner of highways; has been elected Justice of the Peace, but would not accept; wife was Louisa Webster, from New York; married in 1836; has six children.

BEERS CHAS. Farmer, Sec. 11; P.O. Sycamore; owns 151 acres; Rep; from Conn.

BEEMAN O. W. Farmer, Sec. 16; P.O. Sycamore; from New York.

BENTLEY RICHARD, rents Henry Joiner's estate, Sec. 25; 300 ac; P.O. Sycamore; Rep; N.Y.

BENTLEY R. H. lives on C. Joiner's farm, Sec. 26; Rep.

BROOKS GEORGE H. Sec. 9; P.O. Sycamore; Rep; from New York.

BROOKS M. B. Farmer, Sec. 9; P.O. Sycamore; Rep; from New York.

BRASH FREDERICK, lives on Turner Wing's farm, Sec. 33; P.O. Sycamore; Rep; Germany.

BRENAN E. Farmer, Sec. 20; P.O. Sycamore; Rep.

BURCHFIELD S. Sec. 8; P.O. Sycamore; Rep; from Penn.

CARVER JOHN, Farmer on Jno. Tifft's farm, Sec. 1; P.O. Sycamore; Rep; from Penn.
CALHOUN A. H. Farmer, Sec. 31; P.O. DeKalb.

CARLISLE A. W. Farmer, Sec. 11; P.O. Sycamore; born in New York, in 1844; came to state in 1854; Dem; owns 40 acres, value $2,000; value of personal property $250.

CAMP FRANKLIN, Farmer, Sec. 35; P.O. Sycamore; born in Hanover, N. H. in 1824; came to Illinois in 1847; Rep; Bapt; wife was Eliza B. Dow, from Hanover, N. H; was married in 1848; has five children.

CAMP CHARLES, lives on Geo. Clark's farm, Sec. 35; P.O. Sycamore; Rep; from Ill.

CAMPBELL H. G. Sec. 17; 80 acres, val. $3,200; Rep; from Scotland.

CARNES GEO. Sec. 1; 108 acres; val. of prop. $4,320; Rep; from Ill.

CARNES R. S. Sec. 1; 108 acres; val. of prop. $4,320; Rep; from Ill.

CARPENTER WILLIAM, Sec. 16; P.O. Sycamore; 80 acres, value $4,000.

CHRISMAN DELOS, Farmer, Sec. 32; P.O. DeKalb.

CHEASEBRO CHARLES D., P.O. Sycamore; Rep; from New York.

CLARK WILLIAM F. Farmer. Sec. 18; P.O. Sycamore; born in LaSalle Co. Ill. in 1843; came to this county in 1874; Rep; owns 150 acres, value $6,000; value of personal property $1,000; wife was Annie Read, born in Mayfield; married in 1873; has 3 children.

CLARK WM. lives with his father, Sec. 29; P.O. Sycamore; Rep; born in county.

CLARK ERNEST, lives with father, Sec. 29; P.O. Sycamore; Rep; born in county.

CLARK GEORGE, Farmer, Sec. 29; P.O. Sycamore; Rep; from England.

COONFRE DANIEL, Farmer. Sec. 10; P.O. Sycamore; born in Schuylkill Co. Penn. in 1802; came to Illinois in 1856; Rep; Wes. Meth; owns 80 acres, value $3,000; value of personal property $500; wife was Elizabeth Dewalt, born in Penn; married in 1826; has four children.

CORNELL LEROY. Farmer, Sec. 7; P.O. Sycamore; born in Illinois; Rep.

CONDON JOHN, Farmer, Sec. 22; P.O. Sycamore; born in Cork, Ireland, in 1801; came to Illinois in 1830; has lived in this county twenty-six years; Dem; Cath; owns 145 acres, value $8,000; value of personal property $1,500; wife was Eliza Davelin, born in Ireland in 1827; has three children.

CONDON HENRY F. Farmer, Sec. 2; born Will Co. Ill. 1850; came to county 1851; Dem.

COAFERY OWEN, Farmer, Sec. 18; P.O. South Grove.

COOPER WM. lives on H. Draper's farm, Sec. 21; Dem.

COLEMAN H. lives on H. Mackey's farm, Sec. 1; 80 acres; val. of prop. $3,200; Dem; N.Y.

CROSBY WILLIAM, rents farm of E. P. Nichols, Sec. 8; P.O. Sycamore; Rep; from Vt.

CRANE JOHN, Laborer, Sec. 2; P.O. Sycamore; Rep; from Illinois.

CRANE THOMAS, Farmer, Sec. 2; P.O. Sycamore; born in England, June 24, 1815; came to state in 1842, has lived in county since; Rep; owns 120 acres, value $6,000; personal property $1,500; wife was Catharine Lanan, born in Belgium in 1825; married in 1847; has five children.

CRAMPTON THOMAS, Farmer, Sec. 34; P.O. DeKalb; Epis; 80 acres, val. $3,200; England.

D ECKER D. Sec. 15; 180 acres, value $4,800; Rep; from N.Y.

DENNIS J. D. Sec. 22; 120 acres, value $8,000; Rep; from N.Y.

DENNIS G. H. Farmer, Sec. 17; P.O. Sycamore; born in New York in 1831; came to Ill. in 1852; Rep; owns 130 acres, value $6,500; value of personal property $2,000; wife was Louisa Oosterhout; married in 1856; has five children.

DICK J. H. Farmer, Sec. 15; P.O. Sycamore; born in DeKalb Co. in 1851; Rep; wife owns 83 acres, value $4,000; personal property $800; wife was Miss Mattie Judd, born in DeKalb Co. in 1853; married in 1873; one child.

DICK JNO. Sec. 22; 120 acres, value $4,800; Rep; from Scotland.

DOYLE ARTHUR, Sec. 27; 160 acres, value $6,400; Dem; from Ireland.

DOUGLASS IRA, Farmer, Sec. 12, P.O. Sycamore; born in Genesee Co. N. Y. in 1814; came to Illinois in 1851; Rep; Meth; owns 225 acres in Mayfield Tp. and 160 in Kingston Tp. value $10,000; value of personal property $2,000; first wife was Cyrena Goodrich, born in Chenango Co. N. Y. in 1812, by whom he had three children, died in 1855; second wife was Hannah J. Powell, born in Clearfield Co. Penn. in 1825; married in 1856; has three children.

DUNMORE L. M. Farmer and Blacksmith, lives on Sec. 10, with B. W. Dunmore; P.O. Sycamore; born in Monroe Co. Michigan, in 1851; came to Iillinois in 1863; Dem; value of property $650.

DUNMORE B. W. Farmer, Sec. 10; P.O. Sycamore; born in Mich. in 1846; came to state in 1864; Dem; Adventist; 85 acres; value $4,000; personal property $800; wife was Miss Mary Nichols, born in Mayfield Tp. in 1847; married in 1866; two children.

DRAPER BENEDICT, Farmer. and Breeder of a superior Breed of Horses, suitable to all this western country, Sec. 21; P.O. Sycamore; born in Canada in 1815; came to this county Jany. 1874; Rep; Meth; owns 360 acres of land; wife was Mildred Rench, from England; married in 1842; has seven children.

DRAKE CHARLES, Farmer, Sec. 28; P.O. Sycamore; born in Windsor Co. Vermont, in 1827; came to DeKalb Co. in 1841; Rep; owns 40 acres of land, value $1.500; value of personal property $250; wife was Lucinda Decker, born in Delaware Co. N. Y. in 1841; has three children.

DRAKE HIRAM, Farmer, Sec. 22; P.O. Sycamore; born in Vermont in 1819; came to this state in 1843; has lived here ever since; Rep; Meth; owns 134 acres, value $6,000; value of personal property $3,000; has been Commissioner of Roads, and Collector two years; wife was Maria Walrod, born near Utica, N. Y. in 1822; married in 1841; 8 children, all living.

DRAKE H. A. Farmer, Sec. 21; P.O. Sycamore; born in Mayfield, DeKalb Co. in 1849; has lived in this county ever since, with the exception of one year in Iowa; Rep; Meth; owns 75 acres, value $3,700; value of personal property $1,500; wife was Rose Chesbro, born in Erie Co. N. Y. in 1852; has no children.

DRAKE ORLANDO, Sec. 20; 88 acres, value $4,000; Rep; from N.Y.

DRAFFIN DAVID, lives on Jas. Byer's farm, Sec. 7; from N.Y.

DRAFFIN DAVID, lives on A. Partridge's farm, Sec. 22; Rep; from Ireland.

F LEMMING E. Farmer, Sec. 31; P.O. DeKalb.
FOX ALLEN, Sec. 16; 80 acres, value $2,200; Rep.

G UTTSCHALK ROBERT, lives on Sec. 18; P.O. South Grove; Dem; from Germany.
GARDNER DAVID, Farmer, Sec. 3; P.O. Sycamore; born in Connecticut in 1824; came to Illinois in 1843; owns 100 acres, value $5.000; personal prop. $1,500; wife was Miss Kezia Call, born in Ohio in 1835; married in 1856; family of three children; Rep.

GLEASON WILLARD, lives on V. Hix's farm, Sec. 2; Rep; from Ill.

GRAHAM HOOTEN, Sec. 23; 300 acres, value $12,000; P.O. Sycamore; Dem; from Ky.

GRAHAM JAMES R. Farmer, Sec. 11; P.O. Sycamore; born in Kentucky in 1832; came to DeKalb Co. in 1835; has lived in Co. since; 204 acres, value $10.000; personal prop. $2.000; School Director; wife was Miss Nancy Stillwell, born in Kentucky in 1830; married in 1858; family of six children; Rep; Meth.

GROSS WILLIAM, Farmer, Sec. 8; P.O. Sycamore; born in Luzerne Co. Penn. Dec. 5, 1835; came to Ill. in 1855; own 120 acres, value $6,000; personal prop. $1,200; wife was Miss Julia Fague, born in Penn. in 1833; married in 1871; Rep; Meth.

GROSS JOS. K. Sec. 4; 160 acres, value $8,000; Rep; from Pa.

H ALLETT JAMES, Farmer, Sec. 30; P.O. DeKalb; value of prop. $5,000; Rep; England.
HUNTER JAMES, P.O. Sycamore; Rep; from Mass.

HELSON R. J. Farmer, Sec. 1; P.O. Sycamore; born Kane Co. 1851; Rep; rents farm of Jno. Tifft; wife was Phoebe Richardson, who was born in Kane Co. Ill. 1853; married 1873.

HERSON R. J. Farmer, Sec. 1; P.O. Sycamore; born in Kane Co. in 1851; rents farm of John Tifft; wife was Phoebe Richardson, born in Kane Co. Ill. in 1853; married in 1873; Rep.

HURD C. H. Renter on Sec. 34; P.O. DeKalb; Rep; from N.Y.

HUNTER JAMES, works Mrs. A. Nichols' farm, Sec. 7; P.O. Sycamore; Rep; from Mass.

ILES HENRY, Farmer, Sec. 19; born in Bristol, England, in 1822; came to this state in 1849; 80 acres, value $4,000; personal prop. $500; School Director; wife was Susan Talbot, born in London, England; married in 1856; family of eight children; Dem; Epis.

ISRAELSON JOHN A. Farmer, Sec. 12; P.O. Sycamore; born in Sweden in 1841; came to this state in 1868; 63 acres, value $3,000; personal prop. $500; wife was Emma Agrall, born in Sweden, in 1836; married in 1866; no children; Rep; Luth.

J OHNSON JOHN, lives on John Black's farm, Sec. 36; Rep; from Sweden.
JOHNSON ANDREW, lives on W. Wright's farm; Sec. 33; P.O. DeKalb; Rep; Sweden.

JOINER CYRUS S. Farmer, Sec. 26; P.O. Sycamore; born in 1813; came to Illinois in 1837; owns 107 acres, value $4.900; personal prop. $1,000; wife was Almina Lyon, from N. Y.; has three children; Rep.

K ING PHILIP, Farmer, Sec. 9; P.O. Sycamore; Rep; from Ohio.
KNAPPENBERGER N. lives with father, Sec. 7; P.O. Sycamore; Dem.

KING W. M. Farmer, Sec. 9; P.O. Sycamore; born in DeKalb Co. in 1854; value personal prop. $500; Dem.

KNIGHT SAMUEL, Farmer, Sec. 9; born in Frederick Co. Md. in 1816; came to this state in 1837; owns 172 acres, value $8,600; personal prop. $2,000; Commissioner of Roads; wife was Mary Tower, born in Vermont in 1815; married March 20, 1839; has seven children; Ind; Christian.

KNIGHT SAML. Sec. 9; 160 acres, value $8,000; Rep; from Penn.

KNAPPENBERGER B. Farmer and Cooper, Sec. 7; P.O. Sycamore; born in Penn. May 15, 1818; came to Ill. in 1856; rents farm of 320 acres of A. H. Arnold; value of personal prop. $1,000; wife was Anna Storfor, from Penn. born in 1820; married in 1842; has eight children; Dem; Luth.

KNAPPENBERGER JOHN, P.O. Sycamore; Dem.

KOONS J. L. Laborer on Sec. 15; P.O. Sycamore; Rep; from Maryland.

L ANAN NICHOLAS, Sec. 22; 160 acres, value $6,400; Dem; from Germany.

LEROY DANIEL, Sec. 26; P.O. Sycamore; 40 acres, value $1,200; Rep; from N.Y.

LANAN CATHARINE Mrs. Sec. 12; born in Germany in 1832; came to Ill. in 1853; 160 acres, value $8,000; personal prop. $100.

LAMAN HENRY, Farmer, Sec. 4; P.O. Sycamore; born in Belgium, in 1821; came to America in 1833; 207 acres, value $10,350; personal prop. $800; wife was Miss Mary Ann Gregory, from Germany; married in 1854; four children; Dem; Cath.

LONDON W. W. Farmer, Sec. 11; P.O. Sycamore; born in Clearfield Co. Penn. in 1841; came to this state in 1855; 190 acres, value $9,000; personal prop. $500; Rep.

LISTY ANDREW, Farmer, Sec. 34; P.O. Sycamore; born in Germany in 1842; came to U.S. in 1852; owns 159 acres, value $5,000; personal prop. $500; wife was Julia M. Thomas, from N.Y.; married in 1870; has two children.

LYONS MARY Mrs. Sec. 33; 80 acres, value $3,200; P.O. DeKalb; from N.Y.

M cCLELLAND E. P. Sec. 11; P.O. Sycamore; Rep.

McCLELLAND BYRON D. Sec. 11; P.O. Sycamore; Rep.

McCLELLAND M. Farmer, Sec. 11; P.O. Sycamore; born in Crawford Co. Penn. in 1826; came to Ill. in 1844; owns 64 acres, value $3,000; personal prop. $1,000; has been Collector two years, and Assessor one year; wife was Mrs. Mary Osterhout, born in Wyoming Co. Penn. in 1817; married May 8, 1850; has six children; Rep; Christian.

McCARTY DAVID, Farmer, Sec. 17; P.O. Sycamore; 160 acres; value $4,600; Dem; Ireland.

McCARTHY THOMAS, Farmer, Sec. 19; P.O. Sycamore; Dem; from Newfoundland.

McCARTHY JOHN, Sec. 20; P.O. Sycamore; born in Ireland.

McMILLIGAN ALEX. Sec. 30; P.O. Sycamore; 80 acres, value $2,400; Rep.

MACKEY H. Sec. 11; P.O. Sycamore; 150 acres, value $7,500; Dem; from N.Y.

MACKEY JAS. lives on Henry Layman's farm, Sec. 4; from Penn.

MARTIN JNO. lives on Henry Layman's farm; Sec. 4, from Md.

MITCHEL H. H. Farmer, Sec. 23; P.O. Sycamore; born in N.Y. in 1818; came to Ill. in 1837; owns 300 acres, value $15,000; personal prop. $2,000; wife was Mary A. Atwood, born in Penn. in 1833; married in 1852; has six children; Rep.

MITCHEL FRANK, Sec. 23; P.O. Sycamore.

MOYERS JOHN, Farmer, Sec. 4; 80 acres, value $4,000; Rep; from Penn.

MOSES J. H. Farmer, Sec. 7; P.O. Sycamore.

MOORE PETER, Farmer and Blacksmith, Sec. 26; P.O. Sycamore.

MULLEN JOHN, Farmer, Sec. 15; P.O. Sycamore; born in Ulster Co. N.Y. in 1802; came to Ill in 1839; has lived in this Co. ever since; owns 26 acres, value $1,200; personal prop. $500; third wife was Rachael Deyo, born in Columbia Co. N.Y. in 1812; married in 1875; is her of ten children; Rep; Wes. Meth.

MULLIGAN M. Farmer, Sec. 19; P.O. Sycamore; value of prop. $4,000; Dem; from Ireland.

N EWTON FRANK, lives on H. Rote's farm, Sec. 6; 120 acres, value $6,000; Rep; Ohio.

NICKERSON D. Sec. 6; 40 acres, value $2,000; Rep; from N.Y.

NICKERSON M. Sec. 5; 40 acres, value $2,000; Rep; from N.Y.

NICHOLS E. P. Farmer, Sec. 8; 200 acres, value $9,000; P.O. Sycamore; Rep; from N.Y.

NICHOLS STEPHEN, Sec. 26; 120 acres, value $6,000; P.O. Sycamore; Dem; from Ill.

NICHOLS ARDILLA Mrs. widow, Sec. 7; P.O. Sycamore; from Ill.

NICHOLS A. C. Mrs. lives on Sec. 7; P.O. Sycamore; owns 120 acres, value $4,800.

NIC JACOB, Farmer, Sec. 18; P.O. South Grove; Dem; from Germany.

NICHOLS L. Farmer, Sec. 10; P.O. Sycamore; born Sullivan Co. N.Y. 1820; came to state 1837; Adv; 119 acres, value $5,000; personal property, $1,000; wife was Miss Armenia Jackman, born N.Y. 1828; married 1845; two children.

NICHOLS M. S. Farmer, Sec. 9; P.O. Sycamore; born Town Mayfield, 1851; Rep; Wes. Meth; wife was Miss Luella Grant, born Town of York, DuPage Co. Ill. 1860; married March 27, 1876.

NICHOLS C. R. Farmer, Sec. 35; P.O. Sycamore; born in Vt. 1815; came to Ill. Oct. 1875; Dem; owns 36 acres of land, value $2,000; per. prop. val. $500; wife died in 1874; has five children.

NORRIS S. P. Farmer and Blacksmith, Sec. 10; P.O. Kingston; born Bath, Steuben Co. N.Y.; came to Ill. in 1867; Rep; Wes. Meth; owns 8 acres, value $3,200; value personal property, $500; wife was Miss Helen J. Hullett, born in N.Y.; married 1863; has three children.

OSBORN H. Farmer, Sec. 14; P.O. Sycamore; born England, 1834; came to Ill. 1855; Rep; owns 75 acres, value $3,000; value personal property, $1,000; school director; wife was Miss Hattie Bayley, born New York; married in 1863; no children.

OSTERHOUT A. F. Farmer, Sec. 12; P.O. Sycamore; born DeKalb Co. 1842; Dem; rents farm of W. A. Miller; was in 105th Ill. Inf. three years; wife was Miss Celia Carnes, born Kingston, DeKalb Co. 1848; married 1870; two children.

PETERSON F. A. Farmer, Sec. 11; P.O. Sycamore; value property, $5,000; from Sweden.

PARKER CHARLOTTE Mrs. Sec. 37; P.O. Sycamore; 90 acres, val. $3,600; from Vt.

PARKER JOHN, Farmer and Mason, Sec. 16; P.O. Sycamore; born in Ireland, 1807; came to U. S. 1830, but did not come to Ill. until 1867; Dem; Pres; owns 80 acres land, value $4,000; value personal property, $1,000; wife was Miss Mary Anderson, born Ireland, 1823; was married in 1849; has four children.

PATRIDGE HORACE, lives on J. D. Dennis' farm, Sec. 22; Rep; from N.Y.

PETERS N. Sec. 27; P.O. Sycamore; 80 acres, value $2,400; Rep; from N.Y.

REID S. B., P.O. Kirkland.

RAWSON L. W. Farmer, Sec. 34; P.O. DeKalb; Dem; from N.Y.; owns 80 ac. val. $3,200.

RAY GEO. lives on Alex. Ray's farm, Sec. 17; 160 acres, value $4,800; Rep.

RENWICK GEORGE, Farmer, Sec. 29; P.O. Sycamore; born Scotland, 1823; 160 ac. val. $6,000.

RENWICK W. F. Farmer, Sec. 36; P.O. Sycamore; Rep; from Kane Co; value property, $400.

READ WM. Farmer, Sec. 14; P.O. Sycamore; Rep; Wes. Meth; from N. B.; 240 ac. val. $12,000.

RICH WILLIAM, lives on Pat. Keegan's farm, Sec. 28; P.O. Sycamore; 120 acres; England.

ROBINSON WM. Farmer, Sec. 6; P.O. Kirkland; born Summerhill, Cayuga Co. N.Y. 1811; came to Ill. 1849; has lived on this farm ever since; Rep; belongs to M.E. Church; owns 114 acres, value $5,000; per. prop. $800; has been Town Trustee and Road Com; wife was Amanda Nickerson, from Conn; married 1835; two children.

REMALA W. Farmer, Sec. 5; P.O. Sycamore; born in Penn. 1830; came to Ill. 1855; Rep; owns 109½ acres, val. $3,475; wife was Miss Mary A. Rote, born in Penn. 1846; married 1866; two children.

ROCHE THOMAS, Farmer, Sec. 18; P.O. South Grove; born DuPage Co. Ill. 1851; Rep.

ROTE SAMUEL, Farmer, Sec. 26; P.O. Sycamore; born in Penn. Aug. 14, 1844; came to this state in 1859; Rep; owns 80 acres of land, value $4,000; wife was Anna Youkan, born Penn. 1847; married Jan. 18, 1869; has two children.

ROTE HENRY, Farmer, Sec. 6; P.O. Sycamore; born Lycoming Co. Penn. June 20, 1817; came to Ill. 1856; Rep; 124 acres, value $6,200; personal property $500; has been Road Commissioner; wife was Miss Ester Carpenter, from Columbia Co. Pa.; married 1840; seven children.

ROCHE HENRY, Farmer, Sec. 18; P.O. South Grove.

ROSS PETER, Farmer, Sec. 14; P.O. Sycamore.

SIVRIGHT J. Sec. 16; 40 acres, value $1,600; Rep; from N. S.

SNYDER GEORGE, Sec. 32; P.O. DeKalb; 150 acres, value $6,000; Dem; from N.Y.

SAFFORD E. P. Farmer, Sec, 27; P.O. Sycamore; born in N.H. March 14, 1837; came to this Co. in 1858; was in the 105th I. V. I. one year and two months, and was then transferred to the 14th U.S. Colored I. as Captain; resigned in April, 1865, on account of wounds received in action; owns 200 acres, value $10,000; personal prop. $1,500; has been Sheriff of Co.; is now Supervisor of town; wife was Sarah F. Safford, born in Maine in 1843; married in 1866; has three children; Rep; Cong.

SCHMOLDT OSCAR, Farmer, Sec. 24; P.O. Sycamore; born in Penn. April 13, 1833; came to Ill. in 1844; was in California six years; owns 270 acres, value $13,500; pers. prop. $1,500; wife was Mary Townsend, from Sullivan Co. N.Y.; married April 11, 1866; has two children; Rep.

SENSKA F. O. Farmer, Sec. 1; P.O. Sycamore; born in Rockford, Ill. in 1843; owns 40 acres, value $2,000; personal prop. $800; wife was Miss M. A. Ratcliffe, born in England in 1842; married in 1872; family of two children; Rep; Meth.

SHERWOOD H. Farmer, Sec. 11; P.O. Sycamore; rents farm of D. Tower; born in Ill. in 1853; 80 acres, Sec. 10, value $4,000; wife was Miss Matilda Read, born in Kane Co. Ill.; married in 1874; Rep.

SHAW JOHN, Farmer, Sec. 9; P.O. Sycamore; born in Penn. in 1823; came to Illinois in 1846; Dem; owns 100 acres, value $4,000; value of personal property $1,000; wife was Ann Sivwright, from Nova Scotia; married in 1850; has five children.

SHEWEY E. O. Farmer, Sec. 23; P.O. Sycamore; born in Maryland in 1848; came to Illinois in 1864; Dem; Wes. Meth; owns 33 acres, value $1,600; value of personal property $1,0 0; wife was Clara M. Barnard, born Illinois; married in 1873; has two children.

SHEWEY JOHN W. Sec. 23; P.O. Sycamore; Dem; from Maryland.

SHEWEY JAMES, Sec. 23; P.O. Sycamore; Dem; from Maryland.

SHEWEY ALEXANDER, Sec. 23; P.O. Sycamore; Dem; from Maryland.

SHERWOOD C. W. Farmer, Sec. 9; P.O. Sycamore; owns 60 acres, value $3,000; Rep; N. Y.

SHEWEY THEODORE, Sec. 23; P.O. Sycamore; Dem; from Maryland.

SHAW W. H. Laborer, Sec. 11; P.O. Sycamore; Rep; from England.

SIVWRIGHT N. S. Farmer, Sec. 15; P.O. Sycamore.

SIVWRIGHT A. Farmer, Sec. 15; P.O. Sycamore.

SIVWRIGHT JAMES, Farmer. Sec. 2; P.O. Sycamore; 80 ac. $3,000; Rep; Dem; Nova Scotia.

SMITH SIDNEY, Farmer, Sec. 30; P.O. Sycamore; Rep; from N.Y.

SMITH RICHARD A. Farmer, Sec. 26; P.O. Sycamore; born in N.Y. in 1828; came to this Co. in 1856; owns 135 acres, value $9,000; personal prop. $2,000; has been Co. treasurer eight years; went into the 13th I. V. I. as private, and came home as captain; wife was Miss Roxana Gault, born in N. Y. in 1838; was married in 1852; has three children; Rep; Meth.

SMITH EDWIN P. Farmer, Sec. 35; P.O. Sycamore; born in DeKalb Co. in 1843; owns 300 acres, value $15,000; personal prop. $3,200; wife was Flora Joiner, born in DeKalb Co. in 1845; was married in 1870; has one child; Rep.

SMITH N. D. Farmer, Sec. 31; P.O. DeKalb.

SMITH MONROE, lives on Sec. 30; P.O. Sycamore; Rep; from N.Y.

SPARROW S. Farmer, Sec. 12; P.O. Sycamore; born in England in 1848; came to Ill. in 1864; 30 acres, Secs. 24 and 25, value $4,000; personal prop. $1,500; wife was Louisa Brisbe, born in Canada in 1849; married in 1866; has one child; Ind; Meth.

STARK D. W. Farmer, Sec. 3; P.O. Sycamore; 180 acres, value $9,000; Rep; Meth; Penn.

SULLIVAN MICHAEL, Sec. 19; 160 acres, value $6,400; Dem; from Ireland.

TAYLOR JNO. Sec. 3; 154 acres, value $7,700; Rep; from Ind.

TAYLOR JAS. Farmer, Sec. 3; P.O. Kingston; val. prop. $7,000; Rep; Meth; from Ind.

TEEPLE CHARLEY. lives on R. Wilkinson's estate, Sec. 28; P.O. Sycamore; 400 ac; Canada.

TIFFT S. L. Farmer, Sec. 1; P.O. Sycamore; born in Grafton Co. N.H. in 1824; came to Ill. in 1842; owns 207 acres, value $8,000; personal prop. $800; wife was Charlotte Selts, born in N.Y. in 1834; married Sept. 26, 1850; has eight children; Dem; Meth.

TIFFT JOHN, Farmer, Sec. 1; P.O. Sycamore; born in Grafton Co. N H. in 1814; came to Ill. in 1836; has lived in Co. ever since; owns 200 acres, value $10,000; personal prop. $800; wife was Miranda Dunning, born in Orange Co. N.Y. in 1825; married in 1861; has three children by first wife; Rep; Meth.

TIFFT JNO. S. Farmer; P.O. Sycamore; Meth; val. $700; from Ill.

TOWER G. W. Farmer, Sec. 11; P.O. Sycamore; born in DeKalb Co. in 1853; Dem; value of property $1,000; has been Road-master; wife was Carrie Lanan, born in DeKalb Co; married April 11, 1876.

TOWNSEND EDWIN. Farmer, Sec. 15; P.O. Sycamore; born in DeKalb Co. in 1839; Rep; Adventist; 90 acres; value $4,500; personal property $1,000; was in 9th Ill Cavalry; wife was Miss Lorinda N. French, born in Geneva, Ill. in 1851; married 1868; two children.

TOWNSEND CHARLES, Farmer, Sec. 14; P.O. Sycamore; born in Schoharie Co. N. Y. in 1808; came to Illinois in the Fall of 1837, and has lived in this county ever since; Rep; 240 acres, value $12,000; personal property $2,000; has been Road Commissioner; wife was Phebe Nichols, born in Sullivan Co. N. Y. in 1810; married in 1834; has eight children.

TOWNSEND W. H. Farmer, Sec. 13; P.O. Sycamore; owns 35 ac; val. $875; Rep; born in co.

TOWNSEND STEPHEN, Sec. 14; P.O. Sycamore; 163 acres, value $8,150; Rep; from N.Y.

TOWER D. Farmer, Sec. 11; P.O. Sycamore; value of property $1,800; Dem; Vermont.

TREFREN M. B. Carpenter, Sec. 6; P.O. Kirkland; born in Vermont in 1833; came to Illinois in 1865; Rep; was in the 98th N. Y. I., as ward master in the hospital; wife was Ann Snow, born in Maine, in 1832; married in 1854; has six children.

TREFREN G. N., P.O. Kirkland; from New York; Rep.

VANDEBURGH ISAIAH, Farmer, Sec. 32; P.O. Kingston; Rep; born in county.

VANDEBERGH A. Sec. 4; 160 acres, value $8,000; Rep; from Ohio.

VEDDER H. B. Farmer, Sec. 25; P.O. Sycamore; born in N. Y. in 1839; came to Illinois in 1870, has lived here since; Rep; Meth; owns 240 acres of land, value $15,000; value of personal property $5,000; wife was Mira Keeney, born in N. Y. in 1839; married in 1861; lost one child.

WALROD GEORGE, Farmer, Sec. 29; P.O. Sycamore; Rep; from this town.

WALROD J. Farmer, Sec. 28; P.O. Sycamore; Rep; 120 acres, value $5,000; N. Y.

WALL JOHN, Farmer, Sec. 22; P.O. Sycamore; born in Ireland, in 1832; came to U. S. in 1858; Dem; Cath; owns 120 acres, value $6,000; value of personal property $500; wife was Margaret Farell, born in Ireland in 1851; married in 1872; has two children.

WEEDEN W. Farmer, Sec. 33; P.O. DeKalb; value of property $4,000.

WHITMORE H. O. Farmer, Sec. 34; P.O. Sycamore; owns 160 ac; val. $6,000; Rep; Vermont.

WHITMORE HOWARD, Sec. 34; P.O. Sycamore; 160 acres, value $6,400; Rep; from Vt.

WING TURNER, Sec. 33; P.O. Sycamore; 179 acres, value $6,265; Rep; from Canada.

WIKE WILLIAM, lives on Martin Wike's farm, Sec. 5; 160 acres, value $8,000; from Ill.

WINIANS F. Farmer, Sec. 11; P.O. Sycamore.

WILKINSON W. Farmer, Sec. 30; P.O. DeKalb; value of property $10,000; Dem; Canada.

WRIGHT W. Farmer, Sec. 33; P.O. Sycamore; Rep.

WRIGHT JOSEPH, P.O. Kirkland; Dem; from New York.

WRIGHT LUCIUS, Farmer, Sec. 35; P.O. Sycamore; born in New York, Jany. 8, 1846; came to Illinois in 1871; Rep; owns 312 acres of land, value $18,360; value of personal property $5,000; wife was Lucy A. Smith, born in this county; was married Dec. 26, 1870; has two children.

YONKIN HENRY, lives on Jno. Taylor's farm, Sec. 3; Rep; from Penn.

YONKIN WM. Sec. 5; 160 acres, value $8,000; Rep; from Penn.

YOUNGSTRON ANDREW, Laborer, Sec. 12; P.O. Sycamore; Rep; from Sweden.

YOUNG M. J. Farmer, Sec. 12; P.O. Sycamore; value of prop. $9,000; Rep; Meth; Ills.

ZENNER PETER, Farmer, Sec 18; P.O. South Grove; born in Germany, Sep. 29, 1832; came to Illinois in 1852; Dem; Cath; owns 160 acres, value $6,400; value of personal property $2,000; wife was Anna Nic, born in Germany; married May 8, 1855; has 9 children.

20

VICTOR TOWNSHIP.

ALLEN IRA, works for Geo. J. Herrick. Sec. 17; P.O. Victor Center; Rep; Lib.

AMES JAMES, Farmer, Sec. 10; P.O. Victor Centre; owns 60 acres; Rep.

ARNOLD WILLIAM, Farmer, Sec. 20; P.O. Victor Center; born in town Dyke, Lincolnshire. England, June 13, 1846; lived there about five years; came to this country in 1851; lived in N.Y. State two and a half years; came to Batavia, Kane Co. this State and lived there three years; has lived in this town and county eighteen years; Rep; Lib; owns 80 acres land; val. $5,000; has been Road-master several years; married Miss Elizabeth Woodcock, Oct. 3, 1871, she was from town of Belton, Suffolk Co. England; they have two children, one boy and one girl.

ARNOLD ALFORD, Farmer and Stock Raiser, Sec. 27; P.O. Somonauk; importer and breeder Leicester sheep; born Lincolnshire, England, Dec. 10, 1826; came to Co. in 1851; has family of eight children living, four sons and four daughters, three sons and one daughter dead; wife was Miss Lucy Hales, from Norfolk, Eng., born Feb. 8, 1828; married Feb. 25, 1854; 160 acres land, val. $7,500; per. prop. $1,500; Rep.

ARNOLD EDWARD, Farmer, Sec. 27; P.O. Somonauk; born Lincolnshire, Eng. Oct. 10, 1825; came to this Co. in Spring of 1851; has three sons and one daughter; wife was Miss Mary Tinsley, of Lincolnshire, Eng., born May 11, 1827; married Feb. 17, 1848; 160 acres, real estate val. $8,000; per. prop. $1,000; Rep.

ARNOLD ALFRED, Sec. 34; P.O. Somonauk; 160 acres, val. $8,000; Rep; from England.

ARNOLD E. Sec. 27; P.O. Somonauk; 160 acres; val. $8,000; Rep; from England.

ARNOLD JOHN, Farmer, Sec. 20; P.O. Victor Centre; Rep; Lib; from England.

ARNOLD JOSEPH, lives with father, Sec. 20; P.O. Victor Centre; Rep; Lib.

ARKILLS JAMES W. Farmer, Sec. 15. P.O. Victor Centre; Rep; Meth; from Ill.

ARKILLS JOHN W. Farmer, Sec. 15; P.O. Victor Center; Dem; Meth; from N.Y.

BAUMCHEN C. Mrs. Sec. 35; P.O. Somonauk; 80 acres, val. $4,000; from Germany.

BAVIS JAMES, Tenant Farmer, Sec. 22; P.O. Victor Centre; Rep; Meth; from England.

BENNETT NELSON W. Farmer, Sec. 33; P.O. Leland; born in Chemung Co. N.Y. July 11, 1814, and came to this county March 10, 1860; lived in Lowville Tp. Columbia Co. Wis. eight years, previous to settling here; Rep; Bapt; has 320 acres land, value $16,000; personal property $500; had been Captain of a company in state militia in New York for four years; married Harriet D. Rowley, Feb. 25, 1836, she was born in Chemung Co. N.Y.; has six sons and two daughters.

BENNETT SAMUEL, Tenant Farmer; P.O. Victor Center; Rep; Meth; from N.Y.

BELDING O. Farmer, Sec. 30; P.O. Leland; five children; Rep; Luth; born Norway.

BERGERSON BERGY, works for Mrs Stephenson, Sec. 34; P.O. Somonauk; Rep; Norway.

BEVERIDGE JOHN C. Farmer, Sec. 13; P.O. Somonauk; born in Greenwich, Washington Co. N.Y. Feb. 3, 1826; lived in that state 36 years; came to Town Victor, DeKalb Co. in 1862, has lived here 14 years; Rep; U. Pres; owns 200 acres land, value $13,000; has held the offices of Supervisor and Town Assessor, and is Town School Treasurer; married Miss Mary McCleery, Jan. 10, 1865, she was from Ohio; they have four children, all boys.

BOSSONG GEORGE, Farmer, Sec. 14; P.O. Somonauk; born in Lorraine, Germany, Jan. 1, 1840; lived there about 16 years; came to this country in 1856; came to LaSalle Co. this state same year; lived in Northville 10 years and in that county 16 years; came to this county in 1872; Dem; Cath; owns 160 acres land, value $9,600; was in state service three months during war; married Miss Sophia Sherman, Jan. 21, 1867, she was from Town Northville, LaSalle Co. Ill; has six children, three boys and three girls.

BREESE AUGUSTUS, Farmer, Sec. 23; P.O. Somonauk; born in Basking Ridge, Somerset Co. N. J. Oct. 25, 1812; lived in that state 44 years; came to this town, county and state in 1856, and has lived here 20 years; Dem; Pres; owns 160 acres land, value $12,000; has been School Director in his district; married Susan Ann Doty, in May, 1836, she was from Somerset Co. N. J.; they have five children, all daughters; have lost two children, one boy and one girl.

BREWER J. Tenant Farmer, Sec. 17; P.O. Victor Center; Rep; Meth; from N.Y.

BRECHBID JOHN, Sec. 35; P.O. Somonauk; 120 acres, $6,000; Dem; from Germany.

BUCKHART J. Laborer, Sec. 8; P.O. VanBuren; Dem; Luth; from Germany.

BUCKHARDT CHARLES, Farmer, Sec. 16; P.O. Victor Center; Dem; Pres; from Prussia.
BUCKHARDT JOHN A. Farmer, Sec. 16; P.O. Victor Center; Dem; Pres; from Prussia.
BURNHAM A. P. Farmer, Sec. 21; P.O. Victor Center; 80 acres, $4,000; Rep; from Me.

CAREY MICHAEL, works for Cole, Sec. 2; Dem; Cath; from Ireland.
CARSON D. G. Farmer, Sec. 4; P.O. VanBuren; 280 acres; three children; Rep.
CAIN JAMES, lives with his brother Jos. H. Sec. 1; P.O. Freeland; Dem; Lib; from N.Y.
CAIN JOSEPH H. Farmer, Sec. 1; P.O. Freeland; val. $5,000; Rep; U. Pres; born N.Y.
COOK ARAMENTA Mrs. Farmer, Sec. 14; P.O. Somonauk; Meth; from N. H.
CORNELL STEPHEN N. Farmer, Sec. 24, Somonauk; val. $4,000; Dem; Meth; from Ohio.
CONDILL JAMES, Sec. 27; P.O. Somonauk; 120 acres, val. $6,000; Ind; from England.
CONDILL WM. lives with father, Sec. 27; P.O. Somonauk; Ind; from Ill.
COX JOHN, Farmer, Sec. 4; P.O. VanBuren; 120 acres; one child; Rep.
COX JOSEPH, Sec. 25; P.O. Somonauk; 160 acres, val. $8,000; Rep; from England.
COLE R. J. works for Wm. McCleery, Sec. 11; P.O. Sandwich; Rep; U. Pres; from Can.
COLE JOHN R. Farmer, Sec. 2; P.O. Waterman; born in Prince Edward Island, Oct. 22, 1833; lived there 17 years; came to U. S. 1852; followed the sea for 12 years, and sailed all over the world; was in the U. S. Navy 5 years and 8 months, was on the frigate Congress during the war 32 months and on the sloop of war Constellation 3 years; Rep; Bapt; married Mrs. Betsy A. Webster, Oct. 5, 1869, she was formerly Betsy A. Riddle, from Grafton, N. H. she married James S. Webster in 1848, he died in 1864; she owns 100 acres land, val. $6,000; they have two children, both boys.
CRAIG A. Farmer, Sec. 29; P.O. Leland; 320 acres; Rep; Pres; from N.Y.
CRAIG WM. O. Farmer, Sec. 32; P.O. Leland; 160 acres; five children; Rep.

DAVIS ALBERT, Farmer, Sec. 7; P.O. VanBuren; Rep; Lib; from Canada.
DAVIS WILLIAM G. Farmer, Sec. 8; P.O. Victor Center; Rep; Lib; from Canada.
DAVIS JOHN W. Sec. 36, P.O. Somonauk; lives with father; Rep; from N.Y.
DAVIS J. M. Sec. 36; P.O. Somonapk; 100 acres, value $8,000; Rep; from N.Y.
DALE FRANKLIN, Farmer; res. Sec. 31; P.O. Leland; owns 80 acres; Rep.
DARMODY WILLIAM, works for Frasier, Sec. 3; P.O. Waterman; Dem; Cath; from Ireland.
DEACON GEORGE, works for Thompson, Sec. 10; P.O. Victor Center; Rep; Meth; Canada.
DEAN D. L. Farmer, Sec. 23, on farm of Breese; P.O. Somonauk; Rep; Pres; from N.Y.
DENST PHILIP, Sec. 25; P.O. Somonauk; 160 acres, value $8,000; Rep; from Germany.
DEMING JOHN G. Tenant Farmer; P.O. Victor Center; Dem; Meth; from N.Y.
DOBBIN JOHN, Farmer, Sec. 2; P.O. Waterman; born in Ireland, near the "Giant's Causeway," in month Sept. 1796, lived there twenty-three years, emigrated to this country in 1819, came to N.Y. lived in Washington Co. N.Y. thirty-five years, came to this state and county in 1854, and has lived here twenty-two years, and he is now over eighty years of age; one of the oldest men in DeKalb Co; Rep; U. Pres; owns 51 acres land, value $3,500; married Miss Margaret Thompson in 1857; she was from Washington Co. N.Y.; they have two children—one boy and one girl; have lost three children, one son killed battle Vicksburg during war.
DOWNEY J. Farmer, Sec. 4; P.O. VanBuren; from Ireland; Dem; Cath.

ECKERT I. L. Sec. 34; P.O. Sandwich; 160 acres, value $8,000; Ind; from N.Y.
EHNKE JOHN, Sec. 35, Somonauk; works for Mrs. C. Baumchen; Ind; from Prussia.
EDOUX JOSEPH, Farmer, Sec. 12; P.O. Somonauk; born in France in 1807, March 19, came to this country in 1855, and has lived here twenty-one years; Rep; Cath; owns 80 acres land, value $5,000; married Miss Maggie George, Jan. 28, 1854; she was from France; they have two children—Joseph, twenty years of age; Mary, sixteen years of age.

FAULK SIMON, Sec. 26; P.O. Somonauk; 80 acres, value $4,000; Dem; from Germany.
FISK N. L. Farmer; res. Sec. 32; P.O. Leland; owns 80 acres; Rep.
FINAN PATRICK, Farmer, Sec. 24; P.O. Somonauk; Ireland; 210 acres, $10,000; Dem; Cath.
FOX THOS. lives with Cain, Sec. 1; P.O. Freeland; born Ireland; Dem; U. Pres.
FRASIER HORACE, Cheesemaker, Sec. 1; P.O. Sandwich; Rep; Bapt; from Ill.
FRAIN CHAS. Laborer for Martin; P.O. Somonauk; born France; Dem; Cath.

FRANK ADULPH, Farmer, Sec. 2; P.O. Waterman; born Prussia, March 24, 1849, came to this country the same year, lived in New York City twelve years, came to this county about 1862, and has lived here fourteen years; val. per. prop. $2,000; Dem; U. Pres; married Miss Caroline Schafman in Oct. 1870; she was born near Milford, in this state; they have three children—two boys and one girl.

GIBBONS ALVIN. Farmer; res. Sec. 10; works for Wm. Gibbons; Rep.

     GIBBONS WM. Farmer; res. Sec. 10; P.O. Waterman; 120 acres; seven children; Rep.

GLETTY WM. Farmer, Sec. 1; P.O. Freeland; per. prop. $500; born France; Rep; U. Breth.

GOODELL DAVID M. Farmer, Sec. 1; P.O. Freeland; val. $2,500; born N.Y.; Dem; U. Pres.

GOODYEAR JACOB, Laborer for Moore, Sec. 1; P.O. Freeland; born Penn; Lib; Lib.

GOTES FRED. works for Meyer, Sec. 24; P.O. Somonauk; Rep; Luth.

GRADDY EDWARD, Laborer; P.O. VanBuren; works for T. McCormick; Cath; Dem.

GRADY R. J. res. Sec. 5; P.O. VanBuren; Ind.

GRADY THOMAS, Blacksmith; res. Sec. 5; P.O. Van Buren; two children.

GRADY THOMAS, Blacksmith, Sec. 5; P.O. VanBuren; Lib; Lib; from Canada.

GREEN HARVEY, Farmer, Sec. 5; P.O. VanBuren; Rep.

GREEN HARVEY L. lives with his father, James Green; P.O. VanBuren; Rep; Meth.

GREEN J. A. Farmer, Sec. 5; P.O. VanBuren; wife and two children; Rep.

GREEN JAMES, Farmer. Sec. 5; P.O. VanBuren; owns 240 acres; Rep.

GREEN JAMES, Farmer, Sec. 5; P.O. Van Buren; Rep; Meth; from N.Y.

GREEN MARTIN. Painter, Sec. 5; P.O. VanBuren; Rep; owns 22 acres, value $1,100.

GREEN PELEG, Farmer, Sec. 5; P.O. VanBuren; Rep; own 200 acres; has four children.

GRAHAM ANDREW, Farmer, Sec. 12; Sandwich P.O.; born in Reynoldsburg, Franklin Co. Ohio, Dec. 9, 1845; lived in that state five and a half years; came to this county in 1851, and has lived here 25 years; owns 200 acres land, value $12,000; Rep; Pres; holds office School Trustee. Married Miss Mary R. McEachron, Dec. 26, 1873; she was from Washington Co. N. Y.; has two children, a boy and girl.

GRAHAM JAMES, Farmer, Sec. 12; P.O. Sandwich; born in Franklin Co. Ohio, July 27, 1849; lived there only a short time; came to this state and county 26 years; value personal prop. $3,000; Rep; U. Pres. Married Miss Anna McEachron, Nov. 25, 1875; she was from Washington Co. N. Y.; she was born Dec. 27, 1854.

GRAHAM ROBERT, Farmer, Sec. 12; P.O. Sandwich; Rep; Pres.

GRIFFIN WM. Laborer, Sec. 5; P.O. VanBuren; Cath; Dem.

GUNNISON OLE works for Harmonson, Sec. 16; P.O. Victor Centre; Luth; from Germany.

HARMONSON M. Farmer, Sec. 16; P.O. Victor Centre; born in the year 1845, July 14; lived in LaSalle Co. 15 years; lived in Kansas City, Mo., one and a half years; came to DeKalb Co. 1871; lived in town of Paw Paw; Rep; Luth; owns 110 acres land, $5,500.

HARMONSON ISAAC, was born in Norway, 1842; came to this country 1845; lived in LaSalle Co. 19 years; lived in Oregon three years; was in army 18 months, against Indians on Pacific coast. Married Marinda Erickson in 1871; she was born in LaSalle Co. in this state.

HANNEMAN JOHN, Farmer, Sec. 16; P.O. Victor Centre; Rep; Luth; from Germany.

HARRIS FRANK, works for — Sterns, Sec. 5; P.O. VanBuren; Rep; Lib; from Illinois.

HERRICK GEO. J. Farmer, Sec. 17; P.O. Victor Centre; Rep; Lib; from Vt.

HENRICH JOHN, Farmer, Sec. 36; P.O. Somonauk; 140 acres, val. $7,000; from Germany.

HERDERSON J. W. Sec. 26; P.O. Somonauk; 160 acres, val. $8,000; Rep; from Penn.

HERZOG CHAS. Sec. 36; P.O. Somonauk; 180 acres, val. $9,000; Dem; from Germany.

HILL N. Farmer, Sec. 30; P.O. Leland; owns 205 acres; Rep; Luth; from Norway.

HILL OLEYM, Farmer, Sec. 22; P.O. Leland; Rep; Meth; from Norway.

HINES JOHN G. Farmer, Sec. 2; P.O. Freeland; Rep; Meth; from Germany.

HOLSTEIN C. Farmer, Sec. 9; P.O. VanBuren; works part of farm of W. H. Keene.

HOUGH W. Farmer, Sec. 4; P.O. VanBuren; owns 120 acres; Rep.

HUSTON SAMUEL, Farmer; resides on Sec. 1; P.O. Freeland; born in Cumberland Co. Penn. Feb. 13, 1803; came to Illinois, DeKalb Co. in 1861; Rep; Luth; owns 300 acres, value $20,000 Married Ann Smith, Feb. 1831, who was born Penn. 1804; Mrs. H. died Jan. 1841, leaving two sons and two daughters; married for his second wife Mary Reed, Feb. 1844, who was born York Co. Pa. Dec. 12, 1821, and died Dec. 27, 1875, leaving five children, two sons and three daughters.

HUSTON JAMES, lives with father, Sec. 1; P.O. Freeland; born Penn; Rep; Luth.

HUSTON WM. lives with father, Sec. 1; P.O. Freeland; born Penn; Rep; Luth.

HUBBARD LORENZO, Farmer, Sec. 14; P.O. Somonauk; Rep; Meth; from Maine.

KIEHL JOHN. Sec. 25; P.O. Somonauk; 80 acres, value $4,000; Dem; from Germany.

KEENE W. H. Farmer, res. Sec. 4; P.O. Van Buren; Rep; 240 acres; wife and six children.

KOFFMAN DAVID, lives with Jas. H. Cain, Sec. 1; P.O. Freeland; Rep; U. Pres; from Penn.

KULP JOSEPH, rents of John Parisot, Sec. 35; P.O. Somonauk; from France.

KUTZNER FREDERICK, Farmer, Sec. 14; P.O. Somonauk; born in Prussia, Dec. 31, 1819; lived there about thirty-four years, came to this country in 1855, lived in Chicago one winter; came to Kendall Co. this State. 1856, lived there two and a half years, came to DeKalb Co. and has lived here nineteen years; Dem; Lutheran; owns 160 acres land, val. $10,000; married Miss Henrietta Sonnoman, March 12, 1857; she was from Prussia; has three children, two boys and one girl.

LABOLE JULIA Mrs. Sec. 23; P.O. Somonauk; 160 acres, val. $8,000, from France.

LAMB CHAS. works for —— Thompson, Sec. 10; P.O. Victor Centre.

LABEND, Farmer, res. Sec. 29; P.O. Victor Centre; owns 298 acres; born Eng.

LEGNER JOSEPH T. Farmer, Sec. 17; P.O. Victor Centre; born in Nassau, Germany, Jan. 27, 1852; came to this country 1854, lived in N. Y. one year and three months, came to Plano, Kendall Co. this State, and lived there eighteen years; Dem; Cath; val. per. prop. $1,500; has father and mother, three brothers and three sisters.

LEGNER C. Farmer, Sec. 17; P.O. Victor Centre; Dem; Cath; from Germany.

LEGNER FRED. Farmer, Sec. 9; P.O. Victor Centre; Dem; Cath; from Germany.

LOUCKS H. Farmer, Sec. 24; P.O. Somonauk; Rep; Meth; val. estate $10,000; from N. Y.

MARTIN JNO. Farmer, Sec. 13; P.O. Sandwich; Rep; Pres; born N. Y.

MASON JOSEPH, works for —— Thomas, Sec. 10; Rep; P.O. Victor Centre; Rep; Ill.

MARTIN DAVID, lives with Jno. Martin, Sec. 13; P.O. Sandwich; Rep, Pres; born N. Y.

MAUL FRED. works for John McCleery, Sec. 10; P.O. Victor Centre; Rep; Luth; Germany.

MARKLEY W. H. Farmer, Sec. 1; P.O. Freeland; Rep; U. Breth; born Pa.

MERCER ROBT. J. works for Graham, Sec. 12; P.O. Sandwich; Rep; Pres; born Pa.

MERCER JOSEPH, works for Graham, Sec. 12; P.O. Sandwich; Rep; Pres; born Pa.

MEYER FELIX, Farmer, Sec. 24; P.O. Somonauk; born in Alsace, France, Sept. 14, 1838, lived there about fourteen years, came to this country in 1852, lived in Northville, LaSalle Co. one year lived in LaSalle Co. fifteen years, came to this town in 1869, has lived here seven years, Dem; Cath; owns 200 acres land, val. $12,000; married Helen Huprecht, Feb. 3, 1862; she was from Naperville, DuPage Co. Ill; has six children, four boys and two girls.

MEYER L. works for Kutzner; P.O. Somonauk; Dem; Cath; from Germany.

MILLER ALEXANDER, Farmer, Sec. 9; P. O. Van Buren; Rep; wife and four children.

MILLER C. Sec. 34; P.O. Somonauk; 80 acres, val. $4,000; from Germany.

MILLER HENRY, Farmer. Sec. 33; P.O. Leland; owns 160 acres; Ind; seven children.

MONTAGUE G. W. Farmer, P.O. Victor Centre; Rep; Lib; from Penn.

MORENUS W. H. Sec. 5; P.O. Van Buren; Dem.

MORTON CHARLES, Farmer, Sec. 28; P.O. Victor Centre; Dem; 130 acres; two children.

MORTON GEORGE B. Farmer, Sec. 21; P.O. Victor Centre; Dem; Univ; from Mass.

MORTON GEORGE E. Farmer. Sec. 21; P.O. Leland; Dem; Univ; from Mass.

MOORE IRVIN J. Farmer, Sec. 1; P.O. Freeland; Rep; U. Pres; N.Y.

MORRISON JOHN, Farmer. Sec. 3; P.O. VanBuren; Rep; U. Pres; from Scotland.

MORRISON WILLIAM J. Farmer, Sec. 3; P.O. VanBuren; Rep; U. Pres; from Scotland.

McCORMICK THOS. Farmer; P.O. VanBuren; Dem; Cath.

McCLEERY JOHN. Farmer, Sec. 10; P.O. Victor Centre; Rep; U. Pres; from Canada.

McCLEERY WILLIAM D. Farmer, Sec. 11; P.O. Sandwich; born in Wayne Co., Ohio, June 10, 1848; lived in that state 3 years; came to this town, DeKalb Co., Ill., in 1851; lived in the county 25 years; one of early settlers; Rep; U. Pres; owns 200 acres land, value $12,000; married Miss Jeanette Randles in Dec. 1870; she was from Washington Co., N.Y. they have two children, both boys; have lost one boy.

McKEE SAMUEL. Lives with his father, Sec. 11; P.O. Freeland; Rep; Lib. from Ohio.

NELSON SAMUEL, Farmer, Sec. 9; P.O. VanBuren; Rep.

McKEE WILLIAM. Farmer, Sec. 11; P.O. Freeland; born Jefferson Co., Ohio, Sept. 28, 1803; lived in that state 54 years; came to this state and county in 1862; lived here 14 years; owns 60 acres land, value $3,500; Rep. U. Pres; has been School Director; has been elder in Presbyterian church 25 years; has been married three times; Samuel C. McKee, his son, was born Dec. 6, 1850, in Ohio; lived there 12 years; came here in 1862; married Hannah Coates Feb. 4, 1875; she was born in England; they have one child, little girl.

NEWSCHUFFER F. Farmer, Sec. 8; P.O. Victor Center; Rep; Luth; from Germany.

OLSEN JOHN, Farmer, Sec. 31; P.O. Leland; Rep; Luth; from Norway.

OLSEN L. Farmer, Sec. 31; P.O. Leland; Rep; Luth; Norwegian.

OBRECHT AUG. Laborer; P.O. Somonauk; Dem; Cath; from France.

ORR E. Laborer, Sec. 7; P.O. VanBuren; Rep.

O'BRIEN DENNIS, Farmer, Sec. 13; P.O. Sandwich; Dem; Cath; from Ireland.

O'BRIEN MICHAEL. Lives with father, Sec. 13; P.O. Sandwich; Dem; Cath; from Ireland.

PARKS M. Farmer, Sec. 28; P.O. Leland; Rep; from Ireland.

PARKS E. Farmer, Sec. 26; P.O. Leland; Rep; from Ireland.

PARKS EDWARD. Farmer, Sec. 28; P.O. Leland; born in Niagara Co. N.Y., Feb. 12, 1837; located in this county in Oct., 1856; owns 214 acres land, value $10,700; personal property value $1,600; Rep; Meth; Mr. Parks commenced on 50 acres land with but little personal property, but has accumulated rapidly; married Margaret Gould Feb. 20, 1866; she was born in Prince Edward Island; they have four sons.

PARKS R. Farmer, Sec. 32; P.O. Leland; Rep.

PARISOT A. Farmer, Sec. 35; P.O. Somonauk; from France.

PARISOT JOHN, P.O. Somonauk, Sec. 35; from France.

PARISOT JOSEPH, P.O. Somonauk, Sec. 23; from France.

PARISOT PETER, P.O. Somonauk, Sec. 26; from France.

PARKER R. W. works for Fred Legner, Sec. 9; P.O. Victor Center; Dem; Cath; from Mass.

PARRIS JAS. Tenant farmer, Sec. 22; P.O. Victor Center; Rep; Meth.

PENCIL CALVIN, works for Hines, Sec. 2; P.O. Waterman; Rep; Luth; from Ireland.

PETERSON J. works for Graham, Sec. 12; P.O. Somonauk; Denmark; U. Pres.

PETTINGER EMIL, works for Rossong, Sec. 14; P.O. Somonauk; Dem; Cath; France.

PICKMAN HENRY, P.O. Somonauk, Sec. 25; Dem; from Germany.

POTTER WILLIAM, lives with father, Sec. 1; P.O. Freeland; Rep; U. Pres; from Ill.

POTTER PLATT, Farmer, Sec. 1; P.O. Freeland; val. of farm $9,000; Rep; Lib; from N.Y.

PRICE JAMES R. lives with father, Sec. 15; P.O. Victor Center; Rep; Meth; P. E. Island.

PRICE RICHARD. Farmer, Sec. 15; P.O. Victor Center; Rep; Meth; Prince Edward Island.

PRICE S. Farmer, Sec. 27; P.O. Sandwich; 160 acres; no politics; from Prince Edward Island.

PULVER A. Sec. 4; P.O. VanBuren; works W. H. Keene; Rep.

RASPILER ALEXANDER, Sec. 26; P.O. Somonauk; 160 acres; no pol; from France.

RATTKE CHARLES, works for A. Stewart, Sec. 2; Rep; Luth; from Germany.

REESE JACOB, Farmer, Sec. 22; P.O. Victor Center; Rep; Lib; from N.Y.

RIMSNIDER AUGUST, Sec. 35; P.O. Somonauk; 80 acres, val. $4,000, Dem; from Germany.

ROCHFORD JOHN, Farmer, Sec. 5; P.O. VanBuren; 185 acres; Dem; Cath.

ROBINSON HARVEY, works Wm. McCleery, Sec. 11; P.O. Sandwich; Rep; U. Pres; Iowa.

ROMPF ADOLPH, Sec. 36; P.O. Somonauk; 80 acres, val. $4,000; Rep; Germany.

ROMPH GEO. Sec. 35; P.O. Somonauk; 80 acres. val. $4,000; Rep; from Germany.

SAWYER K. Farmer; P.O. VanBuren; Rep; Lib; from Norway.

SCHRADER ALBERT, lives with father, Sec. 23; P.O. Somonauk; Ind; Germany.

SCHROEDER A. lives with father, Sec. 23; P.O. Somonauk; Bapt; Rep; Germany.

SCHRADER JOHN, Sec. 23; P.O. Somonauk; 120 acres, val. $6,000; no pol; Germany.

SCHROEDER JOHN, Farmer, Sec. 23; P.O. Somonauk; born in Prussia, April 18, 1821, lived there about thirty-six years; come to this country 1855; came to LaSalle Co. Ill. the same year; has lived in this county about eleven years; Rep; Ger. Bapt; owns 120 acres land, value $7,200; married Wilhemina Reaseback in 1843, she was from Prussia; have seven children, three sons and four daughters.

SCOTT LUCAS V. Farmer, Sec. 16; P.O. Victor Center; born in Oswego, N.Y. Oct. 21, 1844, and lived in that state eleven years, then sailed on the lakes for twelve years, sailed first from Ogdensburg to Chicago for some time; has been in every position from cabin boy to first mate; came to this state and county in 1869; Rep; Meth; 80 acres land, value $4,000; married Miss Harriet Wiltse in 1867, she was from Oswego Co. N.Y.; they have three children, two girls and one boy.

SCOVILL JOHN H. Farmer, Sec. 20; P.O. Victor Center; born Tolland Co. Conn. Oct. 31, 1827; lived there twenty-one years; came to this state in 1848; came to this county in 1849, and has lived here twenty-seven years, and is one of the oldest settlers; owns 122 acres land, value $7,500; Rep; Bapt; has been School Trustee and School Director; married Miss. Sarah Suydam in December, 1850; she was from New Jersey; they have seven children, four boys and three girls.

SMITH FRANK W. works for G. J. Herrick, Sec. 17; P.O. Victor Center; Rep; Meth; N.Y.

STAFFORD O. Farmer, Sec. 32; P.O. Leland; owns 80 acres; wife and four children; Rep.

STEPHENSON MERANDA Mrs. Sec. 34; P.O. Somonauk; 160 acres, val. $8,000; Norway.

STERN MICHAEL, Farmer, Sec. 5; P.O. VanBuren; born in Cumberland Co. Penn. November 28, 1848, lived there about seventeen years; he enlisted in the army in the 79th Reg. Penn. Volunteers; was in Newberne, North Carolina; the regiment was in severe battle at Raleigh, and lost great many killed and wounded; came to this county in 1865; Rep; Lib; owns 144 acres land, value $7.200; married Miss Cleora Merritt in June, 1872; she was from the Town of Paw Paw, this county; they have three children, girls.

STEWART ALEX. M. Farmer, Sec. 2; P.O. Freeland; prop. $10,000; Rep; U. Pres; Ohio.

STICKEL M. Laborer, Sec. 14; P.O. Somonauk; Rep; Meth; Germany.

STOUT M. F. Farmer, Sec. 15; P.O. Victor Center; Dutch Ref'd; Ind; from N. J.

STOTT DAVID H. works for Beveridge, Sec. 13; P.O. Somonauk; Rep; U. Pres.

STRATTON GEORGE, works for Warren, Sec. 22; P.O. Somonauk; Rep; Meth; Ill.

STRATTON GEORGE N. Farmer, Sec. 17; P.O. Victor Center; born in East Hampton, Suffolk Co. N.Y. June 11. 1810; removed to this county July 2, 1853; Dem; Pres; owns 160 acres land, value $11,200; personal prop. $1,500; he married Mary B. Hand in June, 1837, and had one son, Jonathan M. Stratton, who came to this county with him; Mrs. Stratton died in Oct. 1841; Mr. Stratton again married Nancy Edwards, Oct. 5, 1847; she was born in East Hampton, Suffolk Co. N.Y. August 18, 1817; has one son.

SWEET R. Farmer, Sec. 5; P.O. Van Buren; Rep.

SWEET R. lives with his father on Sec. 17; P.O. VanBuren; Rep; Meth; Illinois.

SWEET PELEG, Farmer, Sec. 17; P.O. VanBuren; Rep; Meth; N.Y.

SUYDAM H. Mrs. widow of H. S., Sec. 29; P.O. Leland; Meth.

SUYDAM SIMON, Sec. 27; P.O. Somonauk; 80 acres, value $4,000; Rep; N. J.

SUYDAM S. B. Sec. 22; P.O. Leland; 160 acres, value $8,000; N. J.

THOMAS AUGUST, Sec. 24; P.O. Somonauk; 80 acres, val. $4,000; Rep; Germany.

THOMPSON DAVID, lives with his brother, Sec. 6; P.O. VanBuren; Dem; Lib; N.Y.

THOMAS AUGUST H. Farmer, Sec. 8; P.O. Victor Center; born in Grand Duchy Nassau, Germany, May 2, 1837; lived there sixteen years; came to this country in 1853; came to Somonauk, DeKalb Co. this state, the same year, and has lived here twenty-three years; Rep; Luth; personal prop. $1,500; had two brothers in the army; married Miss Bertha Brewer Dec. 4, 1867; she was born in Grand Duchy Nassau, Germany; has three children, one girl and two boys.

THOMPSON A. N. Farmer, Sec. 6; P.O. VanBuren; Dem; Lib; N.Y.

THOMSON SAMUEL, Farmer, Sec. 10; P.O. VanBuren; 150 acres; Rep.

THURBER THOMAS C. Farmer, Sec. 11; P.O. VanBuren; born in Saratoga Co. N Y. May 1, 1827; lived there about twenty-two years; came to Aurora, Ill. in 1849, and has lived here in this state about twenty-seven years, and in this county twenty-two years; Rep; Meth; owns 80 acres land, value $4,000; married first to Melvina Eldridge, Jan. 1, 1850; she was from N.Y. State; married Miss Marinda Ash Sept. 27, 1874; she was from N.Y. State; has three children, one son and two daughters.

TROUPPE HENRY, works for John McCleery, Sec. 10; P.O. Victor Center; Rep; Bapt; Ger.

VAN OHLEN HENRY, Farmer, Sec. 29; P.O. Leland; 80 acres; Rep; Luth.

VAN OHLEN C. Farmer, Sec. 29; P.O. Leland; 160 acres; Rep; Luth; Germany.

VAN OHLEN L. Farmer, Sec. 31; P.O. Leland; 160 acres; Rep; Germany.

VORHEES H. S. Farmer, Sec. 21; P.O Victor Center.

WARREN D. J. Farmer, Sec. 22; P.O. Somonauk; Rep; Meth; Vermont.
    WARREN THOMAS, Sec. 22; P.O. Somonauk; 160 acres; Rep; England.
WATSON ROBERT T. Farmer, Sec. 8; P.O. Waterman; Rep; Pres; N.Y.
WEBER JOHN, Tenant Farmer, Sec. 15; P.O. Victor Center; Rep; Luth; Germany.
WELCH WM. Laborer for Finan, Sec. 24; P.O. Somonauk; Dem; Cath; Ireland.
WESSON J. W. Farmer; P.O. Victor Centre; Rep; Lib; from Vt.
WILSON THOMAS T. Farmer; residence Sec. 20; P.O. Victor Center; born in England, March 8, 1834; came to state in the Fall of 1857; Rep; owns 80 acres land, value $4,000; personal prop. $800.
WILSON THOMAS, Farmer, Sec. 20; P.O. Victor Center; 80 acres; Rep; England.
WIRTZ JOHN, Sec. 26; P.O. Somonauk; 160 acres, val. $8,000; Rep; Germany.
WOOD O. Sec. 29; P.O. Leland; Rep; born Victor Center.
WRIGHT MILES, works for John McCleery, Sec. 10; P.O. Victor Center; Rep; Lib; Mich.

ZELLER CHAS. Sec. 25; P.O. Somonauk; 160 acres, value $8,000; Dem; Germany.

GENOA TOWNSHIP.

ABREHAM STEPHEN, Laborer, Genoa; Rep; from N.Y.
    ADAMS E. Sec. 18; P.O. Genoa; 57 acres, value $2,280; Ind; from Canada.
ANDERSON PETER, works for S. Slater, Sec. 21; P.O. Genoa; Rep; from N. J.
ANDERSON FRANK, works for Jesse Wing, Sec. 21; P.O. Genoa; Dem; Sweden.

BALDWIN W. C. Carpenter; P.O. Genoa; Rep; from N. J.
    BALDWIN RALPH L. Blacksmith; P.O. Genoa; Rep; from N. J.
BALDWIN GEO. W. Blacksmith; P.O. Genoa; Rep; from N. J.
BAILEY CLARK, Carpenter, Genoa; Rep; from Illinois.
BARRY THOS. works for R. McCormick, Sec. 17; P.O. Genoa; Dem; from Wis.
BEACH C. H. rents farm of A. P. Stone, Sec. 27; P.O. New Lebanon; Rep; from Ill.
BEARDSLEY GEO. W. works for R. McCormick, Sec. 17; P.O. Genoa; Dem; from N.Y.
BEEBEE DANIEL, rents from J. G. Smith, Sec. 35; P.O. Sycamore; Rep; from Ill.
BECK ROBT. Plasterer, Genoa; Rep; from England.
BLAKSLEY JAMES, works for A. A. Olmsted, Sec. 16; P.O. Genoa; Rep; from Mich.
BLAGDEN A. D. Clerk; P.O. Genoa; Rep; from Illinois.
BLAGDEN WARREN, Farmer; P.O. Genoa; Rep; from Maine.
BLANCHARD ROSWELL, Sec. 5; P.O. Ney; 80 acres, value $4,000; Rep; from N.Y.
BOTHAMY ELLIS, rents of Geo. Lawrence, Sec. 22; Dem; from Germany.
BROWN D. P. Farmer and Stock Raiser, Sec. 30; P.O. Genoa; born in the town of Baldwin, Cumberland Co. Maine, May 19, 1809; came to this county in October, 1837; has six children living, one dead; wife was Miss Charlotte Griggs, of Ashtabula Co. Ohio, born Oct. 7, 1814; married March 27, 1839; has 349½ acres, value $17,450; personal property $2,500; Rep.
BROWN J. L. Farmer, Sec. 29; P.O. Genoa; born in the town of Scarborough, Maine, April 17, 1805; came to this county in the Fall of 1837; married August 17, 1830; wife died March 4, 1848; five children by first wife; married again in June, 1850; four children by second wife; has 400 acres, value $20,000; personal prop $8 000; is Justice of the Peace; Rep.
BROWN J. W. Farmer, Sec. 33; P.O. Genoa; born in LeKalb Co. August 7, 1846; has a family of four sons and one daughter; wife was Miss Mary M. Wright, from DeKalb Co. Ill. born Oct. 8, 1847; married May 14, 1866; has a farm of 160 acres, value $8,000; personal prop. $1,000; is School Director; Rep.
BROWN J. P. Farmer, Sec. 29; P.O. Genoa; born in Johnstown, N.Y. Jan. 31, 1833; came to this Co. in Sept. 1837; has a family of four sons and seven daughters; wife was Miss Susan M. Pratt, from Nassau, Mass., born May 12, 1824; married April 8, 1854; has 354½ acres, value $17,500; personal prop. $5,000; is School Director; Rep.

BROWN GEORGE W. L. Sec. 26; P.O. New Lebanon; 120 acres, value $6,000; Rep; Ill.

BROWN D. S. lives with his father, Sec. 29; P.O. Genoa; Rep; from Illinois.

BROWN JAMES L. lives with his father, Sec. 29; P.O. Genoa; Rep; from Illinois.

BRESEE ALBERT, Sec. 16; P.O. Genoa; 120 acres value $6,000; Dem; from N.Y.

BURBANK GEO. W. Farmer. Sec. 17; P.O. Genoa; born in Erie Co. N.Y. Dec. 9, 1835; came to this county in the Spring of 1857; has a family of one son; wife was Miss Mary Richardson, from N.Y.; married Jan. 1, 1856; has 80 acres of real estate, value $4,000; personal prop. $2,500; Rep.

BURZELL GEO. Sec. 7; P.O. Genoa; 140 acres, value $7,000; Rep; from Canada.

BURZELL J. Sec. 7; P.O. Genoa; 40 acres, value $2,000; Rep; from Canada.

BUCK CHARLES, works for E. Q. Sumner, Sec. 7; P.O. Genoa; Rep; from Illinois.

BUCK GEO. W. Sec. 5; P.O. Ney; 200 acres, value $10,000; Ind; from Penn.

BURROUGHS I. Q. Sec. 11; P.O. Ney; 160 acres, value $8,000; Rep; from N. J.

BURROUGHS W. M. Carpenter, Genoa; Ind; from N. J.

BURLEY T. Mrs. P.O.Genoa; from Canada.

BURINGTON R. S. Merchant; P.O. Genoa; Dem; from Vt.

BURINGTON E. H. Pastor Advent Church, Genoa; from Penn; Rep.

CALDWELL JOSEPH Rev. Pastor M. E. Church; P.O. Genoa; Rep; from Ireland.

CARL JOHN, rents of A. Wager, Sec. 31; P.O. Genoa; Dem; from Ireland.

CHAMBERLAIN ORMAN, Laborer; P.O. Genoa; Rep; from Penn.

CHASE C. Sec. 36; P.O. New Lebanon; farm 103 acres, val. $5,150; Rep; from Ill.

CORSON PETER, Farmer, Sec. 5; P.O. Ney; born in Lycoming Co. Penn. Oct. 6, 1819; came to this county in March, 1869; has a family of five children, three dead; wife was Miss Sarah Newman, from Lycoming Co. Penn; born July 27, 1822; married Jan. 29, 1843, died Dec. 27, 1875; has 80 acres of real estate, value $3,200; personal $1,500; Rep.

CORSON HORTON, lives on father's place, Sec. 28; P.O. Genoa; Dem; from Penn.

CORSON JOHN R. Sec. 9; P.O. Ney; 260 acres, val. $7,800; Ind; from Penn.

CORSON D. B. Mrs. Sec. 4; P.O. Ney; 100 acres, $4,000; from Penn.

CORSON MILTON, rents from E. Depue, Sec. 13; P.O. Ney; Rep; from Penn.

CORSON HENRY, Sec. 3; P.O. Ney; 140 acres, value $5,600; Dem; from Penn.

COOK A. rents farm of A. Crawford, Sec. 23; P.O. Genoa; Rep; from N.Y.

CONNEISS JOHN, Sec. 36; P.O. Burlington; 80 acres, value $4,000; from Germany.

COHOON A. R Sec. 18; P.O. Genoa; 101 acres, val. $5,150; Rep; from Penn.

CRAWFORD ALEXANDER, Dealer in Butter, Eggs, and Poultry; P.O. Genoa; born in Lawrence Co. Penn. Dec. 22, 1822; came to this county Nov. 24, 1839; has family of four sons and one daughter; wife was Miss Laura Shurtliff, from Stansted, Canada, born Jan. 3, 1825; married Dec. 25, 1845; owns 560 acres of real estate, value $33,000; personal prop. $3,000; has been Justice of the Peace, also Assessor; Rep.

CRAWFORD HENRY, lives on A. Crawford's farm, Sec. 26; P.O. New Lebanon; Rep; Ill.

CRAFT GEO. with his father, Sec. 13; P.O. New Lebanon; Dem; from Penn.

CRAFT HENRY, lives with father, Sec. 13; P.O. New Lebanon; Dem; from Penn.

CRAFT THOMAS, with his father, Sec. 13; P.O. New Lebanon; Dem; from Penn.

CRAFT S. G. Sec. 13; P.O. New Lebanon; 160 acres, value $7,200; Dem; from Penn.

CRAFT JOHN, Sec. 14; P.O. New Lebanon; 80 acres, value $3,600; Dem; from Penn.

CROCKER A. A. Sec. 7; P.O. Genoa; 127 acres, value $6,350; Rep; from N.Y.

DAVIS J. M. Painter; P.O. Genoa; Rep; from N.Y.

DANO JOSEPH, rents of H. Haskins, Sec. 34; P.O. Sycamore; Rep; from N.Y.

DAVIES SAMUEL M. Hardware Merchant; P.O. Genoa; born in England, in 1841; came to this county in February, 1875; has family of one daughter; wife was Miss Jennette Spoor, from Newark, N. J.; value of real estate $2,500; personal prop. $3,000; Rep.

DAILEY C. S. Carpenter; P.O. Genoa; Rep; from N.Y.

DALBY D. Sec. 1; P.O. Ney; farm 160 acres, val. $4,800; Dem; from England.

DEWOLF GEO. Butcher, Genoa; Rep; from Penn.

DEWOLF EDWARD, Laborer, Genoa; Rep; from N.Y.

DEPUE JOSEPH, rents of N. Preston, Sec. 29; P.O. Genoa; Rep; from Ill.

DEPUE EPHRAIM, Farmer and Stock Raiser, Sec. 13; P.O. Ney; born in Sussex Co. N. J. Oct. 11, 1815; came to this state in 1849, and to the county in 1861; has family of two sons and three daughters; wife was Miss Catharine Dennis, from Sussex Co. N. J. born Sept. 21, 1817; married April 2, 1838; has 520 acres, value $20,800; personal $3,000; also has 160 acres in McHenry Co. Ill. val. $4,000; Rep.

DOUD JESSE Mrs. Sec. 34; P.O. Sycamore; 47 acres, val. $2,350; Christian; from Ohio.

DRAKE FRANK, Laborer, Genoa; Rep; from Ill.

DUMSER D. F. Horse Trainer, Genoa; Rep; from Ill.

DURHAM A. H. Sec. 10; P.O. Genoa; 269 acres, value $13,450; Dem; from Ill.

DURHAM E. H. Sec. 18; P.O. Genoa; 80 acres, value $4,000; Rep; from N.Y.

DURHAM W. R. Mrs. Sec. 29; P. Genoa; 160 acres, value $8,000; from England.

DURHAM MILTON, lives with father; P.O. Genoa; Rep; from N.Y.

DURHAM MICHAEL, retired; P.O. Genoa; 200 acres, value $10,000; Rep; from N.Y.

EICHLER ALFRED, lives with father, Sec. 10; P.O. Ney; Rep; from Ill.

EICHLER GEO. Jr. lives with father, Sec. 10; P.O. Ney; Rep; Ill.

EICHLER GEORGE, Farmer, Sec. 10; P.O. Ney; born in Prussia, Germany, Jan. 4, 1816; came to this county in 1852; has family of four sons and two daughters; wife was Miss Sophia Geisler, from Prussia, Germany, born in 1812; married in 1844; has 360 acres, value $17,000; personal $1,000; Rep; Luth.

EICHLER HERMAN, Sec. 3; P.O. Ney; 120 acres, value $6,000; Rep; fr m Germany.

EICHLER GODFREY, Sec. 3; P.O. Genoa; 80 acres, val. $4,000; Rep; Germany.

EVANS WM. Carpenter; P.O. Genoa; Rep; from Canada.

FLINT WM. Sec. 33; P.O. Sycamore; 160 acres, val. $8,800; from Penn; Rep.

FOX HARRY, works for Geo. Buck, Sec. 5; P.O. Ney; Rep; from Penn.

FORCE THOS. M. rents of Peter Waters, Sec. 28; P.O. Genoa; Rep; from N. J.

FRANTZ WM. rents of Geo. Preston, Sec. 29; P.O. Genoa; Rep; from Penn.

FRAREY ROBERT, Carpenter; P.O. Genoa; Ind; from Canada.

GALLOWAY JAMES, Laborer, Genoa; Rep; from Ill.

GEITHMAN B. Sec. 6; P.O. Genoa; 90 acres, value $3,600; Rep; from Germany.

GEITHMAN LEWIS, Sec. 6; P.O. Genoa; lives with B. Geithman; Rep; from Germany.

GREGORY E. S. Farmer, Sec. 30; P.O. Genoa; born in Danbury, Conn. April 3, 1803, came to this county in the Fall of 1837; has a family of two sons and one daughter; wife was Miss Jane Brown, from Buxton, Maine, born Oct. 26, 1802; married June 17, 1828; she died Feb. 18, 1873; he has 72 66-100 acres, value $4,355; personal property $700; has been Township Treasurer twenty years; is an unbeliever of Christian religion; Rep.

GREGORY W. G. Sec. 30; P.O. Genoa; lives on E. S. Gregory's place; Rep; from Ill.

GRIFFIN WALTER, Sec. 29; P.O. Genoa; rents farm of Mrs. W. R. Durham; Rep; Mass.

GRONQUIST C. F. Genoa P.O.; Shoemaker; from Sweden.

GWINNUP J. Genoa P.O.; Wagonmaker; Rep; from N. J.

HALLECK ADDISON, Sec. 7; P.O. Genoa; rents of P. Halleck; Rep; from Wis.

HALLECK HENRY W. Sec. 7; P.O. Genoa; lives with Addison Halleck; Rep; N. Y.

HALLECK PARKER, Sec. 7; P.O. Genoa; 40 acres, value $2,000; Rep; from Wis.

HALLECK E. J. Laborer, Genoa; Rep; from Mich.

HASKINS H. Sec. 34; P.O. Sycamore; farm 80 acres, value $5,000; Rep; from N.Y.

HANN WM. Sec. 17; P.O. Genoa; works for A. H. Olmsted; Dem; from Md.

HARRIS R. Blacksmith, Genoa; Rep; from Penn.

HARRIS L. C. Sec. 27; P.O. Genoa; 120 acres, value $6,000; Rep; from Penn.

HALL ELI, Sec. 6; P.O. Genoa; works O. E. Wilbur's place; Rep; from N.Y.

HARRINGTON E. S. Sec. 5; P.O. Genoa; rents farm of Joseph Sturges; Rep; from Ill.

HAUSLEIN M. Sec. 11; P.O. Ney; farm 160 acres, val. 8,000; Rep; from Germany.

HEPBURN WILLIAM, Sec. 10; P.O. Ney; farm 160 acres, value $8,000; Rep; from N. J.

HEPBURN JOHN J. Sec. 10; P.O. Ney; lives with his father; Rep; from N. J.

HEATH JOHN, Farmer, Sec. 34; P.O. Genoa; born in the Town of Argyle, Washington Co. N.Y. Feb. 19, 1817, came to this county June, 1846; family, two sons and five daughters; wife was Miss Hannah Shurtleff, from Canada, born Oct. 5, 1827; married Jan. 24, 1860; has farm 160 acres, value $8,000; personal property $2,000; is Supervisor; Rep.

HEATH WEBSTER, Sec. 34; P.O. Genoa; lives with his father; Rep; from Ill.

HIGGINS PATRICK, Farmer; P.O. Genoa; Dem; Cath; from Ireland.

HILL A. M. Dr. P.O. Genoa; Rep; from Ill.

HOLLEMBEAK A. N. Farmer and Stock Raiser, Sec. 7; P.O. Genoa; born in Genesee Co. N.Y. Feb. 5, 1816, came to this county in the Spring of 1840, and settled in Genoa Tp; has a family of four sons and two daughters; wife was Miss Pamelia Decker, from Genesee Co. N.Y. born May 7, 1817; married Jan. 12, 1838; has 160 acres of real estate, value $8,000; personal property $600; has been Supervisor two terms, Assessor two terms, and Road Commissioner one term; has a patent on a Barbed Wire Fence, also one on a Wind Mill; Rep.

HOLLEMBEAK H. C. Sec. 7; P.O. Genoa; lives with his father; Rep; from Ill.

HOLLEMBEAK R. W. School Teacher; P.O. Genoa; lives with his father, Sec. 7; Rep; Ill.

HOGEBOOM DAVID, Farmer, Sec. 25; P.O. New Lebanon; born Sept. 14, 1839, in N.Y. came to this county 1844; Rep; Free Thinker; owns 40 acres, value $2,000; value of personal property $2,000; wife was Miss Hattie J. Brown from N.Y. born 1841.

HOGEBOOM S. D. Mrs. Sec. 25; P.O. New Lebanon; 340 acres, value $16,000; from N.Y.

HOLT LEE, Laborer, Sec. 32; P.O. Genoa; rents of A. Sowers; Rep; from Kansas.

HOLT L. W. Sec. 33; P.O. Genoa; works for J. P. Brown; Rep; from Kansas.

HOLSHER JOHN, Farmer, Sec. 8; P.O. Genoa; born in Oldenburg, Germany, June, 1826; came to this county in 1853; has family of one son and four daughters; wife was Miss Elizabeth Murphy, from Ireland; married March 18,1860; has 166 acres, value $7,470; personal $2,000; was Road Commissioner and School Director; Ind.

HOLROYD STEPHEN, Farmer, Genoa; Rep; from England.

HOLROYD HENRY, Farmer, Genoa; 120 acres, value $6,000; from Canada,

HOLROYD ALONZO, Farmer; P.O. Genoa; Rep; from Ill.

HOLROYD FRANK, Carpenter, Genoa; Rep; from Ill.

HOAG JOHN L. Blacksmith; P.O. Genoa; Ind; from N.Y.

HOLLAND EDWARD, Sec. 32; P.O. Sycamore; lives on A. Sower's place; Ind; from Ill.

HOLSHER JOHN, Sec. 8; P.O. Genoa; 166 acres, value $7,470; Ind; from Europe.

IDE SARAH; P.O. Genoa; from Mass.

IDE WILLIS, Laborer, Sec. 32; P.O. Genoa; Rep; from Ill.

IDE GEO. Mechanic, Genoa; Rep; from Ill.

IDE D. C. Laborer; P.O. Genoa; Rep; from Ill.

IDE E. D. Sec. 19; P.O. Genoa; boards with Wm. F. Oursler; Rep; from N.Y.

JEWELL WM. Sec. 20; P.O. Genoa; works for Mrs. Wager; Rep; from Kansas.

JOHNSON S. Sec. 34; P.O. Sycamore; rents of J. V. Kelsey; Rep; from Sweden.

JACKMAN K. Dealer in Lumber, Coal and Machinery; P.O. Genoa; born in Franklin Co. N.Y. Sept. 24, 1824; came to this county in June, 1838; family of three sons and two daughters; wife was Miss Mary R. Holcomb, from Genesee Co. N.Y. born Sept. 11. 1828; married Oct. 20, 1869; value of real estate $6,000; personal property $4,000; Ind.

JOHNSON GEO. Barber, Genoa; Rep; Illinois.

JOHNSTON FRANCES E. Mrs. Sec. 1; P.O. Ney; widow of John Gilkerson, who died March 29, 1864; he was born in England Nov. 8, 1820; he left a family of three children; wife was Miss Frances E. Williams from Canaan, N. H; born July 8, 1832; married Dec. 9, 1852; he left an estate of 380 acres, value $13,200; Mrs. Johnson has 160 acres in her own name, value $3,400; Mr. Gilkerson was a member of the M. E. Church; her oldest son, Hiram Gilkerson, owns 40 acres adjoining said farm, value $800.

JONES ISAAC H. Butcher; P.O. Genoa; born in Sullivan Co. N. Y. Oct. 31, 1833; came to this county in October, 1859; married Sept. 3, 1863; wife was Miss Lizzie Gordon, from Sullivan Co. N. Y. born June 26, 1833; died July 1, 1872; married again Sept. 20, 1874, to Miss Annie M. Brown, born March 1, 1839; three children by first wife, none by second; value of real estate $1,500; value of personal property $500; is Justice of the Peace, also Notary Public; Dem.

JONES OSCAR, P.O. Genoa; boards with Isaac Jones; Rep; from N. Y.

KANOKO LEWIS. Sec. 19; P.O. Genoa; 40 acres, value $1,500; Rep; Prussia.

KARL JOHN, works for Mrs. E. Thompson, Sec. 34; P.O. Genoa; Rep; Illinois.

KESLER GEO, Sec. 16; P.O. Genoa; 160 acres, value $8,000; Rep; from N. Y.

KESLER F. lives with G. Kesler, Sec. 16; P.O. Genoa; Rep; from N. Y.

KELLOGG LESLIE, lives with his father, Sec. 3; P.O. Ney; no pol; Illinois.

KELLOGG L. P. Sec. 3; P.O. Ney; 160 acres, value $6,400; Rep; from Vt.

KELLOGG H. Mail Carrier; Sec. 3; P.O. Ney; Rep; Illinois.

KENEDY DAVID. works for Wm. Strong, Sec. 18; P.O. Genoa.

KELLEY D. H. Sec. 34; P.O. Genoa; 80 acres, value $4,000; Rep; from Vt.

KITCHEN THOS. Sec. 4; P.O. Ney; 120 acres, value $6,000; Dem; from Penn.

KITCHEN ROBT. lives with his son, Sec. 4; P.O. Ney; Rep; from Penn.

KINYEN OLIVER, works for Mrs. E. Thompson, Sec. 34; P.O. Genoa; Rep; Illinois.

KUNZLER J. J. Sec. 18; P.O. Genoa; 160 acres, value $8,000; Rep; from Switzerland.

LAMBERT PAT. Sec. 28; P.O. Genoa; works for J. P. Brown; Rep; from Ireland.

LEWIS REUBEN, works for A. H. Olmsted, Sec. 17; P.O. Genoa; Rep; from N. Y.

LAIRD W. H. Hotel and Restaurant; P.O. Genoa; born on Prince Edward Island, June 1847; came to this county in Sep. 1872; no family; wife was Miss Jane Murray from Prince Edward Island; married Sep. 15, 1874; value of real estate $1,800; no politics.

LEWIS JOHN, Sec. 8; P.O. Ney; 80 acres, value $4,000; Dem; from New York.

LISTY JOSEPH, rents of T. T. Wing, Sec. 22; P.O. Genoa; Rep; Switzerland.

LORD R. D. Butcher; P.O. Genoa; born in Saratoga Co. N. Y. Sep. 9, 1817; came to this county in the Spring of 1842; has family of two sons and one daughter; wife was Miss Olive Hogeboom, from Greene Co. N. Y., born April 24, 1820; married March 17, 1840; has 84 acres of real estate, value $7,000; personal property $1,500; served three months in the late war in Co. A, 105th Ill. Regt; Rep; is Justice of the Peace.

MANUEL GEO. works for P. N. Blanchard, Sec. 5; P.O. Ney; Rep; Illinois.

MAUDE WM. rents of D. Dalby, Sec. 1; P.O. Ney; no pol; from N. Y.

MATHEWS W. H. Jeweler; P.O. Genoa; Rep; from N. Y.

MERRIMAN JAMES, business Real Estate; P.O. Genoa; born in Westmeath Co. Ireland, March 9, 1826; came to this county in the Spring of 1849; no family; two children dead; wife was Miss Ursula M. Durham, born in Delaware Co. N. Y. May 10, 1831; married Dec. 25, 1851. has 350 acres of real estate, value $26,250; Dem; Cath; is Corporation Trustee.

MEAD ARTHUR, Grain Buyer, Genoa; Rep; Illinois.

MILLEN E. B. works for J. L. Brown, Sec. 23; P.O. Genoa; Rep; from Wis.

MILLER L. W. rents farm of Wm. King, Sec. 34; P.O. Sycamore; Rep; Ohio.

MINER I. N. Billiard Hall, Genoa; Rep; val. of prop. $2,000; from N.Y.

MORROW JAS. Sec. 25; P.O. New Lebanon; works in Cheese Factory; Rep; from N. Y.

MOORE HENRY. Laborer, Genoa; Rep; Illinois.

MOAN FRANK A. Farmer, Genoa; Dem; from New York.

MUSGRAVE WM. H. rents from E. Depue, Sec. 13; P.O. Ney; Rep; Penn.

McCORMICK R. Farmer and Stock Raiser, Sec. 17; P.O. Genoa; born in Westmeath Co. Ireland, Nov. 11, 1835; came to this county in July, 1857; has family of one son and two daughters; wife was Miss Frances Wager, from DeKalb Co. born May 22, 1844; married Sep. 22, 1862; has 205 acres of real estate, value $13,500; value of personal property $2,500; is School Director; Dem; Cath.

McELROY DANIEL, works for Wm. Flint, Sec. 33; P.O. Sycamore; Rep; Illinois.

McCLAIN JOHN Dr. Physician; P.O. Genoa; Rep; from Ireland.

NAKER A. Sec. 35; P.O. Sycamore; 160 acres, value $8,000; Dem; Germany.

NAKER M. Sec. 35; P.O. Sycamore; 240 acres, value $12,000; Dem; Germany.

OAKS ASA, lives with Thos. St. John, Sec. 2; P.O. Marengo; Rep; from N. H.

OAKLEY M. E. Sec. 25; P.O. New Lebanon; 160 acres, value $8,000; Rep; Illinois.

OFF JOHN. Sec. 20; P.O. Genoa; rents of H. M. Perkins; Rep; Germany.

OLMSTEAD GEO. Sec. 21; P.O. Genoa; 85 acres, value $4,250; Rep; N. Y.

OLMSTED A. H. Farmer and Stock Raiser, Sec. 17; P.O. Genoa; born in Delaware Co. N. Y. Jan. 12, 1835; came to this county in June, 1845, and settled in Genoa Township; has a family of two daughters; wife was Miss Rebecca Jane Eiklor, from Erie Co. Ohio; born Aug. 30; 1844; married Dec. 27, 1859; has farm of 386 acres, value $19,300; value of personal property $3,000; Rep.

OLMSTED N. works for J. J. Kunzler, Sec. 18; P.O. Genoa; Rep; N. Y.

OLMSTED C. H. Sec. 8; P.O. Genoa; 320 acres, value $16,000; Rep; N. Y.

OLMSTED S. L. Sec. 15; P.O. Genoa; 160 acres, value $8,000; Rep; N. Y.

OLMSTED CALEB, Sec. 16; P.O. Genoa; 160 acres, value $4,800; Rep; N. Y.

OLMSTED HENRY, lives with father, Sec. 16; P.O. Genoa; Rep; from Ill.

OLMSTED A. A. Sec. 16; P.O. Genoa; 280 acres, val. $14,000; Rep; from N.Y.

OPH JOHN, Sec. 30; P.O. Genoa; 114 acres, val. $5,700; Rep; from Germany.

OTTMAN WESLEY, Prop. of Pacific Hotel; P.O. Genoa; born in Schoharie Co. N. Y. Sept. 27, 1845; came to this county in the Spring of 1858; has family of two boys; wife was Miss Emily Porter, from Sullivan Co. N.Y., born Dec. 31, 1845; married Feb. 18, 1865; val. of personal prop. $1,000; Rep.

OSBORN HENRY, rents of Gustin Naker, Sec. 34; P.O. Sycamore; Dem; from N.Y.

OURSLER WM. F. rents of H. N. Perkins, Sec. 19; P.O. Genoa; Rep; from Md.

PATTERSON JOHN, Farmer, Genoa; 295 acres, val. $14,750; Rep; from Penn.

PATTERSON JOHN R. lives with father, Genoa; Rep; from Ill.

PADDOCK J. F. Farmer and Stock Raiser, Sec. 24; P.O. New Lebanon; born in DeKalb Co. Aug. 3, 1853; has one child thirteen months old; wife was Miss Sarah E. Trout, from Wisconsin, born May 15, 1857; married March 31, 1873; has 715 acres of real estate, value $35,715; personal $7,000; Rep.

PATTERSON CHAS. lives with his father, Genoa; Rep; from Ill.

PATTERSON HENRY, Carpenter, Genoa; Rep; from Penn.

PATTERSON H. R. Sec. 6; P.O. Genoa; 80 acres, val. $4,000; Rep; from Penn.

PERKINS HENRY N. Merchant; P.O. Genoa; born in New Lebanon, N.Y. Aug. 15, 1833; came to county Oct. 1837; has a family of three daughters and one son; wife was Miss Margaret Stiles, from Fallisburg, Canada, born Oct. 13, 1836; married Feb. 28, 1855; value of real estate $3,000; personal prop. $3,000; has been Supervisor four terms; Rep.

PERKINS HORATIO N. business, Real Estate; P.O. Genoa; born in Groton, Conn. Nov. 6, 1808; came to this county Oct. 1837; has family of one son, two children dead; wife was Miss Eliza Wallace, from New Lebanon, N. Y., born Oct. 15, 1808; married Nov. 1, 1828; has 530 acres of real estate, value $26,500; personal prop. $15,000; is Postmaster; Rep.

PEASLEY FRANK, works B. P. Brown's farm, Sec. 6; P.O. Genoa; Rep; from Ill.

PIERCE M. Sec. 9; P.O. Genoa; 120 acres, value $6,000; Rep; from Penn.

PIERCE JAMES, Blacksmith, Genoa; Rep; from Canada.

PIERCE W. L. Sec. 16; P.O. Genoa; 80 acres, val. $4,000; Rep; from N.Y.

PIPER DAVID, Sec. 3; P.O. South Riley; 135 acres, value $6,200; Rep; from Vt.

POWERS HILAND, Painter, Genoa; Rep; from Ill.

POWERS H. Painter, Genoa; Rep; from Canada.

POND A. H. Farmer, Sec. 32; P.O. Genoa; 200 acres, value $10,000; Rep; from Penn.

PORTER AMOS, Clerk; P.O. Genoa; Rep; from Sullivan Co. N.Y.

PRESTON CHARLES, Farmer, Sec. 29; P.O. Genoa; born in Atwater, Portage Co. Ohio, Sept. 30, 1833; came to this county June 23, 1837; has a family of five daughters; wife was Miss Helen E. Dunn, from Erie, Penn. born Sept. 10, 1834; married July 4, 1855; owns 107½ acres, val. $5,350; personal prop. $1,500; is Township Trustee, also Coroner; Rep.

PRESTON SALLY Mrs. from Penn; Genoa; value real estate $400.

PRESTON N. Farmer, Sec. 29; P.O. Genoa; 215 acres, value $11,855; Rep; from Ill.

PRESTON J. Farmer, Sec. 28; P.O. Genoa; 120 acres, value $6,000; Rep; from Ohio.

RADDUTS HENRY, works for Mrs. F. E. Johnston, Sec. 1; P.O. Ney; Dem; Germany.

REN JOHN, Farmer, Sec 30; P.O. Genoa; Rep; from Penn.

REID ALEXANDER, Sec. 11, P.O. Ney; 160 acres, value $8,000; from Scotland.

READ W. V. B. Sec. 5; P.O. Genoa; 80 acres, value $3,000; Rep; from Penn.

RICE GEO. works for John R. Corson, Sec. 9; P.O. Ney; Dem; from Penn.

RISDON J. A. Blacksmith; P.O. Genoa; Rep; from N.Y.

RISDON JAMES H. Manufacturer Windmills; P.O. Genoa; Rep; from Ill.

RICHARDSON GEO. W. Farmer, Sec. 33; 160 acres, val. $8,000; Rep; from N.Y.

ROSS ALEXANDER, Laborer, Genoa; Rep; from N.Y.

SCOTT WM. Mrs. Sec. 22; P.O. Genoa; 80 acres; value $4,000; from N.Y.

SCHWARTZ D. W. Harness Maker; P.O. Genoa; Ind; from Ill.

SAGER WILLIAM, business is Tinner; P.O. Genoa; born in Leeds, England, Aug. 22, 1825; landed in Philadelphia Nov. 18, 1848; came to this county Sept. 1871; has family of three sons and five daughters; wife was Miss Jane Norris, from Glasgow, Scotland; married May 12, 1851; value of real estate $300; personal prop. $500; no politics.

SENSKA A. C. Mason: P.O. Genoa; from Ill; Rep.

SENSKA ALEXANDER, Mason; P.O. Genoa; Rep; from Ill.

SHAFER FRANKLIN, Proprietor of Genoa Hotel; P.O. Genoa; born in Somerset Co. Penn; June 15, 1847; came to this county Dec. 1874; has family of one girl, born March 30, 1875; wife was Jennie Gutches, from Howard Co. Iowa, born March 23, 1856; married Oct. 17, 1872; owns 700 acres of real estate and thirty-eight town lots, value $6,000; personal property $300; was Orderly Sergeant in Co. C, 32d Iowa Vol. served three years and three months; Rep.

SHUTTS N. Sec. 27; P.O. Genoa; 95½ acres, value $4,750; Rep; from Canada.

SHURTLEFF GEO, Sec. 27; P.O. Genoa; 200 acres, value $10,000; Rep; from Canada.

SIGLIN JOSHUA, Farmer and Stock Raiser, Sec. 35; born in Monroe Co. Penn. Jan. 1, 1844; came to this county April, 1853; no family; wife was Miss Delia Dean, Sullivan Co. N.Y. born May 7, 1842; married Sept. 25, 1866; he served two years in the late war, in Co. F, 17th Ill. Cav; is School Director; value personal property $4,000; Dem.

SIGLIN I. Farmer, Sec. 15; P.O Genoa; 160 acres, value $8,000; Rep; from Penn.

SLATER S. Farmer, Sec. 21; P.O. Genoa; 100 acres, value $5,000; Rep; from N. J.

SLATER H. H. Merchant; P.O. Genoa; born in Hunterdon Co. N.J. Oct. 31, 1840; came to county April, 1855; has family of one son and one daughter; wife was Miss Ammiretta Stiles, from Rutland Co. Vt. who was born June 1842; married Jan. 8, 1868; value real estate $4,000; personal property $3,500; is Corporation Trustee; Rep.

SMIDT FRED, Tailor; P.O. Genoa; Rep; from Germany

SMIDT VALENTINE, works for Geo. Eichler, Sec. 5; P.O. Ney; Rep; from Germany.

SMITH CHAS. rents farm of A. Crawford, Sec. 26; P.O. New Lebanon; Rep; from Mass.

SMITH WM. lives with C. Smith, Sec. 26; P.O. New Lebanon; Rep; from Mass.

SOWERS A. Farmer, Sec. 32; P.O. Genoa; 231 acres, value $10,620; Rep; from Md.

SPANSAIL JACOB, Farmer and Stock Raiser, Sec. 24; P.O. New Lebanon; born in Wurtemberg, Germany, Dec. 16, 1833, came to this county in Winter of 1854; has family of two sons and three daughters; one child dead; wife was Miss Elizabeth Vote from Ohio, born April, 1836; married March 29, 1856; has 280 acres, value $13,000; personal $2,000; is Road Commissioner and School Director; Rep.

STRONG WILLIAM, Lumber and Grain Dealer; residence Sec. 18; P.O. Genoa; born Delaware Co. N.Y. July 24, 1817; came to this county in the Spring of 1840; has family of one son and six daughters; wife was Miss Sobrina Durham, from Delaware Co. N.Y. born March 31, 1825; married Mar. 31, 1845; has 386 acres; value of real estate $21,230; personal property $4,000; Rep.

STRONG W. S. Sec. 12; P.O. Ney; 120 acres, value $4,800; Rep; from Mich.

STEWART ARTHUR, Painter, Genoa: Rep; from Mass.

STEPHENS SAMUEL, Retired; P.O Genoa; has 160 acres, value $9,600; Rep; from Penn.

STOTT J. E. Merchant; P.O. Genoa; Rep.

STOTT CHAS. Merchant; P.O. Genoa; Rep; from Ill.

STEPHENS JOSEPH. Town Clerk, Genoa; Rep; from Ill.

STREETER B. Mrs. Millinery and Dressmaking; P.O. Genoa; from N.Y.

STONE E. D. works Mrs. Hogeboon's place, Sec. 25; P.O. New Lebanon; Rep; from Wis.

STILES E. Farmer and Stock Raiser, Sec. 27; P.O. Genoa; born in Rutland Co. Vt. Nov. 8, 1829. came to this county in the Fall of 1850; has a family of one son and two daughters; wife was Miss M. A. White, of Owego, N.Y. born June 8, 1845; married March 25, 1865; has 160 acres, value $8,000; personal property $2,500; Rep.

ST. JOHN THOMAS, Sec. 2; P.O. Marengo, McHenry Co; 520 acres, value $26,000; Rep; Can.

STANLEY AMOS, works J. Risden's farm, Sec. 6; P.O. Genoa; Rep; from N.Y.

STANLEY LEROY, Sec. 6; P.O. Genoa; 80 acres, value $4,000; Rep; from N.Y.

SUMNER E. Q. Sec. 7; P.O. Genoa; 80 acres, value $4,000; Rep; from Ill.

SURTLEFF HIRAM. lives with his father, Sec. 27; P.O. Genoa; Rep; from Ill.

SUMNER E. Retired; Genoa; 80 acres, value $6,000; Rep; from Vt.

SWANSON JOS. works for Jesse Wing, Sec. 21; P.O. Genoa; Rep; from Sweden.

SWANSON ANDREW, Sec. 23; P.O. New Lebanon; 159 acres, value $7,950; Rep; Sweden.

THOMPSON EMILY Mrs. Sec. 34; P.O. Genoa; 120 acres, value $6,600; from N.Y.

THOMPSON EDWARD, Cabinetmaker; P.O. Genoa; Dem; from Maine.

TOTTEN F. G. Farmer, Sec. 7; P.O. Genoa; 40 acres, value $2,000; Rep; from N.Y.

TRAVIS MICHAEL, works for J. Preston, Sec. 28; P.O. Genoa; Dem; from Ireland.

TUCKER S. S. Editor of *Genoa News*; P.O. Genoa; born in Cayuga Co. N.Y. March 4, 1821, came to this state in 1861; has family one son and one daughter; wife was Miss Nancy Garvey, from Albany Co. N.Y. born Oct. 1822; married April 28, 1850; she died Dec. 31, 1874; value of estate $2,500; personal $800; Rep.

TURNER C. A. Cheese Factory, Sec. 25; P.O. New Lebanon; Rep; from N.Y.

TYLER WM. Merchant, Genoa; Dem; from Germany.

TYDEMAN J. H. Blacksmith, Genoa; Dem; from Ill.

VANDRESSER J. H. Sec. 18; P.O. Genoa; owns 110 acres, value $5,250; Republican; from Ohio.

WAGER WM. H. Farmer, Sec. 21; P.O. Genoa; 147 acres, value $5,400; Rep; from Ill.

WAGER HENRY Mrs. P.O. Genoa; 456 acres, value $18,240; from Ohio.

WAGER ALEXANDER, Farmer, Sec. 21; P.O. Genoa; born in DeKalb Co. Nov. 19, 1850; has a farm of 147 acres; value of real estate $5,880; personal property $1,600; is single man; Rep.

WATERS S. L. Carpenter; P.O. Genoa; Rep; from Penn.

WATERS GEO. lives with S. Slater, Sec. 21; P.O. Genoa; Rep; from N.J.

WATERS LOYD C. lives with his mother, Sec. 10; P.O. Ney; Rep; from Penn.

WATERS JOHN O. rents the Craft farm, Sec. 3; P.O. Ney; Rep; from Penn.

WATERS J. V. Mrs. Sec. 10; P.O. Ney; 240 acres, value $12,000; from Penn.

WESTOVER IRA B. Farmer; P.O. Genoa; Rep; from Ill.

WESTOVER B. G. Merchant; P.O. Genoa; Rep; from Mass.

WHITE JOHN, Farmer and Stock Raiser, Sec. 9; P.O. Ney; born in Weismann, Germany, March 5, 1815, came to this county in 1850; has family of four sons and three daughters; wife was Miss Margaret Hoffman, from Weismann, Germany, born in 1820 and married 1847. has 260 acres, value $13,000; personal $1,000; is School Director; Ind; Luth.

WHITE GEO. lives with his father, Sec. 9; P.O. Ney; Ind; from Ill.

WHITNEY L. Stage Driver, Genoa; Dem; from N.Y.

WHITNEY EDWARD, works Godfrey Eichler's place, Sec. 3; P.O. Ney; Ind; from N.Y.

WHITNEY N. P. Farmer, Genoa; Ind; from N.Y.

WHITCOMB NOAH, rents J. Merriman's place, Sec. 29; P.O. Genoa; Rep; from Canada.

WILBUR O. E. Sec. 6; P.O. Genoa; 80 acres, value $4,000; Rep; from N.Y.

WHEELER OSBORN, works for R. McCormick, Sec. 17; P.O. Genoa; Rep; from Ohio.

WING JESSE V. Farmer, Sec. 22; P.O. Genoa; born in DeKalb Co. Sept. 17, 1852; family of one son, fourteen months old; wife was Miss Bessie Halpin, from the town of Dundee, Scotland, born Dec. 20, 1852; married Oct. 13, 1874; has personal property to the amount of $1,500; Dem.

WING THEO. T. Sec. 22; P.O. Sycamore; 320 acres, value $16,000; Dem; from Canada.

WILLIAMS SIAS K. General Stock Raiser and Dairyman, Sec. 12; P.O. Hampshire, Kane Co. Ill.; born in Lebanon, N. H. June 25, 1818; came to this state in 1842; has a family of two daughters; wife was Miss Mary D. Heafield, from N.Y. City; married Jan. 1, 1846; has two 500 acre farms; has deeded one-half of each to his two daughters; value of real estate $50,000; personal $15,000; Rep; Meth.

WILLIAMS L. Boot and Shoemaker; P.O. Genoa; Rep; from Conn.

WIDGER C. E. works for E. Stiles, Sec. 27; Rep; from N.Y.

WILD WM. Farmer, Genoa; 94½ acres, value $3,780; Rep; from England.

WILLIS S. Sec. 36; P.O. New Lebanon; 240 acres, value $12,000; Rep; from N.Y.

WILCOX JOHN J. Sec. 14; P.O Ney; 160 acres, value $6,400; Rep; from Vermont.

WISNER LAURA Mrs. Sec. 18; P.O. Genoa; 3 acres, value $200; from N.Y.

WILSON L. Sec. 13; P.O. New Lebanon· 100 acres, value $5,000; Re. ; from Canada.

WOOD GEO. E. Farmer; P.O. Genoa; Rep; from Illinois.

WORCESTER F. M. Station Agent, Genoa; Rep; from Illinois.

WRIGHT ELIHU, rents of J. C. Flint, Sec. 33; P.O. Sycamore; Rep; from Illinois.

WYLDE JOHN, Laborer, Genoa; Rep; from Illinois.

YOUNG WM. H. works for Wm. Hepburn, Sec. 10; P.O. Ney; Rep; from Illinois.

YOST PHILLIP, Butcher; P.O. Genoa; Rep; from Penn.

SHABBONA TOWNSHIP.

ABLES E. Farmer, Sec. 29; P.O. Cornton; 80 acres; Rep.

ABRAHAMSEN SALVE, Sec. 6; P.O. Lee; one child; Rep.

ACKERBLAD G. Farmer, Sec. 9; P.O. Cornton; two children; 80 acres; Rep.

ACKERBLAD I. Blacksmith and Carriage Maker; residence Sec. 15, Tp. 38, R. 3; P.O. Cornton; born in Sweden Dec. 18, 1823; came to this state in 1859; real estate $1,000; married Carrie Horty Jan. 17, 1844; she was born in Sweden Jan. 8, 1815; no children; Rep; Luth.

ADAMS B. H. Harnessmaker, Sec. 15; P.O. Cornton; Rep.

ADLER JAMES, Sec. 28; P.O. Cornton; Ind.

ALEXANDER G. M. Drugs; residence Sec. 15, Tp. 38, R. 3; P.O. Cornton; born in Oneida Co. N.Y. in 1823; came to state and county May 8, 1854; real estate $550; personal prop. $2,400; is Supervisor and Justice of the Peace; married second wife, Mary E. Clapsaddle, of Herkimer Co. N.Y. Oct. 19, 1859; has two children—Elizabeth, born Dec. 28, 1849, and Eva, born Sept. 8, 1858; Rep.

ALLEN MARTIN, Sec. 15; P.O. Cornton; born N.Y.; came to county 1845; Rep.

ALLEN CHARLES, Farmer, Sec. 24; P.O. Cornton; rents Terry's estate; Rep.

ARCHER GEORGE, Farmer; residence Sec. 23, Tp. 38, R. 3; P.O. Cornton; born in Suffolk Co. England, August 14, 1847; came to state in 1863; Rep; Meth; owns 25 acres; real estate and personal prop. $1,150; married Elizabeth Carter, of England, in December, 1871; she was born in May, 1854; three children—Sarah, born in 1872; John, born in 1873; and George, born in November, 1875.

ARCHER JOHN, Farmer, Sec. 28; P.O. Cornton; Rep; three children.

ARCHER JOHN, Jr. Farmer, Sec. 28; P.O. Cornton; Rep.

ARCHER SAMUEL, Farmer, Sec. 28; P.O. Cornton; Rep; one child.

ARENT CHARLES, Farmer, Sec. 3; P.O. Cornton; works farm of Wm. M. Whalen.

ATHERTON B. F. Farmer, Sec. 31; P.O. Paw Paw Grove; Rep.

BAILEY ASA, Farmer, Sec. 33; P.O. Shabbona Grove; Rep; four children.

BAILEY FRANK, Laborer, Sec. 33; P.O. Shabbona Grove; Rep.

BAILEY I. L. Farmer, Sec. 23; P.O. Cornton; 12 acres; family of five children; Rep.

BAILEY CYRENIUS Farmer; residence Sec. 33, Tp. 38, R. 3; P.O. Shabbona Grove; born in Schoharie Co. N.Y. June 21, 1823; came to state in April, 1856; Rep; owns 160 acres prop. value $10,000; was Assessor in 1873 and 1875; married Jane A. Morey Dec. 14, 1853; she was born in Saratoga Co. N.Y. March 15, 1826; seven children, four living, viz.: Anna A., born Sept. 24, 1854; Emma F., born August 3, 1856; Asa C., born Oct. 30, 1858; and Jennie N., born April 7, 1863; and three dead; all born in the State of Illinois, except Anna, who was born in New York State.

BAIER FERDINAND, Dealer in Boots and Shoes; residence Lee; P.O. Lee, Lee Co; born in Germany, Sep. 29, 1853; came to state Oct. 3, 1871; Cath.

BATHRICK A. Agent for C. & I. R.R.; P.O. Lee, Lee Co; Rep; family, one child.

BENNETT HARRISON, Proprietor Lee House; residence Sec. 6. Tp. 38, R. 3; P.O. Lee, Lee Co; born in Bradford Co. Penn. Dec. 13, 1822; came to state in 1837; Democrat; Presbyterian; married Mary McEwen Fleming, May 29, 1849; she was born in Mifflin Co. Penn. Aug. 28, 1829; eight children, two dead, and six living, viz: William H., born April 27, 1852; Jennie E., born Dec. 23, 1854; Franklin John, born Nov. 15, 1857; Anna M., born Dec. 20, 1859; Emma M., born Aug. 18, 1861; and Ida B., born Dec. 29, 1865; John, born May 3, 1856, and died Oct. 3, 1858; Lizzie H., born May 29, 1864, and died Sep. 5, 1865.

BEAN JESSE, Sec. 15; P.O. Cornton; five children; Ind.

BECKER EDWIN, Farmer, Sec. 26; P.O. Shabbona Grove; Rep.

BEND RICHARD, Farmer, Sec. 31; P.O. East Paw Paw; Rep; five children.

BEETS FRANK, Saloon, Sec. 6; P.O. Lee, Lee Co; Dem.

BILLINGS J. E. Sec. 15; P.O. Cornton; Rep; four children.

BOSTOCK WILLIAM, Farmer; residence Sec. 30, Tp. 38, R. 3; P.O. Lee, Lee Co; born in Chilwell, England, Feb. 26, 1823; came to county in 1865; Rep; owns 40 acres of land, worth $2,000, together with personal property; married Ann Jane Wood, Aug. 1, 1845; she was born in Derby, March 3, 1823; has two children, Mary Ann, born Nov. 1, 1848, and William, born Sep. 14, 1858.

BOOTH ALLEN, Farmer, Sec. 35; P.O. Shabbona; from England; Rep.

BONSLOUGH SAM'L, Dealer in Grain, etc. Sec. 15; born Penn.; P.O. Cornton; Rep; Cong.

BRANSCOMB S. H. Horse Shoer, Sec. 15; P.O. Cornton; born Can. 1849; Rep; prop. $1,500.

BOWKER WM. Farmer, Sec. 12; owns 40 acres, value of property $2,000; Rep.

BOE THORE P. Sec. 6; P.O. Lee, Lee Co; Rep; works for Christopher & Jorgan.

BRUNSON WM. Farmer, Sec. 12; rents farm of J. B. McIntire; Ind. Dem; Latter Day Saints.

BRANSCOMBE JOSIAH, Sec. 15; P.O. Cornton; Meth; six children.

BRYANT W. H. Agricultural Implements; residence Lee; P.O. Lee; Lee Co.; Postmaster.

BUCKLEY FRANCIS, Farmer, Sec. 36; P.O. Shabbona Grove; Dem.

BURGER C. Farmer, Sec. 22; P.O. Cornton; 80 acres; born in Germany.

BURKE L. C. Farmer, Sec. 21; P.O. Cornton; Meth; Jeffersonian Dem; Anti-mason; Radical.

CADWELL RICHARD, Sec. 15; P.O. Cornton; Dem; two children.

CARLSON C. F. Shoemaker, Sec. 15; P.O. Cornton; Rep; Luth.

CAMERON JAMES, Farmer, Sec. 26; P.O. Shabbona Grove; born in Juniata Co. Penn. Oct. 11, 1824; owns 105 acres, valued at $5,500; Rep; is Road Commissioner; in 1842 was bound to Jesse B. Evans to learn the blacksmith trade, after the time was served bought out Mr. Evans and carried on the business himself; married Melinda E. Wallis, of Juniata Co. Penn. Sept. 26, 1846; moved to McVeigh, Mifflin Co. Penn. in 1847; stayed awhile, then moved to Lewiston, Penn.; is a Methodist, and has been either Leader, Steward, or Superintendent in the church ever since; moved to Shabbona Grove in 1855, lived there till 1865, then moved to Earl, LaSalle Co; in 1866 he moved to Malta, engaged in the grain trade, sold out and moved to Creston, Ogle Co; in 1869 embarked in the hardware trade; in March, 1870, moved to West Shabbona, and stayed till 1874; sold out and bought present farm, in Shabbona Village.

CAMPIN S. M. Clerk; Sec. 6; P.O. Lee, Lee Co; Dem.

COOK GEORGE H. Joiner, Builder, and Dealer in Groceries; residence Sec. 26. Tp. 38, R. 3; P.O. Shabbona Grove; born in Newark, N.J. Nov. 29, 1823; came to state in 1855; Rep; owns 7 village lots, worth $1,000; is now Postmaster; married Catharine Ann Manderville, of Essex Co. N. J. May 4, 1845; she was born Sep. 16, 1824; has two children — John, born Dec. 6, 1847, and Olive, born March 11, 1865.

COOK JOHN B. Carpenter and Joiner, Sec. 26; P.O. Shabbona Grove; Rep; one child.

COOK H. E. Laborer, Sec. 6; P.O. Lee, Lee Co; works for B. H. Skoyles; Meth; Rep.

COX HENRY, Farmer, Sec. 32; P.O. Cornton; works H. Leyson's farm; five children.

COLEMAN E. Dealer Agr. Imp. Sec. 15; P.O. Cornton; came to state 1860; born Mich.; Rep.

COATTS GEO. Farmer, Sec. 18; P.O. Lee, Lee Co; Rep; Meth; rents farm Thos. Wright.

CHALLAND REUBEN, Farmer, Sec. 8; P.O. Cornton; owns 160 acres; Rep; one child.

CHALLAND CHAS. Farmer, Sec. 17; P.O. Cornton; Meth; 120 acres; one child.

CHALLAND JOS. Farmer, Sec. 33; P.O. Shabbona Grove; four children.

CHRISTOPHER C. Sec. 6; P.O. Lee, Lee Co; Rep; Luth; five children.

CLAPSADDLE HENRY, Farmer, Sec. 35; owns 120 acres; Rep; two children.

21

CUTTS SAMUEL, Farmer, Sec. 19; P.O. Cornton; Rep.

DAVIS ISAAC, Farmer, Sec. 2; P.O. Cornton; Rep; Cong; three children.
DAVIS THOS. Laborer, Sec. 6; P.O. Lee, Lee Co; Ind.
DANIELS F. D. Druggist; Sec. 6; P.O. Lee, Lee Co. Rep; four children.
DEACON WILLIAM, Lumber and Grain; lives on Lot 7, Block 5, Sec. 15, Tp. 38, R. 3; P.O. Cornton; born in Ireland, Jan. 6, 1843; came to state in 1867; Rep; Cong; real estate $1,200; personal property $2,400; about four years in the army; married Harriet M. Geoch, of Washington Co. N. Y. Feb. 16, 1868; is a member of the firm of Wm. Deacon & Co.
DEEGIN DORA Mrs. resides on Sec. 12, Tp. 38. R. 3; P.O. Cornton; born in Ireland in 1836; came to state in 1850; Catholic; owns 320 acres; value of real estate $12,000; value of personal property $900; married M. Deegin in 1857; he died April 19, 1875; has had six children, one deceased, five living, John, born June 24, 1857, Malachi, born Jany. 30, 1859; Kate, born Dec. 23, 1861; James, born Jany. 25, 1864; and Eliza, born July 6, 1867.
DODD CHESTER, Farmer, Sec. 1; P.O. Cornton; works for B. Middleton; Rep,
DORR JOHN, Sec. 7; P.O. Lee, Lee Co; works for A. Schall.
DONDLEN JAS. Farmer, Sec. 13; owns 80 acres; val. of prop. $4,500; Dem; Ireland.
DOWNER ABEL, Farmer and Dry Goods; Sec. 6; P.O. Lee, Lee Co; own 120 acres; Rep.
DUFFY MARTIN, Farmer. residence Sec. 13, Tp. 38, R. 3; P.O. Cornton; born in Ireland Oct 11, 1826; came to state in March, 1850; Dem; Cath; owns 401 acres; value of real estate $16,000; value of personal property $1,500; married Bridget Duggan, Jany. 29, 1853; ten children, born as follows: William May 2, 1854; Ellen, Oct. 6, 1856; Catharine, Feb. 18, 1858; Patrick, March 28, 1859; Hugh, Oct. 4, 1861; Lawrence, April 4, 1864; Martin, April 1, 1866; Ann, Feb. 15, 1868; Margaret, June 21, 1869; and James, Feb. 14, 1871.
DUFFY WM. Farmer, Sec. 13; works for M. Duffy; Dem; Cath.
DUNHAM W. Farmer, Sec. 4, P.O. Cornton; owns 160 acres; Rep; Bapt; four children.

EDWARD JAS. Sec. 28; P.O. Cornton; Rep; works for John Archer, Sen.
EMMETT W. H. Sec. 1; P.O. Lee, Lee Co; Rep; clerks for Christopher & Jorgan.
EDWARDS JNO. Mason, Sec. 13; wife and eight children; owns about 75 acres.
ERICKSON JOHN, Farmer, Sec. 20; P.O. Cornton; Rep; Luth; rents farm of Geo. Spray.
ESPE HAAGER, Blacksmith, Sec. 6; P.O. Lee, Lee Co; Rep; three children.

FEIST FELIX, Farmer; Sec. 1; P.O. Waterman; owns 80 acres; Rep; two children.
FINNAN THOMAS, Bartender; Sec. 15; P.O. Cornton; Dem; Cath.
FITZGERALD FREDERICK, Farmer, Sec. 19; P.O. Lee, Lee Co; Rep; rents of S. Storey.
FRITTS JOHN H. Farmer, Sec. 13; P.O. Cornton; born N.Y.; came to county 1855; Rep.
FRITTS JOHN, Sec. 13; P.O. Cornton; born N.Y. 1801; came county 1855; Rep.
FLINDERS GEORGE B. Music Teacher on the Piano and Organ; resides Sec. 26, Tp. 38. R. 3; P.O. Shabbona Grove; born in Nottingham Co. England, Aug. 30, 1852; came to state and county in 1865; Rep.
FROST F. A. Farmer; resides Sec. 27, Tp. 38, R. 3; P.O. Shabbona Grove; born in Schuyler Co. N. Y. April 13, 1834; came to state June, 1868; Ind. hard-money Rep; owns 158 acres real estate, value $8,000. Married Marietta Witherspoon, Nov. 18, 1863; she was born in Somonauk, DeKalb Co. Ills. April 11, 1844; has two children—Frederick J. born Jan. 3, 1865, and Frank W. born Feb. 10, 1867; was a member of the band of the 48th Regt. of Infantry, N. Y.; was enrolled on the 5th day of Sept. 1861, to serve three years or the war; was discharged Sept. 27, 1862, at Fort Pulaski, Ga. by reason of act of Congress, by R. H. Jackson, Capt. 1st Artillery, U. S. Army, mustering officer.
FROST GEO. R. Laborer, Sec. 15; P.O. Cornton; Rep.
FRENCH S. M. Teamster, Sec. 15; P.O. Cornton; Rep.

GARBRAITH JOHN, Farmer, Sec. 19; P.O. Lee, Lee Co; Rep.
GATES ISAAC, Jr. Carpenter, Sec. 38; P.O. Cornton; Rep.
GATES FREMONT, Carpenter, Sec. 38; P.O. Cornton; Rep.
GALLAGHER DAN'L, Farmer, Sec. 30; P.O. Cornton; Rep; owns 40 acres.
GIBBINS JOHN, Farmer, Sec. 18; P.O. Lee, Lee Co; Cath; Dem.
GILBERT FRANK, Carpenter, Sec. 14; P.O. Cornton; Rep.
GLOSSOP GEORGE, Farmer, Sec. 18; P.O. Lee, Lee Co; Dem; owns 80 acres.

GOODYEAR JOHN, Farmer, Sec. 32; P.O. East Paw Paw; Rep.

GORMAN H. Farmer, Sec. 12; P.O. Cornton; Dem; Cath.

GREEN PETER, Farmer, Sec. 4; P.O. Cornton; Rep; owns 246 acres.

GREEN FRED. Farmer, Sec. 3; P.O. Cornton; Rep; rents 40 acres of H. W. Wormley.

GREENFIELD JAS. I. Farmer, Sec. 23; P.O. Cornton; born N.Y. 1821; Rep.

GREENFIELD MONTOLBERT, Farmer; resides Sec. 25, Tp. 38, R. 3; P.O. Cornton; born in Rensselaer Co. N. Y. May 17, 1817; came to state October, 1854; Rep; owns 200 acres; property worth $12,000. Married first Julia A. Willard; had four children, born as follows: Jane, Feb. 13, 1845; Geo. W. July 17, 1847; Julia Alice, March 5, 1850, and Weltha S. Sept. 19, 1853. Married present wife, Jane M. Baker, Jan. 10, 1860; had four children, born as follows: Clara E. Dec. 24, 1860; Burton L. Aug. 2, 1863; DeWitt, May 19, 1870, and Rosa M. Jan. 17, 1872.

GUNDERSON PETER, Sec. 23; P.O. Cornton; Rep; Luth.

GUNDERSON S. Farmer, Sec. 23; P.O. Cornton; owns 20 acres; Rep; Luth.

HALLETT WM. W. School Teacher, Sec. 6; P.O. Lee, Lee Co; Rep.

HARRIS M. P. Live Stock and Coal Dealer, Sec. 6; P.O. Lee, Lee Co.

HALLAM S. C. E. Farmer; resides Sec. 28, Tp. 38, R. 3; P.O. Shabbona Grove; born in Nottingham, England, Sept. 14, 1836; came to state in 1866; Rep; Meth; has 166 acres. Married Elizabeth Challand, of England, Aug. 28, 1864; she was born Aug. 11, 1844; has one child, Emily, born Nov. 16, 1864.

HARPER THOMAS, Farmer, Sec. 26; P.O. Shabbona Grove; Rep.

HARKER SAM'L, Painter, Sec. 15; Rep.

HAYES A. E. Farmer, Sec. 27; P.O. Shabbona Grove; Ind; 103 acres.

HANSON Mrs. E. Sec. 27; P.O. Cornton; owns 60 acres.

HALK ELIJAH, Bartender, Sec. 15; P.O. Cornton; born Penn.; Rep.

HALL ELBERT, Farmer, Sec. 36; P.O. Shabbona Grove; Dem.

HALL ALPHA, Farmer, Sec. 36; P.O. Shabbona Grove; Dem.

HEATH F. Farmer, Sec. 3; P.O. Cornton; Rep.

HEATH CHANDLER, Farmer, Sec. 3; P.O. Cornton; Rep.

HEATH C. D. Farmer, Sec. 21; P.O. Cornton; Rep; owns 80 acres.

HEATH BRADFORD, Farmer, Sec. 11; P.O. Cornton; Rep.

HELM N. R. Farmer, Sec. 21; P.O. Cornton; Rep; owns 120 acres.

HELM W. Farmer, Sec. 24; P.O. Cornton; Rep; owns 160 acres.

HEEG WILLIAM F. Furniture and Coffins; resides Sec. 15, Tp. 38, R. 3; P.O. Cornton; born in Germany, in 1847; came to U. S. in 1853. Married Lena Scholl, Sept. 13, 1873; has two children, Adam and William.

HEEG JOHN Mrs. Sec. 14; P.O. Cornton; widow of John Heeg; Bapt.

HEEG CONRAD Mrs. Sec. 14; P.O. Cornton; widow of Conrad Heeg; Bapt; owns 70 acres.

HEEG CHRISTIAN, Farmer, Sec. 21; P.O. Cornton; Dem; Bapt.

HELLAND HANS, Shoemaker; resides Sec. 6, Tp. 38, R. 3; P.O. Lee, Lee Co; born in Norway, June 16, 1847; came to Shabbona in 1873; Rep; Luth; personal property $500. Married Jengs Salveson, Oct. 6, 1867; she was born in Norway, June 30, 1845; has six children, only five living, viz: Jengs, born Nov. 28, 1868; Sophie, born Jan. 7, 1869; Bertha, born June 8, 1872; Hilda, born Feb. 9, 1874; and Herman, born March 11, 1876.

HELLAND LARS, Wagonmaker, Sec. 6; P.O. Lee; Rep; Luth.

HEDEN FRANK, Mason, Sec. 15; P. O. Cornton; Rep; Luth.

HURST JAMES HENRY, Sec. 1; P.O. Cornton; Rep; works for Levi Hurst.

HINDS A. L. Farmer; resides Sec. 11, Tp. 38, R. 3; P.O. Cornton; born in Redwood, Jefferson Co. N. Y. Aug. 14, 1839; came to state in 1842; Dem; owns 164 52-100 acres; real estate, $8,000; personal property, $1,100. Married Nettie Colley, Feb. 28, 1869; has one child, Alice L. born July 20, 1875.

HINKSTON NELSON E. Sec. 14; P.O. Cornton; works for D. Hinkston; Rep.

HINKSTON ADRIAN E. Farmer, Sec. 14; P.O. Cornton; Rep.

HINKSTON DANFORTH, Farmer, Sec. 14; P.O. Cornton; Rep; Meth.

HILBERBRANT JACOB, Teamster, Sec. 15; P.O. Cornton.

HILTS MIRON, Farmer, Sec. 12; P.O. Cornton; works farm of Mary Jane Hilts.

HOPFT JOHN, works for P. Green, Sec. 4; P.O. Cornton; Rep.

HORTON PHEBE Mrs. resides Sec. 35, Tp. 38, R. 3; P.O. Shabbona Grove; born in Tioga Co. N. Y. Nov. 3, 1816; came to state and county March, 1841; Meth; property $750. Married Miles Horton, from New York state, June 9, 1842; he was born June 2, 1819, and died Aug. 8, 1848; had four children—two living, viz: Darius, born April 15, 1843, and William, born Aug. 23, 1844, and two dead; when she settled in Shabbona Grove there were but seven families, and is one of the oldest settlers.

HOTCHKISS NELSON, Farmer; Sec. 26; P.O. Shabbona Grove; 146 acres; two children.

HOUGHTELEY CHARLES, Farmer, Sec. 17; P.O. Cornton; Meth. Epis; Rep.

HOY PETER, Farmer, Sec. 21; P.O. Cornton; Rep; Cath; rents 50 acres of Thos. B. Reece.

HOWES MOSES, Farmer, Sec. 29; P.O. Cornton; Rep; seven children; owns 80 acres.

HOLBERT AARON, works for John Goodyear, Sec. 32; P.O. East Paw Paw; Rep.

HURST LEVI, Farmer, res. Sec. 1, Tp. 38. R. 3; P.O. Cornton; born in England, Nov. 23, 1823; came to state in 1853; Rep; owns 160 acres; real estate $9,000; personal prop. $700; married Sarah Burdin, May 15, 1849, she was born in England, Feb. 7, 1828; seven children—John, born April 14, 1850; George, born Aug. 10, 1853; James Henry, born Sept. 12, 1855; Sarah Elizabeth, born May 29, 1858; Eliza J. born Nov. 11, 1860; Ann Maria, born Feb. 4, 1863, and Lilly May, born July 22, 1865.

HUNT RICHARD D. Farmer, res. Sec. 30, Tp. 38, R. 3; born in Norfolk, England, April 27, 1830; came to state in 1852; owns 64 acres, worth $2,800; married Sarah Spencer, April 29, 1865, she was born in Ohio, March 5. 1844; six children—Charley D. born Oct. 29, 1867; Thomas H. born Jan. 2, 1869; Nathan E. born Oct. 5, 1870; Mary Ann, born April 5, 1872; Phillip, born Feb. 2, 1874, and Nellie, born Dec. 2, 1875.

HUSK WILLIAM V. General Store; res. Sec. 15; P.O. Cornton; born in Cayuga Co. N.Y. Aug. 19, 1836; came here in 1848; Rep; real estate $3.500; personal prop. $2,500; Postmaster at present; married last wife, Celia Norton, of DeKalb Co. Ill. had by first wife one child, John H. born in 1863, and by last wife two children—Charles, born Dec. 19, 1873, and Nettie, born Nov. 18. 1875.

HUBBELL. C. W. Sec. 15; P.O. Cornton; Rep.

HUSK HENRY, Sec. 15; P.O. Cornton; Rep; two children.

IRELAND THEO. F. Farmer. Sec. 31; P.O. Shabbona Grove; Rep; 160 ac; three children.

IRWIN WILLIE W. Sec. 6; P.O. Lee, Lee Co; Ind.

IRWIN WM. W. Farmer, Sec. 6; P.O. Lee, Lee Co; 210 acres; Ind; Pres; five children.

IRVING FRANK, works for M. Greenfield, Sec. 25; P.O. Cornton; Rep.

IVERSON KNUD, Blacksmith, Sec. 6; P.O. Lee, Lee Co; Rep; two children.

JACOBSON AVER, Laborer, Sec. 15; P.O. Cornton; Rep.

JACOBSON OLE, Laborer, Sec. 15; P.O. Cornton; Rep; two children.

JACKSON GEORGE, works for N. I. Kittle, Sec. 23; P.O. Cornton; Rep.

JACKSON WM. General Store. Sec. 15; P.O. Cornton; born N.Y.; Rep.

JARROW JACOB, General Store, Sec. 15; P.O. Cornton; born Holland; per. prop. $3,500.

JOHANSON HANS J. D. Carpenter, P.O. Lee, Lee Co.; born in Norway, in 1845; came to Illinois in 1871; Rep; Meth; property $600.

JOHNSON ALFRED, Blacksmith, works for I. Ackerblad, Sec. 15; P.O. Cornton.

JONES THOMAS, Sec. 26; P.O. Shabbona Grove; four children.

KELLEY, D. A. Farmer, Sec. 26; P.O. Shabbona Grove; three children.

KELLEY JAMES, Farmer, Sec. ; P.O. Shabbona Grove; Dem; Cath; 5 ac; $1,200.

KELLEY MICHAEL. Farmer, Sec. 26; P.O. Shabbona Grove; born in Kings Co. ireland, in 1811; came to state and county in 1856; Dem; Cath; prop. $450; married Mary McKinney, of Ireland, she was born in 1830; was married to last wife Sept. 10, 1875; had by first wife six children, two living, James and Thomas, and four dead.

KENNEDY JOHN, Farmer, Sec. 6; P.O. Lee, Lee Co; Dem.

KEYES JOHN, works for P. Green, Sec. 4; P.O. Cornton; Rep.

KENNEDY J. W. Farmer, Sec. 19; P.O. Lee, Lee Co; 100 acres; two children.

KITTLE N. I. Farmer, Sec. 23; P.O. Cornton; born Rensselaer Co. N. Y. Oct. 20. 1810; came to state and county Oct. 1849; Ind; owns 174 acres; prop. $11,500; married Maria Quilhot, July 8, 1841, she was born in Cayuga Co. N.Y. Dec. 29, 1817; six children, five living—John N. born Feb. 24, 1846; Margaret A. born Jan. 5, 1848; Cornelia E. born Dec 5. 1850; Cornelius P. born April 28, 1855, and Anna R. E. born Jan. 30, 1860, and one dead.

KITTELL GEORGE W. Physician, Sec. 35; P.O. Shabbona Grove; Rep; nine children.

KNELL GEORGE, Farmer, Sec. 32; P.O. Shabbona Grove; born East Kent Co. Eng. Dec. 27, 1828; Rep; Church of England; owns 242½ acres of land; val. real estate $13,000; is School Director; married Harriet Hooper, of East Kent Co. England, Nov. 19, 1852, she was born Feb. 1825; one child, Elizabeth, born Dec. 27, 1853.

KITTLSON SARAH Mrs., P.O. Cornton; three children; wid. G. Kittlson.

KREG EDWARD, works for Wm. Nicholson, Sec. 8; P.O. Cornton; Rep.

KRUEL FRANK, Farmer, Sec. 9; P.O. Cornton; owns 120 acres.

L AKE OSCAR M. Grain, Sec. 6; P.O. Lee, Lee Co; Ind.

LANDERS MOSES, Laborer, Sec. 26; P.O. Shabbona Grove; Ind; three children.

LALWAY MARY Mrs. Sec. 36; Shabbona Grove; born in Cavan Co. Ireland, March 10, 1831; came to state in 1857; Cath; owns 242½ acres; married Peter Lalway, March 17, 1859, he was born in Ireland 1812, died Feb. 10, 1865; three children, two living—Julia, born June 22, 1861, and Mary Jane, born Feb. 22, 1864, and one dead.

LALWAY MARY JANE Mrs. Sec. 26, P.O. Shabbona Grove; born Ireland, May 8, 1840; came to state and county 1854; Cath; owns 342 acres, valued at $14,500; married Patrick Lalway, of Ireland. Oct. 20, 1864, he was born in 1831, and died Feb. 22, 1872; four children—William, born Nov. 14, 1865; Mary J. born Aug. 6, 1867; Kate. born Aug. 18, 1869, and Thomas, born July 1, 1871.

LANGFORD ROBT. Flour Mill, Sec. 15; P.O. Cornton; Rep; Cong.

LANE G. W. Dealer in Live Stock, Sec. 15; P.O. Cornton; Rep; Meth; two children.

LAMBERT RUSSEL J. Farmer, Sec. 28; P.O. Cornton; Rep; one child; rents Morse's farm.

LEONARD B. C. Painter, Sec. 15; P.O. Cornton; born N.Y.; Rep; Universalist.

LICHER JOHN, Section Boss, Sec. 15; P.O. Cornton; three children; Rep.

LINHON PATRICK, Laborer, Sec. 26; P.O. Shabbona Grove; Dem.

LOVERING GEORGE, Wagon Maker; P.O. Cornton; Boone Co. Ill. 1851; Rep; Ind.

LUCAS T. B. Stock Dealer, Sec. 15; P.O. Cornton; Rep.

M ACKLIN ROBERT, Farmer, Sec. 19; P.O. Lee, Lee Co; Ref. Pres; 120 ac; five children.

MANDERVILLE PETER, Farmer, Sec. 15; P.O. Cornton; Rep.

MARRYOTT JOHN R. Farmer, Sec. 16; P.O. Cornton; born in Cumberland Co. N. J. Nov. 29, 1800; came to state and county in 1850; Rep; owns 120 acres, worth $9,000; personal property $625; served as Constable in 1855; married Margaret Davis, March 11, 1824, she was born in Cumberland Co. N. J. Sept. 27, 1797, and died Feb. 9, 1875; seven children, Susan Ann, born Feb. 1, 1825; Anna Maria, born Sep. 30, 1831; Jonathan D. born Nov. 30, 1833; Margaret D. born Nov. 14, 1836; Juliet. born Aug. 31, 1839, and Sarah Ann, born Oct. 14, 1826, and died Sept. 30, 1830, and Ruth M. born July 14, 1828, and died July 1829; the last two bur.ed in Philadelphia.

MANDERVILLE B. A. Mrs. Dressmaking and Tailoress; res. Sec. 15; P.O. Cornton; born in Chautauqua Co. N.Y. October 20, 1849; Bap; married last husband, Peter Manderville, November 1, 1870; he was born in Penn. February, 1843.

MANDEVILLE SARAH A. Mrs. Washerwoman; P.O. Shabbona; born Pa. 1839; Meth.

MARKS A. W. Boots and Shoes, Clothing; Dealer in Staple and Fancy Groceries. res. Sec 15; P.O. Cornton; born in Shabbona, DeKalb Co. Ill. Jan. 4, 1848; Rep; married Maggie Murry, Sept. 26, 1875; one child, born Aug. 29, 1876.

MARKS L. F. General Store, Sec. 15; P.O. Cornton; born Vt. 1816; Rep; real estate $900.

MANLEY JOHN, Farmer, Sec. 17; P.O. Lee, Lee Co; works farm Mrs. A. McCauley; Ind.

MARRIN D. Farmer, Sec. 6; P.O. Lee, Lee Co; owns 122 acres; wife and six children; Dem.

MACKLIN JAMES, Farmer, Sec. 19; P.O. Lee, Lee Co; Ref. Presb; owns 120 acres.

MATHIAS JOSEPH, Farmer; res. Sec. 24; P.O. Cornton; Rep; Cath; six children; 80 acres.

MALONE MIKE, Section Boss; res. Sec. 15; P.O. Cornton; wife and two children; Dem.

MARSHALL JOHN, Sec. 4; P.O. Cornton; wife and eight children; Rep; Cath.

McCORMICK JOHN A. Proprietor Cornton House; res. Sec. 15; P.O. Cornton; born in Ireland, May 7, 1842, came to state in 1855; Dem; Cath; real estate $4,000; personal property $1,500; three years in Union Army; married Julia Cargan of Ireland, April 24, 1870; four children—one dead and three living, viz: Lizzie, born Feb. 16, 1871; Nellie, born Sept. 12, 1872; and Eveline, born Feb. 9, 1876.

McKINNEY ALEXANDER, Laborer, Sec. 15; P.O. Cornton; Rep; family and one child; Cong;

McGLIN J. C. Sec. 15; P.O. Cornton; Dem.

McCONARCHY JOHN, Farmer, Sec. 18; P.O. Lee, Lee Co; Dem; owns 49 acres.

McCAULEY A. Mrs. widow, Sec. 17. P.O. Lee, Lee Co; owns 40 acres; four children.

McGINNIS JOHN, Jr. Mail Carrier; P.O. Shabbona Grove; Dem; Cath.

McGINNIS JOHN, Sr. P.O. Shabbona Grove; owns 8 acres; wife and five children; Dem; Cath.

MEEK CHAS. Blacksmith, Sec. 15; P.O. Cornton; born Ky. 1849; real estate $2,000.

MENNIS J. J. Mrs. Dressmaking and Millinery; Sec. 15; P.O. Cornton; born in New York State, June 21, 1824, came to state in October, 1859; Bapt; personal property $300; six children—William, born Oct. 6, 1841; James V. born June 7, 1848; Sidney F. born Oct. 25, 1850; Alva P. born May 9 1853; Charles L. C. born Feb. 24, 1856; and Etta E. born July 25, 1860.

MICHAEL P. Farmer, Sec. 5; P.O. Lee, Lee Co; owns 119 acres; wife and three children.

MICHAEL ANDREW, Farmer, Sec. 5; P.O. Lee, Lee Co; Rep; works for P. Michael.

MICHAELSON H. Painter, Sec. 6; P.O. Lee, Lee Co; Rep.

MIDDLETON BURNET, Farmer, Sec. 1; P.O. Cornton; owns 326 acres; wife and one child.

MIDDLETON JOHN, Farmer, Sec. 1; P.O. Cornton; wife and one child; Rep.

MILLER PETER, Farmer, Sec. 24; P.O. Cornton; 168 acres; family and two children; Rep.

MILLER WARREN, Laborer, Sec. 25; P.O. Shabbona Grove; works for M. Greenfield; Rep.

MORSE I. F. Farmer, Sec. 27; P.O. Cornton; Rep; family and ten children.

MOREY H. D. Farmer; res. Sec. 15; P.O. Cornton; owns 25 ac.; Rep.

MORSE FRANK F. Farmer, Sec. 27; P.O. Cornton; Rep.

MULLINS JOHN, Farmer, Sec. 18; P.O. Lee, Lee Co; Rep; family and three children; 154 ac.

MULLINS GEORGE, Farmer, Sec. 7; P.O. Lee, Lee Co; Rep; four children; 140 acres.

MULLINS ROBERT, Farmer, Sec. 17; P.O. Cornton; eight children; Rep.

MURRAY FRANK, Farmer, Sec. 34; P.O. Shabbona Grove; family and four children.

N AU CHARLES. Farmer, Sec. 9; P.O. Lee, Lee Co; owns 206 acres; Ind; Meth.

NAU FRED, Farmer, Sec. 9; P.O. Lee, Lee Co; works for C. Nau; Ind; Meth.

NAU PHILIPP, Farmer, Sec. 10; P.O. Cornton; born in Germany, July 26, 1837, came to state in 1856; Dem; Ger. Evang; owns 40 acres; real estate $2,000; personal property $600; married Anna Hoffman, Aug. 11, 1861; she was born in Germany, April 20, 1840; four children—Dora, born Jan. 11, 1862; Charles, born Sept. 4, 1864; Anna, born Sept. 26, 1869; and Hattie, born Aug. 31, 1873.

NICHOLSON WILLIAM, Meth. Minister, Sec. 8; P.O. Cornton; 200 ac; seven children; Rep.

NICHOLSON KNUT, Tenant Farmer, Sec. 12; P.O. Cornton; Dem; Cath; three children.

NICHOLSON CHARLES W. Farmer, Sec. 8; P.O. Cornton; Rep; Meth.

NORTON DAVID, Farmer, Sec. 14; P.O.Cornton; born N.Y. 1821; Rep.

NORTON SIDNEY. Carpenter, Sec. 15; P.O. Cornton; Ind.

NORTON LYMAN, Carpenter and Joiner, Sec. 26; P.O. Shabbona Grove; born in Washington Co. N.Y. Aug. 4, 1808; came to state and county in 1844; Rep; owns 34 acres; real estate $1,000; one year in the army; married first wife, Hannah Gates, June 1, 1834; seven children, viz: Ann, born July 22, 1835; Melissa, born Sept. 1, 1837; Laura, born Jan. 21, 1839; Edwin, born Aug. 17, 1840; Byron F. born July 4, 1843; William, born Aug. 11, 1845; and Stephen, born Oct. 15, 1849; married present wife, Lydia Ann Weston, Aug. 16, 1853; she was born Onondaga Co. N.Y. Oct. 7, 1832; nine children, viz: Francis, born July 31, 1854; Lillian A. born Sept. 14, 1856; Herbert D born Nov. 12, 1858; Arthur E. born May 20, 1861; Elmer, born Sept. 2, 1866; Byron, born Jan. 23, 1868; Wallace, born May 2, 1870; and balance deceased.

NUTTALL J. A. Sec. 15; P.O. Cornton; Rep; wife and one child.

O 'CONNELL MIKE, Sec. 15; P.O. Cornton; Dem; Cath.

OLSON JACOB, Laborer, Sec. 15; P.O. Cornton; wife and eight children.

OLMSTEAD M. W. Farmer, Sec. 25; P.O. Shabbona Grove; born Ct.; Rep; Meth.

O'CONNOR TIMOTHY, Billiard Hall, Sample Room, Restaurant and Livery, Sec. 15; P.O. Cornton; born in Franklin Co. New York State, June 15, 1835; came to state July 3, 1861; Dem; Cath; real estate and personal property about $3,500; married Ann Lalway, Dec. 31, 1865; she was born in Ireland, Oct. 15, 1838; three children, viz: John, born Oct. 20, 1865; Julia, born June 13, 1867; and William Edward, born April 27, 1870.

OLESON PETER, Laborer, Sec. 15; P.O. Cornton; wife and three children.

OLMSTEAD ISAAC L. Sec. 25; P.O. Shabbona Grove; wife and three children; Rep.

OVERTON M. L. Farmer, Sec. 34; P.O. Shabbona Grove; wife and one child; Rep.

OSHELUND CARL, Mason; P.O. Lee, Lee Co; Meth; Rep.

PADGETT THOS. General Store, Sec. 15; P.O. Cornton; born N.J.; Rep; Cong.

PALM JOHN, Farmer, Sec. 15; P.O. Cornton; Dem; family and two children.

PARKS J. C. Telegraph Operator, Sec. 6; P.O. Lee, Lee Co.

PATTEE ALBION, Farmer; residence Sec. 14, Tp. 38, R. 3; P.O. Cornton; born in New Hampshire Nov. 26, 1837; came to state in October, 1852; Rep; owns 69 acres, value $3,200; held the office of Collector in 1873; married Caroline M. Kilborn Jan. 1, 1861; four children, born as follows: Thomas O., Nov. 17, 1862; Harry W., Dec. 5, 1866; Frank B., April 22, 1868; and Grace E., August 8, 1872; was in the army nearly three years; was wounded in the left breast in the skirmish which took place Feb. 2, 1865, near Blackville, South Carolina.

PATTEE R. Farmer, Sec. 14; 85 acres, value $4,500; Rep; from N. H.; two children.

PARKE GEO. Farmer, Sec. 27; P.O. Cornton; works his father's farm; Rep.

PLANT JAMES, Farmer, Sec. 30; P.O. Lee; works farm of J. L. Greenfield; Rep.

POST A. F. Farmer; residence Sec. 2, Tp. 38, R. 3; P.O. Cornton; born in St. Lawrence Co. N.Y. April 20, 1826; came to state in 1850; Rep; owns 214 acres, value $11,000; perprop. $3,000; married Mariett Hoselton April 26, 1854; five children, one deceased and four living: Ida M., born April 6, 1857; Emery A., born March 2, 1859; Eddie M., born Nov. 29, 1862, and died March 28, 1864; Elma, born Nov. 1, 1869; and Mabel, born Oct. 29, 1872.

POMEROY F. Minister; residence Sec. 26, Tp. 38, R. 3; P.O. Shabbona Grove; born in DeKalb Co. Ill. June 6, 1842; Rep; Meth. Epis; was in the army four years, the last two as Regimental Quartermaster Sergeant; married Mary Tompkins, of Dutchess Co. N.Y. Nov. 29, 1865; she was born Nov. 24, 1846; five children, two dead and three living: Charles H., born August 27, 1866; Edward F., born June 29 1871; and Clarke E., born April 25, 1875.

POTTER OLIVER, Farmer, Sec. 36; P.O. Shabbona Grove; Rep; five children.

POWELL JOHN, Farmer, Sec. 33; P.O. Cornton; Rep; four children.

POWELL T. works old Leyson's farm, Sec. 32; P.O. Cornton; Rep.

PRICE MATHIAS, Farmer, Sec. 32; P.O. Shabbona Grove; Rep.

PRICE JAMES Mrs. widow of James Price, Sec. 32; P.O. East Paw Paw.

PRESTEGAARD OLE J. Sec. 6; P.O. Lee, Lee Co.; Rep; Luth; three children.

QUILLOT P. V. Farmer, Sec. 13; P.O. Cornton; born N.Y; Rep.

RAVER FREDERICK, Farmer, Sec. 20; P.O. Cornton; Rep; Pres.

RAVER HENRY, Farmer, Sec. 16; P.O. Cornton; Rep; Meth. Epis.

RAVER ALBERT F. Farmer, residence Sec. 8, Tp. 38, R. 3; P.O. Lee, Lee Co.; born in Germany, Feb. 15, 1838; came to state in 1865; Rep; Meth; real estate $10,000; owns 160 acres; personal prop. about $2,500; married Lydia Jane Ayres July 4, 1863; she was born in England Feb. 25, 1839, and died June 20, 1874; five children, four living, viz.: Charles, born Sept. 22, 1864; May, born June 27, 1866; Lydia, born March 20, 1868; and Albert, born July 18, 1872; and Anne, born May 29, 1874, and died in March, 1875.

RAVER HENRY, Farmer, rents J. B. Waters' estate, Sec. 20; P.O. Cornton; Rep; Pres.

RANDALL NORMAN, Farmer, Sec. 5; P.O. Lee, Lee Co.; rents from C. Nau; Rep.

RANDALL B. F. Farmer, residence Sec. 5, Tp. 38, R. 3; P.O. Lee, Lee Co.; born in Chemung Co. N.Y. May 3, 1820; came to state in 1842; Rep; U. Breth; owns 120 acres, value $7,000; personal prop. $1,000; married Sarah R. Stickler August 3, 1838; she was born in Steuben Co. N.Y. April 17, 1822, and died in Shabbona, Oct. 28, 1868; eight children: Charles W., born August 2, 1844; Ellen J., born March 18, 1847; Norman L., born Jan. 3, 1850; Manda Ett, born Feb. 18, 1853; Alvaretta, born Jan. 17, 1855; Henry F., born Nov. 30, 1857; John H., born June 21, 1859; Amelia M., born August 12, 1860; and Rhoda Ann, born Sept. 18, 1863.

RAY JOHN, Farmer, Sec. 15; P.O. Cornton; 140 acres; Rep; Bapt; seven children.

RAY BENJ. F. Farmer, Sec. 15; P.O. Cornton; Rep.

RAY JOHN PETER, Farmer, Sec. 15; P.O. Cornton; Rep.

RAY WILLIAM, Agent A. M. Express Co. Sec. 15; P.O. Cornton; Rep; one child.

RICE LYMAN, Sec. 15; P.O. Cornton; Ind; Meth; four children.

ROCHFORD PATRICK, Farmer, residence Sec. 25, Tp. 38, R. 3; P.O. Shabbona Grove; born in Tipperary, Ireland, March 17, 1838; came to state in July, 1863; Dem; Cath; owns six acres, prop. worth $1,500; married Bridget Butler, of Tipperary, Ireland, March 17, 1870; she was born in September, 1846; four children: Thomas, born Sept. 25, 1871; Mary, born March 15, 1873; William, born June 14, 1874; and Frank, born May 20, 1876.

ROCHFORD JAMES, Farmer, Sec. 25; P.O. Shabbona Grove; Dem.

RYAN JOHN, P.O. Shabbona Grove; works for S. C. E. Hallam; from Ireland.

SCHRADER WILLIAM, Farmer, Sec. 10; P.O. Cornton; 80 acres; Rep; four children.

SCHRADER FERDINAND, Farmer, Sec. 3; P.O. Cornton; Luth; Rep.

SCOGGIN HIRAM, Farmer, Sec. 24; P.O. Cornton; Rep; Meth; 125 acres; four children.

SCOGGIN WM. JOHN, works for H. Scoggin, Sec. 24; P.O. Cornton; Rep; Meth.

SHELBURN I. SCOTT, Hotel and Cider Mill; residence Sec. 26, Tp. 38, R. 3 E.; P.O. Shabbona Grove; born in Madison Co. N.Y. August 19, 1813; landed in Chicago Sept. 14, 1845, and came to county Sept. 19, 1845; Rep; owns 13 acres land; real estate and personal property valued at $1,300; served as Justice of the Peace between 1862 and 1870; wife was Maria Groves, of Hampden Co. Mass., born May 17, 1812; married July 6, 1842; no children; one of the oldest settlers of this county; the capacity of his cider mill is forty barrels per day.

SCOTT MILES, Farmer; P.O. Cornton; Rep; rents farm of Mr. J. W. Stevens.

SCHONHOLTZ N. Harnessmaker, Sec. 6; P.O. Lee; Rep.

SCHALL A. Farmer, Sec. 7; P.O. Lee, Lee Co.; Luth; 120 acres; six children.

SCHWARZMANN DAVID, Cheese Manufacturer, Sec. 14; P.O. Cornton; Rep; Cath.

SEELEY HARLEY, Laborer, Sec. 26; P.O. Shabbona Grove; Rep; three children.

SEELEY JOHN W. Laborer, Sec. 26; P.O. Shabbona Grove; Rep; two children.

SEELEY MERCY, widow of Thos. Seeley, Sec. 26; P.O. Shabbona Grove.

SHAW GEO. W. Sec. 35; P.O. Shabbona Grove; Rep; two children.

SHANER WILSON, Sec. 15; P.O. Cornton; Dem.

SHANKS JAMES W. Farmer, Sec. 21; P.O. Cornton; Cong; Rep; works farm L. C. Burke.

SHERWOOD F. O. Carpenter, Sec. 15; P.O. Cornton; Rep; three children.

SIEGEL AUGUST, Farmer, Sec. 31; P.O. Cornton; Ind. Dem.

SMITH JOSEPH, Farmer; residence Sec. 25, Tp. 38, R. 3; P.O. Cornton; born in Saratoga Co. N.Y. Sept. 15, 1818; came to state and county in 1854; Rep; owns 144 acres, value $11,150; served as Assessor in 1869; married Lovina Fritts Dec. 31, 1846; she was born in Saratoga Co. N.Y. Nov. 12, 1827; five children, four living: Emma F., born March 25, 1852; Mary J., born July 27, 1863; Willie, born Dec. 23, 1866; and Jennie E., born Aug. 27, 1868.

SMITH DAVID, Farmer, Sec. 27; P.O. Cornton; Rep; six children.

SMITH J. J. Carpenter, Sec. 25; P.O. Cornton; Rep.

SMITH WARREN, Farmer, Sec. 27; P.O. Cornton; Rep; works for D. Smith.

SMITH HENRY, Farmer, Sec. 27; P.O. Cornton; Rep; works for D. Smith.

SMITH I. Farmer, Sec. 27; P.O. Cornton; Rep; works for D. Smith.

SMITH J. W. of Wm. Deacon & Co. Lumber and Grain; Sec. 15; P.O. Cornton; Rep; Meth.

SNELL MARCELLUS, Carpenter; Sec. 15; P.O. Cornton; Rep; Bapt; four children.

SKOYLES BENJAMIN H. Merchant, Custom Mills; residence Sec. 6, Tp. 38, R. 3; P.O. Lee, Lee Co; born in Filby, Norfolk, England, Feb. 12, 1824; came to state in Jany. 1372; Meth; val. of real estate $12,000; married Anna King of Beccles, Suffolk Co. England, May 2, 1855; she died in the Fall of 1868; built Paw Paw Mills in 1873, and started in Jan. 1874; built Lee Mill in 1876, on improved principles; capacity 100 barrels of flour in 24 hours; Mr. Skoyles was presented $1,630 in money and some land by President of the C. & I. R.R., together with the people of Lee and its vicinity, as an encouragement to start up the above enterprise.

SPRAY GEORGE, Farmer. Sec. 17; P.O. Cornton; Rep.

SPRAY MATHEW, Farmer, Sec. 16; P.O. Cornton; 120 acres; six children.

SPENCER HERBERT O. Agricultural Implements; Sec. 15; P.O. Cornton; Rep.

SPICER JAS. Laborer, Sec. 23; Rep; one child.

SPICER ALBERT, Farmer, Sec. 14; P.O. Cornton; Meth; Rep; rents farm of Jno. Palmer.

SPICER EGBERT, Farmer, Sec. 23; 30 acres, worth $500; Rep; eight children.

SPEARS WALTER Butcher; Sec. 15; P.O. Cornton; Rep; seven children.

STERLING A. W. Proprietor of The Central Meat Market, residence Sec. 15, Tp. 38, R. 3; P.O. Cornton; born in Iowa, Sept. 7, 1852; came to state in 1866; Rep.

STIMPSON SARAH Mrs. widow of Geo. Stimpson; Sec. 17; P.O. Cornton; owns 160 acres.

STIMPSON JOHN, Farmer, Sec. 17; P.O. Cornton. Rep.

STIMPSON WHEIGHT, Farmer, Sec. 17; P.O. Cornton; Rep; one child.

STOPEN PETER, Wagonmaker, boards at McCormick's Hotel; Ind.

STOREY S. Farmer, Sec. 17; P.O. Cornton; Rep; Meth; owns 400; seven children.

STREM PETER, Laborer, Sec. 15; P.O. Cornton; Rep; Luth; five children.

STUBEN P. Wagonmaker, Sec. 15; P.O. Cornton: born Chicago.

STEVENS E. W. Farmer, Sec. 29; P.O. Cornton; Rep; 160 acres; six children.

STEVENS CHAS. works for F. Heath, Sec. 3; P.O. Cornton; Meth; Rep.

STEVENS CHAS. Farmer, Sec. 15; P.O. Cornton; born N. Y.; Rep; Cong.

STEVENS W. H. O. Farmer, Sec. 22; P.O. Cornton; Rep; three children.

STEVENS D. D. Farmer, Sec. 21; P.O. Cornton; Rep; 110 acres; one child.

STEVENS F. O. Farmer, Sec. 30; P.O. Cornton; Rep; 120 acres; two children.

STREETER CHARLES W. Farmer, res. Sec. 10; P.O. Cornton; owns 40 acres; Rep.

STREETER M. J. Farmer, Res. Sec. 10; P.O. Cornton; family five children; 220 acres; Rep.

STEPHEN & PRESTEGARD, Dealers in General Hardware; residence Lee; P.O. Lee, Lee Co.

SWETT JOHN, Telegraph Operator, Sec. 15, P.O. Cornton.

SWEET M. Farmer; P.O. Cornton; Dem; three children.

SWANSON CHAS. works for W. Helm, Sec. 4; P.O. Cornton; Rep.

SWANSON JOHN, works for J. W. Shanks, Sec. 21; P.O. Cornton; Rep.

TEN CHAS. Farmer, Sec. 6; P.O. Lee, Lee Co; Rep.

TEFFRE E. O. Painter; Sec. 6; P.O. Lee, Lee Co; Rep.

TEMPLE E. L. Farmer, P.O. Cornton; born Wis; Rep.

THERBER WM. ORLANDO, Farmer, Sec. 16; P.O. Cornton; Rep.

TODD O. Farmer, Sec. 28; P.O. Cornton; Ind; owns 160 acres.

TODD WM. Farmer, Sec. 28; P.O. Cornton; rents of G. W. Kittel; Rep; two children.

TOWLER JAS. Farmer, Sec. 5; P.O. Lee, Lee Co; 35 acres; Rep; Meth; two children.

TRASK ALFRED B. Proprietor Trask House; residence Lee; P.O. Lee, Lee Co; born in Geauga Co. Ohio, April 22, 1820; came to state in 1844; Rep; Universalist; value of real estate and personal property about $10,000; President of the Board of Trustees; married Temperance E. Bosely, June 9, 1844; she was born in Geauga Co. Ohio, Sep. 13, 1822; has had seven children, only three living—Frank, born Sep. 3, 1851; George, born Jan. 14, 1859; and Minnie E., born Feb. 25, 1870.

TRASK FRANK Farmer, Sec. 9; P.O. Lee, Lee Co; 40 acres; Dem; two children.

TRUBE ERNHT. Farmer, Sec. 1; P.O. Waterman; 80 acres; Rep; one child.

TUCKER JABEZ, Shoemaker, Sec. 15; P.O. Cornton; born New Jersey.

ULLMANN GEO. Laborer, Sec. 26; P.O. Shabbona Grove; Rep; three children.

VAN VELZOR DEWITT, Farmer, Sec. 9; P.O. Cornton; Rep; 160 acres.

VAN VELZOR WM. Farmer, Sec. 11; P.O. Cornton; works for M. VanVelzor.

VAN VELZOR M. Farmer, Sec. 11; P.O. Cornton; Rep; six children

VAN DEUSEN A. V. Farmer, Sec. 34; P.O. Shabbona Grove; Rep; 140 acres.

VAN NESS L. Sec. 15; P.O. Cornton; Rep.

VAN NESS AARON, Shoemaker, Sec. 15; P.O. Cornton; born N. J. 1854; real estate $500;

VROMAN A. C. Agent C. & I. R.R., and C. B. & Q. R.R; Sec. 15; P.O. Cornton.

WAGNER FRED. Farmer, Sec. 9; P.O. Cornton; owns 40 acres.

WALKUP H. H. Farmer, Sec. 11; P.O. Cornton; Rep; works N. R. Helm's farm.

WHITE NANCY Mrs. widow of Lemuel White; Sec. 35; P.O. Shabbona Grove; five children.

WHITE SYLVANUS C. son of L. White; Sec. 36; P.O. Shabbona Grove; Ind.

WHITE CHAS. Farmer, Sec. 35; P.O. Shabbona Grove; Rep; two children.

WHITE OVANDO, Farmer, Sec. 35; P.O. Shabbona Grove; Rep.

WHITEFORD WM. W. Farmer, Sec. 34; P.O. Shabbona Grove; Ind; one child.

WILSON BILLY, Laborer, Sec. 31; P.O. Victor Center; Rep.

WILKIE EDWIN, works for John Edwards, Sec. 13; Rep.

WIGTON CHAS; Carpenter, Sec. 23; P.O. Cornton; Rep; seven children.

WOODBURY JOHN H. Farmer; residence Sec. 34, Tp. 38, R. 3; P.O. Shabbona; born in Tompkins Co. N. Y. Sep. 25, 1834; came to state in 1852; Independent in politics; owns 260 acres, valued at $13,000, and personal property $3,000; married Laura A. Smith, Feb. 28, 1856; she was born in Bradford Co. Penn. Aug. 19, 1833; four children — William W., born Sep. 19, 1858; Elias, born June 4, 1862; Alvin born Aug. 12, 1868, and Minnie, born Jan. 7, 1871.

WORMLEY H. W. Farmer, Sec. 4; P.O. Cornton; 245 acres; Rep; four children.

WRIGHT GEORGE, Farmer, Sec. 7; P.O. Lee. Lee Co; Rep; Meth; six children.

WRIGHT JOHN E. Sec. 7; P.O. Lee, Lee Co; works for Geo. Wright.

YOUNGGREN AXEL R. Farmer, Sec. 8; P.O. Lee, Lee Co.; Rep; Luth.

YOUNGGREN EDWIN, works for J. R. Marryott, Sec. 16; P.O. Cornton; Rep.

YOUNGGREN E. M. Farmer; resides Sec. 8, Tp. 38, R. 3; P.O. Lee, Lee Co; born in Jonkoping, Sweden, March 24, 1823; came to state in 1854; Rep; Luth; owns 160 acres in Shabbona and 80 in Milan Tps; held the office of Collector in 1871. Married Margaretha Sandman, Dec. 26, 1848; she was born in Jonkoping Sweden, Oct. 1, 1817; had five children : Charles W. born Jan. 28, 1850; Axel R. born Jan. 20, 1852; Gustavus M. born Sept. 5, 1854, on Newfoundland Bank; Jenny, born May 20, 1858, and died Dec. 22, 1858; and Melvina C. born Nov. 29, 1859.

YORK H. A. Physician and Surgeon, Sec. 15; P.O. Cornton; born Ill. 1844; Rep.

YOUNGGREN MAGNUS, Sec. 8; P.O. Lee, Lee Co.; Rep; Luth.

YOUNGGREN CHARLES W. Carpenter, Sec. 8; P.O. Lee, Lee Co.; Rep; Luth.

YOUNGGREN GUSTAVUS M. works for E. M. Younggren, Sec. 8; P.O. Lee, Lee Co.; Rep.

CLINTON TOWNSHIP

ABBY LORENZO, Farmer, Sec. 14; P.O. Waterman; property $5,000; Dem; N. Y.

ABBY H. R. Farmer; P.O. Waterman; Dem; from N. Y.

ABBY J. B. Farmer, lives in Waterman; 160 acres, value $8,000; Dem; from N. Y.

ALFORD RUSSELL, lives on rented farm, Sec. 34; P.O. Waterman.

ALFORD CLARK B. Farmer, Sec. 32; P.O. Waterman; Meth; from N. Y.

ALFORD REUEL, Farmer, Sec. 32; P.O. Waterman; Rep; Illinois.

ALLEN AUGUSTUS, Farmer; P.O. Waterman; Rep; Meth.

ALLEN C. F. Farmer, Sec. 4; P.O. Waterman; Meth; Rep; from Vermont.

ALLEN IRA, Farmer; P.O. Waterman; Rep; Illinois.

AMES EZRA M. Farmer, Sec. 33; P.O. VanBuren; Rep; Ind; from N. Y.

ATKINSON WM. Farmer; P.O. Waterman; value of property $5,000.

BAILEY WM. Baker, Waterman; Rep; from N. Y.

BAILEY S. A. Farmer; P.O. Waterman; Rep.

BAILEY DAVID, Farmer, Sec. 28; P.O. Waterman; Rep; Bapt; from Conn.

BALE C. Farmer, Sec. 24; P.O. Waterman; 448 acres, value $16,000; Luth; Germany.

BAXTER HANNAH Mrs. Waterman; value of property $800; Meth.

BATHERS GILES, Druggist, Waterman; value of property $3,500; Rep; Ind.

BARNES MARY Mrs. Sec. 35; P.O. Waterman; 40 acres, value $2,300; Bapt; Ireland.

BALARD H. Farmer, Sec. 6; P.O. Waterman; Rep; Luth; 80 acres, value $2,400.

BERGEN JESSE, Farmer; P.O. Waterman; Rep.

BERMASTER WM. Farmer, Sec. 2; P.O. Waterman; 160 acres, value $7,200; Rep; Luth.

BISHOP DANIEL, Farmer, Sec. 24; P.O. Waterman; Rep; from N. Y.

BIGALOW A. E. Mrs. Sec. 27; P.O. Waterman; 10 acres, value $1,200; Meth; from N. Y.

BIGALOW WM. M. Farmer; P.O. Waterman; property $500; Meth; Rep; from Mich.

BOWERS WM. Farmer, Sec. 5; P.O. Waterman; Rep; Univ; 225 acres, $9,000.

BRADBURY CHAS. Grocer, Waterman; Meth; Rep.

BRADBURY ALFRED, Grocer, Waterman; Rep; Epis; $3,000.

BROWN N. W. Mrs. widow, Sec. 36; P.O. Waterman; 520 acres, val. $26,000; Meth; Canada.

BROWN RALPH, Farmer, Sec. 25; P.O. Waterman; Dem; Meth; Illinois.

BROWN FREDERICK, Farmer, Sec. 25; P.O. Waterman; Dem; Meth; Illinois.

BRYANT ELIAS, Farmer, Sec. 6; P.O. Waterman; Advent; 80 acres, value $2,800; Rep.

BURROWS FREDERICK A. Farmer, rents of T. B. Cole. Sec. 36; P.O. Freeland; Dem; Mass.

BYLAND EDWARD, Farmer; P.O. Waterman; 242 acres, value $10,000; Cath; Dem; Illinois.

CHRONISTER J. Drayman, Waterman; Dem; val. prop. $350.

COLTON F. B. Dealer Musical Instruments; P.O. Cedar Rapids, Ia; 49 acres in Sec. 19.

CHALLAND HENRY, Retired Farmer, Waterman; born in England, Feb. 3, 1823; came to Ill. May 12, 1854; Rep; Pres; owns 5 acres, house and lot in Waterman, value $4,500; personal property $13,000; married Julia Biliney, Oct. 31, 1848, she was born in England, Dec. 30, 1827, died July 23, 1872; they had ten children, eight living; Mr. Challand married Emily Fassett, Jan. 12, 1873: they have one child.

COLTON W. L. Farmer; P.O. Waterman; 49 acres, $2,695; Adv; Rep: from Ill.

COLTON WILLIAM, Farmer, Sec. 17; P.O. Waterman; 128 acres, $7,680; Adv; Rep; N.Y.

COLE TOBIAS B. Farmer, Sec. 36; P.O. Freeland; Rep; U. Pres; from N.Y.

COLLINS EDWARD, Farmer; P.O. Waterman; Rep; Cath; from N.J.

CONGDON G. G. Farmer, Sec. 15; P.O. Waterman; 150 acres, $10,000; Rep; Bapt; from Vt.

COY B. A. Merchant, Dry Goods, etc. Waterman; Dem.

DAILEY MICHAEL, Carpenter, Waterman; Rep; from N.Y.

DAILY JOHANNAH, Sec. 20; P.O. Waterman; 80 acres, val. $3,600.

DEAN E. Butcher, Waterman; prop. $2,500; Dem; Meth; from N.Y.

DEERING ——, Farmer, Sec. 1; P.O. Waterman; prop. $500; Dem; Cath.

DELONG H. A. Farmer; P.O. Waterman; prop. $500; Univ; Dem.

DELONG H. Farmer, Sec. 18; P.O. Waterman; 80 acres, $5,200; Univ; Dem; from N.Y.

DICKEY RUTH A. Mrs. widow, Sec. 30; P.O. Shabbona Grove; 126 acres; Quaker; N.Y.

DOBBIN W. J. Farmer, Sec. 36; P.O. Freeland; 80 acres, $4,000; U. Pres; Rep; from N.Y.

ECKELS WILLIAM, Farmer, Sec. 27; P.O. Waterman; 40 acres, $1,600; Dem; Pres; Penn.

ELMER GEORGE, Farmer; P.O. Waterman; Bapt; Rep; from Canada.

EVANS WILLIAM, Blacksmith, Waterman; Rep; from Wales.

FANCHER MARTIN, Farmer, Waterman; 4½ acres in Sec. 15, $1,200; from N.Y.

FLANDERS C. M. Farmer, Sec. 11; P.O. Waterman; 80 acres, $4,000; Bapt; Rep; N.Y.

FLANDERS JOHN, Retired Farmer, Waterman; val. prop. $3,000; Meth; Rep.

FRASER EDWIN, Farmer, res. Sec. 34; P.O. Waterman; born in Washington Co. N.Y. May 23, 1836; came to this county in 1854; politics Ind; religion Ind; owns 300 acres of land, value $16,000; value of personal property $3,000; has been Supervisor of Clinton Tp. two years; married Mary Gath, March 14, 1864, she was born in LaSalle Co. Sept. 25, 1846; has six children.

FULLER A. M. Farmer, Sec. 17; P.O. Waterman; 120 acres, $6,600; Meth; Rep; from N.Y.

FULLER H. L. Farmer, Sec. 9; P.O. Waterman; 200 acres, $12,000; Rep; Meth.

FULLER OTIS, Farmer, Sec. 11; P.O. Waterman; Rep.

FULLER OTIS, Laborer, Waterman.

FULLER J. B. Farmer, Sec. 16; Waterman; 80 acres, $4,500; Pres; Rep; from Germany.

FULLER W. W. Farmer, Sec. 9; P.O. Waterman; 120 acres, $7,200; Meth; Rep; from N.Y.

FULLERTON JOHN S. Farmer; P.O. Waterman; U. Pres; Rep; from N.Y.

FULLERTON JOHN C. Farmer, Sec. 26; P.O. Waterman; born in Glenville, Schenectady Co. N.Y. March 1, 1807; Rep; U. Pres; owns 160 acres, val. $9,600; val. of personal property $3,000; married Eliza Shelfridge, May 2, 1833, she was born in Argyle, Washington Co. N.Y. Nov. 27, 1811; they came to this state and county April 2, 1859; have nine children, four boys and five girls, all living.

GAHAGAN EDWARD, Farmer, Sec. 1; P.O. Waterman; 240 acres, value $9,600.

GAHAGAN JOHN, Farmer, Sec. 1; P.O. Waterman; 170 acres, $6,800; Cath; Ireland.

GARDNER GEORGE, Farmer; rents of R. Humphrey; P.O. Waterman; Rep; Meth.

GILMORE MICHAEL, Farmer, Sec. 20; P.O. Waterman; 80 ac. $4,000; Dem; Pres; Ireland

GILES F. Druggist, Waterman; Rep.

GILES P. W. Farmer, Sec. 10; P.O. Waterman; 160 acres, $8,000; Rep; came to county 1849.

GILES J. D. Druggist, Waterman; Rep.

GILES J. F. Druggist, Waterman; Rep.

GILCHRIST JOSEPH, Farmer, Sec. 25; P.O. Waterman; 180 ac. $10,800; U. Pres; Rep; N.Y.

GILCHRIST ALBERT L. Farmer and Carpenter, Sec. 25; P.O. Waterman; U. Pres; Rep; N.Y.

GILCHRIST WALLACE, Mechanic, Sec. 25; P.O. Waterman; vat. $4,000; U. Pres; Rep; N.Y.

GRAHAM NATHAN, works for James McCleery, Jr. Sec. 34; P.O. Waterman; Rep; Pres; N.Y.

GREELY JOHN, Farmer, Sec. 3; P.O. Waterman; 160 acres, $7,200; Meth; Rep.

GREELY GEORGE O. Farmer, Sec. 10; P.O. Waterman; 80 ac. $4,800; Rep; Meth; N.Y.

GREELY EBER, Retired Farmer; P.O. Waterman; Meth; Rep; from N. H.

GREELY H. M. Farmer, Sec. 15; P.O. Waterman; 110 acres, $8,000; Rep; from N.Y.

GREENWOOD NATHAN S. Farmer, Sec. 28; P.O. Waterman; 180 acres; Rep; from N.Y.

GREENWOOD GEORGE. Farmer, Sec. 28; P.O. Waterman; 225 acres, $11,500; Rep; N.Y.

GREENWOOD CHAS. F. Farmer, Sec. 33; P.O. Waterman; 160 ac. $8,000; Rep; Lib; N.Y.

GRIFFIN P. Farmer, Sec. 31; P.O. Shabbona Grove.

GRIFFITH J. K. Harnessmaker, Waterman; Ohio; came to state 1850; prop. $1,000; Rep.

HALL S. A. Farmer, Sec. 26; P.O. Waterman; 200 acres, $12,000; Univ; Dem; from N.Y.

HALL R. R. Farmer; P.O. Waterman; Dem; from N.Y.

HALL GEORGE B. Farmer; P.O. Waterman; Rep; from Ill.

HALL WILLIAM, Farmer, Sec. 35; P.O. Waterman; 160 acres, $9,600; Rep; Univ; from N.Y.

HALL SAMUEL P. Farmer, Sec. 25; P.O. Waterman; born in Clinton Township, May 16, 1851; Dem; Meth; owns 240 acres, value $9,600; personal property $2,500.

HATTEREY A. J. Farmer, Sec. 12; P.O. Waterman; 400 acres, value $16,000.

HALBACK SILAS B. Tailor, Waterman; Rep; Pres; from Canada.

HAMILTON WILLIAM, Farmer, Sec. 7; P.O. Waterman; 91 acres, $4,550; Rep; from N.Y.

HANSON JOHN, Farmer, Sec. 21; P.O. Waterman; value property $700; from Sweden.

HARTER J. W. Farmer, Sec. 22; P.O. Waterman; 160 acres, $11,200; Rep; Pres; from Penn.

HAWKINS EARL, Farmer; P.O. Waterman; Rep; from N.Y.

HAYES CHARLES, Farmer, Sec. 12; value of property $1,500; Rep.

HENN WM. Farmer, Waterman; Rep; Evang; from Germany.

HENDERSON WM. Farmer, Sec. 21; P.O. Waterman; Rep; Meth; 80 acres, val. $4,000.

HENDERSON ALEXANDER, Farmer, Sec. 35; P.O. Waterman; Rep; Bapt.

HERRICK GEORGE, Farmer; P.O. Waterman; 200 acres, value $10,000; Ohio.

HILL K. C. son of W. S. Hill, Sec. 20; P.O. Waterman; Rep.

HILL W. S. Farmer, Sec. 20; P.O. Waterman; Rep; 160 acres, value $10,000; from N. Y.

HILL SYLVESTER, son of W. S. Hill, Sec. 20; P.O. Waterman; Rep.

HILL GEORGE, Farmer, Sec. 21; P.O. Waterman ; Rep; 200 acres, val. $10,000; Ohio.

HINDS ALBERT, son of Thomas Hinds, a soldier of the war of 1812; resided in Canada about four years; moved directly to DeKalb Co. where he has since resided, in Clinton township. August 20, 1843, married Fanny Richardson, in Belleville, Canada West; she is now living; the issue of this marriage is four sons—all living—Albert, William R., Carlos W. and Orvis.

HINDS CARLOS W. Farmer; P.O. Waterman; Rep; from Illinois.

HINDS F. M. Farmer; P.O. Waterman; Rep; from Illinois.

HINDS SILAS, Farmer, Sec. 17; P.O. Waterman; Rep; 120 acres, val. $6,000; from N. Y.

HINDS T. H. prop. Livery Stable Waterman; Rep; from Vermont.

HINDS WM. R. Farmer; P.O. Waterman; Rep; Ind; from Illinois.

HIPPLE JNO. H. Farmer, Sec. 23; P.O. Waterman; Rep; 320 acres; from N.Y.

HOLBROOK T. B. Farmer, Sec. 3; P.O. Waterman; Rep; Meth; 160 ac. val. $6,400.

HOWISON WM. Farmer, Sec. 33; P.O. Waterman; Rep; U. Pres; 240 ac. val. $12,000.
HORTON DARIUS, Painter, Waterman; Univ; Dem; val. prop. $1,500; was in 105th Ills. Inf.
HOWISON ROBERT, Farmer, Sec. 26; P.O. Waterman; Rep; U. Pres; 160 ac. val. $9,600.
HUMPHREY ROBERT, Farmer, Secs. 4 and 9; P.O. Waterman; 160 acres, value $9,600.
HUNT J. L. Farmer, Sec. 19; P.O. Waterman; Rep; Pres; 146 ac. val. $8,760.
HURST GEORGE, Farmer; P.O. Waterman; per. prop. $1,000.
HUSTEN GEORGE, Shoemaker, Waterman; Rep; val. prop. $1,200.

I RVING ROBERT, prop. Boarding House, Waterman; Ind; Meth; from Scotland.

J ACOBS CHAS. L. Farmer; P.O. Waterman; Rep; Ind; from N.Y.

K IRKPATRICK HIRAM, Farmer, Sec. 27; P.O. Waterman; Rep; Lib; 280 ac. val. $14,000.
KIRKPATRICK HEZEKIAH, Farmer, Sec. 25; P.O. Waterman; U. Pres; Rep.
KAUFFMAN A. C. Farmer, Sec. 3; P.O. Waterman; born in York Co. Penn, March 4,
1838; came to this state and county March 13, 1868; Rep; Prot; owns 80 acres, val. $4,000;
personal property $1,000; was in the 7th Penn. Reserve four years. Married Caroline
Stern, Nov. 12, 1865; she was born in York Co. Penn. Nov. 16, 1846; has six children, two
boys and four girls; Mr. K. was wounded twice in the army and is now a pensioner.
KIRKPATRICK ISAAC, Farmer, Sec. 16; P.O. Waterman; Rep; Pres; 80 ac. val. $6,000.
KIRKPATRICK JOHN, Farmer, Sec. 25; P.O. Waterman; U. Pres; Rep.
KIRKPATRICK MERVIN H. Farmer; P.O. Waterman; Rep; Pres; from Penn.
KIRKPATRICK ORESTES, Farmer, Sec. 27; P.O. Waterman; Rep; Lib; from Ind.
KIRKPATRICK P. F. Farmer, P.O. Waterman; Rep; Pres; from Penn.
KOPP C. H. Carpenter, Waterman; Rep; val. prop. $1,000.
KIRKPATRICK SMILEY, Farmer, Sec. 22; P.O. Waterman; born in Perry County,
Penn. March, 31. 1825, came to this state and county March 21, 1855; Rep; Pres· owns
245 acres, value $13,000; per. prop. $2,500; has held the office of Town Clerk two years,
and Justice of Peace four years; married Miss A. M. Hipple, Sept. 15. 1853; she was born in
Carlisle, Penn. March 29, 1831; have had ten children, six living, four boys and two girls.

L A GRANGE, J. J. Grocer, Waterman; Rep; Prot; from N.Y.
LAMB HENRY, Farmer, Sec. 10; P.O. Waterman; Rep; Meth; val. prop. $6,000.
LAMB L. Farmer, Sec. 3; P.O. Waterman; Rep; Meth; val. prop. $8,000; from Ohio.
LAMBERT J. R. rents Mrs. S. Woodruff's farm, Sec. 19; P.O. Waterman; Rep; Christian; Ill.
LATTIN SIDNEY, Farmer, P.O. Shabbona Grove; Rep; 77 acres, val. $4,000; from N. Y.
LEIFHEIT AUGUST, Farmer, Sec. 2; P.O. Waterman; born in Germany, Oct. 10,
1843, came to this state Dec. 3, 1854, to the county March, 1860; Dem; Luth; owns 167
acres, value $8,350; per. prop. $2,000; wife was Miss Minnie Baie, born in Germany, July
16, 1846; married Jan. 22, 1865, has five children, four boys living.
LEIFHEIT HENRY, Prop. Billiard Hall, Waterman; Dem; Luth.
LEIFHEIT HENRY, Farmer, Sec. 2; P.O. Waterman; Rep; Luth; 160 acres, val. $8,000.
LEARSON JENKINS, Farmer, P.O. Waterman; Rep; from Canada.
LITTLE A. Retired Farmer, Sec. 8; Waterman; Dem; Univ; 165 acres, val. $10,000; Canada.
LITTLE E. D. lives in Waterman; Dem; owns 160 acres, Sec. 8, val. $8,500.
LOW JOHNSON, Farmer, Sec. 19; P.O. Waterman; Rep; Adv; 120 acres, $6,000; Canada.
LUFFINE HARTWELL, Farmer, P.O. Waterman.

M ACY W. C. Farmer, Sec. 4; P.O. Waterman; Rep; Pres; 100 acres, val. $5,500; from Tenn.
MACKLIN GEORGE M., M. D. Physician; Rep; Pres; came to Ill. 1856; from N.Y.
MAHON WILLIAM, Farmer, P.O. Waterman; Rep; 40 acres, val. $1,600.
MARTIN GEORGE, Farmer, Sec. 18; P.O. Waterman; Rep; val. prop. $2,000; from N. Y.
MARSHALL S. Farmer, P.O. Waterman; Rep; Meth; val. prop. $1,500; from England.
MATTESON O. F. Farmer, Sec. 27; P.O. Waterman; Rep; Lib; 160 acres, val. $9,600; N. Y.
MERCER R. J. works for Andrew Graham, Sec. 12; P.O. Waterman; Rep; U. Pres; Penn,
MERRITT J. H. Farmer, Sec. 5; P.O. Waterman; Rep; Adv; 105 acres, val. $7,350; from N. Y.
MERRITT W. Farmer, P.O. Waterman; Rep; Meth; val. prop. $3,500; from Ill.

MIGHELL, C. F. Merchant, Waterman; Rep; Meth; val. prop. $7.500; from Vt.

MERCER SMITH, Farmer, Sec. 23; P.O. Waterman; born in Beaver Co. Penn. May 12, 1827, came to this state and county June 29, 1856; Rep; United Pres; owns 240 acres, value $11,600; value personal prop. $3,300; has been Collector two years, and Assessor one year; married Margaret Thornburg, Nov. 14, 1850, who was born in Beaver Co. Penn. Feb. 9, 1831; has eleven children, of whom nine are living, seven boys and two girls; settled on his farm June 21, 1856.

MIGHELL, ELLIS W. Farmer, Sec. 23; P.O. Waterman; property $400; Rep; Bapt.

MIGHELL, ELEAZER, Retired Farmer, Sec. 14; born in Vermont in 1792.

MIGHELL, JAS. H. Farmer, Sec. 23; P.O. Waterman; 105 ac; val. $6,300; Rep; Bapt; Vt.

MIGHELL, J. L. Farmer, Sec. 21; P.O. Waterman; 245 acres, value $14,700; Rep; Christian.

MIGHELL, M. P. Grain Dealer, Waterman; value of property $3,000; Rep.

MIGHELL, F. C. Grain Dealer, Waterman; Rep; Illinois.

MILLER ELI, Farmer; P.O. Waterman.

MITCHALL, WM. B. Farmer, Sec. 27; P.O. Waterman; 80 ac; val. $4,800; Rep; U. P; Ohio.

MOORE WILLIAM, Dealer in Lumber, Coal, Lime, Brick, etc., at Waterman; born in England, Nov. 22, 1825; came to Illinois in 1844, and to this county in 1859; Rep; Bapt; owns house and lot in Waterman, value $1.500; value of personal property $600; married Emily H. Morrill, June 28, 1848; she was born in Canada, July 10, 1825; has five children, two boys and three girls.

MOORE S. H. Dealer in Lumber, Coal, and Lime, Waterman; Bapt; Rep; Illinois.

MOORE W. H. Dealer in Lumber, Coal, and Lime, Waterman; Bapt; Rep; Illinois.

MULLIN THOMAS, Farmer, Waterman; Rep; Meth; from England.

MURRAY TIMOTHY, Farmer; P.O. Waterman; Rep; Ind.

McALLISTER JAS. Farmer, Sec. 36; P.O. Freeland; 80 acres, value $4,800; U. P; Rep; N.Y.

McEACHRON THOS. Farmer, Sec. 24; P.O. Waterman; 80 acres, value $3,200; Rep; N. Y.

McEACHRON JOHN A. Farmer, Sec 24; P.O. Waterman; U. P; Rep; from N. Y.

McEACHRON FRANK, lives with his father, Sec. 24; P.O. Waterman; U. P; Rep; N. Y.

McFADDEN PHILIP, rents farm, Sec. 32; P.O. Shabbona Grove; Dem; Cath; Ireland.

McCASKEY AMOS, Farmer, Sec. 23; P.O. Waterman; Meth; Rep; from Penn.

McCASKEY JOHN, Farmer; P.O. Waterman; property $500; Rep; Meth.

McCORMICK PATRICK, Farmer, Sec. 6; P.O. Waterman; 100 ac; value $5,000, Dem; Cath.

McCORMICK WM. lives with his mother, Sec. 31; P.O. Shabbona Grove; Dem; Cath; Iowa.

McCORMICK MICHAEL, lives with his mother, Sec. 31; P.O. Shabbona Grove; Cath; Dem; Ia.

McCORMICK ELLEN Mrs. widow; Sec. 31; P.O. Shabbona Grove; Cath; from Ireland.

McCORMICK MICHAEL Sr. Retd. Farmer, Sec. 31; P.O. Shabbona G.; Dem; Cath; Ireland.

McCORMICK DANIEL, Farmer, Sec. 20; P.O. Waterman; Dem; Cath; 80 acres.

McCLERRY JAMES Jr. Farmer, Sec. 34; P.O. Waterman; U. P; Rep; from Canada.

McNISH JOHN, Farmer, Sec. 27; P.O. Waterman; property $6,400; Dem.

NORMANDIN PETER, Laborer, Waterman; value of property $500; Ind; Bapt; Canada.

OLMSTED DANIEL D. Farmer, Sec. 31; P.O. Shabbona Grove; Rep; Rep; Meth; N. Y.

OLMSTED FRANK D. Farmer, Sec. 31; P.O. Shabbona Grove; Rep; from Ill.

OLMSTED GEORGE J. Short-hand reporter; Sec. 31; P.O. Shabbona Grove; Ind; from Ill.

ORR DAVID, Hardware merchant, Waterman; U. Pres; Rep; from Ohio.

ORR J. S. Son of David Orr, Waterman; Rep; from Ills.

OSTRANDER R. H. Waterman; from Wis.

O'CONNELL D. Farmer; P.O. Waterman; Dem; Cath; from Ills.

O'BRIEN MICHAEL, Farmer; P.O. Waterman; Dem; Cath; from Ireland.

PATTERSON JOSEPH, Farmer; P.O. Waterman; Dem; Lib; from Kentucky.

PERSONS EUGENE, lives with his father, Sec. 30; P.O. Shabbona Grove; Rep; Bap; N.Y.

PERSONS REUBEN, Baptist Minister and Farmer, Sec. 30; P.O. Shabbona Grove; Ind; N.Y.

PEARSON R. N. Dealer in musical instruments, Waterman; Rep; Bap; N.Y.

PERRY JEROME, Farmer; P.O. Shabbona Grove; Rep; from Vermont.

PHELPS L. E. General merchandise; Rep; Bap; from N.Y.

PHILIPS MRS. CAROLINE, P.O. Waterman; owns 80 acres land, value $4,000.

PHILIPS A. H. Stock dealer; P.O. Waterman; Meth; Rep; from N.Y.

PLACE GEORGE, Wagonmaker, Waterman; Rep; from N.Y.

POTTER ISAAC A. Farmer, Sec. 17; P.O. Waterman; born in Dutchess Co. N.Y. May 7, 1831; came to Ill. March 4, 1867; to DeKalb Co. April 13, 1876; Rep; Bapt; owns 165½ acres, value $8,275; personal property $2,000; married Mary A. Robinson May 30, 1855, who was born in Hume, Allegany Co., N.Y. Feb. 18, 1834; they have one child; Mr. Potter moved to Allegany county in 1848, and remained there until coming to this state.

POWELL DAVID, P.O. Waterman; Rep; Latter Day Saints.

POWELL BYRON, works for James McClerry Jr., Sec. 34; P.O. Waterman; Rep.

PRITCHARD I. W. Physician, Waterman; born in Oneida Co., N.Y., Jan. 18, 1842; came to this state in May, 1868; Rep; Ind; owns house and lot in Waterman, value $5,000; also 483 acres of land in Kansas, value $9,600; personal property $6,000; married Debbie I. Coy Jan. 10, 1870, who was born in Otisco, N.Y. April 17, 1853; she died Feb. 23, 1876, leaving one girl; Dr. Pritchard practiced at Kaneville six years before coming to Waterman; graduated at Michigan University, Ann Arbor; attended Long Island hospital, Bellevue Hospital, and the Eye and Ear Infirmary, New York City.

PRICHARD R. M. Farmer, Sec. 30; P.O. Waterman; Rep; Pres; 317 acres; from Malone.

PULFREY E. C. Tinner, Waterman; Rep; Univ.

R ANDLES W. J. Farmer, Sec. 25; P.O. Waterman; Rep; U. Pres; from N.Y.

RASEY JOSEPH, Farmer; P.O. Waterman; Rep; Cong; from N.Y.

RANDLES ANDREW, Retired Farmer, Sec. 25; P. O. Waterman; born in Argyle, Washington Co., N.Y., April 3, 1822; came to this county March, 1866; Rep; U. Pres; owns 160 acres, value $9,600; personal property $3,200; married M. A. McGeochh Feb. 13, 1845; she was born in Washington Co., N.Y., Feb. 1825; has three children, one son, William, who carries on the farm.

REID A. H. Farmer; P.O. Waterman; 120 acres, $7,200; U. Pres; Rep; from N.Y.

REYNOLDS A. H. Farmer, Sec. 10; P.O. Waterman; val. prop. $500; Rep; Meth; from Vt.

REYNOLDS E. A. Farmer, Sec. 10; P.O. Waterman; val. prop. $500; Pres; Rep; from Vt.

REYNOLDS JAY, Farmer; P.O. Waterman; value property $300; Rep; born 1854.

REYNOLDS L. P. Farmer, Sec. 10; P.O. Waterman; 160 acres, $8.000; Rep; Meth; from Vt.

ROBINSON MILES, Farmer, Sec. 35; P.O. Waterman; Rep; U. Pres; from Penn.

ROBINSON THOS. H. the second son of Benj. and Elizabeth (Spangler) Robinson, who moved from Mercer Co. Penn. 1858, to Louisa County, Iowa, where Mr. Robinson died, on the 5th of January, 1861. Thomas H. resided with his widowed mother until 1873, when he removed to his present place of residence. On the 10th of Sept. 1873, he was married to Miss Elizabeth McCleery, daughter of James McCleery, Sr. of Louisa County, Iowa. His mother followed him in March, 1875; he has one son, named James McCleery.

ROBERTS HUMPHREY, Farmer, Sec. 16; P.O. Waterman; born Carnarvon, Wales, Dec. 21, 1823; came to the United States in Aug. 1832, to this state July 22, 1847, and to this county March 3, 1857; Rep; Bapt; owns 390 acres, value $29,250; personal property $10,000; has been Road Commissioner four years; married Catharine Jones, Jan. 7, 1846, who was born Oneida County, N.Y. July 23, 1824; they have six children—four living, three boys and one girl; he also owns a store and house in Waterman, valued at $4,000.

ROBERTS J. DELOS, Farmer, Sec. 21; P.O. Waterman; 320 acres, val. $17,500; Rep; Bapt.

ROBERTS W. W. Farmer; P.O. Waterman; 90 acres, value $5,400; born N.Y. 1845; Rep; Bapt.

ROOT HORACE, Farmer, Sec. 7; P.O. Cornton; 100 acres, value $5,000; Rep; Univ; N.Y.

ROSE H; M. Farmer, Sec. 10; P.O. Waterman; 80 acres, value $7,600; Rep.

ROWLEY E. P. Farmer; P.O. Waterman; 130 acres, val. $7,000; Rep; Meth; from N.Y.

ROWLEY R. P. Farmer, Sec. 18; P.O. Waterman; 101 acres, val. $5,050.

ROWLEY WILLIAM, Farmer, Sec. 7; P.O. Waterman; val. prop. $500; Rep.

S AGE CHARLES, Painter, Waterman; val. prop. $600; Rep.

SAGE JOHN, Painter, Waterman; Rep.

SACKETT, D. A. Farmer; P.O. Waterman; val. prop. $1,000; Rep; Meth.

SCOTT HAMILTON, Farmer, Sec. 13; P.O. Waterman; born in Oneida Co. N.Y. July 6, 1827; came to this State in 1836, to this county in Dec. 1860; Rep; Pres; was in California three years; owns 160 acres, val. $8,800; per prop. $4,000; wife was Julia Shriver, who was born in Dutchess Co. N.Y. Feb. 18, 1833; married Jan. 15, 1862; they have four children, three girls and one boy, all living.

SCHERMERHORN HENRY, Farmer and Mechanic, Sec. 30; P.O. Waterman; $5,450; Rep.
SCHERMERHORN H. A. Farmer, Sec. 19; P.O. Waterman; $3,600; Univ; Rep; from N.Y.
SHANNON JAMES, Mason, Waterman; Rep; from N.Y.
SIMPSON ELMER, Farmer, Sec. 1; P.O. Waterman; val. $6,400; Bapt. Rep.
SPENCER E. G. Farmer, Waterman; Rep; Adv.
SPENCER L. B. Farmer; P.O. Waterman; Adv; Rep.
SPENCER N. W. Rev., Clergyman; val. prop. $10,000; Adv; Rep; from Conn.
SPENCER W. F. Farmer, Waterman; Adv; Rep.
STROM CHARLES, Farmer, Sec. 7; P.O. Waterman; val. $4,000; Luth; Rep.
SWIFT DREW C. Farmer, Sec. 11; P.O. Waterman; 40 acres, val. $1,800; Rep; Bapt.
SWIFT R. K. Farmer, Sec. 11; P.O. Waterman; 40 acres, $1,800; Bapt; Rep.
SWIFT SAMUEL M. Farmer, Sec. 11; P.O. Waterman; 160 acres, $8,800; Bapt; Rep.

TAFT CLINTON, General Merchandise, Waterman; Epis; Rep; from N.Y.
TELFORD D. Teacher; P.O. Waterman; Dem; U. Pres; from N.Y.
TELFORD ROBERT, Laborer, Waterman; val. prop. $600; Dem.
TELFORD F. Farmer, Sec. 35; P.O. Waterman; 120 acres, $7,200; U. Pres; Dem; from N.Y.
TERREL HENRY, Farmer, Sec. 2; P.O. Waterman; 160 acres, val. $8,000; Rep.
THOMAS SAMUEL, Farmer; P.O. Waterman; val. prop. $1,735; Rep; from Penn.
THOMPKINS C. Blacksmith, Waterman; Dem; from Ill.
TOMLIN OSCAR P. Farmer, Sec. 9; P.O. Waterman; Meth; Rep; from Penn.
TOMLIN SARAH Mrs. Waterman; 200 acres in Sec. 9, val. $12,000; Meth.
TUTTLE DAVID, Farmer, Sec. 23; P.O. Waterman; 240 acres; Meth; Rep; from N.Y.
TUTTLE CHARLES L. Farmer, Sec. 23; P.O. Waterman; Rep; from N.Y.

VALENTINE JOHN, Farmer, Sec. 31; 88½ acres, val. $5,800; P.O. Shabbona Grove; Dem.

WAITE LORENZO, Farmer, Sec. 11; 80 acres, val. $4,000; P.O. Waterman; Rep; Meth.
WAITE R. W. Mrs. (widow) Sec. 11; 80 acres, val. $4,400; P.O. Waterman; born Vt. 1824.
WAKEFIELD GEORGE, Farmer, Sec. 8; 260 acres, val. $13,000; P.O. Waterman; Bapt; Rep.
WALKER JOHN, Farmer, Sec. 34; 270 acres, val. $14,000; P.O. Waterman; U.Pres; Rep.
WALLACE E. C. Farmer; P.O. Waterman; Rep; Meth; from New Hampshire.
WEAVER HAMER, Farmer, Sec. 12; 160 acres, val. $6,400; P.O. Waterman; Rep.
WEBSTER FRANK M. Farmer, Sec. 35; 80 acres, val. $3,600; P.O. Waterman; Bapt; Rep.
WHEELER HENRY K. Farmer; P.O. Waterman; Dem; from Vermont.
WHEELER WILLIAM; value of property $400; Dem; from Vermont.
WHEELER W. P. Farmer, Sec. 33; 80 acres, val. $4,000; P.O. Waterman; Ind; from Vermont.
WHITFORD MYRON C. Farmer, Sec. 32; 378 acres, val. $17,500; P.O. Waterman; Rep; Bapt.
WILCOX EUGENE, Farmer, P.O. Waterman; value property $500; Dem; Pres.
WILTBERGER C. L. Farmer, Sec. 11; 320 acres, val. $17,600; P.O. Waterman; Ind.
WOOD C. A. Farmer; P.O. Waterman; value property $300; Rep.
WOOD E. J. Farmer, Sec. 27; 70 acres, val. $3,500; P.O. Waterman; Rep; from N. Y.
WOOD JOHN, Carpenter, Waterman; Rep; value property $200.
WOODS D. H. Farmer, Sec. 3; 120 acres, val. $4,800; P.O. Waterman; Meth; Rep.
WOODRUFF SOPHRONA Mrs. widow, Sec. 19; 80 acres, val. $3,320; P.O. Waterman.
WORBY HENRY J. Farmer; P.O. Shabbona Grove; Ind; Latter Day Saints; from Canada.

YEARNSHAW W. H. Station Agent, Waterman; Rep; Meth; from Rhode Island.

ZIMMER LEVI, Blacksmith, Waterman; value property $500.

BUSINESS DIRECTORY

PATRONS IN DE KALB CO.

DE KALB.

AMOS GEO. Butcher.

ATWOOD J. E. Dealer in Dry Goods, Hats, Caps, Boots and Shoes, Carpets and Oil-cloths.

BRISTOW JOSEPH, Meat Market.

CAMPBELL ALONZO, Blacksmith.

CARTER & ROBERTS, Dealers in Agricultural Implements of all kinds Domestic Sewing Machines.

CENTRAL HOUSE, M. G. Shackelton, Prop. Good Stabling and Livery Accomodations

CROMWELL PHILLIP I. Homœopathic Physician.

DARWIN N. S. Miller.

DURANT & BLAISDELL, Mnfrs. of Harness, and Dealers in Horse Clothing of all kinds.

EAGLE HOUSE, Frank Scriptur, Prop. The Eagle speaks for itself.

ELWOOD HIRAM, Dealer in Drugs, Medicines, Groceries, Paints, Oils, Fancy Articles, etc.

FULLER & HARD, Restaurant, Bakery, and Family Groceries.

HAISH JACOB, Mnfr. Haish's "S" Barbed Steel Fence Wire.

HINMAN C. C. & SON, Dentists.

22

HOPKINS THOS. M. Attorney-at-Law and Solicitor in Chancery, and Notary Public.

LINDSAY D. H. Barber.

LOVE WILSON, Livery.

MACK G. W. Architect, Contractor and Builder.

MAYO E. L., M.D. Physician and Surgeon.

McEWEN L. M. & CO. Dealers in Grain, Lumber, Coal, Stone, Live Stock, Lime, Hair, etc.

MILLER W. H. Billiard Hall.

PERRY E. S. Auctioneer.

POST L. H., Prop. "News." Two Power Presses. Late Styles of Type. Job Printing a Specialty. First Class Work.

RANDALL IRA V. Attorney, Solicitor, and Notary Public.

RUSSELL J. S. Livery, Feed and Sale Stable. Horses and Carriages always on hand. Horses Boarded.

ROBERTS & TYLER, Dealers in Groceries and Provisions, Crockery, etc. Dealers in Live Stock.

SHEA PATRICK, Liquor Dealer.

SHRIMPTON & DORWIN, Mnfrs. of Choice Family and Graham Flour, and all kinds of Feed.

DEKALB — Continued.

TERRY & BRO. Dealers in Grover & Baker Sewing Machines, Stover Wind Mills, Wagons, Buggies, Farm Machinery of all kinds, Pumps, Walter A. Wood's and McCormick's Reapers and Mowers, etc, etc.

UPSON A. M. Constable, Collector and Auctioneer.

WADSWORTH JNO. W. Wagonmaker.

WHEELER & BRADT, Dealers in Fresh, Salted and Smoked Meats, also Lard, Fresh Lake Fish, etc.

WHITMORE J. B. Carriage Painting and Trimming, and Ornamental and Sign Painting.

WHITMORE H. Attorney. Collections a Specialty.

WOOD GEORGE, Blacksmith.

SYCAMORE.

ALLPORT FRANK, Physician and Surgeon.

ARNOLD BROS. Book, Job and Newspaper Printers.

ATWOOD HOSEA W. City Marshal.

BASSETT & WAITE, Props. *DeKalb County Democrat.*

BOIES HENRY L. Editor *True Republican* and Postmaster.

BRYAN O. M. Physician and Surgeon.

BROWN C. & SON, Dealers in Drugs, Paints, Oils, Groceries, Cutlery, and Plated Ware.

CONRAD CASSIUS M. County Clerk.

CARNES DUANE J. Attorney-at-Law.

CURRIER L. M. Homœopathic Physician and Surgeon.

DUSTIN DANIEL, Physician.

ELLWOOD CHAUNCEY, Boots, Shoes, and Leather.

ELLWOOD J. E. & BRO. Wholesale and Retail dealers in Drugs, Medicines, Paints, Oils, Groceries, Pocket Cutlery, Silverware, Crockery and Glassware, Boots, etc.

ELLWOOD R. & CO. Mfrs. Agricultural Implements, Tin and Copper ware. Dealers in Shelf and Heavy Hardware, Wagons, Building and Wagon Material, Iron, Steel, Springs, Axes, Doors, Sash, Blinds, Glass, Putty, Nails, etc.

FLYNN JNO. G. Merchant Tailor.

FLANNERY JNO. J. Attorney and Counselor-at-Law.

GRAVES CHAS. P. Physician and Surgeon.

HARRINGTON JAMES, Lumber dealer.

HOLCOMB R. J. Sheriff.

HOLCOMB SYLVANUS, Justice of Peace and Town Clerk.

HARKNESS & WHITTEMORE, Dealers in Shelf and Heavy Hardware, Agricultural Implements, Stoves.

JOHNSON J. W. & SON, Mfrs. Furniture and dealers in Looking Glasses, Picture Frames, Mouldings, Window Shades, Wall Paper, Coffins, Burial Cases, Children's Carriages, etc.

JONES HARVEY A. Attorney-at-Law.

KELLUM CHAS. Attorney-at-Law.

LATTIN NATHAN, Dealer in Grain, Stock, and Seeds.

LOWELL LUTHER, Attorney-at-Law, and County Judge.

MACK, G. W. Architect and Builder.

MARSH HARVESTER MFG. CO. C. W. Marsh, Pres. W. W. Marsh, Supt. A. M. Stark, Secy. Mfrs. Marsh Harvesters, Riding Cultivators, Wind Mills and Diamond Mowers.

SYCAMORE — Continued.

NESBITT GEO. W. Physician and Surgeon.

PAINE & CARLEY, Dealers and Shippers of Butter, Eggs, Poultry, and Wool.

PERRY ENOS J. Dentist.

PETRIE SAM'L, Brick Manufacturer.

READ GEORGE HENRY, Mfr. Dutton's Cement Air-tight Burial Vaults. Sec. 34, Sycamore P. O.

REYNOLDS, JAS. S. Dealer in Coal and Stone.

ROWE H. H. & CO. Dealers in Groceries, Provisions, Boots and Shoes, Crockery, Glassware, and Notions.

SHROEDER WM. Sash, Doors, Blinds, and Planing Mill.

SHIPPEE E. C. Dealer in Grain, Coal, and Live Stock.

SYCAMORE NATIONAL BANK, J. S. Waterman, Pres., C. W. Marsh, Vice-Pres., P. M. Alden, Cashier.

SMITH JNO. G. Jr. Proprietor Central Billiard Parlor.

SOUTHWORTH J. E. Bazar and Jewelry Store.

STARK MARSHALL, Lumber dealer.

STARK JEFFERSON, Stock dealer.

STARK HENRY J. Stock dealer.

SYME DAVID A. Grain dealer.

SYME JOHN, Dealer in Agricultural Implements.

TAYLOR GEO. W. Photographer.

THOMPSON A. J. Dentist.

VAN GALDER TRUMAN W. Brick Mfr.

WATERMAN & HOYT, Dealers in Dry Goods, Clothing, Boots, Shoes, Hats, Caps, and General Furnishing Goods.

WATERMAN JAS. C. Banker and Real Estate.

WARREN N. C. Dealer in Butter, Eggs, and Poultry.

WARREN GEO. O. Jeweler.

WAITE CAMPBELL W. Editor DeKalb County *Democrat.*

WHALEN JNO. B. Prop. DeKalb Co. Abstract Office, only place in Co. where examinations of title are made.

WHITNEY WALTER J. Manager Livery and Boarding Stable.

WINN LEVI, Hotel and Livery.

MALTA.

BALL ALFRED, Agent C. & N. W. Ry.

GRAHAM SAMUEL, Principal High School.

HOMAN DAVID, Livery and Sale Stable. Open day and night. Charges reasonable.

KINSLOE A. S. Postmaster.

LA BRANT WM. Furniture dealer and Undertaker.

McCREA & LINTLEMAN, Dealers in Lumber, Lath, Shingles, Sash, Doors, Blinds, Salt, Coal, Cement, etc. Highest cash market price paid for all kinds of grain.

PETERS CALEB, Prop. Malta Flouring Mills.

SCHOFIELD WM. H. Proprietor Orient House.

SUMNER JNO., M. D. Physician and Surgeon.

WILLETT J. W. Harnessmaker.

HINCKLEY.

HOLDEHOUSE HENRY, Blacksmith.

MALTBIE H. M. & CO. Dealers in Grain, Ground Feed, Salt, etc.

MILLER SAM'L, Jr. Prop. Livery, Feed, and Sale Stable.

VAN NOSTRAND & WILLSON, Millinery and Dressmaking. All work promptly done.

KIRKLAND.

EDLER FRED. Wholesale and Retail dealer in Lumber. Main office North Branch and Division Sts. (Goose Island), east end of Division St. Bridge, Chicago, Ill. Cars loaded on any R.R. free of charge. Branch yards Kirkland and Fielding, C. & P. Ry.

WELTY H. W. Miller. Prop. Lacey Mills.

KINGSTON.

CHAPMAN JULIUS, Prop. Kingston Flouring Mills.

CHASE W. B. Physician and Surgeon.

MIGNAULT LOUIS, House and Carriage Painter.

SHERMAN I. C. Blacksmith.

TUTTLE W. C. Prop. Hotel.

UPLINGER J. H. Dealer in Hardware, Tinware, Pumps, Lime, Cement, Stucco, Hay, Farm Machinery and Building Material.

SANDWICH.

Bloodgood Henry F. Editor and Proprietor *Free Press*.

Bloom Jas. W. Prop. Transit House.

Bond Wm. Street Commissioner.

Bourne Albert E. Principal Public Schools.

Burdge Washington, Carpenter.

Castle Miles Beach, Banker, Lumber, and Coal dealer.

Close Wm. Carpenter and Joiner.

Culver Amasa J. Cheesemaker.

Dietrich Lewis, Brickmaker.

Doane Enos, Contractor and Builder. Dealer in Building Material of all kinds.

Dyas Joseph, Prop. Sandwich House.

Fairbanks Reuben G. House, Sign, and Carriage Painter.

Graves Henry C. Nursery.

Greenman Alonzo G. Dealer in Stock and Wool.

Harvey Johnsor., Lumber dealer.

Hill Abram H. Boarding House. Dep'. Marshal City Sandwich.

Joles Wm. Blacksmith and Carriage maker.

Kern Jos. D. Jr. Ag't Warder, Mitchel & Co., Mfrs. Champion Reaper and Mower, Springfield, Ohio.

Le Brant Henry K. Painter.

Low Wm. R. Police Magistrate.

Miller Artemus, Livery.

Misick Chas. L., M. D. Physician and Surgeon.

Montgomery J. Ivor, Attorney-at-Law and Collecting Agent.

Munson Frank A. Postmaster.

Parker Raymond P. Prop. Mail and Stage Line between Sandwich and Cortland. Makes round trip every Tuesday, Thursday, and Saturday. Office Railroad Street.

Pomeroy David R. Dentist. Offices Plano and Sandwich.

SANDWICH — Continued.

Ranger Alfred, Carpenter and Joiner.

Richey J. K. Clairvoyant and Botanic Physician. .

Robertson Gilbert H. Editor and Proprietor Sandwich *Gazette*.

Sandwich Bank Loan and Trust Co. M. B. Castle, Pres., Fred. S. Mosher, Cashier.

Sandwich Enterprise Co. Cap. Stock $84,500. Pres. E. Banta; Vice-Pres. E. A. Kennedy ; Sec. B. F. Latham ; Supt. Harvey Packer. Mfrs. of Wind Mills, Feed Mills, Cultivators, Pumps, and Hedge Trimmers.

Sandwich Manufacturing Co. Capital Stock $250,000. Pres. W. L. Simmons: Vice-Pres. G. W. Culver; Sec. and Treas. J. P. Adams; Asst. Sec. W. C. Phelps, Supt. Mechanical Dept. H. A. Adams. Directors, W. L. Simmons, A. Adams, E. Lewis, G. W. Culver, E. Banta, H. Latham, H. A. Adams. Mfrs. Hand and Power Corn Shellers, and Adams and French Harvesters.

Sedgwick Westel W. Attorney-at-Law.

Shepard Amos, Dealer in Stock and Wool.

Smith Nathaniel, Photographer, and General Insurance Agent.

Taylor John C. Furniture dealer and Undertaker.

Thompson & Crawford, Groceries.

Wallace Paul W. Victualer and Meat Market.

Weeks & Tolman, Hardware.

Willis John E. Carpenter, Joiner and House Mover.

Woodward Robt. K. Books, Stationery and News Depot.

SOMONAUK.

Clark John, Cheese Factory.

Molitan Nicholas, M. D. Physician and Surgeon.

Nicholson Chas. Book Agent.

Rosentreter Edward & August, Proprietors Wind Grist Mill.

Ryther Daniel, Bridge Builder and House Mover.

Town Samuel H. Principal Graded School.

Wells Jas. J. Mfr. Centennial Animal Trap.

West Chas. A. Editor and Proprietor Somonauk *Reveille*.

Wright C. E. Druggist and Optician. Dealer in Books, Paints, Cutlery, Jewelry, etc.

CORTLAND.

Bates W. J. Agent Agricultural Implements.

Daly Michael, Prop. Cortland Saloon.

Espey Geo. W. Drugs, Groceries, etc.

Lefler Dr. G. W. Veterinary Surgeon. Treats all Curable Diseases. Office and Infirmary at Hartman House.

Lovell Alonzo L. Prop. Cortland Mills. Flour and Feed at wholesale and retail. Cash paid for good milling Wheat.

Stedman Wm. E. Painter.

GENOA.

Crawford Alex. Dealer in Butter, Eggs, and Poultry.

Davies S. M. Dealer in Hardware, Stoves, and Tinware.

Jackman K. Dealer in Lumber, Coal, Salt, and Farm Machinery.

Jones Isaac H. Butcher.

Laird W. H. Proprietor Genoa Hotel, and Restaurant.

Lord R. D. Butcher.

Merriman Jas. Real Estate.

Ottman Wesley, Proprietor Pacific Hotel.

Perkins Henry N. Dry Goods, and General Merchandise.

Perkins Horatio N. Real Estate.

Sager Wm. Tinner, Repairing, etc.

Shafer Franklin, Proprietor Geneva Hotel.

Slater H. H. General Merchandise.

Strong Wm. Lumber, and Grain Dealer.

Tucker S. S. Editor Genoa *News.*

WATERMAN.

Moore Wm. Dealer in Lumber, Coal, Lime, Brick, etc.

Pritchard I. W. Physician and Surgeon.

SHABBONA.

Ackerblad I. Blacksmith and Carriage Manufacturer.

Alexander G. M. Druggist.

Deacon Wm. & Co. Dealers in Lumber, and Grain.

Heeg Wm. F. Furniture Dealer, and Undertaker.

Husk Wm. V. General Merchandise.

Manderville B. A. Mrs. Dressmaking, and Tailoress.

Marks A. W. Boots, Shoes, Clothing, Staple and Fancy Groceries.

McCormick Jno. A. Proprietor Corn̈ton House.

Mennis J. J. Mrs. Dressmaking and Millinery.

O'Connor Timothy, Billiard Hall, Sample Room, Restaurant, and Livery.

Sterling A. W. Proprietor Central Meat Market.

SHABBONA GROVE.

Cook Geo. H. Joiner and Builder, and Dealer in Groceries.

Flinders Geo. B. Music Teacher: Piano and Organ.

Norton Lyman, Carpenter and Joiner.

Shelburn I. Scott, Hotel, and Cedar Mill.

LEE.

Baier Ferdinand, Dealer in Boots and Shoes.

Bennett Harrison, Proprietor Lee House,

Bryant W. H. Agricultural Implements.

Helland Hans, Shoemaker.

Johanson Hans J. D. Carpenter.

Skoyles Benj. H. Merchant, and Custom Mills.

Stephen & Prestegard, Dealers in General Hardware.

Trask Alfred B. Proprietor Trask House.